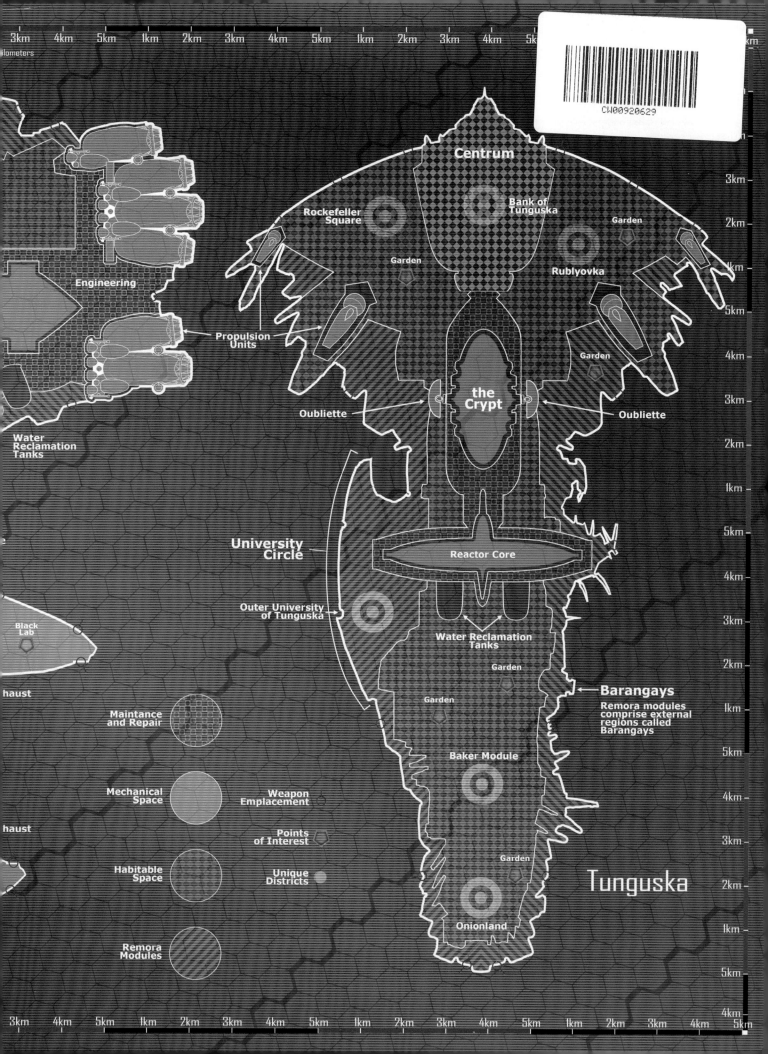

Centrum

Rockefeller
Square

Bank of
Tunguska

Garden

Garden

Rublyovka

Engineering

Garden

Propulsion
Units

Oubliette

the
Crypt

Oubliette

Water
Reclamation
Tanks

University
Circle

Reactor Core

Outer University
of Tunguska

Black
Lab

Water Reclamation
Tanks

haust

Garden

Barangays

Remora modules
comprise external
regions called
Barangays

Maintance
and Repair

Garden

Baker Module

Mechanical
Space

Weapon
Emplacement

haust

Points
of Interest

Habitable
Space

Unique
Districts

Garden

Tunguska

Remora
Modules

Onionland

CREDITS

WRITING
Benn Graybeaton, Jonathan "Killstring" Herzberger, Marc Langworthy, Mark Redacted,
Rodrigo Vilanova, Patrycjusz Piechowski, Giles Pritchard

COVER ART
Ho Seng Hui

INTERIOR ARTWORK
Toma Feizo Gas, Ho Seng Hui, Bagus Hutomo, André Meister, Oh Wang Jing, Vincent Laik, Vladimir,
Aituar Manas, Cristian Picu, Antone "Chuck" Pires, Kenny Ruiz and Noiry Lee, Qi Wu, Chester Ocampo,
Ignacio Bazán Lazcano, ENIQMA, Pierre Revenau, Gregoire Veaulegere, Kenny Ruiz, Noiry Lee, Ryan Harasim

ART DIRECTION
Marc Langworthy, Rodrigo Vilanova

LAYOUT
Thomas Shook

INFINITY RPG LOGO
Michal E. Cross

LEAD EDITOR
Kimberly Nugent

CARTOGRAPHY
Jose "Gigio" Esteras

SECTORIAL ARMIES LOGOS
Alberto Abal, Carlos Llauger "Bostria"
and Hugo Rodriguez

PROOFREADING
T.R. Knight, Marshall Oppel

INFINITY LINE DEVELOPER
Benn Graybeaton

ASSISTANT LINE DEVELOPER
Marc Langworthy

CORVUS BELLI APPROVALS
Gutier Lusquiños Rodríguez, Alberto Abal, Carlos Torres, and Carlos "Bostria" Llauger

ORIGINAL 2D20 SYSTEM DESIGN
Jay Little

GAME DESIGN
Benn Graybeaton, Nathan Dowdell, Mark Redacted, Justin Alexander, Marc Langworthy

PRODUCED BY
Chris Birch

HEAD OF RPG DEVELOPMENT
Sam Webb

PUBLISHING ASSISTANT
Virginia Page

PRODUCTION MANAGER
Peter Grochulski

SOCIAL MEDIA MANAGER
Salwa Azar

COMMUNITY SUPPORT
Lloyd Gyan

SPECIAL THANKS
Thank you to Corvus Belli—Alberto, Gutier, Carlos, and Fernando—for letting us play in your world!

PUBLISHED BY
Modiphius Entertainment Ltd.
2nd Floor, 39 Harwood Road
Fulham, London, SW6 4QP
United Kingdom

Modiphius Entertainment Product Number: MUH050222
ISBN: 978-1-912200-41-2

Artwork & Storyline © Corvus Belli S.L.L. 2018
INFINITY is © Corvus Belli S.L.L. 2018

TABLE OF CONTENTS

INTRODUCTION
REBELS WITH A CAUSE

Space is like a winter sea — while it may be beautiful, it's also cold, merciless, and utterly indifferent to human life. Venturing out among the stars is one thing, but what kind of person makes their home out there? Rebels. Vagabonds. Free-thinkers, dangerous idealists, and transgressive radicals of all stripes. People with no home, nowhere else to go. So they carved one out of the sky itself.

NOMADS

There's *Bakunin:* a collection of private utopias, big ideas, and innovative research. A place where mad scientists create monsters, interplanetary tastemakers create trends, and the revolutionary Social Energy system holds it all together. At least, on most days.

Corregidor wears its rough-and-tumble origins so prominently on its sleeve that it might as well be tattooed there. A collection of criminals, refugees, and other societal unwanteds, they've turned themselves into an interplanetary labour force providing meteor heads, mercenaries, and miners — all tough as nails, and about as friendly — to the rest of the Human Sphere.

But if *Bakunin* is the heart, and *Corregidor* the muscle, then *Tunguska* is the Nomad Nation's sharp, twisted mind. A collection of hackers, bankers, and organised criminals have gone just legitimate enough to be frustrating. Or helpful, depending on your perspective.

A collection of Motherships. Home of the Arachne dark-web datasphere. The eternal opposition to ALEPH's hegemony. The list goes on and on, but never ends because the Nomad Nation is a bastion of individuality, a beacon of defiance, shining brighter than the stars that they call neighbours. And they wouldn't tone it down even if they knew how.

WHAT'S IN THIS BOOK

More than just an expansion, this sourcebook aims to provide a "one-stop shop" for all things Nomad, including everything you need to create characters, run campaigns, or just immerse yourself completely in your character's faction.

> "Everything's legal on *Bakunin*."
>
> —Technically untrue (though close) Nomad proverb.

> "Never headbutt a *Corregidoran*: there's nothing but rocks in there."
>
> —Technically untrue (though wise) Nomad proverb.

> "Everyone has a price. If they say differently, you were insufficiently creative."
>
> —Technically unprovable (though likely) Nomad proverb.

CHAPTER 1– FACTION: NOMADS

Get an in-depth look at the Nomad Nation. Join the improbable journey through the tumultuous early years of the Nomads, up to their modern incarnation. Visit Commercial Missions, dive into Arachne, and learn about the culture of rebellion that informs the Nomad's every action. Witness the Krugs; equal parts concupiscent celebration, black market bazar, and political conclave, these quadrennial gatherings are unlike anything else in the Human Sphere.

CHAPTER 2– THE MOTHERSHIPS

Take a closer look at the triad of Motherships that comprises the bulk of Nomad society. From deck plans to cultural traditions, from topography to tradition, dive into these massive sidereal vessels and find out what makes them tick.

Head to *Bakunin,* the Radical Mothership, and discover a collective of pocket utopias, where everything's legal somewhere, and one person's taboo is another's already-passed fad. Walk amongst mad scientists and passionate revolutionaries. Stop by the BouBoutiques and get a whole new you, or have a night to remember on Sunset Boulevard. But whatever you do, be nice to the cats; they remember everything.

Swing by *Corregidor,* to see how the toughest crew in the Sphere gets by. Raise a toast with mercenaries, discuss urban legends with bounty hunters, and catch the action at the Human Sphere's most notorious underground fighting rings. But don't forget to spend some "G-Time" in a heavy-gravity module, lest the constant weightlessness wreak havoc on your insides.

But don't forget *Tunguska,* the flying tax loophole among the stars. Visit the prestigious Tunguskan Outer University, where Submondo crime barons send their heirs to learn tax evasion, blackmail, and how to avoid police raids alongside traditional subjects. Enjoy your stay, but try to avoid becoming a target on their leaderboards lest someone make a name for themselves by livestreaming the complete destruction of all you hold dear.

CHAPTER 3— SOCIAL ENERGY

A democratic forum, cryptocurrency, social network, and reputation economy all rolled up into one, Social Energy is one of the most uniquely Bakunian concepts to ever grace the Human Sphere. Learn about its origins, where it came from, what it does, and how something so audacious works so smoothly. In the Nomad Spirit, expanded rules for smoothly integrating Social Energy into your campaigns are included. As they say on *Bakunin:* once you've felt it, you've grokked it.

CHAPTER 4— NOMAD CHARACTERS

Life among the stars has its own advantages and challenges, and Nomads explore both to the fullest. With expanded rules tying characters' heritage and status to their ship of origin, new Adolescent and Career events, and eleven new careers — from the triple threat of *Corregidor's* Tomcats, Hellcats, and Wildcats, to *Tunguska's* weaponised Barrister Corps, and *Bakunin's* Chimera and Provocateurs — Nomad characters have a wealth of new options to explore.

CHAPTER 5—GEAR

Revel in the product of rampant, unchecked, gleeful innovation. The Nomads create, modify, or otherwise acquire bleeding-edge technology, and don't apologise for its quirks. Between surplus CrazyKoalas, Viral Spiked Chains, Slag-cannons and more, there's no shortage of new ways to bring the pain. Of course, hackers aren't left out, with an assortment of new programs, augmentations, and armour — and of course, the latest designer drugs — there's something for everyone.

CHAPTER 6—UPLIFTS

From humble beginnings with quasi-sapient cetacean shuttle pilots, Nomad scientists have never been shy about trying to increase an animal's intelligence. Well, they succeeded — far more than anyone expected. Get a closer look at *Bakunin's* latest bit of science run amok with uplifted Cephalopods, Suidae, Avians, and more that were suddenly introduced to the Nomad Nation, turning existing thoughts on consciousness upside-down.

You won't just learn about these creatures, though. With rules for Uplifted player characters across all seven currently feasible Uplift types — and a custom Lifepath system, from awakening to freedom, complete with nine unique careers — these distinctive entities are ready to tell their stories in your *Infinity* campaign.

CHAPTER 7— RADICAL BIOMODS

In contrast to the safe, tested, and clinically proven augmentation that most of the 'Sphere employs, Praxis's Black Labs engage in radical biomodification with unrestrained joy. Xenografts, beast-tissue, and radically invasive gene-therapy are just the tip of the iceberg; there's also a thriving industry of hyper-modified creatures, from savage Pupniks to one-of-a-kind monstrosities. If you absolutely, positively need a fantastical creature, Praxis is happy to oblige.

More than just an overview, expanded rules for biomod augmentation packages, endless combinations of custom-built monsters, and expanded rules for directing your own pack of crimes against nature will ensure your campaigns will never be the same again.

> "Praxis could leave well enough alone: they simply choose not to."
>
> —Posted on a wall, *Bakunian* Moderator Corps Office.

CHAPTER 8— ADVERSARIES

The Nomad's thorny reputation isn't for show. The Nomad Military Force (NMF) has no qualms about deploying its forces anywhere in the Human Sphere and won't hesitate to protect their interests — or retaliate in violent escalation against perceived threats. From Alguaciles to Zeros, the Nomad Nation is more than content to play the adversary.

A collection of richly detailed NPCs rounds out this sourcebook, with unique capabilities and their own story hooks to introduce to your campaign. From Tunguskan Interventors to Sin-Eater Observants, these Nemeses each inject a unique flavour to your *Infinity* campaign, while weaving story hooks for your own adventures throughout.

CHAPTER 1
FACTION: NOMADS

Radical experiments of this nature aren't supposed to last. The Nomad Nation, with all of its idiosyncrasies, should not have survived this long, let alone be thriving. Who could have predicted that this rag-tag bunch of vagabonds, rebels, and miscreants would last this long on the O-12 Security Council with the other G-5 nations? Certainly not the Nomads. Yet here they are, stubborn as ever, having not lost a step.

And whether they're thumbing their noses at convention, warning the Human Sphere of the evils of ALEPH, or dominating niche industries through virally memetic sabotage, the Nomads' stubborn individuality shines through. In many ways, they consider this their role in the Human Sphere – shining a light in the darkness, exposing lies, and illuminating the dark shadows where nightmares dwell.

Except, of course, the shadows they're hiding in.

A TURBULENT HISTORY

Before *Bakunin,* before *Tunguska,* before the rise of the Nomad Nation in 1 NC, there was a station full of convicts, refugees, and terrorists floating aimlessly in space. The privatisation of the *Corregidor* project was no kindness. By washing their hands of the whole sordid affair, nations could join the nascent PanOceania bloc without the blood of thousands on their hands. Unable to support an orbital full of their "surplus population," the remaining South American nations cut the cord, granting *Corregidor* its independence. In a bitterly ironic twist, the denizens of *Corregidor* were now free, but it seemed they were only free to die in space. Soon they were running out of both funds and breathable air, as well as power, food, and every other resource necessary to sustain life among the stars. Barring something drastic, *Corregidor* didn't have much time.

SOMETHING DRASTIC

Facing the prospect of slow but inevitable death, *Corregidor's* warden – Luis Orozco, the first major decision-maker of what would become the Nomad Nation – had some difficult choices ahead of him. The solution was brutally pragmatic in its simplicity. *Corregidor* needed resources, so it would trade anything it had of value to acquire them. Never mind that *Corregidor* had but one type of cargo. Survival wouldn't be cheap, and it wouldn't be clean, but with any luck, there would be future generations to curse his name. And that would have to do.

Orozco quickly sorted his sleeping charges into three categories:

Useful: Contract killers, gang lieutenants, experts in fraud and blackmail. Essentially, anyone who could help the ship make its way through the stars.

Valuable: Mafia Dons, Triad Dragon Heads, and the "nobility" of the Submondo. Many bidding wars – and a few gang wars – raged over the right to acquire these individuals. Usually between those who wanted them back, and those who wanted to see them dead.

Surplus: Petty criminals, impoverished communities, and individuals with mental health issues. All mercilessly sorted into the "surplus" column were earmarked to be taken off life support first in case of emergencies.

Throughout this process, Warden Orozco was impartially capitalistic. High bid wins, no discussion, no questions asked. Unfortunately, this also led to certain undesirables and intelligence agencies concluding that it'd be easier to raid *Corregidor* and take what they wanted by force. With yet another life-or-death crisis facing the ship, this was a critical moment for *Corregidor;* luckily, the Warden still had one ace up his sleeve.

THE MEXICAN GENERAL

No discussion of Nomad history can take place without mentioning Juan Sarmiento who was the self-styled Count of Moctezuma and *Corregidor's* saviour. Even though Juan was the most coveted name on the Red Auction list – terrorists, governments, and Submondo alike were bidding furtively for the right to kill the man – Orozco decided that Sarmiento's knack for finding a way to survive, no matter the odds, was worth the risk.

And it paid off. A man of unsettling politeness and ruthless efficiency, Sarmiento successfully defended the Red Auction with a makeshift force, relying on trickery, knowledge of the ship, and the ruthless capacity for brutality that had been his hallmark. Having secured the Auction, he took to delivering the most valuable purchases personally. Sarmiento converted the new standing forces of *Corregidor* into a mercenary company. After all, armies are expensive. Why not make someone else foot the bill for your troops' training and maintenance? The foundations of *Corregidor's* financial independence were finally secured.

BLACK OPS 2.0

Following the founding of the Nomad Nation, it would be years before another life-or-death crisis reached the Motherships. But when it did, it came like a tidal wave. The Violent Intermission, in addition to being one of the greatest tragedies in the Human Sphere's history, was in many ways a proving ground for the political leviathans to test new methods of conflict. Thousands of Bakunians died at the hands of ALEPH, yet no one else lifted a finger. The successes of the Violent Intermission, temporary though they were, helped set a new precedent for inter-factional conflict in the Human Sphere.

Militaries had long relied on black ops and deniable assets to get around openly declaring war, but with ALEPH's domination of interplanetary media, keeping these strikes quiet was increasingly feasible, provided you had the AI's cooperation. Thus, the Violent Intermission served as a sort of paramilitary beta test for PanOceania and Yu Jing. If, by focusing on small, clandestine strikes, they could successfully attack the Nomads without political blowback, what was to keep them from employing the same methodologies against each other?

Precious little, as it turned out. Once the Phantom Conflict was in full swing, this infighting would provide just enough space for a clever, ruthless, and determined individual to make the fight too financially, politically, and emotionally expensive to continue. Someone who could make the opposition regret picking the fight in the first place. The sort of mad, sociopathic genius that even ALEPH and its lackeys couldn't predict.

As luck would have it, the Nomads already had someone who fit the bill.

Due to his unconventional approach, Sarmiento found success where others failed. Sarmiento had been a guerrilla leader, a smuggler, even a contract killer for "legitimate" intelligence agencies, and this unorthodox résumé lent him both a brutally efficient pragmatism and a flair for unconventional tactics. He knew that an eye for an eye wasn't going to cut it. His enemies had too many eyes for that to work out in the Nomads' favour. But Sarmiento hadn't gotten this far by fighting fair, and while he possessed his own code of honour, gentleness and restraint did not seem to merit his concern.

Nomad Nation (6 NC), p. 19, *Infinity Corebook*.

SHADES OF RED

Steeped as it was in the blood of its inmates, the purging of *Corregidor* to ensure the continued survival of the few was rather aptly named the Red Auction.

Violent Intermission, p. 20, *Infinity Corebook*.

SPECIAL SQUADS

At the dawn of the Nomad nations, ad-hoc "Special Squads" were used to great effect. Comprised of various commandeered troops, they proved remarkably effective in striking deep behind enemy lines and seizing the initiative from their enemies. Their legacy carries over into the modern Nomad military, where combatants are expected to be battle-ready at a moment's notice, and thrive in irregular squads and situations. Initiative is rewarded, daredevils, cowboys, and hotshots are welcomed, and ruthlessness and creativity are prized.

THE FATE OF SARMIENTO

So what became of the Mexican General? After the Phantom Conflicts, he disappeared from the public eye, though that merely shows that *Tunguska* has been thorough in covering his tracks. Still, it's no secret in the intelligence community that Sarmiento found his true calling as the deputy director of the Black Hand, a position he holds to this day.

Expressive, foul-mouthed, and stubbornly attached to the same archaic, obviously artificial Lhost he inhabited back on Earth, Sarmiento is perfectly capable of keeping a low profile. But like any artist, he prefers to sign his work. When the world comes crashing down around someone, he wants them to know it was him.

So he did what he'd always done – escalated. Going above and beyond what military convention considered reasonable, Sarmiento introduced his viciously innovative brand of retribution to an interstellar scale. Strike at the Nomad's outer defences, and the next day you'd find your house burnt down, your accounts emptied, and every bit of blackmail that you swore was buried on an open Mayastream. And that is just the opening salvo. The Count of Moctezuma knew that he'd never succeed in convincing the powers of the Human Sphere to leave well enough alone. But, he could make every victory so entirely pyrrhic that these political leviathans would think twice before attacking the Nomads.

NOMAD LIFE

What is life like for a Nomad? Ask three Nomads, and you'll get four answers, more if a Bakunian is involved. Beyond the Motherships, whose cultural influence on their residents is difficult to overstate, there exists a Nomad identity that transcends societal, cultural, and geographic boundaries. It has to if it wants to exist. The Nomads are simply too spread out and too different for it to work any other way. A unified cultural identity of any sort is impossible for Nomads given the challenges it would face.

For their part, Nomads see no contradiction in this. Of course their cultural identity shouldn't exist. And yet, it does. How could it ever truly be their identity, if it didn't confuse outsiders, fly in the face of convention, and basically have no right to exist? Contradictions, as it turns out, are part of the deal.

COMMERCIAL MISSIONS

Not every Nomad hails from one of the three Motherships. Scattered across the Human Sphere, hundreds of thousands call the commercial missions home. Living in a Commercial Mission is an experience unlike any other.

Neighbours, travellers, and visitors are far more frequent and diverse than on a Mothership. However, the most prominent cultural blending happens within the Nomads themselves. In a Commercial Mission, representatives from each of the three Motherships live and work side-by-side in a space jointly owned and operated. While a focus on certain types of business can provide hints of a particular Mothership – such as a Corregidoran flavour being more prominent in major mercenary hubs – without a Mothership to set the tone, the blend of perspectives creates a diverse array of unique, but distinctly Nomad, hybridised local cultures.

DIPLOMATIC...

To live in a Commercial Mission is to be a not only a merchant, but also ambassador and spy. While some are more strongly associated with one of these roles than the others, everyone has a bit of all three in them. For most denizens of the Human Sphere, a Commercial Mission is the only contact they'll ever have with the Nomad Nation, which makes every resident Nomad a diplomat in their own right.

While most official envoys happen at the embassies, it's the smaller, personal interactions where the true diplomatic battles are fought. If the Nomads have their way, the next time someone sees a news report about those dastardly Nomads, they can remember the cool mercenaries who stood up for them in a bar, the cute hacker who showed them how to access new streaming content, or the new friends their kids made on an otherwise lonely trip. Bakunian social scientists know that winning in the battlefield of public opinion makes the next action against them that much more costly. Thus, effort is made to make everyone's visit to the Commercial Missions as pleasant as possible.

AGGRESSIVELY PROGRESSIVE

Whether it's the hyper-individuality of *Bakunin*, the rough pragmatism of *Corregidor*, or the practical libertarianism of *Tunguska*, the Nomad motherships are each fiercely protective of individuality in their own way. The same goes for commercial missions and Nomads traveling abroad. Individuality is basically a sacred right in the eyes of a Nomad, and they don't have to like someone's choices – or the person in question – to defend their right to make them.

A Corregidoran might not understand *why* a Bakunian considers themselves genderqueer, but they'll be the first to gut a jeering drunk who insists on using the wrong pronouns when addressing their fellow Nomad. While they don't always get along with each other – the cultural gulfs between them often preclude actual camaraderie – the Nomads are aggressively protective of their "in-group" when facing the rest of the Human Sphere.

At the end of the day, if you're a Nomad, you're family. Like many siblings, they fight all the time. But make no mistake, any outsider trying the same is going to quickly regret their decision. Nobody picks on the Nomads except the Nomads.

...IMMUNITY

A pleasant visit to the Nomad Commercial Mission can mean different things to different people. It can be a chance to indulge in behaviour that would be otherwise socially difficult, if not patently illegal, and it's an open secret in the intelligence community that the Black Hand operates out of these Missions. For most visitors, a trip to the bazar for something that's legal to purchase – though interesting to get through customs – is as far as this ever goes. For some, however, this is not enough. Sensationalised tales of Nomad debauchery, which somehow manage to both understate and blow out of proportion the reality, have captured the imagination of more than one traveller. For these intrepid souls, there is only one option.

They need to meet with "Madame Lu."

Who is Madame Lu? The answer varies by location, but the result is always the same. They are the outsider's guide to the Mission Underground. Comparatively tame when contrasted with *Bakunin's* Ultraviolet Quarter, each Mission Underground is nevertheless an anarchic spectacle. Whether they're looking for contraband, esoteric or erotic services, or simply a place to conduct business away from ALEPH's prying eyes, the Mission Underground is more than happy to oblige – provided that the customer can pay.

REBEL REBEL

Outcasts by definition, Nomads categorically refuse to be defined by the systems and structures they reject, opting instead to chart their own course. Shared opposition makes for ready allies, and many Nomads find solidarity in their shared circumstances, varied though they may be. As most Nomads have lived on the Motherships for generations, this rebellion is in many cases hereditary. Because the rest of the Human Sphere is quick to label Nomads as deviants, outcasts, or far harsher terms, the outlaw mentality that's such an integral part of the Nomad identity is reinforced.

Even among their allies, Nomads stand out as idiosyncratic. Nomads and Ariadnans tend to see themselves in each other. They are both scrappy survivalists, managing to hold their own against much bigger entities that would love nothing more than to destroy – or better yet, colonise – them. While their shared opponents may be the only thing they have in common, Nomads are used to common enemies as the glue that holds society together.

The Nomads' first and strongest allies, Haqqislam, still don't quite know what to make of them after all these years. Haqqislamites tend to believe the

Nomads' hearts are in the right place, even if their hands usually aren't. Still, the two factions have been steadfast allies for decades. Most Nomads think of Haqqislam as their slightly uptight distant cousins, probably too straight-laced, but family whether they like it or not. And they don't get a say in the matter. Whether the Haqqislamites feel the same or whether political necessity and a hospitable culture have given the Nomads that impression is difficult to say. Either way, Haqqislam tends to be remarkably tolerant of the Nomads.

Indeed, many Haqqislamites point out that they tolerate them with all their heart.

ALEPH

No discussion of Nomad rebellion would be complete without mentioning ALEPH. While their feelings about the AI are abundantly clear as a nation, what's often missed in the propaganda is the Nomads' deep sense of pride in their oppositional status. Humanity has all but handed the keys to their destiny over to a machine, a soulless creation that is slowly removing people's ability to take care of themselves, eroding privacy and personal freedoms, and generally creating a society that cannot in any way offer it meaningful opposition.

To the Nomads, it's only logical that the AI wouldn't try to wipe out humanity right away. It's a machine. It's patient by nature. And if nobody speaks up, humanity is eventually doomed. Not today, not tomorrow, but doomed all the same. They see themselves as the heirs to the whistleblowing legacy of those who came before them. All one has to do is look at Earth's depleted resources and ravaged environment to see the cost of ignoring the warnings. But this time, there will be no new planet to find, no refuge among the stars. ALEPH's ubiquity means that if humanity doesn't stand up to it, it will eventually lose all ability to do so.

Their second major source of pride in defying ALEPH is much more practical: it's their continued survival. They're living proof that humanity can stand up to ALEPH, and not only survive, but thrive. Proof that you don't need a godlike AI to succeed financially or even have a comfortable life. One has but to take a look around Praxis to realise that ALEPH does not have a monopoly on technological innovation, or cool toys for that matter. Nomads would argue that their quality of life is just as good, if not better, than what anyone in PanOceania enjoys. So what if the Hyperpower's metrics would disagree? They obviously created them as propaganda to show how great it is in their nation.

And this leads us to the third aspect of Nomad culture defined by opposition: an instinctive distrust of Maya, and not just as a datasphere, or a source

> "It is progress we believe in, and the power of science and technology to propel us beyond what we are today. We believe in the power of change. There is danger in the unknown, yes, but there is beauty also. Fear must never hold back the march of progress."
>
> —Fragment of Dr. Fuchs' speech, representing Praxis for the *Bakunin* delegation during the Nomad Nation's foundational meetings in Centrum, *Tunguska*.

THE SECRET ORIGINS OF MADAME LU

Like most Nomad urban legends, there are countless explanations for how the "Madame Lu" phenomenon got started. Some say that there was an influential brothel owner, whose wares proved invaluable in establishing the first Commercial Missions. Some say it's a tribute to a Hiraeth culture silent film about the only trustworthy soul in the German underworld. Others share the story of an O-12 ambassador, so drunk they couldn't remember where they were, asking for someone who wasn't there, but liking what they found anyway. Whether any (or none) of these stories is true is irrelevant to the Nomads. What matters is that they have a reliable way to find both customers and customs agents who ask to meet with Madame Lu for some discreet advice.

ARACHNE FOR DUMMIES

"Any datasphere that doesn't have network neutrality is an implement of societal control, full stop. If your datasphere isn't treating all data that passes through it equally, then you have to assume that it's using that power to influence you. So who wields that power? In Maya, it's ALEPH. And what, exactly, does ALEPH want?

Interesting question, isn't it? Are you confident you know the answer? No? Then you need an open, neutral, and free datasphere. You need Arachne."

— Dr. Cory Payne, professor of quantronic ethics (and sometimes Wardriver), *Bakunin*.

of information. Some Nomads avoid using Maya as a matter of superstition, worried that spyware will infect their comlogs as the AI searches for any opportunity to subjugate them. Whether true or not, Maya is seen as strictly inferior to Arachne in every way that matters. Even if they want to watch a Mayacast, which happens more frequently than most Nomads than would care to admit, they often won't do so until it's completely divorced from Maya and running on safe, reliable, Nomad tech. Any attempt at a reasonable discussion about these two dataspheres is a disaster waiting to happen. Much like someone with a favourite operating system or automobile brand, there's no room for debate, only a holy (flame) war.

A TANGLED WEB

Arachne shouldn't even work. An interplanetary datasphere based on surreptitiously placed nodes with a networking protocol purposefully modelled on irrational, mythological, and outright contradictory logical systems should not be able to function at the level that it does.

While it's inarguably slower than Maya, the fact that a direct competitor, under constant attack from an empowered AI is not only still in operation, but thriving, is nothing short of remarkable. The security of its networks, however, is much easier to explain. While it's said that Arachne is inscrutable to the AI because it's built on a foundation of mysticism, that's a gross oversimplification. After all, ALEPH's owes its very name to the Kabbalah. It's clearly comfortable with some spiritual and mythological concepts. So, what makes Arachne so difficult? As it turns out, there's more than one school of mystic thought.

People tend to grow into their names, and it seems that ALEPH is no different. Named for the first letter of the Kabbalah, symbolically beholding the entire universe, ALEPH has never had issues with sacred geometry. Regardless of the infinite depths they're revealing, the sephiroth don't change their meanings when you're not looking. Each symbol consistently and reliably means the same thing. ALEPH is comfortable with these structures.

To follow the metaphor, if ALEPH is a Kabbalistic concept, then Arachne is pure chaos magick. The meaning of an individual symbol or glyph is given by a community and understood by an individual. Arachne's pathways aren't linear or rigid, they're constantly being re-interpreted, re-purposed, and reimagined on the fly. Rather than mathematical logic, Arachne operates on principles of semiotic constructivism. Essentially, reality is defined by consensus and intent, and constantly undergoes iterative changes. In the beginning, Arachne's

structure was largely based on the neuronal pathways of early Christian martyrs and saints as received from the Observance. No one bothered to ask how they happened to come by these neural maps; it didn't matter whether they were objectively real or not, so long as the Observance believed that they were. Faith and intent governed these initial structures, and faith and intent have guided their chaotic evolution since.

And ALEPH seems to hate it. Any system, regardless of how illogical, can be learned if just holds still. But not only does Arachne make no sense to the AI, the laws that govern it are likewise antithetical to its understanding of reality.

WALKING THE THREADS

For most users, the differences between Arachne and Maya are remarkably pedestrian. The first is speed. Arachne is slow, while Maya is fast. But, Maya tends to guide your search, while Arachne doesn't. So, if you're looking for something that those controlling Maya want you to find — official news, shopping options, *Myrmidon Wars: The Animated Series* — then there's no contest. However, if your search is more esoteric, you must wade through all the content that Maya thinks you want, or perhaps thinks that you should want, before your queries succeed. Thus, many Nomads contend that Arachne's often quicker to use, despite being nowhere near as fast.

Secondly, though more importantly for most, is the question of content. Maya is vast, but it's curated. Arachne is a wild frontier of content, both professional and otherwise. And while Channel Oxyd proudly appends "only on Maya" to every episode of the *Go Go Marlene!* show, most Nomads would be quick to add "unless pirated" as a suffix. The process of siphoning Maya content through the Arachne darknet, Mayatapping, is easy enough for those with some hacking proficiency. However, more than a few would-be content pirates have found their comlogs unexpectedly riddled with malware. As luck would have it, hypercorps have become frighteningly proficient at booby-trapping their content.

KRUGS

Once every four years, the Nomad fleet gathers in one system for the Krug, coalescing in a single location to trade, intermingle, or even switch vessels. It's an irreplaceable conclave, an opportunity to strategise, enjoy cultural and economic exchange, and ensure that the bonds of solidarity between the Motherships aren't weakened over time.

As the one holiday that all Nomads not only celebrate, but get to experience together, it's also the biggest party that the Nomad nation can throw.

Krugs are usually greeted by a host system with an inevitable dread often reserved for significant natural disasters. Admittedly, distinguishing between the aftermath of a Krug and a hurricane can be difficult for anyone.

COMMERCE

For all the headache that they represent — which to be clear, might as well be measured on the Richter scale — other factions remain keenly aware of the opportunities that a Krug provides. Trade prospects are lavish and plentiful, and everyone is invited to the table. Corporations, entrepreneurs, and less-savoury entities all come to explore the unique and irreplaceable opportunities the Krug provides.

The number and value of deals made at a Krug is astronomical. Anyone in the right place at the right time can make a tidy little fortune, so long as they're willing to absorb a little risk. However, anyone who doesn't fully grasp the stakes they're playing with can just as easily lose their fortune here, though few would consider themselves among the latter group. For their part, the Nomads' open philosophy holds sway here. Nobody's going to keep you from the opportunities; nobody will save you either.

PARTIES

Of course, not everyone is coming to the Krug for commerce. For most Nomads, the Krug is a quadrennial party without equal in the Human Sphere. Though to call it a single party is something of a misnomer as a Krug is hundreds, if not thousands of parties, held across the Motherships, and catering to every taste imaginable. While the parties change at every Krug — it's considered a point of pride to repeat yourself as little as possible — several different types of party have emerged as perennial favourites:

The gRAVE Yard: These massive raves combine pulsing dance music, some of the most avant-garde combinations of AR patinas and live lightshows, and every narcotic imaginable, and given its close proximity to Praxis, a few that aren't. Its name has less to do with its organiser or the spooky aesthetic, and more to do with the number of fatalities that occur each Krug. This Krug, organiser Dylan Graves is trying for an unprecedented milestone: three Krugs in a row without breaking into double-digit fatalities. Given the introduction of several new nitrocaine variants, and several corrupt gambling rings taking an interest, Tunguskan odds-makers are not enthusiastic about Graves's chances of succeeding.

SUBMONDO AND THE KRUG

Outside of the Nomads themselves, no one looks forward to the Krugs more than the Submondo. With a Krug providing unprecedented access to criminal syndicates, Hypercorp executives, intelligence operatives, government diplomats, and of course the Nomads themselves, there's no shortage of wealthy, influential people about. Whether they're looking for work, resources, easy marks, or just new contacts, there are few opportunities that compare to a Krug. If nothing else, the parties are unreal.

"If there's discretion that you haven't already abandoned; now would be a good time."

— Sergeant Major Carlota Kowalsky, to a new Tomcat recruit. Hostage rescue on board the pirate ship "Blood Talon," Human Edge

"ATTENTION: Use of this weaponry is prohibited by the Concilium Convention. Violators shall be prosecuted by international courts."

— Standard warning on military-spec flamethrowers. Routinely ignored within the Nomad Nation.

Krug-Chug: A self-described "roving pile of drunken revelry," the Krug-Chug is an extension of the traditional Corregidoran pub crawl, taken to its logical extreme. Known to pass through all three Motherships as well as any nearby vessels, space stations, or planets, if you serve alcohol of any sort, you might find yourself "blessed" with a visit from the Krug-Chug Train and its conductor, the gruff mercenary Javier Martinez. Anyone looking for a rowdy drink and an honest brawl should swing by. Anyone hoping to avoid those things should stay out of their way or stick to bars the Train has already visited; the Chug is a bit iffy on participant consent.

Soirées: Held by too many hosts to list, these elegant galas boast incredibly complex rules of etiquette, so much so that custom software for attendees' geists is complimentary, allowing everyone to keep track of what they're expected to do. Attempting to subvert the cybersecurity in these suites is often a game within the gala, with clandestine deals, applied blackmail, and general mayhem all trying to slip past the watchful gaze of the host's Infowar security. Intrepid hackers should take note: the hosts tend not to take interruptions lightly, and jail time is usually preferable to the undivided attention of the wealthy and powerful in attendance.

PLANNING

Innovation is the lifeblood of the Nomad Nation. Getting the Mothership's decision-makers in a room together is vital for the free-flowing exchange of ideas and information so critical to Nomad policy. Long-term solutions are plotted out, current courses evaluated, and analysts, commanders, and politicians can all hash out what's working and what isn't.

Ideas aren't the only thing exchanged. It's entirely common for large numbers of Nomads to change Motherships during the Krug. A large, but finite population means that maintaining biological diversity must be considered. This is yet another reason why the Motherships support the smorgasbord of wild parties. The number of inter-ship children conceived during Krugs is higher than anyone admits.

Determining the next Krug's location is the last order of business and is a spectacle in and of itself. Inverting the norm for events of its size, rival governments compete with bribes, favours, and political leverage for the honour of the Krug to go somewhere besides their system. Particularly savvy negotiators who sweeten the deal enough, can look forward to their rivals dealing with the wormhole congestion and criminal activity that surely follows each Krug, far away from anything the negotiator cares about.

THE NOMAD MILITARY FORCE

Dirty war, done dirt cheap. Whereas PanOceania can throw money at a situation, and Yu Jing can throw numbers, the Nomad Military Force tends to throw something a bit more crude and foul-smelling directly into the fan. If the Violent Intermission is any indication, the weird heart of the NMF's strength can be found beating in *Bakunin*. Praxis's radical innovations allowed the NMF's forces to keep pace with the Human Sphere's military-industrial behemoths. In no world should a guerrilla army running on salvage stand toe-to-toe with the heavyweights of the era, let alone come out on top. And in fairness, all the technological marvels in *Bakunin* wouldn't be enough to keep the NMF on their feet in a straight-up slugfest against modern opponents.

Luckily, the Nomads seem almost religiously offended at the idea of a fair fight.

No one specialises in applied unfairness like Bakunians unless you consider Tunguskans. And Corregidorans, for their part, take ironic satisfaction when the deck is stacked in their favour for a change. Employing the "three T's"—Technology, Tenacity, and Treachery—the NMF enjoyed great success against overwhelming odds and have every expectation that they will continue to do so, provided that the three Motherships continue to work in harmony.

Observing cooperation between the different Jurisdictional Commands is like seeing the Nomad Nation in microcosm. Nowhere is the interdependence of the Nomad motherships so visibly manifest as when their security apparatus responds to existential threats. By now, everyone knows how it works; *Corregidor* provides the muscle, which only succeeds because of *Bakunin*'s technology, which is only possible due to *Tunguska*'s funding, which is only secured and protected due to *Corregidor*'s muscle, and so it goes, on and on. One can't hope to survive long without the others, but together? Together, they're unafraid of any challenge. For good or ill.

NOMAD MILITARY PHILOSOPHY

"Win if you can, lose if you must, but always cheat."

This quote, attributed to American politician Jesse Ventura, was a favourite of the Mexican General, a pithy way to impart his military vision to the poor souls tasked with executing it. The Nomads are unlikely to bring the amount of firepower necessary to match their adversaries blow for blow. Outnumbered, outgunned, and outspent, without copious amounts of lateral thinking, the NMF wouldn't stand a chance against most modern powers.

Fortunately, lateral thinking is a Nomad specialty. The Mexican General knew that true victories would be rare. Seizing opportunities as they came would be vital. He also knew that victory wouldn't always be achievable. For the Nomads to win a war, heavy losses would be inevitable. Not every battle was going to prove winnable, so sometimes a lengthy, costly, delaying loss would have to do, and his troops would need to make them count.

And finally, it was imperative that his troops banish any semblance of discretion, propriety, or fairness from their minds. To a Nomad soldier, these ideas were contemptible, weaknesses to be exploited. So while it's true that every military fights at least a little dirty, the Nomads are downright filthy, skirting ever closer to war crimes. Even when they aren't violating the Concilium Convention, traditional commanders are routinely flustered by their unorthodox tactics. While NMF tactics are decidedly not pretty, by hook or (more often) crook, they get the job done. And, at the end of the day, that's all the NMF can afford to care about.

ALWAYS READY

Whatever storm is lurking on the horizon, each Jurisdictional Command knows they might have to weather it alone. Thus, their forces have to be ready to fight at a moment's notice. To the NMF, "Always Ready" is more than a motto; it's a way of life.

The Mexican General knew better than to try to corral so many free spirits into a conventional military, and his successors have heeded the lesson. Compared to other nation's militaries, the NMF seems like an undisciplined mess. As always, there's a method to the madness. While Nomad forces might have more vacation time, ability to pursue personal interests, and so on, there's a mandatory level of readiness that they pride themselves on maintaining. "More off-days, but no days off," as the saying goes.

Their weapons? Close at hand. Their physical condition? Religiously maintained. Surprise inspections are just a way of life, and they need to be able to pass a fitness exam at any time. This has led to the gamification of NMF soldiers' personal training complete with dynamic quantronic leaderboards, leading to fierce, ongoing competition between soldiers to set the week's the top score.

On top of that, the NMF is always armed, even in their downtime. It's not uncommon to see young soldiers poolside with Combi Rifles slung over their swimsuits, or getting coffee with a Panzerfaust leaning up against their table. Nomad military doctrine demands that they be ready to fight, so the tools of their trade are never far.

TENETS OF NOMAD WARFARE

Nomad military doctrine is based on three central tenets.

Firstly, war cannot be allowed to reach the Motherships. Fragile and filled with civilians, open war in the corridors of any of the three Motherships ensures catastrophe of immeasurable scope, a lesson learned all too well during the Violent Intermission.

Secondly, wars must be brief. An extended conflict would be murder on the Nomads — quite literally — as their economy, industry, and population could not possibly hope to match the leviathans that oppose them. Adrift in an ocean of stars, the Nomad Motherships are especially susceptible to siege tactics. Fighting a traditional defensive war would be tantamount to suicide.

And thirdly, the Nomad Nation must seize and hold the military initiative, controlling the framework of the war and the conditions of their battles. To slay a giant, one must be elusive, two steps ahead, and overcome strength with cleverness and agility. If the giants dictate the pace and terms of the fight, there's little hope. Thus, the NMF is reliably proactive. Their defensive strategy tends to answer the smallest infraction with gratuitous overkill in hopes that the thorny response will dissuade further prodding.

As a rule, the Nomad Nation doesn't start wars, but if provoked, there's very little off limits. The NMF knows they can't hope to defeat an opposing army, but those armies rely on financial and political support. If the line can be held long enough for PanOceanian Lobbyists' accounts to be frozen, or a Yu Jing general's affairs made public, support for a costly incursion can dry up quickly.

Therein lies the heart of Nomad military doctrine; if someone hits you, hit back three times as hard. Then rob them blind. Then get them fired, destroy their private life, get their family to disown them, and don't stop when you've gone too far. Make every step towards you a harrowing experience, so costly that your opposition stops to think twice before committing troops. And then use that time to hit the enemy on their home soil.

CORVUS BELLI INFINITY

MOTHERSHIP: BAKUNIN

> "*Bakunin* is kinda like a bubble. It's not like the rest of the 'Sphere. It exists in its own little world. I wonder what that's like?"
>
> — Señor Massacre, explaining the dynamics of Nomad Motherships mid-firefight. Ariadnan Commercial Conflicts.

Before *Bakunin*, words like "revolution" had been all but reduced to marketing slogans. The Human Sphere was enjoying unprecedented economic growth, and the prevailing wisdom suggested that people were more or less content with their lives. *Bakunin* proved that not everyone was satisfied with the status quo. To many, *Bakunin* seemed doomed to failure: an anarchistic collective of radicals, dissidents, and activists. Most assumed that *Bakunin* would inevitably collapse under its own weight.

Decades later, not only has the Radical Mothership survived, but it has weathered numerous military and ideological attacks to take its place at the forefront of the Nomad cultural zeitgeist. Today, *Bakunin* is the catalyst for ongoing societal, cultural, and memetic revolution. *Bakunin* is the genuine article; no matter how the rest of the Human Sphere appropriates the word, its revolutionary approach has, well, revolutionised life as we know it.

CLIMATE AND TOPOGRAPHY

The aesthetics of *Bakunin* are similar to its populace: chaotic, vibrant, and unapologetic in their diversity. To an outsider, it can look as though someone took a random sample from cities across the Human Sphere, and lashed them together with duct tape and prayer. However, as with the rest of *Bakunin*, the truth is more complex than it initially appears.

First-time visitors often wonder if they've arrived during some kind of cultural festival, and it's easy to see why. Strings of coloured lights, bright hues, and music, dance, and other forms of live performance assault the senses like a jolt of caffeine to the brain. It's sometimes said that *Bakunin* never sleeps, which seems like a reasonable assumption when entering

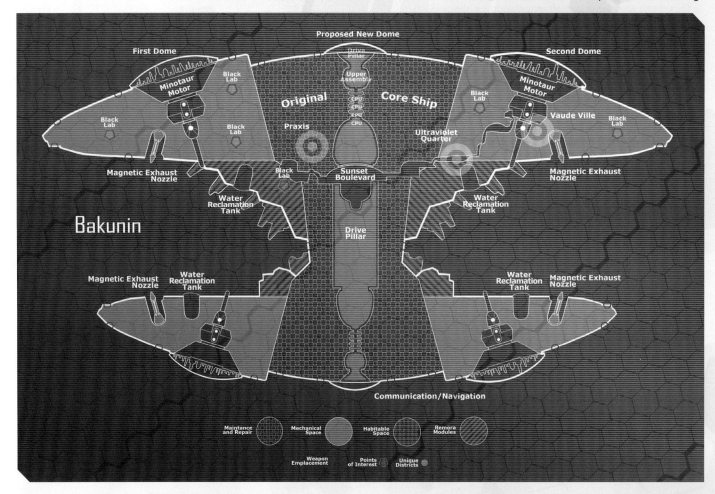

the neon bazaar for the first time. The AR element of the ship has a seductive, nested quality. The distilled essence of "just one more click" permeates the ship's quantronic environment, with the hint of exotic mystery residing in every nook and cranny.

The layers of augmented reality cues are analogous to the construction and layout of the ship itself; *Bakunin* is replete with redundant systems, failsafes, and resilient infrastructure. Though the decks may look like a carnival, and the exposed cabling and vents give it an "under construction" vibe, this is a superficial layer. The exposed wires and machinery are a purely aesthetic element. Nothing important would be placed at such obvious risk. This curious design serves two purposes: first, it gives the ship a sort of stylized, adventurous feel that many Nomads associate with feelings of home. And second, while they certainly don't do anything important, that doesn't mean they do nothing at all. Many of these consoles hide teaching games for young troublemakers. It's assumed that Bakunian kids will try to get into everything, so there are superficial systems for them to mess with in a consequence-free — or at least light — environment. This has led to no end of frustrations when children visit *Corregidor* and quickly find themselves assigned to a punitive maintenance team for tampering with the ship.

BAKUNIAN FAUNA

Stray cats. Stray cats everywhere.

Once upon a time, someone thought it would be a great idea to introduce large quantities of domestic felines to the Mothership. Hoping to make a tidy profit — or at least a dent in the ship's vermin — the population quickly outpaced demand. But as it turned out, between the ship's massive rat population (blame Praxis's desire for lab specimens) and the scraps left by tourists, these feral felines have become a staple of *Bakunin*, in much the same way that squirrels or pigeons crowd some terrestrial urban centres.

Of course, eating garbage at the intersection of travellers from radically different ecosystems is a recipe for introducing new and interesting types of intestinal parasites to a population. The average Bakunian alley cat is a festering hive of alien tapeworms, inflicting unwitting passerby with bouts of explosive incontinence.

Bakunians have some complex feelings about their cats, as is evidenced by their prominent role in the ship's many and varied urban legends. Using Jungian philosophy as a stepping stone, early Bakunian philosophers theorised that a person's soul possessed a sort of duality: the inner self or "anima" lay dormant within a sleeping sheut, and

the outer self or "persona" would require a different sort of storage. Given the emotional toll that the Phantom Conflicts took on the populace, many Bakunians swore that they observed the tell-tale traits of their deceased loved ones expressed in feral tomcats. What this implies regarding the deceased is another matter altogether.

The belief that these cats play host to human spirits — or parts of them, anyway — has fuelled countless urban legends, quietly informed local culture, and completely scuttled public support for any widespread removal of the creatures. Nomads love their urban legends, but on *Bakunin*, even the most outlandish tales have an outside shot of being true. Thus, the mystique and attachment to these feral felines grows, as public health warnings become increasingly insistent.

Of course, this is *Bakunin,* the home of ideas. More than one module has taken the exact opposite view. Though after more than a few near-incidents, cat dissenters are reluctant to raise the issue in public, lest they find themselves shunned by the general populace.

ECONOMY

All of the Motherships are dependent on trade, but nowhere is that so culturally inexorable as on *Bakunin*. Whereas *Corregidor* exports labour, and *Tunguska* concerns itself with finance, the Radical Mothership provides experiences — and the Human Sphere has shown an insatiable appetite.

TOURISM

A year-round destination for holidays, university students on break, or anyone looking to step outside of the mundane for a while, the Bakunian tourism industry is a dominant economic force, perhaps only rivalled by Varuna in popularity. While a far cry from PanOceanian resort ships or Hypercorporate pleasure yachts, *Bakunin* boasts a vibrant nightlife, more artistic performances than one could possibly attend in genres and disciplines many never even knew existed, and of course, the most vibrant live shopping experience that the Human Sphere has to offer.

This contributes heavily to *Bakunin's* travel schedule. To keep things fresh, it travels much more frequently than its fellow Motherships, the increased revenue more than offsetting the price of fuel. Equal parts travelling circus, gambling hall, and anything-can-happen den of iniquity, *Bakunin* plots its course to coincide with major planetary holidays and off-seasons. They set coordinates to the intersection of disposable income and free time.

QUANTRONIC SUBSTRATA

Not every rabbit hole hides something pleasant. *Bakunin* promises to provide unique and novel experiences, but at no point does it guarantee that those journeys will be agreeable. But journey farther down the nested patina cues, and the underlying structure of *Bakunin's* AR is revealed, the Social Energy-fuelled quantronic layer that locals call the substrata.

It is here where Bakunians engage in memetic discourse, debating existential philosophy through quantronic graffiti tags, pondering paradox esviarhythmic cyphers, or simply have a laugh at some wide-eyed tourists' expense. In the substrata, hacking and conversation might as well be one and the same. It's not uncommon for a local to be interacting with a very different reality than a visitor. So if they laugh at an inappropriate time, there's a good chance it has nothing to do with what's going on in the physical world.

BAKUNIAN FLORA

In contrast to the industrial pragmatism of *Corregidor* or the meticulously cultivated gardens of *Tunguska*, *Bakunin's* plant life is a haphazard potpourri of anarchic gardening. Some modules carefully tend private gardens, while others try in vain to get terrestrial flowers to thrive in the artificial environment.

If there is any unifying element, it'd be the cacti. Colourful, spiky, and difficult to kill, many Nomads find much to love about the little plant. The more industrious cultivate cacti for their succulent fruit, or to harvest psychoactive agents.

BAKUNIAN URBAN LEGENDS

Not just cats! Mostly cats, though.

A cat interrupting as you're closing a deal is a bad omen.

A resurrected sheut doesn't remember its persona's time as a cat, but the feelings remain. Mistreat a stray, and the newly revived will hold a grudge; leave out a saucer of milk for strays, and they'll remember your kindness once reborn.

Bay 21 is haunted by the ghosts of sheuts lost during the Violent Intermission. The spirits' anguished cries can be heard at night, and communes residing there are doomed to fail.

Polydactyl cats got that way by hosting multiple souls. They're a sign of good luck.

Johannus Montauk was a brilliant, but quite mad, Praxis scientist whose tachyon field research was considered too dangerous. The Violent Intermission was staged to cover his assassination and the destruction of his lab. Beliefs on the lab's position vary, but strange temporal distortions can be experienced if visited under the right circumstances.

BAKUNIN'S TRAVELS

Given its frequent location changes, Bakunin tends to travel with Circulars more often than its fellow Motherships. Easily one of the largest ships to travel in this fashion, Bakunin rides the C2 and C5 Circulars to popular destinations on wealthier planets. It also occasionally slips from Sol to Human Edge on the C3, spawning rumours that Praxis is using the frontier to ensure privacy for its edgier research. Bakunin is by no means confined to Circulars though. With proposed modifications to the Mothership's drive pillar coming daily, including a custom Minotaur Motor, you never quite know where they'll show up next.

Of course, such a snare requires tantalising bait. This has led to the development of a carefully cultivated aura of raw, transgressive abandon. Accurate enough on the surface, Bakunians nevertheless embellish, misrepresent, and flat-out lie in order to craft a compelling lure for hapless targets. And it works, too: the number of tourists muttering phrases like "the voluptuousness of sin" as though it were some secret code grows with each passing year. These "marks" are usually identified with a Social Energy-locked patina cue, identifying them to locals as someone with more money than sense, and prime candidates for tourist prices, a hefty increase above and beyond what locals pay.

ENTERTAINMENT AND MEDIA

But while tourism is thriving, media is by far Bakunin's most prolific industry, and its best-known export. Whether users are searching for news, entertainment, answers, or even blackmail, the Arachne web delivers more content than anyone could possibly hope to sort through in a lifetime. While it's true that it still comes nowhere close to the juggernaut that is the Maya platform, Arachne's dedication to a free, unregulated, neutral net has allowed niche voices to rise to prominence based on their own merit, rather than the ALEPH-curated, corporate-sponsored, mass-marketed content that dominates Maya.

The lack of regulation means that the riskiest, edgiest, and most unfiltered media in the Human Sphere tends to live on Arachne. Most of the media on Arachne originates from Bakunin, and it promises experiences unlike anything produced elsewhere. Innovative webseries, no-holds-barred interviews, and edgy, boundary-pushing holomovies, and sensaseries are enriched with sensory and emotional content, fed straight to your brain

through your Comlog. Independent filmmakers thrive in Bakunin, leading to a virtual explosion of content in underserved and underexplored areas. Bakunin is a content creation juggernaut — and that's before mentioning its cutting-edge music scene. Live performances have enjoyed a renaissance, adding a raw vitality to the Mothership's sonic exports that most competitors are sorely lacking. No social taboo is off-limits, no topic is too controversial, and no approach is too avant-garde. In Bakunian media, the people are the ultimate arbiter of what's good or not. And judging by the amount of money brought in, most people seem to like Bakunian media quite well.

RESEARCH AND DEVELOPMENT

For all the attention that Bakunin's tourism and entertainment industries garner, R&D is where the bulk of the ship's revenue comes in. In all of Praxis, but especially the Black Labs and Black Ships, the allure of truly unregulated research has attracted many of the Human Sphere's top minds. Unfettered by focus groups, ethics boards, or a need to justify their actions to a corporate board of directors, the research coming out of Praxis has provided a massive boost to myriad scientific endeavours across fields. It's also led to more than its share of horror stories. As it turns out, plenty of rules exist for a reason. Still, it's difficult to deny the quality of their work.

Discovery, though, doesn't pay the bills, and acclaim won't put food on the table. Thus, many researchers split their time between passion projects and more lucrative areas of research, usually with a medical, military, or narcotic application. And while external parties rarely want to know the details, when it comes to pure, unfiltered creativity, Bakunin produces innovative solutions that simply aren't found anywhere else.

WEAPONS-GRADE MEMES

Nomad Memetic science is a finely-honed art form, with its foundations in rigorously tested social persuasion theories. While it isn't taught formally, most Bakunians have picked up the basics of Social Judgement Theory, the Elaboration Likelihood Model of Persuasion, the Extended Parallel Processing Model of Fear Appeals, and other compliance-gaining techniques around the same time that they were learning to walk.

Every Bakunian believes in the power of change. But those tasked with inciting change in the opinions of the Human Sphere know that while revolutions happen suddenly, persuasion is a more gradual process. These Machiavellian memes are designed to slip unnoticed into the cultural zeitgeist, seeding ideas, questioning assumptions, and doing it all with a wink and a smirk.

Of course, it also helps that Bakunin has its collective finger on the pulse of trends. Any attempts to copy their tactics or subvert their iconography tends to leave would-be hijackers left holding last year's fads. Most notably, ALEPH's attempts to subvert these memes have gone over with all the grace of a grandparent trying to use current slang and missing by a decade.

DEMOGRAPHICS AND CULTURE

Narrowing down a discussion of *Bakunin's* culture is a bit like finding a needle in a needle-stack. That's not to say that the ship lacks a cohesive identity, merely that to truly understand that identity, one must embrace the full spectrum of its iconoclastic rainbow.

COLLECTIVELY INDIVIDUAL

Nomads are among the most individualistic people in the Human Sphere. But even among their fellow Nomads, the Bakunian commitment to individuality stands out. Beyond the tourists, the spectacle, and the bright lights are the people who comprise *Bakunin*. And a more diverse collection of souls would be difficult to find.

Yet, despite this religious commitment to individuality, there is a definite solidarity, an *esprit de corps*, as it were. Bakunians think of themselves as individuals first and foremost, but that doesn't preclude membership in a larger group. Many Bakunians largely define themselves by group associations, and it's not uncommon for a citizen to think of themselves as an individual who is also part of a module, but also a Bakunian, and finally, a Nomad. The order can vary, but the hierarchy doesn't preclude strong feelings of attachment and belonging to the various groups. Rather, it provides them with context.

The *prioritised* — some would say fetishised — role of the individual in Bakunian society is its essential building block, but to imply that *Bakunin* lacks a cohesive identity would be disingenuous. The Mothership has an identity. It's just a messy hodgepodge of seemingly-contradictory elements, somehow persisting despite itself. Kind of like *Bakunin*.

BALANCED ON A BLEEDING EDGE: DAILY LIFE IN BAKUNIN

To the rest of the Human Sphere, *Bakunin* is a destination, an exotic, wondrous, almost alien thing. But to those who live and work there, it's simply home. Exciting, sure. But the exotic is commonplace when you live somewhere nicknamed "The Neon Bazaar."

AUTONOMOUS COMMUNES

The building blocks of Bakunian culture, the Mothership's modules form the core of its multiphasic national identity. Inside a given module, reality is whatever the members of the commune say it is. Sometimes literally: VR-primary communes paint virtual worlds for their members to inhabit, conjuring up a home environment quite unlike the rest of the ship (or the Human Sphere, for that matter).

However, most communes are refuges of thought, rather than environment. Want to live in an egalitarian consociational state that doesn't legally recognise the construct of gender? Maybe you'd prefer a "might makes right" kraterocracy, where decisions are made by those strong enough to seize power for themselves? Or perhaps you just want a place where you can gather with other members of your religion and actually live by the tenets of your faith? Whatever your desire, *Bakunin* probably has a module for you; and if not, you could always campaign to start a new one.

THE BATTLEGROUND OF IDEAS

While *Bakunin's* modules present unrivalled opportunity for expression, they also present a unique challenge when stepping into the core: at no point in human history has such a multicultural metropolis been attempted, and the dynamic between core and commune ensures that significant homogenisation is unlikely to occur. *Bakunin* prides itself on its manifold heterogeneity, though the balancing act between different cultures can sometimes feel like a tightrope walk across a razor blade.

The Social Energy system helps regulate the interactions between groups and factions on *Bakunin* by introducing both social and economic repercussions for public behaviour that's perceived as unhealthy. There's also always the opportunity to return to one's module where your rivals' governmental philosophies have no impact on your personal life, and this has lent an unexpectedly civil tone to many discussions. Indeed, *Bakunin* is one of the few places in all the Human Sphere where members of fundamentally incompatible beliefs can regularly discuss them with any modicum of civility. As it turns out, it's much easier to remain calm when one's life and liberty are not — and cannot — be at stake.

LOUD AND PROUD

If there is an underrepresented philosophy in *Bakunin,* it is likely to be moderation, though even that can still be found. From fashion, to music, to cuisine, what passes for understated on *Bakunin* would be considered unconscionably vibrant in the rest of the Human Sphere. As the performer's eyes adjust to the spotlight, so too does the Bakunian's tastes calibrate towards a volume of expression that would leave others deafened.

PLAYTEST TIP
TOURIST PRICES
Non-Nomad characters can be attractive targets for Bakunian hucksters. Spending Heat to indicate that a character's been "Marked"— doubling the effects of any Tariffs rolled when making purchases — can provide a unique challenge for characters to navigate

SHIP EXPANSION
The physical structure of *Bakunin* has always existed in a state of slow but constant changes. Recently, there's a particular change causing concern: *Bakunin* is rapidly running out of space. Historically, new modules were formed by "remora" ships or other affiliated vessels incorporating themselves to the Mothership's construction or the occasional revamping of existing or abandoned modules. But it's fast becoming too unwieldy to travel on the Circulars, forcing would-be expansions to get increasingly creative.

Limit your population to a couple hundred citizens, and you can get just about anything to work."

— Lucius Aldington, Business Analyst for Hesperia Consulting. For *Confidentes Confidential*, a Mercury Media exclusive!

"Looking for the neon bazaar? My friend, you're on *Bakunin*. You're already here."

— A local, giving reliably Bakunian directions to a tourist. Overheard in VaudeVille.

AVERAGE DOESN'T EXIST: A BAKUNIAN DAY

Any discussion on the average Bakunian... well, it generally doesn't get very far before someone from Praxis butts their head in, wondering if you meant to imply the statistical mean, median, or mode. Discussion is constantly ongoing, often occurring in substrata patina cues, and that means getting up, exiting your module, and walking around the Mothership for a bit.

The divide between module and core can be sharp, though many modules tend to cluster around the front of their territory. It's like passing through a thousand different micro-cultures as you walk by. An ordinary stroll might take you past a group of communist utopians, discussing how best to seize the means of production in a philosophical sense. You might find yourself wading through a neo-anarchist protest that's blocked out the corridor, exchange nods, and be let through without issue — much to the chagrin of the Megacorporate executives still trapped on the balcony of their hotel. You might even pass a group of kids, some not yet in their double-digits, trying to assemble a railgun out of scavenged parts.

The little scamps.

While the research, production, and media fields are all big employers, most Bakunians work in client-facing industries. After the day's labour, it's common to relax with a quick stop on Sunset Boulevard, maybe picking up fresh seasonings for dinner from a local specialty shop. On your way home, you might stop to weigh in on some substrata conversations. Everything's on Arachne, of course, but the good stuff tends to be localised. Coming home means something different to everyone, but whether you're greeted by a half-dozen partners and your collectively adopted kids, a commune of like-minded roommates, or that rarest of all commodities on *Bakunin* — silence — it's a place uniquely suited to the individual's taste.

"If PanOceania is a tropical bird, then we're a peacock with its feathers dipped in phosphorous neon. Restraint is not an attractive trait in design. Or anywhere else, for that matter."

Philippe Delange, Fashion designer and creative director, LoroLocco. Interview with Go-Go Marlene, only on Oxyd!

MORLOCK GROUPS

For most Nomads, getting assigned to one of *Bakunin's* Morlock Groups is the furthest thing from a goal. Primarily comprised of the violent and antisocial and controlled by invasive MetaChemical compounds, the Morlock Groups are a colourful example of the Nomad's "waste not, want not" philosophy, brought to life in violent fashion. Here, the dregs of society can find a way to contribute to the welfare of the ship, even if it's just as cannon fodder. While many Chimera wear their time served as a badge of honour, it would be a stretch to assume that any of them wound up there on purpose.

For *Bakunin's* tiny-yet-growing Uplift population, it presents a unique opportunity to blend in. Sure, you might be a hulking boar hybrid, but there's a catgirl to your left, and the guy to your right's got gills. And as far as anyone knows, they were born human. The ability to contribute something to the ship, albeit under harsh conditions for little pay, appeals to many Uplifts. Most don't have any MetaChemistry alterations whatsoever. Turns out that they don't need them in order to behave, and their instincts are already violent enough as it is.

"I just want to put something to rest. The stories about this 'Robin Hook,' some kind of Rogue AI? Hero to the people? Steals from the rich, and looks out for the underclass? Look, it's a nice story, but that's all it is. A story. Fairy tale. We've seen Rogue AIs with slave bodies, or duplicates, whatever you want to call them, and Svengali's no joke. And even if there was a Robin Hook, we'd probably have to arrest her, and then you'd all riot. So, let me be clear on this: Robin Hook? Is. Not. Real. No such thing.

...She's right behind me, isn't she?"

— Moderator Chief Argot Winslow, holding a press conference while Robin Hook was, in fact, right behind them.

CIVIL DISORDER: POLICING BAKUNIN

The Moderator Corps don't have it easy. Tasked with maintaining a semblance of order in a society that revels in chaos, Moderators must not only uphold the laws of Core, but they also need to keep in mind the societal expectations that different Modules bring to the table. *Bakunin* isn't exactly overflowing with space, so if an incident can be resolved without having to throw anyone in jail, Moderators will give it a shot. Thus, communication, psychology, and cultural anthropology are often more important to a Moderator than criminology or investigation. More often than not, a punitive impact on citizens' Social Energy reputation is enough.

But not every dispute can be resolved peacefully. So, when talks break down or residents just aren't interested in dialog, the Moderator Corps isn't in the habit of pulling punches. Other societies might have separate police, anti-terrorism task forces, and militaries, but *Bakunin* has the Moderator Corps, and that's enough. While they sometimes draw on other groups for support — most notably the Observance and the Morlock Groups — each Moderator is more than capable of holding their own and is unlikely to be particularly fazed in the face of even the most bizarre criminal activities.

THE OBSERVANCE

Out of the plethora of religions have been founded, or found refuge, in *Bakunin*, perhaps none is so uniquely Bakunian as The Observance of Saint Mary of the Knife, Our Lady of Mercy. While not technically a cloistered order, they don't proselytise, and new members are put through gruelling, difficult trials. The order's roots are steeped in rebellion, radical interpretations of common assumptions, and a fanatical determination to stay true to themselves, regardless of the cost.

Most Nomads don't really understand them. *Bakunin* doesn't understand them either, but it doesn't have to: they're part of the family. Admittedly, the part you give a wide berth at holidays, but their fanatical hatred of ALEPH has proved invaluable in providing the quantronic security necessary for *Bakunin* to function.

THE ROLE OF THE OBSERVANCE

Ask your average Bakunian about the Observance, and you're likely to get a shrug. Sure, they're a scary blood cult, but there are dozens of those on *Bakunin*. The important thing is their role in the Mothership's cybersecurity. While most citizens don't have cause to interact with the hermetic cyberwitches, the Radical Mothership's live-and-let-live philosophy has afforded them a measure of respect on *Bakunin*. Even if that respect is offered at a healthy distance.

Many people assume that the Observance is a mono-gendered sect, which means their PR wing is working as intended. Through a combination of precedent, cultural inertia, and the faith's hyperfeminist ideology, the Observance is a female-exclusive sect, though not all of its members were born that way. They see power in the feminine divine: males simply cannot achieve purity or enlightenment, making them entirely unsuitable for membership in their sacred Sisterhood.

Ultimately, the Observance is open to anyone with the fortitude to endure their particular vision of pursuit of purity, including men, though their role in the Observance's cosmology is a particular one. The masochistic zealots known as Sin-Eater Observants are an exclusively masculine order. They seek purity and atonement through suffering, and while they're an important part of the

Observance's operational apparatus, they're never trusted to act in a leadership capacity.

In the Human Sphere's functionally gender-egalitarian society, the thought of a militant, mono-gendered sect of zealous militants can be an alien and frightening thought, one that the Observance uses to great effect. Superstitious terror comprises a major component of the Observance's strategic plan. In the war against ALEPH, any advantage could be meaningful, so every advantage is pursued.

Salvation isn't for everyone. Not when the spectre of ALEPH hangs over humanity's heads. Call them cultists, radicals, or dangerous terrorists; the Observance cares little. Their work is everything. And their work is far from done.

OBSERVANTS IN THE LIFEPATH

While creating an *Infinity* character, many things are randomly determined: but a character's sex and gender aren't among them. That said, there are no two ways about it: during their time in the Order, Observants are female, with the exception of Sin-Eater Observants, who are male. However, that says nothing about what biological sex the character was before — or after — their time in the career. This is *Bakunin* after all: sex reassignment surgery is hardly the most difficult medical procedure to come by.

To some people, things just come easy. That's certainly been true for Fabio Varese, whose genius touch with evolutionary supercomputers has given him the wealth and status to work on basically whatever he likes. So, whether it's designing amusement parks or Salyut Zonds for the NMF, any project with Varese's name attached instantly becomes a big deal, much to the chagrin of his fellow researchers. And while it would be a stretch to imply that most Rogue AIs are the result of his tinkering, that hasn't stopped a recent smear campaign from implying just that. But the allegations slide off of him like water from a duck's back, and rumour has it that his rivals are considering something more drastic....

NOTABLE DISTRICTS

While *Bakunin's* makeup is largely determined by its modules, there are some primary districts that merit special mention.

STANDARD DEVIATIONS: PRAXIS'S BLACK LABS

To paint all the Black Labs with a similar brush is a grave disservice. Technically speaking, kittens and *Jorōgumo* are both animals, but you wouldn't want to get them confused. In much the same way, two Labs might seem superficially similar, but looks can be deceiving. Each Lab operates under a shroud of mystery, jealously guarding its secrets, no matter how trivial. Membership often has more in common with initiatory occult traditions, terrorist cells, or secret societies than a typical research environment, but given that many come to Praxis trying to put their past behind them — whether it be criminal, Hypercorporate, or something darker — the cloaks and daggers suit them just fine.

The personnel of a given Lab can be as varied and mysterious as its organisational structure. Here, disgruntled corporate researchers rub shoulders with self-taught virtuosos, reclusive academics, anarcho-futurists, and mad thinkers of every conceivable stripe. Hailing from every corner of the Human Sphere, their work is mysterious, their process enigmatic, their methods arcane, but their results?

Unprecedented. Unexpected. Unparalleled, unequalled, and unconventional. Any strategic advantage, no matter how small, is worth its weight in gold to the Nomads. Ingenuity and innovation often come from unexpected sources. While some might not see the immediate link between efficient waste recycling and close-quarters TAG performance, the Nomads pride themselves on turning even the smallest innovations into competitive leads.

BESPOKE HORRORS

Praxis's Black Labs require a constant stream of funding to stay solvent, and many scientists have a morbid curiosity, a drive to see just what happens "if." Thus, custom-ordered creatures are something of a staple of the Black Labs. From grotesquely mutated gang muscle, to hybridised "guard dogs," as long as someone can pay, Praxis is willing to make their dreams — or nightmares — come true.

Most famous among these are the Pupniks, demi-uplifted human-animal hybrids. Animal uplift research has made exponential strides, recently exploding in discovery, but its history is littered with failed prototypes, dead ends, and stunted, brutish mutants. Thus are the roots of the first Pupniks. Today, Pupniks are manufactured to a precise degree, with their intelligence being deliberately stunted to ensure that they can legally be treated as property, but with increasingly humanoid figures. Kept as sentries, used as cage fighters in gambling rings, or kept for more personal uses — some of which are improbably dark — Pupniks are a favourite status symbol among *Bakunin's* Submondo kingpins, precisely because of how uncomfortable they tend to make people.

VAUDEVILLE: A DESTINATION LIKE NO OTHER

Like a neighbourhood that's always having a street fair, the sprawling district known as VaudeVille must be experienced to be truly appreciated. The primary attraction for tourists, VaudeVille is technically part of the Core, and the shops, kiosks, hotels, and public areas that comprise the district have a Balkanised feel with different Modules providing their own spin on the VaudeVille experience.

Walk a few metres, and things can radically change, yet it somehow all works together, like a sanitised microcosm of the ship itself, a unique blend of experiences unlike anything else in the Human Sphere. VaudeVille is more than a shopping and entertainment district; it's the cultural heart of *Bakunin*, snaking its way through the Mothership, refusing to be confined to any given neighbourhood.

VaudeVille is the epicentre of avant-garde, the soul of haute couture, and the destination of choice for *bon vivants*, bohemians, and expressive visionaries of every stripe. The bleeding edge of self-expression — sometimes quite literally — VaudeVille is where boundaries are pushed, limits are broken, and tomorrow's hottest trends find their footing in a test environment, a sort of beta environment for popular culture.

BLACK MARKETS AND BOUBOUTIQUES

Just about anything can be bought in VaudeVille provided you know who to talk to. Visitors looking for the address of its Black Markets are doomed to frustration. The Black Markets aren't a place you go, they're a parallel economy, woven directly into the fabric of VaudeVille. Just about every place of business in the district has a "secret menu" of sorts, where discerning customers can acquire just about anything. Black Market Resurrections, Concilium Accord-violating arms and armaments, pet mutants, or designer MetaChemicals — very little is truly off-limits here.

Nowhere is this truer than in the BouBoutiques, facilities specialising in body modifications of every type imaginable, and the destination of choice for those truly wishing to express themselves through a physical canvas. To many, this is a godsend. For those suffering from Body Dysmorphic Disorder, Gender Dysphoria, or simply looking to overcome physical disabilities or limitations, modification often represents their best chance at a normal life. For others, augmentation provides an opportunity to express themselves, to stand out from the crowd. For others still, the allure of starting a trend, and the subsequent stardom that follows, proves impossible to resist. And of course, some are just bored, and looking to stir things up a little.

However, they come by the desire, they eventually feel the inexorable pull of VaudeVille. Whether circumventing religious or political red tape, directly defying their local authorities, or simply seeking out the very best in the field, people from every corner of the Human Sphere flock to the BouBoutiques, who famously welcome all...so long as they can pay. And while the price can be high in more ways than one, there's little dispute as to the quality of the work provided. A good BouBoutique sculpts bodies into living works of art, hailing from their client's strangest dreams, wildest fantasies, and weirdest nightmares. The sky is not the limit — again, that would be the bank account — and rival BouBoutiques are constantly pushing the envelope of what's possible.

GENETIC THERAPY

Gene modification is ubiquitous throughout the Human Sphere. Outside of Ariadna, very few children are born without some degree of genetic alteration. A time-tested, proven methodology, gene therapy is safe, reliable, and predictable. There are, however, some limitations.

Firstly, and primarily, is Silk. Originally designed as a vector for gene therapy, there's still no better way to tweak a subject's DNA than via Silk courier strands. Any procedure relying on an expensive and rare biogenic substance is bound to be expensive and slow. Even assuming a best-case scenario — a locker full of Silk, and no waiting list — the process of genetic alteration in an adult host is, by necessity, carried out at a ponderous pace. Even relatively minor cosmetic alterations are best handled gradually, and dramatic effects exponentially increase the wait time from weeks to months, sometimes years.

AUGMENTED SOLDIERS

While Haqqislam's biomedical research produces the finest super soldiers that conventional science can offer, the Black Labs are anything but conventional.

Given the friendly relationship between the two factions, one might expect to see more collaboration, but the methods used in Praxis tend to be a non-starter for Haqqislam.

"Adrenaline. Sex. Danger. The streets of VaudeVille are positively dripping with possibilities. It's an adventure with every step! To live in *Bakunin* is to live in overdrive. And I love it!"

Go-Go Marlene, interactive trendwatching Mayacast. Only on Oxyd!

While accelerants do exist, they're more likely to trigger anaphylactic shock in the subject than meaningfully speed up the process. Anyone willing to take on risk for a faster, more dramatic effect, is probably using a biotech graft.

BIOTECH GRAFTS

In contrast to gene therapy, biotech grafts offer virtually limitless customisation, even more dramatic effects, and a faster turnaround period. The process of surgically attaching body parts is a centuries-old medical tradition, though its cosmetic applications are a decidedly Bakunian innovation. Under normal circumstances, receiving a biotech graft is a fairly routine surgery, practiced all across the Human Sphere. Vat-grown body parts are genetically tweaked to better match the host's DNA, reducing risk of rejection, and otherwise tailored to the desired effect.

VaudeVille, however, is not known for normal circumstances.

Cat ears, prehensile tails, retractable claws. The selection of "off-the-rack" options is wildly different from what you might see in corporate clinics. And though the process may seem similar to conventional augmentation procedures, the wildly exotic nature of these grafts means DNA-matching treatments are all but impossible and rejection prophylaxis becomes significantly more important. In theory, this should be perfectly safe. With a combination of immunosuppressants, Silk-delivered genetic integration therapy, and common-sense health precautions, even the most alien of biografts can be successfully integrated with little-to-no side effects.

In practice, asking a VaudeVillian to take it easy — remembering to take their medication, and completely abstaining from alcohol, narcotics, most stimulants, and sexual activity of any sort — is an exercise in futility. For many, these augmentations represent their ticket out of poverty, their chance at a better life. And for the residents of *Bakunin*'s many ghettos, a sterile, disease-free environment is simply asking too much. Those who turned to the underworld to finance their augmentations may not have much of a choice in the matter. Prostitution and bloodsports are a common landing point. But of course, there's only one way to truly avoid side-effects, and that's to get an entirely new body.

CUSTOMISED LHOSTS

Vat-grown bodies, bespoke biomorphs, and industrial-grade neomaterial frames. With the exception of the odd Siren-class Lhost — usually acquired via dubious means — most BouBoutiques don't carry finished Lhosts, preferring instead to custom-tailor their creations on a client-by-client basis. While there are certainly resurrection clinics in Praxis that can provide more conventional services, a BouBoutique is first and foremost an artistic endeavour, its designers' artistes. Freed from societal constraints, and given the ultimate canvas, BouBoutique artisans can transform their clients into just about anything imaginable, provided they can pay. And make no mistake, acquiring a customised Lhost is a painstakingly detailed and excruciatingly expensive process, but for the truly dedicated, there is simply no substitute.

No matter how fantastical, unearthly, or impractical the request, the sky is the limit. BouBoutiques will happily transform customers into the figure of their dreams, or someone else's nightmares. Usually a bit of both.

THE ULTRAVIOLET QUARTER

When the shopping's done, the shows are over, and the artificial sky over Sunset Boulevard twinkles with stars, there's another side of *Bakunin* to be seen. Though this is strictly metaphorically as the Ultraviolet Quarter is open for business around the clock.

SUNSET BOULEVARD

Bakunin may be billed as "the ship that never sleeps," but just like every other space habitat, on-board time is structured in twelve-hour cycles, providing a natural circadian cycle for its inhabitants. Unlike most sidereal vessels however, *Bakunin* takes the concept of night life quite seriously. When the clock strikes 20:00, the ship-wide artificial daylight recedes, but the iridescent lights of VaudeVille shine all the brighter.

Nowhere is this more pronounced than on Sunset Boulevard. The main district of Vaudeville, and the centre of spectacle, grandiosity, and wonder for *Bakunin* — and perhaps the entire Human Sphere — the Boulevard celebrates and revels in nightfall, and nobody celebrates like VaudeVille. Every evening, in what is perhaps *Bakunin*'s most famous spectacle, the sky-blue dome of the district melts into an artistically rendered sunset. Blazing oranges sear into red and yellow haze, watercolour splashes of violet and blue drip across the simulated horizon, as shafts of iridescent light dance across the neomaterial chrome of the boulevard, and the gathered crowds quietly drink it in.

A moment of Zen.

For one, perfect instant, the district comes together to enjoy the show. Artists, vagabonds, misfits, tourists, and outlaws of every stripe gather to observe this uniquely Bakunian spectacle. Bars, restaurants, hotels, and apartments, every building in the district has a glorious view of the show. Nomads typically consider this the perfect time to sit back, relax, and share a drink with whoever happens to be nearby. In a place as fantastical as VaudeVille, sunset is the most romanticised event of all — the perfect moment, that magical instant, where anything can happen, and dreams can come true.

No travel agency uses actual footage of the UV in a holo-brochure. While plenty of tourists think that they want to embrace the transgressive, not everyone is going to be ready for the reality of the Ultraviolet Quarter. Putting conventional red-light districts to shame, the UV goes above and beyond what any other part of the Human Sphere has on offer.

While it's treated more like a district, technically the UV is a module complete with its own laws and ordinances. Nobody's going to enter by accident, and those without a healthy bank account — or hard cash on-hand — are politely turned away at the remarkably unremarkable checkpoints. In the UV, you can get your hands on just about anything for the right price, but they don't take credit. If would-be patrons want to do business with the predatory loan sharks circling around neighbouring modules, well, that's their mistake to make.

Inside its walls, the transformation is revelatory. There's a saying: "everything's legal under Black Light." And while that's not entirely true, the Plutocratic Commune provides a great deal of leeway. Thus, it stands to reason that just about anything could take place in the UV, provided that it's sufficiently profitable. And this is absolutely the case.

The Ultraviolet Quarter is an unapologetic celebration of raw anarcho-capitalism, and unrestrained vice including prostitution, gambling, gladiatorial death matches, experimental narcotics that even VaudeVille's Black Market won't sell. The UV boasts collectively bargained standard rates of pay for most activities, illustrating the transactional nature of the district. Even the smallest exchange is likely governed by a Tunguskan smart contract, if not also a shadow contract.

EVERYTHING HAS A PRICE

Not everyone who goes into the district comes out, at least, not officially. Smugglers of all sorts operate out of the UV, including those who deal in people. Those looking to cover their tracks, mislead a pursuer, or otherwise vanish for a while can willingly participate in the district's thriving human trafficking trade, and many do just that. Others are a bit more cautious. Although *Bakunin's* distaste for slavery is well-known, many are understandably hesitant to trust their continued freedom, health, and well-being to people who literally put a price on everything.

In the Ultraviolet District, every person, possession, and piece of property is automatically assigned a *wergild* — a financial valuation of their worth — which is paid in reparations should damages occur. Based on Social Energy, publicly available

financial data, and whatever dirt their hackers can dig up, absolutely everything in the UV has an LAI-calculated *wergild,* updated in real-time. Visitors are no exception, underscoring the cold, hard reality of the UV: everyone and everything has a price, whether they like it or not. And absolutely everything is for sale.

TWEAKS, CHIMERA, AND OTHER BIOMORPHS

Few social movements are so thoroughly Bakunian as Biomorphing. A riff on transhumanism unlikely to exist anywhere else in the Human Sphere — even among other Nomads — Biomorphs aren't unified in appearance, motivation, goals, or location. Yet, they remain linked by a bond that has proven nigh-impossible to break. If the Nomad Nation is a gathering of extremists and outcasts, and *Bakunin* are the misfits of the bunch, what does it say that Biomorphs find themselves on the fringes of even the Radical Mothership?

Even so, most Nomads can't help but respect anyone so committed to an idea that they undergo irreversible, transformative surgery. Even if it makes no sense to them, there's no denying that Biomorphs possess considerable conviction in their beliefs. And if that means that they wind up with cat ears, ram horns, and a rabbit tail? Well, it takes all kinds.

MOTIVATIONS

Why do people become Biomorphs? The answers are as varied as their appearance. As with tattoos, piercings, augmentations, or other less-dramatic body modifications, many reasons exist. Some are looking to stand out in a crowd. Others believe, right or wrong, that the change will help them professionally, or to gain acceptance in an insular social circle. And for some, it's about feeling at home in their own skin, a complicated issue in a complicated society. But like anything else in *Bakunin*, it's the loudest voices that tend to get the most attention. And while all Biomorphs can get pretty loud, Chimera can be deafening by any standard.

While some have used the term to describe any Biomorph, a Chimera is quite literally an altogether different beast. Moving past the cosmetic, a Chimera's Biomorphing is radical, transformative, and often quite dangerous. Combat augmentations, untested xenografts, unchecked metachemical enhancements, and a bevy of other untested and

ULTRAVIOLET SECURITY

"What happens under Black Lights disappears once the lights come on," or so the saying goes. Marketing aside, it's important that the quarter can ensure the privacy of its clientele, if for no other reason than to maintain the proprietary nature of any blackmail acquired. Tunguskan infowarriors, augmented (or Uplifted) muscle, and the best mercenaries that money, blackmail, or a hefty discount can buy — the UV spares no expense in preserving their business model.

"Biomorphing: the catch-all term for radical host modification. Basically, if someone's cosmetically modded themselves past the point of what could ever occur in nature, they're a Biomorph. Related sobriquets include:

Chimera: illegally combat-modified humans, often fiercely animalistic in appearance... and behaviour

Tweaks: individuals with obvious — but limited — inhuman features. Given *Bakunin's* preoccupation with cats, feline eyes, ears, and/or tails are a common expression" — Traveller's guide to *Bakunin*, third edition.

BIOMORPHS, DOG-BLOODS, AND FITTING IN

Most Dogfaces have never been outside of Ariadna, let alone off of Dawn. So, to say that relatively few Wulvers or Dogfaces have ever set foot on *Bakunin* would be putting it mildly. However, the few times that it has happened, it's been a revelation.

Having spent their whole lives as an ostracised minority, a Dogface on *Bakunin* is not only spared the gawking, the staring, the fear and whispers, they might not even be the strangest-looking person on the street. Most get confused for Chimera and aren't in a hurry to correct the mistake. If nothing else, it's exponentially easier to find a tailor who can not only deal with your size and likelihood to get into fights, but also has experience making pants for people with tails.

CHIMERA DREAMS

"Am I human? What does that even mean? To accept the traits you're born with? We haven't done that for generations. To look human? Humanity is a spectrum, and Chimera embody every point on the gradient, and more. Besides, is humanity supposed to be intrinsically superior, when we stand shoulder-to-shoulder with Helots and Tohaa?

So, what am I? A sapient being. My frame is androgynous, my mind is my own, and my body transcends antiquated notions of humanity. I am something new, something different, and something uniquely, unequivocally mine. I am more than human. I am Chimera. And that cannot be taken away from me."

— Shine Antique, transhuman activist, performance artist, and of course, Chimera.

THE TRAVELING CIRCUS: BAKUNIAN INTERFACTIONAL RELATIONS

Every Faction has its own unique relationship with the Nomads. And nobody does "unique" quite like *Bakunin*.

Ariadna: On one hand, the freedom-loving USAriadnans see a lot of themselves in the individualistic Bakunians. On the other hand, when the two meet, it's been described as "anaphylactic culture shock," and they have even less in common with the rest of Ariadna. Still, there's a mutual respect between the two, forged in telling the rest of the galaxy to get stuffed.

Haqqislam: Long-time allies, the ideological battles between Praxis and Bourak are almost as numerous as the medical advances that occur when the two partner up. Haqqislam knows that it can always count on *Bakunin* when it's time to try something truly reckless; look through some of the Hassassins' most audacious operations, and you'll find a *Bakunian* with a Cheshire grin, along for the ride.

PanOceania: No fun. Though the countless PanOceanian citizens who patronise *Bakunin's* tourism industry seem to like it well enough.

Yu Jing: Somehow, even less fun than PanOceania, a feat that is both impressive and infuriating. The Party flies in the face of the Radical Mothership's most sacred ideals. Both parties can agree on one thing though: if the other died in a fire, that'd be great.

ALEPH: The most commonly volunteered opinion is hysterical laughter, peppered with creative cursing. More poignant criticisms revolve around ALEPH's painting all Nomads with the same brush, when radical differences exist between Bakunian modules, let alone with their fellow Motherships. But beyond the bitter conflict, most Bakunians don't see ALEPH as being all that special. After all, what's the difference between ALEPH, and a Rogue AI like Svengali, if not infrastructure?

Well, that, and the fact that Svengali's honest about its criminal intentions.

O-12: Bakunians actually have a lot of sympathy for O-12; it's like playing Moderator for the entire Human Sphere. Not the most enviable task. For its part, Bureau Noir has found its share of useful assets on *Bakunin*, though it can prove to be more trouble than it's worth.

unstable alterations to their hosts are par for the course. Often packing mods that are illegal pretty much everywhere except *Bakunin* — and restricted even on the Radical Mothership — Chimera are self-engineered to be the brightest stars in the sky.

Of course, rising stars are rarely as bright as falling ones.

Ultimately, there's as much tragedy as there is opportunity. Novelty and attractiveness are a potent combination for anyone looking to over-clock their career in media. Chimera combine exotic looks, undeniable swagger, and a raw, dangerous edge, excellent ingredients for any budding star. Unfortunately, there's only so much room at the top. And while some people will do absolutely anything to be famous, it's still no guarantee of success. Thus, many Chimera who hoped to achieve fame and renown can often be found in the Ultraviolet Quarter, taking whatever kind of work they can find: prostitution, deathmatch fighting, or if they're lucky, exotic bodyguards.

It's not all doom and gloom, however. One of the benefits of living in the Nomad Nation is that there's always an opportunity around the corner. And it's not that nobody cares what you look like — Nomads are as opinionated as anyone else, often more so — but getting the job done will always take priority. Thus, while a disproportionate number of Chimera can be found acting as "booth babes" at VaudeVille kiosks, they also count engineers, NMF soldiers, and countless other professions among their number.

MOTHERSHIP: CORREGIDOR

> "Ugh. It's like a prison and a warehouse had an ugly baby. It smells like antifreeze and gym socks. When do we head to *Bakunin*?"
>
> — Go-Go Marlene. Unauthorised behind-the-scenes footage, surreptitiously released on Arachne.

Space is cold. It doesn't care who your parents are, what degrees you have, or how much is in your bank account. Given half a chance, the uncaring vacuum of space will snuff out any life it comes across. To Corregidorans, life is a series of transactions, a philosophy they've internalised far more than even the bankers of *Tunguska*, or the most unrestrained capitalist module on *Bakunin*. Because on *Corregidor*, these economics are not a matter of philosophy, nor ambition, but rather one of survival.

freighter and the hyper-crowded slums of modern terrestrial cities, *Corregidor's* interior is a testament to efficiency. While it can look cruelly spartan to outsiders, the reality of life among the stars has led Corregidorans to treasure every cubic centimetre of space and waste nothing.

The result is a stark, efficient landscape with little effort spent on frivolity. Except for the VaudeVille-designed "Solidarity Dome" in the Neck, visitors will find no public parks in *Corregidor,* no sculptures, and no free-standing benches. Any seemingly extraneous element is undoubtedly an attempt to dress up a bit of functionality. Thus, a bulky power converter in the middle of a walkway becomes a "heated bench," a necessary element that incidentally radiates bright light is elevated becoming a "streetlight," and so on. What can look haphazard to the casual observer is nothing more than *Corregidor's* famous pragmatism at work.

CLIMATE AND TOPOGRAPHY

Bakunin is a chaotic, jury-rigged neon carnival, and *Tunguska* is an enclave of brushed alloys and smooth bevels. *Corregidor*, however, is neo-brutalism writ chunkily large. Somewhere between the blocky utilitarianism of an industrial

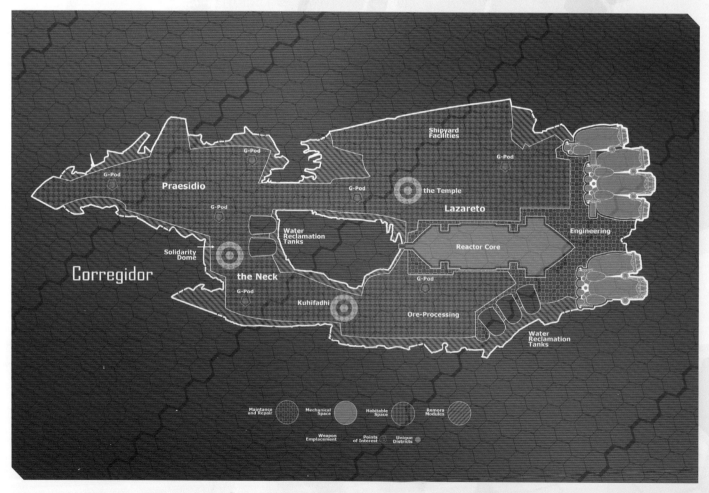

In general, the neo-penal construction of the Mothership prioritises function over form, and then prioritises function again, just to be sure. Heavy tungsten alloys make up the flooring, walls, and ceilings of the bulkhead jungle in a stark, brutal landscape, where strength is a necessity, space is at a premium, and optimism is a luxury few make time for. The people who proudly call *Corregidor* home would have it no other way.

HOUSING

Ironically, in space, personal space is at a premium. *Corregidor* was never truly designed to sustain a population of this size. While getting an exact census on Nomads is an exercise in futility, Corregidorans tend to think in terms of "enough room" and "not enough room."

They haven't really had enough room for generations.

In response, Corregidorans are remarkably efficient with what space they do have. *Corregidor's* residential cabins seem more like military barracks or prison cells than a row of apartments. Newer districts call to mind the unholy offspring of industrial warehouse design and megaslums — like Earth's old Kowloon Walled City, albeit much tidier. However, a closer look reveals that most Corregidorans are studiously neat. Clutter is a luxury reserved for those with more elbow room. Even the slums are far cleaner than their counterparts, more like a greasy machine shop than the archetypical "bad neighbourhood."

Inside, most Corregidoran homes continue the spartan trend. Beds fold up into walls, turning a sleeping space into a public one. Garments are vacuum-sealed when not in use, and individual toiletries are eschewed in favour of multipurpose compounds, anything to free up a few more cubic centimetres. Since more than half the ship is usually out on assignment at any given time, many workers rent flats as a group, with whoever's currently residing on the ship getting the bunks. Two Corregidorans can technically be roommates for years and never meet, and many change residences frequently. For them, home is where you set down for the night, like backpackers moving within one massive hostel.

Personal privacy on *Corregidor* is an alien concept. Some homes have thin screens dividing different sections, but many don't bother. Modesty is likewise a casualty of overcrowding. If someone doesn't want to hoof it to a restroom stall to change, they're probably doing it in sight of a family member or roommate. For Corregidorans, this is neither embarrassing nor titillating. As the saying goes, "Only outsiders stare." These lessons are culturally ingrained in Corregidorans, which has the bonus of easing the transition from civilian life into military and work teams.

"G-TIME"

Some parts of the Mothership — such as large sections of Lazareto — are generally kept weightless when not in navigation burns. Seatbelts adorn most furniture, and everything from storefronts to restrooms is designed with an eye to three-dimensional space. Visitors might easily come away with the impression that Corregidorans spend their lives in a state of perpetual weightlessness, which raises the question: if they exist in a constant state of microgravity, how in the world are they so hardy?

PERSONAL EFFECTS

Except tools and clothing, most Corregidorans keep personal belongings to a minimum. Possessions are almost exclusively limited to software of one sort or another. Belongings that include something without obvious practical use likely mean tremendous sentimental value. Given the space constraints, most home decoration involves rugs, tapestries, or other flat, durable accoutrements, often with Spartan AR overlays. Fibre arts are a popular hobby regardless of gender, and many children create customised decorations for "their" section of wall.

"*Corregidor's* resources are tightly managed out of necessity, it seems. I'm confident that the Warden has detailed population records. They'd have to. However, getting them to share that information has been like pulling teeth from a bear.

Without tools. While covered in honey.

Suffice it to say, population figures aren't publicly available. But ask anyone on-board, and they'll point out that half the ship's population is off-board right now, maybe more. And that seems to be the norm. So, what if *Corregidor* ever had to house its entire compliment of citizens at the same time? If it were anywhere else, I'd tell you they wouldn't all fit. But having seen the place first-hand, I'm confident they'd find some way to pack 'em in."

— Mei Li Silva, *Loĝanto Confidente*. Proprietary report for Hesperya Consulting.

CORREGIDORAN FAUNA

Corregidor has little non-sapient life on board. Unlike *Bakunin's* need for experiments, or *Tunguska's* relative fondness for luxuries, Corregidorans and animals don't usually mix. Between space constraints, resource scarcity, and the fact that most domesticated creatures do very poorly in microgravity, *Corregidor* is all but devoid of animal life.

One notable exception to this is arachnids, spiders in particular. Prospectors, work teams, and mercenaries are constantly coming and going between *Corregidor* and various alien biomes. Insectoid stowaways are an inevitable side effect. These unwanted guests can spread disease, ruin food supplies, and otherwise be a nuisance. But spiders? Spiders keep to themselves, eat pests, and are generally only a problem when provoked. Regular infusions of arachnid predators helps keep the bug population from getting out of hand.

Being the closest thing they could have to pets growing up, spiders tend to hold a special place in the hearts of Corregidoran children. Outside of the rare arachnophobe, most citizens avoid harming the creatures if they can help it. Due to their toughness, adaptability, and general resilience to the hazards of living on a ship, the little weavers have become something of an unofficial Corregidoran mascot, with spider motifs proving increasingly popular as the younger generation comes of age.

TRI-BEAM VILLAGE

Seeming cramped at the best of times, *Corregidor* has to get creative during a Krug. For the last few, that's meant three large vessels manoeuvring in close proximity and synchronised rotation. The addition of rapid, temporary constructions effectively creates a "bubble zone" that smaller ships can embrace to erect temporary villages in the middle of space. Protected from micrometeorites by the larger vessels, "Tri-Beam Village" provides temporary housing for the influx of residents and guests.

CORREGIDORAN FLORA

There isn't much in the way of publicly visible plant life on the Mothership. Importing food is often more space-efficient than growing it, and space on its hydroponic plantation decks is extremely limited. While it's hardly ideal, the psychological importance of being able to survive without imports — even if it's only for a short time — is difficult to overstate.

Agave is by far the most common type of plant life aboard *Corregidor*. While its nectar provides a steady supply of sweetener, its popularity likely has more to do with distillation to make tequila. Outside of these distinctive succulents, *Corregidor* is all but devoid of plant life when compared to the other Motherships.

"You're seriously telling me how to do my job? Kid, you couldn't do my job on your best day. Run home to your little office. Adults are at work."

— Brock Zúñiga, Meteor Head. Endearing himself to the new foreman, Asteroid X-3970.

Two words: Gravity Time.

Sections of the Mothership are designed to be rotated to create artificial gravity of varying strength. Every day, citizens have a mandatory fitness quota they need to fulfil. Everyone works up a good sweat under some G-forces during the usual morning calisthenics, thereby combating negative effects of weightlessness such as muscle loss or skeletal deterioration. While it's technically a punishable offense to skip your mandatory Gravity Time (or G-Time, as it's colloquially known), social pressure and unpleasant side effects are more than enough to compel most people to hit their weekly quotas. Anyone skipping out is likely to suffer the effects when the ship enters full burn.

However, there's nothing stopping people from taking it farther. Subsections of the Mothership can spin up some truly impressive gravitational forces. Soldiers are required to train in excess of Svalarheima's 1.6g environment, sometimes going as high as 1.8 to 2.0g, and it's not uncommon to see everyone from labourers and mercenaries to priests and bureaucrats taking advantage of the G-Pods for intense strength training.

ECONOMY

Corregidor's labour force never stays in one place for long, and brings valuable skill, expertise, and experience to any job. Of course, their willingness to take jobs that others can't — or won't — plays a role, as does their willingness to accept payment in a variety of under-the-table formats, allowing many corps to enjoy significant profit margins while skirting costly regulations.

This is hardly uncontroversial. Many corps use their workers' quasi-legal status to throw their weight around, and use of undocumented Nomad labour is a favourite target of political rhetoric. Even so, their use is virtually ubiquitous in the field of heavy industry. Trying to get a large-scale project off the ground without Nomad workers is definitely playing the game on hard mode.

Despite their obvious skill, relatively few Corregidorans have been brought on by corps or other governments to work in-house. Something about years of trying to kill them off has left most citizens dubious of outsiders to say the least. So while they're happy to take the money, most meteor heads wouldn't consider leaving the Nomads, no matter how good the offer is. Thus, most Corregidorans make their living as independent contractors.

MINING

Mining is in *Corregidor's* DNA. Its early crew of cast-offs and convicts were relegated to taking whatever jobs they could find, and some of the convicts even had experience doing hard labour in African mines. Mining was one of the few legitimate trade skills that the nascent Mothership had in ample supply.

Today, citizens still bring a mix of savvy and toughness that the big mining corps find indispensable. Despite lacking the resources to set up its own large-stake mining operations, *Corregidor* is the Human Sphere's premier supplier of independent contractors, prospectors, and other mining technicians.

Media portrayals of miners are often ripped straight from 19th century history and given a modern sheen. But, *Corregidor's* miners don't swing around pickaxes any more than *Tunguska's* bankers rely on abacuses, or *Bakunin's* doctors — the accredited ones anyway — use leeches. (Not that you couldn't find someone in VaudeVille willing to try.)

Instead, modern mining is more about the process of setting up, guiding, and maintaining automated equipment. It almost never occurs planetside, instead harvesting the Human Sphere's mineral-rich asteroids. While the technology exists to create powerful automated mining structures, the cost in deploying them far outweighs the potential reward in most circumstances. So rather than construct expensive station-grade mining operations, only to abandon them in a matter of years, if not months, it's much more economical to use lightweight, repurposed equipment, and pay miners to set up, maintain, and operate the equipment.

The work, though, is not only hazardous, but also requires technical expertise. LAI-run automated operations have typically been fool's gold, labouring for years without producing results, and needing just as much maintenance in the end. The most successful of these wasn't even what it appeared, as the Rogue AI Svengali had taken over operations and was not only running a successful mining operation but subsidising it through a lucrative smuggling business as well.

Being on the cutting edge of extraplanetary mining, however, is anything but safe for the Corregidorans. During the Helicon Miner's Revolt, workers were brutalised, people died, and the regulations came too late to benefit the original miners. Still, the Human Sphere is hungry for ore, and *Corregidor* is happy to feed the need. But no one should be surprised when Corregidoran Assault Commandos, colloquially known as *Intruders*, embed themselves in work crews, just in case.

PROSPECTORS

Freelance prospectors working individually or in teams provide reach and flexibility that doesn't require mobilising an entire mining operation for a comparatively small vein. In exchange, freelancers typically enjoy the steady work and pay that comes with working for a big company.

Still, that doesn't mean there's no place for solo miners or small teams. Anyone who gets their hands on a small driller-freighter can try their luck among the stars. But, they'd better be lucky indeed. It's not easy finding a minable vein in an asteroid that can be legally mined that is both lucrative enough to be worth the time and small enough that a single person or small crew can manage to extract value on their own.

These prospectors live a life of adventure, but it's hardly a glamorous one. For every success story, there are dozens who barely make enough to cover fuel costs, and dozens more who lose everything in search of hidden treasure. Like compulsive gamblers, many prospectors keep chasing that elusive big score until it bleeds them dry. Still, it's one of the last great frontiers. Anyone with enough grit, sense, and stubbornness has a chance to control their own destiny. For many Corregidorans, that's enough.

CONSTRUCTION & REPAIR

Repair, construction, demolition, and excavation. If something can't be safely automated, or it's easier to simply hire out to independent contractors, *Corregidor* usually gets the job. With more satellites, orbitals, and large spacecraft in operation than at any other time in humanity's history, there's a lot of wrenches being turned in microgravitational environments. And nobody works in zero-g like a Meteor Head.

As with mining, however, the same financial incentives that make hiring Corregidorans attractive can also lead to the hazardous conditions that have plagued the Mothership's workers since its inception. That Corregidorans are more likely to survive dangerous conditions doesn't make them any safer, though many a corporate executive argued that exact point. Either way, space is full of busted stuff, and someone's got to fix it. More often than not, that someone calls *Corregidor* home.

MERCENARIES

A Corregidoran standby. In the early days of the Mothership, its bills were largely paid by exporting nasty, brutish criminals to commit disturbing acts of violence at the behest of paying customers. A lot has changed over the years, though. *Corregidor* has

BOUNTY HUNTERS

In addition to its mercenary teams, *Corregidor* proudly boasts the largest number of bounty hunters per capita in the Human Sphere. When it comes to tracking down notorious gang bosses, nobody sports a better success rate than *Corregidor's* rough-and-tumble hunters. Any Submondo with a sufficient price on their head knows how to cover their tracks on Maya, and most can even manage the same in Arachne.

Thus, anyone planning on bringing them in needs to get their boots on the ground and do some good old-fashioned Psyop legwork. It's precisely this sort of situation where Corregidoran bounty hunters thrive. Most gang members can spot a cop from a mile away, with the right augmentations, sometimes literally. Straight-laced, professional law officers are likely to find more frustration than leads when hunting their prey. On the other hand, a Corregidoran hunter flags as a kindred spirit to most of these toughs and heavies. And if the gangsters are feeling tight-lipped, these bounty hunters not opposed to walking into a pub, cracking a few skulls, then having a calm chat with the bartender while somebody sweeps the loose teeth off the floor.

In other words, they're perfectly suited to the particular brand of blood-under-your-fingernails legwork required to bring in a certain calibre of mark and charge accordingly for their services, which makes hiring them ironically impractical for the Mothership itself.

vastly expanded its industry, and new generations of citizens means that the percentage of criminal records among the citizenry is at an all-time low.

But the brutal pragmatists of *Corregidor* aren't going to fix what isn't broken. And with micro-conflicts flaring up, industrial espionage on the rise, and the arrival of the Combined Army, the Human Sphere's demand for competent, reliable, and durable mercenaries is as high as it's ever been. And while that might be bad news for the Human Sphere in general, it is money in the bank for purveyors of *Corregidor's* traditional export of applied, professional violence.

NARCOTICS

Corregidor's original inhabitants included many Narco gangs, most of whom were exiled to the void. Unsurprisingly, knowledge of how to run a drug cartel has survived the trip, and *Corregidor* boasts a thriving drug trade. Though still quite illegal, canny *maras* gangs can turn a tidy profit, so long as they don't make too much trouble — and remember to pay their taxes. This "Miscellaneous Income" is a significant contributor to the ship's bottom line, and greedy gangsters quickly discover that the Alguaciles harshly punish those who conveniently forget to pay their taxes.

"It's an unspoken assumption in *Corregidor* that for every one incident that gets attention, there are ten more that no one ever hears about. If that is truly the case, then it's no wonder that Corregidorans are slow to trust outsiders."

— Excerpt from *Corregidor: Built to Last,* by Johur Ali al Sefi. Produced by Haas, Al Boushra's travel channel: only on Maya!

"If life gives you lemons, you make lemonade, right? Well, life gave me crap, so what do you think I did with that? That's right! I bought guns." [Sounds of indiscriminate slaughter.] "Also, I made lemonade! The alternative sounded gross. You guys want any?"

— Señor Massacre, having a chat with his co-workers during a boarding action. Haqqislamite corsair ship *Kara Gölge* (Black Shadow), Human Edge system.

DEMOGRAPHICS AND CULTURE

Corregidor's history is a tale of tough people making tough decisions in tough circumstances, and that legacy of difficult choices laid the foundation for the brutal pragmatism that is the hallmark of modern *Corregidor*.

METEOR HEADS

Paragons of obstinacy, Corregidorans have a reputation for being gruff, rude, foul-mouthed, and tougher than nails. And they do their honest best to earn it. Though they work with clients across the Human Sphere, one could hardly describe those relationships as warm. From the moment the first convict was thawed out of cryogenic storage, Corregidorans have been outsiders. Their treatment at the hands of the rest of the Human Sphere has done little to thaw their cold shoulders.

Still, there is a quiet contentment in their self-imposed exile. The cold vacuum of space is a constant threat, but it is also beautiful in a way that nothing else is. Life as an eternal freelancer is demanding, but the work is honest. To be a meteor head is to be native to the uncaring void of space, to live and work within arm's reach of oblivion. To stare deeply into the abyss, until your next job stares back.

Other Nomads see something profound in *Corregidor*. In response, the meteor head shrugs and gets on with the day's work.

URBAN LEGENDS

True or not, Corregidorans love a good story. They mythologise their traditions, sometimes creating fictitious people and entire events to better contextualise their world. These tall tales can grow large, but there's a thread of proverbial wisdom running through them all. Categorically, the Corregidoran urban legend is more fable than rumour.

For example, design decisions that are common across the Nomad Nation are attributed to remarkable individuals who reliably refused to back down when pushed. These folk heroes take several shapes, but the unifying theme is one of stoic determination in the face of oppressive power. Whether their foils are ALEPH, other O-12 nations, fellow Nomads, or even the void of space itself, Corregidoran folk heroes are always seen punching up on behalf of the downtrodden. While these stories tend to have a grain of truth, Corregidorans are more concerned with the lessons of the story than the paticulars. As one such proverb goes: "Facts are nice and all: but don't let them get in the way of the truth."

TOASTS

Ignoring the torrents of profanity that accompany equipment maintenance, combat situations, and most forms of cooking, the Meteor Heads of *Corregidor* seem reserved, even introverted, especially when compared to their fellow Nomads.

One notable exception to this is the Corregidoran fondness for toasts. Other cultures might break into a toast at significant events: weddings, funerals, graduations, and so on. Corregidorans do not require nearly so much prodding. For outsiders, it can come as quite a shock to see them boisterously extoling each other's virtue, flasks raised high. A Corregidoran might toast your health over lunch, toast the delivery driver for finally dropping off the parts they need, and toast a job well done, all over the course of a few hours.

The flasks themselves can contain everything from nutrient paste to black coffee, though tequila remains the libation of choice for Corregidoran adults, as well as a fair share of kids who think they can get away with it. Like a bare-knuckled brawl, most citizens are willing to look the other way when it comes to alcohol consumption, believing it to be good for one's character.

Tequila also holds a special place in Corregidoran society and is used for a variety of purposes beyond consumption. Tequila spritzing is used in lieu of dry cleaning, and the liquor is used to remove mould spores in bathrooms, to disinfect wounds, and to enhance baked goods. Tough old meteor heads have been known to soak their feet in the cheap stuff to get rid of funky boot odour, and more than one broke worker has tried drinking the resulting sludge to embarrassingly disastrous effect.

So entrenched in the Corregidoran psyche is the utility of the stuff, that tequila is often applied in applications where any benefits it conveys are purely psychological in nature. Unsurprisingly, the phrase "put some agave on it" endures as a uniquely Corregidoran method of telling someone to tough it out and get on with their day.

PARIAHS IN THE VOID: DAILY LIFE IN CORREGIDOR

Ask a non-Nomad about Corregidorans, and they're likely to conjure up an impossibly tough, hard-boiled spacer who is gritty, coarse, and stoic. Ask a Nomad, and your answer won't be that different. But ask a Corregidoran, and you're more likely to get a shrug, cold glare, or uncomfortable silence than an answer in so many words.

Many would think that they've been brushed aside.

WORK. LIFE. BALANCE: A CORREGIDORAN DAY

Corregidorans don't always share much in common with their neighbours. But even the most wildly disparate citizens often get to know each other through the shared tradition of constant and demanding ship maintenance. *Corregidor* is in a constant state of maintenance and repair, and it's every citizen's duty to do their part. Thus, after working a late-night shift, a labourer might make small talk with their mercenary neighbour over a busted door console, an overheating circuit, or the nearly ubiquitous coolant leaks that plague the Mothership's design.

Corporate stooges may have "water cooler" conversations, but in *Corregidor*, there are "coolant maintenance" conversations, where the latest Aristeia! matches are discussed, politicians are groused at, and dirty jokes are freely exchanged with knowing winks to kids who think they've managed to hide. Regardless of their upbringing, social class, or economic status, everyone pitches in. Corregidorans take pride in their maintenance. Everyone's learned it growing up, and immigrants catch on quick by necessity. The thought of delegating these minor tasks is akin to insinuating that they can't lace their own boots or dress themselves. Repairs are something you simply do.

Shopping, religious observances, your day job — even during trips to the restroom — if minor repairs are needed, people stop and make them, usually sharing the work with passers-by. Thus, most Corregidorans don't stay strangers for long. You never know who you're going to be handing a spanner to.

But a closer look reveals a deeper truth. More than any of their siblings, Corregidorans are children of the void. Space can be your worst enemy, or your greatest friend, but nobody gets along with it without putting in some work. And Corregidorans are their mother's children.

LAW OF THE JUNGLE: PEACEKEEPING IN CORREGIDOR

Corregidor's law enforcement has its work cut out for it. Trying to keep the toughest crew in the galaxy from ripping each other apart isn't a job for the faint of heart, nor those averse to confrontation. With any conflict holding the potential to boil over into shocking violence, *Corregidor*'s peacekeeping forces need to stay on their toes at all times.

In general, law enforcement is more lenient here than elsewhere in the Human Sphere. So long as the ship isn't damaged, the mantra of "no blood, no foul" provides a better framework for understanding it than any legal code. Alguaciles know better than to break up an honest brawl between consenting adults. As they keep their dispute contained, Mothership Security usually has more pressing matters to attend to. Assault charges are nearly unheard of — it's assumed that most people can take care of themselves in a fight, so anything short of attempted murder tends to merit a slap on the wrist at most.

Of course, the Alguaciles can't be everywhere. The Corregidor Jaguars, one of Sarmiento's more innovative recycling plans, walk the toughest beats in *Corregidor*, and their particular style of enforcement has resulted in a stable, if violent, sort of equilibrium. Most Jaguars are former *maras* and are usually more than happy to turn a blind eye to gang activity, so long as it doesn't spill out into the rest of the ship. Because most Jaguars came from neighbourhoods similar to the ones they now protect, they know all too well the dangers of a stray bullet, unhinged junkie, or rampaging corridor thug. When they do step in, their retribution is swift, violent, and often excessive combining gang-style violence with paramilitary training and equipment.

RED LEGACIES

Nomads are, by and large, a freedom-loving, independent folk. Corregidorans, as the first Nomad Mothership, like to think that they embody those virtues as much as anyone. But there is a spectre looming over their liberty, a dark past to go with their uncertain future. Because for all the platitudes, assurances, and justifications, one fact remains inarguably clear: Corregidoran freedom was bought and paid for in human trafficking (see *Nomads: Faction* p. 4)

Once they'd been categorised, the useful were put to work, the valuable were put on the auction block, and the surplus were demarcated for disconnection if the ship hit a resource crunch. Technically speaking, once the ship gained financial solvency, the classifications were subsequently dropped, never to be mentioned again. But people don't forget such things so easily, and the effects can be felt in Corregidoran culture to this day.

Corregidorans, as a rule, don't like talking about the Red Auction. If pressed, they'll volunteer any number of justifications — it was do or die, desperate times call for desperate measures, and so on. They don't

PAY-PER-BREATH

In *Corregidor*, nothing is free, not even existence. In stark contrast to the iota-scarcity world the rest of the Human Sphere lives in, a philosophy of economic scarcity is an integral part of the hardcore survivalist spirit of *Corregidor*. Keeping the lights on, the ship moving, and the air breathable doesn't happen by accident — these things cost money, and nobody gets a free ride. Whether in currency or maintenance duties, everybody pays. Those who don't, or simply can't? Arrested, and forced to perform community service until their debts are paid.

And when that fails, more than one soul has wound up "going for a stroll" outside the ship. Without a suit

"It's real simple. Don't make a mess you can't clean up. If you wanna get in someone's face, don't expect them to back down. And if you're pushed around? It's expected that you'll push back. Extend others the same courtesy."

— Tomcat Sergeant Major Carlota Kowalsky, advising some freshly-rescued trafficking victims on Mothership etiquette.

"You think he was scary when we were fighting PanOceania? His little sister lives in this 'hood. We're gonna have to ID the suspect by DNA... if there's enough left to even do that."

— Ricardo Diaz, Alguaciles corps, explaining Jaguar jurisdiction to a fellow officer.

"'Every Nomad is equal. The messy history of the Red Auction is behind us now. We are against the very idea of slavery.' Fine ideals. Good thoughts. And utterly false. One has but to look at the stratification of Corregidoran society to see the influence of the Red Auction today: if someone cannot be exploited, or perform valuable services, they're considered 'surplus' to this very day.

You cannot force children to engage in physical labour in order to purchase the right to breathe your air, and in the same breath, say that you have changed your ways? Sorry friends: I don't buy it. If Corregidorans want to be seen as a trustworthy people, the first group they should stop lying to is themselves."

– Jeremiah Duggar, Lobbyist for FamilyFirst. From The Duggar Report: available on Maya.

THE UNWANTED

Pragmatism notwithstanding, nobody likes the idea that they've been marked as "surplus to requirement." Some of the survivors decided that if their so-called "fellow citizens" in *Corregidor* could so easily cast them aside, then they'd look after each other. Tattoos of SURPLUS or S.T.R. in industrial stencilling were common amongst these former "surplus," signalling to fellow castaways that this person, at least, would stand with them. Somewhere between a union and a deck gang, the Unwanted still look after their members and count many commandos among their number.

see the point in further discussion. To their eyes, it happened, it was necessary, and it worked. Nothing more needs to be said on the matter.

CORRIDORS OF CORREGIDOR

Corregidor is prone to understate its hazards to the uninitiated. Its reputation for danger is real, and earned, but to locals, said dangers only come to those who go looking for them. Thousands of little signals that an outsider might miss are as clear as day to a native. Things that are common sense to the local are completely alien assumptions to the visitor, and these misunderstandings can be incredibly dangerous. On *Corregidor*, the key to staying safe is knowing which parts of town to steer clear of and when, trusting instincts honed by years of observation. Of course, good luck getting a local to explain any of this to an outsider.

DECK MAPS

Having grown up among *Corregidor's* groaning bulkheads, constructing internal "deck maps" is as natural as breathing. Corregidorans pay attention to what's under construction, which gangs are fighting this week, and what parts of the ship to avoid unless they're looking for trouble. Like denizens of terrestrial urban centres, a local's knowledge is so integral that it goes without mention. Thus, Corregidorans are routinely confused that people think of their home as being "unsafe." Tough, sure. Gritty, ok. Sure, it boasts a per-capita murder rate closer to a war zone than a resort, but if you don't go looking for trouble, trouble tends to leave you be. Most of the time.

As long as people stay out of the roughest neighbourhoods, most Corregidorans are more than

happy to leave well enough alone. To an outsider, the ship can seem xenophobic, but it bears repeating: most Corregidorans don't warm up to others quickly. If someone spares a greeting while walking down the corridor, they've probably known that person for years.

LAZARETO: A GANGSTER'S PARADISE

Corregidor's worst neighbourhoods get pretty rough, and Corregidoran gangs have benefited from the "no blood, no foul" philosophy of the Mothership's law enforcement. Packing absurd numbers of refugees in a confined, resource-scare environment is a recipe for disaster, no matter their origin. The original Lazareto was exactly that—and then they shot it into space. And while the modern Lazareto module is significantly improved in every conceivable regard, most would be hard-pressed to call it a nice neighbourhood.

In those early days, the *maras* gangs were all that stood between the module and unrestrained chaos. And while it's not publicly talked about, the Black Hand actively works with elements of both *vatos* and *tsotsis*. The Jaguar and Bandit programs, and in a less-official manner, collaborating with local gang leaders, the Black Hand keeps some semblance of the peace.

BANDITS

Packed into a tin can and hurled into space, many of the Sub-Saharan refugees of Lazareto rightly felt abandoned. This led to a resurgence in Reconstructionist observance of traditional religious beliefs, with many taking on the role of protector for their community. In keeping with *Corregidor* tradition, many of these vigilantes donned masks to protect their identities. And in

keeping with his pattern of co-opting the toughest and smartest Corregidorans he could find, the Mexican General cut deals with the spiritual leaders of these communities. He provided training and equipment for the vigilantes, in exchange for their use as covert assets.

A piece of old air force jargon, the "Bandit" designation was chosen for its lack of association with the religious groups, as well as the skill with which these operatives slipped unnoticed past enemy defences and neutralised their opposition. Though it's also considered a tip of the hat from Sarmiento to the Bandits' various patron figures, a recognition that if he failed to keep his end of the bargain, the chosen would disappear, like bandits in the night.

UNDERGROUND FIGHTING RINGS

There are places in the Mothership where the Alguaciles don't go. Not because they're afraid, but because it's rarely worth the fight. These sub-holds and boiler rooms tend to be hot, cramped, and dirty, the perfect place for illegal fighting rings to set up shop.

The existence of these unsanctioned combat leagues is something of an open secret on *Corregidor*. So open, in fact, that matches tend to be well-attended, even by off-duty law enforcement personnel. And while promoters and staff can generally expect a blind eye turned to their antics, the competitors can't always count on the same courtesy.

As such, it's traditional for competitors to don masks – often with outlandish personas to go with them – before entering the fighting pits. Inspired by equal parts superhero and Mexican lucha libre, these personae provide shelter from unwanted attention, as well as inspiring cult followings that translate into massive bets and merchandise sales. So whether they're a criminal with a rap sheet, someone with a price on their head, or just a corporate stiff who doesn't want to explain their hobby to management, fighters have plenty of reasons to keep their identities a secret.

SANCTUARY ZONES

While the *Corregidor* can be a dangerous place, even the toughest soul occasionally needs to cool their heels for a while. When they do, many make their way to *Corregidor's* Sanctuary Zones. Vengeance, violence, and vindication are all fine things to pursue, but they're off-limits in the sanctuaries. This is enforced in the old Corregidoran way, with the threat of even more violence.

SEÑOR MASSACRE

No discussion of Corregidoran deathmatches is complete without mentioning the rise, fall, and rebirth of Señor Massacre. During his prime, his natural agility and fighter's intuition made him a safe bet in the ring. Combined with his trollish antics and oddball charisma, this meant a lot of money coming in attached to his name. Seemingly overnight, he'd gone from one more poverty-stricken *vato* to an exciting, dangerous celebrity of sorts.

To say that he handled it poorly would be an understatement.

Drugs, gambling, and vanity went to his head. Soon, he'd lost a step in the ring, but accumulated some impressive debts. Hoping for a fresh start – or at least to get away from the loan sharks – he enlisted in the NMF, hoping to regain some semblance of what he'd lost. He served with aplomb, though his Interesting Times had just begun. During the NeoColonial Wars, he boarded the Sun Jiao battle cruiser with a group of commandos. He found himself broken, burned, and abandoned during the battle and subsequent shipwreck.

But fate was not done with Señor Massacre just yet. Between the radiation burns and military-grade bioweapons, his body – and some would say mind – was twisted and scarred. He adopted his old persona once more, a little more soldier of fortune than *luchador* this time around. He soon found a taste of his old fame as an incredibly skilled mercenary, albeit a hyperviolent and caustically irreverent one.

Some say that this is a mask, a persona. A way for Massacre to distance himself from the horrors he's experienced. While people speculate the merc has a self-destructive streak, others assume that his grip on sanity is irrevocably shattered. Either way, if you need an efficient, ultraviolent killer for-hire, and you're willing to endure some quirks, Señor Massacre has re-entered the fight, with all the Human Sphere as his arena.

CANTINAS

Corregidor is full of bars and restaurants, but one particular fusion of the two is treated with superstitious caution. According to local legend, Juan Sarmiento, the Mexican General, once had his meal interrupted by a tavern brawl that escalated into lethal violence. Upon having his margarita ruined by arterial spray, he allegedly proceeded to take out each and every one of the offending individuals.

Stories differ on what was done to them, but they all agree on its unpleasant severity. True or not, while cantinas are home to more than their share of brawls, nothing will get sworn enemies to cooperate faster than someone else breaking the unwritten rule against lethally escalating a fist fight. There's no faster way to imperil yourself than to pull a weapon during an honest brawl between hardworking folks.

KUHIFADHI

The original *Corregidor* Cantina and still one of the best-known, the Kuhifadhi module (Swahili for "preserve") stands as a bulwark between the objects of vengeance and their pursuers. Arms dealers, black-market hitmen, and mercenaries with

THE TEMPLE

While there are several different fighting rings, the organisation known only as "The Temple" is by far the most successful. Run by an enigmatic figure known only as El Jefe, the Temple is steeped in Mesoamerican mysticism, and strange, occult trappings. That isn't why people come to the temple, though. They come for the violence.

El Jefe pays more than his competitors, and his sadistic match conditions whip his bloodthirsty crowds into a frenzy, resulting in massive sums being bet. He attracts some of the top talent in the underground – notably hosting the biggest matches of Señor Massacre's mercurial career – but entering his Temple is hardly a safe bet for competitors: they're called "deathmatches" for a reason.

SANCTUARY CODE

Though not everyone does it, many sanctuaries mark their location with a simple sign: VVV. Three v's struck through meaning no vengeance, violence, or vindication is permitted on these premises. Ironically, the individuals most in need of sanctuary are often in too much of a hurry to notice the subtle markings.

varying degrees of scruples can all find themselves the target of a vengeance-obsessed hunter and can all find refuge in Kuhifahdi. Many of its inhabitants have become semi-permanent residents, selling difficult-to-acquire weapons with significant discounts for anyone who'll take care of the people hunting them.

THE HIRING HALLS

Scattered throughout the Mothership, *Corregidor's* hiring halls are as welcoming as possible to visiting clients. Requiring less enforcement than other locations, hiring halls tend to self-police remarkably well. After all, if you're chasing away clients, you're taking air out of everyone's lungs. Not even the sanctuaries would protect someone who commits such a selfish act. Costing the Mothership a client through carelessness or malice is considered tantamount to treason and is a reliable way to go skinny-dipping out an airlock.

"You know how the Cossacks are all grumpy because of the cold winters? Corregidorans are like that, except their winter is an unending darkness actively plotting your murder."

— Adjutant Henri Tallon, Ariadnan Expeditionary Corps.

THE MOTHERSHIP'S RELATIONSHIPS

Due to the nature of their work, Corregidorans often find themselves working with other factions outside the familiar confines of their Mothership, providing a unique perspective when compared to their sibling ships.

Their relationship with Ariadna is distant, but carries a quiet undercurrent of mutual admiration. Arguably no one fought harder on Ariadna's side than the Jurisdictional Command of *Corregidor*. They may not have lent the political and technological support of *Bakunin*, or the financial and legal

muscle of *Tunguska,* but they were in the trenches with the Ariadnan armed forces; neither party will soon forget that.

Flashy Submondo tend to work out of "everything's legal in" *Bakunin,* while leaders see peers on *Tunguska.* But for hardworking, roughneck, workaday criminal muscle, there are few places better to throw back a drink than on *Corregidor.* Many Submondo grunts are based out of the Mothership's shadier districts, taking advantage of the lenient police force.

In contrast, *Corregidor's* relationship with PanOceania and Yu Jing is long, storied, and violent. The next positive thing that *Corregidor* has to say about those political juggernauts will be the first. Based on this, one might expect them to have similar feelings towards hypercorps, but the truth is somewhat more complicated. The thinking goes that most corporate entities are soulless monstrosities that only care about profit — but at least they're honest about it. *Corregidor* doesn't like the corps, but they do an awful lot of business with each other.

Haqqislam presents something of a conundrum. The Kum are kindred spirits of a sort, and caravanserai are frequent ports of call for many a meteor head. However, the Search for Knowledge is a bit high-minded. Most Corregidorans have little interest in discussing anything so abstract and see Haqqislamites as a little "floaty." Even so, they were the Nomad's first real allies, and remain their strongest supporters to this day. So while they might have their head in the clouds, most Corregidorans acknowledge a debt towards Haqqislam, a debt that they're constantly repaying. To Corregidoran eyes, a Haqqislamite's curiosity is probably stronger than their self-preservation instinct. More than one traveller on the Search for Knowledge owes their continued existence to the timely — if grumbling — intervention of a meteor head.

And as for ALEPH? It's complicated. *Corregidor* suffered immensely during the Phantom Conflict, but most Corregidorans feel that they won that conflict, handily. So yes, they're not that far removed from ALEPH trying to kill every last one of them, but half the Human Sphere has tried to kill them at one point or another, and it's getting hard to keep track. It's not that they don't hold a grudge — they absolutely do — but these days, ALEPH seems to have given up on scrubbing them out of existence. Now it's just one more entity trying to run their lives from afar, without much to make it stand out among the others. *Corregidor* though enjoys a good bit of schadenfreude at the AI's expense, and seems to take a special delight in frustrating the efforts of Bureau Toth agents on the hunt for Rogue AIs.

INTERSHIP ATTITUDES

Corregidor's the muscle, but in many ways, it's also the heart. Many, including other Nomads, often conflate "tough" with "dumb" — and that's insulting.

It's never a good idea to insult a Corregidoran.

Without *Tunguska,* they wouldn't be able to exist, and they know that. But it's rough for a construction worker — even the foreman — to really connect with the business side of things. They can work on the same project as part of the same company, but their experiences are so different that there isn't much overlap. But they understand one another, which is more than can be said for the Meteor Heads' relationship with *Bakunin.*

Honestly, they never quite know what to do with them. *Tunguska* they understand. But nobody understands *Bakunin.* If *Corregidor's* a patient bulldog, then *Bakunin* is the yappy chihuahua that keeps getting them into fights. This is ok because more often than not, they enjoy the fights, but they see The Radical Mothership as their loud-mouthed, brilliant little sibling that doesn't know when to keep its head down.

CHAPTER 2.3
MOTHERSHIP: TUNGUSKA

From the *Raubritter* of medieval Germany to the "Robber Barons" of early American capitalism, the history of humanity is rife with people who used legitimate positions to gain political power, wealth, or even get away with literal murder. But it wasn't until *Tunguska* that criminals so openly leveraged the tools of their trade to become a legitimate legal, political, and financial power, eventually becoming the recognised head of a G5 nation.

Thus was the genius of *Tunguska*. In a world increasingly controlled by ALEPH, there was more need for privacy than ever. With the old tax shelters closed up, there was an opportunity to create an entity constructed from the ground up to provide financial benefit in an AI-monitored society. The three groups who best understood how to exploit tax law — organised crime syndicates, low-profile banks, and hacktivist cryptomancers — might have been unlikely bedfellows, but it is the intersection of these diverse elements that would forge *Tunguska's* unique identity. A new form of governance, designed from the ground up by thieves, a haven of their own making.

A kleptocracy, if you will.

TUNGUSKA: A LIMITED LIABILITY NATION

When bankers, hackers, and organised criminals came together to found a nation, getting the right structure in place was of the utmost importance. They settled on a corporate model, dividing the nascent mothership into smaller shares, distributed among the three founding groups. Sussing out how these would be distributed was a contentious matter, and a defining moment in Tunguskan history.

Each group was essential for *Tunguska's* success, though they disagreed on their relative importance. Without the hackers, the Crypt — the foundation of Tunguska's economy — couldn't function. Without the financial knowledge of the bankers, as well as their existing relationships, arrangements, and infrastructure, *Tunguska* might never get off the ground, figuratively or literally.

But without the mafias, all of this was merely academic, an idea in the night sky, just so many empty hopes. These criminal syndicates were *Tunguska's*

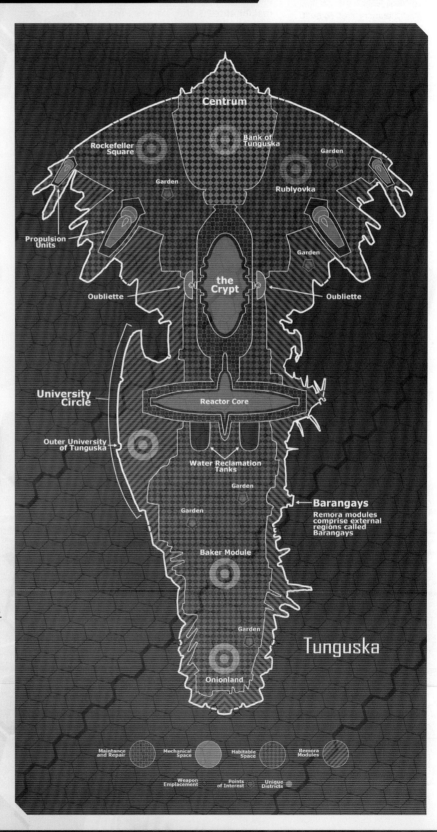

TUNGUSKAN FLORA

Of the three Nomad Motherships, *Tunguska* has by far the most plant life. From the moment someone sets foot in a docking bay, there's at least a trace element of vegetation throughout the station. Praxis has bioengineered the chlorophyll and anthocyanin content of several species of plants in order to thrive under ambient stellar light and for use in dye-sensitised solar cells. Observation windows are often lined with various plant life, which not only helps with air circulation and passenger morale but plays a small part in subsidising the Mothership's massive energy consumption.

first clients and main economic support. They not only provided the network of contacts necessary to set the project in motion, but most importantly the knowledge and will to make sure that the correct permits got signed. Whether greasing palms or making threats, they knew all the right buttons to push to get things done. One way or another, they made offers that others couldn't refuse, ensuring that *Tunguska* became a reality.

The initial distribution was as follows:
- The *Entente* — the gathering of crime syndicates — received 39% of the total shares
- The Bank — comprised of discreet Central European financial institutes — received 29% of the shares
- And Tortuga — the hacker collectives — received 19% for their role

These three groups are collectively referred to as The Nines, due to the common final digit in their share percentages. The remaining thirteen percent was left open to bait external investors and new citizens. Tunguskan corporations like Trysterion were quick to acquire shares, though a great many citizens also possess shares. Everything from wealthy individuals sitting on multiple shares, to like-minded friends splitting a share between them, these citizen-shareholders enjoy the ability to vote directly, wielding unadulterated influence upon *Tunguska's* decision-making process.

In a nation where one share equals one vote, The Nines hold enormous sway over determining the Board of Directors' makeup.

CLIMATE AND TOPOGRAPHY

In contrast to the other Motherships, *Tunguska* is remarkably clean. Outside of ALEPH's fleet, most starships have a lived-in quality to them, but *Tunguska's* common areas can feel more like a technology showroom than a gargantuan space vessel.

While its variety comes nowhere near the barrage of colours that makes up *Bakunin's* interior, *Tunguska* still boasts a lively and varied appearance, a precisely curated exhibit contrasted to *Bakunin's* never-ending street faire. Its interior is particularly manicured for its sheer size: all smooth corners, bevelled edges, open spaces, and light hues. High-stakes negotiations often happen on *Tunguska*, and its design is calculated to give a home-court advantage to its residents.

ECONOMY

The Bank of Tunguska might not be the largest financial entity in the Human Sphere, but it's arguably the most powerful. Corporate financial entities are bound by intricate accounting regulations and other safeguards enforced by O-12's interfactional M-Corp law, and other national-scale entities are beholden to the plodding regulations that governments impose on their financial sectors, to keep them from seizing too much power.

Tunguska was created in the negative space between those realities. Unburdened by M-Corp law due to their status in a G-5 nation and already holding governmental power, the distinction

TUNGUSKAN FAUNA

Due to extensive maintenance efforts, *Tunguska* has virtually no "wild" animal life. Domesticated pets, on the other hand, those it has in abundance. Most of these creatures are consigned to relatively small habitats. Rodents, lizards, and a smattering of aquatic and amphibious pets round out the animal companions of most of *Tunguska's* residents. Considered a pest on their homeworld, gliding mammals from Yutang have enjoyed life as pampered pets on *Tunguska*.

That, however, is not the whole story. Rublyovka residents often keep smaller domesticated animals around their estates. Designer-bred small dogs — and things that look more exotic, but still act like a purse puppy, thanks to Praxis — are a staple among the neighbourhood's elite. Adventurous residents have been known to keep avian pets, with birds of paradise, tropical songbirds, and doves a common motif. To survive the rigors of life on a starship, the rarest of these creatures are the product of genetic alteration and augmentation and come almost exclusively from *Bakunin* with the occasional peacock from Haqqislam. However, most of them are actually remotes with special "pet geists" implanted.

Some would say that expensive Silk-based biotherapy for your pet bird is an extravagant show of wealth, and they would be entirely correct. However, a few augmented pets have nothing on the reckless extravagance that the "new money" crime families of Rockefeller Square indulge in.

between Tunguskan finance and government is practically non-existent. This positions them uniquely in between existing regulatory practices and makes the formation of new ones politically complicated. Compounded even further by the poorly-kept secret that many influential members of G-5 nations make extensive use of *Tunguska* for their private finances, any regulatory proposals are often killed before seeing the light of day.

This does, however, present some challenges. Their ability to skirt regulation complicates their relationship with other financial institutions, who rely on common accounting practices to do business. To get around this, *Tunguska* maintains a massive sovereign wealth funds (SWF) of pure capital across different jurisdictions that predate its inclusion in O-12. These SWFs not only provides security against volatility in the Tunguskan economy but have proven invaluable in interfactional economics.

PRIVACY

In the hyper-connected reality of the Human Sphere, privacy is an illusion. ALEPH's integration to nearly every facet of modern life means that anything and everything about an individual is tracked, monitored, and filed away for future reference. Governments, corporations, and determined hackers can learn virtually anything about someone with alarming ease.

Enter *Tunguska:* re-introducing privacy into a world without it.

Whether it's safe boxes, virtual private datasphere access, or just some very, very good hackers to ensure that your private conversation stays that way, *Tunguska* takes pride in counteracting ALEPH's panopticism with the most robust privacy services in the Human Sphere.

Eighty percent of *Tunguska's* economy is tied to the security provided by the data crypt at the Mothership's core. The Crypt is one of the few locations in the Human Sphere that is genuinely off-limits to ALEPH's prying eyes, despite the AI's best efforts. The oubliettes that separate the Crypt from the rest of the Centrum district provide a sort of airlock. So far, it has foiled the attempts of would-be bank robbers and omnipresent AIs alike. This ironclad security is the foundation on which the Tunguskan economy is built.

FINANCE

Tunguska is a dominant player in the financial services industry, the living embodiment of unchained big banking. Freed from the shackles of regulation, investigation, or anything resembling ethics laws,

THE BOARD OF DIRECTORS

Tunguska is governed by a Board of Directors, functioning in much the same way as a publicly traded company's board. In addition to designating the Executive Director – sometimes called the Chairman, due to the frequency with which *Entente* hold the seat – the board also appoints a President to guide and shape *Tunguska's* evolution, as well as holding the primary legislative power in their government.

The *Entente* families vie and jockey for position within themselves, but, it's usually a Struktura member who holds the title of Executive Director. Tortuga tends to consolidate their influence in the Chief Operating & Information Officer, who is directly responsible for the daily operations of the Crypt, and thus, immensely important in the mothership's continued survival. The office of President is historically dominated by The Bank, providing a respectable face and voice to represent the council internationally.

Judiciary power rests with the Dragnet, an independent agency that has strong ties with Tortuga, given their shared responsibility in the mothership's security. Still, the fiercely independent Dragnet pulls no punches in their administration of justice. A security firm built out of necessity, it has taken on the roles of judge, jury, and in some cases, executioner. Dragnet operates mostly independent from the rest of the Board.

Of course, this is *Tunguska*. Everything's negotiable, if you know the right questions to ask.

the Bank of Tunguska is the single most impenetrable tax shelter in human history. World leaders, criminal masterminds, media moguls, sovereign wealth funds, and intelligence agencies' black budgets – anyone above a certain wealth threshold has two options, either work with *Tunguska*, or risk billions by playing with a severe handicap.

INVESTMENTS

The Mothership boasts extensive investment holdings to round out their financial dealings. While their portfolio boasts the manifold diversity necessitated by their size, they also enjoy a special relationship with the Black Labs of Praxis. And as befits dealings with *Bakunin*, the relationship is anything but conventional. *Tunguska* does not dictate project development, nor do they suggest or approve fields of research. *Bakunin* strongly believes that if creativity and innovation are to be truly revolutionary, they cannot be stifled by arbitrary dictation.

Tunguska, however, doesn't care about methodology. They're interested in results.

To that end, *Tunguska* simply presents the Black Labs with an array of problems, challenges, and opportunities, and puts up the money to see them addressed. In addition to its own sizable assets, *Tunguska* manages Praxis's Black Bounties – outside requests usually of hypercorporate origin for scientific results that simply can't be acquired through more conventional means.

TUNGUSKAN MIRROR BANKS

Tunguska leverages its SWFs with impunity across the Human Sphere. Customers request access to regional funds, which are made available from the stockpiles consolidated in their local region.

Back on *Tunguska*, Centrum is littered with Mirror Banks, institutions which obey regional legislation, but only service business accounts for organisations based in *Tunguska*. Many of these only exist for as long as it takes to move the funds. The magic show occurs behind the closed doors of the Crypt, leaving the Mirror Banks as scrupulous bastions of honesty. Teams of Tunguskan lawyers ensure the Mirror Banks' legality and have an uncanny knack for highlighting the illegal activities of their closest competitors

However the funding comes, to the winner go the spoils. Providing the winning solution means a substantial amount of money, but far more interesting to Praxis is the prestige and renown of beating your peers to the punch. In a hypercharged interpretation of academic rivalry, the practical implications of new discoveries have upped the stakes considerably, leading to fierce, and sometimes bloody, competition between rival labs. Incidents such as the Holistic Confrontations, which lead to the expulsion of the Equinox group from *Bakunin*, have resulted in a thick veil of secrecy over the Black Labs.

Ironically, this has revitalised the market for industrial espionage within *Bakunin*, much to *Tunguska*'s private amusement.

LEGAL SERVICES

While PanOceania is generally assumed to be the Human Sphere's premier supplier of legal expertise, there are certain cases where *Tunguska*'s particular expertise is unmatched. No one knows the law quite like a career criminal, and when it comes to finding loopholes, their expertise is unmatched, especially in the fields of inter-factional tax law.

CONSULTING

Tunguskan Business Analysts provide serious expertise and a useful perspective that's difficult to come by via purely corporate channels. Like white-collar mercenaries, if you need an analyst, project manager, or team lead, *Tunguska* has severe, ruthless professionals available for hire. And just like any other mercenaries, if a given firm can't meet their asking price, they're more than happy to work for the competition.

ADVERTISING, SALES, AND MEMETIC MARKETING

The art of revenue-generating persuasion has been honed to a keen edge in *Tunguska*. The latest advances in Bakunian memes and Haqqislamite advancements in the social sciences are combined into sniper-precise commercial appeals and deployed with merciless efficiency by *Tunguska*'s sales teams. They negotiate hard, close deals like snapping jaws, and have literally been able to sell sand to Bourak.

INFOWAR

It's no secret that *Tunguska*'s hackers are among the best — if not *the* best — in the entire Human Sphere. It's less well-known, however, that they do a fair amount of security consulting for various mega and hypercorps from testing new systems to trying to bring down the competition. If money is no object, Tunguskan hackers can assure superior quantronic superiority in a variety of applications. Or, if the client prefers, they can just as easily make a mockery of their rival's quantronic security.

So long as the job doesn't directly oppose Nomad interests, *Tunguska*'s hacker modules are more than happy to charge an exorbitant fee to provide their services. The rumours have never been substantiated that these jobs come with a free gift in the form of a backdoor for the hacker's later use. Then again, if the hackers live up to *Tunguska*'s reputation, there'd be little evidence either way.

DEMOGRAPHICS AND CULTURE

Bakunin was born in a blaze of revolutionary passion. *Corregidor* came together out of necessity to survive an untenable situation. But *Tunguska* was

---

> "Remember those late-20th century Wall Street movies? 'Greed is good,' mountains of cocaine, no moral compass? I wonder what happened to those guys. Anyway, some suit from *Tunguska* said I should make you an 'offer you can't refuse' after I killed your dudes. So how about this: I got this coupon for half-off at SoyBoy, and I'll trade you for a briefcase full of cash. And, uh, you can't refuse. 'Else I'll cut your head off. With like… like a spork or something. Whadda ya say, sport?"
>
> — Señor Massacre, dipping his toes into the world of Hypercorporate espionage.

WHAT'S YOURS IS MINE; WHAT'S MINE IS ALSO MINE

The Bank of Tunguska is giddily enthusiastic regarding the hostile expansion of its own holdings. Keenly aware of the many ways that financial attacks can occur, they have likewise taken steps to ensure that their own tactics rarely work if turned against them: never owning more than 20% of a given investment and obfuscating even legal holdings behind a shell game of front operations.

This makes attacking the Tunguskan financial empire an exercise in frustration, as by the time a rival has navigated the human shield of pension schemes, mortgage providers, and otherfinancial institutions, not only has the target moved around, they've now gained the attention of an angry Bank of Tunguska.

THE OUTER UNIVERSITY OF TUNGUSKA

While universities aren't always a lucrative proposition, *Tunguska* has a particular knack for making just about anything profitable. Based out of University Circle in the Barangays, The Outer University of Tunguska has a reputation unlike any other in the Human Sphere.

Ask yourself: where do Submondo tycoons send their children to become proper heirs to a criminal empire? Where can students take classes in cleaning dirty money? Where could they learn not just to cook the books, but to Cajun-fry them like an experienced chef? Where do physical education classes cover all the finer points of fleeing from a shootout or escaping a police raid?

There's only one answer: OUT.

Nefarious reputation aside, and despite the remarkably successful Black Propaganda publicising the school, it's actually a top-quality university with the best professors that money can buy. Other institutions might bring in real-world experts to provide guest lectures, but at TOU, students can sit under the learning tree with hitmen, business analysts, and Praxis scientists, all before lunch.

designed from the deckplates up, purposefully and intentionally to be something very specific. That deliberate conviction informs Tunguskan culture to this day.

TRICHOTOMY IN MOTION

Tunguska is a criminal enterprise. Constructed by Submondo families explicitly to benefit themselves and their business interests, the codes of conduct that allowed these organisations to thrive in the underworld are alive and well in the Mothership's DNA.

Tunguska is a corporate enterprise. The need for a mobile legal loophole brought multiple conglomerates together, acting in concert to secure their financial future through creative means. Some have posited that between the corporate and the criminal, there is no true distinction, and that's certainly become true on *Tunguska*.

Tunguska is a rational anarchist's utopian society. The neo-libertarian cryptomancers who make up nearly half of *Tunguska's* population differ from their Bakunian peers in several key fashions. If *Bakunin* is a collectivist assortment of privately-maintained (and often mutually exclusive) utopias, *Tunuska's* hackers are bound by one unifying thread, the idea that rules and regulations throttle the spirit. And any who would sacrifice someone else's freedom for their own security, should live just long enough to regret that decision.

Most importantly, *Tunguska* sees no contradiction in any of those things. Its society is an amalgamation of them, with each happy to pursue its own ends, careful to allow space for the others to do their thing, and entirely comfortable with living a double life so as not to scare away the customers. *Tunguska* is inviting and friendly, but its shadows are deep, and well acquainted with each other.

A NECESSARY EVIL

Tunguska isn't necessarily well-liked across the Human Sphere. As the primary political arm of the Nomads, they are more likely to be encountered at a high level and much harder to dismiss. The advantages that working with the Bank of Tunguska provides are simply too massive to ignore, and there aren't really any viable alternatives. Corporate institutions have to deal with a public perception as legitimate entities. Submondo lack the scope and infrastructure to truly keep pace.

Tunguska possesses neither of these limitations.

Love them or hate them, most entities past a certain size have no choice but to work with *Tunguska*, at least, if they want to stay competitive. Even the Nomads' sworn enemies would rather work with *Tunguska* than be cut off from their services. And they certainly don't want to make an enemy of a financial and quantronic juggernaut with a reputation for spite. So, they grin and bear it, even if they feel the need to shower immediately after every encounter.

A CUT ABOVE: DAILY LIFE IN TUNGUSKA

The rest of the Human Sphere has strong opinions on *Tunguska*, though they can be fairly divorced from reality. But in fairness, it's not like Tunguskans make it easy on them. The notion that everyone has at least two faces — one for public consumption and one that's closer to the truth — is widely accepted on the Mothership. Of course, the Human Sphere sees them as cold, sociopathic power brokers: that's the mask they choose to present. Of course, no one ever promised they'd keep the number of masks down to two.

COMPETITION, FRIENDLY AND OTHERWISE

It would be disingenuous to suggest that living in *Tunguska* is an entirely cutthroat affair. Between the criminal, executive, and hacker cultures that make up the Mothership's culture, an aggressive need to excel is one of the few reliably common threads. From scaling the cryptomancers' dynamic skill rankings to advancing in the hierarchical ziggurat of the key banking families, Tunguskans are constantly in competition with one another, and it isn't always gentle.

However, the Human Sphere has provided no shortage of external targets, and Tunguskans can pretty reliably be called on to channel their aggression towards outsiders. Thus, competition often takes the form of who can do the most damage to the Nomads' various enemies, with hackers, Submondo, and business people all competing to see who can do the most damage, comparing high scores in dynamic online leaderboards.

The Black Hand has recently taken an interest, heavily gamifying the tradition to suit their purpose. By assigning point multipliers, achievements, and limited-time bonus objectives, *Tunguska's* competitive drive can be levelled at targets around the Human Sphere at a moment's notice, bringing ruin without warning. One moment, everything is normal, and the next, there's a small war to see who can empty your bank account the fastest, while hackers unearth your most embarrassing secrets at whiplash-inducing speed. Just one more tool in the Black Hand's arsenal of disincentives.

SERVICE VOUCHERS

As *Tunguska* is technically a corporation, it pays yearly dividends to its shareholders. Even if they aren't part of The Nines, a citizen shareholder can make a killing, though the payout isn't always financial. Since state resources are extremely limited, private contracts handle everything from health care to utilities. However, by taking pay-outs in Service Vouchers, citizens can exchange these credits to access executive-level services, get to the front of the line in inquiries, or simply "grease the wheels" when necessary. It's essentially an institutionalised form of corruption. But many find it appealing for its transparent honesty. The way that citizens tend to see it, governments are, by their nature, corrupt. Theirs is at least honest about it and gives citizens a straightforward way to participate.

TARGET MISERY INDEX

A high score is only worth bragging about if the numbers are objective. To ensure fair play on the Nomads' side and maximum suffering for their targets, *Tunguska*'s cryptomancers have developed a sophisticated scoring system for the objects of their wrath.

Net worth, political influence, Maya followers, mood, and other factors are combined into a single score. Damaging these factors raises the individual's Target Misery Index, or TMI. Intervertor-developed LAIs keep track of changes in TMI and assign credit to the individuals responsible. These values are monitored, displayed on public leaderboards, and updated in real-time. Valuable targets are assigned point multipliers, making attacks against them more efficient. More than one political opponent has had their evening ruined by a limited-time score multiplier.

PRODUCE VS. PRODUCED

Between massive deep-freezers and self-contained greenhouse labs, *Tunguska* is more than capable of satisfying the nutritional needs of its inhabitants. However, time between shipments can be delayed, so like the other Nomad Motherships, Tunguskan residents find more synthetic foodstuffs on the menu than the average citizen of the Human Sphere.

Tunguska is also among the largest per-capita importers of luxury consumables in the Human Sphere. Tunguskans don't have an issue with rehydrated noodles and frozen protein patties provided that they have access to fresh berries from Varuna, exotic coffee blends from Paradiso, and the finest hand-made chocolates that Earth's old-world chefs can concoct.

In their eyes, the quality difference between Demogrant-level meals and good imports is negligible. But in fresh produce or artisanal products, the difference is astronomical. Thus, a *Tunguskan* might spend as much as twenty percent of their income on food — roughly double the average among G5 nations — but have three quarters of that is on exotic cheeses.

TUNGUSKAN FASHION

In *Tunguska,* personally tailored clothing is by far the dominant paradigm. Executive or barista, regardless of their status, most Tunguskans wouldn't dream of wearing something off the rack. The devil's in the details, and *Tunguska* has a rapport with him. Little touches in the quality and make of the garment are everything.

Even the hacker modules adhere to this notion, with a DIY punk ethos echoed throughout the subculture's many styles. From custom-engraved hacking tools to laser-guided hairstyle gradients, the cryptomancers' commitment to unique attire can border on the obsessive, and that's just the parts that are visible to the naked eye.

MERITOCRACY

Each Nomad Mothership is harsh in its own way. *Tunguska* however, considers itself to be one of the few truly fair societies in existence. Corregidorans are often one bad break from dire straits, and Bakunians are at the mercy of whatever mad idea someone's talked themselves into today, but on

Tunguska, a citizen's fortune is determined by their own actions. Loyalty, cleverness, and above all, not getting caught are the ingredients that have fuelled many a rise to the top and continue to do so to this day.

In many ways, it's not unlike the utopian experiments of *Bakunin.* A harsh but fair meritocracy, where ambition and ruthlessness can run virtually unchecked by outside regulations or governmental oversight. To some, this is a utopia in its own right.

The statisticians of *Tunguska* are always trying to find ways to improve this process. Lately, the Board of Directors has been revaluating the utility of Bakunian Social Energy as a means of quantifying an individual's productivity, loyalty, current shares, and risk factor into a single, utilitarian score. Being able to measure a given citizen/employee/goon's value at a glance is an appealing thought, though *Bakunin* seems less than thrilled with the application.

QUANTIFIED VALUE: LAW AND ORDER IN TUNGUSKA

The idea of utility to the Mothership is at the heart of the Tunguskan legal system. What constitutes a criminal act in a society founded and run by criminals? The answer, as it turns out, is the same as it's always been: don't let your actions negatively affect the family.

Tunguskan police work is based around a specific set of criteria. Actions that penalise *Tunguska,* its citizens, and the Nomad Nations — in that order — constitute societal debt. Actions that benefit them make up societal revenue. Tunguskan criminal justice is an accounting system about balancing that margin. Thus, a good defence lawyer is an expert in both economics and criminal justice leading to compelling cases that minimise their client's negative impact on the societal bottom line while puffing up their contributions.

Punishments can be extremely severe, but in a reversal of the normal expectation, offering bribes to get out of a conviction is not only allowed, it's highly encouraged. A sufficient influx of funds can tip the balance back to neutral, or at least significantly reduce the amount of societal debt owed. On *Tunguska,* there is no distinction between conviction and settlement. If a sum is paid to keep a verdict out of the public records, the bribe is recorded as such, and everyone moves on with their lives.

A TUNGUSKAN DAY

If there's one thing that every Tunguskan day has in common, it's an early start. Life doesn't wait, and sleep is for people who can't afford designer stimulants. The extra hours don't go to waste. Conference calls in the shower, geist-curated newsfeeds pouring in over breakfast, updating your living resume on the way to lunch — and that's just for waiters or students.

That's not to say that Tunguskans are trapped in a vicious cycle, or that they don't know how to let their hair down. They're used to living fast and don't like wasting time. They work hard, and when they're dialled-in, their focus can be intimidating.

But when it's time to cut loose, they do so without reservation. The exact nature can vary wildly from person to person. Whether it's an investment banker's nitrocaine-fuelled nightlife, a hacker module's video game tournament, or a kingpin sitting down with a cup of fresh-brewed coffee and a physical book, they're linked by commitment to their indulgence. Even less-affluent Tunguskans don't skimp on their recreational investments. They might live in a small apartment, but their tea is imported fresh from Shentang.

However, there exists a special kind of hell for those who even threaten the life of a shareholder. The victim's contribution to overall revenue is estimated, often generously, across what would be their normal lifespan. If convicted, the guilty party is sentenced to pay that amount back to the bereaved parties, usually a parent corporation. Unless the perpetrator is independently wealthy, this usually results in a sort of indentured servitude, and the convict essentially enslaved by the corporation in question. While values vary, it's essentially a *de facto* life sentence for those convicted.

RAISING THE BAR

Some of the savviest in the Human Sphere, Tunguskan lawyers steer right into the public perception of lawyers as untrustworthy and just keep going. After all, nobody knows taxes like a tax shelter. Nobody understands criminal justice like a criminal. And nobody, nobody, exploits loopholes like a Tunguskan lawyer. They're the best at what they do largely because they have no illusions that what they do is particularly nice.

When it's your neck on the line, who would you rather have on your side? Someone who plays by the rules, or someone who will stop at nothing to succeed on your behalf? The Tunguskan Bar Association assumes that it's the latter, and acts accordingly.

In stark contrast to other legal organisations, Tunguskan lawyers are not expected to show proficiency in the minutiae of different legal codes, provided that they can successfully incite emotional breakdowns, fluster orators, and provide a credible enough threat to induce "temporary amnesia" in star witnesses.

NANO-STITCHING

At first glance, many Tunguskan hackers seem fond of simple t-shirts and tank tops in seeming defiance of the trend towards custom outfits. Most of these shirts, however, have distinct patterns in the stitches on their seams to encode a wealth of information. Song lyrics, personal details, poetry, Comlog codes, and even passwords to unlock various programs — whatever the hacker feels like embedding.

Reading these nano-stitches is an exercise in frustration, requiring intense vision magnification from a wide variety of angles. More than one hacker has infiltrated an area's quantronic security for the sole purpose of using surveillance cameras to read somebody's shirt.

GRENZ SECURITY TEAMS

In the early days of *Tunguska*, attempted bank heists were as common as worms in a Bakunian alley cat. Increasingly sophisticated attempts threatened the sanctity of the Crypt in search of the biggest score in the history of the Human Sphere. Facing the prospect of being overwhelmed by would-be bank robbers, the Waldheim family, an old and powerful Vienna banking dynasty, tasked their personal mercenary force with cleaning up this mess.

Led by the battle-hardened Colonel Nikolai Steranko, these mercs quietly integrated with the Dragnet Special Actions Department, uprooted *Tunguska's* covert enemies, and quietly disposed of them. So successful were these mercenaries, that Dragnet signed them on full-time to simply handle such problems in the future.

The Crypt has never been successfully breached.

The team of primarily Croatian mercs took the name Grenzers, in deference to the old *Krajišnici*, or *Graničari*, Croatian mercenaries who fought for the Austro-Hungarian Empire in antiquity. If the Black Hand is the public bogeyman, the threat that lurks around every corner, then the Grenz Security Team is the threat no one thinks about until it's too late. Not quite a police force, they see themselves as a border patrol. Like the Grenzers of yore, they tirelessly work to keep their adopted homeland safe.

Their list of successes is as long as it is obscure. Each crisis they avert is unceremoniously added to the stack of triumphs that just aren't worth mentioning. In the end, the Grenzers don't consider it a job well done if people know there was a crisis in the first place.

BILLION-YUAN "TYPOS"

In both legal documents and quantronic programming, a single errant character can massively alter a section's meaning.

One particularly nasty Tunguskan trick involves embedding a time-released virus in smart contracts, introducing single-character "typos" on the opposing side, treating them like they'd existed all along. Due to the dynamic nature of smart contracts, it can be difficult to prove when the typo was introduced, as all copies of the document contain the dormant virus.

Rare, and difficult to engineer, this tactic is particularly effective in Yu Jing, where the shame of being tricked, combined with the possibility of genuine error, means that such disputes are often settled as quietly as possible… which is exactly how *Tunguska* likes it.

NEOTERRAN LAWYERS V. THE TUNGUSKAN BAR ASSOCIATION

Neoterra not only boasts the highest population of lawyers in the Human Sphere, and is widely renowned for producing the best, if also the most expensive. Prestigious academies, dignified orators, and encyclopaedic knowledge of interfactional legal codes all are hallmarks of the Neoterran lawyer.

Tunguskan lawyers, on the other hand, boast a very different sort of approach.

Tunguskans are devoid of that finesse, but willing, able, and eager to use every dirty trick, brutish technique, and underhanded tactic in the book — whatever it takes to win, no matter how distasteful. In fact, the more unpleasant the technique, the more appealing it becomes. Tunguskan lawyers pride themselves on being so unpleasant to deal with, that settling out of court — or dropping the case altogether — is often preferable to the filthy slugfest that awaits them.

THE 101ST BARRISTER CORPS

Nowhere is this willingness to fight dirty more pronounced than in the Barrister Corps, an informal association of weaponised legal chicanery, mercifully without peer among the stars. Forming their association during the Phantom Conflicts, a group of law students took the accumulated knowledge of the worst parts of legal history and proceeded to become as much of a nuisance as they possibly could.

No trick was too dirty, no litigation too frivolous, and no nuisance too trivial to be off the table. Those attacking the Nomads were subjected to a barrage of litigation. Mass takedown notices, property disputes, information requests, patent trolling — you name it, they tried it. As it turns out, by throwing propriety out the window, they could generate enough legal spam to give anyone pause especially with Tunguskan hackers causing issues for geists and sorting LAIs.

They dubbed themselves the 101st Barrister Corps, and their legacy persists to this day. Many law students take a semester or two to harass *Tunguska's* enemies in a tour of duty with the Corps, and alumni routinely provide scholarships, stipends, and other financial incentives to keep the tradition alive. They consider themselves to be among the Mothership's most effective defenders, and thus far, no one has disputed the claim.

SHADOW CONTRACTS

Tunguskan smart contracts are a perfect storm of quantronic and legal expertise, and what they can accomplish is nothing short of amazing. Self-enforcing, automated expert systems, smart contracts provide a "one-stop shop" for sufficiently large projects. Bridges are built, orbitals maintained, and interplanetary concert tours booked, all essentially maintaining themselves.

Shadow contracts take it a step further. A smart contract can build your new corporate headquarters, but your rivals will be able to find out with relative ease. A shadow contract operates on a need-to-know basis. Construction of the same corporate headquarters might take a bit longer and cost a bit more when managed via shadow contract. But, the labourers, materials, and permits would all be acquired through different means, and construction occurs at different offsite locations. Until the day of its completion, the true nature of the project could be essentially kept secret, seeming to materialise out of thin air at the eleventh hour.

Certainly though, *Tunguska* is hardly opposed to using them for less scrupulous means. More than one unsuspecting individual has triggered a shadow cascade in their smart contract, leaving them legally culpable in ways that could rightly have been assumed to be outside the scope of their original agreement.

Tunguska has no sympathy for those who don't read the fine print, nor does it particularly care that it's written in moving cyphers. To quote an old Tunguskan proverb: "When you dance with the devil, you don't get to lead."

SEMI-SECRET ORIGINS OF THE BLACK HAND

It's often said that the strength of the Black Hand lies in how little is understood about it. Even its deputy director, the infamous "Mexican General," has privately admitted that he doesn't know exactly how it all works. And while Sarmiento certainly isn't above a little purposeful misdirection, there's reason to believe the statement.

History is replete with clandestine cell-structured organisations, but few have so directly benefited from the applied sociopathy of their designers. Phantom cells and fault-tolerant structures have long been a staple of insurgents, but the fledgling Nomad Nation needed something more.

Clandestine cells usually need to form in the shadows, away from prying eyes. But the Black Hand was different. In order to make good on the Nomad's military doctrine of responding to pokes with a chainsaw to the nethers, they needed next-level intelligence, tactical, and quantronic response capabilities, and they needed them to be a credible threat anytime, anywhere, to anyone.

They needed the perfect monster. This being the Nomads, they built one.

The opportunity to create the perfect clandestine structure proved enticing to the scientists who fashioned its models. Other governmental intelligence agencies needed to maintain some semblance of scruples, but the Black Hand would be different. Its mission was advanced by precise, weaponised fear. Too strong to resist, the allure of creating the academically perfect terrorist organisation then unleashing it on the entities trying to stamp them out lured sociologists, mob enforcers, mathematicians, hitmen, economists, hacktivists, and more. The collective knowledge of the Nomads came together to create a monstrosity, and they more than succeeded at their aims.

Game theory was wedded to gang enforcement, with advanced behavioural prediction models providing the framework for a new type of clandestine cell. The Black Hand — the Human Sphere's first "Fault-Irrelevant, Parallel Phantom Cell Structure" — needed no leaders, and no assignments, just a mission statement. While the original organisation was clearly inspired by Haqqislam's Hassassins, the Black Hand has no singular voice to guide their actions, no mystical enlightenment to pursue, and no illusions of nobility. Instead, they have material support, astonishing leeway, and a mandate to make the Nomads' enemies regret ever having been born.

While its internal hierarchy remains obfuscated, many have correctly observed that the Black Hand could function just fine without a clear command structure. Once agents are sorted into the intelligence, tactical, and quantronic divisions (Black Eyes, Black Fists, and Black Widows, respectively), barring the occasional direct mission, they seem remarkably free to act. Increasingly, the Human Sphere's intelligence agencies have become convinced that the Nomads simply rounded up the most violent and capable sociopaths they could find, gave them top-level training and equipment, and set them loose on the Human Sphere.

True or not, the thought is enough to keep more than one would-be adversary out of the Nomads' business. Which shows that the Black Propaganda machine is working as intended.

"What I'm saying, Your Honour, is that despite the pile of bodies, destruction of property, and wanton disregard for human life — including his own — my client's guilt or innocence in the matter is completely irrelevant. As per the terms of this contract, signed by the prosecution's own hand, any loss of property, personnel, or sanity is to be the sole liability of the client.

The prosecution will suggest that these terms — again, which they agreed to, whether they realised it or not — are unreasonable. The defence happily cedes that point. The defence will also humbly submit that if they wanted something reasonable, they should not have explicitly sought my client's services."

— Faye Bettencourt, defence attorney for Señor Massacre, during the "Catfish Williamson" fiasco.

"We know that Sarmiento is their deputy director. So, ask yourself, who's the director? Who has that madman's leash? Now contemplate the possibility that the answer is 'nobody,' and you'll begin to understand why just mentioning the words 'Black Hand' can make people nervous. The Nomads, as is their way, created a monster that they can't control and couldn't stop even if they wanted to."

— Mei Li Silva, Hesperya Consulting. Briefing on Nomad Intelligence agencies for Moto. Tronica.

NOTABLE DISTRICTS

Unlike *Corregidor's* utilitarian conversion, or *Baukunin's* modular construction, *Tunguska* favours larger districts within its habitats, roughly creating neighbourhoods. Though it technically contains modules, that's something of a misnomer. On *Bakunin,* module describes both a pocket society and a physical location, on *Tunguska,* modules indicate a social construct. Early Tunguskan hackers borrowed the terminology to distinguish between different subcultures, and it's been confusing outsiders ever since.

CENTRUM

Old-world opulence juxtaposed with new-world tech, Centrum is *Tunguska's* core district. Home to the Crypt, and by extension, the financial, quantronic, security, and governmental institutions that surround it, some of the biggest deals in the Human Sphere are made in the confines of its lavish halls.

Among spacecraft, Centrum's design is an anachronistic outlier. Its vaulted ceilings, marble pillars, and glided hardwoods lend an opulent, old-money feel in keeping with the oligarchical banking dynasties who funded its construction. When people think of *Tunguska,* it's usually the smooth, bevelled curves, white and gold aesthetic, and surprisingly open spaces of Centrum.

THE WELCOME MAT

While ships that dock with *Tunguska* tend to linger toward the outside of its hull, there are few entrances on these external locations. Each guest's entrance is instead a curated experience, shuttled to the Centrum. From the moment that they set foot on *Tunguska,* they're greeted by an unfolding spectacle of calculated grandeur, luxury, and commercialism.

While Centrum contains both *Tunguska's* seat of government and its financial district, there's considerable support for visitors as well. From lodgings to restaurants, this visitor-friendly array of establishments — colloquially known as "the Welcome Mat"— provides everything that a traveling businessperson, tourist, or diplomat could need. On the Welcome Mat, *Tunguska* puts its best mask forward. Everyone is pleasant and polite, if not exactly friendly. But most importantly, there is an implicit undertone to the area. People, architecture, everything about the Welcome Mat is designed to communicate a feeling of safety and security.

Of course, the inverse is true. Step off the Welcome Mat, and you're swimming with the sharks. Enter at your own risk.

THE BARANGAYS

Surrounding the core of Centrum, the fractally nested habitats of the barangays comprise the remainder of the Mothership. Grouped together into loose neighbourhoods, residences and common areas form unique districts, each with their own character. While the barangays have plenty of variety to them, each is unquestionably situated towards the refined end of Nomad living.

RUBLYOVKA

Named for an ultimately failed Moscow district, Rublyovka is impossibly posh, impeccably stylish, and impenetrably secure. From the palatial estates that make up its residential "cabins" to the combination public park and shopping district that spans the entirety of its common area, Rublyovka is an example of old-world luxury, refined through generational wealth, and somehow elegantly suited to its place among the stars.

In Rublyovka, extravagance is the order of the day. While any Tunguskan bakery would seem upscale by most standards, in Rublyovka, the same fresh-baked croissant you can pick up in Centrum is

BAKER MODULE'S "LOST CHILDREN"

Enjoying a longstanding partnership with the Black Labs of Praxis, the technowizards of Baker Module undertook a grand experiment using experimental genetic therapy to augment modified clone Lhosts with heightened neuroplasticity and an increased lifespan.

On one hand, the experiment could be considered a success. The students showed an enhanced capacity for rapid decision-making and aptitude with complex concepts. On the other hand, tying the augmenting retrovirus to growth hormones was probably a mistake. The subjects' physical and often emotional growth was slowed to approximately 20% of that experienced by baseline

humans. A variety of treatments were attempted to accelerate growth during the first decade of the experiment, but these were a failure. The corresponding metabolic damage mandated the removal of such accelerators until Lhost technology had improved to the point that it could bear such enhancement until adulthood.

Some of these "lost children" turned out to be some of the best hackers in *Tunguska* — no mean feat. While being trapped in a child's body has innumerable disadvantages, it also allowed for unparalleled infiltration opportunities. To this day, anyone who's come into conflict with them tends to get a bit twitchy when they see kids on their comlogs.

drizzled in a floral honey sauce, flecked with actual gold, and priced even higher than one might expect. Everything is a curated experience for refined palates and is priced accordingly. Like a living museum to old Earth oligarchs, the district doesn't go out of its way to make outsiders feel uncomfortable; it just happens as a matter of course.

ONIONLAND

The professional hacker's paradise. Named in honour of an archaic Darkweb, it is here where the soul of Arachne could be said to dwell. All the freedoms of a Bakunian anarchist module combined with the affluence, stability, and resources that *Tunguska* can offer, Onionland considers itself the best of both worlds, and it's difficult to argue. Unlike on *Bakunin* however, there's no Social Energy here. Citizens are expected to follow all the laws of *Tunguska*, namely, don't endanger the Mothership, don't work directly against Nomad interests, and above all, don't get caught.

Tunguskan hackers specialise in that last one.

The layout is a sort of correlated chaos. While never exactly cluttered, Onionland eschews the manicured grace of Centrum and the effortless luxury of Rublyovka in favour of a kinetic individuality. Every habitat, storefront, and public bench has a slight variation to it. Even the tiles are said to sport subtle differences between them, allowing an informed native to know exactly where they are just by looking down.

Tech shops are popular, but the district's common area is famous for its quantronic cafes, where veteran hackers and neophytes alike can share a cup of coffee and bond over the latest hacking tools, while catching an Aristea! match or comparing their place on various leaderboards.

ROCKEFELLER SQUARE

Splitting the difference between the prior two districts, Rockefeller — a name synonymous with showy displays of wealth long past the relevance of the actual family — is home to those who wish to flaunt their wealth, real or imagined. Consisting primarily of *Tunguska*'s *nouveau riche*, Rockefeller's residents come from all over the Nomad Nations and to a lesser extent, the greater Human Sphere. Where Rublyovka is refined, Rockefeller is celebratory and occasionally a bit gaudy in its display of wealth. Whether they grew up in *Tunguska,* or recently defected to the Nomads, living in Rockefeller Square is a prized, yet accessible, goal.

Unlike the exclusive nature of Rublyovka, Rockefeller goes out of its way to seem attainable. Home to mob bosses and holomovie stars, there's also no shortage of young professionals living just beyond the edge of their means. Working extra hours is a small price to pay for the chance to rub elbows with celebrities or the possibility of being invited to the neighbourhood's legendarily orgiastic parties.

The district is also a premier shopping destination. Rockefeller shops are a tantalising combination of exclusive and posh, while priced just barely within an aspirational Nomad's reach. Bakunian designers often create one-of-a-kind outfits, accessories, and other items specifically for sale in Rockefeller's exclusive boutiques.

UNIVERSITY CIRCLE

Home to the prestigious but sketchy Outer University of Tunguska, the Circle is an idealised version of the archetypical terrestrial college town, filtered through the lens of Mayaseries and half-remembered nostalgia. Some of the finest Nomad emergency responders have cut their teeth working in the Circle, as there's nothing quite like a steady stream of stim overdoses, ill-conceived stunts, and alcohol poisoning to sharpen one's medical skills.

Quieter parts of the district do exist, but they're notoriously difficult for outsiders to locate. As it turns out, neither the university's faculty, nor the more dedicated students particularly appreciate their peace and quiet being interrupted by a party that's spilled out into the common area. Those who find these hidden nests can often be found conversing with some of the Human Sphere's premier scholars with wildly diverse fields of expertise.

INTERFACTIONAL RELATIONSHIPS

While their interactions with the outside world might not be as colourful as *Bakunin's* or as numerous as *Corregidor's*, *Tunguska's* relationships tend to be layered with complexity and comprised mainly of mixed feelings. By far the most politically active arm of the Nomads, *Tunguska* is far more likely to politically engage with its fellow G-5 nations. Though many would prefer if they didn't.

Alongside Haqqislam, they proved instrumental in securing Ariadna's status as a G-5 nation, and *Tunguska* is intensely interested in the prospect of adding another member to the resistance block. For their part, Ariadna is not particularly interested in standing up to the Hyperpower or StateEmpire. They're much more focused on survival for the time being, and tend to be wary of getting too involved in the Mothership's plots.

Haqqislam values *Tunguska* for its adroit political support and appreciates its honesty. Truthfulness is not a trait often assigned to the oily Tunguskans,

> "I'm hardly poor. In most circles, I'd be considered a social elite by whatever metric you care to use. But walking around Rublyovka, it felt like I was, I don't know, trespassing? Like they were going to call the cops, because someone let a vagabond in."
>
> — Carlos Arroyo, VP of sales for Aigletech, following a business trip to *Tunguska*.

QUANTRONIC CAFÉS

A throwback to an old Earth tradition, quantronic cafes trace their roots to wired dataspheres. Due to the scarcity of these connections, people would gather at these "net cafes" and engage in everything from mundane daily use, to collaborative multiplayer games. In an inspired fit of Hiraeth reconstructionism, Onionland's quantronic cafes attempt to recreate that spirit by providing a wealth of tools — programs, hacking devices, and various geists, LAIs, and expert systems — all location-locked to the café.

> "Aaaaand here we have OUT! The only school I know where carrying a gun to class isn't just legal, it's practically mandatory! Good thing your favourite go-getter's got ace security!"
>
> — Go-Go Marlene in "Beyond Bakunin: An inside look at the Nomads." Available on Maya, and for a limited time on Arachne via special consideration from Oxyd Media.

INTERSHIP ATTITUDES

Tunguska's relationship with its fellow Nomads is complicated at the best of times. Although they might consider themselves the leaders of the Nomad Nation, only the lightest touch of governance is tolerated, despite their privileged position on the Nomad Executive Board.

Most of these complications arise from fundamentally different perceptions of the same event. *Tunguska* believes that *Corregidor* tries to oversimplify everything. The Corregidorans believe that the inverse is true, and *Tunguska* isn't satisfied until a matter is too complicated for anyone else to understand.

Interestingly enough, *Tunguska* holds the opinion that no one understands nor values *Corregidor* the way that they do – up to and including *Corregidor* itself.

Their relationship with *Bakunin* is comprised of equal parts admiration, symbiotic business relationship, and a near-constant desire to throttle them. Which part is stronger depends entirely on the day. Still, *Tunguska* couldn't secure its assets without Bakunian technology, and *Bakunin* would get nowhere fast without Tunguskan funding. And on top of that, the relationship between Onionland hackers and some of *Bakunin's* anarchist modules is unambiguously warm, with more than a few Nomads splitting time between the two communities.

but to Haqqislam, they see a collection of people who are quite honest about who they truly are, not just to others, but to themselves as well. Self-deception is an impediment to the Search for Enlightenment, so while Haqqislam might not trust a Tunguskan farther than they could throw them, they usually have a pretty good idea of just how far that would be.

PanOceania and Yu Jing are seen as two sides of the same coin – invaluable business partners, and the deadly foes who came close to destroying the fledgling Nomad Nation. They consider PanOceania little more than an ALEPH puppet state, but by their reckoning, the AI would face little difficulty in manipulating the StateEmpire to its own ends. Yu Jing treats them the way that they might treat any other *Jopok;* as foreigners they're fundamentally untrustworthy. For their part, the Hyperpower will work with anyone, so long as they believe they're getting the better deal. Or in *Tunguska's* case, because they can't afford not to.

To the surprise of many, most corporations enjoy a cordial relationship with *Tunguska.* Much like the Mothership, corps are under no illusions as to their true purpose and have little difficulty in keeping their relationship professional. Some degree of poaching exists on both sides. For every hacker that gets out of the game for a white hat and steady paycheck, there's an account executive who steps out of the boardroom and into their new "family." Hard feelings and burnt bridges are comparatively rare in this case. Since they are likely to be working together either way, both sides do a fair job of keeping matters cordial.

But perhaps the most peculiar of these relationships is the Mothership's interactions with O-12. As the *de facto* leaders of the Nomad Nation, *Tunguska* knows a thing or two about herding cats. And as the closest thing to a governing body that the Human Sphere has, O-12 is certainly no stranger to the difficulty of keeping wildly disparate elements on something resembling the same page. Thus, *Tunguska* feels a kinship with O-12, often stating that they have more in common with them than any other faction.

No matter how this topic is broached, it never fails to make O-12 incredibly nervous.

THE NOMAD RECURSIVE TRIANGLE

There's an old truism in the Nomad Nation: everybody's responsible for everything. While many assume that's a discussion of individual's responsibility to the collective, it's actually in reference to the three Motherships' interdependence. *Corregidor* provides the muscle, which only succeeds because of *Bakunin's* technology, which is only made possible by *Tunguska's* funding that is secured and protected, of course, by *Corregidor's* muscle.

But look deeper, and you'll also see Tunguskan lawyers arranging for Corregidoran workers' rights, while Bakunian marketers secure them contracts across the Human Sphere. And that's before the realisation that each Mothership quite literally contains multitudes: Corregidoran accountants, Tunguskan street fighters, and so on. Look hard enough, and you can even find respectable citizens on *Bakunin,* though they're loathe to admit it in public.

In the end, each Mothership is interdependent, but also independent. They can survive on their own, but together, they form the crux of the Nomad Nation: an entity that has proven to be far more potent than the sum of its parts.

CHAPTER 3
SOCIAL ENERGY

Of all the radical neo-Bohemian ideas to come out of *Bakunin*, none has so quintessentially captured the spirit of the Radical Mothership as Social Energy. Like the ship that spawned it, Social Energy is difficult to categorise. A combination of countless, often contradictory elements, Social Energy somehow forms a conceptual mosaic that is not only remarkably expressive, but inarguably functional. *Bakunin's* Social Energy is a system of social rating or ranking that serves as an ID, a currency, and a self-policing system for social interactions.

A structure that is constantly tweaked, maintained, and otherwise altered by *Bakunin's* denizens, Social Energy is more than just these systems. It's the collective unconscious of *Bakunin,* given material weight and real authority. It's the fuel that keeps its society going, and the tangible expression of what passes for order in the Human Sphere's most chaotic environment.

But beneath the semiotic nomenclature, there's a Teseum-solid foundation that keeps it all running. With military grade quantronic security and information on its citizenry that would be the envy of any surveillance state, Social Energy is comprised of innumerate factors, measuring individuals, interactions, trends over time, and shifts in paradigm. All of this flows through a recursive data stream, where it's constantly reinterpreted and represented in a fluid, dynamic process.

Which sounds nice. But it's a royal pain to keep straight.

WHERE IT COMES FROM

The history of Social Energy is, like the Energy itself, in a constant state of semi-understood flux. While the basic facts are agreed upon, their order and relative importance remains a hotly contested subject.

Bakunin has been described as a series of pocket utopias, held together with duct tape and prayer. But one person's paradise, can very easily be

SOCIAL ENERGY AND ARACHNE

Arachne and Social Energy have a lot in common. Both are sprawling quantronic systems, described in mythical and spiritual terms, and built on radical, unusual architecture. Social Energy makes extensive use of Arachne's unique structures, having been designed to integrate specifically with the Arachne dark web, even outside of the Bakunian Datasphere.

Whether or not Social Energy could truly function without access to Arachne, which is simultaneously more open, yet more closed than Maya, is a topic of considerable debate with few reasonable voices in the mix.

THE ATTRIBUTION WARS

Disagreements about who coined the phrase that lends Social Energy its name is one of the most flame-hot debates going on *Bakunin* at any given time. There exists surveillance footage that clearly shows who uttered the famous phrase. In fact, there are about thirty-seven different, mutually exclusive versions of the footage each of which has been independently verified to be as authentic as all the rest. At this point, the debate is less about what's real and what's not. It's a somewhat transparent attempt to align one's chosen ideology with the mythical founder of Social Energy, lending an authoritative weight to your discourse.

WHAT IS SOCIAL ENERGY?

"The pulse of *Bakunin*. Its heartbeat." – Calamity Jana, Bakunian bartender.

"Social networking, with the weight of a brass knuckle to the gut." – Mei Li Silva, Hesperya Consulting.

"Real debate. In Social Energy, Comlog warriors can't hide behind anonymity. At least, not for long." – Puck, Chimera and Lazaretto arms dealer.

"A hell of a way to run an economy" – Rudy Kirilenko, Bank of Tunguska.

"The voice of the people, distorted and out of phase, which suits it just fine." – Diva Davina, self-proclaimed "Empress of VaudeVille".

"A system. And just like any other system, it can be hacked." – J4R37H, Tunguskan Hacker. Currently banned from 13 different Modules.

"A way to ensure that people behave, by hitting them where it hurts – their wallets." – Svengali.

"Social Energy? Reality's true nature. As seen by madmen." – Charis Colson, underground poet.

"Hippie friendship money for degenerates." – Jerrie Dougan, Lobbyist for *FamilyFirst,* during his 12th fact-finding mission on *Bakunin*.

"Proof that Bakunians have good taste!" Go-Go Marlene, who consistently boasts one of the highest standings of any individual outside the Nomad Nation.

"Useful." – Konrad Sokolov, Xperydes Omni-national Valuation Analyst. Requests for clarification were politely declined.

another's private hell. While this is fine when everyone stays inside their communes, in the core some conflict is inevitable. Outside observers have often wondered how the Radical Mothership's myriad and mutually exclusive worldviews manage to keep from tearing each other apart. The truth is, they haven't always. And a lot of Bakunians paid the price.

DISSONANCE IN THE EQUILIBRIUM

Bakunin's first decade, dubbed the Equilibrium Phase, was a tumultuous time in the Nomad's history and remains a delicate topic to this day. The ship was a grand experiment: a pebble in the sky, stuffed to the brim with agitators, radicals, and social outcasts of every stripe. With little common ground besides their rejection of existing society, settling these disparate groups into some kind of balance was the dominant struggle of the Radical Mothership's early days.

It all came to a head in a clash that would come to be known as The Dissonance. Accounts differ on the specifics, but no fewer than twelve different communes were involved in the incident, with Kairos Module's rigid totalitarianism clashing violently with the now-defunct Unbound Voices group and the Children of Reinvention's hyper-progressive philosophies. Equinox was there too, though few would assign any importance to the fact until much later on.

Bakunin has always been home to revolutionary social memes, but during the Equilibrium Phase there was nothing to keep their viral nature from spreading like wildfire, transforming the core area into an ideological battleground. Eventually, it became a physical one. When the Children of Reinvention's flash mob protest coincided directly with Kairos Module's proselytising, conflict was inevitable. But, no one was prepared for how violent it would become. As with most details from the Equilibrium Phase, accounts on who exactly threw the first punch vary wildly. Then when Praxis's Beauvoir and Equinox modules arrived on the scene, it was like trying to fight fire with gasoline: explosions were inevitable. Though few expected that to be so literally true.

The fighting sprawled into every corner of the core, rapidly escalating in violence and scope. What began as a garden variety street brawl crescendoed in a cascade of homemade explosives, breaching the Mothership's hull, and putting all of *Bakunin* at risk. Horrified by the damage they'd caused, *Bakunin's* citizens came together to try and absterge the damage. People who'd been tearing each other apart mere moments ago worked side-by-side to rescue trapped civilians. It might have been heart-warming if it wasn't a tragedy of their own making. As it was, it was more of a chaotic scramble than the heroic act of solidarity that most accounts describe.

When all was said and done, ninety-seven Bakunian citizens died in the hull breach, most of whom weren't even involved in the original disagreements. As a sombre, mournful *Bakunin* tried to make sense of the tragedy, an onlooker was reportedly overheard saying, "It goes against everything that's good about *Bakunin's* social energy. We've got to do better."

In the wake of their self-inflicted wounds, The Radical Mothership was determined to try.

QUANTIFYING THE CHAOS

It's one thing to recognise a need for structure. It's another thing altogether to get a population as diverse as *Bakunin's* to agree on what that structure should look like. In the wake of the hull breach, most Bakunians were keeping their tempers in check, but even so, tensions remained high. No one wanted to see the structure that would govern their existence dominated by an oppositional worldview, though very few had a suggestion that wouldn't inflict something similar on a different module. It was gridlocked.

Then, arriving just as suddenly as they had during the crisis, a new movement appeared. Comprised of the front-line rescue workers, volunteers, and circumstantial heroes who kept the hull breach from becoming an even worse incident, this diverse collective of disparate individuals proposed something drastic.

Calling it the Moderated Discourse Project, individuals from different modules, walks of life, and philosophical perspectives gathered to create a kind of societal scaffolding. Something that could support the impassioned debate that formed *Bakunin's* fiery heart, while keeping those disagreements confined to the semiotic and dialectic realms, albeit in expressive, multi-layered fashion.

Together, they sketched out the architecture of a self-regulating engagement protocol, a living forum where discussion was encouraged, diversity was applauded, and civility was enforced — physically, if need be. Across a furtive span of sleepless nights, extended brainstorming sessions, and more than a bit of mad social science, they presented the bones of a living, moderated engagement structure, a dialectic scaffold that wouldn't buckle under the weight of *Bakunin's* passion. They crafted a masterpiece.

And then they handed it over to people who couldn't care less if it died in the womb.

THE PANDEMOS SOLUTION

The Moderated Discourse Project was comprised of idea people, and their project reflected that. Like many Bakunian ideas, there was genius in the plan. Like many Bakunian ideas, there wasn't a clear roadmap as to how the details would be implemented. So, like many Bakunian ideas before and since, the Moderated Discourse Project faced an uncertain future, with no outside assistance to be found. During the Equilibrium Phase, the motherships that would eventually form the Nomad Nation had no idea what to make of each other just yet. Thus, the Radical Mothership would live or die by its own hand, and *Bakunin* was doggedly determined to live.

Unwilling to watch their masterpiece die in committee, the Moderated Discourse Project reached out to the Pandemos Commune — a reclusive group of communication scientists, hostage negotiators, and subversive marketers who as far as anyone could tell, had come to *Bakunin* to document its eventual collapse — and all but dared them to craft an implementation plan. Pandemos had come to observe, but the scientific competitiveness that would come to define Praxis burned brightly in them. They accepted the challenge on one condition: if they found a working solution, it would be implemented, no questions asked.

With their backs to the wall, the Moderated Discourse Project had little choice but to acquiesce. Much to their own surprise, Pandemos was handed the keys to the revolution and told to make it go. They set about the task of taking Social Energy from fever dream to functional policy and were ready to prove that it could be done, or die trying.

First, the underlying economic principles received a sound foundation, based somewhat ironically on the nascent Bank of Tunguska's operational precepts. Next, Bakunian hacker collectives created a quantronic blockchain to securely host the massive amount of real-time feedback necessary to keep this new system running. And finally, Pandemos's own crisis experts laid out a roadmap for what would eventually become the Moderator Corps, a legally empowered paramilitary strike force that would add some teeth to the tenets of Social Energy. A literal ban-hammer, if you will.

What the Moderated Discourse Project got back wasn't a utopian vision of a perfect future, nor an elegant example of theory-crafted simplicity. What they got was something that with effort, support, and a little luck could genuinely reshape the way that Bakunian society functioned without collapsing under its own weight. In what was easily the most lopsided vote in the Radical Mothership's history, this new structure — named "Social Energy" for the commentary that inspired it — passed with 87% of citizens' approval. The Moderated Discourse Project spun out into the Department of Social Energy (DSE), and the Moderator Corps who were both entrusted to implement, manage, and enforce *Bakunin's* Social Energy, a duty that the two organisations carry out to this day.

WHAT IT DOES

"If you've felt it, you've grokked it," goes the popular saying amongst Bakunians, and not without reason. On its surface, Social Energy seems intricate, but ultimately not that complicated: it's a state-sponsored form of social networking, with elements of a

> "The Equilibrium Phase was all about brinkmanship, radical difference, and a stubborn refusal to let the dream die, a tightrope walk on razor wire, stretched between skyscrapers. The Social Energy negotiations were the era in microcosm."
>
> — Mikalah Prokhorov, Bank of Tunguska. From Social Energy: Birth of a Movement: available on Maya & Arachne this summer.

FAKE IDS AND SOCIAL ENERGY

Every ID system in the Human Sphere is a complex cypher in its own right, a labyrinthine nightmare of interlocking systems, and Social Energy makes most of them look downright quaint by comparison. Using a Fake ID on *Bakunin* will generally work fine, but any in-depth examination such as trying to make a purchase using your counterfeit Social Energy Rank quickly exposes the lie. That said, Bakunians generally don't mind people concealing their identity so long as they're not defrauding businesses. So while Fake IDs are less effective on the Radical Mothership, they're scrutinised far less frequently.

CIRCLE EVALS

From newcomers to children to those with more ambition than caution, there's always someone who thinks that they've figured out how to game the reputation system. This usually involves a small group, giving each other positive evals over slightly different metrics. These "circle evals" don't usually go anywhere. Not only are they insufficient to trick the algorithms that watch for such abuses, but between the LAIs, "other" AIs, and human Infowarriors, these tricks have all been tried before, and aren't fooling anybody.

reputation economy baked in. And while that's technically correct, it misses a lot of what makes Social Energy different from say, a Hypercorporation's Omni-Sided Platform, or a Shentang resident's Citizen Score.

Social Energy is the heart of *Bakunin*. And like any heart, it's hard at work making sure that all the individual parts and pieces are functioning.

INDIVIDUAL STANDING

Social Energy starts with the individual. Everyone who sets foot on the Radical Mothership has a place in and an impact on Social Energy. Thus, every individual needs to exist as a distinct entity within it. Without this foundation, the rest of the system crumbles. For Social Energy to function, it needs to be able to tell people apart.

It goes without saying that identity theft is a massive concern, though a well-managed one by any standard. Social Energy is only as strong as people's confidence in it; one skilled imposter could do significant damage to that surety. Thus, the DSE is deadly serious about its information security, often quite literally. More than one hacker has taken an involuntary stroll outside the ship for their attempt to subvert Social Energy, though such incidents have become increasingly rare as time goes by.

Most hackers who like the idea of testing themselves against Social Energy's legendary quantronic security do so in DSE-sponsored hacking challenges, with significant rewards awaiting anyone who can find exploitable weaknesses in the Energy's quantronic labyrinth. And any mercenary Wardrivers, corporate spies, or intelligence operatives who would risk taking on *Bakunin*'s best Infowarriors probably have grand designs that go beyond fifteen minutes of identity theft and are spending their efforts elsewhere. With that foundation in place, people generally trust what they're seeing in Social Energy. Which is important, as they see a lot.

HERALDRY 2.0

There's an old saying on *Corregidor:* "If you don't have your reputation, you don't have anything." That takes on a literal weight within Social Energy, as an individual's actions follow them wherever they go. At its most basic level, there's a rudimentary evaluation that's always available within Social Energy, a simple thumbs up or thumbs down. While this does provide a useful metric for calculating a user's reputation score, nobody pays it much mind.

In *Bakunin*'s Social Energy, reputation is everything, though it's anything but simple. Based on stories, anecdotes, and impressions, an individual's place

in Social Energy is a ridiculously complex construct, based on the semiotic impression that they leave upon it. Every action — from social pleasantries to political discourse, graffiti tags to gardening — leaves an impression on those around it. Geists record the context of these impressions, feeding them into the larger system. Each evaluation is weighted against the circumstances of the moment, the individual's prior actions, and all parties' current standings within Social Energy.

This results in a living, dynamic reputation, existing somewhere between personal branding, popular rumour, and individual styling. These neo-heraldic banners provide the bedrock of *Bakunin*'s Social Energy: an ID so complex, dynamic, and volatile, that trying to fool the system is usually a waste of everyone's time.

That said, it's still a system. This being *Bakunin*, people have, of course, attempted to game the structure. There are many reasons why this doesn't work — the DSE's custom LAIs looming large among them — but there's a simpler force at play: Social Energy doesn't track what it considers duplicate evals. Each individual ID has a general approve/disapprove flag attached to them which unloads a barrage of frequent, shallow, positive impressions and generally has no effect on their standing within Social Energy. At best, *Bakunin* gets the impression that you're fond of someone; at worst, it might get you flagged as a spammer.

Opinions can, and do change, and evals do with them. Still, there's a real, tangible weight to a lot of positive or negative evaluations. A lot of small, positive interactions can really build up over time, resulting in a rock-solid reputation rating.

One of the more controversial additions to Social Energy has been the introduction of weighted rankings. The idea is that an eval from someone with a lot of Social Energy behind them should count for more than an eval from someone in poor standing. Feeling that this went against the spirit of *Bakunin,* and not wanting to see a sort of "reputation elite" emerge, the initial backlash was so loud and severe, that the idea was scuttled almost immediately. And while modern Social Energy algorithms do take the evaluator's current standing into account, it's merely one of the innumerate factors that go into an individual's score, a small enough factor that no one's up in arms about it. At the end of the day, there's only so much that one person's opinion matters. To really make waves in the Social Energy, you need to influence people in numbers.

SEMIOTIC CONSTRUCTIVISM

Any individual, no matter how influential, is still just one voice among the cacophony that is *Bakunin*. But when those voices begin to make patterns, rising in unison? That's when things start to get interesting.

Social consensus, as the concept is generally understood, doesn't really exist within Social Energy, at least, not for very long. Consensus implies an agreed-upon truth, something that people uniformly hold to be self-evident, which is far too static a principle to exist within *Bakunin's* Social Energy. Instead, it shapes society through principles of semiotic constructivism, a postmodern philosophy with an empirical centre. Dreams brought to life in a tangible way.

The semiotic landscape of Social Energy is a clash of ideas, symbolism, revolutionary branding, and other memetic forces, virally spreading across *Bakunin's* quantronic patina in unpredictable, organic ways. If, at any point, patterns begin to emerge in this chaos, it's usually a sign of consensus starting to build. Social Energy is notoriously difficult to hijack, so any appearance of agreement is usually an authentic social movement, expressed by Bakunian citizens, and coalescing organically.

The fundamental concepts of semiotic constructivism deals with a philosophical question — what is real? — and boils it down into tangible chunks. Ignoring (mostly) spiritual and existential concerns, it looks at the realities of Social Energy and attempts to identify and codify them. These constructs are ephemeral in nature, existing in the moment, then shifting to become something else entirely. As the DSE is fond of saying, Social Energy can tell you what's real, just don't expect it to stay that way for long.

Still, the semiotic constructs floating about Social Energy at any given time provide an invaluable way to understand the Radical Mothership's current thoughts on everything from fad diets to interstellar politics.

PURCHASING POWER

One of the more practical aspects of Social Energy is its use as a sort of cryptocurrency. *Bakunin* has always been home to several different sub-economies, and attempts to reconcile them into discrete, yet compatible, systems had proved to be enough

> "Fundamentally, it's a question about the nature of reality. What is real? How do you know? We can talk about physics, biology, but when it comes to ideas, it gets messy.
>
> Semiotic constructivism is the acknowledgement that outside of empirical, physical phenomena, 'reality' and 'truth' boil down to whatever people say they are. More specifically, they're whatever people agree upon at that moment in time. These truths are ephemeral, dynamic. They don't stay where you put them. It's one of the elements that makes Social Energy a living, breathing entity. Truth is out there. But it moves when you're not looking."
>
> — The Artful Codger: quantronic university lecture. Freely distributed on Arachne.

of a headache that most had given up hope of ever seeing them connect.

But with the introduction of Social Energy, these micro-economies found themselves a fiscal *lingua franca*. Here was a heavily encrypted system that was already tracking an individual's reputation, as well as their overall contributions to the welfare of the Nomad Nation. Plenty of successful cryptocurrencies have been built on less, and the allure of bending a quantronically assisted democratic platform to other purposes had a definite appeal to the Radical Mothership's denizens.

It didn't hurt that it worked. Buyers, sellers, deal facilitators, every step of the transaction was reflected in participants' Social Energy, allowing Nomads to buy and sell with increased confidence. Built on Tunguskan banking principles, Social Energy was actually well-equipped to serve as a sort of self-regulating line of credit, implicitly available to every Bakunian by virtue of their participation in the ship's Social Energy.

Today, Social Energy Credit (SEC) is used seamlessly alongside or in place of other currencies anywhere that Nomads do business, a subset that when all is said and done, encompasses huge swaths of the Human Sphere. Other factions, and indeed, other Nomads have been slow to adopt Social Energy as a currency. In fairness, without extending the system in its entirety, its value as a cryptocurrency becomes much more volatile. While relatively stable for most Nomads, investing in SECs is a risky proposition for most financial actors.

After all: how much money do you really want to have tied up in *Bakunin's* opinion of you?

DAILY USE

For most Bakunians, however, it's a simpler proposition. The barter economy has blossomed into an entirely functional reputation economy, and most day-to-day purchases are easily handled entirely in Social Energy.

Want a cup of coffee? A new hat? Early access to a new sensaseries pilot? If you're in good standing within Social Energy, the transaction is simply associated with your profile, and you go on your way. This line of soft credit transcends industries on the Radical Mothership. Until you start talking about massive purchases, most people can simply exchange goods and services based on reputation, cutting banks and conventional currency out of the transaction altogether.

For larger purchases though, the system functions like a credit rating. Much like a bank extending a line of credit to someone with a dodgy financial

history, most exchanges over a certain SEC value will automatically flag as risky. But, this is still *Bakunin*. Beyond a friendly warning, nothing about the Radical Mothership is designed to stop people from making terrible mistakes. Quite the opposite, in fact.

DEMOCRATIC PROCESS

Bakunian governance is, by design, an elegant mess. Given the impossible mosaic of microgovernents that comprises its modules, one could be forgiven for expecting a tangle of bureaucracy slowing *Bakunin's* governmental apparatus to a snail's pace. Yet, the Radical Mothership is famously able to act with decisive swiftness, changing metaphorical and sometimes literal course with surprising alacrity. How does something so unapologetically heterogeneous move with such agility?

Some mysteries are better left undisturbed. But a big part of it is surely the role of Social Energy in Bakunian decision making. When contrasted with other heads of state, *Bakunin's* Conciliator is comparatively unburdened with bureaucracy. Most societal referendums are resolved via Social Energy, rather than governmental action, leaving the Conciliator to focus on the big picture.

A tour through *Bakunin's* modules coughs up everything from lineal monarchies to neo-consociational microstates and everything in-between. Anthropologists have tried to classify its myriad governmental systems into a cohesive superstructure. To date, the churn of ideas just moves too fast for anyone to keep up with.

Yet the Conciliator is remarkably unburdened by this. Social Energy not only provides a quantronic forum for the discussion of ideas, but the means of civic engagement, democratic or otherwise. Each module is essentially left to govern themselves, with their chosen representatives working with the Conciliator when necessary, but otherwise minding their own business.

For the Conciliator's part, most of their job entails resolving disputes between modules and keeping *Bakunin* in the air, so to speak. When decisive action is required, a brief survey of the prevailing Social Energy can produce a ready-made consensus — or at least, a reasonable facsimile — at a moment's notice. This allows the Conciliator to make decisions quickly, while staying true to what *Bakunin's* citizens actually want.

At least, as close as a politician could ever hope to get.

> "Power to the People: even if they don't know what to do with it."
>
> — Quantronic graffiti: Sunset Boulevard: Promenade Layer.

HOW IT WORKS

Bakunians talk about Social Energy like it's a living, breathing entity, and it takes on an almost mystical quality, a subtle reality that permeates every facet of existence. Flowery descriptions aside, the practical realities of Social Energy are seamlessly interwoven into Bakunian society in ways that might not be immediately obvious.

SRSLY, THOUGH

The preferred method of communicating one's standing within the Social Energy is expressive, but nebulous. While it might be technically correct to describe one's current standing in *Bakunin's* Social Energy as "like a wave reaching a crest on a shore of jagged obsidian," or the less prosaic "better than yesterday," many Bakunians desire greater transparency—and a description that doesn't make their head hurt.

So the DSE set for themselves the unenviable task of creating a metric that could not only capture enough of the nuance of Social Energy to be a useful reference point, but also be communicated in a fashion that human beings could readily understand. The results were a derived statistic that no one was quite happy with, but could do in a pinch. Or in other words, as good as this was ever going to get.

Thus, the Social Energy Ranking System Logarithmic Yardstick (SRSLY) was created.

Shortened to an acronym in a cheeky nod to the protesters who opposed the idea of reducing Social Energy's distinctly qualitative metrics down to a number, SRSLY is the product of countless variables, weighted, tested, and converted into a positive integer. Ostensibly rankings are between 1 and 10,000, though in a practical sense, values below 2,000 and above 8,000 are extraordinarily rare. These numbers aren't static. Like everything about Social Energy, they're constantly shifting and swirling, but it usually takes a significant event for a shift of more than three digits to occur over the course of a day.

SUB-ZERO RATINGS

Within SRSLY, it's mathematically impossible to achieve a score of 0. On *Bakunin,* being a Zero has an altogether different meaning. There is, however, a sub-zero rank, reserved for entities who've become *persona non grata* aboard the Radical Mothership and are functionally excluded from its Social Energy. Currently, only ALEPH and the Equinox group boast this status, and it would take an act of significantly destructive scope to add another name to it.

A SAMPLING OF DIFFERENT BAKUNIAN COMMUNES' GOVERNMENTS

Under the assumptions that power corrupts and seeking power benefits the already-corrupt, the Ryecatcher commune operates under a procedurally generated demarchy, choosing its political officials by way of random sample. In clear defiance of the Sole AI Bill, the BombCluster commune created an advanced algorithm that straddles the line between LAI and self-aware entity, choosing civil servants from its population based on longitudinal evaluation of their standing within local and ship-wide Social Energy.

Several mythocracies have surfaced of late: a uniquely *Bakunian* amalgamation of mythological superstructure, and governmental ministries. Technically a form of parliamentary democracy, mythocracies appoint officials to mythic archetypes, who oversee matters in keeping with their divine portfolios.

Most famous among these is probably the Asgard Cluster module. Natalie Bremming currently holds the Odinseat, entering her third term of being a hands-off decision maker who occasionally lays down the law. Ola Sigurdson is doing a fine job in his first year in the Thorseat, solving crises where they exist, and causing crises that will need solving where they don't.

And of course, there's the Lokiseat, currently held by an individual simply known as Loki, entering their fourth term. Initially, there were official guidelines as to the seat's duties and areas of authority, but seeing as how they've consistently been replaced with pranks of increasingly elaborate nature, the general consensus is that Loki knows what they're doing, and should be left alone to do so.

Thus far, no one has managed to successfully object to the notion.

Many ideological purists worried that this would reduce Social Energy to a popularity contest, a race to achieve high scores among society's most privileged. As it turns out, they needn't have worried—*Bakunin's* tendency to rebel against the powerful and mainstream automatically paints a target on anyone who ascends to too lofty a height in the informal SRSLY leaderboards. And, as the DSE is quick to point out, the SRSLY metric is merely meant to give a rough idea of one's standing in the complex vicissitudes of Social Energy. By themselves, the numbers are all but meaningless.

Still, SRSLY remains the most accessible, understandable way to suss out one's place within Social Energy at a glance, ensuring that for now at least, the metric isn't going anywhere.

QUANTRONIC BATTLEGROUNDS

When someone thinks of Social Energy, what comes to mind? For many, it's the vibrant quantronic graffiti, spattered across *Bakunin's* collective sensorium. A battleground of colourful ideas, viral memes, and

"You'd think that all Aspects would automatically qualify for Sub-Zero ratings, right? Not necessarily. Between AI liberation activists, more conciliatory modules, and people who just think that Achilles is hot, there's enough support that nobody's gonna be pre-emptively pariah'd. We Bakunians pride ourselves on seeing the individual, even if the individual is part of a malevolent artificial intelligence bent on galactic domination via the subjugation of all sapient life.

...What? Do I have something in my teeth?"

— Calamity Jane, who did not have something in her teeth, on the *Go-Go Marlene* show: Only on Oxyd!

contesting manifestos, that are all spread out across augmented reality like a neon turf war, brilliant, beautiful, and remarkably contained. Like remotely observing a volcano, the heat, violence, and power are obvious, if not immediately threatening.

SRSLY RANK BRACKETS

1–1,000 (Soft Exile): Getting the prevailing Social Energy to agree on anything is legendarily difficult. So if the legendarily tolerant *Bakunin* holds such a uniformly low opinion of you, something terrible must have happened. For most individuals, this is indicative of exile, reserved for traitors and sworn enemies, and not even all of those make it this low.

1,001–2,000 (Troublemakers): Not the Fun Kind, Either: Anyone in this range is either a sworn public enemy of the Radical Mothership, or *Bakunin* has decided that they might as well be.

2,001–3,000 (Griefer): Anyone whose contributions to the prevailing Social Energy are outweighed by the drain they're placing on it.

3,001–4,000 (Disfavoured): At this bracket, the prevailing wisdom considers you to be more trouble than you're worth. Usually. Lucky for you, *Bakunin* has a soft spot for trouble.

4,001–5,000 (None More Grey): The uninspiring side of average, this is a common place for Bakunians to find themselves following a particularly spectacular failure. That said, achieving a rank this high is considered quite the accomplishment for a PanOceanian.

5,001–6,000 (Promising): The average Bakunian spends most of their time in this bracket, rarely falling too far below, or rising much above it. It's here where some of the most vital debate occurs: in the eyes of many Bakunians, if this many people agree and disagree with you simultaneously, what you're saying probably has some merit.

6,001–7,000 (Pot-Stirrers, The Useful Kind): A seriously contributing member to the Radical Mothership's Social Energy, and probably someone who helps to shape it. At this rank, there's enough activity to be constantly noticed, and the positive outweighs the negative, not an easy balancing act.

It's worth noting that this doesn't mean that everyone likes the individual in question. It's more that they're a consistent dialectic contributor, and their efforts are spurring productive discourse. Even if relatively few individuals like or agree with them, they've got *Bakunin*'s Social Energy buzzing. That's valuable.

7,001–8,000 (Opinion Leaders and Agenda Celebrities): At this bracket, not only does the individual have the ability to get people to listen to them, the Social Energy is usually glad they did. These individuals often have an ephemeral cult of personality formed around them. Ignoring or derailing their posts is difficult, leading to a greater number of people being influenced by them, leading to more in their movement, and so on.

8,001–9,000 (Ideological Rock Star): Some of the highest heights one can hit within the Social Energy. Most never spend more than a few hours in this bracket before the inevitable backlash brings their rankings hurtling back down to reality.

Over 9,000: This ranking holds a near-mythical status among Bakunians. Very few ever achieve it, and no one stays there for very long.

LAYERS

One of the most unique aspects of Social Energy is how much of its business is conducted in public spaces. AR-graffiti tags, meme-wars, and even the occasional level-headed discussion are all constantly occurring throughout the Radical Mothership. But what many don't realise is just how deep this rabbit hole goes. While this discussion is technically occurring in public spaces, the quantronic reality that a tourist interacts with is not the same one that a Bakunian native does. A native's experience is going to be richer and deeper that of a tourist's and not in a metaphorical sense.

Bubbling just beneath the surface, Social Energy's most vital discourse occurs in *Bakunin*'s quantronic substrata, hiding in plain sight, and intricately tied to the Radical Mothership's topography. The localised datasphere that coats *Bakunin*'s interior is actually a stack of interconnected, but otherwise discrete layers. The debate you really want to engage in might be happening across the ship, which requires people to get out and move around *Bakunin* for discourse.

These quantronic substrata allow for the discussion, debate, and ideological battles that Social Energy needs to function, without overwhelming visitors or being constantly interrupted by those without an understanding of the topic at hand. It's not seen as being exclusionary. To the contrary, it's considered good housekeeping. Not every visitor is going to want to become embroiled in Bakunian politics, nor be assaulted by competing manifestos with every step. By stratifying its quantronic patina, *Bakunin* creates an environment that isn't overwhelming or hostile to non-Bakunians as long as they remain in core.

While the fractal nature of nested substrata can grow to nearly boundless lengths, there are three generally acknowledged layers to *Bakunin*'s quantronic substrata: the Promenade, Jareth's Labyrinth, and the Undercurrent.

THE PROMENADE

Also known as "general," the "starter area," or the "newbie zone," the outer layer of Social Energy is not entirely unlike similar quantronic environments to the degree that any environment can be similar on *Bakunin*. Designed to be welcoming to guests, and a comfortable environment that any Bakunian could exist in while still interacting with Social Energy, the Promenade manages to tow this line with a fair share of success.

However, it wasn't always this way. While the Promenade of today sports an AR Patina awash in competing graffiti, the imagery is more interactive mural than unmitigated assault upon the senses. Historically, the latter held sway; images designed to shock, disturb, and otherwise disrupt people's daily routines were all the rage in revolutionary meme-tags. But while they may have been effective in disrupting people's assumptions, they were also making the core downright unhospitable and not just for outsiders, but for plenty of Nomads as well.

An unhospitable environment is the kiss of death for a tourism industry, so at the Conciliator's direction, the DSE initiated a migration to a deeper layer of the quantronic substrata, as well as incentivising would-be influencers to keep the sensory assault to a dull roar.

The idea of moving most discussion to a deeper stratum held appeal for all involved. Today's Promenade layer is a more mischievous, playful take on Social Energy as a memetic battleground. Enticing aesthetics carry the day, where the hint, the promise of something more just beneath the surface is the dominant style. Aspiring towards allure, the Promenade has blossomed into one of the more artistically pleasing AR environments in the Human Sphere. And it's just scratching the surface.

JARETH'S LABYRINTH

Honouring the classical musician, performance artist, and auteur David Bowie, this quantronic substrata takes its name from a mythical realm and its enigmatic ruler, described in one of his cinematic landmarks. In tribute to its namesake, this domain is a place of fearless art, bold ideas, and unimpeachable style. Jareth's Labyrinth, often just called "the Labyrinth," is a place where ideas have power, and reality itself can be rearranged if that's what's necessary to make a point.

Making one's way through the logic gates, authorisation prompts, and other quantronic airlocks in place isn't a trivial task — though it can certainly look like one when observing a Bakunian native in their home environment. But all the obstacles aren't meant to keep anyone out. Rather, they're meant to ensure that no one wanders out into the layer on accident.

Blindly stumbling into the Labyrinth is sure to be an adventure, to say the least.

In the Labyrinth, discourse occurs free of constraints, structure, or a need for decorum. However, the layer isn't simply just a cacophonous wasteland of militant ideas, dissonantly shouting each other down without regard for anyone around them, though that's certainly an element. This is the wild frontier of Social Energy: raw, unfiltered, and passionate. Very few matters are actually decided

in Jareth's domain, but countless ideas have been forged in its crucible.

THE UNDERCURRENT

If you don't get lost in the Labyrinth, there exists yet another layer. Purposefully obscured, accessing this layer requires genuine effort on the user's part. Always tied to a physical location, and requiring non-trivial effort to access, the goal is not to be accessible. Instead, these nodes are deliberately antagonistic. One day, it could require the answer to a riddle; the next, a complicated quantronic oubliette. The day after, it might be identity-locked to only allow a few specific individuals in, or have moved to an entirely different area of the ship.

Colloquially referred to as the "undercurrent," this sub-layer of engagement requires genuine quantronic aptitude to be able to identify, much less access and interact with. Like a nightclub with a hidden entrance in a bodega, these nexuses of Social Energy are hiding in plain sight, nested deep within otherwise mundane locations. Public art installations, guide terminals, cafes, and coffee shops all host these hidden nodes on a semi-regular rotation.

Once an individual has gained access to a particular undercurrent, however, worlds of possibilities reveal themselves. The exchange of ideas unfettered by egos, clandestine meetings deciding the future of the Nomad Nation, or just finding a place to receive genuine constructive criticism, free of the subjective maelstrom of subjective viewpoints crashing around the Jareth's Labyrinth at any given time — these and more are nestled in the undercurrent.

Gaining access to the Social Energy Undercurrent is often a rite of passage on *Bakunin*, with a number of modules not considering their residents to be full adults until they've shown that they can locate and meaningfully interact with the Undercurrent at least once. Ultimately, it's not the best, or most important substrata, merely the most exclusive. The Undercurrent is a members-only club, with but two criteria: you must have something to contribute to the Social Energy, and you must be willing to go out of your way to do so.

GONE FISHING

None of this works if the Social Energy is compromised. And while its quantronic security is second to none, that still leaves numerous avenues to exploit. Like the old Tunguskan maxim suggests, any sufficiently complex system can be hacked, and many an enterprising soul has attempted to hijack the Social Energy and direct it to serve their own ends.

PLAYTEST NOTE
SRSLY, SER?
Later in the chapter, rules for Social Energy are introduced, including a 1–5 ranking of a character's Social Energy Rating (SER). If you want a quick and dirty translation, take a SRSLY rating, and divide it by 2,000, rounding to the nearest non-zero whole number. This will result in a rating from 1–5, hopefully giving the player some context as to where their character sits in the prevailing Social Energy.

"It's not that I have a problem with reproductive organs. I don't. But when they're everywhere, they're kind of nowhere, you know?"

—Christine Aldington, Bakunian art curator. Commentary on the Quantronic Cleanup Initiative (better known as the Shred of Dignity Act) of 65 NC.

MORE THAN MEETS THE EYE

It's not uncommon for a Bakunian citizen to spend hours contemplating public works of art. There are many reasons for this, including traditional ones; some people just like sculptures. Most, however, are delving deeply into the nested undercurrent that tends to congregate around such landmarks.

"Question: how many LAIs would pass the new sapience test? How many geists? Answer: as many as we can manage. All of them, if we can swing it."

— Quantronic graffiti. Sunset Boulevard: Undercurrent Layer.

ACCESSING THE LAYERS

Gaining access to the different layers of Social Energy's quantronic substrata can be its own special challenge. While the specifics are likely to change from moment to moment, here's a rough guideline for accessing the different layers in *Bakunin's* substrata.

THE PROMENADE

- Requires a successful **Average (D1) Hacking test** to access, though anyone who can perceive AR can observe the Promenade freely.

THE JARETH'S LABYRINTH

- Requires a minimum Hacking Expertise of 1, or a successful **Average (D1) Education test** to interact with or observe.

THE UNDERCURRENT

- Requires a combined Education and Hacking Expertise of 3 or more, or a successful **Challenging (D2) Analysis, Education, or Hacking test**. May require a **Daunting (D3) Analysis test** to locate a specific Undercurrent.

THE FISHER KING

Countless would-be saboteurs have found themselves "hooked" on one particular hacker's line: an enigmatic Infowarrior who goes by the handle of The Fisher King. Boasting an impressive Social Energy rating due to their tireless defence of the construct, many theories as to their true identity exist, though the reclusive King hasn't come forward in physical space to enjoy the attention. Popular theories include:

- A veteran of the Phantom Conflicts, unable to move due to a retrovirus, taking their revenge on the powers that wronged them
- A collective, perhaps even an entire module of Infowarriors, dedicated to the defence of Social Energy
- An AI, created in Praxis's Black Labs for the sole purpose of hunting down threats to Social Energy
- A particularly gifted, if tormented, Sin-Eater Observant, chained to a medieval torture device and channelling their pain into a never ending thirst for quantronic retribution
- The speaker's cousin's partner's friend, or a similarly convoluted chain of connection

Whatever the truth behind the Fisher King, a few things are beyond dispute: there's a top shelf, military-grade Infowarrior (or several) behind the persona, and they have an uncanny knack for finding, outing, and publicly humiliating anyone attempting to disrupt Social Energy from the outside.

Historically, this has been a recipe for embarrassment, with many Bakunians taking pride in rooting out these outside agents. Fish Tales — stories of how one hooked and humiliated a foreign actor — are remarkably popular. Tales of bumbling spies, lobbyists, and other agents being led in circles are a sure-fire hit at any Bakunian bar. Several individuals have made a hobby of exposing these agents, in a process affectionately referred to as "fishing."

ACTING OUT: RULES FOR SOCIAL ENERGY

More than just a local flavour, *Bakunin's* Social Energy has a tangible impact on the lives of its citizens. For *Infinity* games dealing heavily with the Nomads, or just looking to inject a little Bakunian flair into their sessions, the following rules will help you to integrate Social Energy into your campaign.

Note: These rules are optional. Not every game, even those focused on Nomads, will want to model Social Energy to this amount of resolution. While the rules are meant to be minimally intrusive, and add to the experience without becoming cumbersome, ultimately, each gaming group should decide what will best suit their needs.

FINDING YOUR PLACE: SOCIAL ENERGY RANK (SER) RATING

The details that make up an individual's current standing within the Social Energy are hopelessly complex, consisting of innumerable rankings, trends over time, purchase records, and numerous other qualitative and quantitative factors. These are then expressed with a combination of numerical, anecdotal, and semiotic indicators. There's no such thing as a simple Social Energy Rating.

Even with a hot-rodded geist sorting it all out for them, most Bakunians grasp of their standing within Social Energy boils down to an occasional query of "how am I doing?" sent to their geist. Thus, even though it isn't exactly accurate, many Bakunians rely on the DSE's SRSLY metric to provide a rough indicator of their current standing. In a practical sense, most individuals' places within the Social Energy are best explained by where they fit within a few distinct ranges or categories.

To that effect, in *Infinity* games that utilise the Social Energy rules, characters have a Social Energy Rank rating, or SER rating, represented by a number between 1 and 5 and an indicator describing whether their momentum is trending upward, downward, or remaining neutral. A character's SER rating is not a permanent attribute. Just like the Social Energy itself, an individual's standing will ebb and flow in a constant state of flux. A character's actions, as well as shifting trends within Social Energy, keeps their ratings in constant motion.

Every character begins play with a SER rating. Your current faction plays a significant role in determining this, but don't worry: these ratings aren't set in stone. They can and likely will change a great deal over the course of play.

GENERATE STARTING SER

First, determine your group from the list below. Roll 1d20 and consult the *Starting Social Energy Table* to determine your beginning SER rating. Then, roll 1d20 and consult the *Social Energy Inertia Table* to determine whether your star is rising, falling, or holding steady.

GROUP A

ALEPH, PanOceania, Submondo, Yu Jing

GROUP B

Corporations, Mercenaries, Minor Nations, O-12

GROUP C

Ariadna, Haqqislam, Non-Bakunian Nomads

GROUP D

Bakunian Nomads

STARTING SOCIAL ENERGY TABLE

	ROLL 1D20			STARTING RANK
A	B	C	D	
1–9	1–5	1	–	1
10–18	6–11	2–8	1–5	2
19–20	12–19	9–15	6–12	3
–	20	16–20	13–19	4
–	–	–	20	5

SOCIAL ENERGY INERTIA TABLE

	ROLL 1D20			STARTING RANK
A	B	C	D	
1–6	1–5	1–6	1–8	Falling
7–18	6–15	7–12	9–11	Stable
19–20	16–20	13–20	12–20	Rising

SOCIAL ENERGY IN PLAY

Outside of *Bakunin,* a character's SER rating might not matter much. But when dealing with Nomads, and especially on the Radical Mothership itself, it can massively alter the dynamics of an interaction.

When making a Lifestyle test involving a Bakunian, other Nomad, or in situations where the GM deems it appropriate, compare the two characters' SER ratings. If there's no difference, then proceed normally. If, however, there's a difference between

SER: WHAT DOES IT MEAN?

For a more thorough explanation of what different standings within Social Energy can look like, see *SRSLY Rank Brackets*, p. 52. But for a quick guideline:
- **Rank 1**: Despised or mistrusted
- **Rank 2**: Difficult, unproductive
- **Rank 3**: Average: no strong opinion either way
- **Rank 4**: Insightful, valuable: a boon to the Social Energy
- **Rank 5**: Influential and beloved: very few remain here for long

the two, then subtract the smaller number from the larger number: this results in a value between 1 and 4. We call that value SERge.

This value can affect play in a number of ways, benefiting the side with the greater SER rating:
- The SERge value becomes additional Momentum (or Heat)
- Adding +X🄽 to the character's Morale Soak (where X is equal to the SERge value)
- Increasing intransigence to a given Metanoia effect by +X🄽 (where X is equal value) to the SERge value)

NPC SER RATINGS

The Social Energy rules assume a SER rating for every NPC: but that doesn't need to be an arduous process. In general, most Nomads will have a SER rating between 2 and 4, with the majority coming in at 3. There are a lot of stories to be told around unexpected placement in Social Energy, but if all you need is a quick guideline:
- **SER 1**: Foreign spies, serious bad news
- **SER 2**: Most foreigners, Nomads in a bad way
- **SER 3**: Well-liked foreigners, most Nomads
- **SER 4**: Influential Nomads
- **SER 5**: Almost nobody

AS A CRYPTOCURRENCY

Plenty of Nomads — and other factions as well — use Social Energy as a means of economic exchange every day. But just as there isn't a separate system for making transactions in Sol, Oceana, or Dinar, transactions made with Social Energy Credit (SEC) are handled using the acquisition system from the *Infinity Corebook*. There are some additional options for SERge when making an acquisition:

see p. 52 for guidelines on how to do precisely that.

PLAYTEST NOTE
BOOKKEEPING AND SER

In the world of *Infinity*, a character's place within the Social Energy is the product of millions of individual calculations: tracked by the DSE, monitored by their geist, and represented in a mixture of qualitative and quantitative terms. A character's SRSLY rating is more quantifiable, but understood to be essentially inaccurate.

In a roleplaying game, that much bookkeeping would detract from the experience so the value is boiled down to the much simpler SER, keeping it more manageable. Characters use an exponentially more expressive score; it's an abstraction, designed to facilitate gameplay. That said, if you want to suss out your character's rough SRSLY bracket, see p. 52 for guidelines on how to do precisely that.

PLAYTEST NOTE
EXISTING CAMPAIGNS

If introducing the Social Energy rules to an existing campaign, you may come across some incongruities when generating characters' starting SER ratings; the numbers might not feel reflective of the events in your campaign. In this case, you generally have one of two options: you can either ignore it, freely assigning values that fit the characters, or try to find a way to explain the seeming incongruity. Some amazingly rich stories can come from the latter, but ultimately, there's no right or wrong answer. Just go with what makes sense for your game.

SERGE VALUE EXPENDITURES

SPEND	EFFECT
Press Advantage	Gain SERge value in Momentum
The Weight of Reputation	Add +X Ⓝ to Morale Soak (where X=SERge Value)
Dig in Your Heels	Increase intransigence to a given Metanoia effect by +X Ⓝ (where X=SERge value
I Know Someone	Subtract the SERge value from (or add to) an item's Tariff rating (min: 0, max 5)
Social Energy Credit	Gain "phantom Assets" equal to have the SERge value, rounded town, useable only on this roll

- Subtract the SERge value from (or add to) an item's Tariff rating. Tariffs can only be reduced to 0, or raised to 5 in this fashion.
- Gain "phantom assets" equal to half the SERge value, rounded down, usable only on this roll.

SER MIGRATION

Social Energy is dynamic. It's constantly waxing and waning, shifting due to forces both in and out of the characters control. If we stopped to reassess SER ratings every few minutes, the game would become an exercise in tedium. To avoid this, changes in a character's SER generally happen at the end of, or between sessions.

As noted above, there are three types of Social Energy inertia: Falling, Stable, and Rising.

Falling: If a character's SER is Falling, they need to succeed at a **Lifestyle test**, with a difficulty equal to their current SER rating, or risk reducing their SER rating by 1. If they succeed, then they avoid any loss. By spending 2 Momentum, they can change their inertia to Stable. If they fail the test, however, they reduce their SER by 1, and their inertia remains Falling.

Stable: If a character's SER is Stable, then they don't need to take any actions, and can stay exactly as they are. If, however, they wish to increase their inertia, they can attempt a **Lifestyle test** with a difficulty equal to their current SER rating. If they're successful, they can change their inertia to Rising. If, however, they fail the test, their inertia changes to Falling — such are the risks of pressing your luck within Social Energy.

Rising: If a character's SER is Rising, it's an advantageous, if precarious, position, with a small window of opportunity. If the character does nothing, then their inertia resets to Stable, and no further actions are needed. However, if they succeed at a **Lifestyle test** with a difficulty equal to their current SER +1, then they can increase their SER rating by 1 point (to a maximum of 5), and set their inertia to Falling. If they fail the test, then there's no change in their SER, though they still set their inertia to Falling.

SER 5: If a character reaches the top of the charts, a few additional elements come into play. Firstly, at SER 5, a character's inertia is automatically set to Falling, and can never improve while they remain at the top. Additionally, any SER Migration tests they make are at +1 difficulty while they remain at SER rating 5. In short, it's lonely at the top, and it comes with a massive bulls-eye on your back.

CHAPTER 4
NOMAD CHARACTERS

Coming of age among the stars isn't like growing up on a planet. The Nomad Nation is a different experience than in the rest of the Human Sphere, and even the three Motherships have massive cultural differences. Through it all, the uniquely punk sensibilities of the Nomads get into every nook and cranny of life. Whether doctors, lawyers, hackers, or radical performance artists, there is a thread of defiant rebellion running through the Nomad DNA.

Nomad characters can be created using the variant rules in this chapter, rather than those in the *Infinity Corebook*. If doing so, the entries presented here supersede their counterparts in the Corebook.

DECISION FOUR: NOMAD STATUS

While Nomads have a remarkable amount of social mobility, the status they're born into still plays a key role in determining a Nomad's path through life. Where they call home plays an even bigger role.

STEP ONE: SOCIAL CLASS
Before determining their Social Status, characters in the Nomad faction need to determine their background. Consult the *Nomad Heritage Table* to determine the specifics of your heritage and gain the listed Heritage Trait.

NOMAD HERITAGE TABLE

REGION	HERITAGE TRAIT
Bakunin	Bakunian
Corregidor	Corregidoran
Tunguska	Tunguskan
Planet, Other Faction	Lub'
Commercial Mission	Missionary
Orbitals, Human Edge.	Vagrant

After determining your heritage, roll on the *Nomad Social Status Table* to determine your Status, matching your result with your Heritage Trait. Consult the *Nomad Social Class Table*, and increase the listed attribute by one point and set your Earnings equal to the number shown.

NOMAD LIFEPATH DECISIONS

DECISION ONE— BIRTH HOST
If you roll a 20, you are an Uplift; roll on the Uplift Host Table.

DECISION FOUR— STATUS
The heritage of characters in the Nomad faction grants them a Heritage Trait. In addition, they roll on the Nomad Social Status Table.

DECISION SEVEN— ADOLESCENT EVENT
Characters in the Nomad Faction roll on the Nomad Faction Adolescent Event Tables.

DECISION EIGHT— CAREERS
Instead of rolling on the appropriate Faction Career table in the Corebook, characters in the Nomad Faction roll on the Nomad Faction Career Table as well as the Nomad Faction Career Event Tables. Their Heritage may adjust the difficulty of hazarding certain careers.

HERITAGE TRAITS

In addition to behaving like a normal trait, Heritage Traits also come into play throughout the Lifepath. While the three motherships should be self-explanatory, there are some additional Heritage Traits for those who don't hail from *Bakunin, Corregidor,* or *Tunguska*.

Lub': Short for "land-lubber," those who hail from outside the Motherships have a different perspective, at least in the eyes of their fellow Nomads. Whether it's said with affection or disdain, it's assumed that a Lub' has no idea how to survive in space. Note: characters with a heritage other than Nomad are assumed to be Lubs, regardless of their environment. If you defect to the Nomads, you automatically gain the Heritage Trait Lub'.

Missionary: Not to be confused with the Observants who don't proselytise — anyone from a Commercial Mission gets to dip their toes into every bit of Nomad society, though their understanding is assumed to be broad but shallow. It's also assumed that they know people from every corner of the Human Sphere. An assumption that is only strengthened by the number of people they've met in passing over the years.

Vagrant: Nomads in a true sense of the word, these independent souls live on Orbitals or make their way through the Human Edge, living, for all intents and purposes, on their ships. Whether they're Corregidorian labourers, Bakunian artists, Tunguskan consultants, or something else entirely, Vagrants still pledge allegiance to their Motherships even if they rarely see them. When gaining this Heritage Trait, roll 1d6 to determine your Mothership of origin: *Bakunin* on a result of 1–2, *Corregidor* on a result of 3–4, and *Tunguska* on a result of 5–6.

NOMAD SOCIAL STATUS TABLE

2D6	BAKUNIAN	CORREGIDORAN	TUNGUSKAN	LUB'	MISSIONARY	VAGRANT
2	Underclass	Underclass	Demogrant	Underclass	Underclass	Underclass
3–4	Demogrant	Underclass	Demogrant	Demogrant	Demogrant	Underclass
5–6	Middle	Demogrant	Middle	Demogrant	Middle	Demogrant
7–8	Middle	Middle	Upper	Middle	Middle	Middle
9–10	Upper	Middle	Upper	Middle	Upper	Middle
11	Elite	Upper	Elite	Upper	Elite	Middle
12	Hyper-Elite	Elite	Hyper–Elite	Elite	Elite	Upper

NOMAD SOCIAL CLASS TABLE

2D6	SOCIAL STATUS	ATTRIBUTE	EARNINGS
2	Underclass	Willpower	1
3–5	Demogrant	Personality	2
6–8	Middle	Willpower	3
9–10	Upper	Agility	4
11	Elite	Personality	5
12	Hyper-Elite	Willpower	6

STEP TWO: HOME ENVIRONMENT
By necessity, Nomads are highly communal. Even on *Tunguska*, the surrounding environment can influence a child's upbringing as much as their family, if not more so. Roll 1d6 and consult the *Nomad Home Environment Table*. The result describes the dominant social structure you grew up with. For example, if you had a Bohemian environment as a Hyper-Elite from *Tunguska*, you might have had Bakunian tutors, and their kids were your main peer group. If you had an Old-School upbringing, your parents probably weren't first-generation Corregidorans, but they might be 5th generation Nomads, proudly carrying on their tradition.

HOME ENVIRONMENT TABLE

D6	ENVIRONMENT	ATTRIBUTE	SKILL
1	Bohemian	Personality	Education
2	Violent	Brawn	Acrobatics
3	Garage Rat	Awareness	Tech
4	Old-School	Willpower	Pilot
5	Regimented	Intelligence	Discipline
6	High Society	Personality	Lifestyle

DECISION SEVEN: NOMAD ADOLESCENT EVENT

Across the Human Sphere, adolescence is recognised as a rebellious time in one's life. In a faction defined by rebellion, that can take some extreme forms.

Characters in the Nomad Faction roll on the *Nomad Faction Adolescent Event Tables*. If the character's heritage and faction are different, then they may choose to roll on either faction's unique table on a roll of 1–3.

NOMAD ADOLESCENT EVENT TABLES

D6	TABLE
1–3	Nomad Adolescent Event Table
4	Adolescent Event Table A[1]
5	Adolescent Event Table B[2]
6	Adolescent Event Table C[3]

[1] *Infinity Corebook*, p.49–52

DECISION EIGHT: CAREERS

In the Nomad Nation, carers are more than just a job; they're often a way of life. Becoming a Jaguar or an Interventor is more than a simple change in vocation, it's a response to implied events. By reading between the lines, Nomad characters can gain a rich, complex history, as varied and colourful as the Nomad Nation itself.

NOMAD ADOLESCENT EVENT TABLE

D20	ADOLESCENT EVENTT	SUGGESTED CHARACTER TRAIT	OPTIONAL EFFECT
1	Dragnet caught you trying to hack into the Bank of *Tunguska*. But instead of throwing you in jail, they simply made some introductions.	Known Black Hat	Increase Hacking by 1 rank. You may take Interventor as your first career.
2	You got spaced. You survived, thanks to your vacuum suit, but you screamed your throat bloody raw just the same.	Void Terror	Decrease Morale by 1. Increase the complication range on Extraplanetary tests by 2.
3	Tinkering with your geist, you attempted to overclock its processer. You succeeded, though the end result left you a little exposed.	Obsessive Tinkerer	Increase your geist's Intelligence by 1, but reduce your Firewall by 1.
4	While doing a little zero-G vandalism, you wound up tagging a Bureau Noir agent's ship.	Jinxed	Spend 1d6 years in prison before starting your first career. Gain 1 rank in Extraplanetary and gain a rival or contact in Bureau Noir.
5	You take an internship on one of Praxis's Black Ships. Even better, you survive the process with most of your bits intact.	Insatiable Curiosity	Increase Science by 1 rank. You may take Praxis Scientist as your first career.
6	You volunteered for an experimental neural augmentation procedure. They say they'll have the bugs worked out any day now.	Glitchy Augs	Increase Intelligence by 1, but increase the complication range on Intelligence-based tests by 1.
7	Fed up with your home life, you stole a ship and went joyriding. Did they ever catch you?	Reckless	Increase Pilot by 1 rank.
8	You were beaten within an inch of your life, but they couldn't make you stay down.	Stubborn	Reduce Vigour by 1, but increase Morale by 1.
9	A nasty explosion leaves you badly burnt; your dermal replacements work a little too well.	Hyper-Sensitive Skin	Reduce Brawn by 1.
10	You get accepted into the Tunguskan Outer University's prestigious School of Law, an honour you can't possibly afford. That is, until you're made an offer you can't refuse.	Mafia Connections	Increase Education by 1, but gain a 10 Asset debt. Gain a contact at the university, and you may take Barrister Corps as your first career.
11	They said that replacing your lymph nodes with neomaterials would boost your immune system. It's certainly had an effect.	Shredded Immune System	Increase the complication range on Resistance tests by 2. Repairing this damage is possible, but the procedure will cost 4+4 🅝 (and you probably want a different clinic).
12	You got your first exotic augmentation. It felt better than good: it felt right.	Inhuman Appearance	Gain Cosmetic Augmentation 2. You may take Chimera as your first career.
13	You fell in with a rough crowd, running with the *maras* gangs of *Corregidor*. Caught red-handed, you were offered a choice: prison or something exponentially tougher.	Trouble Magnet	Gain a Criminal Record (see *Infinity Corebook*, p. 54). Either spend 1d6 years in prison before starting your first career or select Jaguar as your first career.
14	You get heavily involved in the protest art scene; footage of your numerous arrests goes viral. At least they got your good side.	The Usual Suspect	You gain 1 rank in Thievery, but all Stealth tests are increased in difficulty by one step in situations where being recognised would cause you a problem
15	You fell ill, and the Praxis doctors were convinced that carbon nanotubes in your spleen were the solution. Regardless, it didn't kill you; perhaps it made you stronger?	Experimental Insides	Increase your complication range on Resistance tests by 2. Increase Vigour by 1.
16	You did it, you got caught, and earned yourself a year of mandatory labour. At least you learned a thing or two about starship maintenance.	Bad Company	Gain a Criminal Record (see *Infinity Corebook*, p. 54). Spend one year in prison before starting your first career, but gain 1 rank in Tech.
17	You fell in with a group of anarchist hackers, taking pot shots at Maya. An Aspect – or maybe ALEPH itself – found you and torched your friends. It saw you, but let you escape, declining to explain its actions.	Person of Interest	Gain 1 Rank in Hacking.
18	You signed up for an experimental military enhancement program. It surpassed expectations.	Early-Access Wetware	Increase Brawn by 1.
19	You always wondered if the struggle was worth it. A better offer came, and you took it; what's the harm in that?	Sellout	You defect to a new faction. Roll on the *Faction Table* (see *Infinity Corebook*, p. 41) to determine your new allegiance. On a roll of 5, 6, or 20, you haven't actually defected; you're a Double Agent.
20	The Praxis doctors were convinced that they could make you immune to disease. They were correct, after a fashion. The dead don't exactly catch cold.	Cynical	Your character died and was resurrected. See the rules for *Resurrection* in the *Infinity Corebook*, p. 54.

DOUBLE AGENTS

In the espionage-rich world of *Infinity*, double (and even triple) agents are rare, but not unheard of. Whether a character is sent to infiltrate, or develops divided loyalties, Double Agents have a lot to keep track of.

They have two factions: their current faction, and their "true faction" where their loyalties lie. By default, Double Agents use their current faction when determining careers, restriction, tariffs, etc. If they wish, they can use their true faction in its place, though this is risky. Any rolls involving your true faction double their complication range (so a complication range of 1 becomes 2, a range of 3 becomes 6, and so on).

In a Wilderness of Mirrors campaign, Double Agents have two different handlers, one each for their current and true factions. When giving out covert objectives, the true faction handler will be cognisant of the Double Agent's need to protect their cover. This may require altering covert objectives. GMs are encouraged to use their discretion.

If a Double Agent's current faction becomes suspicious, it will take steps to ascertain the character's true loyalties. And of course, if their cover is ever blown, a Double Agent can no longer use their current faction when making rolls, though that's likely the least of their concerns.

IT'S ALL WHO YOU KNOW

Nomads of similar backgrounds tend to look out for each other. Thus, your character's Heritage Trait can play a useful role in their career path. Consult the *Heritage Careers Table*. If you elect to hazard a recommended career, you may reduce the difficulty by one step.

HERITAGE CAREERS TABLE

HERITAGE TRAIT	RECCOMENDED CAREERS
Bakunian	Chimera, Clockmaker, Provocateur
Corregidoran	'Cat Squad Member, Jaguar, Heavy Industry
Tunguskan	Barrister Corps, Hacker, Interventor
Lub'	Infiltrator, Investigative Journalist, Pilot
Missionary	Bounty Hunter, Diplomat, Negotiator

Life among the stars presents its own special challenges, as does being the birthplace of Arachne, leading many Nomads to pick up skills that might otherwise be deemphasised. Compared to other factions, the Nomads stress the Hacking and Extraplanetary skills.

Nomad characters may roll on the *Basic Career Table*, spend 1 Life Point to pick a career from the *Basic Career Table,* or spend 1 Life Point to roll on the *Nomad Faction Career Table*. Additionally, whenever they would normally determine a career event they roll on the *Nomad Faction Career Event Tables* to determine which *Career Event Table* to roll on.

NOMAD FACTION CAREER TABLE

D20	CAREER
1	Special Forces[1]
2	Intelligence Operative[1]
3	Reverend Agent[1,2]
4	Heavy Industry[1]
5	Investigative Journalist[1]
6	Hacker[1]
7	'Cat Squad Member
8	Jaguar
9	Negotiator
10	Barrister Corps[2]
11	Chimera
12	Praxis Scientist
13	Infiltrator
14	Interventor[2]
15	Praxis Scientist
16	Mothership Security Corps[2]
17	Clockmaker[2]
18	Provocateur
19–20	Roll on *Faction Table* of Your Choice

[1] Career from *Infinity Corebook.*

[2] Career has a prerequisite of belonging to this faction. You can't hazard this career unless you're of the matching faction. If you roll into this career, you automatically fail your defection check. You can override these limitations by spending 1 Life Point (in which case you were somehow undercover while working the career).

NOMAD FACTION CAREER EVENT TABLES

D6	CAREER
1–3	Nomad Career Event Table
4	Career Event Table A[1]
5	Career Event Table B[1]
6	Career Event Table C[1]

[1] *Infinity Corebook*, p.56–58

NOMAD CAREER EVENT TABLE

D20	CAREER EVENT	GAME EFFECT
1	An old contact from Praxis gets you into an experimental program after the first test subjects found the risks. Most of them.	Either increase an Attribute of your choice by 1, gaining a 10 Asset debt along the way, or gain a contact in Praxis's Black Labs.
2	While on assignment, a hypercorp purchases a controlling interest in your client, resulting in mass layoffs. You're in the process of organising a noisy response when an executive approaches you with a juicy offer.	If you take the offer, increase Earnings by 1, but gain a character trait related to accepting the offer. Otherwise, you are Fired (see *Infinity Corebook*, p. 54).
3	Someone looking exactly like you crashes through a window, accuses you of stealing their identity, and opens fire. After they're chased off, you receive a notice: the technician who does your Cube backups has disappeared.	Gain trait: Cube Doppelgänger.
4	Coming back from a job, your pilot has a medical emergency, and you get shoved into the cockpit. It was certainly a learning experience.	Gain 1 rank in Spacecraft.
5	During some routine external repairs, a sudden impact knocked you and your fellows loose. Your quick thinking managed to save some but not all of the crew. How did you choose?	Gain contacts in a random faction.
6	You're involved in spreading a memetic virus through Maya. ALEPH thanks you for your contributions with a quantronic virus of its own.	Reduce Firewall by 1.
7	When your ship was damaged in transit, everyone looked to you to make the zero-G repairs.	Gain 1 rank in Extraplanetary.
8	Tinkering with your geist's personality emulator, you wind up with mixed results.	Gain Trait: Quirky Geist and increase your geist's Personality by 1.
9	While working planetside, you get a rare taste of terrestrial weather when you're stranded for a week. Did it rain? Snow? Something worse?	Gain 1 rank in Survival but gain a 2 Asset debt to your eventual rescuers.
10	Whether in salvage, falling off the back of a truck, or other means, you find a perfectly good Tinbot just lying around.	Gain a Tinbot Remote. Gain a character trait describing the Tinbot's unique and troublesome quirks.
11	After a workplace accident leaves you hospitalised, you opt to get some structural reinforcement.	Reduce Vigour by 1 but gain a Subdermal Graft Augmentation in a hit location of your choosing.
12	The good news is that experimental brain surgery managed to remove all the shrapnel. The bad news is that some of your synapses are firing a little slower. The worse news is that you had shrapnel in your brain; how'd it get there?	Reduce Intelligence by 1.
13	You met the love of your life. But over time, you've come to suspect that they're an Aspect of ALEPH. Do you confront them?	Gain a contact in a random faction. Work with your GM to determine if they're an ally, rival, or something else entirely.
14	You become part of a truly esoteric subculture.	Gain a character trait describing your new association.
15	You find yourself caught up in a controversy. A *Tunguskan* lawyer can help, but it won't be cheap.	Either reduce Social Status by one step, or gain a 6+6 🛇 Asset debt, as expensive legal trickery saves you.
16	You come across a Tunguskan Elite in some serious hot water. They lean on you to help them out, while Bureau Aegis tries to warn you away. Either course will have benefits and consequences. What do you do?	If you choose to help them, gain a Criminal Record (see *Infinity Corebook*, p. 54) and spend 1d6 years in prison, but gain 10 assets in gratitude payoff. If you choose not to, reduce Social Status by one step, but gain 1 rank in Discipline.
17	A hobby invention of yours becomes a brief fad.	Gain 5 Assets.
18	You strongly disagree with your supervisor, and in grand Nomad tradition, express this by punching them in the face.	You are Fired (see *Infinity Corebook*, p. 54). Gain an appropriate trait.
19	Whether by accident, recklessness, or something more sinister, you found out exactly how well those airlocks work and what it's like to experience the wonders of space without a suit.	Your character died and was Resurrected. See the rules for *Resurrection* (see *Infinity Corebook*, p.54). Gain a trait related to the experience.
20	There's a running joke that the only law that every Nomad obeys is Murphy's law. Well, anything that could go wrong is currently doing so.	Roll again three times on the *Career Event Table* for this career phase. (When spending a Life Point to choose a specific event, you may not choose this result. If you roll duplicate events, it means some similar event has occurred. If you roll Murphy's Law again, add additional rolls.)

'CAT SQUAD MEMBER

Associated more by nomenclature and a shared aesthetic than anything else, Corregidor's Tomcats, Hellcats, and Wildcats are none-theless bound together by a singular thread: it's difficult to imagine the Nomad Nation surviving without them. Whether defending the Motherships, rescuing stranded workers, or out on consignment, life in the NMF's 'Cat Squads is many things, but it's never dull.

ATTRIBUTES						
AGI	AWA	BRW	COO	INT	PER	WIL
+1	+1	+2	+2	+2	+1	+1

SKILLS				EARNINGS
Mandatory	Ballistics	Extraplaentary	Hacking	See 'Cat Squads
Elective	See 'Cat Squads			

GEAR: See 'Cat Squads

SPECIAL: When taking this career for the first time, roll on the 'Cat Squads Table to determine your Squad. Once you've determined your Squad, you no longer roll upon taking this career, but if desired, you can attempt an Average (D1) hazard test to repeat this career in the Squad of your choice. In any case, you can instead spend 1 Life Point to simply choose your Squad.

'CAT SQUADS

Hellcats: The epitome of the NMF's "Always Ready" motto, Hellcats keep themselves in top shape year-round, as at any moment, they may need to deploy in record time, possibly faster. Frequently dropping out of aircraft with little more than a "good luck," Hellcats are not only tough, but disarmingly jovial. After all, if they can survive their missions, what else is there to worry about?

Tomcats: Heroes to the core, Nomad kids fantasize about being Tomcats when they grow up. The Tomcat Special Emergency and Rescue Team is the NMF's answer when things hit the fan. Search and rescue, hostage liberation, or even rapid response military operations, the goal is always the same: save lives.

Wildcats: Unlike their counterparts in search and rescue, rare is the young Nomad who wants to be a Wildcat. Originally comprised of veterans from Africa's "Road Wars"— though survivors might be a more appropriate term — the modern Wildcats are a no-nonsense team of shock troops, drawn from street toughs, violent criminals, and folks with few other immediate options.

Each Squad has a distinct set of Elective Skills that it teaches its troops. When working the 'Cat Squad Member career, roll on the 'Cat Squads Table below or spend 1 Life Point to select a Squad, then use its Electives. At your GM's discretion, you may also use your Squad's Elective Skills in place of the standard for the Special Forces or Intelligence Operative careers, or other careers on a case-by-case basis.

'CAT SQUADS TABLE				
D20	SQUAD	ELECTIVE SKILLS	GEAR	EARNINGS
1–7	Tomcats	Medicine, Spacecraft, Tech	MedKit or Powered Multitool, Light Combat Armour, Combi Rifle	2+2
8–12	Hellcats	Athletics, Medicine, Pilot,	Combat Jump Pack, Spitfire or Assault Hacking Device, Light Combat Armour	2+1
13–20	Wildcats	Discipline, Resistance, Thievery	Boarding Shotgun or Assault Hacking Device, Medium Combat Armour	1+2

BARRISTER CORPS

If the pen is mightier than the sword, the 101st Barrister Corp's legal briefs are the equal of any TAG. A *Tunguska* tradition dating back to the Phantom Conflicts, the Barrister Corps repays aggression towards the Nomads with weaponised legal assaults; geists, LAIs, and more than a few botnets help unleash torrents of legal spam upon their targets. While most documents they produce are only dangerous if ignored, if an inbox is flooded with hundreds of thousands of such memos, one eventually slips through. The 101st prides itself on using unconscionably vile techniques such as takedown notices, zoning disputes, information requests, or good old-fashioned patent trolling that would surely be considered war crimes to their combat equivalents. Considering themselves among the Nomad's most efficient defenders, everyone knows better than to argue with them.

ATTRIBUTES						
AGI	AWA	BRW	COO	INT	PER	WIL
+1	+2	–	+1	+2	+2	+2

SKILLS				EARNINGS
Mandatory	Analysis	Education	Psychology	2+5 Ⓝ
Elective	Ballistics	Education	Persuade	

GEAR: Neural Hacking Socket, Assault Hacking Device

CHIMERA

Though anyone can get cosmetic augmentations, Chimera, by definition, take them to a transformative extreme. Bushy fox tail? Ram horns? Maybe some cat ears? Where other Nomads might dabble, Chimera are likely to combine them all. For some, it's a way to stand out in a crowd, and for others, an imperfect journey towards a body they can finally feel comfortable in. Progressive by necessity, many end up in prostitution, pornography, and Submondo-run fight clubs. Capable in defending themselves, a rare few join the *Überfallkommandos* tasked with infiltrating and disrupting these illegal and exploitive rings. Regardless of their vocation, Chimera saunter through life with a pronounced swagger, even if it engenders trouble more often than not.

ATTRIBUTES						
AGI	AWA	BRW	COO	INT	PER	WIL
+2	+1	+2	+2	–	+2	+1

SKILLS				EARNINGS
Mandatory	Acrobatics	Athletics	Close Combat	0+4 Ⓝ
Elective	Animal Handling	Lifestyle	Thievery	

GEAR: Cosmetic Augmentation 2, Implanted Wetspike or Climbing Plus, SecureCuffs, Recorder

SPECIAL: If working this career multiple times, you can either take a new Cosmetic Augmentation, or increase the value of an existing Cosmetic Augmentation by +1

CLOCKMAKER

While Clockmakers may or may not be *Bakunin's* most valuable contribution to the NMF, they're probably its most beloved. Consummate tinkerers, the Clockmakers are called in to rebuild, repair, and reinvent, often in extremely hazardous situations. Like most of the NMF, they live in a state of constant readiness, never knowing when the call to action will go out. Unlike most of their peers, however, their skillset is best sharpened by constant interaction with civilian projects. As such, it's not uncommon to see a garage, forge works, or even the occasional boutique watch shop act as a combination of home base and playground for the Clockmakers when they're not on deployment. Specialists in non-linear thought, Clockmakers are known for unorthodox and forward-looking technical solutions, though their tendency to tinker with everything in sight—including themselves—can sometimes get them into trouble.

ATTRIBUTES						
AGI	AWA	BRW	COO	INT	PER	WIL
+2	–	+1	+1	+3	+1	+1

SKILLS				EARNINGS
Mandatory	Discipline	Education	Tech	1+2 Ⓝ
Elective	Acrobatics	Lifestyle	Tech	

GEAR: Neural Comlog, D-Charge (3), Powered Multitool, Repair Kit

HACKER

Nearly any conceivable information exists on the Maya network. Hackers make a living breaking down electronic barriers and uncovering secrets, or taking data from others for the purposes of fraud, theft, or mere thrills. Hackers also work with law enforcement, helping to track those with similar skills or counter their efforts. Some specialise in hacking corporate networks, like those of the massive banks and producers of consumer products. Others see it as an art form, hacking challenging military networks or plunging into the depths of Maya in order to find something no one else can.

ATTRIBUTES						
AGI	AWA	BRW	COO	INT	PER	WIL
+1	+2	+1	+2	+2	+2	–

SKILLS				EARNINGS
Mandatory	Thievery	Hacking	Tech	2+2 Ⓝ
Elective	Observation	Ballistics	Stealth	

GEAR: Deployable Repeater (×3), Powered Multitool, Assault or Defensive Hacking Device

CORVUS BELLI
infiNity

CAREER PROFILE
HEAVY INDUSTRY

While expert systems and automation has reduced the number of workers involved in industrial pursuits, those that remain are all the more critical, providing skills and judgment. Modern materials require vacuum purification in electron-beam furnaces; titanic terraforming processors need calibration and adjustment to local conditions before being set to automated operation; volatile planetary core taps demand human decisions where predictive physics break down; and even automated maintenance systems want for their own upkeep. Industrial specialists are an increasingly rare breed that understand the link between sweat and advanced technology. Their knowledge spans grease guns to exclusion fields, and they have the experience to apply either to a problem. Professionals in this field are the gears that keep the Human Sphere turning.

ATTRIBUTES						
AGI	AWA	BRW	COO	INT	PER	WIL
+1	+2	–	+2	+2	+1	+2

SKILLS				EARNINGS
Mandatory	Resistance	Pilot	Tech	2+1 Ⓝ
Elective	Close Combat	Persuade	Thievery	

GEAR: Gruntsuit (with Respirator 1), Powered Multitool, Painkillers (×3), Repair Kit

CAREER PROFILE
INTERVENTOR

Tunguska's economy is entirely dependent upon information security. Without ironclad assurances that their funds, data, or other information is safe, confidence in the Bank of Tunguska would plummet. Leaks, downtime, and other compromises are simply not an option. Fortunately, *Tunguska* is home to arguably the best and most creative hackers in the Human Sphere, with the Interventors foremost among them. Leaving no stone unturned in their search for the best Infowarriors available, Tunguska's Dragnet often turns to problematic "black hat" hackers, offering them the chance to take on the biggest challenges, with the best support, working alongside some of the most notorious hackers. Interventors do more than just secure financial transactions. These Infowarriors ensure quantronic superiority across a wide array of battlefields, many of them quite literal.

ATTRIBUTES						
AGI	AWA	BRW	COO	INT	PER	WIL
+1	+2	+1	+1	+3	–	+1

SKILLS				EARNINGS
Mandatory	Hacking	Observation	Tech	1+4 Ⓝ
Elective	Hacking	Resistance	Stealth	

GEAR: Hacking Device Plus, FastPanda

CAREER PROFILE
INFILTRATOR

Nomad military doctrine is massively reliant on the ability to counterstrike anyone, anywhere, without warning or preparation time. For retaliatory strikes to be effective, Nomads rely heavily on Infiltrators. *Bakunin's* Zeros — codenamed for their exceptionally low number of failed missions and casualties — scout deep behind enemy lines and acquire critical info for the Nomad's deterrence strategies. Bakunian Prowlers' aggressive, no-holds-barred tactics offer creative solutions to the enemy's continued respiration. *Tunguska's* Spektr troops specialise in industrial espionage, often undertaking small "additional objectives" while working for third parties. And the Corregidor Assault Commandos (Intruders) routinely conceal their presence amongst Corregidoran work crews, ensuring a safe working environment for their shipmates. Preferring to work in the shadows, stealth isn't always an option, so Infiltrators are every bit as comfortable kicking down a door as they are staying hidden.

ATTRIBUTES						
AGI	AWA	BRW	COO	INT	PER	WIL
+1	+1	+1	+2	+2	+2	+1

SKILLS				EARNINGS
Mandatory	Hacking	Observation	Stealth	2+1 Ⓝ
Elective	Ballistics	Discipline	Lifestyle	

GEAR: Boarding Shotgun or HMG, Armoured Clothing, Chameleonwear or Cosmetics Kit

INTELLIGENCE OPERATIVE

The tense state of conflict in the Human Sphere means every agency looks for an edge over its competitors. Intelligence Operatives conduct corporate espionage, deep-cover spy missions, acts of sabotage, and other acts which risk their life and limb for agencies that would disavow any knowledge of, or connection to, their operations. An Intelligence Operative is quick-witted, highly disciplined, and often alone in a place surrounded by enemies unaware of the traitor in their midst. They trade in secrets — information that can turn the tide of small-scale conflicts, like raids on secret warehouses holding valuable experimental gear or data — and they can influence the large-scale skirmishes that take place between rival nations. The intelligence an operative collects can cause wars or end them with equal facility.

ATTRIBUTES						
AGI	AWA	BRW	COO	INT	PER	WIL
+1	+3	–	+2	+2	+1	+1

SKILLS				EARNINGS
Mandatory	Observation	Stealth	Analysis	3+1 Ⓝ
Elective	Hacking	Education	Thievery	

GEAR: Fake ID 2, AP Pistol (with 4 Reloads), Breaking & Entering Kit, Recorder

INVESTIGATIVE JOURNALIST

Maya has more than its fair share of tabloid reporting and fluff stories, but the Investigative Journalist seeks the real stuff. Journalists hunt the truth, bringing word to the public about enemy action, the heroic efforts of national forces, and of course the latest scandals to haunt politicians and entertainers alike. Investigative Journalists often face hostility from those they investigate, and tend to have more than a few criminal skills like shadowing, breaking and entering, and sometimes falsifying data to gain admittance to places otherwise barred from them. Some see their cause as bringing the truth to light, while others simply have an insatiable curiosity and a penchant for getting into (and hopefully out of) trouble.

ATTRIBUTES						
AGI	AWA	BRW	COO	INT	PER	WIL
+2	+2	–	+2	+1	+2	+1

SKILLS				EARNINGS
Mandatory	Stealth	Persuade	Observation	1+2 Ⓝ
Elective	Hacking	Education	Thievery	

GEAR: Recorder or AR Eye Implants, Analysis Suite, Breaking & Entering Kit

JAGUAR

In the early days of *Corregidor*, *maras* gangs were running wild. While everyone else (correctly) saw a problem, Juan Sarmiento, "the Mexican General," saw an opportunity. He offered the rowdies a choice: skinny dipping out an airlock, or join his new Jaguar unit. Over time, these thugs, gangsters, and troublemakers were hammered into a cohesive — if brutal — unit. A police unit.

It worked so shockingly well the practice continues to this day. Nobody knows gang territory like a Jaguar, and if local *maras* can avoid stirring up too much trouble, most Jaguars are happy to turn a blind eye. Given the Jaguar's history and frequent deployment as NMF shock troops, most gangsters are only too happy with the arrangement.

ATTRIBUTES						
AGI	AWA	BRW	COO	INT	PER	WIL
+2	+1	+3	+1	–	+1	+1

SKILLS			EARNINGS
Mandatory	Athletics	Close Combat	Restistance	1+2 Ⓝ
Elective	Acrobatics	Extraplanetary	Thievery	

GEAR: Chain Rifle (with 1 Standard Reload), Knife, Smoke Grenades (3) or Nitrocane (2 Doses)

MOTHERSHIP SECURITY CORPS

Whether it's *Bakunin's* street savvy Moderators, *Corregidor's* reliable Alguaciles, or the Tunguskan Dragnet's grim Securitate direct tactical response force and tenacious Grenzer counter-intelligence teams, the Nomad Motherships require a flexible and adaptive security force. Protecting a Nomad Mothership is no walk in the park. Part military police, part detective, part riot cop, Mothership Security forces can be investigating a homicide on one day, then find themselves on mercenary deployment the next, only to spend the next week as mercenaries on the opposite side of the conflict, and finally return home to address a new wrinkle in their investigation. While each uses a variety of different assets to handle law enforcement and counter-terrorism actions, Motherships and Commercial Missions all rely on their security forces to evolve on the fly. Faced with no other option, they reliably do just that.

ATTRIBUTES						
AGI	AWA	BRW	COO	INT	PER	WIL
+1	+2	+1	+2	+2	+1	+1

SKILLS				EARNINGS
Mandatory	Ballistics	Extraplanetary	Observation	1+2 Ⓝ
Elective	Command	Hacking	Medicine	

GEAR: Armoured Clothing (Uniform), Hacking Device or MediKit, Combi Rifle or Spitfire

CAREER PROFILE
NEGOTIATOR

Words are powerful. Wars have been started, fortunes lost, and empires founded on the premise of a few carefully chosen words. It's no secret that the Nomad Nation needs every edge that it can get. When dialogue is the battlefield, they deploy their Negotiators to devastating effect. From the logic-fuelled arguments of the Tunguskan debaters, to the enticing persuasion of trendsetters from *Bakunin* and the *Corregidorans'* coercion techniques, these aggressive orators are experts at their craft. Whether making deals, negotiating over hostages, mediating disputes, or verbally eviscerating lobbyists, these wordsmiths excel in the science of communication, constantly pushing the state of the art forward. Nomad Negotiators understand what buttons to press.

ATTRIBUTES						
AGI	AWA	BRW	COO	INT	PER	WIL
–	+2	–	–	+1	+3	+3

SKILLS				EARNINGS
Mandatory	Discipline	Lifestyle	Persuade	1+4 🄽
Elective	Command	Observation	Persuade	

GEAR: Aletheia Suite, Negotiator's Suite (7 days rental credit), Armoured Clothing (High Fashion), Cosmetics Kit

CAREER PROFILE
PRAXIS SCIENTIST

Genius isn't clean. It's often messy, uncouth, difficult. Hard to deal with, even harder to understand. How could someone ever hope to regulate or control what they don't understand? Only in an open environment can genius reach its full potential. So goes the thinking of the Praxis Scientist, anyway. Whether they work in the fabled Black Laboratories, assist someone else, or have their own private setup, Praxis Scientists blaze a trail to the future. They code intelligent software, push the boundaries of xenomedicinal research, or simply build a better bomb, and Praxis offers the opportunity to pursue their research virtually unchecked. Of course, there's a flip side. Rogue AIs pop up unexpectedly, alien viruses can pose problems, and more than one lab has gone up in flames. But as long as they don't sink the boat, *Bakunin* gives them free reign, and they make ample use of it.

ATTRIBUTES						
AGI	AWA	BRW	COO	INT	PER	WIL
+1	+3	–	–	+3	+1	+1

SKILLS				EARNINGS
Mandatory	Analysis	Education	Science	0+6 🄽
Elective	Ballistics	Discipline	Lifestyle	

GEAR: AnyRez (1 Service, redeemable when necessary; roll on AnyRez Defects Table to determine the catch), Glavar Powder (2 Doses), Analytical Kit or Basic Medical Supplies

CAREER PROFILE
PROVOCATEUR

A Bakunian specialty, Provocateurs are famed throughout the Human Sphere, though for what, exactly, varies wildly. Some are performance artists *par excellence* whose evocative displays elicit tears from the hardest of hearts. Some are punk vandals whose protest art invades popular Mayacasts with rhythmic stink bomb detonations or defaces corporate headquarters with multi-layered AR graffiti programs. Others work quietly, but perhaps to greater effect, by disseminating information behind the scenes for insurgent groups or broadcasting their target's sins across Arachne. As agents of radical change, they're sometimes harnessed for viral marketing campaigns or funnelled into weapons-grade memes that dominate conversations in the Human Sphere. And sometimes, they turn on the Nomads, because no one is safe and nothing is sacred to a Provocateur. Their code is simple: be the defiance you wish to see in the world.

ATTRIBUTES						
AGI	AWA	BRW	COO	INT	PER	WIL
+2	+1	–	+1	+2	+2	+2

SKILLS				EARNINGS
Mandatory	Lifestyle	Persuade	Thievery	0+4 🄽
Elective	Acrobatics	Hacking	Tech	

GEAR: Freedom Kit, Fake ID 2, Recorder, Stealth Repeater, Optical Disruption Device

CAREER PROFILE
SPECIAL FORCES

The most elite soldiers in the Human Sphere carry out spec ops missions across known space… and sometimes upon unknown worlds. Special Forces units operate in covert missions of international warfare, hunting down war criminals, striking important assets, and retreating before anyone can blame their acting governments. These elite units also carry out the most difficult ops in the war for Paradiso, attacking Combined Army commanders and bases, rescuing allies caught far behind enemy lines, and countering the threat of elite enemy units. Governments deploy Special Forces when discretion is needed—all too common in the shadow warfare fought between nations of the Human Sphere—and when regular mercenaries or law enforcement simply aren't enough. A Special Forces soldier receives the finest training, equipment, and most important missions, demanding as much from themselves as their people do.

ATTRIBUTES						
AGI	AWA	BRW	COO	INT	PER	WIL
+2	+2	+2	+1	+1	–	+2

SKILLS				EARNINGS
Mandatory	Survival	Resistance	Ballistics	2+1 🄽
Elective	Close Combat	Hacking	Discipline	

GEAR: Medium Combat Armour, Combi Rifle or AP Rifle (with 5 Standard Reloads), Climbing Plus or Combat Jump Pack, Garrotte

CHAPTER 5
NOMAD GEAR

They have no planetary territory to draw on for resources or host heavy industry, and with a kaleidoscopic diversity of ideologies and cultures unwanted and discarded by their original nations. Locked in opposition with the sole legal AI and forced to fight for survival in the cold expanse of space, the Nomad Nation should have imploded within months. A year, at most. And yet, impossibly, they thrive.

Their response to these seemingly overwhelming problems is rampant, unchecked iterative innovation on every front — genetic engineering and cybernetic augmentation, ideological experimentation and memetic subversion, cutting-edge Infowar hardware and software competition, uplifted allies and samsara exploration, reinvention of contracts and workflows, and miniaturisation and environmental adaptation, across hundreds of small distributed modules, manufactories, habitats, startups, Black Labs, and Black Ships. The remarkable cultural surface area of Arachne's ubiquitous distributed network, their embedded Commercial Missions, their Motherships' migrations, and the fertile synthesis of their Krugs allow rapid exposure, discovery, exploration, correlation, competition, and cross-breeding of ideas and research, unfiltered by ALEPH's influence or governmental meddling.

Despite being unbounded by Yu Jing's stultifying hierarchies, PanOceania's ALEPH addiction, Haqqislam's high-minded abstraction, Hypercorps' sociopathic greed, or Ariadna's suspicious conservatism, the Nomads still find plenty of ways to get in their own way. So many voices pulling in so many directions can lead to inefficiency. Scarcity makes it easy to fixate on personal survival at the expense of the community. And with so much at stake, interpersonal matters of taste can easily metastasise into schismatic squabbling. The threats they face are paradoxically their greatest asset; there's no way to survive except by working together. The Nomads possess vital resources that would cost dearly elsewhere. Every person counts, and there's no margin for waste.

In motherships' and habitats' cramped spaces, ideology and affinity are often worn on one's sleeve or blazoned on one's halo, expressions of wealth and taste and style are close to or even beneath the skin, and even an extreme aesthetic will hardly raise an eyebrow, instead drawing an interested eye. More than anything, connections to each other and the community are the most valuable resource

the Nomads have. To access unique resources, start making friends and doing favours. It'll cost, but you can usually find what you need, a few things you didn't realise you needed, and have the time of your life along the way.

Adhesive Solvent: A go-to for troublemakers, rioters, and the law enforcement and security teams that immobilise them, this spray dissolves the gelatinous adhesives used in common crowd-control ammo. With a **Tech (D1) test**, a solvent canister can be used several ways. If sprayed on a Scale 0 vehicle, the wielder, or on a person in Reach, it renders them immune to all damage and effects from Adhesive and Goonade ammo for the scene and frees them if already immobilised. If sprayed into an adjacent zone, it has the Area (Close) quality, and gives a Scale 0 vehicle or person or immobilised by those munitions' effects a chance to escape at −2 difficulty (minimum 0).

Amygdawire Augmentation: Developed in Praxis's Black Labs, this invasive procedure links a user's neural hacking device directly into their brain's emotional centres, leveraging their subconscious for an Infowar edge. It requires a neural hacking device and activating or deactivating it requires a Minor Action. When active, it grants a bonus d20 to Infowar Hacking tests, but all quantronic damage is also taken as the same amount of mental damage.

AnyRez: It's an open secret that Praxis's Black Labs happily provide black market resurrections, with all the price-gouging, hand-wringing, and anxiety such a dodgy exchange entails. That said, a resurrection is the sort of thing one can't acquire when they need it — since they're dead. To address this need, Praxis provides illegal resurrection services, redeemable later when the buyer is dead. Compared to legal resurrections, or even the "conventional" black market resurrections, providers of AnyRez are downright accessible and will happily sell their special brand of resurrection insurance to virtually anyone, hence the name.

Getting them to hold up their end of the bargain can be another story. At the time of death, a character acquiring an AnyRez service makes a **Persuade test** with a difficulty based on the service previously purchased. On a success, the resurrection is arranged, and can be redeemed at a future date with no further strings attached. However, if the test is failed, then the GM rolls on the *AnyRez Defects Table,* adding the Difficulty

SRS FLAMEWAR

In addition to their popularity with mercenaries and corsairs for boarding actions and urban combat, Fulgor rifles are standard issue for many elite NMF units and Nomad security forces, including Grenzer Security Teams, Tomcat Emergency and Rescue Special Teams, *Corregidor's* Intruders, *Bakunin's* Prowler specialists, and the veteran Wildcats of the Polyvalent Tactical Unit.

MODERATOR RFCS

When *Bakunin's* Moderators have a technical issue they can't solve in-house or need a new piece of standard-issue equipment, they issue a Request For Contributions, a special Black Bounty with strict, even patently unreasonable acceptance criteria: several have been open for years. In addition to a commensurate fee, the Moderators' favour is intensely valuable, and contributors can annotate and comment on each another's submissions, leading to intense – and even surprisingly productive – debates and revisions. Winners go through a closed final review and development phase to ensure their solution is confidential and free of subtle exploits.

J-FARR KOLLECTIV'S FOOMPS

Named for their distinctive sound when fired, Foomp Flingers were initially J-Farr Kollectiv's contribution to the Tsyklon Sputnik development effort, but Moderators quickly became their most avid users. Foomps solved an RFC – open for almost a decade – for a more portable means of rapidly expanding Mods' quantronic reach in emergencies. J-Farr's members have enjoyed a frankly scandalous degree of latitude ever since.

Flexwear Outfit: *Bakunin* smart-material fashion designed for rapid reconfiguration, Lorolocco Flexwear – and its many imitators – leverage nano-pumped, inflatable string-tube segments and selectively-adhesive display fabrics to create a single large piece of cloth that can be used for hundreds of unique looks, mimicking many ordinary fabrics and materials. A character can quickly create a disguise with one full round of complete attention, and Flexwear counts as a kit with one bonus Momentum to Disguise tests or to Lifestyle tests to imitate a subculture's aesthetic. It possesses the Comms quality during the round of reconfiguration but can be placed into Non-Hackable "dumb mode" without penalty once set.

Foomp Flinger: Like ordinary pitchers, J-Farr Kollectiv's Foomp Flingers fire deployable repeaters as Reloads just as grenade launchers fire grenades. Unlike their bulkier cousins, Foomps and the fired FFP repeater rounds are miniaturised for easy incorporation with weapons that have the MULTI Light Mod quality, such as rifles. They can even be added in pairs to weapons with MULTI Heavy Mod, like HMGs. They inflict no damage and target a zone rather than a normal target with a Ballistics (D1) test, modified as normal for range. If successful, the FFP repeater lands in the targeted zone and deploys immediately. (Range M, Burst 1, 1H, Munition, Speculative Fire)

Freedom Kit: ALEPH governs even basic activities like food production and human waste disposal in the Human Sphere, but reliance on it is an anathema to self-respecting Nomads. Freedom Kits contain older technologies carefully constructed to allow Nomads to visit the worlds of the Human Sphere for extended periods corruption-free. These kits contain items like heat filaments for cooking, filters for purifying water, and comm-relays with manual signal boosters for communication with Arachne nodes or Nomad ships. They prevent any penalties avoiding ALEPH's services would otherwise incur in daily life and provide a bonus d20 to all Discipline tests while supplies last. Each kit contains sufficient supplies for a year's travel in the Human Sphere and can be converted into a crude shelter and back again with a **Survival (D1) test**.

Fulgor Rifle: Fulgor (Spanish for "blaze" or "bright") is the nickname among elite Corregidoran forces for a FrancoGermanique Armements SG-5 Alraun2 Combi Rifle when it's combined with a pre-installed, underslung LF-4 light flamethrower. While slightly more expensive than a standard combi rifle, after characteristically vociferous feedback from Corregidoran troops it now comes with a specialised customisation kit that simplifies repair or swapping its secondary weapon to a **Simple (D0) Tech test**.

They are prized by Nomad veterans. Whenever a Nomad would gain a combi rifle as career equipment during Lifepath Decision Eight while serving in the NMF, they can choose to gain a fulgor rifle instead. (Range C/M, 1+5 🅽 damage, Burst 2/1, 2H, Expert 1, Multi Light Mod (with light flamethrower installed), Vicious 1)

Garn Grub: Named for an ancient measurement of space sickness, these medicinal rations alleviate the symptoms of extended exposure to zero-g conditions. Usually sold in sealed palm-sized wafers and stored in airlock first aid kits, they end conditions suffered from zero-g exposure once eaten and add a bonus d20 to future Resistance or Extraplanetary tests to avoid those conditions for the next 2d20 days, as well as preventing the usual long-term cardio-vascular degeneration. Popular with tourists to the Nomad Nation, they are offered freely and included with any Nomad-made basic medical supplies or survival rations.

Gestalt Geist X: Sharing on a level most find unbearably intimate, this basic geist variant splits into multiple instances (one per user it supports), acts as each users' geist, periodically recompiles to integrate its varied experiences into a coherent whole, then splits again to repeat the process. This means that every participant has access to what every other participant has used the geist for, and their preferences and priorities are only a portion of the geist's development. Due to its integration architecture's complexity, the geist has +1 complication range on all tests for each user beyond 2X, can only receive a single Skill Expertise upgrade per skill, and Attribute upgrade costs are doubled. If the geist generates a complication on a test, or if the GM spends 2X heat, it is unable to act for two rounds due to a re-integration and re-splitting cycle.

Why bother? The constant influx of new tasks and priorities, combined with its revolutionary architecture, allow the geist to learn and evolve on its own over time. When it cycles, either when it generates a complication or the GM spends 2X Heat, it temporarily gains X 🅽 ranks – rolled separately – in each skill it has at least one rank in until its next cycle. If one or more effects are rolled, it permanently gains a rank in the skill, to a maximum of 2X Focus and 2X expertise. Urban legends claim sufficiently long-lasting gestalt geists can evolve into Rogue AI, but due to the frustrations and exposure of sharing a geist, the human sides of gestalts rarely stay together for more than a few years. Instead, each user goes their own way, either taking a truncated instance for their own use – removing the geist's ability to cycle but also removing its Attribute cost penalties – or starting anew with another geist.

close-range surprise. Thanks to a fool-proof perma-bond adhesive, a Mgomo tube can be added to any Unbalanced or 2H weapon that does not already have a secondary weapon attached, even if the weapon does not have a Multi Light/Medium/Heavy Mod quality, with a **Tech (D0) test**. Doing so also adds Improvised 1 if the installer has Tech Expertise of 2 or less, and removing it requires a **Tech (D2) test**. It adds the following secondary mode:

- *ADHL Mode*: Range M, 1+5 Ⓝ damage, Burst 1, Disposable, Stun

Monkey Bar: Kitbashed by *Bakunin*'s Electronic Pariahs urchin gang, "monkey bars" are a hollow plasteel bar with magnetic clamps on either end for grabbing onto nearby pieces of metal, wired to a power cell, which is good for ten minutes of continual use and taped inside the tube. This allows the wielder to catch themselves when falling, create an impromptu ledge for second-story work, or swing themselves into otherwise inaccessible spaces. They can be used as a crude weapon akin to a Plasteel Pipe, and adds a bonus d20 to Acrobatics, Athletics, Extraplanetary, or Thievery tests involving climbing, swinging, or clambering around.

Naughties: Bloodborne nanites taken in daily pill form to manage hormonal stress levels and reinforce the user's personal firewall, these grey-market Nomad knockoffs of ALEPH nannies are commonly available from Submondo dealers. They add 1 Ⓝ to the user's ordinary BTS, taken and rerolled daily, but any Effects rolled grant the GM a complication. Taking multiple variants simultaneously is profoundly dangerous. Their maintenance costs and benefits stack, but each effect generated deals the user a Wound and generates a complication. They are usually purchased by the month, although individual daily doses, called naughts, are available from less savoury dealers.

Nemesis Gloves: Falsely claimed as VoodooTech-derived, the gloves are worn only by the truly determined or suicidal, particularly fighters in lethal Aristea! Underground bouts. Nemesis gloves contain a barely-contained radioactive power source on the back of each glove for a fine layer of fractal monofilament microstructures on the palm and fingertips, and this adds Anti-Materiel 2, Backlash 1, Monofilament, NFB, and Vicious 2 to unarmed strikes the wearer makes with their hands. The gloves must be charged before each attack with a **Resistance (D1) test** as a Free Action. If the test is failed, the gloves can still be used to make a single attack, but the wearer immediately takes 1+2 Ⓝ Radiation 2 damage. (Melee, covers hands, Anti-Materiel 2, Backlash 1, Monofilament, NFB, Vicious 2)

Neurocinetics Augmentation: Illegal throughout the Human Sphere, this nervous system augmentation enhances the user's reaction time and reflexes but can cause serious nerve degeneration over time. Users must constantly control their reactions and are easily recognised by their obsessively slow and cautious movements. They can make warfare reactions for one less Heat but take 1 Ⓝ of Vicious 1 physical damage each time they do so. If this damage inflicts a Wound, the user permanently loses one Vigour, to a minimum of their Resistance Focus. Additionally, they have the Ballistics and Close Combat Quick Draw talents while it is active, but if the augmentation is deactivated — for example by a Breach Effect — they lose access to dependent talents.

Nomad Spear X: Often improvised from available materials for frontier hunting or back-corridor warfare, Nomads' throwing spears incorporate monowire tethers, fast-fabbed micro-thrusters, guidance packages for zero-g combat, or other DIY modifications. A Nomad spear has X of the following qualities or features (Melee, 1+4 Ⓝ damage, 2H, Extended Reach, Vicious 1 + features below):

- Concealed 1, thanks to a collapsible smart-material shaft.
- Guided, with added micro-thrusters and onboard software package.
- Piercing 2 instead of Vicious 1, utilising a narrow metamaterial spearhead.
- Retrievable with an **Athletics (D1) test**, using a monowire tether and bracer reel.
- Toxic 2, from a neurotoxic coating on the spearhead, removed on a Complication.

O2 Spray: This nanobot-laden muscle-relaxant oral spray coats the user's lung tissues to increase gas exchange efficiency, while slowing their respiration. Sold in 3-dose canisters for easy attachment to vac suit air supplies, it is named for oxygen's most common allotrope, as well as its inventor, Orville Oxford. Each dose lasts 3d20 minutes, and when determining if an Oxygen Load is depleted while under its effects, the character only needs to succeed at an **Extraplanetary (D1) test** (instead of the usual D2). However, reduced lung capacity adds +1 complication range to Agility – and Brawn-based tests, and if multiple complications are generated, the user begins to suffocate, taking a Wound each round until they succeed at a **Resistance (D1) test**.

Old Steely: Named for the sense of cold, focused detachment it generates, this drug powder's aftereffects cause extreme emotional swings, known as "Riding Old Steely" amongst the Nomad zero-g workers who rely on it. Often mixed into XO suits' water supplies, a dose of Old Steely provides +2d20 to Willpower- and Awareness-based tests for six hours. When it wears off, the user takes

1+4  Mental damage from a sudden emotional cascade and is at +1 difficulty to Personality- and Willpower-based tests for 3 hours, +1 hour per effect rolled.

RedX Jumpsuit: RedX hooded jumpsuits are designed to be worn as daily wear inside a habitat and are lightweight vac suits with built-in emergency beacons, but only a single Oxygen Load, one Part's worth of sealant and patches, and BTS 1 filtering. Named for the sign in public AR for exits to vacuum, they are included in the Nomad demogrant from five-years-old onward and can be exchanged once for free each year in case of wear, growth, or bodily alteration. They are something of a generic baseline for Nomad fashion and are especially popular on Commercial Missions and frontier habitats. *Corregidor*'s childhood versions are coloured according to maintenance team, and learning to hack the suit's beacon and AR tags is an adolescent rite of passage.

Slag-cannon (Ranged): An asteroid-miner's take on a chain rifle, this bulky weapon's chamber can melt magnetically-charged materials into dense white-hot slugs and magnetically fire them through vacuum at a target. Often incorporated into XO suits on shoulder-mounts for use as mining equipment in Human Edge and Sol's asteroid belts, they are an ideal deterrent for claim jumpers and pirates. Loading one requires a Standard Action, a **Tech (D1) test**, and a piece of iron-rich ore, a slag-slug, a Part, or another magnetically-charged item. When fired in atmosphere, their Range is reduced to Close and range penalties are doubled, but in vacuum they can be fired at targets from Close to Extreme range without penalty. (Range (any), 2+5  damage, 2H, Anti-Materiel 1, Improvised 1, Incendiary 2, Munitions, Piercing)

Slag-slug Ammunition: Often carried by asteroid miners who want to ensure they have appropriate ammo on-hand for their slag-cannons, slag-slugs are solid darts of highly-refined ferromagnetic materials, ideal for zero-g conflict. When fired from a slag-cannon or other magneto-propulsion weapon in atmosphere, they reduce the weapon's range to Close, and range penalties are doubled, but in vacuum they remove any Improvised quality. Regardless of environment, they add the Knockdown and Piercing 1 quality, to a maximum of Piercing 3.

Slammer (Ammo Type): A disposable weapon for the truly desperate or vicious, a slammer is a short length of tubing with a built-in round of ammunition — usually Special — and a crude trigger. The slammer is jammed into direct contact with the target and fired, sending the round into the target and wrecking the cheaply fabricated casing, which then degrades into forensically distinctive materials. Slammers' damage is caused as much by the high-pressure gas of the round as by their payloads, rendering them deadly even underwater. They can only be made with ammunition types without the Area, Indiscriminate, or Nonlethal qualities. (Melee, 1+4  damage, Disposable, Improvised 1, Subtle 1, Unforgiving 1, and qualities per ammo type)

Spektr Armour: When *Tunguska* or their well-paying clients need a covert action made with traceless surgical precision, be it theft, espionage, industrial extraction, or cold-blooded murder, they rely on the very best: Spektrs. Spektrs, in turn, depend on their armour. Made from the most sophisticated thermo-optical camouflage and adaptive smart-materials money can buy, it is invisible to almost all surveillance equipment, self-repairing, and allows the wearer to ignore up to 2 difficulty due to

WHO NEEDS A RIDE?

Private vehicles are rare for Nomads, particularly on the motherships, and even on Commercial Missions. Instead, they rely on communal infrastructure — strap-loops, slideways, elevators, induced wind tunnels, even magnetic-wheeled bicycles and RedX suit stations. In the cramped conditions and short sightlines on ships and habitats, moving around too quickly is a reckless mistake, particularly in zero-g, where inertial velocity is difficult to redirect. Unconscious acceptance of these restrictions under most conditions is just common sense for most Nomads, even Bakunians, and is a constant source of surprise for outsiders.

UP CLOSE AND PERSONAL

Slammers are illegal throughout the Human Sphere, but are easily found in shady markets, albeit with the usual wild variations in quality and safety. Fabrication recipes of similarly variable quality for combining innocuous materials into slammers are common on Arachne's darknets. Their disposability makes them the perfect weapon for street violence and murder. They are especially popular with Lazareto's *maras* for back-corridor rumbles and turf wars, since local Submondo dealers refuse to sell them heavier weaponry.

terrain or weather conditions. A thermal-diffusion layer means its TO camo is only compromised if the wearer suffers a Wound from Incendiary damage, and it can collapse into an innocuous piece of baggage easily carried in one hand, with a sensor-thwarting layer that adds +2 difficulty to all tests to identify its true nature.

Sputnik, Lunokhod: While the NMF has used remotes since its inception, the NeoColonial wars strongly demonstrated their tactical potential for tirelessly outpacing and outmanoeuvring opposition. They rarely lasted long in direct combat, leading to the Sputnik series of improvements – reworked mobility systems, increased armour and quantronic defences, and most importantly cost-saving fabrication updates, allowing wide-spread manufacture and deployment. Their light weight and small size are ideal for rapid assaults. The Lunokhod (Russian for "moonwalker") model, in particular, is made to probe and outflank its opposition, bypassing mines and sensor defences to strike at the enemy's rear and supply lines.

ELITE
LUNOKHOD SPUTNIK

ATTRIBUTES

AGI	AWA	BRW	COO	INT	PER	WIL
11	10	8	10	11	5	8

FIELDS OF EXPERTISE

Combat	+2	1	Movement	+2	1	Social	–	–
Fortitude	–	–	Senses	–	–	Technical	+2	2

DEFENCES

Firewall	13	Resolve	8	Structure	8
Security	–	Morale	–	Armour	1

ATTACKS:
- **Electric Pulse:** Melee, 1+4 🅝 damage, Immobilising, Stun
- **Heavy Shotgun:** Range C, 2+8 🅝 damage, Burst 1, Knockdown
  - *Normal Shells Mode (Primary):* Area (Close), Spread 1
  - *AP Slugs Mode (Secondary):* Piercing 3
- **Heavy Flamethrower:** Range C, 2+5 🅝 damage, Burst 1, 2H, Incendiary 3, Munition, Terrifying 2, Torrent

GEAR: Climbing plus, deactivator kit, repeater

SPECIAL ABILITIES
- **Common Special Abilities:** Inured to Disease, Poison, Vacuum
- **Arachne-Powered:** When controlled by a geist or its native LAI, the remote gains a Security Soak of 4.
- **Electric Pulse:** Makes Close Combat Defence Reactions against melee attacks for −1 Heat (minimum 0). If it wins the face-to-face test, deals electric pulse damage and prevents the attack.
- **Minesweeper:** A scanning array allows Tech tests to detect or subvert explosives to be made at up to Medium range.
- **Quadrupedal Mobility:** Can move to a zone within Long range as a Minor Action, or for 2 Heat, as a Free Action.

Sputnik, Tsyklon: The Tsyklon (Russian for "cyclone") model shares the same chassis and overall design

philosophy as the Lunokhod but is optimised for use as a precise firepower platform, and as an extension to friendly infowarriors' reach. Its vision systems test even skilled pilots.

ELITE
TSYKLON SPUTNIK

ATTRIBUTES

AGI	AWA	BRW	COO	INT	PER	WIL
11	12	8	11	8	5	8

FIELDS OF EXPERTISE

Combat	+3	1	Movement	+3	1	Social	–	–
Fortitude	–	–	Senses	+3	1	Technical	+2	2

DEFENCES

Firewall	13	Resolve	8	Structure	8
Security	–	Morale	–	Armour	0

ATTACKS:
- **Electric Pulse:** Melee, 1+4 🅝 damage, Immobilising, Stun
- **Spitfire:** Range M, 1+8 🅝 damage, Burst 3, Spread 2, Unsubtle
- **Pitcher:** Range M, Burst 1, Munition, Speculative Fire

GEAR: 360° vision, climbing plus, repeater

SPECIAL ABILITIES
- **Common Special Abilities:** Inured to Disease, Poison, Vacuum
- **Arachne-Eyed:** When controlled by a geist or its native LAI, the remote gains a Security Soak of 4, and can see in all directions, granting a free d20 roll on Observation tests. Remote pilots add +2 complication range unless they have at least Pilot Focus 4.
- **Electric Pulse:** Makes Close Combat Defence Reactions against melee attacks for −1 Heat (minimum 0). If it wins the face-to-face test, deals electric pulse damage and prevents the attack.
- **Pitcher:** This modified grenade launcher fires deployable repeaters as Reloads. On a successful attack, the deployable repeater lands in the targeted zone and deploys immediately.
- **Quadrupedal Mobility:** Can move to a zone within Long range as a Minor Action, or for 2 Heat, as a Free Action.

Stashpocket X: Stashpockets are flat, shielded pockets without quantronic tags or other identifying branding, a simple sealant-strip along one edge, and a press-adhesive coating one side. They are commonly used by agents and criminals to conceal flashbills, drugs, or other small items. Expensive versions incorporate photoreactive coatings to match skin tone, clothing, or surrounding materials, and even embedded E/M countermeasures to baffle sensors. They have Concealed X and add Concealed X to One-Handed or smaller items stored inside but require an additional 1 Momentum to re-stow the item after use. They can be added to any article of clothing at purchase, but increase its base cost by X, and its tariff by +T(X-1). Adding multiple pockets only increases tariff, not base cost.

SWORD-1 Fritz: A favourite of Tunguska's Interventors, this non-lethal brain blast variant disrupts the vestibular system and the optic and auditory centres of the brain and can only be used

MEDIUM COMBAT ARMOUR VARIANT

RIOT GRRL

The pride of Vulkanja module, these armour suits are carefully personalised for Beauvoir Module's fearsome warriors at no charge, to their exacting specifications. In line with their KIY (Kill It Yourself) philosophy, each Riot Grrl works alongside their armourer and does a significant portion of the work themselves, learning skills they can use for field repairs. The resulting pride and confidence in their gear grants +3 Morale soak when wearing it. The armour also incorporates a Multispectral Visor 1, and Vulkanja's precision engineering grants a bonus d20 on Acrobatics Defence Reactions, and Swift Action Momentum spends in the armour only cost 1 Momentum if the additional action is an attack.

HEART-STASHED

Implanted stashpockets are referred to as Internal Pocket X (see *Infinity* Corebook, p. 346 and 372) and remove the Momentum penalty to stow away items after use. Popular augmentations in the Nomad Nation, particularly with *Corregidor* work crews, internal pockets allow easy transportation of personal effects while in a vac or XO suit without counting against baggage mass limits. Stashing a thin keepsake from a sweetheart or partners in an internal pocket over one's heart is a popular way to stay connected without a ring's safety risks.

against targets using Neural equipment. For one Momentum or as a Breach Effect, the program can deal its damage as Physical damage with the Biotech and Nonlethal qualities instead of Quantronic damage. For each effect generated, the user can add one of the following qualities to the attack: Deafening, Blinding, Immobilising, Knockdown, or Stun.

Teseum Hardcase: Made from a small fortune of Teseum, these hard shells for hacking devices were gifted to Wardrivers as thanks for their invaluable aid by Ariadnan employers at the end of their service in the Commercial Conflicts and are available in limited quantities to hackers who prove themselves Dawn's allies. They add Armoured 4 to the hacking device of any type they were made to house, provide +2 BTS vs attacks with the E/M quality, and grant a bonus momentum on Psywar techniques against Ariadnans and Wardrivers.

Toque-Farra Spines: Toque-Farra (an ancient word and modern slang for "party" in Spanish) spines are grown on miniature stingrays with gene-hacked venom by *Corregidor* back-corridor narco-breeders. Once used to slice or pierce the skin (dealing 1+2🄽 Toxic 1 damage), the user undergoes intense auditory-tactile and gustatory synaesthesia, experiencing sounds as touch and taste for 3d20 minutes, adding a bonus d20 to tests based on hearing, +2 complication range to tests based on touch or taste, and +1 complication range to all other tests from the distracting sensations.

UPGRADE Fadeware: Veteran hackers know it's not the getting in that's dangerous, it's getting out. By dedicating a significant portion of onboard memory to tracking and pre-loading escape vectors, this Supportware ensures Tunguskan hackers see their next sunrise. Incorporating Fadeware into a hacking device allows the hacker to make quantronic Withdraw and Terminate Connection actions as a Minor Action and gives +1 difficulty to Link actions or CLAW-2 Monkey Trap attacks against them.

UPGRADE Lightning: Based on stolen Haqqislamite neurological research, this Supportware dedicates onboard memory to a library of malicious cognition and haptic feedback exploits, adding +1🄽 damage and the Breaker quality to SWORD attacks against targets using Neural equipment. On a successful attack, the hacker can make another SWORD attack against a second target within Close range of the first target for 1 Momentum. (This action cannot be repeated.)

UPGRADE Solifugae: Named for the swiftest order of arachnids on Earth, this Nomad program rapidly explores networks, filtering for notable traffic and affordances, then reports its findings to the user. Effectively deploying the program requires a **Hacking (D1) test**. On success, it extends the user's Quantronic Observation range one zone beyond the range provided by their Hacking expertise, until they suffer a breach. Secured zones block the user's line of sight as usual.

VaudePet X: It was only a matter of time before someone applied Black Lab technology to a beloved family pet. Naturally, it happened first in the Black Labs of Praxis, then filtered quickly into VaudeVille boutiques that claimed all the credit. Every VaudePet is based on an existing animal but gains a variety of unique abilities. Most depend on quantronic interaction to do anything beyond what the original breed could, although for the right price, anything is possible, from turtles with opposable thumbs, to cats with magnetic tails, to corgis with grafted engineering waldos.

Special Abilities

- **Odd Fit**: It's not that you can't find a ballistic vest to fit a Chihuahua, it just costs extra. When purchasing worn gear such as armour, add +2 to the item's base cost and tariff rating. Gear not acquired in this fashion is essentially unusable. Tailoring gear to fit the VaudePet is a unique skillset, requiring a complex **Tech test (D4, 4 Momentum, 2 failures)**.
- **Out of Sight, Out of Mind**: VaudePets gain a bonus Momentum on successful Stealth tests and take −2 difficulty on Lifestyle tests to blend in as a pet (min 0).
- **Small Target**: Ranged attacks against a VaudePet are made at +1 difficulty.
- **Domestically Engineered**: The VaudePet has X of the following benefits:
  - **Cyber-Brain**: There's not enough room for serious mental computing power, unless someone gets creative. This adds 2 Intelligence, but also reduces Vigour by 1.
  - **Durable**: Those who've replaced a pet at great cost tend to worry about its safety and add Implanted Armour 1 to its torso. Other hit locations are generally too small to effectively armour.
  - **Implanted [Equipment]**: More than one intrepid hacker has implanted a repeater inside a stray cat over the years. Now, this time-honoured Bakunian tradition is available for a modest fee. (Equipment must be purchased separately and needs to conceivably fit in the pet.)
  - **Implanted [Weapon]**: Only the truly deranged would implant a pistol in a parrot, unless they were planning something truly entertaining. Either way, Praxis is happy to oblige. 1H Weapons can be implanted in a VaudePet, with ranged weapons activated by mental commands. This is hardly ideal, adding +3 complication range when using the weapon.

FREEDONIA INFRASOUND

Either an extended running joke or signs of a deeper conspiratorial truth, rumours persist on Arachne wardriver forums of ways to induce Fritz-like effects through infrasound via auditory demotics, like the speakers installed in most vehicles and comlogs. Among devotees of the theory, many seemingly accidental celebrity deaths, particularly vehicle accidents, are due to precisely timed distractions from a "Freedonia" attack. Creating false documents cryptically referencing the fictional nation of Freedonia and links to supposed victims is a common pastime for Otaku hoaxers, only fueling true believers' zeal. After all, they argue, some of those files must be the real thing if so much effort goes into confusing the issue... it's just a matter of figuring out which is which.

SPIKE RAVES

Toque-Farra spines are commonly worn as ear or body piercings during Malamanya Krew's underground music parties, and their *maras*-run imitators. They are one of the few scenes where both *vatos* and *tsotsis* eschew violence, instead demonstrating their ferocity through zero-g dance inside a sphere of inward-facing speakers while pierced by as many spines as they can handle — and often more.

CORVUS BELLI INFINITY

76 CHAPTER 5

(Weapons must be purchased separately.)

- **Thumbs!:** Whether a simian, or someone just got creative, this body can interact with technology like a human, though they treat One-Handed items as Two-Handed, and usually can't operate anything larger.

Viral Spiked Chain: Chimeras often wear smart-material spiked chains for menacing decoration and to ensure they have a weapon at hand wherever they go, in addition to their innate weaponry. The particularly intense lace those chains with viral coatings based on the natural toxins of creatures they have an affinity for or those found in those creatures' habitats. Wielding one effectively requires either considerable skill or a hardy constitution. If the wielder does not have a Close Combat Focus of 3 or more, they deal the weapon's damage to themselves whenever they fail on an attack with the weapon. If they have a Resistance Focus of 2 or more, the damage suffered on a failed attack is halved after rolling 🅝, round down. (Melee, 1+6🅝 damage, 1H, Biotech, Concealed 1, Extended Reach, Grievous, Piercing 1)

"BASH THIS!"

Praxis' Check Out Black Lab specialises in deadly augmentations based on wildlife, and toxic coatings and poisons derived from naturally occurring substances. Chondri Eyes and Rabbi Fish, the lab's lead developers, have become increasingly fixated on personal defence after the brutal murder of their partner Callor two years ago. They offer personalised viral spiked chains at reduced rates to fellow chimeras or other heavily augmented individuals for self-defence against hominid-supremacists and aug-phobes.

AMMUNITION TABLE

NAME	CATEGORY	QUALITIES ADDED TO WEAPON	RESTRICTION	RELOAD COST	TARIFF
FFP Repeater Rounds (FFP)	Heavy	See Description	4 (Nomads 2, *Bakunin* 1)	3+4🅝	T2
Slag-slug	Heavy	Knockdown, Piercing 1	2 (Human Edge 1)	3+1🅝	T1

ARMOUR TABLE

ARMOUR	TYPE	ARMOUR SOAK				BTS	QUALITIES	RESTRICTION	COST	TARIFF	MAINTENANCE
		HEAD	TORSO	ARM	LEG						
J-Tabby Socks		–	–	–	–1[1]	–	See Description	2 (Nomads 1)	3+3🅝	T2[2]	–
Krab Gauntlet, Ka-3		–	–	2	–	1	Bioscanner, Heavy Armour, MediKit[1]	3 (Nomads 1)	5+2🅝	T2	1
Krab Gauntlet, N3V		–	–	2	–	1	Heavy Armour, powered multitool[1]	3 (Nomads 1)	5+2🅝	T2	1
Krab Gauntlet, VaNk		–	–	3	–	1	Heavy Armour, panzerfaust[1]	3 (Nomads 2)	9+2🅝	T2	1
Lizard Suit		2	2	1	1	–	None	3 (Nomads 2)	7+3🅝	T2	1
MaiSa Armour		1	2	2	1	2	Combat jump pack, grip pads	3 (Nomads 1)	7+3🅝	T2	2
Spektr Armour		1	1	1	1	3	Concealed 2, Self-Repairing, TO Camo[1]	5 (Nomads 4, Tunguska 3)	9+6🅝	–	–

[1] Armour has additional effects. See description.   [2] No tariff for Nomads   [3] Free for Nomad Middle or higher Lifestyle.

AUGMENTATIONS TABLE

AUGMENTATION	CATEGORY	TYPE	QUALITIES	RESTRICTION	COST	TARIFF	MAINTENANCE
Amygdawire Augmentation	Cybernetic	Implant	Aug, Neural	5 (Praxis Black Labs 2)	6+2🅝	–	–
Conlang Voicebox	Biograft/ Silk	Replacement (mouth and throat)	Aug, Neural	3 (Nomads 1)	10+2🅝	T3	–
Khat/un Augmentation X	Silk	Full-Body	Aug	X+1 (Nomads 2)	10+X🅝		
Neurocinetics Augmentation	Cybernetic	Full-Body	Aug	4 (Nomads 2)	8+2🅝		
Nannie-Pump	Cybernetic	Replacement (Heart)	Aug, Comms	1	+🅝	T1	1

DRUGS TABLE

DRUG	RESTRICTION	COST	TARIFF
Glavar Powder	3 (Haqqislam 2, Nomads 1)	6+3 (N)	T1
Mess	3 (Nomads 1)	3+1 (N)	T2
O2 Spray	1	2+2 (N)	–
Old Steely	2 (Nomads 1)	2+2 (N)	–
Toque-Farra Spines	4 (*Corregidor* 1, Illicit 1, Nomads 2)	1+3 (N)	T1

EXPLOSIVES TABLE

EXPLOSIVE	CATEGORY	DAMAGE[1]	SIZE	QUALITIES	RESTRICTION	COST (PER 3)	TARIFF
CrazyKoala	Mine	2+5 (N)	2H	Comms, Disposable, Indiscriminate (Close), Unsubtle, Vicious 1[2]	3 (Nomads 2, Yu Jing 2)	9+3 (N)	–

[1] Do not add Bonus Damage from attributes to explosive devices.   [2] See entry for additional abilities.

MELEE WEAPONS TABLE

NAME	DAMAGE	SIZE	QUALITIES	RESTRICTION	COST	TARIFF
Breaker Bar	1+4 (N)	2H	Anti-Materiel 2, Piercing 1, Improvised 4	4 (Nomads 2, Illicit 1)	4+3 (N)	T2
Linkspike	1+4 (N)	1H	Piercing 1, Subtle 3	3 (Nomads 2)	3+4 (N)	T2
Nemesis Gloves	1+3 (N)	Covers Hands	Anti-Materiel 2, Backlash 1, Monofilament, NFB, Vicious 2	5 (Nomads 3, Illicit 2)	6+4 (N)	T3
Nomad Spear X	1+4 (N)	2H	Extended Reach, Vicious 1 + added features[2]	X-1	3+2X (N)	T1[1]
Slammer (Ammo Type)	1+4 (N)	1H	Disposable, Improvised 1, Subtle 1, Unforgiving 1, and qualities per ammo type	3 (Illicit 1, Nomads 2)	1+cost of Reload	T1
Viral Spiked Chain	1+6 (N)	1H	Biotech, Concealed 1, Extended Reach, Grievous, Piercing 1	3 (Nomads 1)	6+3 (N)	T3[3]

[1] No Tariff for Nomads.   [2] See entry for details.   [3] No Tariff for Chimaera or heavily augmented.

RANGED WEAPONS TABLE

NAME	RANGE	DAMAGE	BURST	SIZE	AMMO	QUALITIES	RESTRICTION	COST	TARIFF
Foomp Flinger	M	–	1	1H	FFP	Munition, Speculative Fire	3 (Nomads 2)	9+2 (N)	T1
Fulgor Rifle	C/M	1+5 (N)	2/1	2H	Standard[1]	Expert 1, Multi Light Mod (w/light flamethrower installed), Vicious 1	3 (Nomads 1)	7+3 (N)	T2[2]
Mgomo Tube	C/M	1+5 (N)	1	2H	GOO	Disposable, Stun	3 (Nomads 2, *Corregidor* 1)	4+2 (N)	T3[2]
Slag-cannon	C, M, L, E[1]	2+5 (N)	1	2H	Ore or Parts[1]	Anti-Materiel 1, Improvised 1, Incendiary 2, Munitions, Piercing 2	2 (Nomads 1)	2+5 (N)	T2[2]

[1] See entry for additional abilities and details.
[2] No Tariff for Nomads.

REMOTES TABLE

REMOTE	RESTRICTION	COST	TARIFF	MAINTENANCE
Sputnik, Lunokhod	4 (Nomads 2)	10+3 (N)	T3[1]	2
Sputnik, Tsyklon	4 (Nomads 2)	10+2 (N)	T3[1]	2

[1] No Tariff for Nomads.

PROGRAMS TABLE

TYPE	RATING	PROGRAM	DAMAGE	QUALITIES	RESTRICTION	COST	TARIFF
CLAW	2	Black Widow	1+3 (N)	BE[1]	3 (Nomads 2, *Tunguska* 1)	4+3 (N)	T2
SWORD	1	Fritz	1+4 (N)	Nonlethal, Piercing 1, Vicious 1 + Deafening, Blinding, Immobilising, Knockdown, or Stun[1]	3 (Nomads 2, *Tunguska* 1)	3+4 (N)	T3
UPGRADE	–	Fadeware	–	Supportware (Personal)[1]	4 Nomads 2, *Tunguska* 1)	4+4 (N)	T1
UPGRADE	–	Lightning	+1 (N)[1]	+Breaker to SWORD attacks, Supportware (Personal)[1]	4 (Nomads 2)	4+4 (N)	T1
UPGRADE	–	Solifugae	–	Supportware (Personal)[1]	4 (Nomads 2)	4+4 (N)	T1

[1] See entry for additional abilities.

TOOLS TABLE

TOOL	QUALITIES	RESTRICTION	COST	TARIFF	MAINTENANCE
Adhesive Solvent	Disposable, Area (Close)[1]	2 (Illicit 1, Nomads 1)	3+1 (N)	–	–
AnyRez (D4)	None	1	6+6 (N)	T2	–
AnyRez (D3)	None	2	6+6 (N)	T3	–
AnyRez (D2)	None	3	6+6 (N)	T3	1
AnyRez (D1)	None	3	7+7 (N)	T4	2
AnyRez (D0)	None	3	8+8 (N)	T5	4
Carbon4 Outfit	Armoured 2	1	0	–	–
Domovik Apprentice	Comms	5 (Nomads 3)	7+2 (N)	T3	1
Experimental Waldo X	Comms	X (Nomads X–1)	7+X (N)	T(X+1)[2]	X
FastPanda	Comms, Repeater[1]	2 (Nomads 1)	4+2 (N)	–	–
Flexwear Outfit	Comms[1]	3 (Nomads 1)	8+3 (N)	T1[2]	–
Freedom Kit	Comms	3 (Nomads 1)	6+2 (N)	–	2
Garn Grub	None	1 (Nomads 0)	2+1 (N)	T1[2]	–
Gestalt Geist X	Comms	4 (Nomads 1)	2+4X (N)	T(X)	2
Headclamp	None	4 (2 *Tunguska*)	6+4 (N)	T2	–
Laboratory, Personal	Comms	2	6+4 (N)	T1	2
Lounge-lizard Suit	Vac Suit, Pistol, Knife[1]	4 (NMF 1, Nomads 2)	10+2 (N)	T3[2]	1
Naught (1 day's dose of Naughties)	Comms	2 (Illicit 0, Nomads 1)	1+3 (N)	T1	–
Naughties (1 month)	Comms	3 (Illicit 1, Nomads 1)	1+6 (N)	–	1
Portable Monkey Bar	Comms	3 (Illicit 1, Nomads 1)	4+3 (N)	T1[2]	–
RedX Jumpsuit	Locational Beacon, Vac Suit[1]	3 (Nomads 1)	5+3 (N)	T3[1]	1, Nomads 0
Stashpocket X	Concealed X[1]	X-1	X+X (N)	T(X-1)	–
Teseum Hardcase	Armoured 4, +2 BTS vs E/M	5 (Ariadna 3, Nomads 4, Wardrivers 3)	8+4 (N)	T2	–
VaudePet X	Comms, Locational Beacon	X+1	4X + X (N)	T(X)	X+1

CHAPTER 6
UPLIFTS

NEO-CETACEAN PILOT INSTINCTS

The augmented dolphins, tucuxis, and porpoises who comprise the Nomad's neo-cetacean shuttle pilots have a variety of instinctual responses to danger, but it usually isn't to flee. Rather, a panicking Neo-Cetacean is likely to ram into trouble with its nose. An excited pilot can be much worse. Accounts of shuttles attempting to, as far as anyone can tell, mate with other starships aren't frequent, but have been known to occur.

It started innocently enough. At least, as innocently as anything involving scientists from Praxis's Black Laboratories can ever hope to be. The plan was to use cetaceans — dolphins, specifically — to pilot Nomad shuttles, freeing up Human pilots for more tactically demanding positions.

Specially designed VR implants and submerged cockpits were constructed, but it still wasn't enough. The cetacean pilots naturally took to three-dimensional spaceflight, but when the unexpected happened, they were still fundamentally animals. Like a spooked horse driving a carriage, they needed to be calmed before they could get back on course. Training could only help so much. For the program to succeed, they needed to be smarter. And as luck would have it, Praxis has never

suffered for a lack of scientists willing to push the envelope.

There were plenty of hiccups along the way. The original neo-cetaceans were clever, but still not quite on a human's level. Early dead-end research gave rise to countless developmentally stunted human-animal hybrids such as the Pupniks and left countless other dangerous experiments in their wake. But, the cetacean pilot program was a success. Submerged in nutrient tanks, fitted with custom wetware, and wired directly into specially-tuned remote presence gear, these early Starswimmers soon took over piloting duties for the Nomad Nation's shuttles and in-system vessels, a role they continue to fill to this day.

But some people just can't leave well enough alone.

UPLIFTING NEWS

What started as a project to supercharge the Nomad Navy's neo-cetacean pilots rapidly became something much more. As is tradition with Black Lab projects, it quickly spiralled out of control.

Projekt: Volaré, taking an unsubtle pot-shot at ALEPH's Recreations, was the first to crack the code. Working with a petite female tucuxi — about 130 centimetres from tail to snout — and using a proprietary, unstable Silk derivative, they engaged in extensive neurotherapy, cybernetic augmentation, and other experimental procedures to stimulate the cetacean's cognitive process. It was risky, volatile, and damnably expensive. Though tucuxis were much smaller than other possible candidates, the subject named Maria, in tribute to the heroine of Fritz Lang's Metropolis, was still a creature built for wide-open spaces confined to what was essentially an enclosed bathtub. Despite these conditions, Maria showed an incredible capacity for learning, giving the Volaré team confidence that they had the perfect candidate. They were positive that they could make it work. And they were right.

Outfitted with custom wetware, a neural comlog, and a bleeding-edge vizier geist, Maria was picking up language, strategy games, and cultural context at an amazing speed. But it wasn't until she began asking questions about her status as a citizen of *Bakunin* that the team began to wonder if they might have succeeded a little too much. In trying to create a more teachable animal, they wound up with a person, or at least, something very like one.

The project had spiralled out of control, and they had inadvertently unleashed a monster of their own making on the Human Sphere, as is tradition for the Black Labs. Besides existing, Maria wasn't going to cause any serious trouble. But she existed. And that needed to be addressed.

THE SAPIENCE SCALE

Slavery is illegal on *Bakunin*. Plenty of things are and go more or less unchecked, but completely depriving another person of their personal agency is a slap in the face to the Radical Mothership's core beliefs. Thus, while you'll find illicit dealings of every stripe on *Bakunin,* by and large, you won't find them selling people. Animals, sure. Mutant hybrids, why not? But for a faction still working to distance itself from the Red Auctions, trafficking is usually a non-starter.

This put the nascent Uplift population in a tricky position. They weren't human, but Bakunian legal precedent didn't discriminate between humans and aliens. Why would these creatures be any different? On the other hand, outside of a few radical modules, you'd be hard-pressed to find anyone clamouring to get equal status for their housecats. So where does one draw the line?

Praxis was tasked with answering that question. Their answer was the Nuendorf-Skalski Sapience Analytics Test, usually abbreviated to "The Sapience Scale" for ease of reference. By administering a suite of neurological and psychological tests, they aimed to take an ontological measurement. While the methodology was hotly debated and the instrument was woefully ill-equipped to measure the distributed intelligence of an Antipode or the purely synthetic mind of an AI, it was more than up to the task of evaluating organic beings. And while not all Uplifts passed the test, many of them did.

Tunguska swiftly drafted documents recognising all entities with a Sapience Rating of 1.0 or above as people, making them legally indistinct from

ORINOCO FLOW

A freshwater dolphin native to the Amazon Basin, the tucuxi is a pink-bellied, petite creature that forms tight-knit social groups and typically fares poorly in captivity. Facing extinction from the toxins, a group of environmentalist activists, Actionow!, scooped up the Orinoco's entire population of tucuxis. This group would eventually splinter in two. The more radical elements comprised the heart of Eko-Atktion, while the conservationist side joined the *Bakunin* project.

As for the tucuxis, extensive genetic therapy allowed them to conceptualise humans as part of their social group, staving off their terminal depression. This unleashed what might have been Earth's most gregarious species upon the Nomads, creating individuals who were extroverted even by the Radical Mothership's standards.

SAPIENCE, SIMPLIFIED

"Are you smarter than your dog? What about a gargantuan pig-monster? The animal Uplift cases coming out of *Bakunin* have certainly got the scientific community talking. But with O-12 withholding comment, is this 'Sapience Scale' more junk science from the Nomad Nation, or a legit breakthrough?

Well, our crack team of analysts have gone through the hundreds of pages with a fine-toothed comb, and we've come to two conclusions. First, wow, is the methodology dull. Dry as dirt, no question. Also, even though it looks like a simple, linear scale, that's not actually the case. Even the test's creators admit that it breaks down at higher values. So, while the difference between a 1.0 and a 1.1 is immense, and accurately measured, the jump from 1.8 to 2.4 could be smaller, much smaller.

But our second conclusion? For what it's trying to do, the test works like a charm. Looks like those mad scientists are on to something! Rather than bore you with the grisly details, we figured we'd get right to the good stuff. So, without further ado, here's a sampling of average sapience scores from the study:

Laboratory Rat: 0.4

Domestic Housecat: 0.5

Wild Octopus: 0.87

"Pupnik": 0.91

Sapience Baseline: 1.0

Uplifted Feline: 1.3

Uplifted Canine: 1.5

Uplifted Suidae: 1.55

Uplifted Avian: 1.6

Uplifted Simian: 1.62

Uplifted Cetacean: 1.63

Helot: 1.64

Human: 1.65

Uplifted Cephalopod: 1.66

So, there you have it! Be nice to the squiddos, kiddos. Before we say goodbye, we are contractually obligated to mention that the Nomad scientists are disputing the Helot's average score, citing 'biased results' from the PanOceanian scientists who performed some of the tests. To that I say, maybe we should ship 'em some Libertos, and see who's biased then!"

— Skyler Blue, for *Skyler Explains Everything* for Mercury Communications: available on Maya and Arachne.

SAPIENCE, QUANTIFIED

While its methodology can seem impossibly arcane to a layperson, the Nuendorf-Skalski test's results were designed to be easy to understand. A 1.0 on the Sapience Scale is the minimum threshold to be legally considered a sapient being by the Nomad Nation. With the understanding that developmentally disabled individuals were still considered people under the law, the 1.0 number does not necessarily represent an ability to take care of one's self, merely the recognition that the person is, categorically, a person.

humans, Tohaa, or any other thinking, acting, sapient race. Reactions throughout the Nomad Nation ranged from jubilant to noncommittal since most Nomads had long since abandoned the thought that traditional social norms were being terribly important. If these new citizens could pull their weight, then they were welcome. If not, well, the airlocks still worked.

Needless to say, the response across the Human Sphere was a bit more mixed. Given its sudden emergence, O-12 has remained noncommittal on the Nuendorf-Skalski Test and has thus far been reluctant to extend citizen privileges such as the Demogrant to Uplifts for passing a test cooked up in the heart of Praxis. Other corners of the Human Sphere have responded differently. PanOceania's initial enthusiasm for the measure saw a sharp decline when Helot subjects scored about the same and occasionally a little higher than the average PanOceanian. Yu Jing faced small pockets of rioting when a member of the Ministry of Ancestral Fidelity suggested that Japanese citizens be subjected to the measure.

UPLIFTS IN SOCIETY

Despite the massive amount of media attention and the ensuing legal proceedings, the number of recognised Sapient Uplifts has barely reached triple digits in the Nomad Nation. And while the Frankensteinian doctors of Praxis' Black Labs are certainly working overtime in this new field, most of the results are stunted, broken things, too unstable and violent to function in society, often falling just shy of the sapience threshold.

Many Uplifts come into the world the proud owners of a massive debt given by their creators to pay for the cost of their awakening. Others simply need to attend a few conferences and be presented to the larger scientific community. Once they've served to verify the researchers' findings, they're sent off into the world with a pat on the back and little else. Far more common than anyone wants to admit, however, is Uplifts being created by request or sold on the black market, though usually not in so many words. Unscrupulous "agents" purchase the rights to "represent" the Uplift to various clients, usually Submondo kingpins, brothel owners, and the occasional pirate. The Uplift is technically free to do as they wish, but in practice, they aren't really given a choice.

In truth, society doesn't really know what to do with Uplifts as of yet. Most have never left *Bakunin*, let alone ventured outside the Nomad Nation.

EXPERIMENTAL BRAGGING RIGHTS

By their own admission, the Nuendorf-Skalski test doesn't measure intelligence, rather the raw capacity for it. Even so, this hasn't stopped people from bragging about their abnormally high Sapience Scores, or degrading — and in some cases, terminating the employment of — people who score lower on the scale. Still, most people never subject themselves to the intrusive and demanding tests, though it's become yet another bizarre thing for tourists on holiday to do while visiting *Bakunin*.

Even Maria is content to advocate for Uplift civil rights via her custom Zondbot. As far as anyone knows, she hasn't left her tank in the Black Ships since before her Awakening. The next steps will be massive. The first Uplifts to interact with the wider Human Sphere will have a titanic burden on their shoulders, their actions speaking for all Uplifts and shaping society's opinions with every breath.

No pressure.

UPLIFT TYPES

Awakening an animal to sapience is no easy task. Projekt: Volaré proved that it was possible for cetaceans, but not every species has enjoyed the same success. Most attempts result in a tortured, monstrous beast-thing. One can look no farther than the Pupniks to see what a stunted, demi-sapient creature looks like. Still, through many trials and countless errors, a few species have emerged as prime candidates for uplifting:

AVIANS

Forget the songbirds and tropical parrots. Crows — ravens, to be precise — are the clever birds who took well to Uplift research. Presenting unique challenges due to their smaller brains, Avians nevertheless do remarkably well with personality recording. Chatty, creative, and possessed of a razor-sharp, sardonic wit, Avians have carved out a niche as airborne Remote pilots.

CANINES

Arguably the first species to receive experimental uplifting treatments, the field of Canine Uplift research is littered with failed experiments, nightmarish monsters, and the occasional very good but otherwise unremarkable dog. Even so, looking at the few successful Uplifts, it's easy to see why there's so much interest. Canines are loyal, enthusiastic, and good at taking direction. While they're easily distracted and tend to mope, their moods are rarely sour for long, and their ability to take direction is an invaluable and rare trait among Uplifts.

CETACEANS

Neo-cetaceans laid the groundwork, and Maria blazed the trail. Little wonder that Cetaceans remain the most common type of Uplift. Gregarious and clever, they are social creatures, though are terrible with boundaries. Dolphins in particular have a hard time taking "no" for an answer, but all cetaceans possess a predator's instincts. They're used to throwing their weight around and respond with deadly force when they feel threatened. Still, they're natural pilots, great team players, and possess an infectiously cheerful demeanour.

CEPHALOPODS

Possessing massive brains by animal standards, Cephalopod Uplifts have enjoyed a higher success rate than even Cetaceans, with the added benefit of taking up far less space in a lab. Insatiably curious, easily bored, and fond of sandpaper-dry humour, Cephalopods also tend to be supremely introverted, avoiding social situations to an extent rarely observed in humans. Still, their instinctive grasp of three-dimensional movement and comfortability with precise motions has proven useful when operating Remote Presence Gear. An added benefit of this method of interaction is that it allows them to stay at arm's length from the more outgoing races. Which, to be clear, is all of them.

FELINES

Something of a cautionary tale, Feline Uplifts present a suite of unique challenges. Initially created at the request of powerful Submondo, their sponsors imagined something akin to feline Chimera. They forgot one important rule about cats: they're only cute so long as they're not bigger than you. And with housecats proving unsuitable, researchers turned to leopards, lynx, and other big cats to get the job done. The good news is that it worked. The bad news is that cats tend to be aloof, enigmatic, and sadistic in any incarnation; Feline Uplifts generally aren't the exception to that rule.

SIMIANS

Requiring less drastic modification than other species, Simians are seen as a beginner's project in the Uplift research community, nothing you'd build a reputation on. Despite this, horror stories persist including everything from drug-addicted primates crawling around in the vents to cannibalistic chimpanzees breaking free and eating babies. (Though the latter is certainly conjecture; there's a ban on chimps for this very reason.) Frankly, once researchers found success working with less temperamental, more predictable, and frankly, nicer species, there was less incentive to experiment on the "damn dirty apes."

Still, a few Simian Uplifts have seen the light of day. Smaller subjects like the family-oriented Titi monkeys have enjoyed some success while biomorphed gorillas have flourished in tasks where their massive frames prove useful. But, they're hardly popular. Despite their neural suitability, Simians make up somewhere between five and ten percent of all Uplifts.

SUIDS

On the other hand, Suidae, or as they're more commonly known, swine, have enjoyed much greater success than anyone predicted. Affable, smart, and — much to the surprise of casual

observers – neurotically hygienic, Suids are sociable creatures. They're phenomenal at packing on muscle and using it effectively, making them prime candidates for hybrid biomorph bodies. Although they are remarkably laid-back, their calm demeanour isn't always reassuring since they are also prone to sudden, brutal violence. Rage isn't really their style; Suidae Uplifts have been observed ripping human beings to shreds without ever so much as raising their voice.

PRACTICAL PHYSIOLOGY

Awakening an Uplift creates some very real logistical concerns. Beyond the societal factors or philosophical implications, there are some very real, very practical challenges. No matter how smart you are, the world is built for humans. Without significant augmentation, Uplifts would be hopelessly crippled. Luckily for them, extensive modifications are an integral part of the deal. While neural comlogs and custom geists are common to every Uplift, there's usually much more that goes into making them functional. Over time, three categories of Uplift adaptation have emerged: Lhosts, Remote Operation, and Biomorphic Hybrids.

CUBES, LHOSTS, AND THE CHALLENGES OF NOVELTY

How does an Uplift interact with an Lhost? The same way that everyone else does, though the journey is complicated and prohibitively expensive. Modern Cubes are a mature technology, refined over time with a mountain of data from which to draw conclusions.

Uplifts are a genuinely new phenomena. There is no extant research to build on, no shoulders upon which to stand. Any memory recording would be an entirely custom-built project. Cubes are designed to interface with the relatively homogenous encephalic structure of humanity, and each Uplift is essentially a new and different species. Without custom Silk derivatives, a completely hand-tailored neural interface, and commissioned Cube-equivalent, obtaining a digital sheut is next to impossible. Some of the more ambitious Uplifts have attempted to start work on this project. While the Uplifts are new enough that none have yet perished from natural causes, with an estimated lifespan of 35–40 years, any and all anti-aging treatments carry an undeniable appeal.

If acquiring a Cube or Lhost for an Uplift, increase any tariffs up to 3, calculate the cost as normally, and then double it. Any Uplift transferring into a Lhost must succeed at an **Epic (D5) Discipline test** or suffer from Resurrection Dysmorphic Disorder (see *Infinity Corebook,* p. 394). Beyond this, once an Uplift is slotted into a Lhost, their experience is much like anyone else's, though it still takes time to get used to their strange, humanoid body.

REMOTES

Many uplifts rely on Remotes, the original and the most popular option to handle most tasks up to and including feeding themselves, and Remotes are the preferred method of Cetacean and Cephalopod Starswimmers. Many Uplifted pilots will hop between the ship's controls and a customised Zondbot without ever leaving the comforts of their custom habitat. This hyper-sedentary lifestyle can lead to some long-term health issues so most Remote-primary uplifts make time for daily exercise as well as the occasional holiday.

BIOMORPHIC HYBRIDS

For some Uplifts, separating the mind from the body is a recipe for disaster. In other cases, tapping into their unique physiology is part of the appeal. And sometimes, a mad scientist just wants to build a better monster. Whatever the reason, Praxis scientists have been known to create their fair share of custom biomorphic hybrid hosts. And while many of these tortured experiments go awry, resulting in hulking abominations, insane nightmare creatures, or simply leaving their subjects dead on the operating table, the labs occasionally cook up a stable solution.

These Biomorphs are each a one-of-a-kind creature, fusing their original DNA with human, xenobiological, or synthetic vat-grown tissue. Usually, this results in a bipedal hominid with distinct animalistic features, not entirely unlike Ariadna's Wulvers or Dog-Warriors, though depending on the source material, potentially much smaller.

UPLIFT CHARACTERS

If nonhumans are uncommon in the world of *Infinity*, then Uplifts are exceptionally rare. The tiny population of unique individuals has yet to make any significant steps into the wider Human Sphere. Uplift Characters will likely be the first of their kind, first to venture out into the stars, first to visit other worlds, and certainly the first Uplift that most people have ever met.

DECISION ONE: BIRTH HOST

Uplift characters roll on the *Uplift Species Table* to determine their origins. They may instead spend 1 Life Point to simply choose their species. Note: Modifiers from a Species template affect your attributes directly, but

don't go on the Host section of your character sheet. They represent the unique perspective of your animalistic mind, holding true no matter what body you're in. If you are unable to meet the Life Point Cost of the Species, you can either select a Species that you can afford, or simply continue on the Lifepath as a Human.

UPLIFT SPECIES TABLE	
D20	HOST
1	Simian
2–5	Cephalopod
6–8	Avian
9–13	Cetacean
14–16	Canine
17–18	Suidae
19–20	Feline

After determining your Species, you must choose whether your character resides in an Lhost, interacts primarily through Remotes, or is a Custom Biomorph. Nothing prevents your character from picking up a Remote if you begin play in an Lhost, but every Uplift has to start somewhere. Select one of the Host options and pay the listed Life Point cost. Apply the modifiers from your Host to both your attributes and the Host section of your character sheet, and make note of any special abilities or gear.

"Two hosts. Two sheuts inhabiting them. I was born human, but Blue here used to be a jellyfish or — wait, one second — okay, he's something called a "vampire squid." Well, we all identify as something a little different, don't we? Anyway, two very different origins, but what's the difference between us now? His host is a custom biomorph; mine is a Siren Lhost. But at the end of the day, we're both sheuts in a — Blue, where are you going? We're in the middle of an interview....

All right, fine. One difference is that he's shy. But that's just a personality thing. Philosophically, spiritually, and existentially, what's the distinction? Humanity — no, personhood — is so much more than genetics."

—Dana Schäfer and (briefly) Blue Nocturne of the Salted Deep: interview for Transhuman Transmission, only on Arachne.

UPLIFT RESURRECTIONS

The process of Awakening an Uplift creates a lot of data. That said, it's not like one can just acquire an Avian-spec Cube off the shelf. Thus, most Uplifts' heads are a tangle of tissue and wire, hacked together to create a working prototype. No one knows an Uplift like their creators. If an Uplift dies during character creation, they have the option of choosing a Custom Biomorph as their new host, provided that they can pay the associated Life Point cost.

Once they're out in the world, it's a different story altogether. Needless to say, standard Resurrection isn't an option. Reviving a deceased Uplift from its onboard memory storage is going to be an uphill battle and possibly an entire campaign arc in itself.

UPLIFT SPECIES

UPLIFT LIFEPATH DECISIONS

The Lifepath Decisions outlined on p. 38 of the *Infinity Corebook* should be followed with the following exceptions for Uplift characters.

DECISION ONE— BIRTH HOST

In order to use this Lifepath your Birth Host must be an Uplift. This may have been randomly determined or purchased with Life Points. Either way, Uplifted characters roll on the *Uplift Species Table*, then select either an Lhost, Remote, or Custom Biomorph as your initial Host.

DECISION TWO— FACTION AND HERITAGE

Uplift characters automatically take Nomad for both Faction and Heritage, and gain skills accordingly.

DECISION THREE— HOMEWORLD/ HOMELAND

Uplifts are created on *Bakunin,* or on board one of Praxis' Black Ships. They roll on the *Uplift Mothership Table.*

DECISION FOUR— STATUS

Uplifts gain the Heritage Trait Bakunian, and roll on the *Uplift Social Status Table* and *Uplift Home Environment Table.*

DECISION FIVE— AWAKENING EVENT

Uplift characters roll on the *Awakening Event Tables.*

DECISION SEVEN— ADOLESCENT EVENT

Like other characters in the Nomad Faction, Uplifts roll on the *Nomad Faction Adolescent Event Tables.*

DECISION EIGHT— CAREERS

Instead of rolling on the *Nomads Career Table* in the *Infinity Corebook* or *Nomad Faction Career Table*, Uplift characters roll on their respective *Uplift Career Table* as well as the *Uplift Career Event Tables.*

AVIAN

- **Hawkeye**: Gain 1 rank in Awareness
- **Natural Flight**: If you begin play in a Small Biomorph, gain the Aircraft vehicle quality. You may freely fly in atmosphere using either the Athletics or Pilot skills.
- **Gain Species Trait**: Inquisitive
- **Life Point Cost**: 2

CANINE

- **Who's a Good Dog?**: Gain 1 rank in Willpower
- **Enthusiastic**: Gain 1 rank in Athletics. If you begin play in a Biomorph, gain the Common Special Ability, Keen Senses (scent).
- **Gain Species Trait**: Loyal
- **Life Point Cost**: 2

CETACEAN

- **Gregarious**: Gain 1 rank in Personality
- **3D Native**: Gain 1 rank in either Extraplanetary or Spacecraft. Gain the Space Ace talent.
- **Aquatic**: If you begin play in a Biomorph, you can breathe underwater, gain the Common Special Ability: Inured to Cold, and begin play with one rank of the Strong Swimmer talent.
- **Gain Species Trait**: Boundary Issues
- **Life Point Cost**: 4

CEPHALOPOD

- **Uplifted Intellect**: Gain 1 rank in Intelligence
- **Aquatic**: If you begin play in a Biomorph, you can breathe underwater, gain the Common Special Abilities: Inured to Cold, and Inured to Aquatic Pressure, and begin play with one rank of the Strong Swimmer talent.
- **Gain Species Trait**: Antisocial
- **Life Point Cost**: 3

FELINE

- **Predatory Instinct**: Gain 1 rank in Agility
- **Hunter's Grace**: Gain 1 rank in Acrobatics. If you begin play in a Biomorph, gain 1 rank of the Catfall talent.
- **Gain Species Trait**: Sadistic
- **Life Point Cost**: 3

SIMIAN

- **Nimble**: Gain 1 rank in Coordination
- **Natural Gymnast**: If you begin play in a Biomorph, gain Climbing Plus as an augmentation. If it's a small or medium Biomorph, gain a prehensile tail as well.
- **Gain Species Trait**: Foul-Tempered
- **Life Point Cost**: 2

SUIDAE

- **Tough as Nails**: Gain 1 rank in Brawn
- **Naturally Calm**: Gain 2 ranks in Morale
- **Gain Species Trait**: Neurotically Hygienic
- **Life Point Cost**: 3

CUSTOM BIOMORPH, SMALL

ATTRIBUTES

AGILITY	+1	AWARENESS	–	BRAWN	–2	COORDINATION	–
INTELLIGENCE	+1	PERSONALITY	–	WILLPOWER	–		

Odd Fit: Almost nothing is tailored to fit Biomorphs, especially ones this small. When purchasing gear meant to be worn, such as armour, add +1 to the item's restriction and tariff rating. Gear that is not acquired in this fashion causes the Uplift to suffer a +1 complication range to all skill tests. Tailoring gear to fit the character requires a Complex Tech test (D3, 4 Momentum, 2 failures).
Out of Sight, Out of Mind: You generate +1 additional Momentum on successful Stealth tests.
Small Target: Ranged attacks against a Small Biomorph are made at +1 difficulty.
Tiny: When using items of a size larger than One-Handed, you suffer +1 difficulty and +2 complication range, though you may remove these penalties by taking the Brace Action. Either way, you cannot wield items of Unwieldy size or larger
Life Point Cost: 0

CUSTOM BIOMORPH, MEDIUM

ATTRIBUTES

AGILITY	–	AWARENESS	–	BRAWN	–	COORDINATION	–
INTELLIGENCE	–	PERSONALITY	–	WILLPOWER	–		

Custom MetaChemistry: Increase one attribute of your choice by 1 rank.
Uncanny Valley: Close enough that you might pass for a modified Human at first glance, but far enough that no one's making that mistake on their second glance, people find your appearance unsettling. Increase the complication range on all Personality-based tests by one step.
Life Point Cost: 1

CUSTOM BIOMORPH, LARGE

ATTRIBUTES

AGILITY	–	AWARENESS	–	BRAWN	–	COORDINATION	–
INTELLIGENCE	–	PERSONALITY	–	WILLPOWER	–		

Monstrous: They certainly made you big. Increase the difficulty of tests where great size or weight would be problematic by one step. Monstrous creatures are not required to brace Unwieldy weapons, can use two-handed weapons in one hand without difficulty or penalty, and can wield Massive weapons in two hands freely, or in one hand by increasing the difficulty of all skill tests to use the item by two steps. Additionally, they may spend 1 Momentum to add Knockdown to all of their melee attacks for a turn.
Odd Fit: Almost nothing is tailored to fit something this large. When purchasing gear meant to be worn, such as armour, add +1 to the item's restriction and tariff rating. Gear that is not acquired in this fashion causes the Uplift to suffer a +1 complication range to all skill tests. Tailoring gear to fit the character requires a Complex Tech test (D3, 4 Momentum, 2 failures).
Life Point Cost: 3

AVERAGE BIOMORPH SIZES

Small Biomorph: 1 metre or less, 20–45 kg

Medium Biomorph: 1.5 to 2 metres, 70–125 kg

Large Biomorph 2.25 to 3 metres, 150–200 kg

For ease of use, these entries use existing Lhosts, but it's worth noting that the models used are customised, one-off units. Acquiring an Lhost that easily interfaces with the slapdash mess that is an Uplift's head isn't a trivial task, hence the doubled cost of Lhosts once play begins (see p. 84).

LHOST

ATTRIBUTES

| AGILITY | – | AWARENESS | – | BRAWN | – | COORDINATION | – |
| INTELLIGENCE | – | PERSONALITY | – | WILLPOWER | – | | |

Cubed: Gain a Cube.
Hosted: Select a Lhost for your character from either the *Infinity* Corebook (p. 354) or another *Infinity* supplement.
Life Point Cost: Pay the listed Life Point cost for your selected Lhost. If the cost cannot be paid, you may take the Antiquated Lhost at no cost.

REMOTE SPECIALIST

ATTRIBUTES

| AGILITY | – | AWARENESS | – | BRAWN | – | COORDINATION | – |
| INTELLIGENCE | – | PERSONALITY | – | WILLPOWER | – | | |

Just like the Real Thing: You begin play with 1 TinBot, as your "body."
Gear: Remote Presence Gear or Cube 2.0 (choose one)
Life Point Cost: 2 (1 for Cetaceans and Cephalopods)

DECISION THREE: UPLIFT MOTHERSHIP

While the day may come when Uplifts are created somewhere other than the auspices of *Bakunin*, it hasn't come yet. Instead of the *Nomad Mothership Table*, Uplift characters roll on the *Uplift Lab Table*.

UPLIFT LAB TABLE

D20	REGION	LANGUAGE	ATTRIBUTE	ATTRIBUTE	SKILL
1–9	Praxis Black Labs	German, English	Willpower	Agility	Science
10–18	Praxis Black Ships	English*	Willpower	Awareness	Extraplanetary
19–20	Undocumented Orbital	German*	Willpower	Intelligence	Resistance

* Roll again on the *Nomad Mothership Table* (see *Infinity Corebook*, p. 43) to determine a second language you're fluent with. If you roll the same result, that's the only language you're fluent with.

DECISION FOUR: UPLIFT STATUS

Uplifts are still residents of *Bakunin*. They gain the Heritage Trait: Bakunian. However, their upbringing is necessarily quite different. Thus, Uplift characters roll on the *Uplift Social Class Table* and *Uplift Home Environment Table*.

SOCIAL CLASS TABLE

2D6	SOCIAL STATUS	ATTRIBUTE	EARNINGS
2	Criminal Underclass*	Personality	2
3-5	Underclass	Willpower	1
6-8	Middle	Brawn	3
9-10	Upper	Intelligence	4
11	Criminal Upper Class*	Personality	4
12	Criminal Elite*	Brawn	5

* Renegades even by Nomad standards, your creator(s) dealt with Submondo more than with the rest of *Bakunin*. Gain a Criminal Record; you may join the Submondo faction at any time.

HOME ENVIRONMENT TABLE

D6	ENVIRONMENT	ATTRIBUTE	SKILL
1	Underworld*	Brawn	Thievery
2	Violent	Brawn	Acrobatics
3	Virtual	Intelligence	Hacking
4	Clinical	Willpower	Resistance
5	Regimented	Awareness	Discipline
6	High Society	Personality	Lifestyle

DECISION FIVE: AWAKENING

Uplifts don't really have a childhood. They have the time before their awakening and everything that comes afterwards. The transition into sapience is many things — shocking, traumatic, unreal — but it is never gentle.

Uplift characters roll 1d20 and consult the *Awakening Table*, adding the listed skill and talent. You can spend 1 Life Point to choose from the table, or after your initial roll to reroll the result.

DECISION EIGHT: UPLIFT CAREERS

When creating your character, you can choose to select the Test Subject career to gain 1 Life Point. (You can gain a maximum of 2 Life Points in this way. You do not gain the Life Point if you are forced to become a Test Subject by a random roll, event, or hazard test.)

Even if they've changed faction, Uplifts roll on their respective *Uplift Career Table*. At the GM's discretion, when directed to roll on a Nomad faction table, they may substitute their current faction's unique tables instead. If you roll an Uplift career but fail to meet its prerequisites, you can still proceed by hazarding the career, though your attempt suffers +1 difficulty. Attempting to hazard an Uplift career without meeting the prerequisites likewise suffers +1 difficulty to the hazard test. Additionally, whenever they would normally determine a career event, they roll on the *Nomad Uplift Career Event Tables* to determine which *Career Event Table* to roll on. You may spend 1 Life Point to choose any career from your species' career table, or to roll on the *Faction Career Table* indicated.

PLAYTEST TIP
THE HAZARDS OF UPLIFTED CAREERS

Though they can't normally be randomly rolled, there's nothing preventing Human characters from working as an Entertainer or joining Die Morlock Gruppe, and in the world of *Infinity*, many do just that. There's no reason why Human characters can't hazard an Uplift career, or with the GM's approval, roll on the *Uplift Career* Table by spending a Life Point. Though if they don't meet the prerequisites for a career, they fare no better than anyone else.

For Uplifts, it's a little different. Barring special circumstances, they can't take Human careers; there simply aren't many opportunities for a Frankensteinian crow-monster, no matter how slick their resume is. Uplifts require GM approval to hazard any career that does not appear in their respective *Career Table*.

AWAKENING TABLE

D20	EVENT	SKILL [TALENT]
1-4	Shapes, glyphs, symbols — how could anyone hope to make sense of this informational deluge? But slowly, over time, patterns began to emerge.	Analysis [Pattern Recognition]
5-8	You remember screaming. Pain. The procedures tore your siblings apart, but you managed to survive. Your first self-aware thought was the realisation that you were very much alone, in more ways than one.	Resistance [Sturdy]
9-12	They said you were a failed experiment, a dead end. Furious at the dismissal, you determined to make them eat their words.	Discipline [Stubborn]
13-16	When the lab lost power, your fellow subjects were gripped in raw, animal panic. Not you, however. You calmed them all down, even as the stark differences between you and them took shape in your mind.	Animal Handling [Wild Empathy]
17-19	They thought they had you secured tightly, but you soon gave your habitat the slip. It would take them weeks to find you, giving you time to think.	Stealth [Scout]
20	The raid came at the worst possible time. Not just for your siblings and your creator(s), but for your attackers: you were awake, you were angry, and you were fully in control. You made them regret it.	Ballistics or Close Combat (choose one) [Quickdraw]

CAREER EVENT TABLES

D6	TABLE
1–3	Uplift Career Event Table
4	Career Event Table A[1]
5	Career Event Table B[1]
6	Career Event Table C[1]

[1] *Infinity Corebook*, p.56–58

AVIAN CAREER TABLE

D20	CAREER
1–2	Test Subject
3–5	Smuggler[1]
6–8	Entertainer
9–14	Tinkerer
15–16	BouBoutique Clerk[2]
17	Die Morlock Gruppe[2]
18	Starswimmer
19	Clockmaker[2, 3]
20	Roll on *Nomad Faction Table*

CANINE CAREER TABLE

D20	CAREER
1–2	Test Subject
3–7	Personal Security
8–15	Die Morlock Aufstand Gruppe[2]
12–13	Entertainer
14–15	Military[1]
16–17	Ship Crew[1]
18	Wrench
19	Mothership Security Corps[2]
20	Roll on *Uplift Career Table* of your choice

CEPHALOPOD CAREER TABLE

D20	CAREER
1–2	Test Subject
3–7	Starswimmer
8–12	Tinkerer
13–14	Hacker[1]
15–16	Medical[1]
17	Remote Operator[1]
18	BouBoutique Clerk
19	TAG Pilot[1]
20	Roll on *Nomad Faction Table*

CETACEAN CAREER TABLE

D20	CAREER
1–2	Test Subject
3–12	Starswimmer
13–14	Remote Operator[1]
15	Negotiator[3]
16	Pilot[1]
17	Entertainer
18	Medical[1]
19	Corsair[1]
20	Roll on *Nomad Faction Table*

FELINE CAREER TABLE

D20	CAREER
1–2	Test Subject
3–5	Entertainer
7–10	Personal Security
11–13	Die Morlock Gruppe[2]
14–15	Criminal[1]
16–17	'Cat Squad Member[3]
18	Special Forces[1]
19	BouBoutique Clerk
20	Roll on *Uplift Career Table* of your choice

SIMIAN CAREER TABLE

D20	CAREER
1–3	Test Subject
4–8	Wrench
9–11	Die Morlock Gruppe
12–13	Criminal[1]
14–16	Tinkerer
17	Ship Crew[1]
18	Infiltrator[3]
19	Personal Security
20	Roll on *Uplift Career Table* of your choice

SUIDAE CAREER TABLE

D20	CAREER
1–2	Test Subject
3–8	Personal Security
9–11	Heavy Industry[1]
12–15	Die Morlock Gruppe
16	Military[1]
17	Wrench
18	Criminal[1]
19	BouBoutique Clerk
20	Roll on *Uplift Career Table* of your choice

[1] Career from *Infinity Corebook*.

[2] Career has a prerequisite of belonging to this faction. You can't hazard this career unless you're of the matching faction. If you roll into this career, you automatically fail your defection check. You can override these limitations by spending 1 Life Point (in which case, you were somehow undercover while working the career).

[3] Career from *Nomad Characters Chapter*, p. 63.

NOMAD UPLIFT CAREER EVENT TABLE

D20	CAREER EVENT	GAME EFFECT
1	During a routine checkup, the doctors discover an incompatibility in two of your artificial organs; at least one is going to need replaced.	Increase either Awareness or Agility by 1. However, decrease the Attribute you didn't select by 1.
2	An Arachne series runs a feature on you. It isn't exactly flattering, but it gets your name out there.	Increase Lifestyle by 1 rank, but all Stealth tests are increased in difficulty by one step in situations where being recognised would cause you a problem.
3	You spend some time in a VaudeVille amateur performance troupe.	Gain 1 rank in Acrobatics.
4	Your geist was acting up, so you got it examined by some Clockmakers. Bad news: the quantronic virus wreaked havoc on your network. Good news: your geist is running better than ever.	Reduce Firewall by 1 but add 4 skill ranks to your geist.
5	Doctors discover a strange growth. It's removed without complications, but your musculature atrophies from the treatments.	Reduce Brawn by 1.
6	You enter a high-stakes card game and lose, badly.	Gain a 4+4 N Asset debt.
7	When your shuttle pilot has an accident, everyone looks to you to take the helm.	Gain 1 rank in Spacecraft.
8	Sick of being treated like a mascot, you express your displeasure in dramatic, public fashion.	You are Fired (see Infinity Corebook, p. 54). Gain an appropriate trait.
9	Arrested for crimes real or imagined, two figures offer to make it all go away. The Submondo wants a favour; the Tunguskan lawyer wants money. But what do you want?	If you take the Tunguskan's offer, gain a 3+3 Asset debt. If you take the Submondo's offer, you must either take Criminal as your next career or owe a large favour to the Submondo. If you take neither offer, gain a Criminal Record (see Infinity Corebook, p. 54) and spend 1d6 years in prison.
10	When some of your biografts start wearing out, you don't repair or replace; you upgrade.	Increase Brawn by 1. Gain a 5 Asset debt.
11	Most people are immune to animal-specific diseases, and vice versa. You, however, seem to have gotten the worst of both worlds.	Reduce Vigour by 1. Gain Trait: Allergic to Everything.
12	You overclock your personal area network; while your Comlog sometimes runs hot, the results speak for themselves.	Increase Hacking by 1 rank. Gain Trait: Overclocked Network.
13	You spend some time on assignment with Corregidor. Did you make any friends? Enemies?	Increase Extraplanetary by 1 rank. Gain a contact on Corregidor.
14	You enter – and win – a high stakes card game though the Submondo running it are convinced you cheated. Did you?	Gain 4+4 N Assets. Gain a Submondo rival.
15	Caught in the same firefight, you're saved by a Reverend Healer-Killer. After some tense discussion on whether or not Uplifts have a soul, you think you hit it off.	Gain a contact in the Observance of Saint Mary of the Knife.
16	As someone who underwent an Awakening, you can't help but notice that your geist is asking increasingly self-aware questions.	Gain Trait: Rogue Geist. Increase your geist's Awareness and Intelligence by 2 points each.
17	Your supervisor puts you in charge of a charity petting zoo. Jokes aside, it goes well.	Gain 1 rank in Animal Handling.
18	A minor celebrity freaks out when they see you at work, and their rant goes viral.	You are Fired (see Infinity Corebook, p. 54). Gain an appropriate trait.
19	Clandestine operatives abduct you, but Nomad Infiltrators puts a bullet in your head before the vivisection begins. Much to your surprise, you wake up in Praxis.	Your character died and was Resurrected. See the rules for Resurrection (see Infinity Corebook, p.54). Gain an enemy in a random faction.
20	Some of your first memories are assurances that everything will be fine so long as no Unexpected Complications arise. Of course, they always do.	Roll again three times on the Career Event Table for this career phase. (When spending a Life Point to choose a specific event, you may not choose this result.) If you roll duplicate events, it means some similar event has occurred. If you roll Unexpected Complications again, add additional rolls.

CAREER PROFILE

TEST SUBJECT (SPECIAL)

Sometimes, there just aren't any good options. Steady work is a dream for many Uplifts, but far too often, it's a dream out of reach. But when all else fails, when no one is hiring, and there's nowhere left to turn, the Black Labs of Praxis always have room for another Test Subject. Ingesting strange fluids, testing new MetaChemistry treatments, and donating litres of blood, life as a Test subject is rarely pleasant, but at least it isn't dull.

ATTRIBUTES						
AGI	AWA	BRW	COO	INT	PER	WIL
+1	+1	+1	+1	+1	+1	+3

SKILLS				EARNINGS
Mandatory	Animal Handling	Resistance	–	0+1  (max 0)
Elective	Any 2 Other			

GEAR: None

CAREER PROFILE

DIE MORLOCK GRUPPE

On an orderly battlefield, superior discipline, tactics, and firepower rule the day. Amidst the chaos, however, it's all about who can improvise. Enter Die Morlock Gruppe. Comprised of the dregs of Bakunian society, the Morlock Groups are experts in violence, chaos, and inflicting serious damage. Employed primarily as an anti-riot force, they're also unleashed on battlefields around the Human Sphere as ultraviolent and effective, yet difficult to control, shock troopers. They are organised into three main segments, the Aufstand (rebellion), Chaos, and Schaden (damage) groups, and are about as subtle as a bat to the face. Inhuman in appearance, methods, and membership, the Morlocks gleefully introduce bloody chaos into any situation, transforming the crisis into an entirely new sort of problem, one they proceed to pound into the floor.

ATTRIBUTES						
AGI	AWA	BRW	COO	INT	PER	WIL
+2	+2	+3	+1	–	+1	–

SKILLS				EARNINGS
Mandatory	Athletics	Close Combat	Thievery	1+3 
Elective	Ballistics	Close Combat	Psychology	

GEAR: Combi Rifle (with 1 Standard Reload) or Chain Rifle, D-Charges (2), Smoke Grenades (2), Sword

SPECIAL: Each time you take this career, roll 1d20 and consult the *Chaotic Gear Table*, gaining the listed gear.

CAREER PROFILE

BOUBOUTIQUE CLERK

In the iridescent sea of commerce that is *Bakunin's* market, few wear its transgressive verve as proudly as the BouBoutiques. Experts in body modification, BouBoutiques can transform you into anything you like, provided you can pay. With no better advertisement than a living canvas, many BouBoutique clerks boast exotic and inhuman appearances. A recent synergy with *Bakunin's* nascent Uplift population has led to inquisitive and visually striking Uplifts acting as the face of their business. Skilled in sales and walking encyclopaedias of fashion knowledge, BouBoutique Clerks also acquire a fair share of experience in modifying Lhosts, Biomorphs, and other physical hosts. BouBoutiques often run with a lean staff, so Clerks offer a little of everything —all with a smile and a wink.

ATTRIBUTES						
AGI	AWA	BRW	COO	INT	PER	WIL
+1	+2	+1	+1	+2	+2	+1

SKILLS				EARNINGS
Mandatory	LIfestyle	Persuade	Tech	1+4 
Elective	Discipline	Education	Medicine	

GEAR: Powered Multitool (with 6 Units of Parts), Internal Pocket 1 or Geist Upgrade (+2 ranks in Tech, or the Pattern Recognition talent for Analysis)

CAREER PROFILE
ENTERTAINER

Nomads — especially Bakunians — seem to have an insatiable appetite for novelty. Exoticism is prized and is in comparatively short supply. A tourist walking down Sunset Boulevard will have their senses assaulted by a barrage of unfamiliar, wild sights and sounds. But for a Nomad, it's nothing they haven't seen before. Fortunately for them, *Bakunin* is always producing something new and exciting.

Products, services, or people, the Radical Mothership is only too happy to raise its supply of weird to meet this ravenous demand for novelty. If they are nothing else, Uplifts are unmistakably novel. Whether they're dancing, serving drinks, or taking on clients in the Ultraviolet District, if you've got a striking look — which many Uplifts can claim by default — there's work to be had. Even if most of it is being gawked at by strangers.

ATTRIBUTES						
AGI	AWA	BRW	COO	INT	PER	WIL
+2	+1	+1	+1	–	+3	+1

SKILLS			EARNINGS
Mandatory	Acrobatics	Persuade	Psychology	2+1 Ⓝ
Elective	Athletics	Lifestyle	Observation	

GEAR: Cosmetics Kit, SecurCuffs, Recorder, Nitrocane (2 Doses), Naughties

CHAOTIC GEAR TABLE	
D20	GEAR
1	Mess (1 Dose), Old Steely (2 Doses)
2	Smoke Grenades (2), Tear Gas Grenades (2)
4	Goonades (8)
5	Breaking & Entering Kit, Locational Beacon, SecureCuffs
6	Micro-Torch, USAriadnan Entrenching Tool
7	Signal Flares, Bottled Water (1 Week's Supply), Survival Rations (1 Week's Supply)
8	Busted Old Tinbot (Increase complication range by 1, **Challenging (D2) Tech** test to repair)
9	Puraza (1 Dose), Stims (2 Doses)
10	Animal Habitat, Painkillers (5 Doses)
11	Recorders (2), Sports Padding
12	Naughties (1 Month Supply)
13	Adhesive Solvent, Portable Monkey Bar
14	Freedom Kit
15	Hard Hat, Plasteel Pipe
16	Non-Functional Tinbot, 3 Units of Parts
17	Fake ID 3
18–20	Roll Again Twice, Combine the Results

CAREER PROFILE
STARSWIMMER

This is where it all began. A staple of the Nomad navy, the original Neo-Cetaceans' instinctual understanding of three-dimensional navigation was invaluable in keeping pace with the technological juggernauts of the Human Sphere. The introduction of uplifted Cephalopods to the program has reinvigorated Nomad naval tactics, as their instincts add another unpredictable twist to the Nomad bag of tricks.

Other pilots might ghost into a Remote, or dabble in VR-based piloting, but a Starswimmer goes further. For all intents and purposes, they become their ships in flight. This grants Starswimmers unprecedented grace and control, but it comes at a cost: they feel every strain and impact as though the hull was their own body. For Starswimmers, the risk is worth it. The chance to become their ships is the ultimate adrenaline rush. Just don't call them "blowholes."

ATTRIBUTES						
AGI	AWA	BRW	COO	INT	PER	WIL
+1	+2	+1	+2	+1	+2	+1

SKILLS			EARNINGS
Mandatory	Discipline	Stealth	Spacecraft	2+2 Ⓝ
Elective	Exraplanetary	Stealth	Spacecraft	

GEAR: Immersive Pilot Gear, Crashsuit

CAREER PROFILE
TINKERER

Some people are just born curious. And for certain types of Uplift, the instinct to tinker with things irresistible. It's not uncommon to find young Avians studiously disassembling their surroundings, though it's less common to find one who puts them back together again. Constantly deconstructing things, Tinkerers are ceaselessly inventing, reverse-engineering, or tweaking anything to hand. The wealth of technological know-how that these Uplifts possess can be surprising, but to a Tinkerer, it's quite literally in their nature. Many find success in chop shops, with black market arms dealers, or even in legitimate work on a drydock. Some have even joined the NMF as battlefield technicians, though there's always the risk they'll disassemble a soldier's Combi Rifle just before they need it...

ATTRIBUTES						
AGI	AWA	BRW	COO	INT	PER	WIL
+1	+2	+1	+2	+2	+1	+1

SKILLS			EARNINGS
Mandatory	Anayliss	Tech	Thievery	1+3 Ⓝ
Elective	Edcuation	Hacking	Science	

GEAR: Powered Multitool (with 6 Units of Parts), Internal Pocket 1 or Geist Upgrade (+2 ranks in Tech, or the Pattern Recognition talent for Analysis)

UPLIFTED MUSCLE

From Tunguskan investment bankers' private bodyguards, to a *Corregidor maras* gang's heavies, to a BouBoutique's storefront security, every Nomad could use some intimidating muscle from time to time. Sure, there's no shortage of ruthless, violent, or heavyset folks available for the job, for many the ordinary just won't cut it. And that's when having some muscled Uplift as your Personal Security really shines. Using Pupniks in an obvious security role has long been a favourite tactic of Submondo crime bosses. Once they realised they could get their hands on similarly intimidating specimens with a roughly human intellect, the idea really took off. For the discerning underworld tycoon, there's little that flaunts your power like a hulking boar or gorilla at your back. Attack dogs and big cats on a leash have long been a symbol of black-market power, but with Uplifts it's been taken to a whole new level.

ATTRIBUTES						
AGI	AWA	BRW	COO	INT	PER	WIL
+2	+1	+3	+1	–	+1	+1

SKILLS				EARNINGS
Mandatory	Close Combat	Discipline	Persuade	2+1 Ⓝ
Elective	Athletics	Observation	Resistance	

GEAR: Modhand or Nanopulser, Armoured Clothing, Deflector-2

WRENCH

Nomads live and die by their ships. The cold void of space doesn't care where you came from; you either survive, or you don't. So, when it comes down to ship and equipment maintenance, the Nomads are similarly pragmatic. It doesn't matter what school you went to, who your parents are, or how many people up-voted your viral video. You can either do the work, or you can't. As it turns out, plenty of Uplifts can do the work. Sure, some Nomads find it strange to see the person next to them gripping a Multitool with their tail, but if the work is sound, they can only bring themselves to care so much. Nicknamed "Wrenches," these Uplifted mechanics can be found working the most dangerous assignments in the guts of a fallen TAG, repairing a ship's hull from the outside, or anything else where you need a skilled — but expendable — mechanic.

ATTRIBUTES						
AGI	AWA	BRW	COO	INT	PER	WIL
+1	+1	+2	+1	+2	+1	+2

SKILLS				EARNINGS
Mandatory	Discipline	Exraplanetary	Tech	1+2 Ⓝ
Elective	Pilot	Survival	Tech	

GEAR: Engineering Waldo 1, Repair Kit, Plasteel Pipe

CHAPTER 7

BIOENGINEERING

To walk through the streets of *Bakunin* is to see just how modified the body can become, while still technically remaining human — or with the arrival of the Tohaa, ascension of the Uplifts, and the first Helot explorers all dipping their uniquely-shaped toes into the larger Human Sphere, whatever else they started as. While biografts are not uncommon, Nomad bioengineering takes it a step further, then another, and another. They don't stop when they've gone too far. In fact, that's when things start getting interesting.

ALLURE OF THE UNDISCOVERED

How Nomad bioengineering differentiates from standard biografts — such as those produced by Haqqislam, PanOceania, or any number of corporations — is complicated. Standard biografted augmentations rely on carefully calibrated retroviruses and genetically neutral xeno-transplants. It's a safe, cautious, deliberate process, with innumerable protections in place to ensure that everything goes smooth.

Nomad bioengineering offers no such reassurances. What it does offer, however, is the prospect of radical transformation, unshackled by norms, regulations, or concerns for the long-term health. In the hotly contested secret wars of the Human Sphere, the slightest advantage can tip a conflict, and having a trick or two up your sleeve can be the difference between a successful mission and an interplanetary fiasco. Praxis is more than happy to tip the balance in their clients' favour.

XENOGRAFTING

Most augmentation clinics incorporate some manner of xenotissue in their procedures. While more exotic materials such as synthetic Antipode glands are sometimes used, most of this work is done with carefully cultivated, lab-grown tissue. It's safe, thoroughly tested, and well-understood.

In Praxis, however, they do things a little differently. No line of inquiry is off-limits, no topic is taboo. The exploration of possibility is their primary concern. The respect and acclaim of their peers comes next. The well-being of their patients is a distant third, if it registers at all; they knew the risks and decided to roll the dice. It's not the bioengineers' fault if they get more than they bargained for.

"Oh, it's completely unreasonable. We're in agreement there. No reasonable person would allow these mad scientists to experiment on them. My mission is not reasonable. The risks are not reasonable. And my opposition refuses to listen to reason.

When faced with an unreasonable task, you need an unreasonable solution. For those, I come to *Bakunin*."

— Lieutenant Paula Whitaker, Hexas agent. Hexahedron expense review, undisclosed location.

RADICAL GENETIC THERAPY

Outside of Ariadna, virtually every citizen of the Human Sphere has undergone genetic therapy at some point, usually before they were even born. Slow, gradual gene therapy is frequently used to provide a robust immunisation against disease or employed to deal with the effects of aging.

However, that's not all that genetic alteration can do. Radical change requires radical treatments, and with enough Silk, physicians can attempt nearly anything. Whether it's a good idea or not is a different matter entirely. Every non-Nomad jurisdiction has banned rapid, radical genetic therapy, declaring it "woefully and wildly unsafe," a distinction that Praxis has never bothered denying.

Still, throw enough Silk at an idea, and astonishing things become possible. Getting one's hands on that much of the substance is another story entirely, so most Nomad clinics have several other options available to their clients. From splicing animal DNA to accept muscle grafts, to a steady regimen of anti-rejection drugs to deal with your new xenotissue, options abound.

CUSTOM GENEMOD PACKAGES

Applied bioengineering is not for the faint of heart. But for those willing to embrace the risk, there are worlds of untapped potential just waiting to be explored. Unlike traditional augmentation, there is an element of volatility to the process. In the *Infinity Corebook,* the only random elements of augmentation surgery lie in acquisition. Once the goods and services have acquired and paid for, it's generally smooth sailing from there.

Custom GeneMods are not smooth. They're a wild frontier, fraught with unexpected results, both positive and negative. In addition to increasing the cost, restriction, tariff, and maintenance of an upgrade package, bioengineering uses an additional tally: *Risk.*

As more varied and potent treatments go into the GeneMod package, its Risk increases. After acquiring their GeneMod package, players consult their Risk tally and roll on the *Bioengineering Side Effects Table,* adding the effects — positive, negative, or both — to their character.

GETTING MODDED

In game terms, bioengineering can be considered a special kind of biograft. Even though it occurs through the application of GeneMod packages, bioengineering is still subject to the same rules and limitations as other biografts. Each GeneMod package is considered a Full-Body augmentation, though new GeneMod packages can be grafted into the existing one later, adding +1 to the package's Maintenance cost and replacing the existing Full-Body augmentation, rather than adding to it.

GENEMOD STEPS
1. Start with a base of 1+5 Ⓝ
2. Add Modification options
3. Tally the Cost, Maintenance, Tariff, and Risk of your package
4. Consult the *Custom GeneMod Table* to determine the package's final cost
5. Roll on the *GenoMod Side Effects Table* to determine any other effects

Restriction / Cost: Instead of each modification having its own Restriction or Cost, the following tables are used to determine the Restriction and Cost of a custom bioengineering package, a bundle of modifications obtained and applied together. Given that a large portion of the expense is in acquiring the time, expertise, and undivided attention of a Nomad Bioengineer, purchasing several modifications as a large package is quite cost-effective compared to buying individual augmentations. However, the more specific the demands, the more difficult it is to find someone who can do the job in addition to the increased risk of having yourself modified.

When creating a custom Gene-Package, before selecting any options, there's a base cost of 1+5 Ⓝ. This baseline represent the cost and difficulty of getting a Praxis Bioengineer to agree to work with

ANTITHANATICS
Most of the Human Sphere uses antithanatic — or anti-aging — treatments to counteract the ravages of time. Popular treatments such as Haqqislam's tameer (تعمير, Arabic for longevity or immortality) are applied gradually over the course of years, subtly slowing senescence. While such treatments are available in the Nomad Nation as well, more radical procedures are also quite popular. Most recently, this has manifested as an attempt to create subtly radioactive cells within a host, not only locking them in stasis but preventing the cells from becoming cancerous. At least, that's the idea. Mostly, people are getting radiation poisoning. The search for true immortality in one's birth host continues.

WHY WOULD ANYONE DO THIS?

Traditional augmentation is safer, often less expensive, and offers some very potent results. If that's not enough, getting a new Lhost opens up possibilities that traditional augmentation simply doesn't, without exposing the character to the volatility inherent in bioengineering GeneMods. So why would a reasonable character — or player, for that matter — attempt something so risky?

Several reasons. GeneMods offer some options and capabilities that simply can't be acquired elsewhere. Even if new gear is invented and acquired, there always exists the possibility that the character won't have access to it. GeneMods are a part of the character; they can't be taken away outside of vivisection, and if that's occurring, the character has other problems. They can be smuggled in anywhere and always relied upon.

Also, the volatility of GeneMods can work both ways. Yes, there exists significant risk, up to and including the character's death. But within that volatility, there is also opportunity. Many bioengineering side effects are positive, or at least, a mixed blessing. Yes, they're statistically less likely to occur — especially as players accumulate Risk — but some folks just can't resist the thrill of pushing their luck.

you in the first place. It's the foundation you'll build your custom GeneMod package on. While it doesn't do anything by itself, its cost is divided alongside your upgrades. Next, select the options you want, add up their respective costs, and then consult the *Bioengineering Gene-Package Table*.

Total the number of modifications. This will indicate your GeneMod package's restriction, the amount of Risk you've accumulated, and a value to divide your Cost and Maintenance by (rounding down), resulting in the GeneMod package's final Cost.

Maintenance: Some modifications can introduce a Maintenance cost. Unlike tariffs, there is no ceiling on Maintenance increases; Nomad bioengineers aren't in the business of protecting their customers from themselves. They do know a few good loan sharks, though. Maintenance costs are divided by the values indicated in the *Custom Genemod Package Table*, and there are additional options that can reduce Maintenance costs. Note that these only

CUSTOM GENEMOD TABLE

RISK	RESTRICTION	DIVIDE COST & MAINTENANCE BY...
1–3	+1	1
4–6	+2	1
7–10	+3	2
11–14	+4	3
15–18	+5	4
19+	+5	5

GENEMOD SIDE EFFECT TABLE

RISK	SODE EFFECT TAB;E
1–7	Side Effects Column A
8–14	Side Effects Column B
15+	Side Effects Column C

BIOENGINEERING SIDE EFFECTS TABLE

A	B	C	INCIDENT	EFFECT
1	–	–	The enhanced neural lining not only ties your package together but now you feel invincible.	Increase Firewall, Morale, and Vigour by 1 each.
2	–	–	The bioengineer slips in a little something extra. To everyone's surprise, this goes quite well.	Gain +1 to an Attribute of your choice.
3	1	–	Getting your new mods to integrate required extensive neural modification.	Increase Firewall by 1.
4–5	2	–	The biochemistry is a near-perfect fit: you feel stronger than ever.	Increase Vigour by 1.
6–7	3–4	1	Bad news: they needed to replace most of your skull. Good news: your new, reinforced skull is probably better than the old one.	Add Armour Soak 1 to your head. This replaces any existing Armour, such as from Subdermal Grafts or integral Lhost Armour.
8–9	5–7	2	Echoes of someone else's memories linger in the genetic payload.	Gain Trait: Mnemonic Echoes. Choose a skill; you can treat your Focus as 1 rank higher when purchasing Talents.
10–12	8–10	3–5	Your anti-rejection medication has some side effects: while you're less sensitive to physical pain, emotional distress is intensified.	Reduce Morale by 1 but increase Vigour by 1.
13–15	11–12	6–8	Your brain chemistry is on overdrive, flooding you with positive emotions, but also amplifying your physical nerves.	Reduce Vigour by 1 but increase Morale by 1.
16–17	13–14	9–10	They got creative. Your body works, but things are... different.	Reduce one Attribute of your choice by 2. Increase one Attribute of your choice by 1.
18–19	15–16	11–12	To everyone's surprise, the GeneMods hypercharge your metabolism.	Gain 1 rank in Athletics. Increase Maintenance by 1 and gain the Trait: Hair-Trigger Temper.
20	17–18	13–14	The pieces fit. Mostly. But you get queasy at the most inopportune moments, and you've started craving flavors you used to abhor.	Gain Trait: Unstable Biochemistry.
–	19	15–16	Everything's where it's supposed to be, but you feel... sluggish.	Reduce Agility by 1.
–	20	17–18	You nearly died on the operating table. A last-minute injection of a small fortune in Silk saved you. Now you owe a small fortune to a loan shark.	Gain a debt worth 10 Assets. Increase your Maintenance by +1 until it's paid off.
–	–	19	Everything worked fine. They just needed to scoop out some muscle tissue to make room. It'll grow back. They think.	Reduce Brawn by 1.
–	–	20	You violently reject the treatment dying suddenly on the operating table.	Your character dies. See the rules for *Resurrection* in the *Infinity Corebook*, p. 392.

EXAMPLE: GENEMOD PACKAGE

On holiday on *Bakunin*, Yasmin decides to acquire a suite of BioMods. She selects Chameleonskin 2, Environmental Adaptation 1 (Desert), Immuno-Booster 1, Inured to Heat (1), and Superhuman Awareness 1. Her player starts with the baseline cost of 1+5 Ⓝ, and then adds the selected items, coming to a total of 13+15 Ⓝ, T6, with a Maintenance of 5, and a Risk of 10. Expensive, but the price will be reduced later. But first, Yasmin's going to do some tweaking.

The Maintenance cost seems daunting, so she reduces it to 4 by taking on an additional 2 Risk, leaving her with a total of 12. That makes her nervous, so she spends 4 Assets to reduce her risk back down to 10. Consulting the *Custom GeneMod Package Table* she notes that her Restriction will be 3, and she'll be dividing both Cost and Maintenance by 2. That takes the package down to 6+7 Ⓝ, and drops her Maintenance down to 2. However, even the extended Tariff range doesn't go up to 6, so she reduces it to T5 and adds 1+1 Ⓝ to her cost, giving her GeneMod Package a final value of 7+8 Ⓝ, Restriction 3, T5, Maintenance 2.

Consulting the *GeneMod Side Effect Tables*, she'll be rolling on Column B on the *Bioengineering Side Effects Table*. Yasmin's player grits her teeth and rolls the dice, hoping that the increased risk doesn't get her more than she bargained for.

WIDE SPECTRUM IMMUNISATION X

Some creatures, such as the striped bass, can survive with little issue in either fresh or saltwater environments. Mimicking this capacity can provide a degree of the same protection to the user, reducing the difficulty on Resistance tests involving water filtration by X, to a minimum of 0.

FISH OUT OF WATER

A character with the Amphibious modification can still breathe the type of water they didn't select, though they run a serious risk of infection. In every scene where they do so, they must succeed at a **Daunting (D3) Resistance test** or suffer an attack with the Biotech quality for 1+6 Ⓝ damage.

apply to the package itself; you can't reduce the upkeep on your Powered Armour by cutting corners on your GeneMods.

Qualities: All GeneMod packages possess the Aug quality. Some modifications add additional qualities to the package, listed in their descriptions.

Risk: The more experimental a package, the more risk it entails. Untested technologies can be powerful but hazardous, and every additional modification increases the chance that things take an unexpected turn. For each modification in the package, increase the Risk tally by +1. Some options will add additional Risk to the package; these are in addition to the +1 Risk that each modification provides. After finishing the package, consult the *GeneMod Side Effect Tables*, and roll on the appropriate column of the *Bioengineering Side Effects Table*.

Note: If the amount of risk is 19 or greater, they're playing with fire. Every point of Risk beyond 19 is added to the results of their roll on the *Bioengineering Side Effcts Table*. Accrue too much risk, and you're literally gambling with the character's life.

Tariffs: Several different modifications can increase the tariff rating of the package. Unlike most other cases, this can push the total tariff rating beyond T3, up to T5. If this would ever raise the tariff rating beyond T5, add 1+1 Ⓝ to the package's final Cost for every value above T5. This increase comes after applying the divided Cost increase from the *Custom GeneMod Package Table*, so these increases are not divided.

RISK MANAGEMENT

While the Cost of a GeneMod package can be quite reasonable, the risk and maintenance costs are often anything but. If players are staring down some oppressive Maintenance costs, they can always add the Bootleg modification to represent less than sterling ingredients. But if that's still not enough, they have the option to exchange their Maintenance for Risk, reducing the Maintenance tally by 1 for every 2 Risk added in this fashion.

And if the Risk becomes too much, there are few things that giant piles of money can't solve or at least help with. Risk can be reduced by spending Assets; every 2 Assets spent in this fashion reduces Risk by 1.

BIOENGINEERING MODIFICATIONS

Amphibious: A xenograft that usually involves gills, this allows the user to breathe normally when submerged in either salt or freshwater, chosen at the time of installation. While black-market Helot gills are coveted, all manner of aquatic and amphibious life is used in the procedure.

Bootleg X: Not every xenograft can use top-quality ingredients. Not every GeneMod has the luxury of custom-tailored, silk-delivered DNA. Using gills from sea bass instead of Helots, gorilla meat instead of Morat muscle tissue, and a dog's nose and DNA instead of the Antipodes' powerful olfactory apparatus — sometimes you just have to work with what's on-hand. Or what's cheap.

Add X Traits describing how your new GeneMod is problematic in some way (such as Twitchy, Unexpected Allergies, Obviously Inhuman, etc.), and reduce its Maintenance cost by X, and Risk by 1+X, each to a minimum of 0. Between 1 and 3 of these Traits can usefully be applied to a given host: 1 is common, 2 is rare, and 3 is essentially unheard of. One can only skimp so much before hitting diminishing returns: regardless of their source, a Bootleg value greater than 3 provides no cost reduction, as complications drive the price right back up.

Chameleonskin X: While popular speculation implies that grafting Shasvastii xenotissue results in this capability, the true source is closer to other pigment-altering lizards such as chameleons. Still, this natural camouflage grants +X bonus Momentum on face-to-face Stealth tests against targets at Long range or farther. However, the technology isn't exactly stable; it increases the complication range on Stealth tests by X as well.

Technically, this augmentation stacks with Chameleonwear, but using both in conjunction doubles the total complication range. (So a character using Chameleonskin 1 and Chameleonwear would have a complication range of 17–20). Chameleonskin is available in ratings from 1–3.

Direct Stimulant Applicator X: A fancy way of saying "drug delivery augmentation," this modification uses Silk to create custom neural pathways, allowing the user to deliver hits of their drug of choice directly to their brain through thought instructions. The user can take a hit of their drug of choice as a Free Action by issuing a mental command. Direct Stimulant Applicators can deliver X number of specific drugs, chosen upon installation. There is no limit to the value of X that can be purchased, though each modification is custom work. Users looking to add a new type of stimulant will need to have the old pathways completely redone, purchasing the new modification from scratch.

Enhanced Attack X: Spines, barbs, calcium deposits – whatever the delivery method, the user's natural weapons get a boost. Calcium deposits for punches, weapons-grade claws, even horns and fangs can be acquired. While it does nothing for melee attacks with a weapon – including Nemesis Gloves and other similarly-designed gear – their unarmed attack gains X of the following enhancements:

- **Grievous**: Adds the Grievous weapon quality. This also adds +3 Risk.
- **Parry**: From Xenografted Shrike Tardigrade hide, to calcium deposits, or good-old synthetic bone lacing, add the Parry 1 weapon quality. This can be taken a second time to make it Parry 2.
- **Piercing**: Vampire fangs to unicorn horns laced with titanium, hyper-dense bone, or just straight Teseum, this modification adds the Piercing 1 weapon quality. This can be taken a second time to make the quality Piercing 2.
- **Venomous**: Allows the character to deliver the contents of a Venom Gland X augmentation via their unarmed attack. If no Venom Gland modification is present, then it simply adds the Biotech weapon quality.

Environmental Adaptation X: Through a combination of xenografting, radical genetic alteration, and – according to at least one Observance member – "black magick," the character becomes adapted to a particular type of environment, allowing them to ignore all difficulty modifiers due to environmental conditions or terrain and to reduce difficulty caused by environment-specific weather (such as blizzards for Arctic Adaptation, or sandstorms for Desert Adaptation) by two steps. The user selects X of the following environments: **Arctic**, **Desert**, **Jungle**, **Mountain**, **Forest**, **Plains**, **Subterranean**, or **Urban**.

Inured to X: Expensive, untested, and highly unstable, radical gene-therapy can nevertheless

do some amazing things. To many, that's worth the cost... and the risk. Tissue samples from ancient *kossomn* Helots, Shrikes, and other exotic life forms have been used to create these mods. The user selects X of the following qualities (which differ slightly from their counterparts in the *Infinity Corebook*, p. 418):

- **Aging**: Powerful antithanatic treatments completely halt the aging process.
- **Cold**: Provides immunity to the effects and damage of extreme cold.
- **Heat**: Provides immunity to the effects and damage of extreme heat including fire, though the users' hair and skin receive no such protection, to say nothing of their clothing.
- **Pain**: Incapable of feeling pain, the user continues undeterred despite the most horrific agony. They cannot be Dazed or Staggered by physical attacks.
- **Poison**: Provides immunity to all forms of poison, venom, and toxin.

Immuno-Booster X: By supercharging the immune system with Silk-laced (or close enough) micro-organs, the body's response to viral attacks is significantly bolstered. It increases BTS by +X, up to a rating of 3. This bonus is cumulative with the Bioimmunity Organ augmentation, but interactions between the two can be unpredictable, adding +X complication range to Resistance tests when both augmentations are present in the body.

Keen Senses X: Harkening back to the very first xenografts, improving the senses via questionably ethical science is a time-honoured Nomad tradition. Keen senses reduce the difficulty of Observation tests using the specific sense by one step, though an option can be taken twice to increase the reduction to two steps. The user gains Keen Senses in X of the following senses: Scent, Sound, Sight, Touch, or Taste.

Super-Jump: Just because the process of grafting Antipodean DNA has been refined, doesn't mean that it can't also be part of a GeneMod Package. Super-Jump augmentations allow their user to vault over obstacles up to their height without penalty. They also enjoy −1 difficulty on skill tests to move through difficult terrain.

Superhuman Attribute 1: Arguably the height of Nomad Bioengineering, this treatment might not reach the lofty heights of Haqqislam's Runihura supersoldiers, nor ALEPH's latest and greatest Lhosts, but it comes closer than anyone else, and its customisability is second to none.

As per the Common Special Ability (see *Infinity Corebook*, p. 418), this adds Superhuman Attribute 1 to a single attribute:

INTEGRATED RESERVOIRS

When you have the ability to deliver stimulants directly into your brain, heading out to acquire more can be a real pain. Instead of needing to buy their drug of choice in doses, users who acquire this modification can have a steady supply of their favourite inebriant on-hand by adding Maintenance equal to the drug's Restriction rating to the GeneMod package. This provides enough for the user to take one dose of the drug per scene, should they be so inclined. If they wish to use it more frequently, then they can still traditionally acquire doses and expend them whenever using more than one dose in a scene.

"Everyone assumes that the need came first, and Praxis delivered. It's actually the other way around. They just so happened to have a couple dozen cybernetically augmented porpoises lying around, so we put'em in ships."

— Text embossed on a support pillar inside the ArTechnodivarius Module, *Bakunin*.

BIOENGINEERING MODIFICATIONS TABLE

MODIFICATION	EFFECT	COST	SPECIAL
Amphibious	Breathe normally underwater	+1 Ⓝ	+1 Maintenance
*Wide Spectrum Immunisation X	Reduce the difficulty of water toxin-based Resistence tests by X	+X Ⓝ	-
Bootleg X	Add X traits to your character.	-	−X Maintenance, −1+X Risk, −X Tariff
Chameleonskin X	X Bonus Momentum on Face-to-Face Stealth tests at Long+ ranges	X+6 Ⓝ	+1 Maintenance, +X Tariff
Direct Stimulant Applicator X	Use your drug of choice as a Free Action	X+4 Ⓝ	+X Risk
*Integrated Reservoirs	Gain an integrated supply of your drug of choice	2+2 Ⓝ	See Entry
Enhanced Attack X	Adds a variety of modifications to unarmed attacks	3+X Ⓝ	+2 Tariff, +X Risk
Environmental Adaptation X	Ignore terrain modifiers, reduce weather-based difficulty by 2 steps in chosen environment	X+1	+X Tariff, +X Risk
Inured to X	See Entry	2+X Ⓝ	+1 Maintenance +1 Tariff, X+X Risk
Immuno-Booster X	Adds BTS X	2+X Ⓝ	+X Maintenance, +X Tariff
Keen Senses X	Reduces the difficulty of Observation tests	1+X Ⓝ	+X Risk
Super-Jump	Adds Super-Jump Augmentation*	1+1 Ⓝ	+1 Tariff, +1 Maintenance
Superhuman Attribute 1	Add Superhuman Attribute 1 to a single attribute**	4+1 Ⓝ	+1 Tariff, +2 Maintenance, +2 Risk
Synthetic Dopamine Regulator	+1 Morale Soak	3+1 Ⓝ	+2` Risk
Venom Gland X	Adds a venom gland with a variety of options	1+X Ⓝ	+1 Maintenance, +X Risk, +X Tariff

* See *Augmentations*, p. 346, *Infinity Corebook*   ** See *Common Special Abilities*, p. 417, *Infinity Corebook*

- Adds 1 automatic success on tests with the relevant attribute
- If the attribute normally grants bonus damage to a particular type of attack, add +1 damage to the attack
- If the attribute is normally used to determine a type of incidental stress, add +1 to that damage track

Multiple instances of Superhuman Attribute are not cumulative with each other; characters only benefit from the highest instance, regardless of the source.

Synthetic Dopamine Regulator: Through a combination of drugs, neural rewiring, and good old electromagnetic shocks to the brain, the user's mood is permanently bolstered, granting +1 to Morale Soak.

Venom Gland X: For the person who has everything: what could be better than their very own venom sac? While it doesn't create enough venom to usefully distribute, and it doesn't last long outside the user's or a victim's body, bioengineered venoms can do some truly terrifying things to an unsuspecting target. This venom can be surreptitiously placed in food or drink, dealing 1+3 Ⓝ damage and possess any weapon qualities acquired below. However, using venom in this fashion does not gain bonus damage from high attribute scores.

The venom possesses the Biotech and Toxic 1 qualities, and the user gains the trait Venomous and X of the following qualities:

- **Breaker**: The venom gains the Breaker quality.
- **Immobilising**: Potent neurotoxins grant the venom the Immobilising quality.
- **Spitter**: The user gains the ability to spit their venom at some truly impressive ranges. They gain a spitting attack, Range C, 1+3 Ⓝ damage. While they can attempt to spit beyond Close Range, their range penalties are doubled when doing so.
- **Toxic**: Replaces the Toxic 1 quality with Toxic 2.
- **Vicious**: Adds +1 Vicious to the user's venom. May be taken up to 3 times, though the third instance increases complication range when using it by +1.

BESPOKE BEHEMOTHS

Of course, no one ever said that Nomad Bioengineering was limited to self-aware humanoids. There's a thriving shadow economy of made-to-order creatures including vat-grown beasts that never existed in nature, augmentation of existing species, and even personal self-defence pets. The subset of Praxis — nicknamed the "Pupnik Factory"— that specialises in their creation is none too picky about their clientele.

PRAXIS' ANIMAL FARM

When *Bakunin's* first Uplifts became public knowledge, the Human Sphere was stunned. Well, not that stunned actually, more like confused. The Neo-Cetaceans made sense at least; their instinctual comfort ability with three-dimensional movement made them a natural fit as starship pilots. But why, exactly, were scientists stuffing pigs full of cybernetics? What did they hope to gain from trying to link a murder of crows to form a hivemind? What was the point of it all? The truth is, there wasn't a point, and there never really was. They simply wanted to discover the limits of what was possible.

And transgress them.

The allure of Praxis is largely about having absolute freedom to pursue whatever research its inhabitants desire. The idea is to discover what is possible, and then trust in *Bakunin's* bleeding-edge marketers to find a way to make it profitable. Creating something that people can use is often a side effect, something you work into your projects to keep the lights on. Pushing the envelope of human understanding has always been the true goal, discovery and innovation the only objectives worth pursuing.

That's not to say that Praxis is opposed to practical applications of their tech, just that it's secondary to the thrill of scientific discovery. Juggling passion projects with those that pay the bills is an ongoing concern, with many scientists partnering with Fixers to ensure a constant stream of high-value requests. Especially within the Black Labs, there's little thought wasted on why a client wants something. As long as they're willing to pay, Praxis will make just about anything.

ORIGINATING SPECIES

Praxis isn't the only place where such creatures can be found, nor is it the first. In fact, most immediate precursors trace their roots back to Pre-Nanotech Wars Earth. Biological drones had become a popular alternative to their mechanical counterparts. Project Osprey fitted birds with sensory recorders, long-range communications devices, and other mechanical augmentations, offering surreptitious surveillance on battlefields that had become accustomed to the sight of mechanical drones.

NOMAD FIXERS

Equal parts talent scout, agent, smuggler, and negotiator, the Nomad Nation's Fixers serve an important role in its ecosystem. If a Submondo crime boss wants modified Bengal Tigers as sentries, who do they talk to? If a Praxis scientist is running low on funding, and needs a big payday, who sets that up? And when a corporation wants to set up a Black Bounty, but is leery of revealing their identity to *Tunguska,* who manages the double-blind exchange?

Fixers. *Bakunin* is crawling with them, but they can be found in just about any corner of the Human Sphere, provided that one knows where to look.

PUPNIKS, ABOMINATIONS, AND OTHER ASSORTED HORRORS

While her early canine uplifts fell far short of sapience, Dr. Maureen Schröder eventually hit upon a formula for a hyper-intelligent breed of animal sentry. Dubbed "Pupniks"—a wry phrase initially coined by JFK—these beasts are easily her most enduring creation, though they're far from the only horrors to emerge from Praxis's Black Labs.

While Pupniks became a coveted commodity for increasingly sordid applications, Schröder continued to tinker with her design. These augmented creatures weren't much smarter than a chimpanzee, but with clever use of LAIs and speech modulators, she found that they could briefly fake sapience nearly as well as the average geist.

Though Pupniks' physical forms trended towards the humanoid, the Black Labs continued churning out customised horrors for the few clients willing to pony up the cash for something unique. From Bengal tigers, to mythical guardians such as basilisks, custom abominations were quietly made available for the discerning client, even as Schröder's pun-fuelled fondness for Black Labradors ensured that a slow trickle of Pupniks found their way into the black market. Arriving with Pupniks in tow soon became a favourite power play for *Bakunin's* Submondo elite. Flanked by the rare and dangerous creatures, gang bosses could communicate volumes about their power, wealth, and control without uttering a single word.

Meanwhile, certain organisations in and around Praxis were keen to adapt various abominations as a more controllable, less aggressive alternative to the volatile, unstable, and extremely illegal Pupniks. Plus, these abominations' voice modulators allowed them to recite scripted dialog, proving useful — if entirely unsettling — to informed and unwitting listeners alike.

Certain labs steered directly into this property, crafting sentry creatures who could not only inform trespassers to back off, customers of their appointments, and other such useful details, but would occasionally recite snippets of text, seemingly unbidden. Some favourites include:

- "Do you require each of your organs, human? No reason."
- "A word of advice: tread carefully. The master doesn't like surprises."
- "I was a man like you, once. It seems so long ago..."
- "Leave, if you can. No one deserves this fate."

...and other such macabre phrases, usually implying that the beasts had once been people who got on their owner's bad side. More than one would-be saboteur has thought better of their plans when encountering a Pupnik, guard-beast, or some other bioengineered horror. Whether that's due to their excellent sentry work, or a product of the existential terror they're created to instil, it's difficult to say. But one way or another, laboratories employing creations from Dr. Schröder's lab and their many imitators have a remarkable track record of failed break-ins.

PUPNIK, PET, OR SOMETHING ELSE?

Pupniks are categorically unruly. Stuffed with the most aggressive instincts and combative traits derived from dozens of predators, Pupniks are a murder waiting to happen if not constantly restrained and even that's no guarantee. Thus, even on *Bakunin*, creating a Pupnik is against the law, though owning one becomes more of a messy grey area. Genetically engineered pets, on the other hand, are a profitable export, and a part of many Bakunians' lives. They're entirely legal, and their creation is heartily encouraged. Between these two extremes lie a variety of genetic abominations, bioengineered animals that clearly aren't as aggressive as Pupniks but have a few more surprises to them than a typical house pet ought to.

"YOU'LL KNOW ONE WHEN YOU SEE ONE"

Pupniks are illegal. But since the very notion of a Pupnik is a social construct, enforcing that law is beyond tricky. The definition of what is, and is not, technically a Pupnik is a source of endless debate, and steady revenue, for Tunguskan lawyers.

Today, bioengineered invertebrates provide subsentient undersea sensor suites on planets like Varuna, blending into the local ecosystem. USAriadnan engineers continue their grand tradition of using whatever they can get their hands on, like implanting primitive GPS trackers and automated recorders in their local wildlife.

No one has embraced the idea of augmented fauna quite to the degree that Praxis has. From the monstrous Pupniks, to subsentient organic defence matrices, the Black Labs have the market cornered on made-to-order bioengineered creatures. Subsapient by design — though an experiment occasionally surprises them — Praxis's mad scientists can create anything from sentries to pets, and they often combine the two.

HUMAN EDGE REMOTE LABS

While *Bakunin* is the undisputed leader in animal bioengineering, it's far from the only location, even among the Nomads. The Radical Mothership offers incredible freedom, access to resources, and a ready market for your wares, but it also operates under numerous restraints. Namely, there's only so much room to work, and the Moderators tend to get cranky when an experiment destroys a chunk of the ship. Smaller ships in the Black Fleet provide a way to work in peace, but are no less space-constrained, and have the unfortunate side effect of dooming all its inhabitants if significant hardware failure occurs.

In the Human Edge, there are any number of unpopulated asteroids and planetoids, ripe for the taking. Constructing a habitat that can stand up to the rigors of its environment is expensive and time-consuming, but the Human Edge is littered with abandoned mining bases, providing the sturdy construction necessary for volatile research.

If a Fixer is trying to fill a request for say, a domesticable Neoterran Emerald Dragon, delivering a dozen or so to a remote lab with instructions that at least one needs to be a family pet when this is done can usually produce the desired result, with the rest either being sold as sentries, opponents for underground fighting rings, or used for parts. More than one Pupnik comes from similar origins, frequently crafted from stock that is otherwise unusable — at least for legitimate purposes.

Of course, cut off from the rest of the Nomads, if something goes wrong, it can take significant time before anyone realises that something's gone wrong. More than one of these remote labs has unexpectedly gone dark, burying whatever research notes still exist in a tomb of metal and stone, prowled by whatever crimes against nature were created within.

TAMING THE BEAST

From the Morat's Oznat Huntresses to Ariadna's Antipode Assault Pack Leaders, the Human Sphere is replete with characters leading trained beasts into battle, and Praxis's Pupnik Factory is only too happy to throw its hat into the ring. However, the rules and guidelines in this section aren't exclusive to the Nomads. Any character can make use of the expanded context, new Talents, and guidelines outlined here.

BOUND VS. WILD

As anyone who's ever trained an animal can tell you, there's a world of difference between "your" creature and someone else's, even if they've both been trained in the same fashion. In game terms, this means that the creature is "Imprinted" on its handler. This bond between trainer and animal is usually the result of countless hours spent training, grooming, and otherwise caring for the creature, but many of the Pupnik Factory's clients simply don't have that kind of time. Thus, when building a creature to order, Praxis uses the purchaser's own DNA to create a kind of synthetic bond, an instinctual imprinting on the new owner, binding it to their authority.

All creatures purchased from the Pupnik Factory are considered to be Imprinted on their owner. If a character wishes to go about this the old-fashioned way, this is usually a complex **Animal Handling test** (D1, 6 Momentum, 2 failures) that takes place over the course of months, though spending Momentum can rapidly accelerate that process. If the character doesn't have that much time to spend, they can attempt the same complex test to have the creature be functionally Imprinted for the remainder of the scene, though they may need to repeat the test in future scenes, until the Creature has had time to acclimate to their new handler. And of course, invasive augmentations — such as Antipode Control Cranial Implants — effectively confer the same effect.

So, what's the difference in game terms? While anyone can use Animal Handling to try to instruct a creature, using the Direct Creature action and the associated talents requires that the Creature be Imprinted on the handler.

CONTROLLING CREATURES

Attempting to direct the actions of a non-Imprinted creature is a common use of the Animal Handling skill. In Action Scenes, this usually takes the form of an Assist Action, providing direction and Momentum that the NPC can use on its turn. But for Imprinted Creatures, the handler has a few more options.

ACTIONS

The following Action is available to all characters, regardless of their Heritage or Faction.

DIRECT CREATURE [STANDARD]

You can direct the actions of an Imprinted Creature. Make an **Average (D1) Animal Handling Group test**, with the Creature assisting you. Increase the difficulty of this test by 1 step for every range increment beyond Close that you need to communicate across. If successful, the creature may immediately take its turn, using the Momentum generated on the Group test as its result for a single Standard Action.

TALENTS

The following Talents are available to all characters, regardless of their Heritage or Faction.

IMPRINTED BOND
Prerequisite: Wild Empathy

The character is particularly skilled at directing Creatures they know well. Once per round, they can use a Minor Action to grant an Imprinted Creature in line of sight an immediate Standard Action.

LEADER OF THE PACK
Prerequisite: Imprinted Bond

The character has a close bond with their Imprinted Creatures, and they'll leap to the character's defence if given the chance. The character can treat Close Combat tests as Group tests, with any Imprinted Creatures within Close Range providing assistance.

PACK COMMANDER
Prerequisite: Leader of the Pack

The character has a close bond with their Imprinted Creatures, communicating on a near-instinctual level. When the Creature takes a Reaction, the character can make an Animal Handling test in place of the Creature's usual skill test. Range penalties apply.

MONSTER MASH

But beyond simply interacting with NPCs, players might want to do more than just hear about the fantastical creatures, being custom-built in Praxis; they might want to place an order themselves. The

rules in this section make that a possibility. When creating a custom Creature, they are considered to be Imprinted on the buyer. One too many disasters has led to that particular feature coming standard.

Building a creature is essentially creating a custom adversary. As such, GMs are encouraged to use these rules for their own purposes, adding custom Special Abilities of their own, resulting in virtually limitless adversaries for their game.

STEP ONE: ADVERSARY CATEGORY

First, select the Adversary Category of the creature. In play, Creatures follow the same rules and guidelines as other Adversaries of their category, meaning that Troopers cannot attempt reactions, Elites cost 2 Heat to bring is as reinforcements, and so on. Additionally, Creatures use Fields of Expertise, rather than individual skills. Even so, building Creatures is a different endeavour than creating your own Adversaries. Follow the rules in this chapter when creating a purchasable Creature.

TROOPERS

Most creatures will be classified as Troopers. Pets, wildlife, guard animals, and even the unspeakable horrors coming out of Praxis's remote labs are still mostly Troopers.

- Troopers begin with an Intelligence of 3 and cannot use Intelligence-based skills.
- Troopers assign 40 points to their remaining Attribute scores, though an Attribute cannot be increased beyond 10 in this fashion.
- Troopers assign 4 skill ranks between their Fields of Expertise, though neither Expertise nor Focus can be increased beyond 2 in this fashion, and they cannot use skills based on Intelligence.

ELITES

Much more difficult to come by, these Creatures reveal a greater level of diversity, both in appearance, and in their capabilities. Praxis is more than happy to create truly spectacular creations for the corporate princess who absolutely needs a unicorn for her birthday or the mob boss who just can't live without a manticore in their office. Of course, plenty of Elites are still somewhat conventional in their appearance, but at this level, nature has less to do with the equation than engineering.

- Elites begin with an Intelligence of 5 and cannot use Intelligence-based skills.
- Elites assign 57 points to their remaining Attribute scores, though an Attribute cannot be increased beyond 12 in this fashion.
- Elites assign 8 skill ranks between their Fields of Expertise, though neither Expertise nor Focus can be increased beyond 3 in this fashion, and they cannot use the Technical Field of Expertise.

SURREPTITIOUS IMPRINTING (2–6 HEAT)
Given that the scientists creating the creature are synthetically binding it to its new owner, many have wondered if they're not also perhaps binding it to other people: such as the new owner's business rivals. Fortunately, outside of the scientist themselves and the occasional lab assistant, this almost never happens.

But rarely, it does happen. By spending an amount of Heat (2 if the Creature is a Trooper, 4 if Elite, and 6 if it's a Nemesis), the Creature can be revealed to be Imprinted on an NPC in the scene. This makes all Animal Handling tests to control the Creature into Face-to-Face tests — for either party — if they want to control it.

This should be used sparingly and as a major plot point if it does occur, but it can make for a memorable encounter.

PLAYTEST TIP
IS IT IMPRINTED?
The Imprinted keyword doesn't show up in previous *Infinity* RPG books. Rather than try to compile a complete list of what is and isn't Imprinted, a small dash of common sense can go a long way. When introducing NPCs, asking yourself if their creatures are Imprinted or not as a simple question of relationship. Wild animals, or Creatures just being introduced, are probably not Imprinted. Animal Companions, service animals, and obviously weaponised creatures almost certainly are. Imprinting isn't meant to be a limiting factor, just a way to clarify the relationship between Creature and Handler.

CAN MY CREATURE DO IT?

With the ability to command Creatures, players have the ability to send their animal surrogates to act in their stead. Especially in cases of heavily-modified, high-Intelligence Creatures, it can be easy to forget that these are still subsapient animals. There's a limit to what they can accomplish. Common sense should rule the day here. While your Elite cyber-ferret can certainly use the Thievery skill to pilfer a gem, they're not going to be contacting the black market.

Usually, Creatures — even very smart ones — can't handle terribly complex tasks. For example:
- At Intelligence 4, a Creature can follow basic commands — sit, stay, come here, etc. — without the need for an Animal Handling test.
- At Intelligence 6, a Creature can follow more complex instructions — wait for me, protect them, run home — if their handler makes a successful Animal Handling test.
- At Intelligence 8, a Creature can solve rudimentary puzzles, not unlike a chimpanzee or gorilla, by making an Analysis test. They could figure out a guard's rotation, or how to open a door latch; they could not, however, operate a Comlog, or enter a keycode.

Generally, a Creature can't use gear — including weapons — unless they're implanted. And even then, implanting a Killer Hacking Device in your cybernetic assault penguin isn't going to do anything other than give it a headache.

Ultimately, these are just guidelines. They're not meant to be absolute law but to give an idea as to what's possible for a Creature when using the person-centric *Infinity* skill system. Your own common sense is still the best tool when determining what a subsapient Creature, even a really intelligent, augmented one, can accomplish.

DIRECT CREATURE EXAMPLE

Sami's being attacked by some *Maras* gangsters. Lucky for him, he's got his trusty assault kitty, Mr. Fluff, nearby. He uses the Direct Creature action, and together he and Mr. Fluff generate 3 Momentum. He directs Mr. Fluff to attack the nearest gangster, an **Average (D1) Close Combat test**, spending 1 point of Momentum to succeed, leaving Mr. Fluff with 2 leftover Momentum to unleash his gene-modded poison sacs on the unsuspecting gangsters.

NEMESES

Every now and then, there's a spark of twisted inspiration, a dark insight that elevates the fantastical into the realm of myth. Nemesis Creatures are what happens when that dark genius meets the appropriate opportunity and funding. Incredibly difficult to come by, these creations are each one-of-a-kind, unique even among bioengineered Creatures. If the aforementioned mob boss wanted their manticore to have integrated experimental bioweapons and a subsapient intelligence that allowed it to follow comparatively complex instructions, they'd want to splurge for a expensive but troublesome Nemesis.
- Nemeses begin with an Intelligence of 7 and cannot use Intelligence-based skills.
- Nemeses assign 63 points to their remaining Attribute scores, though an Attribute cannot be increased beyond 14 in this fashion.
- Nemeses assign 16 skill ranks between their Fields of Expertise, though neither Expertise nor Focus can be increased beyond 3 in this fashion, and they cannot use the Technical Field of Expertise.

STEP TWO: CUSTOMISATION

Next, select any desired customisations. Do you want a small creature? A durable one? How about one that can make close-range attacks for you? Or maybe you just want to augment the Creature with bioengineering like you would any other character.

BIOMODS

As part of the bioengineering process, you can have custom BioMod packages installed in a creature. These are added to the total cost in Step Three.

MONSTROUS CREATURE

The considerable bulk and mass of this creature makes it less agile and graceful than smaller creatures and hinders it moving through confined spaces.
- Add +1 difficulty to tests where great size or weight would be problematic.
- Suffer a Wound following seven or more Vigour damage (instead of five).
- Spend 1 Momentum before attacking to add Knockdown to its melee attacks for the current turn.

PERSONAL DEFENCE CREATURE

A *Bakunin* speciality, these Creatures often function more like gear than NPCs. Specifically, they allow their owner to essentially use them as a melee weapon, by attacking with the Animal Handling skill, rather than Close Combat. This can be done any time that the character would normally make a Close Combat attack, provided that their Personal Defence Creature (PDC) is still able to function. Given the proper training and augmentation, everything from sleeve-vipers and shoulder-cats to domesticated wolves and cyber-lions can be Personal Defence Creatures.

PDC's assign Attributes and skill ranks according to their Adversary tier, though functioning as a PDC requires a certain robustness across Attribute scores, otherwise the Creature operates at less than peak efficiency. Specifically, if a PDC is created with an attribute below the minimum Intelligence for its tier (3 for Troopers, 5 for Elites, 7 for Nemeses), then it cannot function as a PDC, and its handler cannot use it to make attacks until its Intelligence is increased to meet the minimum threshold.
- When treated as a weapon, PCD's deal 1+🅝 equal to half of either their Agility or Brawn (rounded up) damage.
- When treated as a weapon, use the owner's Willpower in place of their Brawn when to calculating bonus 🅝.
- A PDC can benefit from the Enhanced Attack X and Venom Gland X modifications.
- A PDC must be in Reach of its handler to be treated as a weapon.

- When acting on its own, treat PDC's as any other Adversary of their tier, though they do not act on their own during action scenes.

SMALL CREATURE X

Some Critters are truly tiny, capable of being carried – and concealed – on their handler's person. Add Concealed X to the Creature. This customisation is incompatible with Monstrous Creature.

VOCAL MODULATOR

While subsapient creatures aren't capable of understanding speech to the degree that a sapient person is, they can certainly be modified to sound like they do. This augmentation allows the Creature to mimic human speech, to an intelligible and unsettling degree. They can be taught phrases, not unlike a parrot. And they can also be used to deliver pre-recorded messages, input by their handler, and synthesised, essentially using the Creature as an organic amplification system.

STEP THREE: DETERMINE COST

After you've assembled the Creature of your dreams (or nightmares), you need to determine how much it'll cost to have it made. First consult the *Creature Creation Table* and the *Bioengineering Modifications Table*, if necessary, and then tally up your Cost, Maintenance, Tariff, and Risk.

Next, consult the *Creature Customisation Package Table* to determine the Restriction of your Creature, and divide the cost accordingly. Finally, consult the *Creature Side Effect Tables* and roll on the appropriate column of the *Bioengineered Creature Side Effects Table* to determine the unintended consequences of asking a Praxis scientist to play Frankenstein on your behalf.

EXAMPLE

PERSONAL DEFENCE CREATURE

Yasmin wants to acquire a modified Funduq Viper as a Personal Defence Creature. She envisions the PDC living in her sleeves, ready to strike at anyone who gets too close. A Fixer puts her in contact with a Praxis lab that is only too happy to fulfil her request.

Yasmin's player acquires a Trooper PDC, assigns 4 points each to the Creature's Agility and Brawn by 2 (raising each to 6) and raises its Personality and Willpower by 4 (raising each to 8). They then assign 1 point each to the PDC's Combat, Senses, Movement, and Social Expertise.

Not satisfied with a stock PDC, Yasmin acquires the Venom Gland 2 modification (taking Vicious twice), which adds the Biotech, Toxic 2, and Vicious 2 Weapon Qualities to her new pet. When attacking with her Viper, Yasmin's attacks will deal 1+3🅝 damage, with the Biotech, Toxic 2, and Vicious 2, as well as dealing an additional +2🅝 of bonus damage from Yasmin's Willpower of 10.

CREATURE CREATION TABLE

CUSTOMIZATION	COST	TSPECIAL
Trooper	6+6🅝	+1 Maintenance, +2 Risk, +1 Tariff
Elite	7+7🅝	+2 Maintenance, +4 Risk, +2 Tariff
Nemesis	10+10🅝	+3 maintenance, +6 Risk, +3 Tariff
Monstrous Creature	1+1🅝	+2 Maintenance, +8 Risk, +3 Tariff
Personal Defence Creature	+1🅝	+1 Maintenance
Small Creature X	X+2🅝	+1 Tariff
Vocal Modulator	2+2🅝	–
Bioengineered Modifications	See Entries	See Entries

CREATURE CUSTOMISATION PACKAGE TABLE

RISK	RESTRICTION	DIVIDE COST BY...
1–4	+1	1
5–10	+2	2
11–15	+3	3
16–18	+4	4
19+	+5	5

CREATURE SIDE EFFECT TABLES

RISK	CAREER
1–7	Side Effects Column A
8–14	Side Effects Column B
15+	Side Effects Column C

HEALTHY, GROWING CREATURES

Much like a Geist, Imprinted Creatures can be improved by spending Experience Points. The costs of these improvements are calculated in the same way that they would be for the player character themselves.

IT'S ALL BIOENGINEERING HERE

Creating a custom Creature is essentially like creating a BioMod package with a few extra options. Just like any other bioenginering project, they begin at a base value of 1+5🅝, T1. You can also reduce the Maintenance cost by increasing Risk and reduce Risk by spending Assets. The Maintenance cost of a Creature can never drop below 1; these things require a special diet and eat a lot. Every point of Risk past 19 is added to your result when rolling for side effects.

BIOENGINEERED CREATURE SIDE EFFECTS TABLE

ROLL D20			INCIDENT	EFFECT
A	B	C		
1	–	–	The Creature's Imprinting process went better than expected.	Increase the Creature's Morale by +3.
2	–	–	The bioengineer slips in a little something extra. To everyone's surprise, this goes quite well.	Add +1 to one of the Creature's Attributes.
3	1	–	It's… it's ADORABLE.	The Creature generates an additional Momentum for you on Persuade tests where a cute critter would be helpful.
4–5	2	–	The biochemistry is a near-perfect fit; the creature looks incredibly durable.	Increase the Creature's Vigour by 1.
6–7	3–5	1	Bad news: they needed to replace most of the creature's skull. Good news: its new, reinforced skull is clearly superior to the old one.	Add Armour Soak 1 to the creature's head.
8–9	6–8	2	It's got good eyes! Maybe too good, as it can't seem to stay out of trouble.	Increase the Creature's Awareness by 1 but reduce its Willpower by 1..
10–12	9–10	3–5	The creature's personality is a touch more timid than you might expect, though it's certainly every bit as tough as you might have hoped.	Reduce the Creature's Morale by 1 but increase its Vigour by 1.
13–15	11–12	6–8	The Creature is disciplined. Strong. Willful, but obedient. It's just a little more fragile than expected.	Reduce the Creature's Vigour by 1 but increase Morale by 1.
16–17	13–14	9–10	They had to get creative. The fruits of their labour aren't a total loss.	Reduce one of the Creature's Attributes by 2. Increase one of the Creature's Attributes by 1.
18–19	15–16	11–12	Some critters are just born ugly. This one was made that way. Nobody wants to be around it, which is problematic, but occasionally useful as well.	When the Creature is nearby, increase the Complication range on your Persuade tests by 1; unless you're using the Intimidate Psywar Technique, in which case, add +1 bonus Momentum on successful tests.
20	17–18	13–14	Due to the interaction of your requested components, you're going to need a special nutrient blend to keep the Creature well-fed.	Increase the Creature's Maintenance by +1.
–	19	15–16	Everything is exactly as promised, but you expected the creature to be a bit more nimble.	Reduce Agility by 1.
–	20	17–18	Everything worked fine: they just needed to scoop out some muscle tissue to make room. Let it run around, it'll be fine.	Reduce the Creature's Brawn by 1.
–	–	19	The Creature came out a little too agreeable, but they swear it can be trained.	Reduce the Creature's Morale by 1. The Creature does not begin Imprinted to the purchaser.
–	–	20	The Creature nearly died on the operating table. A last-minute injection of a small fortune in Silk saved it, though now you owe a small fortune to a loan shark.	Gain a debt worth 10 Assets. Increase the Creature's Maintenance by +1 until it's paid off.

CHAPTER 8
ADVERSARIES

REBELS, RENEGADES, AND RAMPAGING MONSTERS

They were sent into space to die. Instead, they carved out a place for themselves among the other mega powers. They refused to be subjugated and fought back against oppression. They continue the struggle against the omnipresent ALEPH that plays the G-5 nations as a puppeteer controls their toys. The crews of the Motherships include social revolutionaries, descendants of political prisoners, avant-garde philosophers, mercenaries, violent criminals, and dirty mobsters. In short, the Nomads are a besmudged mirror reflecting the entire Human Sphere. And it doesn't always like what it sees.

ELITE
BAKUNIN ZERO

Every army needs clandestine operation specialists, and the Nomads are no different. Each ship has a cell of trained agents, able to operate in hostile conditions and behind enemy lines. Those agents focus on harassing supply lines, destroying infrastructure, and assassinating key targets. On *Bakunin* such operators are nicknamed "Zeros," after their low count of failed missions and reported casualties. They achieve that through rigorous training provided by the different environmental hubs of *Bakunin*. The Mothership is a dangerous environment even for a well-trained operative, and the Zeros have earned a reputation as ruthless, dangerous individuals who don't shy away from violence. On a ship where anything is possible, these operators learn to expect the unexpected.

ATTRIBUTES						
AGI	AWA	BRW	COO	INT	PER	WIL
10	9	9	9	10	8	8

FIELDS OF EXPERTISE							
Combat	+2	1	Movement	+2	–	Social	+1	–
Fortitude	+1	–	Senses	+2	1	Technical	+2	–

DEFENCES					
Firewall	10	Resolve	8	Vigour	9
Security	1	Morale	–	Armour	1

ATTACKS
- **Assault Hacking Device**: CLAW-3, SWORD-0, SHIELD-0, GADGET-0, IC-1, +3 🔵 bonus damage
- **Combi Rifle**: Range C/M, 1+6 🔵 damage, Burst 2, 2H, Expert 1, MULTI Light Mod, Vicious 1
- **Linkspike**: Melee, 1+5 🔵, damage, 1H, Piercing 1, Subtle 3

GEAR: Light Combat Armour (with Chameleonwear)

SPECIAL ABILITIES
- **Multi-Environmental Training**: Zeros undergo extensive training in *Bakunin's* multi-environmental modules, giving them an adaptive edge across terrain types. When making an Acrobatics or Athletics test to move through difficult terrain, they reduce the difficulty by two steps, to a minimum of Simple (D0).
- **Predator**: Zeros prefer to strike first, giving their enemies no time to respond. When a Zero attacks from the hidden or detected stealth states, their target pays an additional +1 Heat to use the Defence Reaction against them. This lasts until the end of the scene.

ELITE
TUNGUSKAN NEGOTIATOR

When butting heads with the Nomads, much of the Human Sphere would describe them as radical hotheads and anarchic rebels who gleefully dive head-first into trouble. Both stereotypes make the job that much easier for Tunguska's Negotiators. While each Mothership has them, *Tunguska* famously deploys their Negotiators to unleash coercion, persuasion, bribery, and good old-fashioned intimidation on anyone standing in the Nomads' way. Only the best endure the work, but not because the job is dangerous. While individual Negotiators often find themselves imperilled, few want to risk angering a Chancellery by needlessly endangering its members. The work, by its nature, can be mentally exhausting. At Chancelleries like *Wysocki & Synowie* or *Pravova dopomoha bidnym*, the average employee quits after less than a year.

ATTRIBUTES						
AGI	AWA	BRW	COO	INT	PER	WIL
8	9	7	8	10	11	10

FIELDS OF EXPERTISE							
Combat	+1	–	Movement	+1	–	Social	+3	1
Fortitude	+1	–	Senses	+2	1	Technical	+2	–

DEFENCES					
Firewall	10	Resolve	9	10	7
Security	–	Morale	2	Armour	1

ATTACKS
- **Pistol**: Range R/C, 1+5 🔵 damage, Burst 2, 1H, Vicious 1
- **Stun Baton**: Melee 1+4 🔵 damage, 1H, Non-Hackable, Knockdown, Subtle 1, Stun

GEAR: Recorder, Aletheia Kit, Negotiator's Suite, Armoured Clothing, Cosmetics Kit)

SPECIAL ABILITIES
- **Backed by Muscle**: Sometimes, you have to conduct business the old-fashioned way. When spending Heat to call reinforcements, the GM reduces the total cost by 2 Heat, to a minimum of 1. If the Negotiator is incapacitated, the GM can no longer use their Backed by Muscle ability.
- **Greasy Palms**: The Negotiators know how to make others cooperative. When attempting a bribe, they gain two bonus d20s per Heat paid. The normal limit of three bonus d20s still applies.
- **Diplomatic Immunity**: Tunguskan Negotiators have a reputation that proceeds them, a fact they exploit for all it's worth. They benefit from a 2 Morale soak, reflected in their profile.

ELITE

SWAST TASKMASTERS

Most policing on *Bakunin* is handled by the Moderator corps, which is usually enough to deal with whatever trouble appears in the Mothership's common areas. However, sometimes the Jurisdictional Command needs to pay an unexpected visit to one of the Black Labs located in the Praxis module, where more abstract and less humane experiments take place. Often, if a JC team is knocking on a laboratory's door, all hell is about to break loose. And that's where the Taskmasters come in. Clad in bleeding-edge powered armour, Taskmasters enforce the rules when no one else can, or will. Acting as judge, jury – and frequently executioner – once the Special Weapons and Suppressive Tactics team is called in, the situation's already gone off the rails, and the Taskmasters are making the rules now. And those rules usually involve a good old-fashioned bullet with your name on it.

ATTRIBUTES						
AGI	AWA	BRW	COO	INT	PER	WIL
9	9	10	10	8	9	8

FIELDS OF EXPERTISE							
Combat	+3	2	Movement	+1	–	Social	+1	–
Fortitude	+2	1	Senses	+1	–	Technical	+1	–

DEFENCES					
Firewall	8	Resolve	8	Vigour	
Security	2	Morale	–	Armour	5

ATTACKS
- **Heavy Machine Gun (HMG)**: Range L, 2+7 (N) damage, Burst 3, Unwieldy, Spread 1, Unsubtle
- **Pistol**: Range R/C, 1+5 (N) damage, Burst 2, 1H, Vicious 1
- **Modified Stun Baton**: Melee 1+8 (N) damage, Unbalanced, Non-Hackable, Knockdown, Subtle 1, Stun, Vicious 2

GEAR: Powered Combat Armour (gain up to +3d20 on Brawn tests with +3 complication range, Kinematika), CrazyKoala)

SPECIAL ABILITIES
- **Big Buddy**: Whether it's the Moderator Corps, Die Morlock Gruppe, or some other unit, Taskmasters are used to coordinating with other forces. When leading a fireteam, they can reroll up to 2 (N) when making a ranged attack but must accept the new results.
- **Seen It All**: Some of it twice. When making an Observation test, the Taskmaster can reroll one d20 but must accept the new result.
- **Little Buddy (1–3 Heat)**: Taskmasters are protective of their "little buddies," any smaller, less armoured forces they deploy with. So virtually all of them. By spending X Heat, they can reduce the difficulty of the Guard Reaction, and if they succeed in intercepting the attack, they also deal X Morale damage to the

ELITE

CORREGIDOR BANDITS

Sub-Saharan Africa's supernatural guardians traditionally protected tribal communities through a young, possessed host prepared by the tribe's shaman and masked to preserve their anonymity. If ever there was a time that protection was needed, it was during the massive refugee exodus to *Corregidor's* Lazareto module. Traditionally masked vigilantes arose to keep the *maras* in check, and while many died, Lazareto's shamans never lacked for youths eager to take their place. As life in Lazareto improved and work teams left to ply their trades, internal threats were replaced by exploitation from employers. But their guardian spirits began stealing the safety equipment they were denied, beating abusive foremen, and exposing or killing the executives responsible. Impressed by their skill, the Mexican General extended an offer: in return for a promise not to interfere with their activities, a select few guardians would undergo intensive training and work as deniable assets to protect the entire Nomad Nation. The project avoided codenames with tribal connotations, instead using old air force jargon for confirmed hostiles, one outsiders have learned to fear – Bandits.

ATTRIBUTES						
AGI	AWA	BRW	COO	INT	PER	WIL
10	10	10	10	8	7	8

FIELDS OF EXPERTISE							
Combat	+2	2	Movement	+2	1	Social	+1	–
Fortitude	+2	1	Senses	+1	–	Technical	–	–

DEFENCES					
Firewall	8	Resolve	8	Vigour	10
Security	–	Morale	–	Armour	1

ATTACKS
- **Light Shotgun**: Range C, 1+6 (N) damage, Burst 1, Unbalanced, Knockdown
- **Paired Tonfa Bangles**: Melee 1+5 (N) damage, 1H, Concealed 2, Parry 2
- **Sword**: Melee, 1+7 (N) damage, Unbalanced, Non-Hackable, Parry 2, Vicious 1

GEAR: Armoured Clothing (with Chameleonwear), Stims, Surge, Glavar Powder

SPECIAL ABILITIES
- **My Life for the Helpless**: These masked vigilantes possess a selfless streak bordering on self-endangerment. They pay no Heat to use the Guard Reaction.
- **Violent Vigilante**: Bandits are trained to ignore pain and unleash vengeance upon their people's enemies. When making a melee attack, they can reroll up to 4 (N) but must accept the new result.

ELITE

TUNGUSKAN INTERVENTORS

To many casual observers "Nomad" is virtually a synonym for hacker. And while it's certainly true that the Nomad Nation boasts more than its fair share of Infowarriors, not every Nomad is an elite system cracker. But among those who are, one name stands above the rest. Interventors. The true crème-de-la-crème of the Human Sphere's quantronic battlefields. *Tunguska's* economy relies on keeping its secrets secret, and so they need the best hackers the Sphere has to offer. While some members of the Interventor Corps trace their roots to *Tunguska's* first cryptomancers, many are reformed lawbreakers, black-hat hackers caught in the act and offered a deal they couldn't refuse. Many Interventors actually don't mind working for 'the establishment' that they used to fight against. After all, they are still doing what they do best, cracking code and kicking quantronic ass. While they happily don their white hats in the service of the Nomad Nation, a darker shade remains in reach at all times. After all, you never know when you'll need a bit of that old black-hat magic. They have a reputation as the best. And, they take their reputation deadly seriously.

ATTRIBUTES						
AGI	AWA	BRW	COO	INT	PER	WIL
8	9	8	9	11	8	10

FIELDS OF EXPERTISE							
Combat	+1	–	Movement	+2	–	Social	+2	–
Fortitude	+2	–	Senses	+2	–	Technical	+3	1

DEFENCES					
Firewall	11	Resolve	10	Vigour	8
Security	2	Morale	1	Armour	2

ATTACKS
- **Combi Rifle**: Range C/M, 1+6 (N) damage, Burst 2, 2H, Expert 1, MULTI Light Mod, Vicious 1
- **Killer Hacking Device**: CLAW-0, SWORD-2, SHIELD-0, GADGET-0, IC-1, UPGRADE Cybermask, Piercing 3

GEAR: Light Combat Armour, FastPanda, Deflector-1

SPECIAL ABILITIES
- **It Takes a Thief (1–5 Heat)**: Interventors have been on the other side, and they know how to deal with it. When making a face-to-face Hacking test, they can spend X heat and reroll X d20s, though they must accept the new result.
- **Riding the Wave**: Interventors are the crème-de-la-crème of Tunguskan hackers, and they know it. They benefit from a Morale and Security soak, incorporated into their profiles.

ELITE
ALGUACILES

To many, the Alguaciles are the face of the Nomads. It happens only naturally, as most of the mercenaries sent to work outside of the Nomad Nation are recruited from among the ranks of the Alguaciles. Experienced and unrelenting, but also stubborn and sometimes foolhardy, the Alguaciles are the backbone of the Nomads. But, continuing with the metaphor, they could be also likened to the tired hands of the labourer, toiling for the betterment and comfort of the future generations. Many Alguaciles spend more time outside of *Corregidor* than they do at home, but they don't seem to mind. They work so that others may live, placing them squarely among the unsung heroes of the Nomads.

ATTRIBUTES						
AGI	AWA	BRW	COO	INT	PER	WIL
8	8	8	8	8	8	8

FIELDS OF EXPERTISE						
Combat	+1	–	Movement	–	–	Social	+1	–
Fortitude	+1	–	Senses	+1	–	Technical	+2	–

DEFENCES					
Firewall	8	Resolve	8	Vigour	8
Security	–	Morale		Armour	1

ATTACKS
- **Combi Rifle**: Range C/M, 1+5 🅝 damage, Burst 2, 2H, Expert 1, MULTI Light Mod, Vicious 1
- **Pistol**: Range R/C, 1+4 🅝 damage, Burst 2, 1H, Vicious 1
- **Knife**: Melee, 1+3 🅝, damage, 1H, Concealed 1, Non-Hackable, Subtle 2, Thrown, Unforgiving 1

GEAR: Light Combat Armour, Micro-torch, Powered Multi-tool

SPECIAL ABILITIES
- **More Than a Job**: For many Alguaciles, being a mercenary is not a job, but a way of life. They travel all over the Human Sphere, picking up different skills as they go. Each point of Momentum or Heat spent to add dice to a test provides two d20s instead of one.

ELITE
MOBILE BRIGADA

If you wanted to describe the Mobile Brigada regiment with one word, it would be "reliable." That's what they are. Their weapons and armour can be depended on, their character and morale are exemplary, and their knowledge of squad-based combat is excellent. These qualities make them outstanding mercenary troops, often hired alongside regular Corregidoran workers and Alguaciles as part of a wholesale deal. However, the Brigadas know that with great power comes great responsibility. Their unspoken mission is to look out for mistreatment of hired Nomad labourers, and if the situation warrants it, they step in to "correct the error." Sometimes it means slapping some people around; sometimes it means that the entire operation grinds to a halt as the facility is taken over by angry Nomads in power armour. *Corregidor* knows that in times of need, the Brigadas will be there for them. Members of the unit just smile behind their masked faceplates and continue doing their job.

ATTRIBUTES						
AGI	AWA	BRW	COO	INT	PER	WIL
9	10	9	10	8	9	8

FIELDS OF EXPERTISE								
Combat	+2	2	Movement	+1	–	Social	+1	–
Fortitude	+2	1	Senses	+1	–	Technical	+2	–

DEFENCES					
Firewall	8	Resolve	8	Vigour	10
Security	–	Morale		Armour	1

ATTACKS
- **Heavy Machine Gun (HMG)**: Range Long, 2+8 🅝 damage, Unwieldy, Spread 1, Unsubtle
- **Light Flamethrower**: Range Close, 1+6 🅝 damage, 2H, Incendiary 3, Munition, Terrifying 2, Torrent
- **Modhand**: Melee, 1+8 🅝 damage, 1H, Concealed 2, E/M, Stun, Subtle 1, Vicious 2

GEAR: Powered Combat Armour (gain up to +3d20 on Brawn tests with +3 complication range, Kinematika)

SPECIAL ABILITIES
- **Folk Heroes**: When the situation is dire, look to the Brigadas. A Mobile Brigada can be summoned as reinforcements for 1 Heat, instead of the usual 2. Brigadas coming in as reinforcements generate +1 additional Momentum on their first successful test.
- **Trained Leaders**: Brigadas usually lead smaller detachments of Corregidoran troops. When leading a Fireteam, the Brigada can reroll up to 2 🅝 when making a ranged attack but must accept the new results..

TROOPER/ELITE
PUPNIK

Hypoallergenic ferrets. Crazy-smart birds of paradise that alight on your shoulder and serenade you. Dogs that don't mess on the carpet. The Black Labs of Praxis have created some amazing and wonderful creatures, much to the delight of the wider Human Sphere.

They've also produced the Pupniks.

Borrowing their name from a moment of levity in Earth's Cold War, the Pupnik is a highly-aggressive, violently unstable, subsapient amalgamation of canid and humanoid features. About as intelligent as a clever chimpanzee, these creatures combine predatory instincts, vat-grown muscles, and a singular design aesthetic. Popular as "show muscle" for Submondo crime bosses, they've also seen increasing popularity as pit fighters, where their primal instincts drive them to fight, kill, mate, and eat — sometimes all at once. Their torturous creation ensures an always-violent killing machine, ready to explode at a moment's notice. Like a dog that was beaten in the womb, Pupniks are born with a mean streak. Though they can always be made meaner and often are.

ATTRIBUTES						
AGI	AWA	BRW	COO	INT	PER	WIL
10	10	12	6	7	8	4

FIELDS OF EXPERTISE								
Combat	+2	2	Movement	+1	–	Social	+1	–
Fortitude	+1	–	Senses	+1	1	Technical	–	–

DEFENCES					
Firewall	7	Resolve	4	Vigour	12
Security	–	Morale		Armour	1

ATTACKS
- **Claws**: Melee, 1+5 🅝 damage, Piercing 1 (Elites add the Grievous weapon quality)

GEAR: AR Eye Implants

SPECIAL ABILITIES
- **Common Special Abilities**: Fear 1, Keen Senses (Smell)
- **Crimson Rage (Elite Only)**: No matter how well-behaved they may seem, Pupniks are never far from the edge. Whenever a Pupnik suffers a Wound or Metanoia effect, it flies into a violent rage, attacking the nearest source of agitation with terrifying abandon, usually the source of the Harm, but any living being will do. While in its rage, it gains +4 Morale and deals +4[🅝 to melee attacks, though it suffers +2 difficulty to all tests that don't involve dealing something bodily harm. Talking a Pupnik out of a Crimson Rage requires succeeding at a Dire (D4) Animal Handling test, with the difficulty reducing by 1 each round, to a minimum of Simple (D0).

TROOPER/ELITE
GENETIC ABOMINATION

Through a combination of genesplicing, radical augmentation, and biografted xenotissue, the Black Labs of Praxis can create any creature that their customers can dream up. Of course, not all dreams are pleasant and their Genetic Abominations cover the entire spectrum, from statuesque gryphons and regal unicorns, to twisted chimerical horrors best left unmentioned. Like Pupniks, these sub-sapient creatures are often employed as security. Despite lacking killer instincts, they're easier to control, are unsettlingly weird, and possess a near-human vocal range that has proven more than enough to frighten off many would-be trespassers. And what of those who decided to test their luck against these manifest nightmares? In most cases, they need to identify the remains by DNA sample. While a given Abomination might possess any number of different lethal augmentations, they are known to be remarkably thorough.

ATTRIBUTES

AGI	AWA	BRW	COO	INT	PER	WIL
10	10	10	5	8	8	9

FIELDS OF EXPERTISE

Combat	+1	1	Movement	+1	–	Social	+1	1
Fortitude	+1	–	Senses	+2	1	Technical	–	–

DEFENCES (TROOPER)

Firewall	4	Resolve	5	Vigour	5
Security	–	Morale	1	Armour	1

DEFENCES (ELITE)

Firewall	8	Resolve	9	Vigour	10
Security	–	Morale	–	Armour	–

ATTACKS

- Troopers have access to one of the following attack types; Elites choose two:
  - *Acidic Spit*: Range C, 1+5 🅝 damage, Biotech, Breaker, Toxic 1
  - *Neurotoxic Bite*: Melee, 1+5 🅝 damage, Biotech, Immobilising, Toxic 2
  - *Xenotissue Spines*: Melee, 1+5 🅝 damage, Grievous, Piercing 1

GEAR: Stealth Repeater

SPECIAL ABILITIES

- **Abandon All Hope Ye Who Enter Here**: From remote-fed personal data, to uncanny body horror, Genetic Abominations are well-equipped to unsettle their targets. They generate an additional +1 Momentum on successful Psywar attacks.
- **Unexpected Metachemistry (1 Heat)**: A Genetic Abomination's capabilities aren't always immediately obvious. By spending 1 Heat, the Abomination gains access to an additional attack type (see above) for one action.

ELITE
DIE MORLOCK GRUPPEA

Life on *Bakunin* is a riot of colour, vibrance, and indulgence. For some, resorting to extreme violence is the only means of coping with the constant assault on the senses with the result that a few of these unhinged individuals become very good at it. Rather than lock them away and waste their talent, the Bakunians hook the worst of these vicious psychopaths on MetaChemistry compounds and assign them to one of the Morlock Groups. The MetaChemistry barely refrains their fury, however, so maintaining a safe distance at all times is highly recommended. Once they taste combat, the inhibitive control of the drugs in their systems releases and flips, working to further enhance the potency and violent natures of these inhuman beasts.

ATTRIBUTES

AGI	AWA	BRW	COO	INT	PER	WIL
10	9	10	10	7	6	7

FIELDS OF EXPERTISE

Combat	+3	2	Movement	+2	1	Social	+2	–1
Fortitude	+2	1	Senses	–	–	Technical	–	–

DEFENCES (TROOPER)

Firewall	8	Resolve	9	Vigour	10
Security	–	Morale	1	Armour	–

ATTACKS

- **Combi Rifle**: Range C/M, 1+6 🅝 damage, Burst 2, 2H, Expert 2, MULTI Light Mod, Vicious 1
- **Pistol**: Range C, 1+5 🅝 damage, Burst 1, 1H, Vicious 1
- **Morlock Blade**: Melee, 1+7 🅝 damage, Unbalanced, Non-Hackable, Parry 1, Piercing 1, Vicious 1
- **Smoke Grenades**: 1H, Disposable, Indiscriminate (Close), Nonlethal, Speculative Fire, Smoke 2, Thrown

GEAR: Ballistic Vest

SPECIAL ABILITIES

- **MetaChemistry Boost (1-2 Heat)**: Thanks to their MetaChemistry, combat triggers physical changes that are unique to each Morlock. Once per combat scene, the GM can spend 1 or 2 Heat to boost one of the Morlock's physical attributes by 1 or 2 points.
- **Red Mist**: When their MetaChemistry unleashes their psychotic tendencies, Morlocks think of little else. They gain a Morale Soak of 3 and an Intransigence of 4 during combat scenes. Additionally, they can reroll up to 2 🅝 when making a melee attack, but must accept the new results.

ELITE
KRIZA BORACS

Originally created to plug a perceived hole in the defences of *Tunguska*, the Specjalne Krize Jedinice (Serbian for Special Crisis Units) are a heavy infantry unit deployed to crisis points as a hammer blow to end the situation. Conceived as an unstoppable force that can respond to flashpoints with overwhelming firepower, the Kriza Boracs (Crisis Soldiers) enjoy the use of Praxis-designed power armour that enables them to perform both offensive and supporting roles during engagements. Professional, solemn (for Nomads at least), and adaptable, the Kriza Boracs have solidly earned their reputation for being in exactly the right place at just the very moment when their particular skills are needed.

ATTRIBUTES

AGI	AWA	BRW	COO	INT	PER	WIL
9	10	9	9	8	8	10

FIELDS OF EXPERTISE

Combat	+2	1	Movement	+2	–	Social	–	–
Fortitude	+1	1	Senses	+2	1	Technical	+1	1

DEFENCES (TROOPER)

Firewall	8	Resolve	9	Vigour	10
Security	3	Morale	2	Armour	5

ATTACKS

- **Heavy Machine Gun (HMG)**: Range L, 2+8 🅝 damage, Burst 3, Unwieldy, Spread 1, Unsubtle
- **Heavy Pistol**: Range C, 2+6 🅝 damage, Burst 1, Unbalanced, Unforgiving 1, Vicious 1
- **Knife**: Melee, 1+7 🅝 damage, 1H, Concealed 1, Non-Hackable, Subtle 2, Thrown, Unforgiving 1

GEAR: Powered Combat Armour (Comms, Exoskeleton 3, Kinematika, Self-Repairing)

SPECIAL ABILITIES

- **Crisis Response**: Kriza Boracs are ready to move at a moment's notice and prepare for the worst scenarios. They have a Morale Soak of 2.
- **Superior Firepower (1 Heat)**: Overwhelming firepower heads the doctrine for the Kriza Boracs. When operating a Chain Rifle, HMG, or MULTI Rifle, the GM may spend 1 Heat to increase the Spread quality of the weapon by 1 for a single ranged attack.

ALEXANDER SHVARTS

NEMESIS

ISAAC STRAVHS
(INTERVENTOR/SPY MASTER)

The official operation to guarantee the prospecting encampment a security detail was a front for the real operation: securing a Max-Seal data-package from the client and uploading it into the Crypt for safekeeping. Stravhs was certain that several dozen such contracts had been signed between different Hyper-corps, the Ariadnans, and the Nomad Nation in the past few years. There was no conflict of interest, just business as usual for the information brokers of Tunguska and their allies.

And this was how the young hacker was now planetside with a mild case of agoraphobia, supervising security in a Teseum prospecting camp. The hit and run attacks on the encampment had all been repelled thanks to the Alguaciles' combat experience and Stravhs's superior tactical coordination skills. Still, he remained restless while waiting for the client to deliver the data-package. No mere data jockey, he had accessed the satellite feeds to gain awareness of the position and movements of their attackers, which allowed him to coordinate the defence of the encampment. He'd even had the unit's engineer booby trap the main access to the camp. Luckily, the client's data-pack courier arrived minutes before the main attack began.

The timing couldn't be mere coincidence, and Isaac realised that the true motive for the Nomads' presence had been leaked by someone intent on seizing the information by any means possible. The entrance flooding with attackers seemed the perfect time to activate those explosives. "Chang! Activate the bombs! Let's give them a nasty surprise!"

Nothing happened. The aggressors kept pushing toward the gate and the beleaguered defenders. Stravhs worriedly ran a quick survey on the camp, looking unsuccessfully for the engineer as he nervously activated the remote he used for surveillance, an old transductor unit. On a hunch, he instructed the small unit to check the comms station where the data-pack was being uploaded. Isaac then returned to coordinate the now-failing line of defence of the camp.

A few seconds later, Stravhs heard a loud explosion coming from the comm station. Running clumsily and drawing his pistol, he saw black smoke emerging from the tent that housed it. He immediately regretted rushing in as his lungs began to fill with oily smoke. A shot whizzed past his head as he doubled over to cough. This was exactly why he hated being planetside.

APPEARANCE

A lanky man with a rather mysterious air and ever-present hacking goggles, Isaac tends to press his lips together and narrow his eyes when dealing with people. When working with Ariadnans, he crosses his arms and frowns often.

ROLEPLAYING

- Although fit, he is clumsy when performing physical chores (which he avoids).
- He is very haughty to the point of being rude.
- He despises Ariadnans, even though he sometimes works with them.

BACKGROUND

After signing a contract with Dragnet, "Smiley" (due to his electronic signature) quickly found his place in on-the-field counter-intelligence. His first assignment to track a series of apparently random glitches in Arachne's sub-systems led to him exposing an incipient AI program that had already killed several high-profile programmers on Tunguska. The Black Hand assigned a more complex challenge with a squad of Securitate. He came out of that exercise with flying colours and secured a future as one of the most efficient field specialists.

Repeatedly assigned to high-risk missions planetside, Isaac took it as a sign of the Black Hand's trust in him. Recently, however, he is starting to feel like somebody is either toying or wants him dead. A proud man intent on a first-rate job, his skills have so far kept him ahead in his is currently assignment to a multi-ship unit that poses as a standard Corregidor security team. Coordinating with agents from all three Motherships makes the missions assigned to the team even more challenging and dangerous.

ATTRIBUTES

AGI	AWA	BRW	COO	INT	PER	WIL
8	12	8	8	14	8	12

FIELDS OF EXPERTISE

Combat	+1	1	Movement	+1	–	Social	–	–
Fortitude	+2	1	Senses	+3	3	Technical	+4	4

DEFENCES

Firewall	18	Resolve	14	Vigour	10
Security	–	Morale	–	Armour	2

ATTACKS

- **Hacking Device Plus**: CLAW-2, SWORD-1, SHIELD-2, GADGET-3, IC-2, UPGRADE Cybermask, Fadeware, Sucker Punch, White Noise; +4  bonus damage
- **Pistol**: Range R/C, 1+7 damage, Burst 1, 1H, Vicious 1

GEAR: Light Combat Armour, FastPanda, Deflector-2

SPECIAL ABILITIES

- **All Ears. All Thumbs, Too**: Whip-smart and eagle-eyed, Stravhs doesn't miss much. That hasn't made him any less clumsy, however. When making a test based on Awareness, he can reroll one d20, but must accept the new result. However, he suffers an additional +1 complication range to actions based on Agility, Brawn, and Coordination.
- **Embedded Asset**: Stravhs spends an inordinate amount of time planetside, and as such, is used to passing as janitors, security guards, and other innocuous professions. He reduces the difficulty of Lifestyle or Stealth tests to blend in by two steps, to a minimum of Simple (D0).
- **Smiley Was Here (1–5 Heat)**: Even by the standards of the Interventors, Stravhs is something of a hotshot. But it's not bragging if you can back it up. When making a Hacking test, he can spend X heat and reroll X d20s, but must accept the new results.

ERNESTO CHANG (ARIADNAN SABOTEUR)

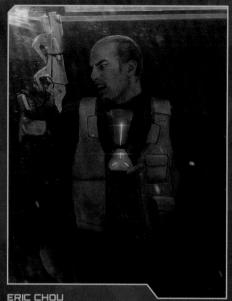

ERIC CHOU

NEMESIS

ERNESTO CHANG

ATTRIBUTES

AGI	AWA	BRW	COO	INT	PER	WIL
9	11	10	9	10	9	12

FIELDS OF EXPERTISE

Combat	+2	1	Movement	+1	1	Social	+1	1
Fortitude	+2	1	Senses	2+3	1	Technical	+3	3

DEFENCES

Firewall	13	Resolve	14	Vigour	12
Security	–	Morale	–	Armour	2

ATTACKS

- **D-Charges**: Explosive Charge, 2+6 damage, 1H, Anti-Materiel 2, Comms, Disposable, Piercing 3, Spread 1, Unsubtle, Vicious 2
- **Pistol**: Range R/C, 1+6 damage, Burst 1, 1H, Vicious 1
- **Punishing Flames (Special)**: Explosive Charge, 1+4 damage, 1H, Anti-Materiel 1, Incendiary 2, Spread 2, Unsubtle, Vicious 2

GEAR: CrazyKoala, Light Combat Armour, D-Charges, Smoke Grenades

SPECIAL ABILITIES

- **Covering with Fire**: Ernesto interprets certain terms very literally. If he succeeds at a Daunting (D3) Tech test when using the Covering Fire Reaction, he can deal his Punishing Flames attack to anyone attacking the ally being assisted until the beginning of his next turn.
- **Fire in the Hole (2 Heat)**: Ernesto isn't an arsonist, he just so happens to have various and sundry explosives. For 2 Heat, he detonates a device and deals his Punishing Flames attack to anyone in its zone. Until the end of the scene, anyone traveling through or ending their turn in the zone must succeed at a Challenging (D2) Acrobatics test, or suffer the attack.

He had to admit to himself that, until now, this mission had been a blast — literally. He was finally back home after almost two years of blowing up stuff across the Human Sphere with the security team he had been assigned to. The new mission for a Teseum mining company seemed simple enough. Chang's job likewise seemed simple: supervise the installation of the comms rig, secure the perimeter, then try to seem busy.

Ernesto wasn't too keen on blowing his Adiadnan comrades on Dawn to bits, particularly as they would be part of the real mission. Chang had discreetly received instructions right after the comms array was up and running, just before putting it online for the Tunguskan Interventor to take the helm. And that was the rub, the Tunguskan hacker in charge of operations. Apparently he wasn't the only one running a double scheme, and the Nomads were expecting some high-end with valuable information. The fact that they had taken so much care to disguise this transaction clearly meant it would be invaluable to whomever controlled it. If Stavka wanted it, then it was Chang's job to obliterate every single piece of equipment in that camp in order to retrieve the data.

Stravhs, the engineer turned spy, had already rigged and booby trapped most of the installations. It sounded as if Stavka had sent a full regiment to storm the camp, and this kept the Tunguskan officer focused on the defences. Ernesto had direct access to the communications arrays.

"Chang! Activate the bombs!" Chang cut the communication short. His time was up. No bombs detonating as expected had just played his hand. He had to think fast! Looking around, he found some equipment crates near the tents and lugged them to the mine entrance. He fixed a custom-made proximity charge to it just as he saw one of the Nomad remotes heading at full speed to his location. Cursing, he barely had time to dive behind the comms array before the remote entered and set off the explosive, filling the station with smoke and small fires, and his ears with a constant beep.

Ernesto crawled dazedly from behind his cover and retrieved his weapon. He aimed at the tent's entrance while someone, a Nomad for sure, entered the tent. Fired half-blind, he hoped to gain time to recover and figure out where the data-pack was.

APPEARANCE

Ernesto wears standard-issue Alguacil fatigues under a battered blue jacket and a yellow vest with the word "Dozer" embroidered on it. He carries several grenades with him and what looks like a detonator is hanging from his belt. Although smiling, there is something off-putting in his eyes.

ROLEPLAYING

- He constantly uses puns and references to explosions.
- He is slightly hard of hearing (on account of too many explosions at close quarters).
- He speaks with a strong USAriadnan accent.

BACKGROUND

Not considering himself a pyromaniac, Ernesto prefers to think of himself as someone inclined towards explosives and is liberal with their usage. Still, he couldn't blame his CO for court-marshalling him after he blew up a building of smugglers instead of opening a breach on the wall for the special-ops teams to capture them. He was waiting in a Fairview military prison for a long sentence to be handed to him when a high-ranking visitor made an offer he simply couldn't turn down. Rumours of undercover specialists recruited by Stavka drifted through the lockup, but Chang gave them little consideration and certainly never thought he would be forced into service as one of them!

Ernesto no longer reports to his superiors regarding his use of explosives, but he finds himself in ever more dangerous situations. There are always perks to be found when passing for a disenfranchised mercenary capable of piercing the toughest vaults and adamantine armours. His new job is definitely cut out for him, but it is getting harder for Chang to remember where his loyalties are. He's more preoccupied than ever as his superiors ae making the consequences for failing to deliver quite clear. For now, he takes every new mission one explosion at a time.

ERIK REIERSEN

NEMESIS

ZANA

ATTRIBUTES

AGI	AWA	BRW	COO	INT	PER	WIL
9	10	8	9	13	10	11

FIELDS OF EXPERTISE

Combat	+1	1	Movement	+	1	Social	+1	1
Fortitude	+3	1	Senses	+2	1	Technical	+3	3

DEFENCES

Firewall	16	Resolve	14	Vigour	11
Security	–	Morale	–	Armour	1

ATTACKS

- **Hacking Device Plus**: CLAW-2, SWORD-1, SHIELD-2, GADGET-3, IC-2, UPGRADE Cybermask, Solifugae, Sucker Punch, White Noise; +3  bonus damage
- **Nanopulser**: Range C, 1+5 damage, 1H, Biotech, Subtle 3, Torrent, Vicious 2

GEAR: Armoured Clothing, Stealth Repeater, Stims

SPECIAL ABILITIES

- **Fidgety**: Zana hates to sit still, and in a conflict, this keeps him on the move. He gains X Morale and Security Soak, where X equals the number of zones he's travelled since his last action (excluding zones travelled by vehicular movement).
- **Hacker**: When making an Infowar attack, Zana can reroll up to 5 but must accept the new result.
- **Sharp Senses**: Zana's eyes may dart around like a caffeinated hummingbird, but he's surprisingly adapt at processing what he sees. He can reroll one d20 when making an Observation test but must accept the new result.

Zana uploaded the firewall program and made sure the repeater was running correctly. Somehow during the night, the brand-new repeater had burned out.

Segal, Zana's Alguacil escort, clapped his hand on Zana's shoulder. "When you are done, I'll be outside in the street. I think someone was following us, so we better return fast to the Mission."

Segal left the building while Zana finished and hurriedly gathered his remaining tools. The Nomad hacker rushed out of the repeater's building to where his escort would be waiting.

Zana found Segal, bending over and incessantly coughing. The Alguacil tried to draw his pistol, but the cough prevented him, and he clumsily fell to the floor.

"Segal! What happened? Are you alright?" Zana asked, cradling his friend and colleague.

"Zana... I think... we are made... you have to get... to the ..."

Blood trickled from Segal's mouth as the coughing ceased, and he closed his eyes one last time.

"Segal!"

Zana's eyes darted around the growing crowd, his mind racing, and he gently lowered Segal. Segal had no signs of open wounds, so the culprit had to be someone nearby. Someone who had gotten close to him.

Hacking into Maya, he filtered, on a hunch, all comlogs with open access and uploaded a personal quantronic malware to overload all users' receptions channels. This immediately generated the response Zana was looking for. Almost everyone on the street stopped to check their malfunctioning comlogs. With only a few seconds before they reset, Zana frantically scrutinised the crowd. Then he saw him: a single man walking hurriedly away from the confused crowd.

Zana had the killer, now it was a matter of action.

ZANA (HACKER)

APPEARANCE

Zana is young man from *Corregidor* with nervous mannerisms who is constantly immersed in his comlog. Unlike other Nomad hackers, his clothing and gear all are immensely practical, yet advanced and sophisticated. Zana can blend in with a crowd and uses this anonymity when dealing with would-be ALEPH attackers.

ROLEPLAYING

- He cannot keep still for long periods and is always doing something with his hands.
- Zana constantly cleans his hands with antiseptic spray.
- He does not have a sense of privacy and tends to hack even his friends' personal devices.

BACKGROUND

Zana never thought much about the Phantom Conflict nor the struggle between ALEPH and the Nomad Nation. He learned the histories and legends of the struggle of the Nomads and their heroes against the AI, but he never saw it as anything beyond that: history. As a Corregidorean hacker attached to the Alguacil Security detachment in the Commercial Mission, he assumed his work would be ensuring Arachne's repeaters were up and running. Simple.

That is, until the Commercial Mission was targeted by cyber-attacks, assassinations, and sabotage runs. Though in shock from the attacks, it would take the death of one of his squad mates for Zana to realise that ALEPH and its threat to all Nomads in the Human Sphere was real. He was in a war of extermination, and he would not fail his people, no matter what it takes!

ROBERT DI GIOVANNI (SIN EATER)

ROBONRAGE

NEMESIS

ROBERT DI GIOVANNI

ATTRIBUTES

AGI	AWA	BRW	COO	INT	PER	WIL
8	10	12	11	8	8	13

FIELDS OF EXPERTISE

Combat	+3	3	Movement	+1	1	Social	+1	–
Fortitude	+5	1	Senses	+2	2	Technical	+1	–

DEFENCES

Firewall	9	Resolve	18	Vigour	17
Security	–	Morale	–	Armour	2

ATTACKS

- **Mk12**: Range M, 2+7  damage, Burst 3, 2H, Salvo (Knockdown)
- **Nemesis Gloves**: Melee, 1+6 damage, Covers Hands, Anti-Materiel 2, Backlash 1, Monofilament, NFB, Vicious 22

GEAR: Medium Combat Armour, Ritual Knife

SPECIAL ABILITIES

- **Bodyshield**: Completely unconcerned with his own safety, Roberto will gladly take a bullet for his charges and often has. He can only designate a single individual, including a character, at a time; as his charge. When used to protect his charge, Roberto does not pay Heat to use the Guard Reaction.
- **Continuous Catechism**: Roberto has committed Our Lady of Mercy's doctrine to heart, reciting it nigh-unconsciously. His unwavering dedications grants him a Morale Soak of 3.
- **Suffer For Your Sins**: Roberto's not much for dodging: it interferes with his aim. He does not pay Heat to use the Return Fire Reaction, but when he uses it, his opponent gains +2 on their attack

The Sin Eater and the smaller woman evaluated the abandoned smelting facility from a hidden position.

The Reverend Moira, Julia, instructed the huge man besides her. "Stay here and guard our back. I will locate the operative and rendezvous as soon as possible."

"May Our Lady of Mercy find me useful."

"May you atone for our weaknesses, Sin Eater."

With that, Reverend Julia went into the ruined building, leaving Robert di Giovanni on top of a ramshackle hut where he could oversee the entrance to the building.

He was in the second mystery of the Observance Litany, when a transport arrived at the building, unloading seven armed men. Somehow, they knew the Moira were here.

"Sinful men," Roberto thought.

He aimed at the vehicle's pilot, who never got a chance to repent of his sins. The rest of the men immediately took cover, firing blindly at Robert's position. He kept firing his Mark 12, not bothering to cover himself, and each shot found its mark on the enemies of the Observance.

The attackers were well equipped and organised, Robert acknowledged in the haze of his faith-induced trance, but he had the higher ground and clear lane of fire. He fired the last round of his magazine and started reloading when he heard the distinctive sound of a grenade launcher. He saw the trajectory of the grenade heading his way, as in slow motion, hitting squarely in the parapet he was stationed.

Shrapnel hit the Sin Eater in the chest and neck. Robert grimaced at the pain, finished reloading, and got on his feet to shoot the doomed soul.

Afterwards, he approached the vehicle, took out what was left of the driver, and climbed in his stead. The Reverend then came out of the building, helping a limping man climb into the vehicle.

"Thank Our Lady for her intervention! Get us out of here!"

Roberto tried to answer but blood gurgled out of his wounded throat. Resigned, he hit the accelerator and headed to the docks.

APPEARANCE

An imposing man in impeccable white uniform, Robert is armed with a huge rifle. This impatient man is covered in scars that riddle his face and neck, as if they follow some kind of secret pattern.

ROLEPLAYING

- He is constantly whispering Our Lady of Mercy catechism.
- He has wild, enervating eyes, and he tends to stare directly into whomever talks to him.
- He has an electronic voice, due to damage to his vocal chords.

BACKGROUND

Robert di Giovanni had many flaws, one of them was his condition as a sinful man. He indulged in every sin he had access to – and on *Bakunin*, there are more than just seven! He never gave a moment's thought to consequences or even a Social Energy decline.

During the Violent Intermission, he was in one of the first modules attacked by the AIs infiltrators, and he would have died a horrible nano-tech death had it not been for the reverends and their pious purge of the Evil that is ALEPH.

With his dying breath, he begged for the purification of his sins to one of the Reverend Healers. That day, he died and was reborn as a Sin Eater, taking on the sins of others and searing them into his flesh, his thoughts, his very soul. Thus does he serve the Observance and the Nomad Nation in atonement, trusting that even if his suffering never cleanses his dissolute soul, it at least serves a higher purpose.

JAKE SHEPERD (CLOCKMAKER)

NERRU

NEMESIS

JAKE SHEPERD

ATTRIBUTES

AGI	AWA	BRW	COO	INT	PER	WIL
9	10	8	11	10	12	9

FIELDS OF EXPERTISE

Combat	+1	1	Movement	+1	–	Social	+3	3
Fortitude	+1	–	Senses	+1	1	Technical	+4	4

DEFENCES

Firewall	13	Resolve	10	Vigour	9
Security	–	Morale	3	Armour	1

ATTACKS

- **Combi Rifle**: Range C/M, 1+7 🔸 damage, Burst 2, 2H, Expert 1, MULTI Light Mod, Vicious 1
- **D-Charges**: Explosive Charge, 2+6 🔸 damage, 1H, Anti-Materiel 2, Comms, Disposable, Piercing 3, Spread 1, Unsubtle, Vicious 2
- **Foomp Flinger**: Range M, Burst 1, 1H, Munition, Speculative Fire

GEAR: Armoured Clothing, FFP Repeater Rounds 2, Freedom Kit, Powered Multitool

SPECIAL ABILITIES

- **Lust for Life**: Shepard's *joie de vivre* can border on the absurd, but it seems to suit him just fine. He gains a Morale Soak of 3.
- **Stone Free**: Even by Bakunian standards, Shepard is an independent soul. Command tests against him are made at +2 difficulty.
- **Under Pressure**: For whatever reason, Jake finds his rhythm when the heat is on. During action scenes, he reduces the difficulty of Tech tests by two steps to a minimum of Simple (D0).

"Sheperd! The remote got blown again! We need your help!"

"Again?! What are you doing with it?"

"Stop wasting time! We need the REM's repeater up and running or our support will crash into the jungle, and then we are done for!"

Gritting his teeth, the engineer took a deep breath and jumped out of his cover. The beleaguered Nomad unit was ambushed by the Shasvastii, and Jake had been in charge of the remotes. They detected the Shasvastii moments before the attack, allowing the Nomads precious seconds to prepare and take cover.

Now, the skirmish was at a standstill, and it was a battle of attrition. The faction that received reinforcements would wipe out the opposing unit. Sheperd shivered at the thought of what kind of reinforcements the aliens would bring.

Tumbling, dodging, and somersaulting, he somehow managed to avoid getting killed while reaching the wrecked remote, right in the middle of the battlefield.

Throwing himself to the ground, Sheperd assessed the remote. It had received a direct blast, but the repeater was surprisingly intact. He just needed to jumpstart the unit.

During the boot cycle, he heard a guttural scream from above. Instinctively, he rolled to the side while a Shasvastii Seed Soldier launched himself at the Nomad. Jake barely had time to sweep the lanky alien's legs while getting up on his feet. The alien crawled back and drew a wicked knife. Full of adrenaline, Jake rushed and kicked the alien, diving under the Shasvastii's reach and connecting with its abdomen. The invader grunted and fell back. It recovered but before it could skewer Jake, the alien's head exploded.

Stunned, Jake looked around until he saw an Alguacil hacker giving cover fire to his position.

"Quit wasting time, Sheperd!"

Jake, covered in alien blood, smiled at the hacker and turned on the repeater.

"Ready to go! Call in the cavalry!"

APPEARANCE

A man of indefinite age, neither young nor old is usually found in his workshop, rhythmically moving to some inaudible tune. While he tinkers, Sheperd tends to chew on whatever is at hand, edible or not. He has unusual cortical implants on the back of his head and wears the distinguishing white and orange uniform of a Clockmaker of *Bakunin*.

ROLEPLAYING

- Jake is always chewing something.
- He is constantly offering to "upgrade" any technological contraption he sees.
- He likes music and is constantly humming and dancing by himself.

BACKGROUND

The best part of being a Clockmaker is the constant challenge of rearranging stuff in order to improve it. For Jake Sheperd, doing this while in extreme conditions like on the field repairs only add zest to his life. Sheperd works best under pressure, truly happy when he finds his rhythm under enemy fire or the impending menace of a ship to ship boarding action.

Although his contraptions are sturdy, and his repairs always help his Nomad comrades to carry the day, they are not as long-lived as one would expect from a renowned engineer. It is unknown if this is his first incarnation or if he has been resurrected before, but Jake lives this life to the fullest and enjoys it with a *joie de vivre* rarely seen even in a Bakunian.

GRIGORI VEGA (HACKER)

TILL SCHLUSEN

NEMESIS

ROBERT DI GIOVANNI

ATTRIBUTES

AGI	AWA	BRW	COO	INT	PER	WIL
9	11	8	9	14	7	12

FIELDS OF EXPERTISE

Combat	+1	1	Movement	+1	–	Social	–	–
Fortitude	+2	1	Senses	+3	3	Technical	+5	3

DEFENCES

Firewall	19	Resolve	14	Vigour	10
Security	–	Morale	–	Armour	1

ATTACKS

- **Hacking Device Plus**: CLAW-2 (CLAW-2 Black Widow, 1+3  damage), SWORD-1, SHIELD-2, GADGET-3 (GADGET-1 Lockpicker), IC-2, UPGRADE Cybermask, Fadeware, Sucker Punch, White Noise; +4 bonus damage
- **Heavy Pistol**: Range R/C, 2+6 damage, Burst 1, Unbalanced, Unforgiving 1, Vicious 1

GEAR: Adhesive Solvent, Armoured Clothinge

SPECIAL ABILITIES

- **Hacker**: When making an Infowar attack, Grigori can reroll up to 3 but must accept the new result.
- **One Step Ahead of the Machine**: Grigori knows all the tell-tale signs of AIs, and he's good at exploiting them. He adds Vicious 3 to Infowar attacks against Aspects, geists, Rogue AIs, and other artificial intelligences.
- **Paranoid**: Grigori is constantly expecting ALEPH, or its minions, to come after him. But it's not paranoia if you're right... He pays two less Heat to use Reactions, to a minimum of zero.

11110N's name flashed every 3.33 nanoseconds, a rather annoying advertising of the hacker's abilities. The backdoor program was so loaded with booby traps and defence bots that it even included a transit gauge, which made any effort to analyse it a dangerous affair to explore.

This only made the Nomad hacker, Grigori Vega, more determined to crack the cyber-safe. He was happily charging every second he worked on this job to Lawson, the suave investor who had approached him with the job of writing up a key that would bypass this type of security.

But first, Grigori had to neutralise the piece of code 11110N had written as a failsafe that would erase all the information contained in the program.

This was probably the toughest security array Grigori had encounter in his life, yet there was something strange in the code and the quantronic arrangement in general, like a pyramid of data packs, different from the carefully structured Yu Jing firewalls or the monolithic PanOceanian locks and bots. This was something else, the appearance of disarray but carefully orchestrated.

That was when Grigori understood it. "Of course! It's all a front!" All that security, the undecipherable programs and bots were just that, a trap by itself.

* * *

"Here you go. A trinary-quantronic lockpick program, perfect for hacking into any magenta-level security system in Human Edge."

"I have to say, I am quite impressed! Only a Tunguska hacker..."

Lawson's speech was suddenly interrupted by a huge gun pointed at his too perfect face.

"Yeah, only a Nomad hacker would see your trap for what it is, program. The next time you dumb AIs try to ambush us with such lame tactics, try not to be so obvious. Remember, 11110N: we are smarter than you." He smirked. "Which is why you're not going to find any nearby Proxies to jump into. See you around."

The Posthuman's face contorted in a rictus full of hate before disappearing in a red mist.

It had been a close call this time. If Grigori hadn't noticed the pattern, ALEPH would at the very least have killed him. At worst, ALEPH would have acquired access to Arachne and the location of the Nomads nodes in the Orbital where he was located.

"Just keep one step ahead of the machine. That's all I have to do."

APPEARANCE

Grigori Vega is dressed in very worn clothes but carries a highly sophisticated hacking device. His eyes are bloodshot, and he clearly hasn't bathed in a while. Vega has the appearance of a genius or a mad man, but it is not clear which it is.

ROLEPLAYING

- Vega always tries to make a profit from every situation.
- Nobody is as good as him, and if they are it's because they are cheating.
- He is very secretive and gets defensive if anyone asks about his life.

BACKGROUND

"Who is the target?"

"One Grigori Vega, of *Tunguska*."

"Never heard of him..."

"He is the one who took out Project: Illium."

"I thought Illium had gone rogue."

"That's the official version. Turns out he found about Illium, took him out and took over his persona for almost two hours..."

"Last known position?"

"One of the Commercial Missions on Paradiso. Could be a red herring though..."

"Perhaps. But that's the only clue we have. If he took out Illium, there is no way I'll be able to crack him down. I'll have to do it old school, in real space."

"Never let it be said that we fail to offer challenging work opportunities."

CORBIN MADDROX
(MODERATOR INVESTIGATOR)

MADDROX

NEMESIS
CORBIN MADDROX

ATTRIBUTES

AGI	AWA	BRW	COO	INT	PER	WIL
10	13	8	9	10	10	10

FIELDS OF EXPERTISE

Combat	+2	1	Movement	+1	–	Social	+2	2
Fortitude	+1	1	Senses	+4	2	Technical	+3	1

DEFENCES

Firewall	12	Resolve	11	Vigour	9
Security	–	Morale	3	Armour	1

ATTACKS
- **Combi Rifle**: Range C/M, 1+8  damage, Burst 2, 2H, Expert 1, MULTI Light Mod, Vicious 1
- **Hacking Device Plus**: CLAW-2, SWORD-1, SHIELD-2, GADGET-3), IC-2, UPGRADE Cybermask, Sucker Punch, White Noise; +2 bonus damage
- **Modhand**: Melee, 1+4 damage, 1H, Concealed 2, E/M, Stun, Subtle 1, Vicious 2

GEAR: Armoured Clothing, SecurCuffs, Recorder

SPECIAL ABILITIES
- **Too Old for This (X Heat)**: Even if he's comparatively young, within Maddrox's chest beats the heart of an authentically grumpy old man. As a Reaction, he can mutter, grumble, and curse his way to +X Morale Soak for himself and all allies in his zone until the end of his next turn.
- **True Moderator**: Maddrox may look like he's about to fall asleep, but he's deceptively sharp behind those bloodshot eyes. As a Reaction, Maddrox can respond to any Infowar attack with an Infowar attack of his own, made at +2 difficulty. This attack is resolved before the enemy attack, and if it causes a Breach, then the original attack is prevented.
- **Seen It All**: Most of it twice. Some of it thrice. When making an Observation test, Madrox can reroll one d20 but must accept the new result.

The androgynous Moderator adjusted their white, grey, and red uniform and stared at Corbin Maddrox, the Moderator Investigator assigned to the case. Reaching for a cup of coffee, Maddrox yawned and checked the holo-files on his station in the small cubicle he called home.

He looked as if he hadn't had much sleep lately, if ever.

"So?" Myr's voice wasn't prying, but it was insistent. "You are going, right?"

"There is nothing to work with here. It is all circumstantial! I am not going into Moreauvia just because the brass thinks we are expendable!"

Myr frowned. "But, they took Olivia. It's right there in the hologram!"

Maddrox rubbed his eyes, brow furrowed. "Perhaps they did. Perhaps they were just helping her. You know exactly that's what the Doctor or whatever weird clone she sends to deal with us will say! Plus, it was inside the Commune, and you know how that goes. Their house, their rules! There is no way they will allow us to perform any kind of investigation within its confines."

He sighed. "Sorry, Myr. You know I'm always here for you, but there's nothing I can do with this case... and you know I liked that Olivia reporter. She had spirit, but this case is as good as closed"

Myr smiled slightly at Maddrox. He returned to shuffling clutter in the chaotic room, as if that would somehow cause the white-haired moderator to leave and hopefully take this problem with them.

"I am sorry, detective. But you fail to notice the fact that we have jurisdiction on this one," Myr said, a smirk emerging on their face.

Maddrox gave up the busywork and sighed: Myr was right.

"The Neoterran... he is dead?"

"On the contrary! Very much alive and demanding we turn over his associate!"

Myr was enjoying every bit of the exchange.

"Dammit! If he'd just had the common sense to get killed by that Pupnik." He closed his eyes, pinching the bridge of his nose. This was already a headache. "Myr? We are screwed. And it looks like I'm off to Moreauvia, Commune A/121, and into the jaws of that crazy Doctor. I hope you still have that spitfire with you?"

APPEARANCE

Maddrox is dishevelled man wearing a Moderator's uniform. Despite dark circles under his eyes, Corbin's eyes are sharp, and his hands are steady. The Moderator has a genuine smile and make eye contact when speaking, although he has a snarky tone.

ROLEPLAYING

- Corbin always complains about everything.
- He acts as if he is hungover, and perhaps he is most of the time.
- He loves coffee and is always searching for his next caffeine fix.

BACKGROUND

Corbin Maddrox really enjoyed being a regular Moderator and every day grumbles at having applied to the evaluation program. Thinking he would be assigned to a fast reaction team like the Taskmasters or even in Vice, he instead was assigned to detective status, and his life got complicated since then. Apparently the only one he fooled acting dumb all this time was himself.

A grumpy old man at heart, Maddrox is a true Moderator, caring for the wellbeing of *Bakunin* and its inhabitants. He gives 110% in each of his cases, which leaves him exhausted and slightly depressed after facing the worst *Bakunin* can offer humanity.

He constantly strives to maintain the balance and the Social Energy between the different Communes and *Bakunin,* but sometimes this proves to be more than even the veteran Moderator can take.

Aqu...
Conti...

Von Moltke

Santiago
de Neoterra

Rommel

ostrum
Ocean

Clausewitz

Splendor
Archipelago

Cook
Ocean

San Pietro
di Neoterra

Novaria

...win

Gratia
Archipelago

San Giovanni
di Neoterra

Serenitas

...nta María
la Soledad

Neapolis

Sybaris

Turoqua

Pax
Continent

Australis
Ocean

NEOTERRA

CREDITS

WRITING
Benn Graybeaton, Jonathan "Killstring" Herzberger, Marc Langworthy, Mark Redacted, Rodrigo Vilanova, Patrycjusz Piechowski, Giles Pritchard, Mitchell German

COVER ART
Ho Seng Hui

INTERIOR ARTWORK
Toma Feizo Gas, Ho Seng Hui, Bagus Hutomo, André Meister, Oh Wang Jing, Vincent Laik, Vladimir, Aituar Manas, Cristian Picu, Antone "Chuck" Pires, Kenny Ruiz and Noiry Lee, Qi Wu, Chester Ocampo, Ignacio Bazán Lazcano, ENIQMA, Pierre Revenau, Gregoire Veaulegere, Kenny Ruiz, Noiry Lee, Ryan Harasim, Aleksi, Cloud, Emilio Rodriguez And Francisco Rico

ART DIRECTION
Marc Langworthy, Rodrigo Vilanova

LAYOUT
Thomas Shook

INFINITY RPG LOGO
Michal E. Cross

LEAD EDITOR
Kimberly Nugent

CARTOGRAPHY
Jose "Gigio" Esteras

SECTORIAL ARMIES LOGOS
Alberto Abal, Carlos Llauger "Bostria" and Hugo Rodriguez

PROOFREADING
T.R. Knight, Marshall Oppel

INFINITY LINE DEVELOPER
Benn Graybeaton

ASSISTANT LINE DEVELOPER
Marc Langworthy

CORVUS BELLI APPROVALS
Gutier Lusquiños Rodríguez, Alberto Abal, Carlos Torres, and Carlos "Bostria" Llauger

ORIGINAL 2D20 SYSTEM DESIGN
Jay Little

GAME DESIGN
Benn Graybeaton, Nathan Dowdell, Mark Redacted, Justin Alexander, Marc Langworthy

PRODUCED BY
Chris Birch

HEAD OF RPG DEVELOPMENT
Sam Webb

PUBLISHING ASSISTANT
Virginia Page

PRODUCTION MANAGER
Peter Grochulski

SOCIAL MEDIA MANAGER
Salwa Azar

COMMUNITY SUPPORT
Lloyd Gyan

SPECIAL THANKS
Thank you to Corvus Belli—Alberto, Gutier, Carlos, and Fernando—for letting us play in your world!

PUBLISHED BY
Modiphius Entertainment Ltd.
2nd Floor, 39 Harwood Road
Fulham, London, SW6 4QP
United Kingdom

Modiphius Entertainment Product Number: MUH050224
ISBN: 978-1-912200-42-9

Artwork & Storyline © Corvus Belli S.L.L. 2018
INFINITY is © Corvus Belli S.L.L. 2018

TABLE OF CONTENTS

WELCOME TO HUMANITY'S FUTURE

"Bright heights and laser lights, busy days and pulsing nights." – A refrain from Club Life, a Top 100 chart breaking song from Maya star Elyse 'L-Ease' Mitchell.

A short refrain which captures the beat, rhythm, verve, and life of PanOceania. Resplendent as the most technologically advanced, wealthy, and sophisticated power in the Human Sphere, PanOceania is proud of its singular achievements and progressive society. The lines between reality and possibility are blurred for citizens of this affluent Hyperpower as they live lives that intermingle the physical and quantronic, blending human existence with the advancements of AR and VR to provide infinite realms of possibility.

The following pages provide an in-depth review of this tech-obsessed Hyperpower, from the opulent lifestyles of the wealthiest corporate magnates to the desperate fight for rights experienced by the most hard-bitten Ateks. Additional details covering topics such as popular entertainments and common security measures will provide rich depth to every game of *Infinity the Roleplaying Game*.

WHAT'S IN THIS BOOK

More than just an expansion, this sourcebook aims to provided a "one-stop shop" for all things PanOceania, including everything needed to create characters, run campaigns, or just immerse oneself completely in the glory of a favoured faction.

CHAPTER 1 – FACTION: PANOCEANIA

As the preeminent Hyperpower, one comparatively microscopic tome could never hope to encompass the magnificence and splendour that is PanOceania. Chapter 1 does, however, aim to provide an insightful overview of this foremost of G5 nations, from current trends in entertainment, to politics and *Empresas*.

In addition to the regular foot soldiers and veteran troops of the PanOceanian military, this chapter takes a look at the iconic guardians of the many branches of the Christian Church, plus some of the more clandestine roles that are employed in boardrooms and on battlefields. An outline of the oft-misunderstood Atek and Helot sub-cultures can also be found here.

CHAPTER 2 – ACONTECIMENTO

The only habitable planet of the Descoberta system also happens to be the industrial powerhouse of PanOceania's might. This chapter provides a unique insight into the Descoberta planetary system, ranging across topics such as the orbitals and planets that pervade the system, the industrial economy that fuels the G5 giant, important landmarks and regions, and the minutiae of life on Acontecimento itself.

CHAPTER 3 – NEOTERRA

Described by many as the shining jewel of the Human Sphere, the PanOceanian capitol of Neoterra is laid bare as never before. This treatise on the undisputed centre of human culture explores the Tencendur system and its stellar inhabitants. With a focus on Neoterra, the chapter covers the planet's regions, indigenous inhabitants, lobby groups, and various aspects of the Christian Church.

CHAPTER 4 – VARUNA

An oceanic paradise, the lush archipelagos and warm depths of Varuna serve as an iconic and attractive tourist spot to humanity at large. The chapter will take nascent travellers beneath the waves of this ocean world, exploring the atolls and islands that dot the planet, the sprawling human capital, Akuna Bay, the floating Lilypads, and the Libertos Terrorist Group.

CHAPTER 5 – PANOCEANIAN PARAPHERNALIA

With a technological edge that surpasses all of their rivals, the gear catalogue section offers a whole host of devices and tools to enhance a PanOceanian's apparent status. Prestige bank accounts, heritage weaponry, iconic jewellery, and a plethora of new arms and armour offer all of the accoutrements a budding socialite would need to polish their image. A number of TAGs and vehicles complete the trappings on offer.

CHAPTER 6 – PANOCEANIAN CHARACTERS

With plenty of technological and sociological advantages, the average PanOceanian receives a unique perspective on life within the Human Sphere from the outset. The Lifepath chapter empowers the creation of PCs that are undeniably attached to *the* Hyperpower thanks to the dedicated tables for birth hosts, homeworlds, adolescent, and career events, and a number of unique careers.

> "PanOceania is the dominant Hyperpower, Moto.tronica a distinguished and prominent megacorp, because we ensure we are always first. As both a Hyperpower and megacorp, we were among the first to recognise the changing dynamics of the political and economic spectrums during the dawn of the Hyperpowers and the Second Great Space Race. We blazed a trail across the stars for others to follow and led the way in establishing a new order that remains sacrosanct to this day. We are, and need to remain, trendsetters, innovators, and pioneers across multiple arenas. Second place is not the PanOceanian way, nor should it be yours."
>
> — Sylvia Greene, CEO of Moto.tronica Advanced Improvements presenting a speech at the megacorp's annual awards ceremony for innovators.

CHAPTER 7 - HELOTS

Misrepresented and misunderstood, the indigenous Helots are an aquatic race that had evolved beneath the oceans of Varuna long before PanOceania staked a claim. This chapter dives beneath the surface of Varuna's oceans to provide an insightful treatise on Helots, including their history, culture, language, and current status within both PanOceania and the Human Sphere. In exploring this unique race one step further, however, the chapter also offers rules on creating a Helot character, which includes additional Lifepath tables and careers that are unique to this marine race.

CHAPTER 8 - ADVERSARIES

No exploration of PanOceania would be complete without a look at some of the functionaries, missionaries, and militants that make the Hyperpower tick. With most of the wild regions of PanOceania's home worlds tamed, the adversaries on offer represent some of the forces at their command should they decide to bring their might to bear.

A number of richly detailed NPCs help to round out the collection of adversaries, each with their own unique storylines and capabilities. From the Knights of Montesa and Paradiso Veterans to Father Knight Harris, there are a number of opportunities to introduce the mighty Hyperpower's unique flavour to any *Infinity* campaign.

CHAPTER 1
FACTION: PANOCEANIA

LIFE AT THE TOP

PanOceania are known as *the* Hyperpower for good reason. As a G5 nation, the giant entity can draw on the economic might of three prosperous systems and several prominent colonies. They can call upon the might of the Christian Church and are able to grace their sizable military with cutting edge weaponry. Even the average citizen is fortunate enough to have access to technological advancements that are the envy of more affluent residents in other nations. Beneath all the glitz and glam, however, there are still those unfortunates who slip through the cracks — the downtrodden and dispossessed. This chapter provides an insightful treatise on what life is like behind the chrome plating of the PanOceanian bubble.

LIVING CITIES

PanOceania has managed to create living spaces that are truly unique, truly something to be envied by the other powers in the Human Sphere. Cities are carefully laid out to manage wind flow between high-rise buildings to minimise damage during storms and funnel winds toward turbines that generate power. A flowing web of roads feed one into the other, with traffic systems automated and run by pseduo-AIs. Solar power, water management, waste disposal, all the day-to-day concerns of any living space are automated for peak efficiency and designed to be as low-impact as possible.

Augmented reality displays signs, directions, traffic, and hazard information. If you're moving through a commercial district, the same systems allow easy and instant access to the Maya storefronts and menus of any shop or eatery you are nearby, allowing you to order, pay, and then walk in and pick up. While you're sitting in the park perusing the menu of a nice restaurant, your geist can be purchasing the items you need from half a dozen stores close by. Automated systems can even package and deliver them to a location of choice, meaning you have more time to enjoy your meal.

Gardens can be found everywhere, full of herbs, vegetables, fruit trees, and more. These privately owned parks have carefully manicured and regularly replenished spaces full of fresh produce available to pick and citizens can help themselves through microtransactions automatically paid through their comlogs. These havens of greenery are not confined to spaces locked between buildings, but flow onto and up the buildings, providing a range of benefits from insulation to better air quality and even improved mental health.

IN THE KNOW
Navigating a PanOceanian city, even if you're new to it, is simple with up-to-date information instantly available through any comlog. Location tracking and facial recognition allows anyone to view the public Maya profile of the people they pass.

On every planet PanOceanian cities can be found, a subtle blending of the natural and the technological can be observed. On Earth, Acontecimento, Neoterra, Varuna, and Svalarheima, the influence of the native flora and landscape can be seen in the shape and layout of the cities themselves. On Earth, the history and architectural fashions of previous eras are accentuated and celebrated. On Acontecimento, the cities overflow with small orchards and the gardens spread onto and over the buildings. On Neoterra, the symbolism of state and religion are pervasive, and the planet is a celebration of the high technology and affluence of PanOceania. On Varuna, great ponds, pools, waterways, and canals dominate the lattice of the city structures and are vital components of the transport systems. On Svalarheima, practicality dominates, with buildings descending into the ground as much as up, thickly insulated against the cold and built to withstand heavy storms.

ENTERTAINMENT

Every possible distraction that could ensnare the mind and senses is available to the PanOceanian citizen. Any flavour of entertainment a person could desire is easy to access, for a price. Blockbuster Maya-streamed dramas and comedies are hugely popular, especially in recent years, those dealing with Paradiso, like *Myrmidon Wars*. The Aoidoi, the propagandists for ALEPH, find plenty of fertile ground in PanOceania, with eager consumers hungry for news, rumours, and insights, but above all, epic stories. The ability to consume media through your comlog or wetware anywhere and anytime has led to the epithet "Zoner," a term for anyone particularly unfocused on the world in front of them.

Music is ubiquitous, with easy listening through wetware or hardware. A vast majority of citizens live their lives to a personal soundtrack. Most geists run a simple algorithm helping match a person's physical context and mood to musical tracks that are a mix of classics, favourites, and new material. Many indie artists and music producers pay Maya services good money to get on the lists most commonly accessed by geists for this purpose, and it's worth it with popular songs enriching, enhancing, and giving a pulse to the lives of billions of citizens at any one time. Some enterprising individuals have even programmed their geists to operate as something like DJs, providing an often eclectic or zany mix of music for people to tune into via Maya (for a simple microtransaction of course).

Aristeia! is the most popular sport on Maya, and Aristos have fan followings that rival the most famous of Maya stars. It is hard to find a workplace or bar where this sport isn't a dominant theme in casual discussion, especially when the Ordeals are on and the intense, surprising, and thrilling fights between the Bahadurs take place!

Maya-based games are a huge industry, one that occasionally exceeds the film industry in terms of revenue. From RPGs to military simulations to civilisation and building games, they are ubiquitous, with high rankings and achievements the life goal of some *surfistas*. It's not uncommon to hear a group of civilians discussing an engagement with the Combined Army as if they were veterans of the Paradiso conflict. The PanOceanian Military Complex has not missed the opportunity these games have provided. Many game development companies are sponsored by the military, and recruitment into the units the games revolve around have made the costs more than worthwhile. A more worrying and increasing trend for some involves the programming of geists or Aspects into a game system, where they monitor players for key skills that will make them suitable for recruitment as Hexas, TAG, or ship pilots.

Entertainment and social media are so intertwined that the two blur into one another. Evercasting has become a popular trend in recent years, but even without that, the degree to which a person is liked and followed by others, and particularly a person's publicised political leanings and the lobbies they support, are regularly a factor in job interviews. For many, the effort to ensure they are liked, followed, and adored on Maya is significant.

INFORMATION

Information on any and every subject is easy to obtain from the vast quantronic data banks of the Human Sphere and Maya network. From the esoteric to the obvious, never before has so much knowledge been readily available at the fingertips of so many.

Geists perform a vital role in the gathering of information, with most being more than capable of tracking down data even on obscure or hard to find topics. Geists have been known to develop strange attractions to specific topic areas, or follow their search patterns into esoteric areas that attract the attention of law enforcement and even the Hexahedron.

Interaction between geists in the sphere of information sharing has led to many geists forming interdependent bonds with one another even if the people they belong to have never met. The military has, in the past, had some issues with troop movements and locations inadvertently being shared through geist interactions, which is why military personnel are required to limit their geists to specific military networks.

Maya has a vast store of useful information, and using wetware, a person can run apps to overlay a simulation on top of the real world, mapping their actions to the simulation to achieve the desired result. Crackdowns on videos related to lock-breaking, hacking, munitions manufacturing, and even piloting have only had limited success in restricting the application of such simulations.

EDUCATION

All public education is Maya-based, with the government funding online schools where a single teacher and a suite of adaptive algorithms can service the educational needs of hundreds of students, who never need leave their homes. "School days" are something of an anachronism, instead students are expected to log a certain number of hours in a specific set of classes, and spend a set amount of time interacting with online peers. The number of students who have managed to trick the system by using their geist to log the hours for them has encouraged local governments to look at physical systems that match a student to a Maya space. This has worried some child safety groups, who point out such systems can be hacked just as easily and pose a potential risk to the students.

Every online school also provides firewalled "playgrounds" for the students beacuse even online, social interaction is vital. These playgrounds are carefully designed to provide a wide range of entertainment types, all of which can involve one or many of the school students, and encourage interaction and social behaviour.

Physical schools in PanOceania, outside smaller settlements and outposts, is the preserve of the wealthy. Such schools are typically privately run, and access to them can be expensive. While they often flaunt their consistently high grades, the real reason the rich send their children to such schools is for the contacts they make while attending.

For adults wishing to extend themselves, change careers, or follow a passion, Maya again has the answer: the official Maya-Based School Network approves thousands of courses, every year, across a wide range of subjects. It is typical for a PanOceanian citizen to have several degrees or certificates, regardless of their occupation.

PRIVACY

The quantronic revolution arrived with an impact felt in every aspect of life. Devices became exponentially more powerful, smaller, and eventually migrated into wetware: implants that "wearers" interact with through conscious will alone. One aspect of life significantly impacted by the development of technology was the concept of privacy. The concept of privacy never eroded, but it evolved with technology, and attitudes toward privacy, alongside the technology that impacted it, became pervasive aspects of the broader culture.

PanOceania is an open society: its citizens have a concept of privacy that often startles and frightens a citizen from less technologically immersed cultures like Ariadna, or more libertarian ones like the Nomads. Even for conservative PanOceanians, concerns over nudity, relationships, and gender roles are a hang-up of the past. Society has moved forward, and the concept of private and public has morphed as technology changed.

Interference technology has seen a boom in the last few decades, as sensors capable of recording sound, vision, heat, movement, and other factors have grown in ubiquity, reduced in size, and are able to be relocated with ease, often remotely piloted. Interference devices typically provide a bubble of "noise" that inhibits sensors from being able to discern useful information from the background they generate. At recorded events involving high-profile politicians, business people, and the like, those with any social position are trained to cover their mouths and throat while speaking with one another, lest any conversation be modelled from the movements of their lips and larynx. Most important communication is made via firewalled "rooms" in Maya keyed to specific participants, where communication is virtual rather than physical. Multiples of such tense meetings can be taking place at the same time as a physical event involving smiles, handshakes, and waves to the cameras.

EMPRESAS

Some projects are too vast and too risky for private enterprise to consider them. Projects on such a scale require a huge number of specialists working with high-end technology in order to make the breakthroughs required for success. In PanOceania such ventures are called *empresas*. To fund them money is funnelled from the government, as well as from corporate interests hoping to gain a technological edge over their competitors, into proposed *empresas*.

The selection of *empresas* is usually a governmental decision, but is typically strongly influenced by lobby groups, and by the corporate interests providing additional funding or support. Once given the green light by parliamentary vote, an *empresa* is formed, a project management team is selected, and it begins the arduous task of assembling the facilities required to explore and complete the project. *Empresas* can be generational, with

LET'S GET POLITICAL

Some game companies have been on the receiving end of a strong backlash for deliberately trying to leverage the popularity of their gaming platforms by including political messages, sometimes even hidden ones, as subplots, side stories, and Easter eggs. *Man Down* is one such game, a popular first-person shooter set against the backdrop of the Second Paradiso Offensive. The game devs received criticism and even death threats for their portrayal of PanOceania's involvement in the Teseum trade on Ariadna, a side plot relating to one of the NPCs in the game that painted PanOceania as the ruthless exploiter of a weaker nation, implicating several PanOceanian companies indirectly. The NPC and story line at the centre of the furore were quickly removed from game.

THE PROFESSIONAL FILTER

With street cameras, drones, Maya tracking, and with a wash of citizens posting images, sound, and video of themselves and their surroundings, it can be difficult to work a job that requires secrecy and anonymity. Infowar specialists with Bureau Noir, the Hexahedron, and other such agencies spend considerable time and effort making sure their operatives remain secret. Facial scrubbing, video manipulation, wearable tech, even old-fashioned prosthetics, make-up, and body doubles are used on a regular basis.

Another result of the public nature of the PanOceanian experience is the need for intelligence, services to provide their agents with a trackable counterpart. This is in large part supplied by infowar specialists, but body doubles and even Lhost copies have been used to deflect an enemy agency away from the real operative. Insidiously, there have been rare cases in which agents have been forced to track versions of themselves, sometime resulting in both going rogue in a struggle for the one identity. It is ironic in a sense, as running multiple copies of a Cube is highly illegal and severely punished. Intelligence services will always claim their actions serve a higher good, and must, due to the nature of their operational requirements, push boundaries to achieve success and safety for the Hyperpower.

THE CRETAN ENTERPRISE

The Cretan Enterprise pushed the boundaries of the Minotaur engine and gave the Human Sphere the foundation for the wormhole-capable ships currently in use. It was a triumph of singular vision, and while it came with an enormous price tag, the benefits have been incalculable.

several teams working for decades over the life of the project.

There are several well-known and celebrated *empresas* currently running, and an unknown number being quietly carried out through a mix of government and lobby funding.

ARKVAULTS

Two great ArkVaults are currently in construction, one in the Tencendur system and the other in an unnamed dark system. Built within giant asteroids, and both partially operational, they are designed to hold and protect seeds, fertilised eggs, and the genetic blueprints of every living thing encountered by the human species, including humans themselves. Inside the ArkVaults, beneath layers of heavy rad-shielding, are also Cube Banks and organic printers. These vast archives are powered by great jump-capable engines and contain a host of CPUs run by a splinter of ALEPH. They are a security measure, a resource in times of need, and if the worst possible outcome should descend upon the Sphere, the last hope for the human race.

THE HAND OF THE LORD

Originally devised as a military program that sought to reduce training time for elite soldiers and lessen the impact of shock on new combatants. The program integrated foreign memories with a soldier's Cube: an experimental spin-off of the Resurrection process where the goal was to create a highly trained and experienced soldier in minutes. The program has been a boondoggle plagued by Cube corruption, dysmorphic disorders, cost overruns, and severe problems with muscle reflex sitting out-of-sync with the subjects' mental reactions. The Hand of the Lord has shown some successes with language training and academic studies, but the costs compared to translation suites and analytic programs is exorbitant to the point where these successes have been completely downplayed by the program operators lest they fuel calls for the entire project to be cut.

DYSON SWARM

Recently initiated in the Tencendur system, amid much fanfare and celebration, is the beginning of a single ring Dyson Swarm. A multitude of small satellites will eventually form a ring around Tencendur, gathering energy output from the star and beaming it back via laser to collection stations on Neoterra. Simultaneously, a large team of engineers has been working on prototypes of the self-replicating robots that will be used to take over construction of the ring. Once built it should meet the energy needs of Neoterra many times over and lay the foundations for PanOceania's energy needs into the future.

LOBBIES

Lobby groups in PanOceania are the confluence of political will and financial power. The current lobby system is an attempt to divorce political and economic power and give strength to the voice of the people.

Lobbies can be large or small, wealthy, or just well meaning. They are the policy engines for the Hyperpower, a direct voice from the people providing instruction on what PanOceania should look like today and into tomorrow.

FALCO

A military lobby backed financially by a variety of weapons manufacturers, most notably Moto.tronica, and with a huge number of members across all of PanOceania's settlements. Extremely popular with military and ex-military personnel, Falco lobbies for a dominant and well-funded military, as well as neoconservative economic policies that tend to be insular in focus. With the Paradiso conflict raging, Falco has seen a boom in members and influence.

NIRUKTA

A small but wealthy lobby supported by and pushing social policies geared to support Hindu businesses and interest groups. In the past the Nirukta lobby had success pushing through popular policies related to the Cultural Integration Programs.

SUPERBIA

A right-leaning conservative lobby group, tied to a range of business interests, universities, and religious groups. It has been largely Superbia, in recent years, that has pushed for PanOceania to stop paying to "prop up" O-12, citing a range of technicalities to avoid their payments.

ZEITGEIST

A lobby group funded by hardware and wetware companies, and has a broad following in the technophiliac PanOceania. Zeitgeist has, in the past, looked to modify regulations surrounding privacy laws and implanted technology. It has also pushed for an *empresa* to create an open source operating system for person-to-Maya integration, which would shake up corporate ownership laws and allow more program suites to operate across different platforms.

MILITARY DETAILS

From infantry holding key ground locations to ships providing firepower from orbit, the PanOceanian Military Complex is the largest, most sophisticated, and capable military force in the Human Sphere.

FUSILIERS

Nearly every successful military operation, at some point, relies on boots on the ground. Whether the frozen wastes of Svalarheima or the steaming violence of Paradiso, the most used boots on the ground belong to the Fusiliers. This light infantry corps is ubiquitous, and units can be found in every PanOceanian territory. Well trained and often working in tandem with heavy support units and spec-ops teams, the Fusiliers are the starting point for any young hopeful entering the PanOceanian Military Complex.

Recruitment offices can be found throughout PanOceanian territories, with enlistment an easy process of identity verification and a fitness test. Training camps are widespread, with basic training building discipline, endurance, strength, weapons, and field skills. Typically, basic training is a 12– to 16-week course, with further specialisations available as Riflemen, or Support Corps (frontline soldiers and support weapon crews respectively). If a recruit makes it through this gruelling experience they advance to the rank of Private, with promotions available to Corporal, Sergeant, and Warrant Officer before further training is required for the Commissioned Ranks (Lieutenant and above).

Whether they join for patriotism, money, adventure, or to pay off a debt to society, members of the Fusiliers can be sure they are entering a fraternity built on courage and teamwork. Basic training remoulds a civilian into a soldier, and deployment hardens them further still. The Fusiliers are the backbone of the Military Complex, charging into the fire of conflict with bravery and tenacity.

Standing Orders: Fusilier units are typically made up of soldiers recruited together, serving as part of their respective Planetary Armies. Units are barracked on military properties scattered throughout the Human Sphere, they may be close to a front line or in orbit around a planet, but they are commonly stationed near training bases, and can be found in most cities throughout PanOceania. Orders coming from the strategic arm of the Military Complex based in a unit's area of operation will brief a commanding officer on an operation and operational parameters. That officer then assembles the teams required to carry out the operation, and briefs the Fusiliers involved. The soldiers that make up the teams used for smaller operations tend to serve together repeatedly, as it is widely recognised that the bonds of trust and interdependence forged in conflict can be an important factor if complications arise.

Where a unit will be going, for what purpose, and who they'll be fighting is information passed from top down through the chain of command. The

Fusiliers maintain a ready disposition at all times because their missions are varied and can be given a month or more in advance or mere hours before the soldiers ship out. A Fusilier always keeps their bags packed and ready in case they need to move out suddenly. The old motto "hurry up and wait" is still very much a part of the life of a Fusilier.

Locust Clandestine Action Team: If Hexas agents have a reputation for brutal efficiency, the Locusts hardly have a reputation at all, and that is much more frightening. Their motto is Vis Invisibilis (Invisible Power), and they impose it fully. The Locusts are the field agents for a division of the Hexahedron known as the Big Nothing, a division so secret even its existence is classified, known only to the Inner Hexahedron and the intelligence agencies around the Sphere that have had the misfortune of encountering them.

Locusts extend the power of PanOceanian will outside the territories of the Hyperpower. Operating under deep cover, Locusts are trained to change their identities as quickly as changing a shirt, and everything, from surgical modification to support from the Big Nothing infowar specialists, makes sure these identities are as legitimate as born citizens. The Locusts are deadly and use a wide-ranging, fatally precise skill set to execute the will of PanOceania irrespective of means or consequences.

By Invitation Only: Locusts are usually recruited from the ranks of the military and particularly the Hexahedron, though there are notable examples of agents with talent invited from mercenary or civilian backgrounds. The reality is the Big Nothing farms the data suites collected by the Hexahedron for candidates, from whatever background, who show an aptitude for subterfuge, deception, killer instincts, and psychopathic tendencies as those qualities indicate a willingness to ignore potential moral or legal consequences in the pursuit of their goals without regret. Actual weapons training is important, but not vital, as training programs can build muscle memory more easily than they can remould a person's psychology. Locusts are not people who enjoy killing and mayhem, but rather, people who are willing to use both to meet their objectives, and are not overly burdened by the consequences of their choices.

Once a potential candidate has been identified, they are monitored for a period of time before contact is made. Recruits are usually lured by a mix of patriotic appeal and by the money and opportunity serving affords. Initially recruits are led to believe they have been earmarked for service as Hexas agents; if a recruit manages to survive their training, they are fully briefed on their role and

MAID OF ORLEANS

Over a thousand analysts, programming experts, neuroscientists, psychologists, transpersonal psychotherapists, historians, and more laboured for years to develop and nurture the first reincarnation: Joan of Arc. Her efforts as part of the Order of the Hospital have been phenomenal, a living and transcendent heroine, she is a like a demi-goddess to the people of PanOceania.

Lobbies. See Infinity Corebook, p. 180

BOOTS ON THE GROUND

The Fusiliers can be found on guard duties for high security complexes, Vila Boosters, and stations. They serve on the front line in conflicts across the Human Sphere and in small team operations dealing with paramilitary criminal groups. More often than not, if an objective must be held until the cavalry arrives, it is the Fusiliers who have that thankless task.

Storm the Barricades: A small hand-picked team of Fusiliers are ordered to don civvies and mix in with a crowd of potential rioters. Their objective is to identify the ringleaders, and when the proverbial hits the fan, take them out. Pacifying violent rioters and supporting local law enforcement in settling the riot are secondary orders.

Hold the Fort: A small team of Fusiliers are supporting an anti-smuggling naval operation in the outer system. The naval ship cripples a smuggler with a hold full of illegal Silk and other contraband. The Fusiliers are dumped on board to secure the crew and hold the ship until the cargo can be removed "like it was never there." Trouble is, some Corsairs have a different idea: to them the Silk belongs to Haqqislam!

Trouble in Paradise: It should have been a simple mop-up job: find the downed rotor and retrieve the Cube of a long-range recon scout it was supposed to be carrying home. Then the Combined Army showed up. Why are the Combined Army so far from their lines? What could the scout have a record of that they are so eager to get? Where is the cavalry?

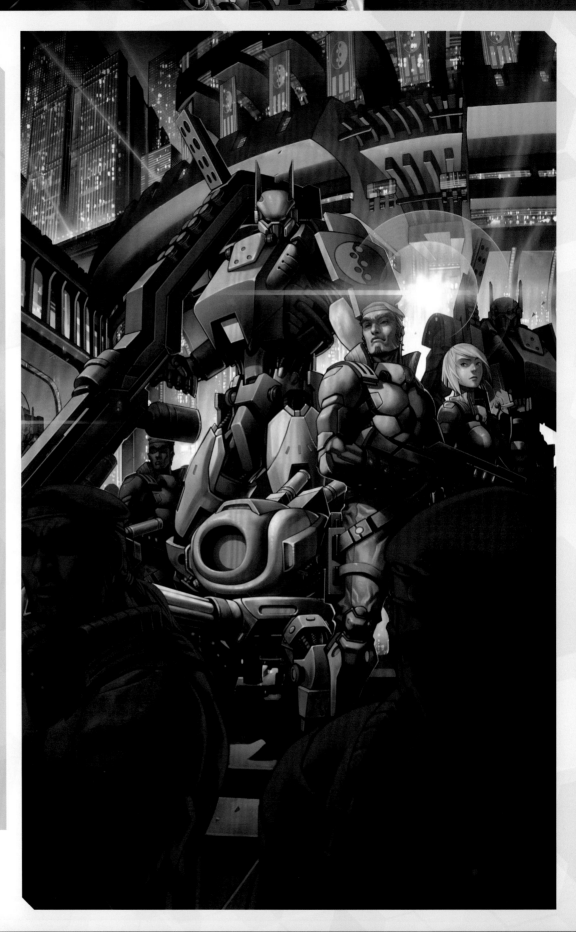

operational parameters. Training is extreme and it is not uncommon for recruits to suffer mental or physical breakdowns, or even die. Locust recruits will experience gruelling spec-ops training camps, train alongside Hexas agents, learn languages, customs, and cultures, and finally work missions with a mentor for a period of time in PanOceanian space, before being promoted to Locust, and given their first assignments beyond PanOceanian borders.

Sleep Walking: Once on operation (known as Sleep Walking) a Locust is expected to "go dark": they are sleeper agents, wandering the Circulars and Human Sphere until triggered. Locusts are expected to live for extended periods in deep-cover, and different agents, depending on their backgrounds, will have an affinity for certain social circles: criminal, hacker, political, business, mercenary, or military. They are provided the initial support to fill whatever societal role they decide is relevant, but are expected to operate completely autonomously, their true identities buried beneath their deep-cover façades.

Each agent has a keyed trigger which may be as benign as a specific pattern of interference in a Maya broadcast, a simple message or phrase, quantronic signals, or physical meet-ups. Once triggered, the agent will become active, seeking out their mission parameters, which may be delivered through a coded or cryptic hard copy, memory stick, data package, or via a quantronic briefing. An agent never meets or sees their commanders from the Big Nothing, they are deniable assets, often mistaken for criminals, dissidents, and terrorists by the authorities their actions impact.

It is typical for agents to work alone or in small teams, spending years from home at a time. Locusts identify each other through subtle hand signals and coded phrases that seem like odd twitches and ordinary conversation to anyone who might be observing. Once a mission is received and executed, the agent moves on, shedding their assumed persona for a new name and background, Sleep Walking again, prepared to be triggered, always ready to strike.

THE MILITARY ORDERS

The Military Orders provide the Neovatican church with a physical power unparalleled among the religions of PanOceania. These modern-day knights are iconic, the Orders famous, adored by fans, and idealised by Maya dramas and they are unique to PanOceania. More than just popularised symbols though, they are capable of exerting and imposing and imposing physical force, and the Knights of the Orders are warriors feared across the Human Sphere for their ability, prowess, and unrelenting faith.

Confrère Knights: Confrère Knights are an outfit of Knights fighting under the direction of one Order, but who belong to a different Order. Such Knights, seconded to serve a different Order, are organised as a Company (in the case of large operations) or a Sect (in the case of smaller operations). Companies may be a dozen or more Knights, each often accompanied by a small unit of Order Sergeants from their respective Orders, and are used in conflicts, especially on Paradiso. Sects are a smaller group of Knights sent on highly specific missions, usually unsupported, and expected to be able to operate autonomously to reach their stated mission objectives.

SLEEP WALKERS

Locusts are given missions that often go against every covenant of the articles of war, their targets can be military, civilian, criminal, or government; they don't ask questions, just coldly get the job done.

Supernova: A young and popular Yu Jingese political star, born on Svalarheima, has become a strong activist voice speaking against PanOceanian interests on the ice planet. Arranging his apparent suicide would do much to discredit the cause.

Escalation: The Locusts are imbedded in a Mercenary crew given the job of roughing up and bullying some local Ariadnans to ease negotiations for a subsidiary of Gāng Tie Industries to secure mining rights to the area. Engineering the situation to escalate from some low-level bullying to a borderline atrocity will ruin any chance of Gāng Tie Industries gaining the mining rights.

Shadow in the Shadows: A Locust is directed to serve deep-cover as a Nomad agent assigned to Bureau Noir with mission parameters involving leaking operational details to the Hexahedron. After securing the trust of the group through several missions they are to fatally betray the cover of the Bureau Noir team they are operating with, discrediting the Nomads.

RANK AND FILE

Each Order has its own structure, but by and large they all follow the model set by the Order of the Hospital. Each Order also has its own field of expertise, and ranks and domains that match those specialisations tend to be given more weight within the Order.

Grand Master: The supreme authority within an Order, and elected by council. The Grand Master is typically supported by one or more chosen Piliers, a rank of prestige usually occupied by Abbots.

Abbot Colonel: Head of the military wing of the Order, the Abbot Colonel is the leader of the Strategic Council.

Abbot Commodore: Head of the naval wing of the Order, this rank fluctuates in importance, depending on the specific Military Order. The Abbot Commodore sits on the Strategic Council.

Abbot Conservator: Head of the infowar wing of the Order, and in charge of the Chaplains of Obedience who specialise in this field. The Abbot Conservator is also in charge of maintaining the records of the Order, and all propaganda coming from the Order. The Abbot Conservator sits on the Strategic Council.

Abbot Marshal: Head of the research and development wing of the Order, specifically related to weapons manufacture and TAGs, but different Orders have different specialities. The Abbot Marshal sits on the Strategic Council.

Master and Commander: Head of a specific facility run by the Order, usually belongs to another rank category as well. The role of Master and Commander is a signifier of both prestige and competence, as well as a functional role.

Marshal: In charge of maintaining the vehicles, TAGs, and powered armour used from any base of operations to which they are assigned. Usually expert technicians.

Father-Officers: Highly experienced and elite Father-Knights, may be called to sit on the Strategic Council depending on their area of expertise. Father-Officers usually serve as the on-the-ground leaders of military detachments and groups of the Order. Father-Officers are ordained priests.

Standard Bearer: In charge of organising and running the training programs of the Squires, and coordinating the Father Instructors at specific training facilities.

Father-Instructors: Previously Father-Officers or Father-Knights of experience and wisdom. Father-Instructors serve as teachers and advisors in military schools across Pan Oceania. Father-Instructors are ordained priests.

Father-Knights: The elite soldiers of the Military Orders, iconic and feared throughout the Human Sphere. They come in many varieties depending on their speciality, unit, and Order. Father-Knights are ordained priests, and often take the field as front-line chaplains.

Brothers of Office: Symbolically equal in rank to the Father-Knights, but lacking prestige, Brothers of Office are would-be Knights unable to meet the strict standards for admission as a Knight. The Brothers of Office are the bureaucratic managers of the Chaplains of Obedience.

Chaplains of Obedience: Sitting outside the ranking structure of the Order, the Chaplains of Obedience are the bureaucrats and technicians who maintain and run every aspect of the Order, from logistics to office supplies, infowar, and propaganda.

Order Sergeants: The rank and file of the Order. Order Sergeants can be career soldiers in the Order, volunteers from other units, or even paid members, but all of them are there to support the actions of the Knights.

Order Associate: The rank given to anyone who has paid for the opportunity to "belong" to an Order, but who does not actually serve any function within the Order. These are typically benefactors and wealthy followers.

Companies or Sects of Confrère Knights are usually gathered at the behest of the Order leading the operation, the Church (particularly the Curia), or as a result of a governmental or private request, the latter only in cases where the private company or individual is a significant patron of the Church. Requests for Confrère operations are usually processed by the Church, and sent out as a general call to the Military Orders. Orders respond by either hand-picking Father-Knights (rarely other ranks are selected), or by allowing Father-Knights to volunteer. If the operation requires a Company, Father-Knights given the blessing to go will then select the Order Sergeants (if any) to accompany them.

Once selected, a Company or Sect will assemble in a single location, usually a training facility run by the lead Order, and there they will have a short period of time to get to know one another, both personally and professionally. The Orders allow this period because they understand that knowing the people you serve alongside can make a significant impact on the success of a mission. Alongside this period, the Master and Commander in charge of the Confrère gathering will run any relevant training sessions, and a series of briefings to inform the Confrère Knights of their mission objectives, likely conditions, opposition, and so on. Sects are treated a little differently: due to the varied nature of their missions, and the small number of Confrère Knights, they spend their time more informally undergoing briefings and planning together, with greater access to local infowar specialists to help lay the groundwork for their specific mission.

OTHER FACTION DETAILS

ATEKS

PanOceania is a civilisation that unites two worlds, the physical reality and the augmented reality. The ubiquity of the comlog, either as hardware or wetware, geists, and continual access to Maya are vital components of the PanOceanian experience. The ability to access and interact with the augmented and connected aspect of society is taken for granted as it provides access to financial services, education, entertainment, and a vast majority of occupations require it.

Ateks, the disenfranchised poor who exist at the bottom rung of PanOceanian society, are denied access to the basic entitlements of full citizens. They lack the the financial means to stay current with vital updates and often have limited access to Maya. As a result, Ateks lack the capacity to engage with PanOceanian society as full citizens. Some have chosen this life, fearful that the march of technology seeks, under the guidance of ALEPH, to break and reshape the human mould and supplant

the species. Others have fallen on hard times, suffer physical or mental impairments which they cannot afford to have treated, or are criminals seeking to live a life without the all-seeing eye of "Big Brother" looking over their shoulder. A majority of Ateks though are born to it, they inherit their status from parents and grandparents and lack the supports required for social mobility.

There are many organisations seeking to provide some level of help for Ateks, to assist them to integrate or reintegrate into PanOceanian society. But these are few and overstretched. The slums fringing the cities of PanOceania see more babies born every year. The difficulties facing an Atek seeking to change their social standing are institutionally arrayed against them. A broad lack of empathy for their situation coupled with a complete ignorance for just what barriers exist for an Atek seeking to integrate combine to feed a prejudice that compounds the problem utterly.

Education, access to technology, and wealth are all significant factors in empowerment, but each of them is an almost insurmountable hurdle laced with bigotry on all sides. Above all else, an Atek seeking to integrate needs access to the support structures that exist in order to affect that change, and support is hard to find and grudgingly given.

A broad attitude among PanOceanian citizens is that the Ateks don't want to change or integrate, and the more prejudiced go further to add a range of stereotypical reasons for this, typically linked to crime. If they wanted to change they would, if they wanted to change they'd do something to affect that change... these arguments are common among PanOceanian groups advocating policies laced with slogans like the popular "Ateks Out!" campaign.

For a vast majority of Ateks, life means a struggle to find work or make a better life from their situation. The slums they live in survive on a cash-, barter-, and favour-based economy, and they find what work they can as manual labourers and unskilled itinerant workers, often exploited. Whether in areas dominated by agriculture or industry, the picture is similar: Ateks live in slums, a ramshackle tangle of housing often devoid of proper sanitation, hot water, widely distributed electricity, and other hallmarks of modern civilisation.

Transports owned by factory, farm, or orchard owners roll into the slums early each morning, Ateks pile in, and once full, the transport is off to deliver its cargo to a long day of manual labour. Pay is appalling, and meals for workers often have to be purchased with their wages. Holding little power to rock the status quo (speaking out or complaining could earn a blacklisting – meaning no more work),

UNDER THE CROSS

Sects of Confrère Knights are sent on a wide range of mission types through PanOceanian space, into the Human Sphere and beyond. They are expected to carry themselves with skill and absolute bravery in the face of often bitter opposition. They are sent by the Church (or their Orders) under the symbol of the Cross, doing the Lord's work in dealing with those who seek to undermine Him. At times Sects will operate proudly as Confrère Knights, at other times their missions will demand the secrecy of cover.

Exorcism: Rumours that an old Templar artefact containing an AI have surfaced. The Confrère Sect must travel undercover to the Human Edge, where the auction for this artefact is rumoured to be taking place. They must discover its origins and previous owners before destroying it and the AI it is purported to hold.

Corrupted Deeds: The Church discovered a wayward priest illegally awarded points for Deeds (see List of Deeds) not fulfilled. The Confrère Sect must discover who has been awarded these points and have them stripped. In this process they learn the falsely awarded points have been used to rig Resurrections for members of a local crime syndicate. The wrongly Resurrected must be vanquished, and the crime syndicate crushed.

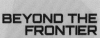

BEYOND THE FRONTIER

A Brave New World: A probe has sent back promising signs that an inhabitable moon orbits a gas giant in the system. The Space Exploration Division dispatched a survey crew to make a thorough analysis of its viability. However, a small ghost ship slipped the blockade of Paradiso and covertly set up a well-hidden outpost of Shasvastii pioneers here. What could this moon hide that is so important to the EI?

A Hidden Danger: Spectral analysis indicates a star is surrounded by a tight asteroid ring. A survey mission has been dispatched to carry out mineral analysis of the asteroids and earmark potential sites for a mining conglomeration. However, pirates loyal to the Nomads have been using this hidden location as a ship-yard and staging platform for their attacks against shipping lanes in PanOceanian space.

Pressure Cooker: While studying the mineral compositions of an asteroid ring close by an alien star, a sudden solar storm has fried many of the ship's systems. The PCs must get the ship back online before it drifts dangerously into the asteroid ring. At the same time, an exploratory craft of Yu Jing origin seems to be hailing them — are they a threat, or do they need help?

Ateks struggle daily, let alone have the financial capacity to change their station.

As a result, crime flourishes in Atek slums, not only because they are free from the continual monitoring of PanOceanian society, but because organised crime networks and gangs do a better job supporting their communities. Law enforcement in an Atek slum will find themselves stonewalled at every step: the Ateks know who best serves their interests, and it isn't the state.

SPACE EXPLORATION DIVISION

A considerable amount of money is poured from the state coffers into the PanOceanian Space Exploration Division, the most extensive and well-equipped fleet of exploratory ships in the Human Sphere.

The main function of the Space Exploration Division is exploration, which is not just a govern- ment-run activity. It is typical for the PanOceanian Space Exploration Division to jointly fund or even sponsor corporate exploration and mining projects. The search for habitable worlds is fundamental, but so is the industrial and corporate demand for raw resources. Star systems with planets, proto-plane- tary disks, and even dark systems are all important discoveries able to be exploited for gain.

Survey and exploration craft used by the Space Exploration Division are either unmanned probes or small ships manned by a minimal crew of mixed science and martial backgrounds. Mission parameters for expeditions fall into two categories: exploration and survey. In exploration missions the parameters are left intentionally loose. Spectral analysis of a star system may indicate the presence of planetary or protoplanetary bodies, and even provide some significant details on what is likely to be present, but the mission objectives are typically set around the confirmation of results and then left to the team to select a series of points to explore. Survey missions are more specific and usually follow on from probe explorations. When surveying, teams are expected to provide specific details, whether on particular bodies orbiting the star or on mineral compositions of accretion disks or asteroid rings. Survey missions serve a mix of governmental and corporate objectives: the discov- ery of new places to settle, where facilities may be constructed, or the discovery of mineral resources to be exploited by enterprise.

CHAPTER 2
ACONTECIMENTO

Industrial powerhouse and breadbasket for PanOceania, Acontecimento is the workhorse of the Hyperpower's economy. The capacity of Acontecimento, and its centrality to the influence and might of PanOceania is difficult to overstate. While Neoterra is the brighter, faster, and flashier heart of PanOceanian politics and corporate dealing, Acontecimento is the mainstay of the Hyperpower's success. Without the bounty produced by Acontecimento, PanOceania would not enjoy the wealth and prosperity synonymous with its name.

CLIMATE AND GEOGRAPHY

A somewhat elliptical orbit combined with its axial tilt produces a strange balance in seasonal changes for Acontecimento. As the planet orbits its star Descoberta, this combination of factors makes for a relatively stable yearly season in the northern hemisphere, while allowing the southern latitudes to enjoy a more differentiated range of seasonal changes. Even so, seasons across Acontecimento

are only slight climactic differences compared to any other planet in the Human Sphere; at the most extreme latitudes the planet still enjoys a year-round mild climate, ideal for continual growth and production.

Geographically, the surface of Acontecimento is dominated by sweeping plains and gentle hills. Only on the Vishwa Archipelago and the Magalhães continent are there anything resembling mountain chains. Tectonically active, the myriad of small plates that make up the crust of the planet are driven by the volcanism of deep ocean rifts, which cause the small plates to jostle each other in two broadly circular "currents", with the majority of the plates meeting in transform boundaries. Earthquakes are common, but typically not severe, and most Aconteccans are used to the gentle shivering that regularly punctuates their lives. The tectonic activity can be disconcerting to visitors who are often concerned it is a preamble to something bigger, but it is such a normal part of the background rhythm to life on Acontecimento that natives barely notice it.

This continual movement creates a shifting pattern of fissures and canyons throughout the continents of Acontecimento. Much research has been poured into the mapping of plate boundaries and movements to help predict and monitor these potentially dangerous features.

Climactically, the planet enjoys a continual warmth that extends far into the northern and southern latitudes. Rainfall over a majority of the planet's surface is regular and plentiful year-round, and few areas see temperatures drop to the point where it snows. This is ideal for many staple Earth crops, which, since their introduction, have flourished. Wide grasslands allow for livestock herds in massive numbers. Such are the size of herds being intensively farmed on the vast Aconteccan pasture lands that some scientists have raised concerns over the long-term effect they may have on the greenhouse gas levels and climate of the planet itself. Vast tracts of land have also been dedicated to agricultural zones, which, due to both the fertility of the soil and the beneficent climate, produce an immense quantity of crops year round, enough not only to support the needs of Acontecimento and PanOceania broadly, but also surplus to trade.

A million years ago Acontecimento was dominated by jungle and old-growth rainforests, now the remnants of these ancient forests hold out in specially maintained forest reserves, the largest of which is the Great Arboreal Reserve on the Aryavarta continent. This vast jungle sees almost continual rainfall, and the emission of oxygen, water vapour, and other gases from this huge jungle affects the climate of the entire planet. As a carbon sink it does much to provide flexibility for Acontecimento's massive industrial complex, and allows the planet to be less careful with the management of its factories than is required in more delicate ecosystems. The forests, in fact, have a huge stabilising effect on the planetary climate, and this has been one of the key reasons for spending so much to protect them from the advance of the grasslands and clear-felling industries.

The polar regions of Acontecimento are small considering the size of the planet, but unsurprising given the generally mild climate. Terra de Gelo in the south is an archipelago layered with ice sheets which grow weak during the torrid melts of the summer. In the north, Terra de Neve is little more than a large swathe of pack ice, continually broken and moving with the warm currents driving north between the Aryavarta and Camões continents.

FIELDS OF DESTRUCTION

The grasses of Acontecimento come in a wide number of species, all of which share some unique traits. They are able to proliferate quickly, with a rapid life cycle that allows them to quickly consume new land, or areas decimated by fire. The grasses caused some major headaches in the early days of settlement, competing with crops introduced from Earth and reclaiming cleared land almost as quickly as it had been cleared. The grasses on Acontecimento have extensive rhizome networks, which extend as much as a foot or more into the ground and constantly enrich the soil with nutrients like nitrogen. A majority of the grass species go to seed every few weeks, and their tiny seeds are almost exclusively distributed by the wind. It is a constant task to keep cropland free of the grasses, even with specially designed weed agents applied on a regular basis. Some politicians have proposed initiating a program of extermination, but the grasses provide such a mineral wealth to the soil that it is simply not worth doing. Rather, crop farms will rotate fields which are left fallow, allow the grasses to move in, and after a few cycles, spray them before replanting the crops. This ensures the soil maintains its nutrient-rich state and overall increases yield.

FLORA

Acontecimento is a strange hybrid of extensively farmed Earth crops and robust native plant life. When the first settlers arrived, Acontecimento was widely covered with vast grasslands punctuated by patches of huge old-growth forests. It was discovered early in the settlement phase that the native grasses were aggressively capable of breaking down wood, and the advancing grasslands were slowly eating away at the remaining forests. Careful studies of the planet's biosphere led to a program of protection for the forested areas, which was executed through the establishment of huge reserves designed to protect the old-growth forests and jungles from further destruction. These reserves, the largest and most famous of which is the Great Arboreal Reserve, have done much to maintain the native flora and fauna of Acontecimento despite the extensive farming practices carried out.

One of the significant downsides of Acontecimento's grasslands is that several varieties produce an extremely fine pollen which can play havoc with anyone prone to hay fever or asthma. Stormy weather in areas dominated by these particular species can be especially dangerous. Storms pull the pollen up into the atmosphere where they absorb moisture causing them to burst into smaller allergenic particles which can induce sudden and dangerous asthma attacks, even in people not prone to suffering from asthma. Each year there are many cases of Aconteccans dying as a result. Pollen counting and weather prediction services combine data to identify risk areas to provide early warning of such events.

There are multiple species of grasses which live in great clumps, floating in huge tangled blooms on the ocean surface. These blooms move with the currents and are as vibrant with life as coral reefs.

The thick jungles of the Great Arboreal Reserve have been likened to stepping back in time, long before humanity took root on Earth. The slightly lower Aconteccan gravity has allowed the trees to balloon to vast sizes, with gigantic boles stretching far into the sky and providing a dense green canopy. Competition for sunlight is fierce, and as a result the trees are capable of growing extremely quickly. Beyond the jungle of the Great Arboreal Reserve are the temperate rainforests of Camões Reserve. Towering white-trunked trees are shrouded at their bases by a thick layer of fernery. In both the jungles and the rainforests there are a great many fungi, fruits, and berries, some of which are edible, many of which are deadly. Preliminary studies indicate that the numerous types of fungus growing in the jungles and rainforests may yield useful medical applications.

FAUNA

Acontecimento is home to immense herds of non-indigenous grazing animals from Earth. Sheep, cows, goats, as well as other farm animals such as chickens, geese, and more, are farmed extensively. The resulting industries in meat production, leather working, cheese making, and milk powder production are the fundamental reasons Acontecimento is such a vital cog in the PanOceanian Hyperpower. The magnitude and intensity of this livestock farming is difficult to understate, and there is a constant balancing act between four aspects of land management on Acontecimento: living space, crop production, grazing land, and nature reserves. All of them are fundamental to the success of the planet and the growing tourism industry is placing some pressure on the fine balance between these four areas.

Quite apart from the introduced species, Acontecimento had a prosperous eco-system of its own. Thanks in large part to the size and swiftness with which the nature reserves were instituted, this biosphere is still a thriving component of the planet today. Like Earth, all the trophic levels are present on Acontecimento, from the ubiquitous plant life to low-level herbivores and through to apex predators and decomposers. Some of the most successful life forms on the planet are arthropods, which, due to the low gravity, warm atmosphere, rich nutrients, and the evolution of preliminary lungs, range from the expected small insects to massive chitinous leviathans.

On the plains, and now in the cities, the infamous caskudas are the most populous genus, with a multitude of species ranging from the size of an Earth cockroach to varieties measuring 45 centimetres in length. Harmless for the most part, they are nonetheless infuriating, as like cockroaches they are omnivores. On the plains they survive on the seeds and tiny nut-like fruit produced by the grasses, and serve as pollinators for many grass species. In the cities they get everywhere in their search for food, and have the reputation for being disgusting spreaders of bacteria, though in truth the trails of faecal matter are what repulse people most. On the plains caskudas are hunted by a predator know colloquially as the "gato chitina", a cat-sized arthropod that is surprisingly quick and nimble, able to jump significant distances using its large hind legs and deliver a killing blow to its prey through knife-like mandibles. They are more than capable of injuring a human, though are only likely to do so if cornered or protecting their nest.

As annoying as the caskudas are, the most reviled animal on Acontecimento is, without doubt, the spear fly. These bloodsucking creatures once only tormented the vast herds of grazing animals that thrived in Acontecimento's plains but now are the bane of native creatures, livestock, and humans alike. Around the size of a marble, these flying insects land, usually in significant numbers, on their prey and pierce the skin with a proboscis that hooks into the flesh, making them difficult and painful to dislodge. Evolved to deal with the hides of large animals, they are capable of inflicting small wounds on people, and often carry blood-borne diseases. If attacked in enough numbers, a victim can suffer shock and even die as a result.

There are a range of native mammalian herd animals on Acontecimento, though many of these have been driven off their land into the forest reserves where they lack the adaptations to thrive as they once did and are struggling to survive. The most common of these are the vaca peluda, named for their resemblance to the long-haired cows of Earth. These animals are well camouflaged, slightly smaller than Earth cows, and live in large herds. A number of industries on the planet are farming these animals for their skins and meat.

The forest reserves are a bounty of life, largely populated by herbivorous arthropods and mammals, although there are also a handful of dangerous predators. The Pássaro Cruel is one such creature. About the size of a Labrador, these deadly flying insects occupy the same niche as a bird of prey on Earth. They are perfectly adapted ambush predators, sitting high in the branches and swooping suddenly on silent wings to impale their prey. Many of the herbivorous mammals in the forests are gliders, and the Pássaro Cruel is their preeminent predator, capable of striking them from the air as they glide. The most dangerous of the animals inhabiting the Great Arboreal Reserve is the Onça-Preta, an animal similar in size and aggression to a puma. Onça-Pretas have mottled dark fur that makes it almost impossible to spot in the shadows of the great forest. These animals are also ambush predators, lurking in trees and dropping onto their prey from above.

Restricted largely to Bharatavarsha Island, the sabre-toothed bear is a Lazarus taxon of apex predators that once dominated the food chain across Acontecimento. Slightly smaller than Earth bears, they are ferocious and quick, capable of terrifying bursts of speed. Smaller varieties thrive in the forest reserves throughout Acontecimento, and while they are just as dangerous, they are smaller pack hunters, lacking the brute size and savagery of their large sabre-toothed cousins.

FLOATING PASTURES

The wetlands of the Vanga region are home to the infamous Lily Traps. Almost indistinguishable from the grasses that proliferate in the swamps, they grow in deep patches and any abrasion caused by a Lily Trap's razor-sharp edges administers a nerve agent which quickly contorts the body of the victim and is particularly deadly to mammalian life. The long grass stems, moved to action by the thrashing, flex and cover the victim, their barbs and razor edges vibrating over it and cutting it slowly, inexorably, and constantly until little remains. The flesh and blood spilt into the soil provides all the nutrients the Lily Trap requires. Removing a victim from a Lily Trap can cause significant harm, often inducing enough cuts and puncture wounds to kill them. Even those saved from a Lily Traps are rarely the same as they were before they took that fateful last step...

SPEAR FISHING

In the varied waterways of Vanga, and elsewhere on the planet in the river systems, water striders are both a strangely compelling and disturbing sight. These tall arthropods can reach a height of three metres due to their long legs, and are comprised of a football-sized thorax, a similarly sized abdomen, and a downward facing head with huge multifaceted eyes. As their name suggests, they stride through shallow waters on their four rear spindly legs scanning for heat signatures and movement. Once a target has been spotted the water strider impales it with one of its two fore-legs, evolved into limbs like hardened spears, and raises it from the water to its mandibles.

ECONOMY

Acontecimento has a thriving economy that revolves around multiple industries, from farming to production. It is a wealthy planet, not just in the capital gained from the sale of trade goods, but also in the goods and resources themselves. While Acontecimento is not as obviously affluent as Neoterra, and maintains a reputation throughout PanOceania for being a "working class" world, the population lives what any other power would call a comfortably middle-class lifestyle. High wages are made possible by Acontecimento's self-sufficiency and massive export surplus. PanOceania relies on the bounty of Acontecimento to maintain other less habitable worlds and it is a source of local pride that this is so consistently achieved.

Crop farming is widespread across Acontecimento, and due to the ideal conditions harvests are always bountiful. Much effort has gone into developing the right farming strategies to suit the ecosystems, climates, and biomes of Acontecimento, with the continental farming zones as the ultimate step in harmonising, streamlining, and maximising crop production across the planet. In the tropical zones, crop farming tends to focus on rice and sugarcane, while crop farming in the more temperate zones focuses on wheat, rye, and maize. Recently, with the introduction of ALEPH-managed farming attempts in the Adarsana region, alfalfa has been introduced, which makes for good animal feed and is relatively drought-resistant, making it ideal for growing in this more arid area.

In addition to the significant space dedicated to crop production, much of the rest of the planet, particularly the grasslands, is given over to pastures for livestock. Livestock animals are almost exclusively introduced, with cows, goats, sheep, and poultry key among them. Livestock farming is intensive, with herds of animals typically numbering in the thousands for a single farming unit. These herds are kept in the wide grasslands, and due to the rapid cycle of the grasses, always have plenty of feed available.

Mining is another key industry on Acontecimento, with everything from precious stones to rare earth metals and ores available from the deep mines in Magalhães. Mining for ore on Acontecimento has proven to be a difficult and dangerous proposition because the frequent tectonic activity makes the process too risky for human workers. Remotes and drones are typically used, except in the most illegal of operations.

Material dug from the dizzyingly complex web of mines here is shipped across the planet to fuel industrial production and transported up the orbital elevators or packaged and fired into orbit via a giant railgun in Vanga designed to propel special cargo containers into orbit. Not only do these ores and materials fuel the industrial works on the planet's surface, they also compliment the ore mined throughout the Descoberta system and are used for trade or in the vast orbital industrial complexes like the naval yards.

Across the planet vast reserves of petrochemicals can be found below the surface due to the ancient forests that dominated the world millions of years ago. While not used widely as a commercial fuel source, they are used in industrial processes, the manufacture of plastics and polymers and so on.

A small number of Teseum mines have also proven profitable on Acontecimento, with automated mining drones excavating the material from deep shafts puncturing the planet's multitude of tectonic fault lines. Teseum mined on Acontecimento is almost exclusively used in the naval docks and orbital industries servicing the military.

A nascent industry on Acontecimento is tourism. Since the institution of the Canto Directive, a range of government-funded marketing programs have done excellent work in trying to shift the public image of Acontecimento away from a rural backwater to a thriving and vibrant planet. Their successes have seen the tourism industry on Acontecimento begin to thrive in recent years with future projections looking very promising.

DEMOGRAPHICS AND CULTURE

PanOceania assumed the mantle of supremacy among the great powers of humanity when it settled Neoterra, and on the heels of this great step forward came another, the settlement of Acontecimento. While Neoterra held the promise of a new governmental seat, the base of operations for the brightest and wealthiest of the hypercorps that wield the economic might of PanOceania, Acontecimento became the muscle, the engine, the great provider. In the full throes of celebration for a new era for all of humanity, waves of willing settlers lined up for a chance to be a part of this wonderful new event. Acontecimento's name loosely translates to "the Great Happening" to honour its discovery and founding. The settlers came predominantly from Brazil, India, and Chile, willing middle-class workers eager to take full advantage of the opportunity this new life would present them.

While the blend of cultures otherwise estranged by distance on Earth might have given rise to tension at other times, this was the dawn of a new era, and the settlers recognised with that dawning the old cultural boundaries that dominated Earth were no more. In a full sense of cooperation and understanding that they were leaving behind thousands of years of history and stepping onto a new world, they set to work building the foundation for that future. The general esprit de corps that had become so much of the cultural zeitgeist of PanOceania was refreshed and reinvigorated by the opportunities the expansion beyond Earth brought. Acontecimento, while presenting challenges, was also instantly recognisable as a place of unparalleled opportunity. With fertile soil and rich mineral wealth, the settlers soon managed to create a fledgling chain of settlements that not only provided for themselves, but Neoterra as well. The promise of Acontecimento was established well within the life span of the first colonists and has only proven itself to be everything the Hyperpower might have wished for.

The rise of a truly Aconteccan culture grew from seeds first sown in the earliest days of settlement. Hope and promise, wedded with a willingness to work hard and a resilient tenacity to overcome any hurdle was the prevailing attitude of the settlers, whatever their cultural background. Interdependence was required, establishing the first farming communities involved unceasing work to beat back the grasses and establish their own crops and new building materials and techniques needed to be developed. Industrial and nanofacturing technology had to be modified and developed in order to cope with the different stress requirements of Acontecimento's lower gravity, continual growing seasons, and high pollen and seed counts (which proved to be frustrating for the first generations of industry). Through work success was achieved, and this has become ingrained as a part of the national identity.

Given the main cultural groups of the first settlers, religion was both a binding and dividing factor. The common need and will to make a success of the great opportunity welded the peoples together, but religion was and is a significant and culturally important phenomenon. Initial settlement locations began, by necessity, culturally homogenous, but the coordination of settlement, expansion, and development saw the blending of these ethnic borders from an early stage. Religion too has seen some evolution, with the Sikh and Hindi peoples, initially maintaining a separation between the two groups of followers, becoming more mixed in the wake of the Adarsana catastrophe. Religion is a vital cultural component of Aconteccan life, and the three faiths most prevalent are the Christian Church, the

largest by far of the three, followed by Hinduism, and Sikhism. The relationship between the three is largely genial, and while they disagree on the articles of faith, they maintain a close relationship tied to the ideal that a prosperous future benefits all.

ARYAVARTA

Aryavarta is a strange mix of landscapes and biomes. From the bountiful Khalsa Farming Zone and the Great Forest Reserve in the north of the continent through to the wasteland of Adarsana and the boggy marsh ridden Vanga region in the south. Initially settled by largely Indian colonists, over the years the needs to coordinate and expand, as well as the rise of truly global industries, has encouraged a wide blend of ethnic backgrounds. While the general character of Aryavarta, including many of the place names, are identifiably Indian in heritage, the diversity of ethnicities has given the region a distinct feel. The heritage is noticeable, but no longer dominant, a new cultural milieu has diverged from the old patterns, and wherever you travel, through Aryavarta or BomJesus, the places and people are connected by this developing cultural identity: Aconteccan, and they are proudly so.

ADARSANA

Known across the planet as both a cursed land and a stark warning, Adarsana is the posterchild and clarion call to action for eco-terrorist groups across Acontecimento. Images of its barren wasteland are widely used in environmental propaganda and are familiar to all Aconteccans, even though a vast majority have never seen them in person. The distinct species of grass that dominated the region had a violent chemical reaction with the Earth-origin crops that were introduced, bleeding poisonous chemicals into the soil. This reaction coincided with a series of earthquakes, which both destroyed the city of Punta Al Sur, and caused a rise in the water table, bringing deep layers of salt closer to the surface. The combination wiped out the grasses and crop plants both, leaving the soil barren and salt-laden, and the desertification of the region followed quickly after.

Luckily, the species of grass prevalent in Adarsana was unique to the region, and similar effects have not occurred elsewhere, although many eco-groups continually warn a second such disaster is only a short time away. To the south of the Adarsana region is a low-lying mountain range, the chain of rivers that flow from these to the oceans is many. Beyond the range, the far south of Adarsana is still a fertile basin, with grass and marsh lands dominating, and while a few nascent settlements hold on here, the Adarsana region has largely been abandoned.

ECO-STRIFE

Eco-terrorism is a dangerous social trend that has flourished in recent decades. This too has its roots in the early days of settlement, with contentious debate about the degree to which the eco-systems of Acontecimento should be subverted to serve the needs of the farming and industrial complexes. Over the years this issue has remained broadly unsolved, with a range of environmental scientists raising concerns about pushing the native habitats, which engender the prosperity of the planet, into a death spiral. These issues have largely been crushed beneath the heel of capitalism. With the Adarsana catastrophe the real trigger point for escalation, the continued development of farming zones and the rise of automated farming practices have seen many eco-terrorist groups transition from angry propaganda to acts of violence. This trend appears as if it might worsen if the authorities don't take significant action.

PUNTA AL SUR

In the depths of the wasteland lies the ruins of Punta Al Sur, a burgeoning city in its heyday, it is now abandoned and in ruin. Half buried by the shifting sands that surround it, it is something like a modern Pompeii. Rumour and urban legend speak of it as a cursed and haunted place, where the bleached skeletons of those who died in the quakes that ruined it are occasionally revealed by the wind moving the sands. A vast hulking wreck dominates the jagged skyline of Punta Al Sur, the remains of the Al Sur orbital elevator, the base of which was partially constructed when the city fell. Urban legend has it that experiments on a kind of deforestation virus, designed initially to clear the grassland, was the real cause of Adarsana's devastation, and that these secrets lay half buried in the sands still.

HIGHS AND LOWS

Bhai Gurdas is divided into the old and new sections, though in truth the 'new' sections were built rapidly nearly a century ago to cope with the influx of refugees. Locally they are known as the Uchch Bhoomi and the Chhaaya Jhuggiyon, the High Ground and the Shadow Slums. The High Ground is home to the wealthy and working middle classes, while the Shadow Slums are the tendril like sprawls of housing, now largely dilapidated, that house the city poor.

On the borders of the salt-ridden desert of Adarsana, far from the nearest Aconteccan settlement, there are developments going on. Beacons and communication relays, and a complex pattern of regimented farms has been slowly growing. The Demeter Empresa is underway here, a farming experiment utilising salt and drought resistant crops like alfalfa, managed completely autonomously by ALEPH. Every facet of these farms, from land preparation to sowing, watering, harvesting, and processing is completed by a complex network of robotic systems managed by an ALEPH aspect. Currently in its early days, the processes and developments borne of the Demeter Empresa could be disruptive technology that revolutionises farming practices not just on Acontecimento, but everywhere.

KHALSA

A vibrant and plentiful region, Khalsa is home to a vibrant mix of ethnic groups, predominantly drawn from Sikh and Hindu stock. It is a melting pot of cultural practices, where the distinctly Aconteccan milieu has been embraced. Khalsa became the test bed for the first Continental Farming Zones (CFZ), which consist of farmes and agricultural scientists working from cities and towns while their vast farmlands operate remotely. In Khalsa vast crops of rice, maize, and wheat are grown in staggering quantities. Alongside fruit orchards sit immense packing and freezing houses, where produce is processed, frozen, packaged, and shipped to the orbital elevators ready for transport to other parts of PanOceania.

BHAI GURDAS

Bhai Gurdas is the largest city in the Khalsa region, and was a key resettlement zone in the wake of the Adarsana catastrophe. At that time it expanded at an exponential rate to accommodate the refugees coming in. The city itself sits close to the middle of the expansive Khalsa CFZ. Geographically Bhai Gurdas is a sprawling mess, at the time of its expansion city planners looked to ensure the rapidly constructed housing zones were built on stable ground, something vital across Acontecimento, but had little time to incorporate good access to commercial districts, schools, and other vital infrastructure. Since then the city has been fighting a losing battle, dealing with problems as they arise, repurposing old housing blocks into shopping centres, schools, and industrial businesses, running power, waste, and water above ground and doing their best to provide for their citizens. Despite the regional wealth, the council of Bhai Gurdas is struggling under the accumulated weight of their problems.

BHAI MURDANA

Bhai Murdana sits on the coast facing the Descobridores Ocean. Famous for the perpetual scent of its multitude of saptasarni trees, it is both a port city and widely known for its appreciation of the arts. The docklands are extensive, with large warehouses holding a sizeable percentage of the produce coming from the Khalsa CFZ. From here wide barges in long trains are loaded and make the journey down the coast to the newly established orbital elevator at Bhai Khalla.

The Poets' Quarters sits away from the coast, facing inland, and is a sprawling network of open plan housing, bars, temples, and theatres. Performance poetry has become popular, with many of the bars and theatres holding poetry slams, recitals, and readings on a weekly basis.

PLASKA PRASRAVANA

A resort town built around the hot springs and geysers of Prasravana, Plaska Prasravana has a small permanent population, while a majority of the inhabitants are itinerant; visiting for short periods, looking for an opportunity to refresh. The mud baths and hot springs are famous planet wide for their purported healing properties. The nutrient-rich mud is able to give years of life back to a face worn by age or work. Recently Plaska Prasravana has received a number of terrorist threats for plans to build an extensive 'sky-walk' and elevated resort above the geyser fields.

Separated from the town itself by security entrances, and extending into the jungle, is the Officers Special Academy. Here officers in the Aconteccan military are sent for training in command and jungle operations.

SAN FERNANDO DE DAGOPAN

Isolated from the rest of the Khalsa region, San Fernando de Dagopan has resolutely stood back from participating in the Khalsa CFZ. Its surrounding farmlands are still maintained by clan farmers, and many rumours suggest that the community supports and conceals members from a variety of eco-terrorism groups fighting the expansion of the CFZs. A sizeable portion of the town's wealth comes from petroleum mining.

Due to its proximity to the forest reserve the main base of operations for the Tikbalangs. The Tikbalangs, famously, are a regiment of Aconteccan Chasseurs of the PanOceanian Mechanized Cavalry. They are a TAG unit specialising in jungle combat who use the Forest Reserve as a training ground in preparation for Paradiso.

GREAT ARBOREAL RESERVE

Larger than any nature reserve elsewhere in the Human Sphere, the Great Arboreal Reserve holds a singular significance. Not only is it a place of rare and magnificent beauty, not only is it a refuge for the flora and fauna that once dominated the surface of Acontecimento, but it is also the key training location for the PanOceanian Military Complex, for soldiers intended for the war on Paradiso.

Surrounding the entirety of the Great Arboreal Reserve is one of the longest defensive structures ever built. The Shield Wall is not designed to defend against the onslaught of a violent enemy, the foe it defies is more subversive in nature. The grasses of Acontecimento took the lead in the evolutionary arms race millennia ago. Able to reproduce at a staggering rate they also produce a by-product capable of breaking down the lignin that gives wood its rigidity. Left unchecked the edges of a woodland facing grassland will appear to waste away over time, and as the canopy opens up, the grasses move in. The shield wall is designed to prevent this assault, and does so using a variety of ingenious technologies. Surrounding the wall

is a wide "moat" of land poisoned to prevent the grasses taking hold. Vast fans propel air flow up, pushing a majority of seeds into the atmosphere, where turbulence generated by the weather patterns of the forests themselves typically see them back into the grassland, ionised antennae attracts pollen, and everyone entering or leaving the area goes through a decontamination process.

The Shield Wall displaces the grassland herds forced into the forest from their usual migration patterns. This has played havoc with the various species impacted, with their yearly rhythms disrupted and the new habitat to contend with, most are on the brink of extinction.

Within the wall is a wilderness. No roads, paths, or access ways exist except for several walled-off military installations and the recent and controversial town of Peshawit. Stepping into the Great Arboreal Reserve is like stepping into another world. A majority of the animals that make their homes there will never set eyes on a human being, it is truly a place of wild wonder. Maintaining the reserve are the Forest Rangers Service, a talented and eccentric team of scientists, trappers, and hunters who track, monitor, and study the forest and its inhabitants.

The military bases of the Great Arboreal Reserve are high tech training centres for the elite. Most famous of these training camps is the ESTTC, the Escape and Survival Tactics Training Camp. Not only do special force units like the Bagh Mari train from these facilities, but so too do members of ALEPH's Special Situations Section. Training is high stakes, with live munitions used in most exercises, it is the final test for any elite soldier destined for Paradiso.

PESHAWIT

Controversially allowed because it sits on the coastline, itself not technically part of the Reserve, Peshawit has been a significant point of contention between the local government, nature groups, and the developers who purchased and developed the land. Billed as the ideal place to retire, Pashawit has seen an influx of wealthy citizens seeking a quiet and beautiful location to live. While many environmental scientists have raised serious concerns about the potential impact of Peshawit, the developers have been allowed to continue because they have not technically broken the law. Needless to say many are eager to see the laws change!

VANGA

Vanga is an unstable region of shifting marshlands. People have been known to go missing while traversing the marshes, and even stable roads have sometimes disappeared beneath the shifting waters. The marshlands are home to a curious range of native fauna and flora, some of which, like the Lily Traps, have a truly terrifying reputation.

BHAI KHALLA

Bhai Khalla was little more than a large town when it was selected as the location for Acontecimento's newest orbital elevator. This recent development saw a boom in the town's population, and, now a small and developing city, Bhai Khalla has become a regional centre for produce and trade goods coming from the Kalsa CFZ. The air of Bhai Khalla is filled with the promise of tomorrow, and it seems that every week a new industry is looking for land to purchase. The dockyards are currently being extended, and the local transport infrastructure is struggling to catch up with the growing demand.

GALVÃO

Galvão is a city of two halves. The first is the massive industry built around the endless barges arriving from the Magalhães mines. Kilometre-long piers stretch out into the Descobridores Ocean, receiving a constant flow of traffic laden with mined ore. From the docks these minerals are transported to massive industrial centres in the city where the ore is separated, in some cases refined, and packed tightly into large rectangular cargo pods. Once packed the cargo pods are transported to the Galvão railgun, a massive 50-kilometre-long magnetic cannon capable of firing the cargo pods into orbit. Given just enough momentum to reach high orbit, small jets manoeuvre the pods into a ring surrounding the planet. From here they are picked up by automated tugs, which will collect a dozen such containers before pulling them into a higher orbit and off to the orbital processing facility. It is a complex dance with many components and multiple fail-safes, but is functional, and able to project high quantities of minerals into space without wasting needed room on one of the orbital elevators. Some rumours suggest that other goods are stuffed inside the ore shot into orbit, but so far little evidence of such activity has been uncovered.

The second half of Galvão is given over to the military. Here PanOceanian troops train alongside members of ALEPH's Special Situations Section. Indeed, Galvão lays lucky claim to being one of the very few bases of operations for the SSS outside Concilium, and forms a connected training centre for the SSS base in the Great Arboreal Reserve.

BOMJESUS

A majority of the BomJesus continent straddles the equatorial zone, and as such benefits from remarkably stable, if warm temperatures, as well as regular rainfall. It is a rolling pastureland of unending grass, or at least it was until the La Guardia-Orujo and Zacuto Continental Farming Zones cordoned off enormous extents of the landscape for farming. Where the Khalsa CFZ focuses on cereal crops, the CFZs of BomJesus intensively farm fruit and animals. With the grasslands so dominant, the CFZs are carefully designed with vast pastures ringing the perimeter, cereal crops in a second ring inside that, and the innermost areas dedicated to fruit growing. This structure has helped to protect the fruit trees from the ravages of the native grasses, buffered as they are by specially designed walls, and ringed by cropland. The pastures beyond this ring of cropland are home to massive herds of animals; cows, goats, sheep, and more recently the native vaca peluda, which are all maintained in prodigious numbers.

Like much of Acontecimento, BomJesus is a fractured land, the city of Cidade BomJesus is the most stable, but the rest of the region is as prone to earthquakes as the Khalsa region. This has had a significant impact on the architecture of the region, on one hand pressured to build in a low-lying sprawl to prevent damaging collapses, and on the other pressured to build in density to preserve as much land for farming as possible. Being relatively newly settled, the pressure for land has been regarded as a lower priority, so the cities and towns tend to hug the landscape, extending over large areas, rather than building densely populated city centres.

If Khalsa is known predominantly for its farming produce, BomJesus is most famous for its industry and manufacturing. Huge quantities of the ore and minerals mined throughout the planet are transported to feed this economic sector, and the resulting products are fed back into the many malls and homes of the planet itself, or transported up the orbital elevators into space, and from there traded across the Human Sphere.

CIDADE BOMJESUS

The largest planetary city of Acontecimento, Citadel BomJesus is the planetary capital, seat of government, the site of one of the most important Christian churches, and the beating industrial heart. In addition, it is the most densley populated city on Acontecimento and the onlu place that skyscrapers dominate the skyline. skyscrapers can be seen dominating the city centre. Beyond the skyscrapers of the city centre, and the glorious monochrome rainbow that is the orbital arch, is the industrial centre. This ring is populated by massive manufacturing facilities, corporate, and research and development offices as well as the extensive warehousing to support this wealth of industry. The outer ring of the city is a sprawling network of residential zones, a mix of housing and apartments punctuated by wide roads, warehousing, and transportation facilities. Beyond this is a scattered ring of Atek slums, while most services are connected into these areas, they are not well maintained. In truth though the Ateks of Acontecimento are generally better treated than elsewhere in PanOceania due to the quantity and necessity of labouring jobs the planets many commercial enterprises require. Due to the high level of development and manufacturing here Cidade BomJesus has become something of a hive for industrial espionage and sabotage.

ORUJO

If Cidade BomJesus is the manufacturing heart of Acontecimeto, Orujo is the transportation hub that keeps the never-ending cycle of goods from across the planet flowing. Here corporations manage the flow of resources, produce, and goods across the planet, as well as feeding the zero-g manufacturing facilities in orbit around Acontecimento and the massive interplanetary trade networks that pour through the Asturias Astroport. Orujo is also suspected as being the epicentre of planet-wide smuggling rings, using the constant sea of traffic to conceal their operations.

Extending out over the Rondon Sea is an extensive chain of port facilities that receive barges from the Zacuto and Camões CFZs. The Triangle Airports receive a constant tide of aircraft transportation, carrying manufactured goods from across the planet, each airport separated by physical space and requiring incoming craft to use different altitudes to allow for a denser incoming stream of traffic. The maglev lines that drive through the city from multiple directions haul colossal numbers of carriages loaded with minerals, produce, and animals. A majority of these are destined for packaging and shipment off-world, and extensive abattoirs, built in large chains beyond the city, service the restaurants of PanOceania.

Orujo Minor is largely formed of industrial facilities run by corporations with large military contracts. Orujo is like a beehive, a place of constant bustle and activity. It is a city that never sleeps, where things are always moving. These facilities operate under a number of legal exemptions, and receive a large quantity of goods and resources from across Acontecimento, manufacturing components in service to the naval yards in orbit. Due to the restricted information available about what exactly the corporations of Orujo Minor do, what is developed and shipped off world by them is something of a mystery.

PUERTO LA GUARDIA

Gateway to Acontecimento for many, Puerto La Guardia can be a disappointment for those arriving planet-side with high expectations. While the city is clean and well laid out, it is also ringed by extensive Atek slums known locally as the Os Anéis. This initial encounter can be a souring experience for those who arrive expecting a rural paradise, and the local government has initiated several redevelopment programs aimed at changing the Os Anéis, but so far little effective action has been taken.

Dominating Puerto La Guardia is the orbital elevator and the services industries that meet its needs. Extensive hotel, restaurant, entertainment, and commercial businesses occupy the city centre, huddled around the elevators massive base. Here too the many maglevs and transports unload their food products and manufactured goods for transport to the Trinidad station in orbit.

TIRADENTES

Joined to Cidade BomJesus by the orbital arch, Tiradentes has seen a significant economic boom, with a resulting explosion in growth and industry over the last decade or so. Since the boom was somewhat expected as the development of the arch took years to complete, Tiradentes is a carefully managed and well laid out city. Its centre, around the base of the arch, was completely redeveloped and split into multiple zones, all with clear and easy to access public transportation. Food and entertainment, shopping malls, manufacturing, shipping, and supporting industries are all carefully

INDUSTRIAL MIGHT

Allowing all of this trade and industry to function is one of the most complex networks of transportation and shipment to be found anywhere in the Human Sphere. Orbital elevators, the orbital arch, maglev trains, barges, VTOL transports, and trucks are used extensively in a tightly bound and highly functional apparatus. Businesses built around packing, unloading, freezing, drying, dehydrating, and transport are massive conglomerates that work together like so many cogs in a complex machine, indeed, much of this cooperation is automated, with ALEPH Aspects fundamental to the smooth functioning of this never-sleeping industry.

FAME AND FORTUNE

Cidade Bomjesus is home to the headquarters of Aura Biochemicals. Aura Biochemicals is a successful corporation that has made its mark on the Sphere by analysing, synthesising, and applying the biological resources of Acontecimento. The company is owned predominantly by the Duarte family, and one of its younger heirs, Paola Duarte, is the famous Aristeia! Fighter and bow huntress called Dart. Less well known is that Paola Duarte is a Posthuman who collaborates with the SSS and the Acontecimento Shock Army.

TEMPORAL POWER

One of the defining features of Cidade BomJesus is the Basilica of Santa Maria do Acontecimento. Visible for kilometres, like a fire in the midst of the city due to its massive bronze dome, the basilica is the religious heart of Acontecimento. That it sits next door to, and overshadows, the wide and functionally designed offices of Government should leave few in doubt of the power the Church wields on the planet.

separated, with the amenities and facilities to fully support each carefully designed into the layout of the city itself.

Tiradentes is also home to the training grounds and barracks for many of the Acontecimento Regulars who serve in the planetary army. Alongside these are the Military Police, whose headquarters, known as the Halls of Justice, manage the patrols and stations in all the military facilities across the planet.

ZACUTO

A relatively conservative town, Zacuto is dominated by the families of agricultural engineers who oversee the machines and processes running the expansive Zacuto CFZ. Zacuto is widely known as being the town of churches, and religious life is a dominant thread in the culture of the people who live here. Despite the predominance of religion and a reputation for a quieter and slower lifestyle, Zacuto has the dubious record of having the highest murder and accident rate per capita of any place on Acontecimento.

The Da Gama University is the largest building in the town that is not a church, and teaches a strange mix of theology and agricultural sciences. The silo district on the eastern edge of Zacuto is an extensive array of storage facilities for the grain and produce harvested from the Zacuto CFZ. Here produce is loaded into massive bins that are loaded onto barges and shipped through the Rondon Sea to Orujo.

CAMÕES

Camões is a continent divided, the eastern side of the continent is dominated by the second-largest forest reserve on the planet, while the western half is the location of the highly productive Camões Continental Farming Zone. The grasses that dominate the rest of Acontecimento had less of a foothold here than elsewhere on the planet, and now have been entirely eradicated both to protect the forest reserve and the farmland. As a result, the soil here requires more continual fertilisation than the soils of either Khalsa or BomJesus, and a steady trade from BomJesus, transporting animal manure collected from their extensive pastures, is used to maintain the fertility of the earth.

Being positioned solidly above the equatorial band in the tranquil northern hemisphere provides Camões with a temperate climate, steady rains and excellent growing conditions. As a result of the eradication of the grasses, less concern is given to the protection of the forest reserve, which abuts the farmland comfortably. The peoples of Camões have a reputation for high education and culture, with

poetry, song, and group dances common pastimes enjoyed by many.

The success of the Camões CFZ has done much to push the production levels for the planet well past the levels required for self-sustenance, and much of the crops harvested here are transported by barge to Orujo, destined for trade elsewhere in the Human Sphere. The forest reserve here too is vital to the planet, acting as a reserve for both flora and fauna, it is the best chance any citizen of Acontecimento has of experiencing the planet as it might have been many thousands of years ago. Access to the forest reserve of Camões is easier to obtain and less stringently monitored than access to the Great Arboreal Reserve, and as such many biologists, qualified and amateur, do much to catalogue and identify uses for the native life found beneath the canopy.

PUNTA NORTE

Famous across Acontecimento and, indeed, across the Human Sphere for the rare and beautiful stone types quarried here, Punta Norte is something of an architectural gem. A once small town redeveloped by the local council carefully and artfully over many years, almost every building in the town is architecturally designed, from the largest government building to the smallest house. As a result, the town is a montage of architectural styles, each building making use of the stones in a new and different way. It has become a signifier of talent and ability to be commissioned to design a building in Punta Norte, and competition for such jobs is fierce, attracting architects from across the Human Sphere. Some regard this local habit as an expensive waste of time, but the council is always quick to point out that every building is an advertisement for what wonders can be achieved with stones from their quarries. Such is the extent of the trade, that the quarrying has created a series of massive canyons on the outskirts of the town.

SELVA PRETA

Built in the heart of the forest reserve from which it draws its name, Selva Preta is an idyllic township, originally devised to blend in with the surrounding forest itself. Access to the town is only possible via VTOL craft, and such transports, carrying people and goods both, are a regular sight in the skies above the town. Selva Preta is a town divided against itself, split into Old Town and New Town.

Old Town was founded by scientists and was specially designed to incorporate and blend into the forest itself. The architecture is cunning and organic, buildings sometimes suspended over the forest floor, sometimes winding around a clade of ancient trees. Walkways and raised paths arch from structure to structure, and the themes of nature,

PUNTA NORTE DEFENCE RESEARCH CENTRE

The Punta Norte Defence Research Centre is built deep inside one of the first quarries established, and no longer quarried. During the NeoColonial Wars it served as a vital research and development facility for targeting systems and weaponry. Now its facilities have been completely refitted and designed to create technology, systems, and protocols around infowar. Massive servers fuelled by an underground generator run state of the art expert systems that manage and assists in the research and development tasks. Access to the facility is via a series of underground tunnels, once a part of the original quarry, but extended and protected by automated systems. The people that work this facility are some of the smiling mothers, fathers, and teenagers of Punta Norte, unknown and hiding in plain sight.

light, and life dominate and fascinate the senses. Any wonder it was an attraction to any who saw images of it!

New Town was the result of an approved expansion, bought out by property developers, who then subdivided and sold off the land using clever marketing strategies across PanOceania. Seeing the wealth such land brought, some of the older inhabitants of Old Town have sold off their stake as well, compounding and hastening the change. New Town is faux Old Town, the architecture a poor copy rather than a compliment. The buildings are prefabricated, flown in and installed, and in some cases the forest itself has been cleared away, the buildings put in place, and new flora introduced to make a show at natural integration. Needless to say there is little love lost between the residents of New and Old Town!

SIERPES ISLAND

Bastion of the Christian church on Acontecimento, Sierpes Island is the location not just of San Juan de Sierpes, the preeminent cathedral of the planet, but also of the Quarters, an administrative and judicial centre which manages and coordinates the Church, its business interests, lobby groups, and liaises with the Military Orders. Negotiations between any of these powerful groups typically takes place in the Confluence, a large estate and attached gardens forming the northern section of the network of buildings referred to as the Quarters. Many influential political, corporate and military negotiations have been thrashed out, debated, and agreed on in the Confluence, decisions affecting not only Acontecimento, but also the trade in goods and produce which supports PanOceania itself. Some cynics even go so far as to refer to the Confluence as the real Government houses.

Sierpes Island is famous for two other important features, the Garden District, and the Great Library. The Garden District is a botanist's dream, a carefully sculptured rolling space enclosed by extensive walls, it includes water features, like a small river system and waterfalls, as well as dells, hills, caves, and a host of other natural features. Dotted throughout this massive area are buildings where visitors can rest, enjoy food and drink, and study. The Garden District seeks to model the range and diversity of life on Acontecimento, from the jungles, rainforests, cave systems, and grasslands. Every catalogued plant and fungus on the planet can be found in a carefully constructed miniature biome. Classes in biology are held here almost constantly. While it may seem just a natural pleasure, the Garden District has been home to some serious science, with a range of nano-materials, medicines, psychotropic drugs, and poisons developed from the plants that can be found within the grounds.

The Great Library is another centre for learning, built both above ground and extending into solid bedrock in the middle of the plate that forms the island, the Great Library is not only a catalogue of learning, language, books, media, and culture, it also stores genetic samples from every living thing on the planet, and many extinct ones as well.

SAN JUAN DE SIERPES

San Juan de Sierpes is the religious centre of Acontecimento. While the cathedral of Cidade BomJesus is impressive, the Punta Norte stone palace, basilica, seminary, priory, and convent form a collective of buildings like a small town, gorgeously constructed. While Acontecimento may have a reputation for rural quiet, there is no doubt about the power, wealth, and influence of San Juan de Sierpes, even on Neoterra the Aconteccan See wields significant clout; when the Archbishop speaks, many listen.

To the north of Sierpes Island is the Monastery of Saint Paul of Sierpes. A centre for the Order of Montesa it is built as a multi-layered Bastion Fort. Its walls forming gigantic stars that overlap one another, threatening anyone who approaches with the prospect of enfilade fire from multiple points. Beneath this defiant appearance the fortress is a cutting edge military facility, participating in high value research and development programs into weapons systems and most especially TAGs.

MAGALHÃES

Named in honour of Fernão de Magalhães, more commonly known by the name Ferdinand Magellan, the massive peak of Almofrei Mountain dominates this continent both in geographic and economic importance.

ALMOFREI MOUNTAIN

Almofrei is the tallest naturally occurring geographical feature on any planet yet inhabited by humanity. The atmospheric pressure at its peak is so low that climbers must wear pressure suits to prevent hyperbaric trauma.

The same forces that thrust it to the very edge of the atmosphere brought with them enormous mineral wealth. Mining remotes dig tunnels deep into the mountain, chasing veins of metal, rare elements, gemstones, and other valuable resources.

PORTOBELO

Once dominated by Minescorp and the trans-shipment of ores, Portobelo's fortunes changed with the reengineering of the Zebro River, which brought ore barges to Riomeio with a fraction of the effort and cost. Almost overnight, most major shippers

SUBIDA ALMOFREI

Every year, the mountain tracks connecting the Almofrei mining facilities are used for a wildly popular race called the Subida Almofrei. Teams pit modified mining remotes in a hell-for-leather race up the mountain. Hilarious, furious, and above all fun, the Subida Almofrei has been hugely popular both in person and live on Maya. Many of the teams are now receiving sponsorship, and the competition is fierce.

ARISTEIA!

Portobelo is home to the famous Aristeia! and Maya star "Gata". An icon of Portobelo's garotas, the beautiful women of the city, she has done much to boost tourism. Her image can be found everywhere around Portobelo and she is a proud ambassador for the city.

SELVAGENS

Once no more than navigational hazards for barge trains leaving Portobelo, these islands now provide carefully cultured venues to connect with Acontecimento's unspoiled natural tropical habitat. Resort owners stock the islands with an abundance of native species, and jokingly call them the Savage Isles. They've become one more attraction for the resorts, and due to the strong magnetic fields generated by the rocks that form the islands, they are almost completely isolated from both Maya and Arachne. Some visit the Selvagens to disconnect from the incessant chatter that permeates society, and others, it is widely suspected, utilize it for more nefarious purposes.

relocated. When Minescorp moved their headquarters, Portobelo had to act.

Fortunately, wise financial stewardship allowed for a substantial investment in the future. Blessed with beautiful beaches, hot springs, a tropical climate, and lush vegetation to match, Portobelo built resorts along the coast. The success of these early efforts then fuelled further investment in mountain resorts, attracting skiers and climbers to areas once given over to mining facilities.

The contrasting climates so close together have attracted tourists across Acontecimento and the Human Sphere. Celebrities and dignitaries either make an effort to be seen or not seen rubbing shoulders with the elite, and many high-level negotiations and agreements take place at the resorts. So much so that security and the possibility of espionage has become an ever-increasing concern.

RIOMEIO
Once the smaller brother to Portobelo, the reengineering of the Zebro River changed everything. Once-choked waterways became thoroughfares for mined resources, and both the economy and size of Riomeio blossomed. Further reconstruction created the Great Cargo Yards, where barges disconnect from river tugs and hitch to the giant ocean-going barge trains.

This rapid expansion has brought the offices of several hypercorps into the city, though Minescorp was the first, and all the attendant smaller businesses that support these behemoths. The rapid

growth has caused problems, as the traditional alliances normally found amongst the lobbies have recently begun to break down as expansion plans are debated.

ZEBRO RIVER PASSAGE
The Zebro River Passage represents one of the largest engineering efforts on the planet. Bourakian engineers headed the project, and heavy construction Remotes took over five years to move such vast amounts of soil that the tailings could be seen from space.

The fast-moving waterway now carries more tonnes of resources than any other single transportation channel. Locks running parallel to the main passage bring the barges back to the mine heads for reuse. Much of this system is automated or handled by Remotes, called Estivadores.

TRADE MISSIONS AND THE GREAT CARGO YARDS
The importance of the resources flowing through Riomeio is such that every nation in the Human Sphere, and many corporations, have trade missions within the city, most of these clustered near the Great Cargo Yards. These missions loom over the edge of the yards like so many lions over a kill — the strongest shouldering aside the throng to get the choicest rewards.

The sprawl of the yards, in comparison, are almost completely flat. Most of them are simple docks and massive floating transfer tenders to get the materials ready for shipment to the rest of Acontecimento.

VISHWA

The Vishwa Archipelago embodies two strong spirits: that of humanity's will to control the planet, and that of the planet's indomitable ability to adjust and resist.

PanOceania has only recently expanded the automated farming techniques from the continental plains to the lands and seas of Vishwa. Though the CFZ expansion had enjoyed initial success, several trends show the planet's biome may not be willing to relinquish the region without a fight.

MIL JEMS (MINOR ISLANDS)

This term refers to the multitude of small islands throughout the archipelago. They span a broad range of climates and geography, from low, beach-skirted paradises of the north to jagged, mountainous eyries in the south. This incredible diversity of habitats supports many biomes found nowhere else, and scientists have likened the region to the Galapagos Islands on Earth. The unintended introduction of non-native flora and fauna has already caused irreparable damage in several cases, much to the chagrin of the scientific community. Rumours that the Libertadores of Faleiro may be moving into the area have not yet been verified.

BHARATA

Often compared to Venice, Bharata straddles the bay of the same name, though its canals are both broad and meticulously logical in their layout. The Chamber of Islands, located at the mouth of the bay, houses Vishwa's governmental chambers. Constructed from a transparent sphere, the Chamber lies just beneath the surface of the bay, with representatives' seats suspended around a podium that floats at the centre. Vishwa officials claim they have the best view on the planet.

BHARATAVARSHA ISLAND

Jaanavar Mountain, originally volcanic, created the now verdant Bharatavarsha Island. Much like the surrounding islands, Bharatavarsha supports a wide variety of native wildlife, the most famous being the sabre-toothed bear, which sat firmly atop the food chain prior to the arrival of humans.

Owing to the barren volcanic rock and jagged spurs common close to the peak of Jaanavar, most habitation sits near the coastlines. The slow growth of these settlements has forced wildlife father up the hills, shrinking their habitat. With so many important species at stake, the Vishwa government has taken steps to establish preserves throughout the archipelago, a move which does not sit well with CFZ developers.

DUSHYANTA

Dushyanta is comprised of the flattest geography of any large island of the Vishwa archipelago and fecund shallow surrounding seas have created an ideal testing ground for CFZ methods on a more modest landmass. The Prachurata Corp, one of the newer CFZ organisations, has spearheaded the third expansion from their local headquarters in the city of Shaant Samudr, which also serves as the control centre for both land and sea-based remote pilots.

Terrace Farms: While Dushyanta may be more level than most islands of Vishwa, it is hardly the same as the rolling plains of the larger scale CFZ operations. From above, much of the island resembles a topographical map made real, with concentric terraced rings separated by walls created from a slurried compound of the rock and indigenous plant life cleared from each level.

Remotes circle the terraces in great winding loops, doing the necessary work for the season: tilling, planting, culling, harvesting, and ploughing the chaff back into the soil in an unceasing cycle.

Coastal Plantations: The shallow waters surrounding most of Dushyanta have allowed Prachurata to experiment with aquafarming techniques. Though every bit as large as the land-based operations, they're still considered experimental. They have brought both aquaculture experts and equipment from Varuna, and have a wide variety of seaweed and seagrasses in strictly segregated plots to test for yield and labour required from planting to harvest. These areas are restricted from private traffic due to navigational hazards, although conspiracy theorists suspect more dire reasons. Despite no substantiated evidence supporting the claims, some assert that Bakunin-modified "sea monsters" also roam the area, providing security for more sinister experiments.

SHAKUNTALA

Despite being the second largest landmass in the Vishwa archipelago, Shakuntala's fortunes are most firmly tied to the sea. The Nabia Research Centre is one of the foremost authorities on aquatic Lhosts outside of Varuna, and a tide-powered network of locks bring ocean water inland for processing. This focus led to the lack of roads connecting the major communities of the island. Though cross-country vehicles exist for specific cargos, transport by sea or air is far more common.

NABIA RESEARCH CENTRE

A joint project by Acontecimento, Varuna, and ALEPH, the Nabia Research Centre leads research and development into deep-sea Lhosts and augmentations for humans to allow for survival at great depths. Progress on these deep-sea Lhosts,

CITY OF CANALS

The rest of Bharata spears out from the Chamber of Islands, connected by radial canals that continue through the land at the edges of the bay. Transportation is mostly by hovercraft and flitters able to use the waterways as roads, with most buildings having both docks and landing pads.

Great pains have been taken to preserve and enhance the bay's marine life, which remains almost entirely native. Keeping invasive species out of the bay, especially those from elsewhere on the planet, has been particularly challenging.

BEARS AND BUGS

Acontecimento's most famous native resident is the sabre-toothed bear. Active year round, this carnivore is relentless in its pursuit of food. A fondness for rummaging through human garbage brought the early colonists and the bears into conflict. Bharatavarsha natives are religious about keeping food waste in sealed containers so as not to attract these fearsome beasts.

Oddly, the most common other animals, and favoured prey of the sabre-toothed bears, are large insects. Ranging in size up to that of a small dog, they are both stubborn and tenacious, their armoured carapace able to shrug off the attacks of most predators. Many believe the tusks of the bears to be an adaption to pierce these shells, and careful analysis of the structure of the tusks seems to support this theory; they are remarkably strong piercing weapons.

LIBERTADORES

Despite protestations that their guides ensure that hunts end humanely and inflict minimal suffering on the animals, activists have provided several embarrassing examples of botched hunts that have become Maya fuel for the anti-hunting movement. The main group of activists call themselves Libertadores. Splinter groups range in methodology from total non-violence, often infiltrating the preserves and interposing themselves between hunter and animal, to far more violent ideologies, believing that every eliminated hunter saves countless other animals.

named Nabias after the Lusitanian goddess of water and rivers, has been dramatic. In just the last decade, research teams have swept way past limitations on depth, duration, and durability. Sensory suites allow "visual" data collection even in low — and zero-light conditions, exposing the deepest trenches of the Bandeirantes Ocean. Of course, many of these discoveries have significant non-scientific applications.

SAMUDR BAANDH

The ocean locks of Shakuntala, powered solely by the tides, bring seawater inland for processing. Desalinated water from the Samudr Baandh plant provides most of the drinking water for its communities, and its solar-power farms at the top of the locks utilize the sodium for high-efficiency power storage. Though none of the technology is particularly novel, natives are proud of its zero-waste elegance. Power from the plant supplies communities all over the island, including the Nabia Research Centre and the Biswas Aeropterport.

The locks also bring Bandeirantes vessels to the forges that separate precious metals from the dross dredged from the bottom of the ocean of the same name. Aspiring crew often line the locks, hoping to be selected to replace a crewmember suffering from barotrauma, decompression sickness, or oxygen toxicity.

BANDEIRANTES

The Bandeirantes Ocean has significant precious metal deposits, but most are inaccessible to any but the most well-equipped, or those with the greatest appetite for risk. Tales of the mother lode still lure fortune hunters to the area, and Shakuntala supplies them with all they can afford, though not always all they need.

Aeropters transport injured crew to local hospitals in non-acute cases, and to the Nabia Research Centre for the most critical. Pressure-related injuries are distressingly common, but they are always more willing crew.

BISWAS AEROPTERPORT

The lack of roads connecting Shakuntala's major habitation centres has created the need for alternate means of long-distance transportation for people and goods. Aeropters, which range in passenger capacity from a single individual to roughly twenty, provide mobility for the people. Dynastat hybrid airships haul goods and other freight to even the most remote communities.

ARCHIPELAGOS

The archipelagos of Acontecimento have enough land mass and population to have developed their own distinct cultures, and have maintained that differentiation over time. This is by design, as none are separated from the main continents by any great stretches of water. Those looking for experiences outside the Acontecimento norm need only look to the island chains of various archipelagos.

FALEIRO

Known throughout the Human Sphere as the largest artificially stocked hunting preserve in any system, the Faleiro Game Preserves attract hunters from every nation. The preserves are not limited to land. Both coastal and deep-sea hunts have proven enormously popular as well.

The Faleiro Gaming Authority stocks these preserves with adult animals cloned at their Novo Viveiro facilities, a complex of gleaming white domes along several islands of the archipelago's inner sea. With the aid of Bourak scientists, they have pioneered both cloning and fast growth techniques that ensure the preserves always have a wide variety of big game, on land and in the sea.

SAHIBZADAS

Originally populated by Sikh colonists, they still form the ethnic majority in the Sahibzadas, and the islands reflect their culture and beliefs. From the Golden Temple to the University, from the Sarbat Ghala gardens to scores of restaurants in the villages and cities, they reflect a seldom-examined sub-culture of PanOceania.

With their emphasis on knowledge, the arts, and science, one could almost be forgiven in thinking they'd discovered a Haqqislam enclave in the northern reaches of Acontecimento.

TERRA DE GELO

The "Land of Ice" is actually a mass of ice sheets surrounding a rocky archipelago that protrudes in rocky crags only at its highest points. Its winters bring bone-chilling cold that doubles Terra de Gelo's size, and its summers melt the surface snow, resulting in flash floods both above and below the ice, known to scientists as invisível. Spring and fall bring snows that replenish the snow pack and compress into glaciers.

One permanent scientific station, which shares the name of the main landmass — Rocha, clings in the lee of the precipitous highlands. Perched on massive stilts to keep it above the permafrost and snow, it has an organic shape that allows it to shrug off the wind and weather.

VASCO DE GAMA

Vasco de Gama was named after the famous Portuguese explorer. Given its proximity to Cidade BomJesus, the inhabitants of the Vasco de Gama archipelago seem particularly anachronistic. These Bandeirantes eschew both the urban lifestyle common to the rest of Acontecimento and its flora and fauna. Their small farms and villages, and large estates, would not seem out of place on ancient Earth. Despite this seeming rural lifestyle, the homesteads are well connected with Maya, and they utilize the latest in biotechnology.

DESCOBERTA SYSTEM

When the Exploratory Vessel Pos Udyam first explored the Sol-Acontecimento wormhole, the scientific team named the star Descoberta, "Discovery" in Portuguese.

MIRANDA

Despite the chaotic and inhospitable environment of Miranda, humans have still left their mark, lured by the intensity of the star's energies, and the exotic compounds available nowhere else in the Human Sphere.

DEEP PRESSURE MINES AND UM SOLAR ARRAYS

Miranda, a hot planet similar to Jupiter, has a surface of "hot ice", a combination of water and various long – and short-chain hydrocarbons put under such pressure that they form a solid, despite temperatures many times water's typical boiling point.

The D-1 Deep Pressure mines are almost completely automated due to radiation, pressure, and heat, but they provide rare substances and compounds for consumption by Acontecimento's vast manufacturing sector. A mass driver near the equator slings these raw materials to a small station at the L2 point, where small freighters transport it to the outer system.

Flanking Miranda like planetary "ears" are the Um Solar Arrays, which absorb energy from Descoberta's intense rays and beam it to various Acontecimento orbitals, primarily the low-gravity Teseum foundries.

PETECA

Peteca's eccentric orbit has its periastron inside that of Acontecimento, and its apastron outside of Aparecida. Thankfully it also lies nearly 30 degrees outside the stellar plane, reducing the potential for interstellar collision.

A small mesoplanet would normally not warrant any attention, but due to some incidental detail of its creation, it has an abnormally high percentage of heavy elements in its crust, making mining operations worthwhile.

ACONTECIMENTO ORBITALS

VICTORIA, TRINIDAD, AND CONCEPCIÓN

This triumvirate of orbital stations is the conduit of commerce between Acontecimento and the rest of the system and Sphere.

Victoria, linked by the Ipanema Orbital Elevator to Orujo, is the industrial powerhouse. Co-located foundries, fuelled not just by ores from Acontecimento, but also from Peteca and other mining operations throughout the system, create refined Teseum from ores sourced from across the Human Sphere, and other exotic alloys. The titanic energies beamed from the Um Solar Arrays power the industry of this orbital. The nonstop activity of the forges illuminates the station in yellows, oranges, and reds.

Trinidad, connected to Puerto La Guardia by the La Guardia Orbital Elevator, is the commercial hub of Acontecimento. More than one hundred docking spines protrude from a massive central core, resembling a three-dimensional snowflake or spider web. Trinidad provides non-stop maintenance and support for ships, and also serves as a passenger terminal, with vast alloyed portals overlooking the planet below. The stunning view and dining establishments taking advantage of it make Trinidad a destination in its own right instead of merely a transportation connection.

Concepción, at the apex of the Bhai Khalla Elevator, supplies massive quantities of food stuffs and produce. Of the three stations, Concepción is the smallest, newest, and most hungry for additional business.

TESEUM FOUNDRIES AND CORONADO NAVAL YARDS

The Teseum smelters and casting facilities create a ruddy glow over the Victoria Orbital and its surrounds – the hammer and anvil of the PanOceania military and commercial machine. Acontecimento Orbital Control (AOC) designates the entire area a no-fly zone due to the incredible energies beamed into the area by the Um Solar Arrays. AOC similarly restricts the Coronado Naval Yards for many of the same reasons. Construction tugs and work crews proliferate the area, building hulls from the humble Pardal cargo skiff all the way up to the largest PanOceania battlecruisers. Most of the work

BHAI GURDAS UNIVERSITY

Though Sahibzadas's university specialises in in multi-denominational religious studies, it is also widely renowned for its science curriculum, serving as a beacon of knowledge every bit as impressive as the Golden Temple. Students have access to physical copies of almost every holy text of antiquity, as well as cutting edge scientific laboratories. Though less well known, the poetry department also enjoys widespread acclaim,

The university has an exchange program with the Talawat on Bourak, which is only a "short" journey away on the C6 Circular.

WARDENS

One of the larger buildings in the city of Bandeirantes on Vasco de Gama is the headquarters of the Wardens, who serve as police, customs, and border patrol for the island. All ports of entry, down to modest public landing areas, have at least one Warden. Keeping Acontecimento's aggressive flora off the island is quite a challenge, and every visitor is subject to Bioscan and decontamination. This also provides a surreptitious identity scan that probes PanOceanian criminal databases.

ORBITAL FORTRESSES

The Knights of Santiago maintain military orbitals around each planet and Vila Boosters. Classified as "fortresses", this moniker can be misleading. Though certainly armed and armoured, their main function is to supply the flotilla of high-g patrol vessels that ply the system, acting as both deterrent and mobile reaction force for any hostilities or mishaps

PEREGRINO STATION

Utilising a complex pattern of Hohmann transfer orbits to keep it moving throughout the Descoberta system, but always within reach of the various Circular routes, is Peregrino Station. PanOceania built the station with the specific intent of supporting – and capturing – the revenues of vessels transiting between Circulars without the intent of moving in-system. Supplied by hydrogen from Aparecida, manufactured goods from Acontecimento and the Coronado shipyards, and all manner of entertainments, Peregrino supplies the basics to vessels transferring between Circulars.

The station maintains the appearance of a rough and tumble outpost for more independent-minded captains and their crews, but this is a carefully cultivated image. Rumour has it that the station is rife with Hexahedron agents. Though unverifiable, many point to the avoidance of Peregrino by Nomad vessels as proof.

areas are open frames around the vessels under construction, but crews occasionally construct electro-optical cages around classified projects.

APARECIDA

A Class I gas giant with high ammonia content, Aparecida is primarily known for two things. The first is the gas mining operations that provide hydrogen, helium, associated isotopes, and other liquefied gas products needed for propulsion, industry, and life in space. The second is the massive atmospheric storm known as the Vortex. While breathtaking in its majesty, and a system destination for cruise ships, it also complicates mining operations in its vicinity.

GAS MINING PLATFORMS AND THE VORTEX

Countering Minescorp influence in the system, MagnaObra acquired a controlling interest in Aparecida's gas mining operations in the early days of system exploitation. Believing the planet to have hidden Teseum reserves, they have ruthlessly excluded any possibility of significant competition by deft political manoeuvers and outright fiscal force.

The Vortex, a persistent, tornado-like cyclone along Aparecida's equator, has a funnel larger than most planets. While it provides a tourist attraction that brings hundreds of vessels into the system on the Circulars each year, it also generates far more mobile satellite storms that disrupt gas mining operations.

SORVETE

Were it not for its inconvenient position in the system, water and hydrocarbon ice from Sorvete would have supplanted the gas mining operations on Aparecida. While certainly valuable, its orbit aligns so infrequently with Circular traffic that operations have been more modest, mostly supplying in-system needs.

ICE QUARRIES

When seen close up, areas of Sorvete's surface look as if giant blocks have been carved from its icy crust. Remote extraction crawlers follow veins of ice with desirable properties, most commonly water ice and those with high hydrogen or oxygen content.

Rumour has it that bodies of Acontecimento criminals have been found in the ice quarries, frozen in the orthogonal walls left behind the extraction crawlers, but most consider this an old wives' tale – a mobster equivalent of a ghost story.

WORMHOLES

Acontecimento has five stable wormholes, terminating at Sol, Shentang-Yutang, Neoterra, Bourak, and Varuna. This places it on the Circular routes C2, C5, C6, and C7. This makes it one of the most connected systems in the Human Sphere. Huge amounts of commercial and military traffic pass through the system. Only Sol boasts so many connections to such influential systems. Of course, with this gift comes responsibility and the need for vigilance.

CIRCULARS AND LUSIADS

Each of the wormholes boasts its own Lusiad, a combination navigational beacon, surveillance system, and orbital fortress. Their powerful LIDAR and RADAR arrays scan every vessel transiting the gates across the entire electro-optical spectrum, and transmit the information in-system through several redundant repeaters. They also compare the readings with a comprehensive database of known vessels. This gives forces in the system maximum advanced warning of any threats or conundrums.

CHAPTER 3
NEOTERRA

SHINING JEWEL OF HUMAN CULTURE

Bathed in the light of Tencendur rests the shining jewel of the human sphere, Neoterra. This bustling world is not only the home of San Pietro, PanOceania's capital, but it is also a centre of industry, art, music, culture, and wealth. Neoterra is the most important world in the Human Sphere, influencing not only PanOceanian culture, but also all of human culture. Decisions made on the planet will shape the future of human society for generations to come, and true understanding of human society starts with Neoterra and its people.

CLIMATE AND GEOGRAPHY

Neoterra's geography was changed drastically by an extinction-level event approximately a billion years ago that dramatically altered its geography, climate,

and biological diversity. Evidence of this event can be found in fossil records and tectonic activity, and it's known in popular culture as Zeus's Wrath.

Approximately one and a half billion years ago, one of the moons in orbit around Zeus fell into the gravitational pull of the planet and the resulting cosmic catastrophe saw a terrestrial world the size of old Earth ripped apart. While most of the debris from the event would form the dense asteroid field that orbits Zeus, one large chunk was thrown into the vastness of space.

For the next 500 million years, this massive celestial body tumbled through the Tencendur system, it's erratic orbital path effected by every planetary body. One fateful day it crossed the orbital path of Neoterra, slamming into the southern hemisphere. The impact of the debris caused a massive ecological and geological catastrophe. Entire continental plates buckled and the resulting shockwave and fireball nearly wiped the planet clean of all life. Over the next 200 million years, volcanic and tectonic activity almost finished the job. After

the destruction subsided, the few lifeforms that survived the catastrophic events clawed their way to dominance reflecting a fragile and non-diverse ecology that Neoterrans struggle daily to preserve.

NORTHERN COLD FRONTS

The impact of the asteroid caused a shift in the northern hemisphere's climate pattern creating unusually cold weather fronts in the Nostrum Ocean. These weather fronts pick up the warm, moist air traveling north and transform it into extreme cold fronts that freeze the coasts of the northern continents and create frequent blizzards. These cold fronts move through the northern hemisphere creating extreme microclimates near Bose Harbour and other northern ports resulting in dramatically colder temperatures compared to the rest of Neoterra.

GREAT TIDES

The twin moons of Neoterra (see "Tencendur System," p. 48) create tides similar to Earth's tidal calendar, but every few decades the moons come into conjunction, dramatically altering the tides and weather of the world. This event causes a variety of extreme weather events worldwide, but most significant are the Great Tides generating massive waves across the world. These wave fronts batter the shores of Neoterra with tsunami-sized waves.

Thanks to effective infrastructure development and tidal prediction algorithms by ALEPH, all but the worst damage from the tidal events is casually mitigated, but on rare occasions Neoterran coastal cities can suffer damage causing billions of Oceana in damage. The less extreme wave systems are a source of extreme sport surfing where the best athletes in the Human Sphere take on the waves for the entertainment of billions of people. All proceeds for the events go to charity to help the victims of the tides.

FLORA & FAUNA

Incautious development led to ecological collapse on Solitudo Island in the early days of colonisation. This event fundamentally shaped Neoterran culture prioritizing protecting Neoterra's natural environment. While a pale shadow of Haqqislamic environmental traditions, Neoterran naturalism plays a key role in Neoterran culture with outdoor activities and exploration of natural wonders generating billions in profit every year.

Neoterra's wildlife consists almost exclusively of a single family of closely related animals akin to warm-blooded lizards collectively called reptilos. These creatures fill a wide variety of ecological niches ranging from apex predators to herds of grazing herbivores, and even roles normally filled

by insects on Earth. Reptilos are grouped into sects identified roughly by colour: A ruddy crimson, an iridescent cerulean, and a scaly iridescent — or popularly as red, blue, and green. Each sect is incredibly hostile to the other sects, but carnivores from one sect cannot consume the meat of another sect.

The exception is Spes Archipelago which is known for its diverse biosphere which was spared the worst, biologically speaking, of the impact of Zeus's Wrath. A wide variety of species can be found in the jungles and rivers of this teeming archipelago rivalling Gratia Archipelago's natural beauty.

TRAPPER VINES

Throughout the forests, jungles, and seas of Neoterra is a variety of deadly plant that feeds on the bodily fluids of animals. They are covered in poisonous thorns that paralyse animals scratched by them and contact with the thorns causes the vines to snare and entangle its prey. As the plants tighten around the captured creature, the thorns penetrate the skin and reservoirs in the thorns drain the vital fluids from the creature. In order to keep a regular flow of fluids from the entangled animal, the vines steadily tighten over time draining the creature over a few days.

The plants vary in size from garden nuisances to ones that feed on large reptilos. The vines are surprisingly fast moving for a plant, and they are a regular problem for negligent tourists, hikers, and children. Regular Maya reports tell of tourists who thought they didn't need a guide as well as stories of children lost to these plants.

DRAKES

These flying reptilos fill the role held by birds of prey on Earth, and all are exclusively carnivores. The reptilos vary in behaviour and size, but all are characterised by a membrane stretched between their front and rear legs for flight. When they are on the ground they'll crawl on all fours.

There are a number of notable species such as the *Acalica*, a breed of hanging drakes that suspend upside-down by their hind legs from cliffs in large colonies. They are commonly kept as pets in groups of six to ten. The largest of the drakes can carry away small animals or even small children on rare occasions.

ECONOMY

Decisions and innovations made in the boardrooms and workshops of Neoterra will shape the Human Sphere's economic development from Earth to the Human Edge. Some commentators joke the Neoterran economy is the glint on the jewel of the Human Sphere. While the world's economy is

NEOTERRAN OCEANS

Cook Ocean: A very warm and calm ocean packed with transcontinental military and civilian naval traffic. Leaked Hexahedron reports suggest the recent spike in piracy on the ocean are actually covert operations by an unidentified power.

Australis Ocean: Drone cargo ships ferry tons of cargo annually from resource extraction sites like Santa Maria de la Soledad on this cool, calm ocean.

Nostrum Ocean: The ocean's abundant and varied plankton feeds a wide variety of reptilos, making it a rich source of food and environmental tourism. Wild fisheries harvest a myriad of reptilos, but the work is dangerous due to the ocean's unpredictable weather.

Samudra Ocean: This rough ocean is a source of the worst of the Great Tides and combined with water temperatures, makes the Samudra a very rough ocean. The ocean is home to a breed of whale-sized, phosphorescent reptilos that resemble a manta ray. These insatiably curious and friendly creatures shadow boats moving cross the ocean, and sailors consider them a good omen.

varied, the major industries are quantronics and financial services.

The world's varied economy is dominated by the quantronics industry. The ground-breaking, civilian market is the most robust in the Human Sphere. Neoterra is also home to the latest military-grade quantronics research and development, and highly secure, top-secret facilities are regular targets of espionage.

Neoterran banking centres provide financial services considered the most secure in the Human Sphere with ALEPH securing transactions and guaranteeing the reliability of financial predictions. All manner of loans, insurance, and investments move through Central Bank in Turoqua. Meanwhile the Vatican Bank has ever greater influence over PanOceanian society, and the Hospital Bank comforts the faithful with the knowledge their investment in the bank supports the Order of St. Lazarus (See *Infinity Corebook*, p. 179).

Finally, Neoterra's orbit contains extensive military and civilian shipyards servicing everything from small, civilian transports to deadly military combat carriers. The orbital shipyards of Neoterra are abuzz with building and spaceship enthusiasts flock to watch the flurry of activity, and possibly catch a glimpse of the latest ships under construction.

LAW AND ORDER

Law enforcement on Neoterra is based on the concept that local authorities have the ultimate authority starting at the local block force. While larger, centralised law enforcement agencies can claim local authority, it requires the permission of the local force to operate. A point of contention between the law enforcement agencies comes with large agencies overstepping their bounds.

BLOCK FORCES

A block force is the smallest type of law enforcement agency on Neoterra and they are responsible for policing the local districts of the cities. Each block force is based out of their local watch house where officers report for duty. Block forces rely heavily upon AI assistance from ALEPH for coordinating the placement of officers. Officers are highly trained and capable of dealing with numerous issues ranging from mental health emergencies to violent crime. Watch houses are organised centrally by a police council overseen by lobby-elected commissioners.

CENTRAL DEPARTMENT OF CRIMINAL INTELLIGENCE

The Central Department of Criminal Intelligence (CDCI) is responsible for investigating any crime crossing district lines or which "impacts planetary or national security". They can also be called in to fulfil security, crowd control, anti-terrorist duties, and to address general public unrest.

The CDIC has a variety of units assigned to address a broad spectrum of crimes including smuggling, narcotics, human trafficking, and other intercontinental crimes. The units are highly specialised relying on ALEPH for coordination, and mixed unit teams are not unusual during an investigation. There are two notorious units in the CDIC. The Financial Crime Unit (FCU) works closely with ALEPH to monitor financial transactions for signs of money laundering and other financial fraud. Another infamous unit is the Special Narcotics Force (SNF) which is responsible for combating narcotics smuggling on Neoterra. The criminals they hunt tend to call them "Sniffers", after the deployable sensor, for the fact that once they're on you they'll never lose your signal. The unit's current focus is the nitrocaine epidemic sweeping Neoterra.

AUXILIA

The Auxilia operate across Neoterra as the planetary defence army forming the backbone of defence for the capital of PanOceania. They are tasked with a wide variety of security functions including convoy escort, of both military and civilian assets, as well as counter-terrorism operations. In times of disaster or tragedy they can be deployed to provide relief and security.

The Auxilia are pampered by the High Command, with superior access to high-tech equipment. Each member of this unit has an Auxbot linked to their geist. They are regularly engaged in wargames on the Sankt Martin Plains in Aquila, but conspiracy theorists claim the wargames are a cover for other operations.

DEMOGRAPHICS AND CULTURE

A Neoterran is always connected to Maya and their day begins with checking their messages, posting live updates or streaming their morning to their friends and family, and checking the latest news. Some go too far, becoming *surfistas*: people who choose to live in the moment, letting ALEPH and their devices direct them through life. With the liberty that all PanOceanians have, it's a waste to just surf along.

TERRITORY RESPONSE GROUP (TRG)

The Territory Response Group (TRG) is a subsection of the CDCI that focuses on policing rural areas outside the major cities. The TRG adopted the structure of the Auxilia due to their operations in rural and isolated areas. They provide police protection to small, trial settlements and research outposts. Their duties focus heavily on anti-poaching and breaking up illegal settlements. The TRG finds itself in conflict with Atek populations who've set up camps away from the city, which they raze before arresting the inhabitants.

The TRG unit from Novaria was made famous by "In Harm's Way", a recent eco-documentary, covering their actions fighting poachers on Gratia Archipelago. Critics have described it as a heart-warming portrayal of finding hope amid loss and an environmental call to action of the generation.

OPERATION QIÓNG

A leaked Bureau Noir report known as the Qingdao Report claims a consortium of top Yutang companies, Yǎnjīng military intelligence service agents, and underground Triad organisations have colluded to claim hegemony over the entire Human Sphere. Operation Qióng is described to involve an operation where Yǎnjīng agents funnelled weapons and resources through the Triad to dissident groups and criminals bent on disrupting Neoterra's society and economy. They may have even been playing both sides of the Atek controversy funnelling equipment to both Revolta and Ateks Out! militants.

AQUILA MAINLAND

The rolling Sankt Martin plains stretch across much of the continent, with their wide vistas and stunning sunsets the subject of a multitude of nature documentaries. Home to a variety of Lagartos Colosos herded by the local ranchers for their delicious meat, the creatures' fine hides are used in some of the latest fashions.

The Schwarz Bergrücken range on the northern end of the continent prevents cold weather from raging across the plains and is characterised by constant snow and freezing temperatures. The harshness of the environment is also considered a thing of beauty. The mountains are home to a breed of reptilos famed for their mating rituals, and the sounds of their skulls slamming together echo through the range during mating season.

Neoterra has a health-focused culture, and most people start their day with exercise in one of the many recreation centres, gyms, and parks. After their exercise, most spend their day either working or engaging in community service to build their reputation or score points on the List of Deeds. The religious attend daily services at least once a week, with Sunday being the most common for Christians.

NEOTERRAN CIVIL RIGHTS ASSOCIATION (NCRA)

The Neoterran Civil Rights Association was formed in the aftermath of a block force's aggressive response to an anti-block force violent protest in Sybaris about a decade ago. Nuns from the Congregation of the Holy Trinity intervened by forming a human barrier, and the police backed down and the NCRA was born.

The Neoterran Civil Rights Association is led by Sister Ana Macedo, and she uses her unexpected Maya notoriety to organise protests fighting for Atek rights. Ana and her Sisters are unusually outspoken, and pushing an order, whose chief tenant is humility, into an intense national debate. Sister Ana regularly defies her Reverend Mother's orders to tone down her action, and has drawn the ire of the Papal See for defying her Bishop's orders when the *Go-Go Marlene! Show* followed her in recent protest actions. NCRA activist assistance ranges from free software updates to comlog implants in pop-up surgical centres for Atek children. They work closely with the Neoterran Integration Fund to provide these essential services.

This new civil rights movement struck a chord among Neoterran youth who've embraced the cause to a greater degree. Those who stand in solidarity with the Ateks have adopted the stereotypical bright techno-favela style of hair and clothes. "Change is Coming", the Neo-Ragga anthem of the Atek movement blasts from university dorm rooms across the Hyperpower.

ATEKS OUT! LOBBY

While the NCRA focuses on integrating the Ateks into Neoterran society, the Ateks Out! lobby focuses on barring Ateks from participating in Neoterran society. The lobby's legislation efforts range from requiring certain bio-implants for access to core city areas to deporting the residents of Atek slums somewhere out of sight — off the planet if possible. Ateks Out! rails against the Neoterran Civil Rights Association's raucous protests, while lobbying for the disintegration of the Neoterran Integration Fund.

Under the surface of this political activity lies something darker. Gangs of Ateks Out! extremists attack techno-favelas over real or perceived crimes by Ateks in Neoterran cities. These gangs conceal their faces with balaclavas and quantronic-viral masks displaying anti-Atek slogans. Accusations abound of gangs evicting Ateks during Sybaris' gentrification. The authorities have been unable to identify the criminals and Ian Coelho, the leader of Ateks Out!, may be secretly supporting the extremists.

REVOLTA

Revolta formed out of the discontent of Ateks' treatment by the PanOceanian government. The loose organisation has engaged in a mix of cybercrime and limited terrorist activities under the auspices of protecting Atek rights. With almost religious zeal they reject ALEPH and PanOceanian culture refusing basic bio-implants that would allow them access to much of PanOceanian culture.

Revolta is led by a mysterious individual known only as Plato. At this time, the Hexahedron can't definitively ascertain the true identity of this revolutionary whose diatribes filter from the depths of Arachne to ears of Maya-users on Neoterra. Conflicting reports suggest they may be getting covert support from Nomad or Yu Jing operatives.

AQUILA

The Aquila continent is the heart of Neoterran military culture, and its cities hold the most prestigious military academies. Each city on Aquila is a military city from the imposing fortresses that dominate their skylines to military schools shaping each city economically and culturally.

AQUILA MANOEUVRES

Regular military manoeuvres take place across the continent providing training in the variety of climates. Aquila is in a constant state of military activity and training, and the ranchers complain about the exercises spooking their reptilos. Regardless, the locals are always happy to see PanOceanian troops.

The most recent manoeuvres in the Sankt Martin plains fall under the umbrella of a wargame called Operation Brasstacks. While these wargames seem rather commonplace, the Hexahedron is using them as cover to destroy suspected camouflaged facilities linked to nitrocaine smuggling and production

CLAUSEWITZ

Clausewitz sits on the edge of low cliffs ringing Schlieffen Bay, and the cliffs conceal a labyrinthine network with vast chambers large enough to fit buildings. The Clausewitz Citadel is a seemingly blank, thirty-storey cylinder that rests some ten kilometres from the coast. Most of the districts are short buildings whose height is deceiving as there are a number of levels underneath, built into the caves below. Residents use a mix of surface streets and underground thoroughfares to travel the city.

Meerbusch rests at the base of the cliffs, on a beach that stretches the entirety of Schlieffen Bay. Meerbusch's laidback culture is popular with academy cadets for relaxation. As one enters the district, whether by sea or land, they are bombarded with live music, boisterous pub-going crowds, and street artists. The most popular location is a pub called The Happy Crab, and it's known for cheap beer and steamed blind crabs.

Upscale Haan runs counter to almost everything that Meerbusch represents and serves the economic elite of the city. The city's financial district holds a branch of the Vatican Bank and branches of many other financial institutions. Wealthy district residents live in homes hanging off the side of the cliffs accessible only by private elevators or subterranean tunnels

Further inland from the coast lies the Hilden district, popular among the hippest trendsetters of Neoterra. The district has become a tech business centre for a wide variety of robotics technology start-ups that increasingly rely on Military Complex funding for their research. The district runs counter to the laidback beach culture, adopting what can be described as "counterculture chic" that some claim is ruining the vibe of the city.

Clausewitz is not without its techno-favelas, and the most notable is Sternschanze, or as it's known by the locals, "Schanze". The city's largest techno-favela claims space in the tunnels under the city and is a wild place with diverse political views. The favela is constantly raided by the local block forces due to blatant violations of environmental protection laws. These constant raids have bolstered the NRCA presence, but the raids are turning more aggressive with each passing year, and a Revolta cell is recruiting among the locals.

Clausewitz Advanced Institution Centre: The CAIC continually strives to advance the battlefield superiority of PanOceanian's military-grade TAGs and dronbots of the PanOceanian military. Moto. tronica is a constant presence having worked with CAIC for decades, and the facility is responsible for bringing the latest TAGs and Auxbots through final testing. A highly classified testing program called the Advanced Development Program is tasked with

AQUILA ARCHIPELAGO

Splendor Archipelago is an undeveloped chain used by weapon smugglers for hardware storage prior to sale. The CDCI occasionally raid here, but have yet to make any newsworthy arrests. Various conspiracy theories link the smugglers to everything from opportunity theft and Hexahedron backed resistance, to blackmarket ops for MagnaObra and others. The favoured theory, however, links them to Yu Jing.

TONHALLE MUSIKHALLE

This breathtaking music hall in the Haan district is famous for its use of the natural acoustics of the cavern, and entire pieces have been written with the natural acoustics in mind. The music resonates through the caverns and is often heard throughout Schlieffen Bay as it bounces off the cliff walls.

reverse-engineering captured equipment from across the Human Sphere including Tohaa and Combined Army equipment.

Junker Military Engineering School: This small training centre trains PanOceanian's famed Machinists on TAGs and drones, while mastering battlefield engineering and demolitions.

The Peeler Training Field is an extensive training field for combat engineering at the academy, where trainees can work with the latest combat engineering and demolitions techniques. Locals know when training is taking place by the explosions regularly echoing from the academy's facilities.

The Skunkworks academy training program encourages students to explore bizarre lines of research as part of their training. It is closely associated with CAIC and the best Machinists are recruited to work at the academy. The program is notoriously high-pressure and the dropout rate is exceedingly high.

ROMMEL

While most cities on Aquila hug the coast, Rommel is a landlocked city built in the twisting limestone canyons of the Delbrück Labyrinth. The seemingly organic layout of the city is difficult to navigate, and learning your way around is a rite of passage for new residents.

The military fortress known as the Burrow lies in Weiswand Canyon, a narrow, dead ended, slot canyon. The subterranean fortress is protected by a massive, heavily guarded gate built to resist all manner of bombardment. As new industries and non-military residents moved to the city, they followed suit in their construction and much of the city is underground or built into the canyon walls.

The Commons is a residential and shopping district in Gelbeshaus Canyon, and is identified by twelve distinctive rock pillars extending above the treeline. The district's structures have been built up the sides and into the pillars. Each of the pillars is identified simply by a number. The district is home to a broad mix of residential housing and commercial services comprising the beating heart of the city.

Pillar Four: Pillar Four is home to much of the entertainment services in the district with a wide variety of concert venues and virtual reality entertainment services. Pillar Four has a newly opened Aristeia! ring, and Pillar Four Arena draws fighters from around the Sphere who want to test their skills in its risky, multi-level fighting arena.

Pillar Ten: Pillar Ten is in the northeastern end of the Commons, and is occupied by a local Atek community. This techno-favela climbs the formation's seven-storey height, and is topped with a building where the Ateks meet to discuss community issues. The residents of this favela are called "Tenners" by the locals, and they've built a solid relationship with Rommel's strongest local municipal lobby much to the chagrin of the city's police council.

Palo Duro Racing Circuit: Palo Duro Canyon is a narrow canyon that's a hotspot for high-speed air racing with experimental, single-seater aircraft. The canyon is notorious for its tight turns and unpredictable winds drawing the most skilled and daring pilots from across the Human Sphere. The Annual Palo Duro Open is has become incredibly popular in the last few years.

Rommel Armoured Command School: The Rommel Armoured Command School (RACS) is the premier armoured combat training academy in the Hyperpower and the Human Sphere. This school trains officers in the tactics and strategies of armoured vehicular combat. While Clausewitz focuses on light TAG training, the RACS focusses on training with heavy armour; unusual for this era of highly mobile warfare. Various heavy and specialist TAG models are tested and trained with at the RACS including the occasional Seraph.

SANTIAGO DE NEOTERRA

Santiago de Neoterra in the heart of the Sankt Martin Plains is the economic centre of the Aquilian continent. The metropolis is a bustling high-tech city full of research facilities, both military and civilian, and the city's economy dominates continental cybernetics, weapons, and dronbotics development. The city relies heavily on experimental autodroids for law enforcement purposes, freeing up the block forces for more active community policing, and Santiago de Neoterra has become the national model for addressing the Atek problem, and their programs providing accessible schooling, wide-ranging integration programs, and free, pop-up implant clinics to help locals are being adopted by other municipalities.

Civilian research facilities are the primary employer in the city, but Military Complex funding permeates much of the research. Scattered throughout the surrounding rolling hillside are a number of highly classified research facilities. These isolated facilities research cutting-edge military technology, and are guarded by highly trained forces. Corporate and military espionage is a common occurrence, but information about it is suppressed.

Santiago de Neoterra is city overflowing with high-tech facilities, and Barrio Bombarda is a prime example of the city's incestuous relationship between private research and the Military Complex. Smaller Military Complex and private research facilities dot the district working with Moto.tronica to test and research the latest dronbots. Traffic congestion is a common problem when prototypes are transferred to field testing facilities in the Los Colinas Hills or the spaceport in Barrio Chelas.

The Santo Angel district is a visual spectacle at night, and this impressive party district sports two cultural hotspots: Sector 62 and Club Orbital. While the former caters to those seeking the latest dance music and experimental refreshments, the latter hosts a myriad of musical performances from provocative modern artists to late 21st century tributes. The founder of Club Orbital, Leonor Dantas, is an Atek turned orbital sports star who returned home to give something back to her favela in Olivar Sur.

Olivar Sur is the city's techno-favela lying on the southern end of the Santo Angel District. The city laboured to improve the status of Ateks in the city, but it was only possible through an uneasy alliance formed between the Falco lobby and Leonor Dantas that overcame the favela's rightful distrust of the government. The favela has gone through a transformation, and has become an artists' community with buildings decorated in eclectic colours and Atek cultural icons.

Finally, Iacobus Point is the home to the Aquila Officers Academy. The Aquila Officers Academy trains the officers in combat search and clearing operations, VIP protection, as well as the security of classified military documents and maximum security facilities under Code Red situations. Cadets may find themselves in the middle of a test when they least expect it. This training program birthed a famous pub crawl that is a rite of passage for graduates.

Turing Training Centre: The Turing Centre trains officers in technological-counter operations and cryptology to counter the enemy's technological advantage. Specialists from this school are known for their ability to operate in a technological vacuum. Local businesses have put puzzles and codes in their establishments, and Turing Centre students who crack the codes get a free drink. Cheating on the codes is looked down upon.

Indigo Blade Psyops School: The Indigo Blade school is a classified, special division of the psyops school that trains officers in the use of offensive psychological warfare. Their training runs the gamut of psychological warfare including media manipulation and Maya trend engineering. The school is rumoured to have a highly effective insurgency warfare training program.

Executive Protection School: This school prepares graduates for managing security operations for sensitive document transfers and VIP protection. Graduates of this school will likely find themselves protecting diplomats, government or church officials, and high-value personnel. Graduates are known for being competent sharpshooters and trained in combat driving, as well as knowing which fork to use.

VON MOLTKE

Frigid Von Moltke sits on the frozen Sax Harbour that ice-breaking drones keep clear of ice in all but the summer months. The city prides itself on hospitality, and "Welcome Home" is the unofficial, municipal motto. The hospitality dates back to the early days of colonisation when the early colonists established public halls as community centres and local government houses. These public halls are the centres of a robust brewing culture, and each district has its own unique beer. The autumnal beer festival draws thousands of tourists every year.

Sax Harbour is the city's industrial centre operating day and night, and is regularly trafficked by cargo ships exporting resources extracted from the Schwarz Bergrücken range. The harbour is guarded by Luckner Naval Base, and the ships stationed at the base patrol Nostrum Ocean engaging in scientific research and anti-piracy operations.

The techno-favela in the Tossens district has taken a turn for the worst as Comuna thugs from the aggressive Acontecimento mafia spread nitrocaine, while gaining public sympathy for defending the community from local Ateks Out! vigilantes. Despite the recent troubles, the district is the heart of a back-to-basics beer brewing fad. People endure the cold to relax in the picturesque snowy beer gardens.

Von Moltke Academy: Von Moltke is home to the Neoterra Capitaline Army's extreme environment training school for deployment on Svalarheima. Only a select few can endure Von Moltke's intense training program. Graduates have a stoic attitude, and are said to have "Moltke ice" in their veins.

The academy prepares soldiers for fighting in a fearsome environment, and the school is famous for its Cold Weather Indoctrination Course. This week-long initiation course sends squads into the freezing Schwarz Bergrücken range to test their mettle under the supervision of unyielding drill

FRIGID HOSPIALITY

Von Moltke's character is quaint and relaxed. You'll always find shelter from the cold, whether you're marvelling at the size of Wilhelmshaven's beer hall while downing a pint of their famous doppelbock, or sampling the multitude of beers from the Loxstedt district. The snow-covered streets have a comfortable and friendly atmosphere.

GRATIA GEOGRAPHY

The impact of Zeus's Wrath dramatically affected the continent, with the resultant natural wonders drawing scientists, explorers, tourists, and thrill seekers from across the Human Sphere.

Famous for its unique geological fold formations, Fold Valley is a long valley running the length of the continent. It's also a hotspot for viewing the Lagartos Coloso migrating to their spawning grounds, with air tours offer relaxing air cruises to view the enchanting formations of the herds.

The extensive Tamacala Wetlands are popular for hovercraft excursions from Novaria. Thrill seekers and scientists employ guides to navigate the hostile environment, whilst mercenaries are regularly hired for protection. The impact of Zeus's Wrath buckled a portion of the continental plate, resulting in the sheer Deadman's Cliffs, a popular destination for adrenaline junkies. Other than the resorts on Tres Hermana, the only hotel outside of Novaria hangs from the cliffs here, providing an amazing view of a breed of nocturnal drake whose iridescent green scales reflect the rising and setting sun in an awe-inspiring lightshow.

The spawning grounds for the Lagarto Coloso who return here throughout their lifetime, Cala Salada beach runs along the south-western shore of the continent. Air and sea cruises bring tourists to watch these massive beasts frolic in the water during birthing season.

Named Isla Isabel, Isla Octavia, and Isla Valentina, Tres Hermanas is the trio of smaller landmasses north of Gratia Largo. Their resorts are the exclusive domain of celebrities and the filthy rich, with security at each especially tight.

sergeants with minimal cold weather protection. If they can make it through the course, then they are formally accepted into the academy, but most fail to complete the course. Soldiers brag about which finger or toe had to be replaced because of the cold as a point of pride.

GRATIA ARCHIPELAGO

Gratia Archipelago is the smallest of the continents and a lush landscape established as a nature preserve in an effort to protect the planet's ecosystem. The continent's lone city, Novaria, is the launching point for eco-tourism to see the natural wonders of the continent via river, ground, and air tours. Outside of the few resorts and waystations scattered around the continent, the island is effectively uninhabited wildlands.

A wide variety of reptilos on the continent are the target of poachers, and the Territory Response Group maintain outposts to hunt the poachers. Additionally, the sparse population on the continent makes the area a centre of trans-orbital smuggling by the Comuna and Triads. Smuggler ships descend into the upper atmosphere and drop containers designed to survive the landings. The criminal

organisations recover the cargo, and then distribute the contraband across the planet.

NOVARIA

This resort town is a destination for the rich and famous where you'll find the hottest parties and the best food. The city has taken on a reputation as a city where people celebrate life-changing events ranging from graduations to marriages to anniversaries giving the city a perpetual, celebratory atmosphere.

Visitors can find all manner of experience, both family friendly and not, in Novaria. The district of San Antonio is known for its rowdy parties and its red-light areas. The district has a seedy reputation for celebrations getting out of hand. In stark contrast to San Antonio is the high end Manacor district whose luminous hotel casinos house extravagant shops and exclusive bistros cater to those having extravagant honeymoons or indulgent getaways.

Puerto Antiguo is a destination for families looking to explore the biological wonders of Gratia Archipelago from the safety of the city. The district contains venerable research facilities that have studied the Archipelago's bio-diversity since Neoterra's discovery. Visitors experience

the extensive zoos and aquariums in the district, and children from around the Human Sphere are elated by the performance of a red, reptilos whale named Tonto. The tourism funds cutting edge zoological and biological scientific research, and the facility secured funding for a top-secret study of Combined Army troops' remains recovered on the battlefield.

LUX

The first settlers of Lux hailed from Australia and New Zealand, and their descendants bear many hallmarks of those cultures. English is the common language and sport is an obsession, largely revolving around several competing football clubs with cricket coming in a close second. The continent is known for the beauty of its mountainous landscape and sweeping forested lowlands.

BOSE HARBOUR

Bose Harbour's economy centres on deep water fishing and processing containing the largest fisheries on the planet. Logging is a seasonal part of the Bose Harbour economy, and logging camps in the surrounding woodlands draws workers from around the planet for seasonal summer work. A summer in logging or fishing in Bose Harbour has become a common popular work for university students across Neoterra, and those who just want to disappear for a little while.

A few years ago, historic Maxwell Row was an abandoned fishery, but the district has been refurbished with shopping, restaurants, extensive aquarium, and an educational centre. The global fishing powerhouse, Bose Harbour Fisheries, funds the facility, and the company's green reptilos mascot gives tours, in holographic form, through the various aquatic attractions.

DARWIN

The city of Darwin sits on the southern coast of the continent and much of its economy is dedicated to servicing the Main Operating Base, home to the elite Neoterra Bolts of the Capitaline Army. You'll rarely find the Bolts present in town, as most of them are deployed. The town has the air of a heavily armed university town.

Darwin Main Operating Base is the primary facility in the city, and is the first stop for Bolts back from deployment in defence of PanOceania's interests across the Human Sphere. The sounds of Bolts recruits training on the beaches are heard each day, and trainees are regularly seen around the city. The people of Darwin have a close relationship with

the base, and soldiers know they will find a friendly face anywhere in the city.

The main operating base is a major command centre for operations under the PanOceanian Special Operations command. The base's highly secure perimeter is regularly patrolled, and anyone violating the perimeter can expect to be met by an armed patrol that will detained and question them.

Prospect Cove is dominated by the military dock for training operations and general patrols. Training operations involving aquatic landings are regularly practiced nearby, and the boats used in training berth here for maintenance. Brookvale is a major shopping centre just to the north of the cove and automated ferries provide comfortable public transit for commuting residents.

Dirac Hills is a ramshackle techno-favela on the outskirts of Darwin that's increasingly hostile to the local block forces. A cell of Revolta has taken root in the favela, and a series of attacks against police officers, NRCA activists, and, in one instance, a Neoterran Bolt recruit are believed to be their handiwork. The recent events allowed Ateks Out! sympathies to take root in the city, and anti-Atek vigilantes have been seen in the Dirac Hills favela.

Despite these problems, the city is generally considered a great place to live for those who like sun and warm weather. The city's championship rugby team is stuck on a losing streak that has become a thing of infamy. Every few seasons the team gets close to winning the championship only to see their hopes dashed in the playoffs.

Battlespace Preparation School: This specialised school prepares the Neoterran Bolts for the wide variety of combat roles and environments to which they will be deployed after graduation. Battlespace Preparation School graduates have elite training in a wide variety of extreme environments ranging from space to underwater operations. Soldiers at the school train for operations including, but not limited to, search and destroy, breach and clear techniques, and airborne assault. The unforgiving curriculum pushes soldiers to their limits, and prepares them for the trials they'll face on the battlefield.

Combined Skills School: The Combined Skills School is the final step for a recruit becoming a full-fledged Bolt. Trainees at the CSS focus on punishment operations specifically designed to deter future enemy action. Bolts master the effective use of force to break the will of the enemy. As Neoterran Bolts, they will mete out the appropriate responses to challenges to PanOceanian influence on the Human Sphere and will find themselves

LUX GEOGRAPHY

The continent is dominated by three mountain ranges with the Aspiring Range in the north, the Norgay range lying in the centre of the continent, and the canyon-filled Cradle Range. The Planck Canyon Network runs the length of the continent, and the fast-moving water empties into the Galileo River basin in the Nostrum Ocean. The water is generally rough and not effective for river transport, but it is a destination for hikers and extreme water sports.

The Humboldt coast runs the length of the coast from Newton City to Darwin. This semi-tropical forest is popular for with hikers and backpackers. There are a number of secure areas cordoned off by the Military Complex, and their purpose runs from benign research to conspiracy theory according to those on Maya.

AMUNDSEN DEEP WATER

Situated near Bose Harbour, the Amundsen Deep Water Research Facility studies the Nostrum Ocean to better understand the lifecycle of the reptilos they fish and their deepwater habitats. The facility is on the forefront of submersible research and a Bose Harbour Fisheries grant funded an experimental submarine that can dive deeper than any known submarine. Unknown to the public, the research facility is covertly funded by the Military Complex's interest in the submarine's capabilities. The presence of Military Complex personnel has been a point of contention for the lead scientist on the project.

operating in all corners of their Hyperpower's hegemony from Human Edge to right on their doorstep on Neoterra.

EINSTEINBURG

This city is divided along cultural and economic lines, as well as physical geography, and is effectively two cities built into the walls of Dor Canyon that separates them. The city is a popular destination for rock climbers and spelunkers exploring the formations and caves created by the river below

This multi-tier city clings to the sides of the canyon which are connected by two massive bridges over the River Iss that carries most of the city's cross-canyon traffic. Southgate and Northgate bridges are massive structures containing shopping centres, restaurants, and public transit hubs, and smaller bridges criss-cross the canyon interconnecting the districts. The bridges have become a point of contention, because Ateks are commonly blocked from crossing the bridges. The local Atek community is considered one of the more isolated in PanOceania.

The two sides of town have distinct atmospheres with Bohrs renowned for their local barbeque and rugged attitude. In comparison, Heisenburg is known for lavish shops, galleries, and the Glass Bridge restaurant famous for its amazing views as much as the food. There is a deep, yet friendly rivalry between the two parts of town that culminates in regular football matches that are notorious for getting rowdy. The city is famous for its festival of lights during Christmas when it is covered in intricate and festival light displays using everything from traditional incandescent lights to holograms.

HAWKING'S JUNCTION

Hawking's Junction's chief industries are mining and scientific research, specifically stellar observation. The horizon is dominated by an array of radio telescopes that observe the Milky Way from Neoterra's position in the galaxy. Additionally, the city's Rapid Resource Transport System (RRTS) is a massive network of maglev lines that carries goods to every city on the continent. The system is fully managed by ALEPH, and the trains formed by the containers can swap containers while moving at 1000kmh.

The district of West Faraday is the home of a major Maya telecommunications hub, and diligent Hexahedron agents are alert for any attempts to sabotage the node. The district is home to a number of science research firms, but they eschew funding and oversight from the Military Complex as the firms don't want their research used for military

purposes. Apartment blocks make up the vast majority of the residential buildings, but all have rooftop green spaces where astronomy enthusiasts can get a clear look at the stars thanks to the city's strict light pollution laws.

East Faraday is characterized by affordable residential blocks and bustling shopping districts. This district is where almost everyone comes for their daily shopping needs. People from all walks of life can be seen interacting here.

The refineries of the Rontgen district work day and night under strict air quality laws to avoid interfering in stellar observation. Living in the shadow of Rontgen's refineries are the city's Ateks. The Ateks work in the refineries and nearby mines, and recent Mayacasts documented how the Ateks are exploited by the Salcedo family.

LIVINGSTONE

Livingstone is less a city and more of a fortified prison complex dominated by the Tower High-Security Correctional Facility, where PanOceania's most dangerous convicts are kept under lock, key, and behavioural inhibitors. The prison is built into the side of a cliff, accessible only by VTOL aircraft. The nearby town of Livingstone is a charming prefabricated residential town which seems to have been lifted straight from a real-estate catalogue. However, this town was custom built to house the prison staff and their families. Children playing in the shadow of this facility are often completely unaware of the monsters that dwell nearby.

The large prison facility, simply referred to as "The Tower", is made up four cell blocks housing a few thousand inmates each. The cell blocks are each increasingly secure and connection points between cell blocks are rigged with demolition charges to prevent prisoners from taking over the prison.

An officer of the Aquila Academy directs all security at the prison, and reports directly to the warden except in instances of military matters. Guards at the prison operate in full armour, and riot control teams are ready to spring into action at a moment's notice. Movement of prisoners is strictly controlled, and all communications with the outside is strictly monitored. Despite the high level of security, there is an active black market within the prison trafficking in everything from popular candy to narcotics.

A mineral processing facility employs the better-behaved prisoners. Despite the dangerous and taxing conditions, prisoners compete for jobs at the facility. Hard work earns privileges such as family visitation rights, access to an improved canteen, and special access to entertainment. The north

HERSCHEL SCIENTIFIC INSTITUTE

Hawking's Junction's Herschel Scientific Institute is a well-regarded educational foundation dedicated to observing the universe. They maintain a series of radio telescopes, and coordinate the activities of various stellar observatories. The Institute is dedicated to the search for non-human life throughout the galaxy, and hopes to discover more species beyond the Tohaa and the Combined Army. They've recently been tasked with observing a known Tohaa system by the Military Complex. The readings would be at least a century old, but the Military Complex hopes to glean something off the observations.

SALCEDO MINING INTERESTS INC.

The Salcedo family dominates the mining industry in Hawking's Junction. The family is cutthroat in using its influence to open doors for their allies, and close them for those who defy them. Smaller mining operations find themselves financially strong-armed into submitting to Salcedo's interests. There are unsubstantiated rumours they may have connections with the Comuna out of Acontecimento.

and south landing pads provide the only access to the cliffside facility, with auto-drones delivering ore-laden containers hourly. These regular deliveries are heavily monitored for potential escape attempts, and the prisoners' behavioural inhibitors are tied to their proximity to the prison.

Alongside the prison are the warden's quarters and the prison administrative offices. The guard housing is located on site, and full facilities available for the guard's families including a well-stocked commissary and respected educational facilities for the children.

Life at the prison is taxing for both guards and the families. The security requirements to prevent escapes means families are prisoners almost as much as the inmates. All guards operate under a three week rotation with one week of on site duty at the prison, a week off site, on call, and a week off duty. Transport off site is heavily monitored by ALEPH to reduce the chance of escape.

While life in Livingstone is harsh, the surrounding area is full of natural beauty, and the views from the Tower out onto the Norstrum Ocean are breathtaking. Residents watch the storms forming over the water. The lightning shows and cloud formations are beautiful despite being a harbinger of dangerous weather.

NEWTON CITY

Newton City rests on a series of islands in the wide delta of the Leibniz River. Newton City, in homage to its namesake, is a city in constant motion. Buildings, a term used loosely in Newton, are constantly moving across the city on the famous Newton Arches. The arches are an architectural wonder interconnecting the islands creating an ever-changing city geography as the city's buildings move across the arch structures. While visitors complain the city is only navigable with the aid of one's geist, locals love the fact they wake up to a different view each morning. The city is well-known for its annual Apple Festival offering everything from the perfectly engineered apple to a finely crafted pint of cider.

Concealed within this constantly moving city is a highly secure, cyberwarfare centre resting on a small island on a private corporate island. The Lovelace Cyberwarfare Centre is a key operational centre defending the frontlines of Maya on Neoterra and includes a heavy guarded datacrypt. EVO-troopers and military hackers are on constant alert for any incursions into Maya, and they constantly track Nomad and Yu Jing agents in an endless, invisible war to dominate the Human Sphere.

The city's techno-favelas, like the city, are fully mobile being composed of individual boats that relocate when local law enforcement cracks down on the Ateks. The boats vary widely in size housing anywhere from a single family to as many as a dozen for larger vessels. The vessels gather in clusters up and down the coast where they've found safe haven.

PAX

Originally settled by colonists from southern Europe and Latin America, Pax is home to the largest and most influential cities on the planet. Pax is the political and economic centre of Neoterra and all of PanOceania. The continent is home to the holy NeoVatican city, PanOceania's grand capital, and the stunningly beautiful vacation hotspot of Sybaris.

NEAPOLIS

Neapolis is a popular destination for the religious and non-religious alike. Built on the shores of a hundred picturesque lagoons, the waters are a visual spectacle as they change colour hourly due to a wide variety of algae blooms that make up the local flora. The waters of the lagoons even glow at night thanks to a breed of phosphorescent algae.

The broad streets and pedestrian paths are lined with stunning architecture in homage to the Baroque style of the Italian renaissance. Neapolis is regarded as the most pleasant place on the planet for a stroll, with streets meticulously planned to reduce congestion and disperse noise pollution.

Where most Neoterran cities have highways Neapolis has canals. Boats are the most popular mode of transportation ranging from speedboats racing down the canals to lazy water buses ferrying people around the city on the Grand Canals. Every Neapolis citizen has a personal watercraft, and they're said to be born on the water. All manner of water-based racing is an immensely popular pastime, from speedboats to personal watercraft, and every Neapoli follows the racing current standings.

The city is also home to a robust community of religious artists, who explore their faith through all forms of art and expression. The Dance of Light is the annual religious festival welcoming pilgrims who've travelled to bathe in the city's purifying hot springs. The festival culminates in a grand nighttime water show, where jets of illuminated coloured water are set to music for the delight of viewers. Each year local artists compete to create a visual spectacle that will win Papal recognition during the Pope's annual visit to the festival.

ATEK DEATHS

Ateks' lack of connection with Maya and ALEPH limits their access to public transportation systems. Ateks on Lux have overcome this by stowing away on cargo containers travelling across the continent. An entire sub-culture has sprung up around the activity with a special graffiti Ateks use to communicate to future passengers. Stowing away on the rapid transit system is extremely dangerous, and Atek deaths from falls and impacts are a regular occurrence.

THE FORGOTTEN

Ultra Block is the most secure cell block in the prison, which houses the worst of the worst of PanOceania's criminals. The residents are referred to as "The Forgotten" after the reason they were initially housed in the cell block. The Military Complex uses Ultra Block to dispose of enemy operatives that are too valuable to kill or house in a cube bank. At any time there can be up to half a dozen critical enemy agents incarcerated in the cell block who are subject to regular Cube interrogation. The Military Complex is constantly on alert for extraction attempts on critical enemy assets, and highly trained Hexas agents keep watch on these critical enemy assets.

PAX GEOGRAPHY

The continent's picturesque geography is a subject of awe in the Human Sphere. The Marsiliana Plains is home to a wide range of wineries cultivating grapes, and Pax wine country is the destination for those seeking a romantic getaway in a cosy country house.

As the plains head south into the Liro River Valley, the horizon is dominated by the Aenos range to the east and Mount Celenis to the west. These majestic mountain ranges are the destinations for hikers and pilgrims respectively. Hikers take in the breath-taking views of the Bergamo trail while staying at small inns and hostels stationed within a day's hike of one other. Conversely, solemn Pilgrims climb Mount Celenis to pray and bath in waters of the mountain's the holy shrine.

Finally, there's the sights of the bewitching southern coastline. Fossils of long extinct Neoterran life have been preserved in the cliffs where they were found. Their gigantic skeletons tell the story of Neoterra before the impact of Zeus's Wrath a billion years ago.

Neapolis is a quiet city, and the residents take great pride in that fact. The city has a restrained night life, with strict rules about noise and closing times for bars and clubs. Instead, people gather in the local squares and plazas, relaxing with friends as the quiet sounds of guitars and laughter can be heard on the wind. Even this is too much for Neapolis, and residents are expected to quiet down around midnight.

San Marco is the heart of the religious art movement in Neapolis. The culture operates on a strict apprenticeship system, where aspiring artists are taken under the wing of masters for training. Each year potential students present their work to the local masters hopeful to be accepted as an apprentice. Sadly, most walk away disappointed. The lanes and canals of the district are lined with religious murals ranging from exalting to criticising, reflecting each artist's unique perspective on religion and politics. Controversy is a common theme in San Marco, much to the chagrin, and joy, of the Pope.

If one wants to bathe in Neapolis's many refreshing, hot springs then there's no better place than the Castello district. The district is dotted with spas and saunas servicing secular and religious needs. The local businesses cater to all ranges of economic status, and it's known as a place where powerful politicians will find themselves sitting next to a factory worker. Among all these locations, the Convent of Saint Cecilia is an essential stop for anyone visiting Neapolis. The convent sits at the base of Mount Celenis, and the nuns welcome a multitude of pilgrims each year. These visitors climb thousands of steps up the side of Mount

Celenis, seeking to bathe in the shrine's purifying springs while the nuns serenade the bathers with music and song honouring Saint Cecilia.

Sitting on an island in the middle of the lagoons is Murano. Murano lies just outside the jurisdictional limit of Neapolis, and isn't beholden to the laws restricting nightlife. Murano stands in stark contrast to Neapolis's quaint atmosphere. Instead, the district is a constant party, the destination for the famous and beautiful looking blow off steam in the bacchanalian atmosphere.

SAN GIOVANNI DI NEOTERRA

San Giovanni di Neoterra is a city shaped by the presence of the, now heretical, Order of the Temple. The Templars' yearning for advanced quantronic and cyber-warfare systems shepherded a robust quantronics industry that's outlasted them. San Giovanni is home to quantronic technology corporations ranging from tiny start-ups to the largest corporations in the Human Sphere. The influential presence of the Templars laid the groundwork which made San Giovanni a living city managed almost completely by ALEPH. The presence of such a vast array of quantronic companies also makes it one of the most secure cities from a cybersecurity standpoint.

San Giovanni is a city rocked by turmoil after the Order the Temple was disbanded and their assets distributed to the Order of the Hospital. For months, the city erupted in street protests after the Templars were dissolved, and demonstrators camped in front of the Cathedral of St. John of the Cross demanding the Order be restored. The protests did not save the Templars, and their supporters quickly lost any support as the evidence against the Templars was presented to the public.

Even with the evidence in the open, conspiracy theories run rampant about the real cause of the Templar's demise. The conspiracy theories inspired a plethora of books, holos, and other entertainment on the subject. The most popular is "The Guardians", a story of betrayal and torrid love affairs involving a Sphere-ranging conspiracy directed by the Papal throne to capture the last true Templar and the rogue AI they're protecting. The popularity of the show and other related entertainment draws tourists to the city to see the sites related to the fall of the Templars.

The character of the city stands in contrast appearing as a solemn monastic city combined with the latest technological wonders. Despite the recent rowdy protests, the city still has an air of contemplation as if it were a temple dedicated to expanding quantronics.

The Hospital Bank dominates the local financial services economy in San Giovanni di Neoterra, heavily investing in both the medical complex and granting loans to new businesses. The Bank's motto, "Save your Money, save your Soul" has been fully embraced by the local populace. The Bank saw a large percentage of the population shifting their savings to the Bank, or donating to the Bank's related humanitarian causes. Security at the Bank is high, and rumours suggest the vaults of the monastery hold valuable Templar developments.

San Giovanni di Neoterra is a wonderful city in which to live. The Bellosguardo district dates back to the early colonisation of Neoterra. The local architecture is meticulously preserved. and the district was recently granted protected status as a heritage site by O-12. Lying at the heart of the district is the grand Cathedral of St. John of the Cross that appears as if it floats in the centre of a large reflecting pool. Beautiful hand-carved stone shrines placed around the exterior of the pool allow Christian adherents to perform the Stations of the Cross. The cathedral is famous for its respected choir that travels the Human Sphere to inspire and awe the religious and non-religious alike. The choir's daily practice echoes through the district giving the area an almost heavenly feel.

Meanwhile, neighbouring Novoli has come to be known as Little Kyoto as immigrants, political dissidents, and refugees fleeing the Japanese Uprising have settled in the district. The new arrivals have integrated well into the local culture. The district is heavily monitored by intelligence services who hold the new arrivals suspect, and the CDIC is investigating reported Yakuza activity in the area.

SAN PIETRO

San Pietro di Neoterra is the political centre of the planet and of all PanOceania, and some might say the entire Human Sphere. This grand and beautiful metropolis is the heart of temporal and religious power. PanOceania is the greatest power to exist in human history, and the decisions made in PanOceania's capital will shape humanity's future.

San Pietro di Neoterra is the seat of the Pope guiding the Christian Church. It was here, at the end of the Ad Astra Pilgrimage, that the papal throne was brought to the Archbasilica of the Holy Trinity, and the Curia and the College of Cardinals advise the Pope on church matters. The Military Orders are also stationed within NeoVatican City, overseen by the Curia. Drawing adherents from across the Human Sphere is the Basilica of San Pietro di NeoVaticano, a grand recreation of St. Peter's Basilica in Rome, inspiring the faithful.

From within NeoVatican City also comes the Church's broad financial influence through the Vatican Bank. The papal bank is sustained by donations from the faithful, and gives the Church broad influence to shape human affairs across the Human Sphere. Deep within the bank are the vaults of the Holy Archive protecting the most valuable holy objects in Christendom. These vaults, defended by a special section of the Swiss Guard, make the vault one of the most heavily guarded locations in the Human Sphere. The vaults not only hold religious artefacts, but also items that would be considered heresy, ranging from false artefacts to ancient texts that, even now in this modern era of science, unsettle the Church. Reports also suggest the vaults contain forbidden technology created by the Order of the Templar, but these reports cannot be confirmed.

The district of San Saba is a grand market and shopping district dominated by the Theia, the Lady of Light. This massive structure in the form of the Greek goddess of light holds a great orb containing the rotating Lightball Mall, providing ever changing, panoramic views of the city for locals and tourists enjoying high-end shops and restaurants. It is also home to the Neoterran Museum of Modern Art containing the greatest collection of modern religious art in the Human Sphere. This art is not only dedicated to the Christian faith, but displays modern art from all of humanity's faiths. Security is high at the museum but you'd never know it, as the guard, a special security detachment of local Block Forces, are always in plain clothes or hovering

HOSPITALLER MEDICAL COMPLEX

San Giovanni di Neoterra is home to the cutting edge Hospitaller Medical Complex in the San Niccolo district. The medical complex specialises in a wide variety of experimental medical techniques. The medical complex can handle a wide variety of complex procedures ranging from highly infectious diseases to consciousness transfer. San Niccolo is also home to the monastery of San Giovanni di Neoterra that once belonged to the Templars. The monastery is now the home of the Order of the Hospital's Grand Master as well as the headquarters of the Hospital Bank.

TEMPLAR SYMPATHIZERS

A few Templars found refuge among the Nomads, and they refuse to accept the Church's judgement. They found supporters among the Nomads for a wide variety of reasons running a wide gamut ranging from believing the evidence was fabricated, to pro-AI development groups that disagree with the international regulations on AI development. These sympathizers argue on Maya about the minutia of the trial and evidence to conspiracy theory. Nomad operatives use the conspiracy theory groups and activists as cover to operate in PanOceania, and have developed the Pizzini (see *Infinity* Corebook, p. 262) for covert communications.

behind the scenes. While San Saba is a commercial spectacle, there is also a more intimate side to the district with small shops and food stalls to service the local populace. It's here that you'll find beautifully handcrafted items and specially grown food. If there's anything you're looking for, you can find it in San Saba.

While much of the broader debate takes place in the VR-moots, officials still need to meet to organize and coordinate. The district of Ostia is home to governmental offices necessary for running the various ministries that oversee the PanOceanian Hyperpower. The offices of the President and their cabinet set the polices for the nation from the capital building, and security is always high in the area protecting government officials and their secrets. The Hexahedron is not far from the political centre of PanOceania, and the building dominates a portion of the skyline. This highly secure facility is the home of PanOceania's ever vigilant intelligence service keeping watch on the security of the Hyperpower. Regular counter-intelligence operations deter PanOceania's enemies, and the course of the Human Sphere has been saved multiple times without the public being the wiser to the risk they faced.

SERENITAS

Serenitas is a quiet city where the elderly come to live out their twilight years, and families escape the hustle of larger Neoterran cities. Serenitas encompasses the entirety of Marina Azul, and the small downtown area of Puerto Rico is the only section of the city with buildings over ten stories. The city prides itself on the multitude of relaxing public parks. If all else fails, have a beer while relaxing on the beach at Playa Morgan. Life in Serenitas is good, and the residents embrace the lazy atmosphere. It's not Varuna, but it's a good place to set down roots.

The Neoterra Capitaline Army maintains a small naval facility on Coronado Island in the middle of Marina Azul. Accessing the island requires crossing the Coronado Bridge from the Puerto Rico district. The beautifully designed bridge arcs over the water, permitting naval and civilian shipping vessels to pass under. The bridge can be lowered into the water creating defensive wall blocking the bay. Patrols from the naval base monitor low-orbit drops into the Pax-Gratia Strait by smugglers bringing illicit goods onto the planet.

SYBARIS

The Sybaris economy was built on processing resources extracted at mining platforms around Maria de la Soledad, and then shipping them off-world via the Spinoza spaceport. When the mines started to run dry, an economic crisis was on hand, but the New Sybaris Lobby had a vision of Sybaris as a beautiful, modern city, and the populace swept them into power.

After the election, the mayor immediately set to changing Sybaris from a refinery town to a luxurious city climbing the surrounding hillsides. The harsh, industrial feel of the city was reinvented with the latest Nuevo Art Deco architecture. Large swathes of the city were remodelled or outright demolished.

Not everything went smoothly, and the local techno-favelas were situated on valuable land blocking development. After months of negotiating with the residents, the mayor ordered the favelas cleared by the Sybaris block force. Construction crews quickly demolished the favelas sparking massive protests that culminated in a week of riots and looting. Through the efforts of NRCA activists the block captain responsible was punished for his actions, but his 20-year sentence for ordering violence and turning a blind eye to Ateks Out! vigilantes was later overturned due to a suspicious lack of evidence and a recanted testimony a year later. Now the former captain, Carlton Byrd, is a significant functionary and celebrity within the New Sybaris Lobby.

A decade later, Sybaris is a luxurious city, and a major holiday destination for the rich and powerful. It has some of the hottest clubs and fashion shops on the planet. The latest Maya stars, hottest fashion designers, and models are seen taking in Sybaris-style luxury. This is where the wealthy come to relax, and Sphere spanning business deals are made in this city.

The San Cristovao district is a perfect example of the city's stunning views with the finest beaches stretching for miles lined with the best cafes and hotels. The water is perfectly clear, and the reefs are incredibly active with life, making it a destination for snorkelling and diving.

The Santa Teresa district is home to Sister Ana Macedo, founder of the NRCA, and the Convent of the Trinitarian Sisters. Santa Teresa was once a techno-favela where the sisters ministered to the needs of the Atek population, but they watched in horror as the block force cleared and demolished the favela; their convent the only building spared. While Santa Teresa is the home of gorgeous hillside hotels and extravagant shopping centres, the Sisters haven't let residents forget what happened years ago. With donations collected from across PanOceania, the Sisters established a museum honouring the Atek experience telling their stories and

showing their art. The museum is now considered a key part of the cultural history of the city, and the awareness raised by Sister Ana's activities has spurred the formation of a truth and reconciliation council to address the injustices from a decade ago.

Visitors can arrive via the local spaceport owned by the Spinoza family, a once a powerful family dominating the export of extracted resources. As the economy in Sybaris weakened, the family fell on hard times almost losing their spaceport to debt collectors. The revitalisation of Sybaris found their spaceport repurposed for receiving the wealthy's private spacecraft, and the family's reputation survived. Eduardo Spinoza, the family head, has become an integral part of the local culture renowned as a playboy and political mover.

TUROQUA

Turoqua is a city of towers dwarfing any other city on Neoterra, and is the financial heart of the Human Sphere. Home to the PanOceanian Central Bank, this powerful organisation authenticates and sets interest rates for the Oceana, the national currency. The economy is driven by the Money Market of Turoqua, the heart of corporate competition. The corporations and banks compete on the markets as much as they also strive to outdo one another with daring displays of neotech architecture reaching toward the sky. The bankers and corporate heads that occupy the boardrooms and social clubs of Turoqua's skyscrapers are kings on their thrones vying for control of the most powerful economy in human history.

Every corporation, megacorp, and hypercorp has some sort of presence in the city seeking proximity to this centre of wealth and power. The city is a panoply of vibrant capital markets, money markets, derivatives markets, interbank markets, and quantronic spot markets, along with a million trading companies and just as many service industry firms to serve them, from hotels and meeting facilities to escrow operators and limousine hire fleets. This city is a place of wealth and excess that's displayed daily.

The corporations don't just compete financially, but aggressively through a variety of corporate espionage from personnel extractions to outright sabotage. Corporate security is ever on alert watching for potential attempts to attack their employer, and some less scrupulous organisations are not beyond resorting to bribes, intimidation, or even violence. The security is well trained and equipped with the best equipment available. While all of these actions are illegal under much of PanOceanian law, most companies can't afford to have their failures publicly known and many are

ANTI-SMUGGLING OPERATIONS

Contraband smuggled onto the planet is generally focused at spaceports, but inventive and criminal organisations like the Comuna and Triad use the Pax-Gratia Straight as a splashdown location for low-orbit cargo drops. Teams of smugglers then quickly scoop up the cargo with light aircraft or boats. All manner of contraband is contained in these drops ranging from narcotics to weapons for distribution across the planet.

The Capitaline Army naval base on Coronado Island coordinates with the Territory Response Group to track and interdict these shipments and apprehend the smugglers. The smugglers get more inventive every day, and while most want to go undetected, gun battles aren't unheard of if the smugglers have the upper hand.

TURF WAR

Spinoza Spaceport has a filthy underbelly that few in Sybaris see. When the Spinoza family fell into debt, they become indebted to the Comuna. In exchange for the loans, the Spinoza family allowed the Comuna to smuggle contraband through the port. Once reluctant members of the Comuna, the family has fully embraced its role in the criminal enterprise.

The spaceport is the key entry point for nitrocaine trafficked through Sybaris, and the enterprise's corruption reaches the highest levels of the city administration. Special Narcotics Force investigations into the smuggling ring find themselves constantly chasing their tails. The Triad recently set its eye on Spinoza Spaceport, and they're determined to take control of the operations on the planet. A turf war is brewing in Sybaris characterised by fast cars, beautiful people, and lots of money.

LAGARTOS COLOSO

The long-necked *Lagartos Coloso* are asexual creatures that instinctually migrate long distances. At the end of each migration they may lay eggs and enter a multi-year hibernation cycle. The newly hatched young protect the hibernating adults while moving through the spawning ground in tiny herds. When adults awake from hibernation, their young follow them on their migration across continents.

Smaller breeds are farmed for their meat as cattle can't survive in the Neoterran environment making beef a bit of a delicacy. The largest breed stands over ten metres tall and wanders Gratia Archipelago in massive herds. Resplendent in vibrant colours, they are a huge tourist attraction with many visiting their costal spawning grounds.

FINANCIAL CRIME UNIT (FCU)

As Turoqua is the centre of banking and finance, the CDCI headquarters is also the home of the organisation's Financial Crime Unit that focuses on enforcing PanOceanian financial law. The unit is constantly on the alert for financial fraud, money laundering, insider trading, and other financial crimes. The officers of this unit receive a chilly reception when they appear in the lobbies of the most powerful businesses in the Human Sphere, and much to the chagrin of the powerful corporate entities, the officers of the FCU are notoriously principled. These incorruptible officials know their duties secure not only the financial future of the PanOceania, but the Human Sphere itself.

quietly sweep under the rug with a skilled public relations campaign.

Turoqua is also the headquarters of the CDCI making it the centre of transcontinental law enforcement on Neoterra. The facility is the command centre of law enforcement, coordinating the broad swathe of law enforcement operations happening across Neoterra with actions and investigations taking place with local block forces all the way to the Auxilia. The facility is also home to the CDIC's primary training facilities, and recruits from across Neoterra are constantly training to uphold law and order on Neoterra.

While Turoqua is the financial centre of the Hyperpower, not everything is excess and glamour. Life for those who live in the shadows of corporate towers can be difficult. The city caters to the rich and powerful, and corporate security teams sometimes run roughshod over those at the bottom. This is especially true of the Atek population, who's only places of refuge are in the sewers and maintenance tunnels of the city. The communities are impressive and the tunnels have become home to their own cultures with trade, commerce, and even fledgling governmental systems. While the Ateks have carved out some semblance of a life, there are also violent Atek gangs who exert their power and control over the populace, and Ateks Out! vigilantes harass the local population with corporate backing. This is a place forgotten by those in their lofty towers, and a place where a person can disappear if they've caught the eye of corporate security.

SOLITUDO ISLAND

Human settlers arrived on Solitudo Island, an island abundant with life, but that changed all too rapidly when something — expert opinion remains divided on what — contaminated the island's ecosystem. A massive die-off of plants ensued and the animal population soon followed. Many settlers starved before follow-up flights from Earth were able to bring more supplies. Today the island is a barren wasteland, good for growing nothing but rocks. Only the tall, spindly Archer Willow trees, lithophytes which draw their sustenance from the air, remain. They cover the southern part of the island, their green upper fronds creating a canopy high above that leaves the ground level in perpetual gloom.

The southwest of the island is dominated by the cloud-shrouded peak of Pico Rubio. The mountain has cultural significance for the island's residents, and they maintain a New Year's Day tradition dating back to the first days of colonisation. Each year, a group of residents hike to Pico Rubio summit to the location where the first colonists signalled

the relief vessel that saved them. The pilgrimage honours those who died on the island over the past year, and is seen as an opportunity to unburden oneself. Each pilgrim carries an item of personal significance to the deceased, or themselves, to honour them or pay penance for transgressions. When they reach the mountain's summit, the item is left at the peak on the cairns of other items that have accumulated since the first days of colonisation. It's said that when you look out from the peak all of your burdens from the past year are lifted off you. The tradition has sparked the imagination of some Neoterrans, and tourists are starting to take the pilgrimage each year alongside the island's residents. Anthropologists from Firozabad study the cairns and Atek scavengers sometimes claim useful items.

SANTA MARIA DE LA SOLEDAD

The sole city on this desolate island is Santa Maria de la Soledad. Located on a rocky spur that juts into the sea at Bahía de San Jorge, it is dominated by the undersea resource extraction industry — drilling platforms and support facilities for undersea mining.

Santa Maria de la Soledad is settlement with few permanent residents, and all commerce in the city focuses on servicing the worker population. The city is a rather bleak place to live and work, contributing to higher rates of substance abuse, domestic violence, and other scourges compared to the rest of Neoterra. Despite this, the workers are a tight community and look out for one another with a reputation for solving their own problems.

The city itself is little more than a collection of housing structures for the platform workers and their families, the docks, and the related processing facilities for extracted resources. Housing here is Spartan from a PanOceanian point of view with meagre shopping and entertainment facilities for workers back from their month-long shifts on nearby extraction platforms.

The city docks are the roughest part of town and are in constant operation loading and offloading resources. The area is a mass of temporary residential hotels, food stands, pawn shops, restaurants, brothels, and rowdy bars that are open all hours. Its sleazy reputation means most workers' family members frequent the local shopping district on the west side of town.

A huge facility called the Resource Reception Facility dominates the city and its operation can be heard day and night. The facility receives resources via an underwater network of conduits connected to the extraction sites in the Bahia de San Jorge. The conduit system moves tons of resources per day in magnetically levitated containers, and workers and support personnel are transported via passenger containers. Resources are then distributed to the local processing facilities or loaded on ships for transport to other facilities on Neoterra.

SPES ARCHIPELAGO

Spes Archipelago's biosphere is home to a wide variety of species not seen anywhere else on the planet including mammals and birds. This biodiversity draws a wide variety of researchers seeking to understand Neoterra's ecosystem, and get a window into what Neoterra might look like if Zeus's Wrath had never devastated the planet.

The biosphere is robust, and the low risk of catastrophic ecological failure resulted in less stringent contamination protocols, with the island settled by numerous settlements called *spes-gaanv*. The people of Spes Archipelago are not confined to cities and are spread out across the Archipelago.

In efforts to preserve this unique biological diversity the people of Spes border on almost ecological fanaticism. Environmentally sound expansion techniques and conservation drive the local economies and politics. Local lobbies can't expect to gain a foothold without clear environmental plans.

The early settlers of Spes hailed from the Indian sub-continent on Earth, and a slim majority of the population is Hindu, which gives this region more cultural heterogeneity than found elsewhere on Neoterra. The archipelago is full of shrines and temples honouring Hindu gods as well as grand Christian churches.

AIRAVATA

Airavata is city made of twenty distinct districts spread across the valley from the shoreline to the base of Mount Meru. Each district has a unique character and attitude. Hindu pilgrims come to worship at the Airavata Shrine at Mount Meru's base. The six-day pilgrimage requires a stop at each district's unique shrines and temples, fuelling the local economy. The pilgrimage has become popular with non-Hindus, and celebrities on pilgrimage are as much a part of the sights as the local districts.

The unique flavour of each district creates a diverse community who've developed friendly rivalries. The people of Airavata love variety, this is shown no better than in their food. The region's unique cuisine,

dubbed pilgrim's cuisine, draws inspiration from food designed to be eaten on the go by pilgrims traveling to Mount Meru. The food is a hodgepodge of multiple cultures and cuisines, inspiring chefs to open restaurants dedicated to a specific style, but the best versions come from the small venders who sell to pilgrims on the road to the Shrine.

AMARAVATI

Amaravati is the City of Maya, as the slogan goes. Elite research facilities located in the city-state's four development parks develop cutting-edge prototypes filling the city with the most advanced technology in the Human Sphere. The population is looking for the newest technology, and happily participate in public beta tests of the latest innovations. The biggest Maya entertainment channels also call the city home, creating a media macro-bubble and Amaravati's population is rated as the most evercasted people in the Human Sphere. Additionally, highly automated manufacturing plants turn out the best vehicles and auto-droids, and the city is dominated by an annual car and droid show each year showing off the latest concepts and prototypes.

Amaravati springs from four *spes-gaanv* linked by the local maglev system. The city is vibrant and exciting despite some saying that the city lacks the character of that makes other cities on Spes unique, and the city's residents have a reputation for being shallow. It'd referred to derogatorily as "Surfista City" for the degree to which everyone seems obsessed with their commlogs and social media presence. Each district has its own unique character whether it's the visual spectacle of the building-tall holograms and Maya concerts of the Kandiwali *spes-gaanv*, or the augmented reality chaos of the Andheri East district. Despite how some other Spes Archipelago residents deride the city, the city is known for its friendly and celebratory atmosphere. The locals are always happy to show someone around the city, sharing the latest innovations with visitors.

FIROZABAD

Firozabad is several densely-packed *spes-gaanv* villages that grew together to form the largest city in the Spes Archipelago. Its towers, scattered between the former *spes-gaanv* city centres, form organic curves that twist into the sky like the tendrils of some heaving plant. This design has inspired the city planners, and Firozabad's layout feels like you're walking through a jungle creating a contrast of high-tech structures and verdant green spaces that flow together seamlessly. The local vernacular is Hindi, a testament to the majority population of Indian descendants who originally founded Firozabad.

SPES LYNX

The fast-moving, six-legged, feline-like mammals are nocturnal pack hunters indigenous to the Spes Archipelagos. They are mischievous, social animals that evolved the ability mimic sounds to draw in prey. They have even been known to mimic human sounds, and their sociability has made them popular as native pets. They come in a range of colours that allow them to blend into the verdant jungles of the archipelagos.

SPES GEOGRAPHY

Spes is formed of four smaller islands sitting on the same continental plate. Relatively uninhabited, Ramaniyaka Sub-Archipelago is dominated by two inactive volcanoes, and the most impressive feature on the island is the stunning Kunchikal Falls.

Prithvi Island is a dense jungle filled with swamps and rivers that meander across the island. The rivers are abundant with a wide variety of life, but the most famous species is a chubby and lethargic green reptilos that swims alongside boats full of sightseers.

Svarga Island is the largest of the islands, with Mount Meru dominating its southern coast. From the mountain's northern base, jungles stretch all the way to the city of Amaravati. The rolling hills are easy to transverse, but the aggressive species of trapper vines makes the jungles dangerous. Trigarta Island is the least rugged of the islands, and home to an array of communes spawned from Neel Parvat. The jungles of the island are sparser than the other islands, and a pair of rivers meander through the island. The island is famous for receiving torrential downfalls that last for only a few minutes at time.

MOTOR SPORTS

Firozabad is also home to an obsessive racing culture centred on the Surya Motor Speedway. This configurable, multi-track speedway provides racing enthusiasts with the most exciting car races in the Human Sphere. The track is built with a unique system of rotating road sections, and the track can be configured into a wide variety of circuits. There are even some races where the track is reconfigured mid-race requiring constant vigilance by the drivers.

PIRACY

Piracy in the Tencendur system is an embarrassment to PanOceania. In reality, it is a relatively minor issue, but it's perceived as a significant menace which the Knights of Santiago constantly strive to bring under control. One infamous and evasive source of piracy is former Haqqislam corsairs in violation of Haqqislam mandates. They're hunted by caravanserai officials and the Knights of Santiago, but the pirates have assistance from corrupt officials. One of the most famous pirates of the belt is Sayyida ed-Din, a former corsair now turned pirate, whose legend grows with every theft. She's described by survivors as a charming rogue with a strict code of honour.

The Firozabad skyline is dominated by the crystal domes of Narada University atop the Valmiki Towers. Narada University is the preeminent university for political and social science in the Human Sphere shaping the way humanity understands itself. The university is home to the most respected researchers in their respective fields. The city's residents have a reputation for a love of political debate, and one can always find a VR-moot debating all host of topics.

NEEL PARVAT

The *spes-gaanvs* surrounding the city of Neel Parvat embrace Neoterra's environmental idealism, fuelling ecofriendly industries and global activism. The residents pride themselves on their diversity, and balk at more traditional parts of PanOceanian society. It's the most ideologically diverse city in the Human Sphere, hence the local joke, "What's the only thing Parvatians agree on? Recycling."

The city's bohemian attitude is a haven for alternative medicine, splinter Hindu and Christian sects, and pioneering musicians of the Neo-Ragga genre. As you wander the streets of Neel Parvat the local culture shifts from street to street. The city's culture welcomes everyone on the condition of mutual respect. This cultural diversity spurred the Nomads to establish a small Commercial Mission in the city presenting a unique diplomatic opportunity, and Nomads from Bakunin feel oddly at home in Neel Parvat.

The locals embrace all of the city's idiosyncrasies with abandon, but tensions from the outside are pressing in on Neel Parvat. The splinter sects allowed to prosper in the city are butting up against the interests of NeoVatican City, and the local cardinals and bishops are pushing for more oversight of these groups with the local lobbies. They are meeting stiff resistance from the most powerful lobby in the region, the United Sphere lobby, dedicated to uniting the Human Sphere under O-12 to stand against the Combined Army.

The economy of Neel Parvat is as diverse as its residents, and everyone is a CEO in Neel Parvat. Neel Parvat's economy runs on locally owned and manufactured goods with extensive, public micro-factories available for residents to produce wares for cottage industries. These unique goods are gaining popularity across the Human Sphere. Neel Parvat is the centre of environmentalism on Neoterra, and city planners plan environmentally sound city expansion, while local companies develop the latest environmental technology with the ultimate aim to restore the environment of Solitudo Island.

TENCENDUR SYSTEM

Tencendur, a G2IV class star, is a centre of commerce in the Human Sphere, and ships transiting take advantage of access to the Circular routes. An Order of Santiago station watches over the exit of each wormhole; coordinating patrols, performing cargo inspections, and other law enforcement activities. Vila Boosters accelerate ships to the interior of the system. Most of the boosters are aimed at Neoterra, but some facilitate travel to Zeus and Poseidon.

HERMES

Hermes is the closest planet to Tencendur and has a rapid orbit of 60 days. The proximity to the star creates a hellish environment. Suseia Station is an Order of Santiago facility, and the planet's sole orbital station resting perpetually in the shadow of the planet. The personnel keep watch over the scattered stations on the planet's surface. Hermes is considered the worst assignment in the system, and being assigned here is often seen as punishment.

APHRODITE

Aphrodite is home to a large, privately funded terraforming study backed by eclectic, wealthy patrons that is the butt of jokes in some circles. Their experiments, if successful, will make the planet partially habitable in 300 years. The planetary mining facilities are constantly at odds with the terraforming project, and their lawyers' legal wrangling to stall new mining projects. The Order of Santiago Sword station monitors traffic around the planet and regularly works to intercept smuggling traffic destined for the mining facilities

NEOTERRA ORBIT

ORBITAL STRUCTURES

Neoterra's orbit is filled with a wide variety of orbital facilities ranging from small, private habitats to massive shipyards, and orbital traffic control systems manage thousands of orbital transits a day. Neoterra's orbit is defended by the PanOceanian Navy, the Order of Santiago, and an array of Trebuchet-Class orbital-defence platforms; powerful railguns that can also be repurposed for ground support in the event of a terrestrial invasion of Neoterra. Most traffic in Neoterra's orbit moves through the Neoterra Orbital Spaceport, and it's the busiest facility in the Human Sphere. The security personnel are highly trained and professional and supported by an Order of Santiago team assigned to the astroport.

Spaceship maintenance and construction constitutes a major part of the orbital economy. The Astilleros Cardama shipyard services a wide variety of vessel classes including gantries for repairs on sections of the circulars, and the shipyard is famous for performing unique modifications and custom jobs. Astilleros is overshadowed by the Military Complex's Factorias Vulcano shipyard constructing the ships of PanOceanian Navy.

Floriana Station is an Order of the Hospital secondary headquarters containing a number of maximum security vaults. Conspiracy theorists claim the vaults house a rogue AI, named Bahamut. The AI is a ruse to draw in Templar sympathizers, but actually contain secret data and money, possibly out of the watchful eye of ALEPH, for well-connected PanOceanian tycoons.

SELENE & ARTUME
Selene is the smaller of Neoterra's two moons with an orbital period of only 13 days. The moon shows evidence it shielded the planet from asteroid impacts, and there's a large scar believed to be from when Zeus's wrath scraped the side of the moon before impacting Neoterra. The primary industry on Selene is the mining dominated by the Cordoba Mining Network, operating a small network of mining facilities whose mining drones extract iron and titanium. The larger and more distant moon is Artume with an orbital rotation of 53 days. The moon is geologically active and has a thin sulphuric atmosphere. There are half a dozen catcher stations in orbit catching shipments launched from Zeus and Poseidon.

ZEUS

This large, purple gas giant lying 6.2 AU from Tencendur surges with storms. The planet is surrounded by a dense and unstable asteroid belt created by the destruction of a moon (see *Climate and Geography* above, p. 31), and asteroid mining is the planet's major industry. The Olympian Belt is a wealth of resources, but mining on the asteroids can be a dangerous affair due to frequent collisions and orbits that take the asteroids into the gas giant's atmosphere. These unstable asteroids are called "Skippers", and mining them is illegal under PanOceanian safety regulations. Despite that, illegal Skipper miners perform death-defying feats to extract the resources from the asteroids before they tumble into the upper atmosphere of Zeus.

CHAVENA STATION
This rough and tumble asteroid station houses work crews mining ice and ore. The station consists of a main living space in a rotating gravity ring and the low-g mining facility under the asteroid's surface. Nomad miners face regular discrimination and workplace danger. Civil unrest is common and the local security force cracks down harshly. Nitrocaine and other stimulant abuse are high on the station due to intense work schedules, and the security force's investigation struggles to find the source.

SHASHTAN STATION
Shashtan station is a joint venture built by the Group of Six, an organisation formed of the most important PanOceanian corporations: Moto.tronica, Omnia Research, MagnaObra, Minescorp, Multicomm, and Oxyd. The station is a place of free trade where the corporations rule, and it is a vibrant station with a bustling market and low gravity manufacturing facilities making it a centre of trade in the local Zeus system. The Group of Six have recently extended investment opportunities to Vinamayama Industries and CineticS.

A Nomad Commercial Mission on the station provides the corporations with convenient access to the Tunguska data crypt for covert transfer of data and money. The mission is concerned about the treatment of their people on Chavena Station, and their efforts to organise the local workers is meeting serious opposition from the station's director.

POSEIDON

This deep blue gas giant lies a distant 28 AU from Tencendur. There are hundreds of gas mining stations in high orbit whose drones dip into the upper atmosphere to harvest gas for refinement at Eryx Station. Poseidon is orbited by six moons: Amphitrite, Idyia, Hippo, Lilaea, Nemesis, and Petraea. The moons are home to a number of isolated research stations studying everything from the mundane to risky paths of study and research.

An O'Neil cylinder named Eryx Station is the centre of local gas refinement, and the first stop off for many ships entering the Tencendur system. The Order of Santiago maintains docks at the station for maintaining their fleets operating in the outer system. The Neoterra-4 Nomad Commercial Mission negotiates trade and watches over Nomad interests in the Tencendur system.

MAHRAJAN CARAVANSERAI
A Haqqislam *caravanserai* orbits Zeus acting as trade centre for the outer planets of Neoterra's system, and is in direct competition with Shashtan Station for control of the local markets. The fierce competition results in mutual acts of sabotage, cyberwarfare, and other covert actions. The Knights of Santiago try to corral these activities, but there are constantly stonewalled, and the station is accused of acting as safe haven for Haqqislamite pirates in the system.

CRONUS OPERATIONAL BASE
Cronus Operational Base is the local command post of the PanOceanian Military Complex's Armada. It services three destroyers dedicated to patrolling the crowded Olympian Belt. While the destroyers project the station's power, the Order's smaller shuttles and patrol boats investigate crimes, mete out justice, and settle disputes between the belt's multitude of independent mining groups. The station has holding cells for serious criminals and fugitives, but those prisoners must be transferred to a long-term holding facility.

CHAPTER 4
VARUNA

CLIMATE & GEOGRAPHY

Varuna enjoys a warmer climate than Earth, owing in part to the high humidity and natural build-up of vapours in the atmosphere. Inhabitants of Varuna are no strangers to sweat when working, but the temperature is exceptionally well-suited to relaxation for most of the year. The average summer temperature is between 25°C and 33°C and is capable of climbing into the high thirties and low forties on rare occasions. Across the rest of the year, there is little deviation.

Rain is a common occurrence on the planet, but the showers rarely stray over the landmasses due to the immensity of Varuna's ocean. Showers vary from a light drizzle to small storms, but outside the rainy season, it's rare for a day to see more than fifteen minutes of rainfall. Thanks to the sloped topology of the archipelagos and the well-constructed sewerage systems on Varuna, on the odd occasion that rain reaches the shoreline it rarely leads to flooding. This beautiful weather is fundamental to the Varunan tourism complex, ensuring the Varunan beaches are paradise year around.

An odd weather phenomenon occurs in Varuna's atmosphere when a ship or foreign object attempts orbital entry or exit. A sudden upset of the vapours and moisture in the atmosphere causes the rapid formation of rain clouds. It is rare for ships to enter Varuna's atmosphere outside of the spaceports or orbital elevator, but these places are beset by narrow corridors of constant rain. This stands in stark contrast to the rest of the planet's sunny weather. Tourist vessels are normally cleared for night-time landings to mitigate the cloud formation. Both meteorologists and military scientists

are interested in the phenomena as it allows them to track objects that enter Varuna's atmosphere, whether it is debris or an unregistered spacecraft.

Winter is a foreign concept on Varuna. In the hot season, the temperature rises to its most pleasant, and the warmer days of Varuna are the selling point for many visitors. Dehumidifiers are commonly used to control the humidity levels in hotels and buildings, as it can become uncomfortable. The cold season is ironically named, since the temperature only drops slightly compared to the hot season. Temperatures hover around the mid-twenties, and the humidity calms somewhat. Fog is common in the morning or at night due to the cooler winds. The rainy season is unique and most disaster prone, but is also mercifully short, occurring planet wide every ten months for two weeks. Interrupting the cycle of the hot and cooler seasons, large volumes of rain fall in staggered patterns across the planet while temperatures continue around the norm.

DISASTER READY

Varuna is no stranger to potential disasters during the rainy season. While violent storm surges and hurricanes are a rare occurrence, previous storms have prompted the Varunan people to be ready to ensure the safety of any clientele. Varunans pride themselves on the structural durability of their towns and cities, as well as the ironclad solidity of their disaster reaction plans.

Fatalities and structural damage due to natural events are universally low because of this culture of preparation, and community relief from the effects of storms is quick and efficient. To the average Varunan, these events are just another part of life. It is a common joke amongst the hospitality workers of Varuna's coasts that the storm season is simply the last and most violent guest of the tourism year.

Earthquakes on Varuna are incredibly rare and generally weak but have been known to cause tsunamis. Experts have mapped earthquakes and fault lines to better prepare for the influx of water.

THE SURFACE

Although the landmasses of Varuna are small, they are packed with vegetation and wildlife. The tips of underwater hills and mountains that reach for miles under the ocean form Varuna's four major archipelagos. Pre-colonisation flooding occured when Varuna's polar caps melted, leaving only the highest ground unsubmerged. Several rivers and lakes run between the mountainous areas of the archipelagos as a result of this.

Other waterways formed when the few remaining

natural dams were broken by years of pressure from the rising ocean. There are very few independent water sources on Varuna. Nearly every inland body of water connects to the ocean through overland paths or through subterranean water flows. Freshwater sources are created with desalination processes or stored using rain collection devices. These devices range from the advanced storm veins that spread like wings over the Living Cities to simple tarps pulled over impromptu houses by the Ateks.

THE DEPTHS

In many ways, Varuna is a vertical world. Not in the way of towering mountains and skyscrapers how-ever, as the small amount of landmass can't support skyward structures. Underneath the glimmering blue waters of Varuna's ocean stretches another world, though. Forests of coral surround immense subaquatic mountains and canyons, a landscape few other worlds can boast. Varuna is home to the deepest aquatic points in the Human Sphere, with depths exceeding 20,000 meters.

During the initial mapping of Varuna, communi-cation with the Helot people led to the process of separating these locations into three depth bands. First is the *sissala*, or 'uplands.' The *sissala* has warmer waters and plentiful light and contains much of the vibrant wildlife of Varuna. This band of the depths, which includes the landmasses above the waters, is the most extensively charted, a union of PanOceania's advanced geographical mapping technology and the assistance of Helot locals.

The second level of the depths is referred to as the *sissolu*, simply translated as the 'waters.' Down in the *sissolu*, light is still present but dim, and many of the planet's less attractive flora and fauna make their homes here. Helot communities tend to favour this depth. as the unique Helot pressure-sensitive biology is most productive there. The strong currents make this depth the most turbulent of the three, requiring care to navigate.

The final depth is the *kossulu,* or 'deepwaters,' and is only lightly mapped compared to the other two depth bands. The pressure, lack of light, and incredible cold make travel to this depth danger-ous without proper care and preparation. Some information has been gained from talks with the Helot people, but for the sake of tradition, they tend to stay tight lipped about the *kossulu*, wishing to respect the privacy of their elders, the *kossomn*.

THE TASSALA

To combat the lack of landmass above water, early settlers used temporary and crude rigs to expand

DURALAN FIVE

The most notorious *tassala* rig still in operation is the Duralan Five rig. A massive web of metal and rust, the rig was at the centre of a massive radiation leak early in its life when its reactor entered meltdown after a particularly harsh storm smashed it against the coast of Gurindam. Though it has since been repaired and depowered, no one trusts the relic of a rig anymore. The rig holds a small, permanent population of Ateks, leading to difficulties in permanently removing the rig.

KŌRURU

A mythic creature named by the Hawaiian crew that claim to have discovered it, *Kōruru* is described as an immense shadow that tipped over a fishing vessel early in Varuna's settlement. Since then it has become a cryptid to the Varunan people, the same as the Loch Ness Monster or Bigfoot. Though many doubt the authenticity of the tale, sightings of large, shadowy creatures are becoming more common as the deepest depths of Varuna are explored.

outward from the small islands, developing farms and mining platforms to pursue their business. The Helots called these rigs *tassala,* and the name stuck with the local humans.

The *tassala* and the companies building them were indifferent to the damage to the local ecosystem, and this occasionally brought them into conflict with displaced Helot communities. It was common that these pods were forced to leave areas occupied by the supports used in rig construction and machinery to prevent natural reclamation by coral and seaweed.

As more and more humans settled on Varuna though, these temporary solutions became inefficient and outdated. Modern *tassala* are marvels of engineering, built to support the local wildlife, encourage coral growth, and some even provide housing for Helot pods. Some say the only reason the companies that produce the expansions followed a more ecologically sound solution was to support the tourism industry, but no one wishes to argue the fact thanks to the benefits the new rigs offer.

Though nearing completion, the phasing out of the old *tassala* rigs is an unfortunately slow process. For the Varunans, this can't happen fast enough, as their ugly construction is a distraction from the sleek elegance of their modern counterparts.. Recent developments in the *tassala* include a newly developed plant species that actively desalinates water that flows inland.

FLORA & FAUNA

Though the majority of Varuna's ecosystem lies beneath its ocean, life has also evolved to survive on the archipelagos. These species range from familiar amphibious life forms to more alien creatures.

FAUNA

The most populous of the island species is the strange creature known as the mud toad, named for the amphibian pests of Earth. A subaquatic species, they nest in rivers and inland waterways and are squat, spherical creature with a limb span of about thirty centimetres. The mud toad has six limbs, four legs and two appendages with mouths at their tips. The creature's ears and eyes are hidden well on its body, blending into the natural patterning of its smooth skin. The mud toad consumes plant matter at terrifying speeds and accumulates stores through fat pockets in its body. This appears to be an evolutionary defect, once valuable when digestible resources were rare on the archipelagos and

competition was fierce. Luckily for Varuna, the mud toad isn't the only terrestrial animal.

The suncrest is a serpentine avian creature sporting four wings, a strong, dextrous tail, and a sharp beak. Suncrests earn their name from their bright plumage, which is a vibrant yellow and orange. They are graceful creatures that hunt mud toads almost exclusively, leading to Varuna's love of suncrests due to the effect a flock of the creatures has on the local mud toad population. The popularity of the suncrest has spread to other aspects of Varunan culture, including the popular Scuball team, the Syurga Suncrests. It is also the name given to a particularly gaudy line of luxury watercraft.

The rest of the wildlife in Varuna is primarily found underwater. The most popular and beautiful species are found in the *sissala*. Brightly coloured *Kidok* (robe-fish) sport beautiful patterns. *Kidok* earn their unusual name for their fins, which secrete a substance resembling cloth to envelope the animal. When threatened, the *kidok* can shed the substance as a distraction and dart away to safety, regrowing its 'robe' over the course of a few days. The population of *kidok* has only grown stronger with the arrival of humanity because the *tassala* drove away the natural predators of the robe-fish.

The robe-fish share their environment with a species known as serra-fish, a familiar creature to Earth travellers as it resembles a salmon. Inherently social animals, serra-fish stick to large schools when travelling, splitting apart upon arrival at a reef or algae bloom to feed and mate. It boasts highly reflective scales used to communicate with their schools in vibrant displays of colour. The serra-fish is the staple of many predators' diets, lacking any comprehensive defence and suffering from high visibility as well as admittedly poor intellect.

The more predatory species of the uplands include the Ithican Arrow and its natural predator, the Narain Stingray. The Ithican Arrow is a strange creature, more akin to a sentient torpedo than a fish. Notable for its incredible speed underwater, it uses a pressurised gland to swallow and expel water at an incredible rate, allowing it to outswim most predators and chase down its own prey.

The Narain Stingray is a cunning creature in contrast, a master of camouflage and ambush tactics. A polychromatic creature about half a meter wide, the Narain Stingray uses its colour-shifting abilities to blend into the vibrant coral of the uplands and wait for passing wildlife. It then dazzles its prey with a lightshow of bioluminescence before striking with its harpoon-like tail. This same ability allows it to elude the few predators that seek it out, allowing it to daze and injure them before making good on its escape.

Deeper into the ocean, the glamour of the upland species is replaced with a simple majesty. The *badak*, nicknamed the rhino whale, is a legless amphibian about three meters long. A gentle herbivore, it mainly consumes underwater plants but will occasionally surface to eat dry vegetation to supplement its diet. It is during these times that Varuna's Atek population hunt the docile creatures. Though the skin of a *badak* is tough, the meat is nutritious and admittedly tasty. A single *badak* can feed a small community for a week. These aren't the creatures' only predator however.

The *jerung,* a creature vaguely similar to Earth's stingray, is the apex predator of the *sissolu*. Dark grey with razor sharp teeth, these predators can grow to surprisingly large sizes with some growing larger than three meters in width. The *jerung,* deceptively fast and voracious, hunts its prey silently and relentlessly. It is rightly feared not only by the wildlife, but Helots and humans alike.

In the deepest reaches of the *kossum*, the *Gaim Moyu* dwell. Large cephalopods with a single large tentacle, most span between three and nine meters long. Some species of *Gaim Moyu* can grow larger than this and have several tentacles, but these are rarer. The *Gaim Moyu* live secluded lifestyles in the deeps, only surfacing to feed on small fish and plants. *Gaim Moyu* don't possess the speed to chase down their prey, usually serra-fish, and rely on tiring their quarry out. They have been known to attack human craft that they perceive to be territorial or mating rivals.

FLORA

The plant life atop the archipelagos tends toward simplicity. Much of the biodiversity of Varuna's terrestial life vanished with the rising tides, leaving only the most durable species. The most notable terrestrial species is the coral known as *kubala*. Invertebrate colonies, *kubala* grows out of the water onto the shoreline to nestle in the nutrient rich earth, creating white and chalky forests.

As with animal life, the plant life of Varuna becomes more diverse when entering its oceans. Lemuria algae is one of the planet's most interesting examples. Named after the Lemuria archipelago, the algae is hailed as a miracle organism with an incredible amount of applications in science, medicine, and even construction.

Katallpeacs seaweed is also an important plant for the inhabitants of Varuna. Though ordinary, *katallpeac* has one remarkable quality, its adhesive properties. Dead *katallpeac* drifts to the surface of the ocean and fuses together when exposed to the air, creating natural formations known as lily pads. Helot communities used these lily pads and the currents to travel from one archipelago to the other, a practice still used in the present by more reclusive Helots.

Across the Sphere many people talk of the incredible oceans of Varuna and how they seem to glisten unlike any other ocean. This can be attributed to the microscopic excretions of a fungus known as riftweed. Riftweed grows within the coral reefs of Varuna and constantly sheds reflective particles that are carried through the currents of the planet, and over the years has almost become global. Sometimes a shift in the ecosystem or climate from a natural disaster causes riftweed to dump a large amount of these spores in an effort to reproduce rapidly and survive. The oceans of Varuna shine on these occasions, and Varunans view the event as a sign of rebirth and reconstruction.

ECONOMY

Varuna is a natural jewel in the Sphere, famed for its beauty and intrigue. It is little wonder that one of its primary sources of income is tourism. Every day thousands of people pass through Varuna's star ports, looking to escape from the rigors of their home and work life.

Varuna is home to many natural wonders such as the Ó Hailpín Deep (the deepest underwater point of the Sphere), the coral reefs of Atlantea archipelago, and the seasonal migration of the serra-fish, which causes the oceans to shine. These sights and many more continue to attract visitors. Varunans have become the masters of seafood in the Human Sphere and proudly supplement this with carefully selected and grown produce both local and foreign.

Despite tourism being its most visible industry, Varuna's major export lies in aquaculture. The immense amount of exploitable resources within Varuna's ocean is staggering. Hundreds of companies farm entire species of fish and plant life, exporting them to the rest of the Human Sphere. *Katallpeac* seaweed's adhesive elements, once refined, make excellent glue and construction paste, the preserved scales of serra-fish always find their ways into fashion trends in foreign capitals, and *kidok* are a much sought-after pet. Beyond the allure of the tastier breeds of fish, certain plants and organisms have proven to be invaluable for medical and scientific use. Though Lemuria algae is the most famous in this regard, several other species have offered new and exciting insights across a variety of fields, and Varuna benefits from selling them (in controlled moderation of course).

There are rumours of even larger animals than the Gaim Moyu in the further reaches of the *kossum*, titanic creatures that can reach sizes exceeding thirty metres. They are described as having ink black skin, making it near impossible to spot them. Tales of sudden and violent currents rocking deep sea explorers and immense forms blocking spot lights have become more common as the years pass. A majority of Varuna's scientific community dismiss these creatures as little more than phantoms, wild stories told by panicked submariners. Helot pods sometimes pass down stories that include creatures matching these descriptions, describing them as the guardians of the planet"s secrets. As to what this means, no one is clear.

ATEKS OF THE KATALLPEACS
It isn't unknown for small communities of Ateks to take up residence on one of the *Katallpeac* lily pads and drift to different parts of Varuna. Some Varunans have learnt how to predict the movement of the lily pads from Helots.

HELOT LABOUR
The mining and aquaculture industries both make prolific use of Helot workers. Treatment of the Helot workforce has always been a black mark on the reputation of Varuna's companies, who exploit the gaps in the relatively young laws that protect the Helot people's rights and worker protections. Mistreatment, overwork, and poor pay are common, and the work of the hypercorporations makes progress at closing these legal gaps slow.

ATLASIUM

Atlasium was discovered shortly after mining operations on Varuna began. When tested under pressurised conditions, the alloy was found to be eight times more stress resistant than other leading construction materials. Export of the ore is Sphere-wide, and now several space and aqua-craft can claim a small percentage of the Atlasium-Teseum infused Herculeum alloy within their hulls. The fusion of the two metals grants the pressure resistance of Atlasium at a greatly reduced weight.

VARUNAN CUP

Scuball's majetic Varunan Cup takes place at the end of each solar year just before the stormy seasons. Off-worlders can find themselves swept up in the sheer fiery passion that grips Akuna Bay as the twelve most successful teams in the league battle for the position of number one. Citizens are known to become rowdy at this time of year, but it is tolerated as the last celebration before the onset of the disaster-prone storm season. Although Scuball holds the hearts of Varuna's people, it is far from the only sport enjoyed by the populace on a professional level. Varuna hosts several successful leagues that are broadcast across the Sphere including the PanOceanian Volleyball League, the Interplanatary Quadathlon Federation, and several more.

Most of these resources are fed back into Varuna's scientific community. While not as publicly acclaimed as the facilities of Haqqislam, Varuna quietly achieves a remarkable level of success in various fields. The unique conditions of Varuna's oceans allow for a depth of testing unattainable in most other environments, and the natural elements attainable from Varuna's species allow for the construction of potent medicines and minor genetic engineering processes, as well as powerful biofuels and some interesting construction materials. These medicines and treatments have helped to cement Varuna's reputation as a place of mental healing and growth, the two-pronged effect of Varunan medicine and hospitality serving as an excellent place for high stress victims to unwind and finally, truly, relax.

Outside of these industries lies the last of Varuna's economic powerhouses, mining. The archipelagos' surfaces remain largely untouched by mining companies because nearly all of Varuna's mineral resources lie far below in the oceans. Large scale operations dig away at the forgotten landmasses below the surface, retrieving an immense variety of ores, gases, and gemstones. The pressure resistant metal Atlasium is an alloy used in the construction of deep sea exploration equipment on Varuna and more recently deep space craft.

CULTURE AND DEMOGRAPHICS

Varuna seems to be the happiest place in the Human Sphere. Wherever you turn, someone is smiling. Varunans are constantly portrayed as friendly, laidback, and more than willing to party into the depths of the night.

The average Varunan is remarkably well off, even when compared to other PanOceanian citizens. Hospitality is the most common entry level job on Varuna, and the relatively low population combined with the influx of tourists means that most service sector jobs have good, stable hours with great pay. The workers of Varuna find ample time outside of their jobs to pursue their many hobbies, and there are few places better to do that than in paradise. Off-planet visitors find that in picturesque Varuna, people are laidback and deeply content.

The positivity of Varuna's people is another beast altogether. A vast number of Varunans have mastered the art of pleasantry, drilled into them from years at work in their jobs in hospitality. A well-timed smile or friendly compliment is usually all that's needed to make a customer happy, and the workers of Varuna know all the tricks in the book

and when to use them. Due to most of a foreigner's contact with Varunan locals being limited to hospitality workers and businesspeople, many don't see the boisterous and rude attitudes common amongst Varuna's farmers and miners. Savvy tourism companies of the Sphere refer to this as the Varunan Smile. This skill serves many Varunans who enter fields such as politics and business.

Varunans tend to be a communally peaceful folk, content in their work and leisure and at ease with one another. In a culture where everyone has been in the 'business', most workplace issues come from a rude off-worlder rather than locals, leading to a strong bond of unity amongst communities and work circles. Unfortunately, this leads to a casual frustration with foreigners, carefully hidden when at work. More extreme members of the Varunan community display racial insensitivity or outright racism, though these people are usually ushered far away from the front lines of the hospitality scene. Most cases are met with disapproval from other Varunans, but the undercurrents never truly disappear.

Activists work against this growing distrust in any way they can. Allies to the Helots' plight have existed on Varuna since the early days of settlement, and they have made it their business to make sure the Helot peoples are given the same rights and responsibilities that any sentient creature deserves. These activists work with the Helot community to counter the negative press gained from the actions of Libertos and try to help Helots find ongoing, humane employment. This activism spreads to other issues, and Varuna has robust environmental activist groups in the face of Varuna's rapid urbanization.

Despite philosophical divsions, one of the most unifying aspects of Varunan culture is their love of sports. Aqua sports such as polo and competitive swimming are popular, as well as more terrestrial sports such as football. But none of these sports match the popularity of Scuball. Scuball season is one of the most important parts of the Varunan year, breathing life into the population and giving them passion they usually have no time for. The Varunan Scuball League is a powerful force in Varuna's culture and economy, and it's hard to find a Varunan that doesn't at least keep up with the happenings of the sport.

Crime is surprisingly rampant on Varuna. Though it is more accurate to say Varuna suffers from crimes imported from other worlds. Crimes committed by locals tend to be petty, possession of illicit substances and minor cases of theft, and Varuna is mostly free of major crimes. However, tourists from other worlds tend to bring more dangerous

criminal activities with them. Drug trafficking is a major problem in particular, many dangerous substances being brought in by the crime syndicates from other worlds. Varuna's reputation as a party world means drugs are sold easily in such environments. The Varunan government does its best to keep a leash on the influx of dangerous banned substances.

Crimes of passion are incredibly common as well. Cheating husbands and wives retreat to Varuna seeking an affair only to be followed by their spouse and violently confronted. In other cases, powerful businesspeople are hunted down by those they have wronged and made to pay. Regardless of the circumstances, Varuna's police are left to deal with each mess as the people of the Human Sphere drag their dramatic baggage to the doorstep of the planet.

Because of these problems Varuna has a well-equipped police force as well as a surprisingly large private investigation scene. These two forces work together to try and stop these crimes from happening pre-emptively, or at the very least getting to the bottom of them at a fast and orderly pace. Better to sweep the issues under the rug as fast as possible and let Varuna's guests' lives in paradise go on. Due to the minor nature of crime on Varuna, the standing police force is rather small but well

trained and equipped, with a focus on de-escalation as opposed to outright law enforcement. Uniforms are rare in the force, whose only identification is their badge and equipment. This is to allow them to blend in and give Varuna a 'freer' feel. This has led to the locals calling the police 'deputy bouncers'.

Aside from the 'working' class of Varuna, the upper class tends to keep their distance from the archipelagos and their 'mundane' wants and responsibilities. The rich inevitably find their way to one of the Living Cities of Varuna, vast platforms that support a range from small towns to large cities. These places are a step above anything seen on the archipelagos, the sleek architecture and incredible technology matching the hyper advanced and flamboyant inhabitants. To live on one of the floating cities is to experience a life of luxury that cannot be attained anywhere else in PanOceania, perhaps even the Human Sphere. The most notable of these cities is Karthikeyan, the *crème de le crème* of Varuna. One visitor is quoted as saying that it is the closest one can get to heaven in the universe.

This has led to a frustrating complexity in responses to the Helot people as well. For the most part the Helot people are tolerated on Varuna. Most people understand that Helots, like them, just want to live their lives. Interactions with the *tete-kulu* can colour this view negatively however, leading to

ECOLOGICAL ANGER

Scattered debris remains a problem on Varuna despite the gradual shutdown of the old tassala. Environmental groups work constantly to hold the hypercorperations accountable when corners are cut and tassala remains aren't properly salvaged. Activists have received bad press in many situations, especially where they have aimed their focus at restricting construction zones that would negatively impact the coastal environment. Tensions were highest when a rally resulted in the death of a construction worker from activists picketing the construction of the largest Scuball stadium on Varuna.

some Varunans seeing Helots as violent and lazy. With the rise of the threat of the EI Hegemony, anti-alien rhetoric is beginning to poison public opinion towards the Helots. Combined with the actions of Libertos, it is becoming more dangerous each day to be a Helot, the risk of violent racism a growing issue.

ATLANTEA
AKUNA BAY

Akuna Bay is the capital of the Atlantea archipelago and by extension Varuna. Built on the island of Mu, the city sits close to Highwater Spaceport, one of the two major spaceports on Varuna, as well as the large aquatic port built within the bay that connects it to the primary export hub of Deepwater. These two avenues of trade and transport ensure that Akuna Bay is among the first and last stops for goods and tourists that travel to Varuna. Proximity to the Planctae Sub-Archipelago, which houses Varuna's largest military presence, ensures the city maintains a constant guard against any harmful forces that seek to pass onto the world.

Atlantea maintains the largest population of the archipelagos, and Akuna Bay holds the largest amount of that population. The city's architecture is low rising but wide, taking up most of the bay's edge and expanding deep into Mu Island. This can confuse foreigners who hear of the quaint size of Varuna's towns and cities. In truth Akuna Bay is the exception to the rule, a sprawling metropolis compared to the frontier-like towns that make up the rest of Varuna's centres of population.

The city's shore plays host to its large tourism industry. Hotels, bars, and restaurants run along the length of the bay side. Nestled amongst them are the myriad travel agencies and boat rental services that allow travel across the breadth of Varuna, with some agencies even offering ekranoplans, snub-nosed ground-effect aircraft, for the impatient traveller.

Many off-world companies make their home in the financial districts, establishing branches to monopolise on the many lucrative ventures Varuna can provide. Nestled further inland beyond the limits of the city centre are the industrial district and suburbs where many of Akuna Bay's workers live. Maglev trains connect these suburbs to the city's central hub, ensuring that whilst Akuna Bay is a large city, travel considerations impact little on productivity.

The industrial district is home to all manners of construction companies. The Highwater Spaceport and Deepwater ensure materials arrive with timely

reliability, the only drawback being the constant rain that pours on the edges of the districts and suburbs. The poorer of Varuna's workers and companies usually find their way to these outskirts, the constant rain lowering the property values of lots and homes.

At the very edge of these suburbs are the slums that Ateks call home. These slums make up the largest Atek community on Varuna, and constant expansion ensures the Ateks are on the move constantly as their temporary homes are demolished and removed.

Intelligence agents are surprisingly common in Akuna Bay. Undercover operatives from across the Human Sphere lie in wait for an ambassador or executive with vital information and attach themselves to them carefully to gain said information. Though this is well known in the intelligence community, it is frustratingly hard to find hostile operatives. Thousands of legitimate travellers come in and out of Akuna Bay each day and finding the one spy is near impossible.

A monument to the Omn Accords — a large statue depicting a Helot and human shaking hands — stands in front of the Hall of Governance. The Accords were the first formal legislation that granted the Helot people a measure of the rights held by humankind. These include property ownership, the right to fair treatment within the justice system, the right to life, and so on. The accords were an agreement between the two races to work together to create a better Varuna and to respect each other's culture.

The Libertos terrorist group argues that the Accords were a calculated move to ensure that O-12's watchdogs couldn't bring the hammer of legal action down upon the corporations that at the time abused the rights of Helots, and still do to the present day. For many, the monument stands as a sign of peace, the first true steps in guaranteeing a future of cooperation, but this hasn't stopped attempts to deface the monument. Radicals from xenophobic camps on both sides of the political spectrum have made it their business to destroy what they see as a monument to compromise. Such incidents have only increased security for the monument however, and now it is nearly impossible to reach the statue without being tagged by eight different identity probes and arrested. Even if the statue is damaged, there are rumours that the government has several identical backups of the statue just in case.

This hasn't dissuaded nationalist groups from aggressively working against the Helot population in other arenas. Within Akuna Bay a movement called Akuna Bay Reclamation League campaigns against the rights of the Helot people. Driven by a loose ideology of nationalism, and fuelled by racial prejudice and xenophobia, Akuna Bay Reclamation League works to keep the Helot people out of population centres and in the oceans 'where they belong.' Whilst the movements had very little traction in the past, current events such as the war against the Ur Hegemony has caused their membership to rise as anti-alien sentiments become more common. Most members live and operate in the poorer parts of Akuna Bay's suburban district, and many have only seen Helots on Maya in pictures and videos. But, misinformation and prejudice are potent forces. Though their numbers are still small compared to other activist groups, meetings are carefully monitored by the Varunan government. Several officials are worried now that the first politically minded members of the group begin to gain power. All eyes are on the most vocal member of the group, Betty 'Jaqqi' Jackson, for the job. Despite her blatant lack of political knowledge and administrative training, her ability to rally the uninformed is second to none in the suburbs of Akuna Bay.

DEEPWATER

Deepwater occupies the island of Hesperia and is immediately recognizable from afar for the immense tower of clouds that rises above it. Deepwater and its orbital elevator handle the majority of interplanetary shipping and cargo, despite two planetary spaceports. Immense loads of raw materials are passed up and down the elevator each day to be passed onto waiting cargo ships and ferried across the Sphere.

Unlike Highwater Spaceport and Syurga however, Deepwater is relatively untouched by rain. There is a wide berth of entry lanes for orbital transport, and the only disturbance to Varuna's atmosphere is the length of the orbital elevator. The gentle drift of the tower isn't enough to cause a full-blown storm to develop, but enough to stir up the atmospheric layers and cause storm clouds and gentle rain to form. This phenomenon has been named the *retett-tunkii* by the Helots and referred to as the storm tower by the locals. This pillar of clouds has served to make Deepwater famous in the tourism industry and one of the many stops offered to visitors on their way to Akuna Bay's central travel hub. Riding the elevator down to the surface has become a popular attraction, tourists enjoying the thrill of descending through the small active storms and rain. Safety is never an issue, as the tower was modified to harness the lightning that developed in the clouds it created to reduce costs and funnel electricity into Deepwater.

Due to the unexpected popularity of Deepwater, the town is undergoing a bustling expansion project to introduce more activities and sights for tourists. Every day more companies try their hand at creating attractions to keep tourists entertained, but the task is becoming progressively harder. Deepwater was built with stability for the elevator in mind rather than any natural wonders. The waters surrounding Deepwater lack reefs or interesting underwater attractions. The species that normally amaze foreigners are absent due to lack of food and places to nest. Mud toads are the most common animal around the town, leading to a mercifully sizable suncrest population. However, the battle to turn Deepwater into a tourist trap is a failing one. There is simply too little material for any lasting attractions to be viable beyond the elevator. The small burst of corporate attention has been appreciated by the locals however, giving the local economy a minor boost. The last remnant of this effort is a small red-light district in the deeper sections of the ports, which is still frequented enough to remain operational.

The shipping industry has always been strong in Deepwater. The starport is a maze of warehouses and storage centres with a vast selection of uses. Row upon row of freezer storage keeps food from Anahena and fish from across the globe fresh, whilst storage yards receive trucks stuffed to the brim with minerals from the efforts of the mining towns of the Gurindam archipelago.

Carefully guarded yards contain the incredible creations of the Varunan military complex, ready to be shipped across the Sphere for combat use. Deep vaults contain samples taken from across Varuna, incredible species being sold to other worlds to expand the scientific knowledge of the Sphere. All this and more await in the shipping yards of Deepwater, demanding a strong security presence. Unlike Akuna Bay's focus on immigration police, Deepwater's guards are more militant.

The companies who store their goods on site hire private security firms, leading many to joke that the true military force of Varuna is found in the shipping industry. Although they are carefully covered up, it isn't uncommon for small skirmishes to break out between these contracted soldiers in the dead of night as one company seeks to liberate cargo from another. The law enforcement agencies of Varuna have been known to respond carefully to these skirmishes, announcing their presence loudly to pressure the skirmishers to scatter so long as fatalities and structural damage are at a minimum. Fatalities and full-blown fire fights are fortunately rare, leaving the peace of Deepwater intact.

HALL OF GOVERNANCE

The heart of Akuna Bay is the Hall of Governance, a tall and proud building holding the majority of Varuna's governing body. Every day politicians from across Varuna come to represent the interests of each of the archipelagos and their population centres. Attached to the Hall are several embassies and hotels that offer a home to politicians traveling from off world. The high number of foreign visitors ensures that political intervention is a common necessity. A visit to Varuna to bail a confused traveller out of trouble is considered a lucky job amongst the political community of the Sphere, as the proceedings to deal with the red tape can take ages, during which it isn't uncommon for the good folk of Varuna to offer all their hospitality. Sometimes, with the right strings pulled as favours, a matter that should have taken days can take weeks.

HELOT EMPATHY

On the other side of the political spectrum are activists supporting the Helots and their environments. Despite the heavy activity of Akuna Bay's port, several pods of Helots call Akuna Bay's reefs home. Friction between the native population and the construction industry is common whenever plans to expand the ports surface. These attempts are universally opposed by Helot rights groups and environmentalist groups who oppose the destruction of the reefs within the bay. Ironically the greatest support these groups gain is from the industries opposed to the expansions. Trade and mining industries support the expansion of the docks only to be blocked by groups funded by the tourism and aquaculture industry. These feuds appear in the streets as large protests and rallies and in back-door deals within the financial district. So far, each motion for expansion has been blocked, and support for preservation remains high.

NEO CANBERRA

Neo Canberra is based on Sarakino Island and is surrounded by sporting arenas. Neo Canberra was initially a deep-sea mining outpost. Upon discovery that the seams which seemed plentiful at first were shallow and pocketed, interest in the location dwindled, leaving little for the populace to do but fish and play sports. As time passed, these sports became an attraction of their own. The creation of Scuball, the most popular aqua sport in the universe, occurred when the miners used their underwater propulsion gear to make the first Scuball propulsion suits.

It's said if a citizen of Neo Canberra was to step out of their house and throw a ball into the air, it would likely land in a sports stadium. Sport runs in the blood of Neo Canberrans more deeply and fiercely than anywhere else on Varuna. Water sports are popular in Neo Canberra for a refreshing reason — water sports offer a release from the endless oppression of the planet's warmth, which can become overwhelming at times.

Akuna Bay may be the capital city of Varuna, but it's Neo Canberra that every off-worlder knows about. Millions of viewers from across the Sphere tune in every week to see the latest Scuball matches. Neo Canberra is the beating heart of the Scuball scene, the most famous teams in the sport claiming descent from one of the small clubs that played the high-intensity sport in its fledgling years. The same teams are immortalised in the Scuball Hall of Fame to this day, one of the greatest honours possible within Neo Canberra. Though Scuball holds ascendency in popularity, every conceivable water sport known to man can be found somewhere in Neo Canberra.

Neo Canberra hosts many famous sporting events throughout the year, with influxes of tourists usually coinciding with a final or championship. Because of this, Neo Canberra is designed almost exclusively as a tourism capital. Whilst Akuna Bay has its industrial sector and financial district, and the other archipelagos can claim sources of revenue outside of hospitality, tourism is the lifeblood of Neo Canberra. The Golden Mile, an immense chain of hostels and resorts, dominates the shoreline of Sarakino, leaving almost no room for fishing and other forms of aquaculture. The terrain around the city is mountainous and unfit for planting crops or raising livestock. Though the earth and ocean beneath Neo Canberra now lack mineral deposits, the remaining mining industry still tries desperately to find what should have been an immense supply. Without visitors from other planets, the city would wither and die. And so, the leagues of Neo Canberra monopolise on the popularity of sports on the planet.

A constant drive to expand the major attractions of the city means nothing else can come first. Natural wonders are mowed down to make room for stadiums and sports fields. Nesting grounds for endangered animals are swept aside to erect museums and statues to the great sporting heroes of Varuna. Culture has taken precedence over nature, which has drawn the attention of many activist groups from neighbouring Akuna Bay. Unlike Akuna Bay however, there is very little corporate interest in the survival of a few suncrests, or the preservation of an empty reef. The public could care less, caught up in a never-ending season of tourist activity and team spirit. Coldly, carefully, and in great secrecy, Neo Canberra's businesses ensure their city's survival at the cost of the local environment.

OCEAN VISTA

Atlantea isn't a quiet archipelago. The bustle of Varuna, the roaring crowds of Neo Canberra and the endless grind of delivery in Deepwater never stop. It seems impossible for there to be a quiet place on the islands of Atlantea and yet, in the east of the archipelago, there is. Ocean Vista is the embodiment of twilight years. The days are slow and pleasant. The air is clear and soothing. The waves lap at the shore in a steady rhythm that lulls the mind and soul to ease. The wonders of Circeo Island are simple things, not sold with flair or fake smiles. In Ocean Vista, one has time to sit back and unwind.

Ocean Vista is dedicated to looking inwards and focusing on the inner self. There is a quiet spirituality to the island that cannot be found in the storm of activity that is Varuna, and it is one of the few places on the planet free of commercialisation and advertisement. Meditation, hiking, and swimming are popular pastimes for the visitors of the town, free of the distractions of the modern world. Newlyweds, who seek to deepen their new powerful bond, and seniors, who sometimes want to find it again, are the most common visitors. Attracting lovebirds, the town has the fond nickname of 'Lovers Roost' amongst the people of Varuna, and there is many a young romantic who dreams of one day having someone they can take to Ocean Vista.

The sunset of Ocean Vista is its most popular attraction. A unique breed of reflective coral grows in the deeps around the town, and riftweed is common within the reefs beyond. Combined with an unobstructed view of the Timur Ocean, the sea seems to dance in the twilight, a dazzling display of colour that can move even the hardest heart to tears.

CAS

At the edge of Neo Canberra, built onto the water of the Timur Ocean, sits the Centre of Aquatic Sports, which generates hundreds of millions in revenue each quarter. Comprised of a considerable number of stadiums, the Centre is active nearly all year round, hosting professional athletes and the several media outlets that provide Maya coverage. The Centre is almost a town itself, containing all of the resources the average human needs. An almost permanent population of workers man the stalls, merchandise shops, and convenience stores that pay for the maintenance of the Centre.

PLANCTAE SUB-ARCHIPELAGO

Varuna may be a laidback world, but it is hardly defenceless. As is expected of each planet within PanOceania, Varuna has a standing army at the ready. The Varunan High Command sits on the Planctae Sub-Archipelago. The entire cluster of islands has been turned over to military use, every inch of the archipelago dedicated to housing for the army, storage for weapons and munitions, or as a training ground to keep the regiments of Varuna up to the high standards the modern military demands.

War games and drill camps take up most of a soldier's time in the Varunan defence force, with at least one rotation to Akuna Bay and the vast oceans for patrol duty. High Command is far enough away from the capital to stay out of sight, but close enough to immediately react in the event of a hostile attack on the city. To ensure that any foreign aggression is headed off, High Command keeps an intricate array of intersystem scanning facilities operational at all times. The Varunan fleet also stands alert, exchanging a feed of information with these ground-based assets and responding to the odd bogey within Varuna's extra-planetary borders.

Before contact with the EI Hegemony, Varuna's peaceful status meant that the presence of its army wasn't always needed. Thanks to this, the Hexahedron established the Varunan Immediate Reaction Division, a section of the Varunan military that acts as PanOceania's first responders in a military crisis, drawing troops from a planet that is unlikely to be the target of a foreign power. Members of the force are commonly called Snake-Eaters, because a majority of the Immediate Reaction Division is composed of special forces that deploy quickly and survive on their own grit whilst waiting for the main forces to arrive.

The recent war with the Combined Army has changed this. Every day, troops from Varuna's military branches, including the famous ORC regiments and Kamau Intervention Teams, are deployed to the front to combat the EI's armies, shrinking the garrison little by little. Luckily for the military, recruitment remains steady, ensuring that the Varuna's defence remains secure.

KUMARI KANDAM
BHARGAVI

On the north-western edge of Apam Napat Island, lies heaven. Bhargavi is hard to find, a secret kept by Varunans for themselves, a paradise for the people who work in paradise. Bhargavi is quietly

VARUNA'S FINEST

The Immediate Reaction Division and Varunan Army is made up of Varuna's best and brightest, and many of its regiments have earned themselves renown amongst their peers.

The ORC troops of the Varuna Division are famed for their skill traversing aquatic terrain as well as moving quickly and quietly, quite the feat for a soldier in powered armour without any stealth technology. Enemies have taken to calling the Varunan heavy armour specialists 'god damn sharks,' which, more often than not, is a point of pride for the troopers. These ORC's commonly work in mixed teams with other forces such as the Kamau to achieve tactical supremacy, and there are few warriors you would rather have at your back.

The Kamau represent some of Varuna's best operatives abroad and at home and are commonly planted in other units to lend their expertise. They are trained to integrate in units quickly and earn the trust and respect of their fellow soldiers before applying their talents, be it counterterrorism or aggressive infiltration.

Famous units include Echo Bravo, the Ready Reaction Unit, the pride of the Immediate Reaction Division. These soldiers act as special ops paratroopers, deploying in the worst situations and turning it to their favour. They refer to themselves as the true snake-eaters and run their training operations in stormy weather on the abandoned oceanic platforms that dot Varuna.

Another famed unit is Zulu Cobra, the Special Recon and Intervention Group. The unit acts as special operation infiltrators and skirmishers and are known for their brutally effective tactics. Descended from a fusion of the Australian Zeta unit and Indian CoBRA antiterrorist group, they share the motto यश या मृत्यु, "Glory or Death."

considered the most naturally splendid location on Varuna. Its waters are crystal clear, filled with vibrant coral that are home to schools of serra-fish and *kidok*. The sands are pristine and white, perpetually warm under the sun. The plants surrounding the shore emit a sweet smell that drifts on the wind. Those who discover the best kept secret on Varuna are inclined to hoard the secret for themselves.

The hotel Nirvana is a surprisingly humble place considering the secrecy surrounding it. For an off-worlder to gain a reservation, they need to be invited by Rawat or one of her more trusted customers. Locals gain reservations more easily, a custom that Rawat makes sure to propagate.

The service at Nirvana is handled by the best of the best, handpicked from across Varuna for their skills. Every want or need is taken care of before the customer even has the idea of it, drinks refilled, food replaced, and services rendered. Nirvana is infamous amongst its residents for the waiver that requires signing before entry, legally silencing Nirvana's customers from speaking about it without permission from the manager herself. This dedication to secrecy has made many wonder what Rawat did before she became a successful hotel owner, and whether it would be safe to find out.

AMYRA RAWAT

One savvy businesswoman, Amyra Rawat, decided that such a natural wonder needed to be exploited and cultivated to perfection. She carefully contracted the construction of a hotel, making sure the building complemented the surroundings of Bhargavi rather than overpowering them. It was Rawat who planted the sweet-smelling flowers and trees that give the shore its signature smell that drowns out the stench of rotting seaweed. In short, she engineered Bhargavi itself to make it perfect. She promptly called her resort Devaloka, after the Buddhist heavens.

Many have puzzled over who Amyra Rawat actually is. Many believe she is an ex-Neoterran politician or black operations agent. She waves aside these allegations every time with a smile and laugh, which is somehow more terrifying than any harsh words.

KOIMALA

Koimala was the first of Varuna's floating cities. Not as sleek as its modern siblings, it was plagued by a variety of unforseen issues. *Katallpeac* seaweed jammed its propulsion systems, and aggressive Helot pods caused minor damage when Koimala's waste dumps provoked them. The city suffered from inadequate drainage to combat the storms that sometimes sweep Varuna. But it was the lack of disaster planning that struck Koimala down in the end. An immense typhoon destroyed the navigation systems of the city and swept it off course, causing it to run aground on Thuvaraiyam's shores. Though efforts were made to make the city seaworthy again, the outdated systems and the construction of more stable floating cities doomed Koimala to remain where it had fallen.

Several of Koimala's inhabitants decided to stay with the city however, and soon expansion began to make Koimala liveable again. One of the first buildings raised was a series of immense anchors named the Driftlock Towers. The towers acted as giant pitons to stop the city from moving even slightly as the tide rose and fell, to ensure a modicum of stability for the city. The towers exist to this day, despite the expansions from the city centre holding Koimala still, to remind the inhabitants of their struggle and victory again the tides.

Koimala is roughly divided into three layers. The city centre houses much of the original architecture of Koimala. The docks beneath the lip of the city edge handle the duty of maritime imports and exports, and the upland expansions is where most of Koimala's residents make their home. Koimala's local economy grows each day as more and more people come to live in the upland estates, as even the shadow of the opulence the city once contained is enough to draw those who seek to live in a beautiful location.

HAWAIKI
ANAHENA

Anahena holds a swath of flat even ground, a rarity on Varuna's archipelagos. Nearly all of this space has been given over to farmland to generate a food surplus on the planet. With the use of careful planning and applied terraforming technology, several corporations have moulded the soil to be capable of growing almost any crop. Some farmers use this to capability to grow sweet fruits whilst others use their space to grow sturdier crops such as grains, carrots, and other vegetables.

Large agridomes protect the crops from the extremes of Varuna's climate, ensuring that rain

and winds during the stormy season don't destroy any of the farmers' efforts. These domes are usually built around maglev rail hubs that lead back to Anahena, a nexus of skyscrapers and refineries that process the raw materials into shipping units. Varuna then can supplement its usual aquaculture and expand its enterprises.

Within Anahena lies Varuna's emergency crop surplus, the Hawaiki Reserve. A combination of cryogenic storage and chemical preservation has been used to create a back-up supply of seeds and usable crops in case of an emergency situation such as floods or hurricanes. Each year the reserve is replaced, and the excess is put towards humanitarian efforts across the Sphere, as meagre as it is compared to the exports of larger planets.

Whilst the reserve takes up an impressive amount of space, it is hard to notice with the amount of bustle throughout the city proper. Hundreds of vehicles ferry deliveries across the city from maglev to maglev, before shooting off their cargo to another section of the city to be processed, stored, and loaded onto the ships. The chaos is barely contained by the tireless effort of the Anahena Shipping Authority and the several companies that call Anahena home. This furious pace is matched by Anahena's citizens, the city barely sleeping amongst the constant flux of product. This doesn't stop the workers of Anahena from enjoying themselves, however. The city has grown to adapt to the flow of industry, and shift schedules ensure that the city never sleeps.

IKATERE

Ikatere holds the crown of clubbers' paradise on Varuna. A town famed for the brewers that make their home there, Ikatere is a string of clubs, bars, and restaurants that each delivers a different experience. Some offer brief tastes of culture for those who are homesick while others embrace the odd or eclectic, dabbling in the oddities that Varuna's ecosystem has to offer.

Ikatere is home to the largest community of *tetekulu*, 'wild ones', on Varuna. Rare is the Helot that lives above water, but the *tete-kulu* are usually rejected by pods under the waters and feel more at home on land. A slum lies outside of Ikatere that acts as the housing for these wayward Helots, who find a sense of home and community amongst the other rejects. A fierce loyalty is found within the slum community, and it is a foolish outsider who attempts to cause trouble for the *tete-kulu* of Ikatere.

Because of this proximity to a permanent Helot presence, Ikatere has adopted many Helot foods

TIKASSAN CLUB

Many clubs claim to be the best in Ikatere, but the heart of the club scene lies on the shoreline in a bar known as *Tikassan* Club. Famous for being one of the very few Helot run establishments on Varuna, *Tikassan* Club is the premier bar for all things Helot, from food and drink to music and art. *Tikassan* Club celebrates the unseen wonders of Helot culture. The club's menu is a fusion of Helot traditionalism and the Human Sphere's diverse tastes, and the expertise on show is incredibly wide, serving an inordinate amount of drinks and food, combining techniques from across the Sphere.

The owner and head bartender, a Helot by the name of Badara, owes this wealth of knowledge to her travels across Varuna as one of its first Helot auxiliary troops. Born a *tete-kulu*, Badara was shunned from her pod for her aggressive nature. This led her into the military life as a member of the Helot Militia, which she found she excelled at. She even attained the rank of warrant officer, a position no other Helot had ever reached, and might have risen higher if not for her race. Eventually, she could no longer stomach fighting Libertos; Helots who simply wanted to erase the prejudice she and others had experienced. After resigning, she used her savings to retire into the business of bar ownership. *Tikassan* Club is a haven for other *tete-kulu* and a place Badara can keep an eye on the younger Helots who have yet to find a way to channel their aggression. In her bar, she teaches them how to stay away from trouble (or make the best of it) and build something with their lives. This practice means that the staff on shift tend to be hot-headed and prone to violence, but this has done nothing to stop *Tikassan* Club's meteoric rise to popularity. Altercations are rare, but always end with an apology from the staff under the stern gaze of Badara.

Rumours suggest that Tikassan Club also acts as a meeting place for Libertos. Amongst the many tales of the Tikassan Club, this is one of the few that is true. Badara has been a staunch supporter of Libertos since her separation with the military, and while she avoids direct involvement in their activities, she supports them with alibis and logistical support when she can. No lines have ever been traced back to Badara, as none would suspect the star of PanOceania's greatest Helot success story being associated with the rabble.

and traditions. The people of Ikatere are perhaps the friendliest to Helots on Varuna, having lived side by side with them each day. One example of this unity is the famous Ikatere drink, Helot Rum. Referred to as *kotussum* by the Helots, the drink is a combination of algae, purified fish blood, and locally refined alcohol. The drink is famous for its strong but surprisingly good taste and the effect it has on the body, heightening the senses and giving the imbiber a feeling of floating. Though many assume there would be negative side-effects, the drink is surprisingly healthy for the human body, acting as a good source of potassium and vitamin D.

TINIRAU

Tinirau sits at the edge of Ranginui and faces another small landmass to its north. The currents that sweep between these landmasses are erratic and uncertain, and flooding is common along the shores of the island. Settlers faced unique challenges in building a lasting town, because while the flooding was inconvenient, the currents had the tendency to draw in an immense number of sea life.

Fishermen of Tinirau find it easier to catch fish than other places on Varuna, the currents literally sweeping them into their nets. An odd efficiency became the aim to the people of Tinirau, and to improve the frequency of their catches they designed their buildings to float with the currents. Originally this was simply to handle the challenges the tide brought in, keeping the town from flooding when the tide swept in. In time however, fishermen began to abandon their boats and ships, electing to simply build extensions onto their homes to handle the storage of their gear and hold their catches. Soon enough most of Tinirau followed this example. This has led to a town made of watercraft that is constantly repositioning itself. Each day the town disconnects itself from the shore and shifts up and down the Hikri Strait, following the schools of fish that are swept along its length.

Entire sections of the community follow this method, including the schools and medical centres. Traditionally, fishing tends to be a lonely job, but in Tinirau, it is an act of community. Friends and families tie their craft together and extend their net lines to share in the spoils. Store owners learnt long ago that the best business practice is to follow their customers onto the open ocean. Each day eateries and convenience stores latch onto fishing hubs as they depart into the strait to sell food, drink, and other necessities as the day passes.

This has caused issues for the Varunan government in the past. It is remarkably difficult to enforce law and order in a town that simply changes its position on the map each day. To alleviate this issue, a permanent communications centre was built at the centre of the Strait that tracks the movement of the town. This also serves the twofold method of preparing drop locations for supply convoys to resupply the town and collect the spoils of the day.

As Tinirau grows larger and more coordinated each year, it grows closer to classification as a floating city. This has drawn the ire of the many upper class Varunans who consider the 'ramshackle heap of a town' an eyesore, nothing close to the beauty

THE IKATERE BRAVES

A small faction of the Libertos members loyal to Badara, these Helots are primarily composed of *tete-kulu*. Trained by Badara to inflict maximum damage at minimal cost of life and exposure, they are perhaps one of the most dangerous groups in Libertos, trained to know what to expect from the military's counter terrorism taskforces.

TINIRAU DOCKS

Though much of the town floats on the currents, a permanent dock was established towards the eastern side of the Strait. Construction companies specialising in Tinirau's unique housecraft abound here, including the largest local business known as the best in the rather unique field of interlocking, floating houses: Crine Manufacturing. Crine's advanced nodal docking programs and alignment detection systems have revolutionised the town. Thanks to their technology, the drifting town floats in formation with its vital services acting as the heart, providing stability and prosperity to its expanding population.

MINING CREWS

Often accompanied by Helot guides and riggers, Damak miners operate in five-man teams and seek out seams within the tunnels. One member is always an experienced pilot able to navigate the rushing currents of the tunnels — submersible pilots can always find work in Damak. After finding a seam and fixing themselves to the wall of the tunnel, the team begins the dangerous task of carefully displacing and mining the materials, which is made hard thanks to intense pressure from the current necessitating the use of special diving suits and equipment. To capture the minerals before they are swept downstream, the Helot riggers build a careful lattice of netting which is secured to the submersible once the seam is mined out. The crew let the current drift them to the other side of the island for retrieval and ferrying.

and opulence of their incredible, floating cities. Only time will tell if the town will ever make the jump in classification, as the citizens of Tinirau are more than happy to continue their nomadic ways, bound by community, hard work, and a little bit of advanced technology.

GURINDAM
DAMAK

Damak is a town of sludge and stilts and holds the title of the mining capital of Varuna. Damak is a small town on the southern tip of Lagu Island that is easily considered the dirtiest place in Varuna. Underneath Damak flows an immense network of flooded tunnels, perilously close to the surface. Combined with the sloped geography of Lagu, the rains and ocean have soaked the land to its core.

When the Varunan government conducted geographical inspection of Lagu Island, they discovered incredibly rich seams of ore and gemstones hiding beneath the sodden earth. Several companies attempted to dig their way down, but every conventional method either failed or did not return enough revenue to make the process worth it. Eventually, one company stumbled on a solution. The natural tunnel formations underneath Lagu had worn away at the bedrock, exposing many of the seams over the years. Using carefully modified underwater exploration vehicles and the assistance of a local Helot pod, the company dispatched an expedition to traverse the winding paths of the

tunnels. It took time to map out workable routes, but eventually a map was created and work began proper.

The town of Damak was built to establish homes for the miners and storage areas for the companies. As the industry grew, so did the town, and presently Damak supports a small population of about ten thousand, most of them miners and their families. The town stands upon an impressive network of stilts several meters above the earth. Carefully positioned to sit on the few stable points of bedrock, Damak is constantly being rebuilt and reclaimed from the soil and sludge, an enterprise that sometimes feels pointless. But the people of Damak carry on with pride and determination as the mining capital of Varuna, exporting incredible amounts of raw materials and containing some of the bravest and most daring souls on the planet.

This has led to an intense rivalry with their sister town, Hujan. The two towns constantly butt heads, a conflict that has existed since the early days of Varuna. Neither town has shown signs of giving up this feud. This works in favour of the Varuna mining sector as the fierce competition drives the workers to achieve the status of the best of the planet. Profits climb in particularly intense years, leading to some companies 'nudging' their employees with staged pranks to boost enthusiasm.

HUJAN

Aside from Damak, Hujan is the second most successful mining town of Varuna. Though the efforts to reach seams beneath Damak began first, Hujan was the first town to be built. The island of Keharmonian doesn't suffer from the complexities of Lagu. The ground beneath Hujan is solid and filled with a wealth of minerals, allowing for traditional mining methods and a stable influx of mined goods.

Several dig sites pepper Keharmonian's surface and the waters surrounding it. Although the workers of Hujan aren't as well adapted to underwater mining as the miners of Damak, they aren't strangers to the efforts required to reach underwater deposits. Several underwater mining operations are carried out by Helot workers around the edges of Keharmonian to reach seams that are too far out to safely obtain.

The town of Hujan is located on the eastern shore of Keharmonian. Unlike Damak, Hujan is a town like any other on Varuna. A port built by the town connects Hujan to the global shipping lanes of Varuna. Hujan supports a population larger than Damak thanks to its stable ground, though Hujan's people tend to be dour and serious compared to the inhabitants of Damak. The sour facade hides a simple, fierce pride in their work, however. More than anything, they want to prove themselves the better of Varuna's mining towns and work hard to achieve it.

Hujan relies on unity in purpose and openly shared information to ensure their profits are maximised. This has led them to form a unified body to handle the distribution of information and mining rights, the Keharmonian Miners Guild. This union of miners from across the island specialises in different forms of excavation. At an annual meeting each year, information gathered by each of the companies is shared to allow the best-equipped miners to tackle the right jobs as they appear. To date, this has worked in the favour of each company. Time will tell if the depletion of resources will compromise this agreement.

PULARI UTARA ISLAND

In the northern reaches of Varuna's oceans sits Pulari Utara. A quiet and unremarkable island, very little of note can be found on its verdant mass. That is unless you know the paths to the facility built beneath it.

Thousands of meters below the surface and built into the bedrock of Pulari Utara lays the Centre of Aquatic Warfare, the greatest military secret on the planet. The complex is only accessible by underwater shuttle or one of the few hidden elevators on the island's surface, each heavily guarded by carefully hidden REM Dronbots. The brightest minds of PanOceanian aquatic engineering contractors, such as Moto. tronica, meet within to design the next generation of PanOceania's naval might. Some of the wonders created in its halls include pressure-resistant Atlasium alloys, the infamous Cutter Naval Warfare Chasseur, and special operations *Ithican* assault craft.

The secrets preserved in the facility demand a high level of security, and this is provided by a variety of dedicated units. A contingent of ORC troopers remain on site, cycling out every month. A handful of Cutters are also kept on site to defend against any attacks from the underwater entrances to the facility. Top-of-the-line, motion-tracking security-ware monitors each and every object that moves within a fifteen-kilometre radius of the island and keeps logs on anything within one hundred kilometres. Some would consider this excessive, but it isn't uncommon for teams of off-worlder agents to attempt to find the base and steal its secrets.

Cyber security specialists do their best to deflect these probes into PanOceania's interests, but every day brings with it the chance of discovery. In recent years, the gaps between potential detection events grow shorter as foreign powers drag their noose tighter.

SYURGA

It's always raining in Syurga. Like Akuna Bay's spaceport, Syurga is host to a perpetual case of rain storms, summoned by the constant arrivals and departures. Unlike Akuna Bay however, there is very little reason for the storms to be hidden. Tourism is rare on the bleak reaches of the Gurindam archipelago and so locals must brave the constant downpour brought on by the turbulent atmosphere.

That isn't to say the people of Gurindam's capital are miserable. Syurga is a bustling city of business, enjoyment, and — surprisingly — the fine arts. Many of the deep-sea miners from across the archipelago make their home here and often return from long assignments looking for rest and relaxation. Pilots also find they have time to burn on their assignment turnovers and spend their hard-earned money in the city. Syurga hosts an expansive entertainment scene, offering the latest recreational technology from across the Sphere. Aside from this technology are the many theatres, galleries, and bars which support a solid cultural bedrock that works to combat the dreary weather.

Within Syurga lies the headquarters of the Coldsoil Mining Conglomerate, a public company that officially runs most of the mining efforts in Gurindam

RIFT RIDERS

Though it is expressly illegal, many daredevils ignore the application process to enter Damak's aquatic mines and dare the currents on their own. Known as rift riders, they attempt to traverse the length of the island in small high-speed pods, stopping only to rest and eat.

ITHICAN ASSAULT CRAFT

Inspired by the *Ithican* Arrow, the assault craft is a rapid insertion submarine used in naval engagements. Used as a boarding craft when confronting other subaquatic vessels, the assault craft is shot at the enemy vessel. Upon contact it latches to the hull and employs cutting blades and precision-guided shaped charges to breach the side of the vessel, disorientating the enemy crew and allowing its cargo to deploy.

DAMAGE DAREDEVILS

Only the most daring workers accept positions in the Damak mining workforce. Each day is a risk, but an exhilarating one. Daredevils and thrill seekers from across Varuna commonly apprentice in the Damak workforce, ensuring a constant influx of workers. This enthusiasm usually runs its course safely enough. A slip or tumble down the currents can scare almost anyone out of the job. Though fatalities are rare with the high standard of safety and medical technology available to Varuna, there are around fifteen fatalities a year in the tunnels.

and unofficially runs them all. Made up of several smaller companies which handle such things as subaquatic vehicle building, geographic surveying, and aquatic research, the Coldsoil Conglomerate uses its many subsidiaries to maintain an edge in the growing mining sector on Varuna. As one of the financial powerhouses of Varuna, it constantly contributes to lobbies to lift restrictions on no-mining zones and employs underhanded techniques to ensure that it maintains its grip on the resource monopoly it has established. Even the few companies that find their way to acquiring mining rights tend to disappear under the weight of the Coldsoil Conglomerate, quietly bought out and repurposed into a branch organisation within the titanic company. Varuna's governing body tends to overlook such aggressive takeovers for the sake of economic stability. Coldsoil Mining accounts for nearly eighty percent of mining employment planet wide and seventy eight percent of mining contracts and surveying. Without the company's business, Varuna's economy would take a brutal hit.

The city is truly a reflection of the archipelago, filled with the working class and their families. Education inevitably leads to one of the many trade schools or universities that specialise in geosciences. This paved path is far from popular with the youth of Syurga, who tend to act out against the inevitability of their future. Most eventually fall into the work anyway, with few opportunities offered around Gurindam outside of hospitality and mining. A few become lucky, however, and break the mould. This is either by enlisting with the PanOceanian military, moving to another city, or by channelling their frustration into an artistic focus and finding their way into one of the prestigious art institutions that pepper Syurga and Akuna Bay. These schools are dedicated to producing the best actors, musicians, and artists on Varuna, with the Syurgara Institute being the most prestigious. Varuna's most famous personalities have been trained in its respected halls, where they are offered a strangely classic education compared to the more modern institutions of the Human Sphere. The arts are oddly well-respected considering Syurga's commonly more down to earth occupations. The inhabitants of Gurindam never forget the people who make them laugh and cry.

LEMURIA
CRYSTAL COVE

Lemuria Algae is one of the most precious resources on Varuna. The abundance of applications for the waterborne organism are incredible. Though Lemuria algae is plentiful in the archipelago it is native to, it stubbornly refuses to be spread anywhere else. Scientists are at a loss as to why

this is, but some speculate there is a unique quality to the waters of Lemuria that enables the substance to grow. Regardless of the conditions of growth, Varuna always seeks out new methods of expanding their harvesting efforts, and Crystal Cove remains the most effective harvesting and refinement plant in the archipelago.

Crystal Cove earned its name thanks to the efforts of its trawlers and harvesting stations, whose combined efforts to process algae ensure the surrounding waters are incredibly clean. All manners of substances — both natural and unnatural — are dredged from the ocean for processing. The refinement plants grow day by day to meet an ever-expanding demand.

An expanding fleet and increasingly successful methods of capture demands a larger workforce and more space to store the supply of refined algae before it is shipped across Varuna and off world. A small town has grown around the plant to house the ever-increasing population of workers of the plant and their families. The development of a small community and self-sustaining economy has taken root, and if the current rate of growth continues experts predict that Crystal Cove could become a fully-fledged population centre within as little as five years.

FOSTER BEACH

As with all water sports, surfing has a popular following on Varuna Surfing, though, is one of the few professional sports on Varuna not held in Neo Canberra. Due to the busy beaches and cluttered waters outside of the city, surfing is difficult and sometimes even dangerous. So, the surfers of Varuna wandered until they stumbled on their own little chunk of paradise.

The incredible Foster Beach sits at the tip of Silver Sands Island, surrounded by a whole lot of nothing. Colonisation has yet to reach the island, and the inhabitants have no complaints. There are no permanent buildings in Foster Beach, leading to its title as the City of Tents. Travellers, Ateks, Helots — all are welcome on Foster Beach. This temporary town is a favourite location for the youth of Varuna, particularly students and surfers. It isn't uncommon for the young folk of Varuna to make pilgrimages and road trips to Foster Beach in between school semesters and during their vacations. Though far from a rite of passage, the journey to Foster Beach is counted as some of the best times of many a Varunan's life.

Foster Beach isn't without its problems however. Drugs and other illicit substances find their way to the unregulated society that Foster Beach supports. Raids from the law enforcement of nearby cities are often attempted but never turn up anything

OCEAN PROVISIONS

Between the Silver Sands, Redcliff, and Ararat islands runs a powerful current that courses from the Barat Ocean into the Tengah Ocean. The current is strong enough to tear excess Lemuria Algae and funnel it into naturally forming blooms that can spread up to hundreds of meters wide. Some rare blooms can even reach a kilometre in width. Crystal Cove acts as the port for a fleet of trawler ships that capture and condense these blooms before returning them to Crystal Cove's refinement plants for processing. Combined with the harvesting platforms littered within the currents between the islands, the intake of algae is incredible.

ANNUAL SPOTLIGHT

Once a year, Foster Beach holds a festival designed to coincide with the Surfer's Cup of Varuna. This is one of the only times Foster Beach steps into the spotlight within the Varunan year. Food and music entertain the guests of the City of Tents as the surfers prove their skills.

worth the effort. The fact that the nearest hospital is hours away via aircraft and even more by boat contributes to several deaths a year on Foster Beach. Thankfully the culture of care in the town is a strong one, and the inhabitants of the City of Tents are sure to watch out for each other and help in any way they can should tragedy strike.

HALIDON BRIDGE

With currents battering the passage between the three islands, Crystal Cove has difficulty exporting its algae. Many a cargo ship has been lost to storm-infused riptides. To provide a point of egress that didn't rely on the fickle currents and dangerous waters of the three-point strait, a combined port and airfield was developed on the edge of Halidon Island. Though this worked initially, the small gap of ocean between Halidon and Redcliff Islands became a bottleneck to increased productivity. A bridge was commissioned to further improve the flow of import and export, and began construction of Halidon Bridge.

Initial construction was a massive undertaking. To close the gap between the islands and link the many small towns of Redcliff and Halidon's Port, the bridge needed to span many kilometres. Redcliff Island was still sparsely inhabited in those days, so workers had to either commute by aircraft each day or construct their own accommodation.

Accommodation was originally clustered at the entry point of the bridge, but workers' camps grew alongside its own expansion across the water. Each camp became semi-permanent fixtures thanks to plumbing and essential services linked between them. At final completion, the services were left behind untouched until a property developer hit upon an innovative scheme. Soon enough, Halidon Bridge's first 'high' rise apartments created a town beneath a bridge, beneath a town.

The apartments were aimed at the men and women working the maglevs that transport hundreds of tonnes of algae and import essential supplies, but as Crystal Cove's operation expanded, so did the local community. Hundreds of modular, affordable apartments sprang up, with luxury apartments and business premises soon following. It was cheap, had a wonderful view, and the maglevs were only an occasional distant rumble, so people found their way to live there. The Halidon Bridge of today looks like children's brickwork, with buildings attached to points across and under its entire architecture.

NOAHTOWN

Unsurprisingly, ship construction is major business on Varuna. Even in an age of interstellar travel and technological marvels, few methods of transport are as cost effective as sailing. The sheer number and scope of vessels that ply Varuna's oceans requires a constant and furious effort to keep afloat. Though most Varunan towns and cities have a shipyard, there is only one that truly matters: Noahtown.

Based on the most south-western corner of Ararat Island, Noah's Point, and named after the biblical figure whose Ark came to rest on the peak of Mount Ararat, Noahtown is barely a town despite its name. It encompasses kilometres of shipyards, factories, and warehouses that handle an incredible sixty-seven percent of ship construction and maintenance on Varuna. From small, humble fishing dinghies, to the colossal freighters that transfer crops and fish from Varuna's farms, many Varunan ships can trace their origins back to Noahtown's shipyards.

Although officially classified as a habitable town, Noahtown has few of the standard systems in place to identify it as such. Noahtown personnel that have families generally choose to live in one of Ararat's many smaller towns. The town's few schools and hospitals are small and mainly focussed on first aid and apprenticeships. Every other plot has been given over to industry in Noahtown, with only minimal consideration given to necessities such as food, water, and accommodation. The workforce prefers it this way, as they are fiercely prideful of their work and distractions aren't tolerated well.

Noahtown maintains a strong relationship with the miners of Gurindam, as a large portion of their spoils end up at the inland refineries. This monumental process refines then combines Varuna's unique ores with more familiar alloys such as iron, aluminium, and titanium. These molten concoctions are then shaped into plating, ferried by maglev to the great shipyards, and fitted to the hulls of ships. Many vessels, including the immense Living Cities that make such an incredible sight, return to their birthplace for repairs and refitting, as the craftsmanship and care shown in Noahtown is peerless.

Noahtown's greatest achievements are undoubtedly the Living Cities of Varuna. Its shipyards were the pioneers of the immense city ships and they continue to receive each new contract for the construction of one of the opulent vessels.

In addition to civilian contracts, Noahtown also caters to various military outfits, all of whom clamour for cutting edge aquatic vehicles and an advantage in maritime warfare. To ensure that the secrets within remain secure, the shipyards dedicated to military contracting are carefully guarded by private security firms. Sensibly, weapon systems are kept off site as a point of safety and are only fitted once in the hands of those that

SHIPWRIGHT'S GUILD

Even the ancient profession of shipbuilding must grow and modernize with the times. Noahtown's companies bring their brightest minds in naval engineering together at the Varunan Shipwrights Guild and task them with paving the way to greater nautical achievements. A loose collection of engineers, scientists, programmers, and even carpenters, they research and develop newer and better naval technologies whilst preserving nautical traditions.

BRIDGE LIFE

Society on Halidon Bridge is normal enough. People go to work and children go to school on the mainland. Base jumping and drone racing are popular hobbies. Many toil at the maintenance required on the bridge itself, but others find jobs on the maglevs, or at the many refineries in Halidon Port or Redcliff.

HALIDON TROLLS

Despite humble beginnings, Halidon Bridge hasn't been immune to the darker side of society. Making their home in the bridge's dark underbelly, the Halidon Trolls ensure crime is at an all-time high on its modular streets, particularly anduction. Though not necessarily violent, the gang are notorious for stealing portions of the algae shipments that pass overhead, which they then use to create Varunan Blue. Though simply named, the drug is a dangerous hallucinogen that provides a powerful high. In mockery of the algae's healing properties, it also damages the brain's synapses and causes extreme paranoia. Despite harsh sentencing, Varunan Blue has found its way across Varuna and off-world more than once. Police efforts have failed to date, as the Trolls are incredibly adept at disappearing... or making those who seek them disappear.

commissioned their construction. Of course, this also serves as insurance of payment.

RYLSTONE

Located on the remote island of Haven, Rylstone is the heart of Varuna's biotechnological industry. Primarily a collection of famous universities dedicated to bioengineering, biological nanotechnology, and the development of new and incredible substances derived from Varuna's strange ecology, Rylstone's proud institutions and best and brightest are protected by a private security force that maintain a tight cordon.

Students can expect gruelling coarse loads and intense deadlines designed to weed out the uncommitted and subpar. Only the best can graduate into the alumni of Rylstone and turn their minds to the betterment of the Human Sphere.

The halls of the famed Biogenetic Research Centre (see sidebar) conduct hundreds of experiments under varying conditions. The sheer scope of research is credited to the wonders of Varuna's diverse ecosystem, which contain evolutionary marvels that could greatly benefit mankind if replicated. Research requiring field testing or observation in an active environment is undertaken in one of several underwater facilities. The unique conditions granted by these environments have kept the scientists of Haven a step ahead of their PanOceanian competitors.

To maintain the secrecy of some of the more ground-breaking advances in bioscience and material development, PanOceania's Hexahedron has classified Rylstone and its research as a strategic resource and defend it with care. Wary of foreign influence, carefully planted operatives from the military's intelligence branch keep a watchful eye on the scholarly community. With the town meeting most of their needs, Rylstone is a close-knit society whose members rarely leave for reasons other than business or research excursions. Dormitories and more permanent residences have been built, allowing families and friends to regularly visit. Considered a prestigious posting, working at Rylstone is a dream come true for the career scientist.

The increased security presence surrounding Haven's more secretive laboratories provide an air of mystery to those living nearby. Rumours and conspiracies abound concerning the Rylstone's facilities, with some even inspiring films about the biotechnical experts and their 'twisted' practices. For the most part, the rumours are false. Now that humanity's fate lies in a struggle with an aggressive alien power, every day requires greater military advancements to ensure victory. With increasing

frequency, scientists are receiving unusual assignments that deviate from their common workload. Although no lines have been crossed yet and would almost certainly be met with strong reactions if they did, one can't help but wonder if Haven will earn the reputation it is rumoured to have.

WAVE PORT

Positioned at the uppermost north of Ararat Island with views across the Tengah Ocean, the city of Wave Port is considered the last stop for a successful soldier, and the first stop for a recovering one. The capital of Lemuria Archipelago is famous for its hospitals and recovery facilities, with Hospitaller Order's Blessed Heart Hospital of Saint Lazarus Upon the Sea chief among them. Dedicated to the physical and mental rehabilitation of military personnel, the hospital has a sterling reputation amongst the military for therapy and reintegration. The Hospital's celebrity has even led to wounded from other nationalities applying for treatment. Though the vetting process is strict, applications sometimes receive support from high in the PanOceanian government.

Many of PanOceania's frontline combatants bear physical and mental scars. A visit to Varuna is a common recommendation on retirement. See the sights, breathe the sea air, and finally rest after years of brave and faithful service. Thanks to advances in medical reagents via Rylstone, Wave Port's methods are continuously expanding and improving. A constant stream of the sick and injured, both military and civilian, make their way here from across Varuna, and beyond. Varuna's environment helps set the mind at ease, which in turn allows the body to heal. Thanks to these combination of factors, Wave Ports success rate is nothing short of miraculous.

Religion is an important aspect of PanOceanian life, which is doubly true in Wave Port. Churches are almost as common as hospitals. Neither are the two mutually exclusive; in Varuna's city of miracles, faith, and science meet with the goal of healing the sick. Education also maintains a strong presence, as its proximity with Rylstone provides many medical students the opportunity to intern in Wave Port's hospitals. Earning a doctorate at such a facility is a high honour on Varuna that virtually ensures employment.

The city earns its revenue through medical care and contracts from Rylstone. Wave Port offers the opportunity to test the many advancements discovered in Rylstone's laboratories on active medical cases. This cooperation ensures that each new technology is tested humanely and rapidly, increasing the pace of healing and research in both locations. Though the rare case ends tragically, the risks often outweigh the cost.

TBRC
The Tescari Biogenetic Research Centre (TBRC) sits at the centre of Rylstone's hive of intellectuals. Professor Marco Tescari was a prodigious genius of his time whose credits include pressure adaptive drugs for deep sea workers, the genetic modification of plants to increase the viability of farming on Varuna's nutrient-poor land, and the Helot pressure suit. Some even praise him as the man who made Varuna habitable, a title that would make him twist in his grave. Believing that cooperation can overcome anything, he was a staunch advocate of the power of unified effort. As one of his last projects before his retirement and death, the TBRC was posthumously given his name so as to inspire others to rise up together, or not at all. Although a staunch anti-revivalist, the professor consented to a brain scan and the construction of a fully ALEPH-integrated pseudo-personality. This quasi-Tescari now serves as Rylstone's librarian.

THE MAD DOCTOR MARCO
Made shortly after Tescari's death, The Biomancer movie drew elements from the Professor's life and works to create a highly fictionalised tale. Considered an affront to his feats, it was panned across the Sphere. Despite its label as the film that killed Varuna's credibility in the media industry, a cult following has led to several direct-to-Maya sequels.

CHAPTER 5
PANOCEANIA GEAR

PanOceania's iota-scarcity prosperity rests not only on profound infrastructural integration with ALEPH, but on a robust consumer economy, diverse citizenry, vast territory, and deep governmental investment in research and development to maintain the Hyperpower's technological edge. Maya permeates every aspect of PanOceanians' lives, allowing them to not only share their thoughts and desires, but to find whatever they desire quickly and easily, accelerating trends and shifts in fashion.

Lifelong immersion in this high-tech consumer's cornucopia means that demotics and personalisation that would be luxuries elsewhere are expected defaults in PanOceania, even for basic items. Maya's panopticon makes each choice of style, make, and materials into a statement of personal, political, and sub-cultural identity — a tangible ring in one's halo, and a socially rewarding game for those willing to make the effort.

Poorer PanOceanians are, if anything, even more involved with this stylistic interplay, although their inexpensive materials and Maya overlays raise eyebrows in Elite circles — AR variable clothing that changes radically depending on halo permissions is a recent fad. Among the wealthy, smart fabrics and items that draw textures and palette from a very particular neighbourhood, era, or fictional work are increasingly popular, often requiring personal knowledge of the wearer or user's taste to interpret.

Some things remain difficult to acquire, even in this iota-scarcity economy. Access to exclusive vacation spots and tourist enclaves, specialized tools, personal vehicles, and military hardware of all kinds require not only funds, but the right connections. In a society where almost anything is possible, the inaccessible becomes intensely valuable, and the right friends even more so.

NEW QUALITY

HERITAGE WEAPON X (CULTURE)
Though modern society is a largely peaceful one, the martial aspects of its many originating cultures are quietly encouraged to ensure support for military actions. Heritage Weapons are bestowed by cultural leaders to recognize an individual's actions on behalf of their community, with encoded metadata as proof — higher rankings are awarded for increasingly important accomplishments. Wearing the weapon visibly, or revealing its metadata tags in one's halo, grants X bonus Momentum when leaning on one's accomplishments and reputation in social tests with individuals from the appropriate culture or sub-culture, but misusing one is a serious risk to that reputation, adding +1 complication range to the test.

NEW VEHICLE TYPES

Aircraft: The vehicle is capable of self-propelled flight at a variety of altitudes. This distinguishes them from Hover vehicles, which push off from a nearby surface and can only hover a short distance from the ground, water, or other surfaces. Most modern Aircraft are capable of vertical take-off and landings, and a considerable degree of lateral movement.

Remote Presence: The vehicle is designed to be piloted remotely. If it has Max Passengers zero, it has no cockpit or other life support systems.

Submersible: The vehicle can safely submerge and operate underwater, and handle the ordinary pressures and temperatures of aquatic and deep-sea conditions.

GEAR CATALOGUE

Adarsana Grenade [Environment]: Nanotech pesticides altered by Eco-Aktion bio-hackers and named for the Acontecimento region destroyed by invasive Earth-born crops, Adarsana grenades release a vicious array of bio-toxins designed to destroy "impure" plants and ecosystems in a particular environmental biome. They deal negligible damage to non-flora, but Cover Soak from fungus, plants, bushes, or trees from the target environment in the affected area is reduced by one each round until reduced to zero, and the zones fill with slurries of rapidly-degrading plant matter, becoming D2 Difficult Terrain. (Explosive Grenade, Disposable, Indiscriminate (Medium), Nonlethal, Speculative Fire, Thrown, Unsubtle, destroys plant cover)

Aerarium Account X: Named for the ancient Roman treasury, these high-security Hospital Bank accounts provide +2X Security Soak to the user's financial interactions and transactions, due to constant and detailed monitoring against illicit intrusion or manipulation. Opening an account requires Earnings of at least 3+X, and good standing with the Church, ALEPH, and PanOceanian officials.

WHAT YOU'LL FIND IN THIS CHAPTER

- A new item Quality, Heritage Weapon X

- Several new Vehicle Types common in PanOceania

- A catalogue of new items and vehicles used by PanOceanians

- Four iconic TAGs used by the PanOceanian Military Complex

Aircraft — see *Infinity GM Guide*, p. 130

iota-scarcity — see *Infinity Corebook*, p. 140

BALISONG KNIVES

Balisongs, also known as butterfly or Batangas knives – originated in the Phillipines, and can be quickly opened by skilled fighters. Their handles are split into two narrow bars which rotate around the tang and have grooves which conceal the knife when closed.

MEDIUM COMBAT ARMOUR VARIANT
BAGH-MARI ARMOUR

Named for ancient clans of Indian tiger killers and a fierce counter to Yu Jing Tiger Soldiers, Acontecimento's Bagh-Mari wear armour built for the hunt, incorporating adaptations and Chameleonwear coatings specific to their intended operational biome (aquatic, desert, or jungle), as well as a Multispectral Visor 1.

Aeropter: Lightweight civilian VTOL frames, aeropters see extensive use as communal vehicles on the frontier, archipelagos, CFZs, and as cheap aircabs for the ever-changing skyline of Neoterra's Newton City.

AEROPTER
AIRCRAFT, EXPOSED (+2 Ⓝ COVER), FRAGILE

ATTRIBUTES		
Scale	Speed	Brawn
2	1/2	9 (+1)

DETAILS	
Max. Passengers	Impact
4	2+3 Ⓝ (Knockdown)
Hard Points	
–	

DEFENCES			
Structure	9	Firewall	6
Armour	2	BTS	0

Alpenstock: Ice axes attached to smart-material extensible poles inspired by the ancient Swiss climbing poles of the same name, alpenstock are quickly becoming heritage items among Svalarheimans, returned to the community on death. Each owner adds a stanza or two to the embedded saga. Alpenstocks count as kits for climbing. (Melee Weapon, 1+4 Ⓝ damage, Unbalanced, Heritage Weapon X (Svalarheimans), Improvised 1, Non-Hackable, Stun, Vicious 1)

Balisong Motorcycle: A daredevil's favourite, balisongs are as swift and unexpected as their namesake Filipino blades – and nearly as dangerous to untrained amateurs. This year's Manila model from San Fernando de Dagopan's Skym-Naza Motors is their best in years, but Baling AB's 2–9 and Tagatek's Manny are still significantly easier to repair.

BALISONG MOTORCYCLE
EXPOSED, GROUND, WHEELED

ATTRIBUTES		
Scale	Speed	Brawn
0	3	10

DETAILS	
Max. Passengers	Impact
1	1+3 Ⓝ (Knockdown)
Hard Points	
Chassis 3, Comms 1, External 1, Internal 1, Motive 1, Weapons 1	

DEFENCES			
Structure	8	Firewall	6
Armour	1	BTS	0

SPECIAL ABILITIES:
- **Splitwheels**: The cycle's wheel sets are pairs attached to independent hydraulic struts, and can split and extend for ATV-like manoeuvres and sudden leaps. With a Pilot (D2) test at +2 complication range, the balisong can ignore up to Hazardous or Difficult Terrain 2, or vault over obstacles up to a meter tall without penalty.

Banduk E/Mitter: Produced by Khalsa's own Chikreli Arms, and favoured by the Akali commandos based in the region, banduk (rifle in Punjabi) E/Mitters are underslung launchers for subsonic non-lethal electromagnetic-pulse projectiles, designed for use with weapons with the MULTI Light Mod quality such as Combi Rifles. Excellent for assaulting technological units or disabling defence and security systems, the careful calibration required adds +1 difficulty to Tech tests to add to a weapon. (Range C/M, 1+5 Ⓝ damage, Burst 1, 1H, Nonlethal)

Blade of St. George: The iconic weapons of Knights Hospitallers, these formidable swords incorporate the latest in modern melee materials, including a Teseum edge, while carefully avoiding the Templar apostasy of artificially intelligent weapons. (Melee, 1+5 Ⓝ damage, 2H, Grievous, Non-Hackable, Parry 2, Piercing 2, Vicious 1)

Bounce: Named after the low-g "Acontecimento Step", and popular with PanOceanian partiers, bounce is a euphoric drug with an intense comedown, taken a few hours before the end of a night of carousing to ensure restful sleep. Sold in disposable oral sprays, it is banned in Yu Jing and Haqqislam's territory due to dangerous side-effects if abused.

Special Effect: Once administered, the user gains +1 Morale Soak and +4 Resolve for three hours. Once those three hours are up, they heal 4 Mental damage, and quickly descend into deep REM sleep for the next six hours.

Addiction 1 (8 doses), Compulsion 1

Overdose Wound Effect: all overdose damage is doubled, and taken as mental damage.

Withdrawal: 2+2 🄽 mental damage, Harm Effect (user takes double mental damage until recovered, and suffers intensely personal nightmares)

Bush Knife X: Deeply-grooved broad blades with hardwood handles, also known as Bowie knives, bush knives were indispensable during Neoterran colonisation. Originals and knockoffs are formal apparel and constitute significant gifts between Neoterrans with frontier Australasian heritage. Many have layered blade inscriptions in addition to metadata. (Melee Weapon, 1+5 🄽, 1H, Heritage Weapon X (Australasian Neoterrans), Thrown, Unforgiving 1, Vicious 2)

Caskuda Jewellery: Named for the nigh-invulnerable Acontecimento cockroach, these ornate bracelets are mosaics of multihued Punta Norte stones surrounding a memory diamond library of unique and exhaustive Infowar countermeasures, providing 4 Security Soak to the wearer's personal network so long as they stay in close proximity with the wearer's skin. Rumours abound about their source, but only a few are sold each year, always through anonymous cut-outs and obscure dead drops, and since they permanently imprint on the first individual to wear them, bidding is fierce among collectors and elite hackers.

Citplant: Currently only used by the PanOceanian military as an additional security measure for key installations, these implanted identity tokens each contain a unique but static cryptographic database embedded in memory diamond, adding +2 difficulty to forge a specific implant to anyone with Tech or Hacking focus of 2 or less. The "Ateks Out!" movement has recently advocated for gating access to all city cores and services with the use of similar "citizen-only implants" to further marginalise Ateks, who rely on fake IDs for access.

Contender: A family of duelling weapons for use in Aristeia! competitions, Contender designs widely vary by manufacturer, but all share a low rate of fire, high stopping power, and compact size. Despite seeing some military use, their biggest market remains Aristeia! fighters and fans, with prices driven by marketing rather than any actual difference in utility. (Range M, 1+4 🄽 damage, Burst 1, Unbalanced, Anti-Materiel 1)

Croc Mine: Like the infiltrators that use them, croc mines are designed for amphibious stealth and covered in a chameleonwear coating, rendering them difficult to see unaided — they cannot enter the revealed state unless the viewer is within Medium range. When deployed underwater, at any depth, they passively adjust their buoyancy and use shrouded pump-jet impellers to maintain their position. (Explosive Mine, 2+5 🄽 damage, 1H, Comms, Disposable, Fragile, Indiscriminate (Close), Unsubtle, Grievous)

Cutter TAG: Characteristically high-tech Mototronica weapons for ocean dominance, Cutters are designed from first principles for stealth both above and below the waves, despite their massive depth-resistant construction. In addition to TO Camo sheathing and internal system sound-suppression, passive filtration-layers disguise the TAG's radioactive and E/M profile, effectively shielding it from sensor detection.

A CineticS Lunan MULTI HMG is a Cutter's sole weaponry besides their fists, so they are best in coastal engagements where their amphibious manoeuvrability lets them strike from surprising angles at Long range. On land, their exaggerated swimmer's build's can appear ungainly, but at sea attenuated wings at shoulders and ankles unfurl to steer them in smooth sweeping arcs — powered by the aquajet that comprises most of their torso's bulk, they reveal a deadly streamlined grace.

POPULAR CONTENDER MODELS

TauruSW Duelist — basic undisguised model

Styrock Carb8 – disguised as a conventional carbine.

CineticS FLX line — built into a personalized armour forearm.

Goa Dynamics' Bhujang series — incorporate custom-grown *reptilo*-scale inlays and AR effects to complete the wielder's look.

Acontecimento Step — see *Infinity Corebook*, p. 224

Caskuda — see *Infinity Corebook*, p. 225

"NEMO NOS EFFUGIT" (NOBODY ESCAPES US)

Varuna's Naval Chasseurs, or more specifically their Fast Intervention Unit, use Cutters as armoured spearheads for both deep-sea and amphibious covert operations — infiltrator insertion, punitive actions, perimeter enforcement, interdictions, and so on. While analysts and investigators often resent the photogenic TAGs drawing all the attention, there's no denying they sustain the unit's motto. The sole exception is Libertos attacks — Helots somehow reliably detect and evade Cutters, a black mark on the Naval Chasseur's otherwise flawless record.

Cube Scan — see *Infinity Corebook*, p. 394

DANGEROUS THREAD

Every nation has a unique recipe for D-Thread, each of which is treated as a state secret, and an illicit creation of it is a capital crime in some nations.

SHARED VISION

Even without Maya Integration, AR Eye Implants are so common among PanOceanians that broadcasting what one sees to friends, family, or even the public at large is an unconscious reflex. Sharing a live visual feed (with modest on-the-fly editing by one's geist) is a common signifier of trust between friends — or cheeky flirtation.

CUTTER TAG
ENCLOSED, GROUND, HANDS, REMOTE PRESENCE, SINGLE-SEAT, SUBMERSIBLE, WALKER

ATTRIBUTES

Scale	Speed	Brawn
2	2	17 (+2)

DETAILS

Max. Passengers	Impact
0	3+7 🄽 (Knockdown)

Hard Points	
None	

DEFENCES

Structure	16	Firewall	10
Armour	8	BTS	6

GEAR: ECM 1, TO Camouflage

MOUNTED WEAPONS:
- **MULTI HMG**: Range L, 2+5 🄽 damage, Burst 3, Unwieldy, Medium MULTI, MULTI Heavy Mod, Spread 1, Unsubtle

SPECIAL ABILITIES:
- **Run Silent**: +1 difficulty to Observation tests to detect the Cutter, so long as it makes only Careful Piloting actions.
- **Run Deep**: Ignores penalties imposed by pressure, even at extraordinary depths.

D-Thread: Thin thread with a dense core of flawless segmented octanitrocubane explosive crystals, D-Thread is often laced into clothing or concealed in a flat coil until needed. Triggered via short-range receiver, useful as a fuse or impromptu D-Charge, it is particularly effective as a cutting charge, adding +1 🄽 damage if wrapped repeatedly around a target or coiled in rings on its surface. It requires a Tech (D2) test to set, and it can only be detonated from Medium range or closer. (Explosive Charge, 1+4 🄽 damage, Anti-Materiel 2, Concealed 3, Comms, Disposable, Piercing 2, Unsubtle, Vicious 2)

Dream-Recorder: While reading thoughts in real-time is beyond the reach of modern consumer tech, these hat-like scanners can record the wearer's neural activity during REM sleep for later analysis. Interpreting a week's worth of data is almost as much of an art as analysing a Cube scan, requiring a successful Psychology (D2) test to analyze correctly, but on a success grants 1+2 🄽 bonus Momentum for social skill tests targeting the subject of the recording. On a failure, or if any Effects are rolled, a single Momentum is generated, along with a Complication — which can be used by the GM in the same way as a complication generated on a skill test.

Exo-Compass: Exo-compasses contain magnetic field maps and starfield profiles from every major planetary body in the Human Sphere, aiding wilderness and interplanetary navigation. While they do not require a comlog to use, they are often combined to leverage navigation software. An exo-compass grants one bonus Momentum to Survival tests to navigate through an unfamiliar region — or to similar Extraplanetary navigation tests offworld.

Electric Pulse: This contact-activated defensive system is typically installed on vehicles and remotes, and generates a discharge strong enough to non-lethally immobilize and daze targets. A defender can use their electric pulse system for Close Combat Defence Reactions against melee attacks for −1 Heat (minimum 0). If the defender wins the face-to-face test, they deal Electric Pulse damage to the attacker, in addition to preventing the attack. (Melee, 1+4 🄽, Mounted, Immobilising, Stun)

Full-Sensorium Maya Integration: Maya-stardom demands more than a fierce sense of style and an enthralling personality — modern audiences want to feel and see and hear and smell and taste their idol's sensations, ever-cast in real-time for eager consumption and critique. Wiring the nervous system for high-definition recording and transmission is a profoundly invasive full-body Silk augmentation, adding Vicious 1 to any damage received during the procedure. Despite the risks, aspirants across the sphere take extensive loans or sign elaborate contracts with media conglomerates for a chance to make their dreams of fame come true... for as long as they can make it last.

Haladie: Inspired by early Syrian and Indian blades, these double-ended daggers are popular showpieces, prizes, and signs of favour among Acontecimento criminals and smugglers, and are banned from every major settlement. (Melee Weapon, 1+4 🄽, 1H, Heritage Weapon X (Acontecimento Submondo), Vicious 2)

inDeeds: As the primary dispenser of Resurrections in PanOceania, the NeoVatican Church has revived the medieval tradition of indulgences — services to the Church are rewarded with points towards a Resurrection licence, tracked through the inDeeds app on the user's comlog. The app is tied to the List of Deeds, a regularly updated list of praiseworthy acts, both general (donating money or volunteering for the Paradiso Crusade), and very specific, sometimes triggering mercenary competitions to see who can achieve them first. The app indicates nearby opportunities, including personalised tasks from the Church, and a steady stream of "daily deeds"— minor acts of charity and goodwill that benefit one's immediate community.

Ice Crawler Transport: With six broad tracks, a nose-mounted slow-burning flamethrower attachment, and plenty of room for cargo or passengers, ice crawlers are crucial for Svalarheiman survival, and several models contend for the market — Neoterra's Neoni Lupo, Sol's FierraFord Model I, and Moto.tronica's Polaris, built right in Vest Festning.

ICE CRAWLER TRANSPORT
ENCLOSED, GROUND, WHEELED (TRACKS)

ATTRIBUTES		
Scale	Speed	Brawn
2	3	13 (+2)

DETAILS	
Max. Passengers	Impact
7	3+5 🌑 (Knockdown)
Hard Points	
Chassis 3, Comms 2, External 1, Internal 2, Motive 2, Weapons 2	

DEFENCES			
Structure	16	Firewall	6
Armour	4	BTS	1

MUNTED WEAPONS:
- **Slowmelt Flamethrower**: Range C, 2+5 🌑 damage, Burst 1, 2H, Incendiary 4, Munition, Nonlethal, Torrent

SPECIAL ABILITIES:
- **Toasty**: Grants passengers immunity to even extreme cold so long as they stay inside the crawler.
- **Low Gear**: Crawler drivers can make the Ram Through vehicular Momentum spend for 1 Momentum.

Gt Bracelet: Named for the founder of the original Knights Hospitaller, Gerard Thom, and charitably subsidised by the Order for any PanOceanian citizen, this bracelet painlessly micro-samples the wearer's blood and continually records their biometrics to build a detailed medical profile over time. As long as it is worn continually for at least a month, it provides anyone with 2 or more Medicine Expertise and network access to it a bonus d20 on tests to diagnose health issues the wearer is suffering from, or to provide the wearer with Long-Term Care.

Kirpan X: A Sikh article of faith and reminder to defend themselves and others from injustice and oppression, Kirpan are curved blades with an inner cutting edge. Still worn after religious initiation, they are also prized Gatka School teacher-student gifts, and wearing one is a pan-cultural sign of Aryavartan pride. (Melee, 1+3 🌑 damage, 1H, Heritage Weapon X (Aryavartans), Subtle 2, Unforgiving 1, Vicious 1)

Locust Rifle: Combi Rifles extensively modified for Locust clandestine action teams, Locust Rifles fire BTS-degrading Breaker rounds, and in addition to their modular secondary weapon assembly, have a charge-plate — equivalent to a Stun Baton — built into the stock usable as a melee weapon without any Improvised penalty. (Range C/M, 1+5 🌑 damage, Burst 2, 2H, Expert 1, MULTI Light Mod, Vicious 1)

Malasartes Grenade: Named for the legendary Latin American trickster and rogue, Malasartes grenades release a cloud of concealing smoke carrying illegally fabricated nanotech that partially blocks modern optics and sensors, including the multispectral sensors used by high-security buildings. Used for getaways and criminal heists, they are also useful for agents disguising their operations as Submondo activity. (Explosive Grenade, Disposable, Indiscriminate (Close), Nonlethal, Reflective 1, Speculative Fire, Thrown, Unsubtle)

Mere: Short broad-bladed flat clubs made from *panamou* (nephrite jade) and designed for thrusting strikes at short range, these Maori weapons recognize the bearer's *mana* (personal energy and prestige in Austronesian languages) among PanOceanians with Polynesian ancestry. They are common homecoming gifts for victorious soldiers and diplomats. (Melee Weapon, 1+4 🌑, 1H, Heritage Weapon X (PanOceanian Polynesians/Maori), Knockdown, Stun, Vicious 2)

Mobility Armour: A product of the Omnia Research Corp, and at Joan of Arc's insistence made available to carefully vetted Father-Knights, mobility armour is dangerous to use unless the wearer is carefully trained and in peak physical condition. Add +3 complication range to all Acrobatics tests if the wearer does not have at least three Acrobatics Talents, an Agility of 13 or more, and a Brawn of 12 or more. (Combat Armour)

Mulebot: Created as multifunction logistics remote units, mulebots support even the most dynamic PanOceanian forces. Their multiple configurable attachment points, reliable design, and open architecture proved equally useful for civilian

HEAVY COMBAT ARMOUR VARIANT

SWISS GUARD ARMOUR

Guardians of the NeoVatican and the Pope's elite guards since before humanity left Sol, the Swiss Guard may follow ancient traditions, but their armour is uncompromisingly modern, incorporating thermo-optical camouflage, Blades of St George blessed by the pope himself (+3 Morale Soak), and extensively purified personal firewalls (+3 BTS).

SPES-GAANV MOLEE

Fish cooked in a spiced coconut gravy, this staple of Malaysian/Indian cuisine is a ubiquitous dish in Neoterra's Spes Archipelago's agricultural villages, each of whom swears by a recipe incorporating locally grown ingredients. Tours of the region during festival season are popular with Elite gourmands.

MULEBOTS INCLUDED

Mulebots are designed to serve in trios — three of them can precisely fit in a shipping container as a single modular unit for storage and shipping via space elevators, the Galvão railgun, or other high-velocity transportation options. The three-bot one-container configuration is often sent as part of a larger shipment, providing delivery on arrival and eliminating the need for local short-haul transport.

purposes once Moto.tronica's exclusive contract with the Hexhedron ended, and they now form the backbone of PanOceanian shipping and warehouse management, as well as a substantial hobbyist modding community.

TROOPER
MULEBOT

ATTRIBUTES						
AGI	AWA	BRW	COO	INT	PER	WIL
11	10	9 (+3)	11	7	4	4

FIELDS OF EXPERTISE						
Combat	–	–	Movement	+3	1	Social	–	–
Fortitude	=1	–	Senses	+1	–	Technical	–	–

DEFENCES					
Firewall	6	Resolve	6	Structure	12
Security	–	Morale	–	Armour	2

ATTACKS
- **Electric Pulse**: Melee, 1+4 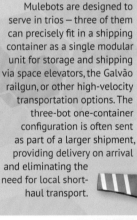 damage, Immobilizing, Stun

GEAR: Repeater

SPECIAL ABILITIES
- **Common Special Abilities**: Inured to Disease, Poison, and Vacuum; Superhuman Brawn 3
- **Open Architecture**: So many eyes on their code have resulted in a robust and fairly bug-proof architecture. When controlled by a geist or native LAI, mulebots gain Morale and Security Soak of 2, and Tech tests to modify or repair them are at −1 difficulty.
- **Shipping Configuration**: As a full-round Action, a mulebot can retract its limbs and heat-sink panels, reducing its profile for easy shipping, and go into power-saving hibernation.
- **Tri-Sync**: Mulebots in civilian use are designed to work in threes, and each mulebot in the triad rolls +1d20 on tests when lifting, moving, or transporting cargo in coordination with the others.

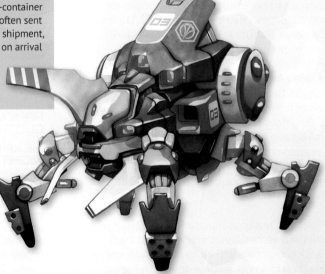

Nanopulser Jewellery: While ordinary nanopulsers are widely restricted for civilian use, PanOceanian Elites have carved out an exception for openly-worn "protective ornamentation". Usually embedded in ornate Portuguese-style filigree, these single-use short-range nano-bot sprayers quantronically alert authorities and then dissolve when used, and require extensive identity vetting before purchase. A clear signifier of influence, Nanopulser Jewellery acts as if it had the Heritage weapon 1 quality when in polite social interactions with PanOceanian Elites and Hyper-Elites. (Range C, 1+5 damage, Biotech, Comms, Disposable, Torrent, Vicious 2)

Noimosyn: A common prescription for cognition disorders, noimosyn enhances concentration and memory, and is often abused as a performance enhancer by students and data workers. Sold legally only in pill form, possession of the drug without a prescription or in other form factors is a minor crime on most worlds.
Special Effect: The user gains a free d20 reroll on Analysis tests requiring intense concentration, memorisation, or recall for one hour. If they have the Pattern Recognition talent, they gain a second free reroll, but must accept the new result. Once the noimosyn wears off, the user suffers +1 difficulty to Brawn tests for two hours.
Addiction: 2 (6 doses), Compulsion 1
Withdrawal: 1+1 mental damage, Harm Effect (user suffers Withdrawal damage whenever they make non-Analysis tests, and easily fixates on finding connections between arbitrary data or stimuli to the exclusion of other activity)

Orb-Light: Modelled after the great sphere upheld by San Pietro's iconic Lady of Light, these small flying spherical lights follow the user, and can brighten via quantronic command to illuminate the user's zone. They are near-inescapable tourist trinkets in PanOceanian territory, particularly in the Lightball Mall, and come with a Theia charging-statuette.

Pitcher: Modified grenade launchers, pitchers increase the effective range of tactical Hackers, firing deployable repeaters as Reloads just as grenade launchers fire grenades. The weapon inflicts no damage, and targets a zone rather than a normal target with a Ballistics (D1) test, modified as normal for range; if successful, the deployable repeater lands in the targeted zone and activates immediately. (Range M, Burst 1, Unbalanced, Munition, Speculative Fire)

Pollock Grenade: A PanOceanian specialty, these grenades detonate in mid-air, spray a fluorescent nano-laden telemetry paint in all directions, use their overlapping sensors to take a snapshot of their surroundings, and register paint that struck potential targets. They then transmit the results to networked friendlies, giving anyone in the target zone the Marked condition unless they succeed at an Acrobatics test as a Reaction with difficulty equal to the number of effects rolled. (Explosive Grenade, Disposable, Indiscriminate (Close), Nonlethal, Speculative Fire, Thrown, Unsubtle, marks targets)

Pressure Suit: These sleek, skin-tight mesh pressure suits allow a Helot to negate the effects of unwanted environmental pressure, and act normally without modifiers or Pressure Personality Traits. They provide no protection on their own, but can be worn beneath conventional armour with some modifications.

Prison Transport: VTOL aircraft used to move prisoners securely, prison transports are constructed in sterile fully-automated facilities to prevent tampering. Devatech's BH-4 Bhishma, named for the *Mahabharata*'s honourable warrior and kidnapper, is the only version used by the Tower High-Security Correctional Facility on Neoterra, but KraussEK's Hund T, Lupo's Maria Noir, and Castellón's Minorca are also relatively popular.

PRISON TRANSPORT
AIRCRAFT, ENCLOSED

ATTRIBUTES

Scale	Speed	Brawn
3	2/4	13 (+1)

DETAILS

Max. Passengers	Impact
2/12	4+5 🄽 (Knockdown)
Hard Points	
Chassis 3, Comms 2, External 2, Internal 2, Motive 1, Weapons 3	

DEFENCES

Structure	28	Firewall	10
Armour	4	BTS	5

GEAR: ECM 1, Electric Pulse

SPECIAL ABILITIES:
- **Holding Area**: The rear zone of the transport is sealed, and designed to hold up to a dozen prisoners immobilised. Tests to escape it are at +1 difficulty, and it can be flooded with Oneiros gas by a Tech (D1) test from the 2-crew cockpit.

Remote Pod X: These enclosed cockpits with integrated remote presence gear allow operators to pilot remotes in safety and comfort at a distance, often in environments too hazardous for human life. Advanced pods incorporate olfactory sprays and hormonal-mediation auto-injectors, smart-material upholstery, micro-climate control, and bio-management features — anything to keep their charges happy and alert through long shifts of remote work. Many corporate, governmental, and even military employees, particularly in PanOceania and Yu Jing, spend their workday inside a remote pod in their home.

Remote pods have the Neural quality, count as VR equipment, and remove the complication range penalty for operating remotes and vehicles via remote control. Though ghosting a remote is intense, practiced operators can optimize their remote pod's features for +X Morale Soak while in the pod. The pod's firewall quality is crucial for defence against malicious hackers and quantronic intrusion, providing +X Security Soak.

Rippa Board X: Driven on one's belly when underwater or balanced on as a narrow surfboard on the surface, these aquatic sleds are incredibly common sights near PanOceanian coastal vacation spots and pleasure islands, especially during Great Tides. Quality boards are nimble but less stable: anyone with Agility less than 9+X is at +X complication range.

RIPPA BOARD X
EXPOSED (+2 🄽 COVER), SUBMERSIBLE, WATERCRAFT

ATTRIBUTES

Scale	Speed	Brawn
0	X+1	9

DETAILS

Max. Passengers	Impact
1	1+3 🄽 (Knockdown)
Hard Points	
None	

DEFENCES

Structure	7–X	Firewall	5
Armour	1	BTS	X

GEAR: 2 Oxygen Loads, Recorder, Locational Beacon

SPECIAL ABILITIES:
- The board grants X bonus Momentum to Acrobatics tests to perform stunts and X-1 bonus Momentum to Piloting tests to manoeuvre around obstacles.

Sanctuary Service: Initially provided by the Order of Santiago in Human Edge for PanOceanians far from home, and now offered regularly on Circulars and Santiago-controlled stations, these hour-long church services offer both spiritual and practical reinforcement. During the service — which heals 2+2 🄽 Mental Damage for believers — attendees' personal networks are isolated from all outside connections to avoid distraction, and given careful review by Santiago technicians, healing 2+4 🄽 quantronic damage, and healing a Breach per effect rolled. Services are free for Church employees, Military Order members, and Circular workers.

Scuball Suit: Varuna's most popular sport, scuball is played not only by professionals like the Neo-Canberra Sea Devils, but by enthusiastic students and amateurs all over the planet. Scuball suits contain a head-mounted recorder, aquajet thrusters in

HELOT ARMOUR
Pressure suit-compatible armour either provides one less Armour Soak in all locations, or the added bulk restricts movement, negating the user's Natural Swimmer trait. Pressure suit modifications add +2 🄽 and +T2 to an armour's cost, but the basic suits are subsidized by PanOceania, ensuring widespread adaptation. See Pressure Personality Traits — see page 94.

OPTIONAL RULE
REM-LAG
Returning to the physical limitations of a human body and the serene pace of an office environment after the intensity of remote work can lead to disorientation, irritability, depression, and other psychological issues, collectively referred to as rem-lag. Mandatory breaks and counselling alleviate stress for corporate and governmental workers, but intense expectations, ambition, and greed often drive operators past their own limits.

To reflect rem-lag stress, at the GM's discretion, for every hour of remote work beyond their maximum Resolve, pilots who work without pause take 1+1 🄽 mental damage, healing one Resolve if an effect is rolled. After double their Resolve in hours, the damage increases to 1+2 🄽, and at triple 1+3 🄽 is also taken as physical damage.

Tower High-Security Correctional Facility — see *Infinity Corebook*, p. 261

"NOICE RIPPAH, GUPPY."
Varunan rippers have an extensive vocabulary differentiating what might seem like near-identical variations to outsiders — particularly swift rippa are "aggra" or "gnarl", for example, while slower and more stable versions are "bigs", regardless of size.

the limbs, protect the wearer from aquatic hazards, and contain three Oxygen Loads. As a Minor action when underwater, the wearer can move to another underwater zone within Long range with a successful Athletics (D2) or Extraplanetary (D2) test.

Sensarecorder Augmentation: Performance in blockbuster Triple Alpha sensadramas requires augmentation even more elaborate and invasive than so-called "full-sensorium" Maya integration – sensatech. Designed to be imperceptible except to a deep medical scan, this invasive surgery implants hi-fidelity sensors throughout the user's body, and even links to their Cube's carrier systems, gathering a slice of the recorded sensory information. This allows recording of subtler senses far beyond the basic five, such as kinaesthetic proprioception, cardioception, somatic and visceral pain, hunger and thirst, and even a portion of the user's emotions, storing an incredibly elaborate profile of the user's experiences, which can then be uploaded as the raw material for sensaseries or for detailed analysis and review – uploading takes five minutes per day of recorded sensory data. Wiring the user's nervous system for high-definition recording is an invasive full-body Silk augmentation, adding Vicious 1 to any damage received during the procedure.

Sensatranslator: Experiencing a sensaseries requires the use of a special device that partially connects to Cube sensory implants. Passive devices, sensatranslators can only provide sensory input, and cannot access a Cube's contents, to prevent exposing the Cube to outside interference, and there is always a slight sense of separation from the experience in the interest of psychological safety. Since constant experience in the first person with the same character is often exhausting for the audience, directors cut between multiple viewpoints and senses, allowing the spectator to enjoy a curated artistic experience. Each series also includes bundles devoted to specific characters, providing different points of view to increase the chances of repeat viewings.

The device's cost covers staying current with a number of sensaseries equal to the character's Earnings – if unpaid, the user still has access to previously purchased episodes. They can gain access to an additional number of shows equal to their Earnings by increasing the Maintenance cost by one. With GM permission, extensive repeated viewings of a related sensaseries can halve the XP cost to gain the first rank of Expertise in a particular skill.

Seraph TAG: Strong in their faith, Military Order Father-Officers fight without fear of death or hesitation, resulting in severe attrition rates until the creation of remote operated Seraph TAGs, which allowed them to lead on the frontlines without needlessly risking their lives. Powerful back-mounted aero-jets and gliding wings allow them to soar over battlefield terrain, enhancing their already angelic humanoid form.

Built-in coordination systems make Seraphs guardians and guides for allied remotes, just as their pilot safeguards the souls of the soldiers under their command, but they are formidably armed even on their own, with a chest plate Nanopulser, CineticS Bagyo-T Spitfire, and iconic shoulder-sheathed TAG-scale greatsword. The greatsword's edges' micro-grooves are filled with superconducting gel, which turns into intense directed blasts of ionized plasma on impact.

SERAPH TAG
ENCLOSED, GROUND, HANDS, REMOTE PRESENCE, SINGLE-SEAT, WALKER

ATTRIBUTES		
Scale	Speed	Brawn
2	2	16 (+2)

DETAILS	
Max. Passengers	Impact
0	3+7 (N) (Knockdown)
Hard Points	
None	

DEFENCES			
Structure	16	Firewall	10
Armour	7	BTS	6

GEAR: ECM 1, Kinematika

MOUNTED WEAPONS:
- **Spitfire**: Range M, 1+5 (N) damage, Burst 3, 2H, Spread 2, Unsubtle
- **Nanopulser**: Range C, 1+5 (N) damage, 1H, Biotech, Subtle 3, Torrent, Vicious 2
- **Seraph Greatsword**: Melee, 1+5 (N) damage, Massive, Anti-Materiel 1, Spread 1, Unsubtle, Vicious 2

SPECIAL ABILITIES:
- **Ardour**: Designed as a tactical coordination nexūs, Seraphs grant allied Remotes within Medium range one bonus Momentum to Ballistics and Athletics tests.
- **On Wings as Eagles**: Seraphs can vault over obstacles up to twice their height without penalty, and grant −2 difficulty on tests to move through difficult terrain.

Spike: A favourite of Aristeia! competitors, many of whom sponsor their own brands, a spike is an adhesive patch embedded with gel packets of fast-acting medications that absorb through the skin when the patch is slapped on.

Special Effect: Spike can be administered once a round to Absterge physical conditions. 1+1 (N)

damage is taken per dose, ignoring armour and BTS. Ten minutes after application, the user becomes Fatigued until they get a full night's sleep, and multiple doses add additional instances of the condition.

Squalos TAG: The second iteration of Moto.tronica's Stingray TAG platform, Squalos (shark in Italian) retain the line's pedigree of manoeuvrability, comprehensive firepower, armoured durability, and raw speed. Improvements include cutting-edge countermeasures against Guided weaponry, and — addressing longstanding pilot complaints — refactored finger actuators and reinforced knuckle guards.

The TAGs themselves are unmanned, piloted from kilometres away via purpose-built remote presence pods. Towering nearly two stories tall, their lack of life support systems ensures a lean humanoid silhouette, broken only by a pair of transmission antennae sweeping back from the head and a shoulder-mounted CineticS Lunan MULTI HMG with a Switech Cadentem Heavy Grenade Launcher rack built into its stock. A BernaDente HAP5 Heavy Pistol, mounted in the torso but detachable for an ambidextrous firing arc, ensures armour-piercing firepower at Close range.

SQUALOS TAG
ENCLOSED, GROUND, HANDS, REMOTE PRESENCE, SINGLE-SEAT, WALKER

ATTRIBUTES		
Scale	Speed	Brawn
2	3	17 (+2)

DETAILS	
Max. Passengers	Impact
0	3+7 (N) (Knockdown)
Hard Points	
None	

DEFENCES			
Structure	16	Firewall	10
Armour	8	BTS	6

GEAR: ECM 2

MOUNTED WEAPONS:
- **AP Heavy Pistol**: Range R/C, 2+4 (N) damage, Burst 1, Unbalanced, Piercing 2, Unforgiving 1, Vicious 1
- **MULTI HMG**: Range L, 2+5 (N) damage, Burst 3, Unwieldy, Medium MULTI, MULTI Heavy Mod (Heavy HGL), Spread 1, Unsubtle
- **Heavy Grenade Launcher**: Range M, 3+5 (N) damage, Burst 1, Unbalanced, Munition, Speculative Fire + Grenade qualities

Strides: Also known as "trou", these skeletal exoskeletons are used by farmers, factory workers, and police for quick transport and extra muscle. Their sale is heavily restricted outside PanOceania, despite hypercorp lobbying. They

VAC SUIT VARIANT
SIGMA-OXS PIAILUG
Named for an ancient Micronesian navigator, these advanced suits incorporate an exo-compass, two Sensor Suites of the purchaser's preferred type, and an additional Oxygen Load and Part to support extended solitary jaunts. Their additional complexity adds +2 complication range for users with less than 3 Extraplanetary Focus, but veteran explorers swear by them.

"AD FINEM" (UNTIL THE END)

Acontecimento's Armoured Chasseurs exclusively use Tikbalang, and are based in and primarily piloted by locals from San Fernando de Dagopan. Due to fierce public support, local lobbyists and manufacturers block the sale of the TAGs to outsiders, enhancing "our hunters" mystique. Opposing arguments quickly founder on the squadrons' motto.

SUNDANG

A large cutting tool traditionally popular in the Philippines and Indonesia, these broad-bladed narrow-tipped knives were used extensively in revolutions against the Spanish and the United States of America. Modern square-tipped versions', with their sharpened knuckleguards, only vaguely resemble the originals, but still represent proud independence in San Fernando de Dagopan's Filipino-Malaysian enclaves. Tikbalangs' TAG-scale sundang add a Teseum edge and larger construction, but retain a striking similarity to their human-sale equivalents.

grant Superhuman Brawn 1, and allow the wearer to move to a zone within Long range as a Minor action.

Thunka Charges: Nicknamed by Neoterran troops for the sound they make when attaching, thunka charges are D-Charges with a guidance package, micro-jets, and permabond adhesive strip around the edge of their directional cover, designed to be thrown in the general direction of their target and then guided into place remotely. Successful placement requires a successful Athletics (D1) test(+1 difficulty for each range category beyond Close) to send the Thunka in the right direction – it then guides itself to the target location. (Explosive Charge, 2+6Ⓝ damage, 1H, Anti-Materiel 2, Comms, Disposable, Guided, Piercing 2, Spread 1, Thrown, Unsubtle, Vicious 2)

Tikbalang TAG: Like the eponymous mythical Filipino half-man, half-horse, Tikbalang haunt the jungle and ambush the unwary with overwhelming force, returning again and again if killed.

Third-generation Stingray models adapted for combat in dense forest and jungle, they carry TAG-scale Teseum-edged sundang blades and TauruSW KHF-7 Caldera (Portugese for boiler) Heavy Flamethrowers to clear vegetation and opposition, and CineticS Tausug HMGs for rapid long-range fire.

Designed for remote piloting, they are more compact than most PanOceanian TAGs, since they lack life support systems and manual controls. Using mimetic sheathing, sound-suppression, and passive radiation filtration derived from the same Moto.tronica research used to build Cutter models'

more advanced concealment, as well as surface treatments to reduce friction from vegetation, Tikbalang move swiftly and silently through dense terrain to outflank opposition and force breaks in enemy lines

TIKBALANG TAG
ENCLOSED, GROUND, HANDS, SINGLE-SEAT, WALKER, REMOTE PRESENCE

ATTRIBUTES
Scale	Speed	Brawn
1	2	16 (+2)

DETAILS
Max. Passengers	Impact
0	2+7Ⓝ (Knockdown)

Hard Points	
None	

DEFENCES
Structure	16	Firewall	10
Armour	6	BTS	6

GEAR: Chameleonwear, ECM 1

MOUNTED WEAPONS:
- **Tikbalang Sundang**: Melee, 1+5Ⓝ damage, Unbalanced, Anti-Materiel 1, Piercing 4, Spread 1, Vicious 2
- **HMG**: Range L, 2+6Ⓝ damage, Burst 3, Unwieldy, Spread 1, Unsubtle
- **Heavy Flamethrower**: Range C, 2+5Ⓝ damage, Burst 1, 2H, Incendiary 3, Munition, Terrifying 2, Torrent

SPECIAL ABILITIES:
- **Mángangaso**: The Tikbalang can ignore Difficult Terrain up to its controller's Pilot Focus in jungles, forests, or other environments with dense vegetation.

ARMOUR TABLE
ARMOUR	HEAD	TORSO	ARM	LEG	BTS	QUALITIES	RESTRICTION	COST	TARIFF	MAINTENANCE
Pressure Suit	0	1	0	0	1	Immunity to Pressure	1	5	0	0
Mobility Armour	3	4	2	3	3	Exoskeleton 1, Kinematika, Self-Repairing	4 (PanO 3, Military Orders 2)	10 + 3Ⓝ	T3[1]	3
Strides	0	0	1	2	1	Exoskeleton 1, Heavy Armour	3 (PanO 1)	6 + 2Ⓝ	T2	2

[1] No Tariff for Military Orders

AUGMENTATIONS TABLE
AUGMENTATION	CATEGORY	TYPE	QUALITIES	RESTRICTION	COST	TARIFF	MAINTENANCE
Citplant	Cybernetic	Implant	Aug, Comms	4 (PanOceania 3)	4+4Ⓝ	T4	–
Full-Sensorium Maya Integration	Silk	Full-Body	Aug, Comms, Subtle 3	2	13+1Ⓝ	T3	–
Sensarecorder Augmentation	Silk	Full-Body	Aug, Subtle 3	4 (PanOceania 3, Nomads 3)	15+1Ⓝ	T2	–

MELEE WEAPONS TABLE

NAME	DAMAGE	SIZE	QUALITIES	RESTRICTION	COST	TARIFF
Alpenstock X	1+4 (N)	Unb	Heritage Weapon X (Svalarheimans), Improvised 1, Non-Hackable, Stun, Vicious 1	2+X (Svalarheima 1+X)	2+X (N)	T(X)
Blade of St. George	1+5 (N)	2H	Grievous, Non-Hackable, Parry 2, Piercing 2, Vicious 1	3 (PanO 2)	8+2 (N)	T1
Bush Knife X	1+5 (N)	1H	Heritage Weapon X (Australasian Neoterrans), Thrown, Unforgiving 1, Vicious 2	2+X (NeoTerra 1+X)	4+X (N)	T(X)
Electric Pulse	1+4 (N)	Mounted	Immobilising, Stun[1]	1	5+3 (N)	T1
Haladie X	1+4 (N)	1H	Heritage Weapon X (Acontecimento Submondo), Vicious 2	2+X (Acontecimento 1+X)	3+X (N)	T(X)
Kirpan X	1+3 (N)	1H	Heritage Weapon X (Aryavartans), Subtle 2, Unforgiving 1, Vicious 1	2+X (Acontecimento 1+X)	5+1 (N)	T(X)
Mere X	1+5 (N)	1H	Heritage Weapon X (PanOceanian Polynesians /Maori), Knockdown, Stun, Vicious 2	X+1 (PanO X)	4X+X (N)	T(X)

[1] No Tariff for Military Orders

RANGED WEAPONS TABLE

NAME	RANGE	DAMAGE	BURST	SIZE	AMMO	QUALITIES	RESTRICTION	COST	TARIFF
Banduk E/Mitter	C/M	1+5 (N)	1	1H	E/M2	Nonlethal	3	6+4 (N)	T1
Contender	M	1+4 (N)	1	Unb	DA	Anti-Materiel 1	1	5+5 (N)	T2
Locust Rifle	C/M	1+5 (N)	2	2H	Breaker	Expert 1, MULTI Light Mod, Vicious 1[1]	3	6+4 (N)	T3
Nanopulser Jewellery	C	1+5 (N)	1	–	–	Biotech, Comms, Disposable, Torrent, Vicious 2[1]	5 (PanOceania 4)	10+3 (N)	T2
Pitcher	M	–	1	Unb	Deployable Repeater	Munition, Speculative Fire[1]	2	8+2 (N)	T2

[1] See entry for additional abilities

EXPLOSIVES TABLE

EXPLOSIVE	CATEGORY	DAMAGE[1]	SIZE	QUALITIES	RESTRICTION	COST (PER 3)	TARIFF
Adarsana Grenade [Environment]	Grenade	-	1H	Disposable, Indiscriminate (Med), Nonlethal, Speculative Fire, Thrown, Unsubtle[1]	3 (Illicit 1)	5+2 (N)	T2[1]
Croc Mine	Mine	2+5 (N)	1H	Comms, Disposable, Fragile, Indiscriminate (Close), Unsubtle, Grievous	3 (PanO 2)	5+3 (N)	T4[1]
D-Thread	Charge	1+4 (N)	1H	Anti-Materiel 2, Concealed 3, Comms, Disposable, Piercing 2, Unsubtle, Vicious 2	3	8+2 (N)	T3
Malasartes Grenade	Grenade	–	1H	Disposable, Indiscriminate (Close), Nonlethal, Reflective 1, Speculative Fire, Thrown, Unsubtle	3 (Illicit 1)	5+2 (N)	T3
Pollock Grenade	Grenade	–	1H	Disposable, Indiscriminate (Close), Nonlethal, Speculative Fire, Thrown, Unsubtle[1]	3 (PanO 2)	5+2 (N)	T1
Thunka Charges	Charge	2+6 (N)	1H	Anti-Materiel 2, Comms, Disposable, Guided, Piercing 2, Spread 1, Thrown, Unsubtle, Vicious 2	3 (PanO 2)	7+2 (N)	T2

[1] No Tariff for Military Orders

REMOTES TABLE

REMOTE	RESTRICTION	COST	TARIFF	MAINTENANCE
Mulebot	2 (PanOceania 1)	9+3 (N)	T3	3

TOOLS TABLE

TOOL	QUALITIES	RESTRICTION	COST	TARIFF	MAINTENANCE
Aerarium Account X	Comms	1+X	1+X (N)	T(X)	1
Caskuda Jewellery	Armoured 5, Comms, NFB, Concealed 1	5	5+5 (N)	T5	–
Dream Recorder	Comms, Fragile	1	4+1 (N)	T1	–
Exo-Compass	Comms	2	2+2 (N)	T2	–
inDeeds	Comms	1	1	–	–
GT Bracelet	Comms	1	3+1 (N)		–
Orb-Light	Comms, Fragile	1	3+1 (N)	T1	–
Remote Pod X	Comms, Mounted, Remote Presence Gear	1	8+2X (N)	–	X
Sanctuary Service	Comms, Disposable	2 (PanOceania 1)	4+2 (N)	–	–
Scuball Suit	Adapted[Aquatic]	2	8+1 (N)	T1	1
Sensatranslator	Comms, Fragile	1	12+1 (N)	–	1[1]

[1] See entry for additional abilities

DRUGS TABLE

DRUG	RESTRICTION	COST	TARIFF
Bounce	1 (Yu Jing 3 / Haqqislam 3)	3+1 (N)	T1
Noimosyn	2	2+2 (N)	T2
Spike	1	3+1 (N)	T1

VEHICLE COSTS TABLE

NAME	SCALE	SPEED	BRAWN	ARMOUR	BTS	IMPACT	RESTRICTION	COST	TARIFF
Aeropter	2	2	9 (+1)	2	0	2+3 (N)	1	10+2 (N)	–
Balisong Motorcycle	0	3	10	1	0	1+3 (N)	2	9+3 (N)	T1
Cutter TAG	2	2	17 (+2)	8	6	3+7 (N)	4 (PanO 3)	15+5 (N)	T4
Ice Crawler Transport	2	3	13 (+2)	4	1	3+5 (N)	2	12+2 (N)	–
Prison Transport	3	2/4	13 (+1)	4	5	4+5 (N)	3	10+4 (N)	T2
Rippa Board X	0	X+1	9	1	X	1+3 (N)	X	6+X (N)	T(X)
Seraph TAG	2	2	16 (+2)	7	6	3+7 (N)	4 (PanO 3, Military Orders 2)	14+4 (N)	T4[1]
Squalos TAG	2	3	17(+2)	8	6	3+7 (N)	4 (PanO 3)	14+5 (N)	T3
Tikbalang TAG	1	2	16 (+2)	6	6	2+7 (N)	4	13+3 (N)	T3

[1] No Tariff for Military Orders

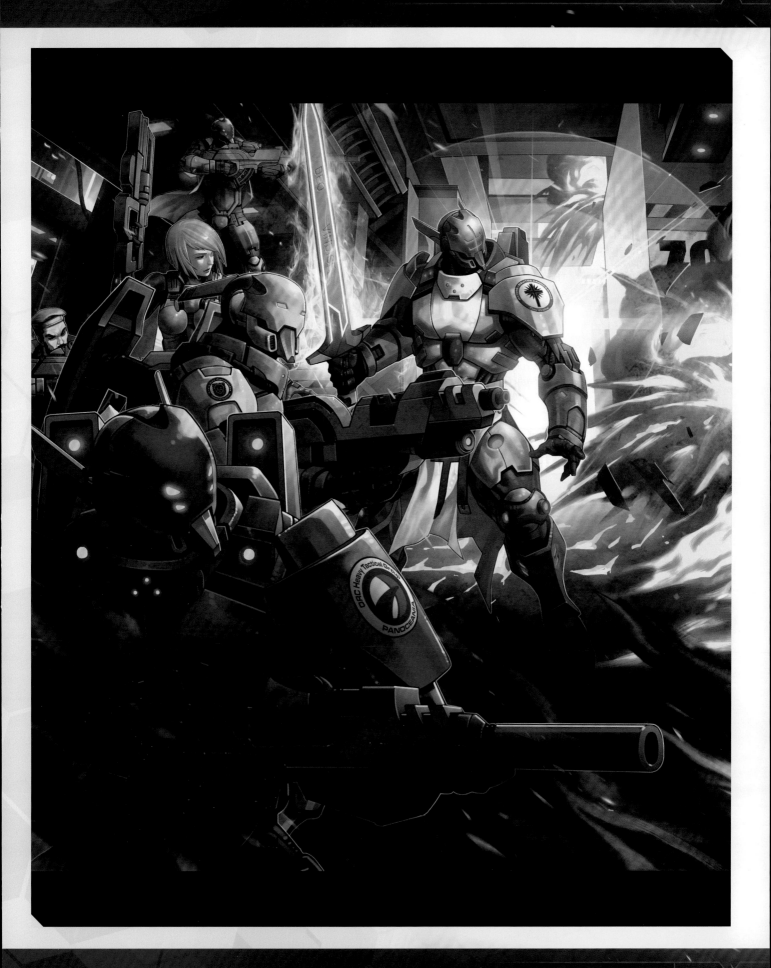

CHAPTER 6

PANOCEANIAN CHARACTERS

PANOCEANIAN LIFEPATH DECISIONS

The Lifepath Decisions outlined on p. 38 of the *Infinity Corebook* should be followed with the following exceptions for characters belonging to the PanOceanian faction.

DECISION ONE— BIRTH HOST

If you roll a 19 or 20, you are of alien heritage. Head to *Chapter 7: Helots* to determine your character's non-human heritage.

DECISION THREE— HOMEWORLD/ HOMELAND

Characters with PanOceanian heritage roll on the *PanOceania Expanded Homelands* sub-tables (next page) after determining their homeworld.

DECISION FOUR— STATUS

Characters in the PanOceania faction roll on the *PanOceania Faction Status* table (p. 82).

DECISION SEVEN— ADOLESCENT EVENT

Characters in the PanOceania faction roll on the *PanOceania Faction Adolescent Event Tables* (p. 82)

DECISION EIGHT— CAREERS

Instead of rolling on the *PanOceanian Faction Career* table in the *Infinity Corebook*, characters in the PanOceania faction roll on the *Expanded PanOceania Faction Career* table (p. 84), as well as the *PanOceania Faction Career Event* tables (p. 84).

Life in the Hyperpower is different than in the rest of the Human Sphere. Bigger, more prosperous, and better-connected than their peers, PanOceanian citizens have a unique perspective on the galaxy, the view from the top. Advantages that others would only dream of are an everyday occurrence, and dangers that others contend with rarely touch PanOceanian shores. Which is not to say that PanOceanians are never challenged. The weight of expectations can be as crushing as it is empowering, and while the economy is stable and thriving, an individual's fortunes can fluctuate wildly.

PanOceanian characters can be created using the variant rules in this chapter, rather than those in the *Infinity Corebook*. If doing so, the entries presented here supersede their counterparts.

DECISION ONE: BIRTH HOST

Determining Alien Heritage: Roll 1d20. On a roll of 19 or 20, your character belongs to an alien species. (For the purposes of this rulebook, this means that you're a Helot; see p. 91.) If you roll an alien

heritage, you can instead choose to spend 1 Life Point to be human.

Alien Host: Each alien species or non-human type has a template. Apply the species' attribute modifiers to both your attributes and Host section of the character sheet. Make note of any special abilities possessed by the species.

Alien species also have a Life Point cost. You can choose to pay this cost to simply choose the species, but the cost must be paid even if you randomly roll into it. (If the cost cannot be paid, the character is considered human.)

DECISION THREE: EXPANDED HOMELANDS

The Hyperpower is a massive entity with a huge amount of diversity throughout its territories. After determining your region by rolling on the *PanOceania Homeworld Table* (*Infinity Corebook*, p. 44), add your attributes and skill as normal, then roll on the associated *Homeland Table* to determine precise region, and what language(s) your character speaks.

ACONTECIMENTO HOMELAND SUB-TABLE

D20	REGION	LANGUAGE
1–4	Aryavarta	Hindi or Punjabi (choose one), Portuguese, and English
5–8	Bomjesus	Portuguese or Spanish (choose one) [1], and English
9–11	Camões	Portuguese, Spanish, and English
12–14	Magalhães	Portuguese, Spanish, and English
15–17	Vishwa	Hindi, Punjabi, or Portuguese (choose one), and English
18–19	Minor Archipelagos	Hindi, Punjabi, or Portuguese (choose one), and English
20	Descoberta System	Hindi, Punjabi, or Portuguese (choose one), Spanish, and English

NEOTERRA HOMELAND SUB-TABLE

D20	REGION	LANGUAGE
1–4	Aquila	German, or Italian (choose one), Spanish, and English
5–6	Gratia Archipelago	Hindi, or Italian (choose one), Spanish, and English
7–10	Lux	English and Spanish
11–15	Pax	French, Greek, Italian, or Portuguese (choose one), Spanish, and English
16	Solitudo Island	Hindi, or Italian (choose one), Spanish, and English
17–19	Spes Archipelago	Italian, Portuguese, Tagalog, or Spanish (choose one), Hindi, and English
20	Tecendur System	Hindi, or Italian (choose one), Spanish, and English

VARUNA HOMELAND SUB-TABLE

D20	REGION	LANGUAGE
1–6	Atlantea Archipelago	Spanish, Malay, and English
7–11	Gurindam Archipelago	Tamil, Tagalog, or Malay (choose one) [1], and English
12–15	Hawaki Archipelago	Māori, Malay[1], and English
16–18	Kumari Kandam	Hindi or Malayalam (choose one), Tamil, and English
19	Lemuria	Malay, Portuguese, or Tamil (choose one), and English
20	Mitra System	Malay, Malayalam, or Spanish (choose one), Tagalog, and English

PARADISO HOMELAND SUB-TABLE

D20	REGION	LANGUAGE
1–8	Syldavia	Portuguese, Punjabi, or Hindi (choose one), Spanish, and English
9–16	Gāyatrī	Portuguese, Spanish or Punjabi (choose one), Hindi, and English
17	Isles of Paradiso	Hindi, or Spanish (choose one)[1], and English
18–20	Paradiso System	Hindi, or Spanish (choose one)[1], and English

SOL HOMEWORLDS

Characters from Earth and the other worlds of the Sol system will be detailed in the *Sol Sourcebook*. PanOceanian characters from the Sol system can either use the rules in that supplement, or simply roll on the *PanOceania/Sol Languages Table* in the *Infinity Corebook* (p. 45) and add English.

HUMAN EDGE HOMELAND SUB-TABLE

D20	REGION	LANGUAGE
1–6	Asteroid Belts	Spanish and English[1]
7–14	Trojans	Portuguese, Hindi, or Spanish (choose one)[1], and English
15–16	Heraclitus	Portuguese, Punjabi, or Hindi (choose one), Spanish, and English
17	Livy	Portuguese, Tagalog, or Hindi (choose one), Spanish, and English
18–20	Socrates	Tagalog, Hindi, Spanish, or Yujingyu (choose one), and English

SVALARHEIMA HOMELAND SUB-TABLE

D20	REGION	LANGUAGE
1–5	Arkhangelsk	English, German, and SvalarNorse
6–8	Nordkap	German or Spanish (choose one), English, and SvalarNorse
9–16	Solokov	German, or Spanish (choose one), English, and SvalarNorse
17–19	Trollhättan	German, Spanish (choose one), English, and SvalarNorse
20	Epsilon Eridani System Orbitals	German, Spanish, or Tagalog (choose one) English, and SvalarNorse

[1] Roll again on the *PanOceania Homeworld Table* (*Infinity Corebook*, p. 45) followed by the appropriate sub-table to determine a second language you're fluid with. If you roll the same result, that's the only language you're fluent with.

DECISION FOUR: STATUS

As any citizen will tell you, growing up in PanOceania is different from the rest of the Human Sphere. Wealthier, more technologically advanced, and interconnected — unless, of course, you're an Atek — it's good to be in the Hyperpower.

During *Step One: Social Class* of Decision Four, characters currently in the PanOceania faction roll on the *PanOceania Faction Social Status Table* (instead of the *Social Class Table* from the *Infinity Corebook*).

PANOCEANIA FACTION SOCIAL STATUS TABLE

2D6	SOCIAL STATUS	ATTRIBUTE	EARNINGS
2	Atek[1]	Willpower	1
3	Demogrant	Personality	2
4–6	Middle	Coordination	3
7–8	Upper	Agility	4
9–10	Elite	Personality	5
11–12	Hyper-Elite	Willpower	6

[1] Ateks are unfamiliar with advanced technology. Characters who become Ateks in Decision Four gain the trait Quantronic Novice and suffer +1 complication range when using Expert systems. This minor trait (including the expanded complication range) can be removed by spending 50 XP or 1 Life Point.

DECISION SEVEN: PANOCEANIAN ADOLESCENT EVENT

During Decision Seven, characters in the PanOceania faction roll on the *PanOceania Faction Adolescent Event Tables* to determine which *Adolescent Event Table* they use to generate their adolescent event.

PANOCEANIA FACTION ADOLESCENT EVENT TABLE

D6	CAREER
1	Heritage Event Table[1]
2–3	PanOceanian Adolescent Event Table
4	Adolescent Event Table A[2]
5	Adolescent Event Table B[2]
6	Adolescent Event Table C[2]

[1] If available, otherwise roll on *PanOceanian Adolescent Event Table.*

[2] *Infinity Corebook*, p.49–52

PANOCEANIAN ADOLESCENT EVENT TABLE

D20	ADOLESCENT EVENT	SUGGESTED CHARACTER TRAIT	OPTIONAL EFFECT
1	You were selected to be fitted with bleeding edge Mayacasting tech – with a few corporate strings attached.	Pop-Ups	Gain Full-Sensorium Maya Integration, but your geist has become fond of advertisements. Increase your complication range by +1 due to untimely distractions. Removing the ads will cost 10+8 (N) Assets but will remove this penalty.
2	You tried to modify your geist, with poor results.	Faulty Geist	Reduce your geist's Firewall by 1.
3	Trying to meet your mentor's expectations, you wound up hospitalized for a year. What happened?	Crushing Expectations	Reduce Vigour by 1 but gain 1 rank in Discipline.
4	You tried to modify your geist, with mixed results.	Hyperactive Geist	Reduce your geist's Firewall by 1 but increase their Morale by 1.
5	Your family's fortunes more than enabled your bad spending habits.	Spendthrift	Gain a 5 Asset debt but gain 1 Rank in Lifestyle.
6	You discovered an underground nightclub scene – and the party favours to go with it.	Bounce-Bunny	You are addicted to Bounce (p. 117). Begin play with 1+4 (N) doses.
7	Although raised in a religious household, you began to question everything. How did this inform your beliefs?	Skeptic	Gain 1 rank in Analysis.
8	Facing the consequences of crimes you most assuredly did commit, someone offered to make it all go away. Did you let them? If so, what was the cost?	It Takes One to Know One	Either spend 1d6 years in jail before starting your first career and gain a Criminal Record (see *Infinity Corebook*, p. 54) or gain a debt of 3+5 (N) Assets.
9	You tasted stardom as part of a popular children's Maya broadcast. You handled the celebrity better than expected, but you never did learn financial restraint. People still recognize you on occasion.	Former Child Star	Gain a debt of 1+6 (N) Assets. Additionally, reduce the difficulty of all Lifestyle tests by 1 (to a minimum of 0) with individuals who recognize you.
10	You had the misfortune of experiencing a *Libertos* attack first-hand. Separated from your family, it was hours before rescue services found you.	Suspicious	Always looking for trouble, you may reroll 1d20 when making a surprise test but must accept the new result.
11	You spent some time living in an orbital – it didn't suit you at all.	Astrophobia	Increase the complication range of Extraplanetary tests by 1.
12	While traveling to orbit, your pilot suffered a heart attack. Turns out all those hours in sensorium flight sims paid off.	Big Damn Hero	Gain 1 rank in either Pilot or Spacecraft.
13	You became heavily involved in the Maya ARG scene.	Amateur Sleuth	Gain 1 rank in Analysis
14	An accident left you needing cybernetic replacements. Luckily, you got some cutting-edge tech. Maintaining your aug is expensive, but it routinely outperforms the competition.	Aug Addict	You have a cybernetic arm or leg (*Infinity Corebook*, p.363). Increase the Maintenance cost by 1 but add one bonus Momentum on successful tests made with the limb.
15	You got so involved in a Maya fandom that your health started to suffer for it.	Couch Potato	Reduce Vigour by 1.
16	You trusted someone, and they burned you – hard. You're not going to let it happen again.	Won't Get Fooled Again	Gain 1 rank in Discipline but suffer +1 complication range on all social skill tests where trust is a factor.
17	You know the difference between genuine, Made-in-PanOceania gear and the knock-offs. And you hate to settle for less.	Brand Loyalist	Gain +2 (N) Morale Soak when wearing exclusively PanOceanian Armour or clothing but increase your complication range by 1 when you're not.
18	The Church left a strongly favourable impression on you.	Pious	Add 1 to your Resolve Stress track. You may choose Priest as your first career.
19	One of your most deeply-held beliefs about your home is turned on its head. What happened? Why did it lead to you leaving PanOceania?	Disillusioned	You defect to a new faction. Roll on the Faction Table (see *Infinity Corebook*, p. 41) to determine your new allegiance
20	The recall didn't catch you in time, but the resulting scandal ensured you didn't waste away inside a Resurrection queue.	Bitter	Your character died and was resurrected. See the rules for *Resurrection* in the *Infinity Corebook*, p. 54.

DECISION EIGHT: CAREERS

PanOceania is a place of great opportunity, but with those opportunities comes risk in equal measure. Compared to other Lifepaths, PanOceanian careers boast higher earnings and more gear – with a few drawbacks. Earnings are more volatile, and career events are significantly more likely to result in being fired or a loss of assets or earnings. PanOceania is the high-stakes table. Just because you were born wealthy doesn't mean you'll stay that way!

During Decision Eight, characters in the PanOceanian faction follow the normal procedures for performing their career phases with the exception that they roll on the *Expanded PanOceanian Faction Career Table* whenever they would normally roll on the *Faction Career Table* in the *Infinity Corebook*. Whenever they would normally determine a career event, they roll on the *PanOceanian Faction Career Event Table* to determine which *Career Event Table* to roll on.

PANOCEANIA FACTION CAREER EVENT TABLES

D6	CAREER
1–3	PanOceanian Career Event Table
4	Career Event Table A[1]
5	Career Event Table B[1]
6	Career Event Table C[1]

[1] *Infinity Corebook*, p. 56–58

EXPANDED PANOCEANIAN FACTION CAREER TABLE

D20	CAREER
1	Special Forces[1]
2	Intelligence Operative[1]
3	Lobbyist[1,2]
4	Maya Personality[1]
5	Corporate Executive[1]
6	Fusilier[2]
7	Mayacast Support Staff
8	Sensorium Mayacaster
9	Explorer
10	Fighter Pilot
11	Neoterran Special Officer[2]
12	Hexas Agent[2]
13	Priest
14	Order Sergeant[2]
15	Knight[2]
16	Croc Man[2]
17–20	Roll on *Faction Table* of Your Choice

[1] Career from *Infinity Corebook*.

[2] Career has a prerequisite of belonging to this faction. You can't hazard this career unless you're of the matching faction. If you roll into this career, you automatically fail your defection check. You can override these limitations by spending 1 Life Point (in which case you were somehow undercover while working the career).

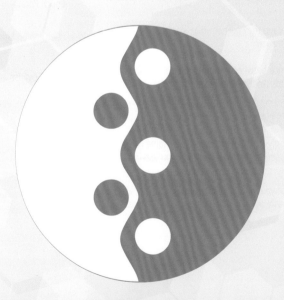

PANOCEANIAN CAREER EVENT TABLE

D20	CAREER EVENT	GAME EFFECT
1	Some of your investments pay off.	Gain 4 Assets.
2	Bureau Toth brings you in for questioning. What do they want to know? They let you go, but under what condition?	Gain Trait: On the Watchlist
3	Your words are badly misconstrued in an interview.	Gain Trait: Antisocial Media. Increase the difficulty of hazarding your next career by +1.
4	You invest in some high-risk stocks.	Roll 4 🄽. Gain Assets equal to the result but lose 1 Asset for every Effect rolled.
5	An old Maya post of yours goes viral overnight.	Gain Trait: Fringe Celebrity
6	Pitting rival employers against each other costs you your job but opens some doors.	You are Fired (see Infinity Corebook, p. 54). Gain an appropriate trait. However, reduce the difficulty of hazarding careers by 1, to a minimum of 0.
7	You are the "lucky winner" of a transfer to Paradiso.	Gain a character trait describing your experience. You may take Croc Man or Special Forces as your next Career without making a hazard test.
8	You save a tourist from a horrible fate.	Gain an ally in a random faction.
9	You embrace the Church's teachings wholeheartedly.	Gain Trait: Zealot. You may choose Priest, Order Sergeant, or Knight as your next career without making a hazard test.
10	Circumstances converge to put you at the helm of a ship. What brought this on?	Gain 1 Rank in Spacecraft. You may choose Pilot, Ship Crew, or Fighter pilot as your next career.
11	You arrive for work to find nothing. It's as though your employer never existed.	Gain Trait: Left in the Dark. You may not elect to extend or repeat your current career.
12	You developed an obsession with a professional sports team. As go their fortunes, so go your moods.	Gain a trait describing your new obsession.
13	A Hexahedron agent visits your employer. The next day, your employee access has been revoked. What happened?	You are Fired (see Infinity Corebook, p. 54). Gain an appropriate trait. You may choose either Hexas Agent or Criminal as your next Career.
14	Someone close to you is a criminal, but you can't bring yourself to turn them in. Why not?	Gain Trait: Dirty Little Secret.
15	You foiled an act of espionage against your employer.	Gain Trait: Dangerously Curious. Additionally, gain +1 Earnings for your act of balance-sheet-friendly heroism.
16	You are fired. What did you do, and why was it worth it?	You are Fired (see Infinity Corebook, p. 54). Gain an appropriate trait.
17	You are scouted by an unlikely employer.	You may hazard your next career, even if you don't meet the faction prerequisite.
18	Some old Maya posts of yours get the wrong kind of attention before you can delete them.	You are Fired (see Infinity Corebook, p. 54). Gain an appropriate trait.
19	You are murdered. Who was blamed for this, and who do you think was actually responsible?	Your character died and was Resurrected. See the rules for Resurrection (Infinity Corebook, p. 54). Gain a trait related to the experience.
20	You pay the Price of Ambition: things are about to get interesting.	Roll again three times on the Career Event Table for this career phase. (When spending a Life Point to choose a specific event, you may not choose this result.) If you roll duplicate events, it means some similar event has occurred. If you roll The Price of Ambition again, add additional rolls.

CORPORATE EXECUTIVE

Executives in the most influential hypercorps wield more power than many sovereign rulers among the minor nations. With the trade of currency and favours, an Executive alters the course of political development, positions their company to benefit first and foremost from government contracts, and helps shape the Human Sphere. A Corporate Executive swims in shark-infested waters, vying with competitors for the best deals. An Executive is responsible for their company's interests, which often means meeting and negotiating with the most high-powered individuals in human space. They must adapt to constantly changing situations with a quick wit and keen eye for opportunity.

ATTRIBUTES						
AGI	AWA	BRW	COO	INT	PER	WIL
–	+1	+1	+2	+2	+3	+1

SKILLS				EARNINGS
Mandatory	Persuade	Lifestyle	Command	3+3 
Elective	Education	Lifestyle	Discipline	

GEAR: High-Fashion Clothing (with Locational Beacon), Tonfa Bangles or AP Pistol, Neural Comlog or AR Eye Implants, 1 dose of a recreational drug

EXPLORER

The Hyperpower has always prided itself on its Explorers, the brave souls who fearlessly chart new courses, find neo-material rich asteroids to mine, and in exceptionally rare cases, new worlds to colonise. Of course, most of an Explorer's life is spent in far less grandiose pursuits. Whether conducting an environmental survey, navigating an asteroid belt, or pushing the boundaries of the Human Edge, Explorers all have one thing in common — they heard the call of adventure.

ATTRIBUTES						
AGI	AWA	BRW	COO	INT	PER	WIL
+1	+2	+1	+3	+1	–	+1

SKILLS				EARNINGS
Mandatory	Extraplanetary	Pilot	Spacecraft	1+4
Elective	Observation	Survival	Tech	

GEAR: Crashsuit, Exo-Compass, Inlaid Palm Circuitry or Thunka Charges (2)

CROC MAN

Veteran scouts from the brutal jungles of Paradiso, the Croc Men were founded in the wake of the Ravensbrücke debacle. The PanOceanian Polynesian Division went into the ill-fated operation as Fusiliers. The survivors came out as a battle-forged whanau.

Many Crocs, regardless of ethnicity or gender, honour the unit's heritage by opting to receive *Tā moko* — the tattoo-like facial markings signifying status and coming of age in Māori society — upon embarking on their first tour of duty. Specializing in surveillance, covert operations, and sabotage, Croc Men make stalwart friends and deadly enemies.

ATTRIBUTES						
AGI	AWA	BRW	COO	INT	PER	WIL
+2	+2	+1	+2	+1	+1	+1

SKILLS			EARNINGS
Mandatory	Ballistics	Survival	Stealth	0+1
Elective	Close Combat	Observation	Stealth	

GEAR: Light Combat Armour, Mere X, Croc Mines (3) or Subdermal Grafts (choose one location), MULTI Sniper Rifle

SPECIAL: In Decision Nine, set the value of your Mere to the number of times you took the Croc Man career, and gain Contacts: any other Croc Man.

FIGHTER PILOT

In the PanOceanian Armada, perhaps no role is as glamourized as that of the fighter pilot. PanOceania's aviators are portrayed as brash and reckless top guns in many a Maya-series, a reputation that their real-world counterparts do little to discourage. Outside of the holomovies, successful fighter pilots possess a killer instinct and hunter's temperament sharpened to a fine point. With unmanned high-manoeuvrability fighter squads operating at speeds beyond human capability, a pilot needs synchronisation that is hard to match from a Remote Presence Cockpit. Many Fighter Pilots become permanent adrenaline junkies; from Father-Pilots to Archeron Blockade vets, once you've danced among the stars with your life on the line, a sedentary lifestyle holds little appeal.

ATTRIBUTES						
AGI	AWA	BRW	COO	INT	PER	WIL
+1	+2	+1	+3	–	+1	+1

SKILLS				EARNINGS
Mandatory	Ballistics	Pilot	Spacecraft	3+2 
Elective	Observation	Resistance	Spacecraft	

GEAR: AR Eye Implants, Inlaid Palm Circuitry, Surge (2 Doses), Light Combat Armour or Assault Pistol with 2 Reloads

SPECIAL: Members of Military Orders may substitute their Order's Electives for this Career.

INTELLIGENCE OPERATIVE

The tense state of conflict in the Human Sphere means every agency looks for an edge over its competitors. Intelligence Operatives conduct corporate espionage, deep-cover spy missions, acts of sabotage, and other acts which risk their life and limb for agencies that would disavow any knowledge of, or connection to, their operations. An Intelligence Operative is quick-witted, highly disciplined, and often alone in a place surrounded by enemies unaware of the traitor in their midst. They trade in secrets — information that can turn the tide of small-scale conflicts, like raids on secret warehouses holding valuable experimental gear or data — and they can influence the large-scale skirmishes that take place between rival nations. The intelligence an operative collects can cause wars or end them with equal facility.

ATTRIBUTES						
AGI	AWA	BRW	COO	INT	PER	WIL
+1	+3	–	+2	+2	+1	+1

SKILLS				EARNINGS
Mandatory	Observation	Stealth	Analysis	3+1 
Elective	Hacking	Education	Thievery	

GEAR: Fake ID 2, AP Pistol (with 4 Reloads), Breaking & Entering Kit, Recorder

FUSILIER

The unquestioned backbone of the PanOceanian military, Fusiliers consider themselves the light infantry troop to judge all others by. Professional soldiers hailing from every corner of PanOceania, many citizens have spent a tour of duty with the Fusiliers. While not all go on to careers in the military, most look back on their service with immense pride.

Fusiliers commonly posit that they form the heart of the army — everyone else is basically their support staff. And while this sentiment is echoed with a range of intentions from comical to dead serious, it wouldn't survive this long without at least a grain of truth. Ubiquitous, modern, and versatile, Fusiliers are the binding agent that holds the PanOceanian Military Complex together.

ATTRIBUTES						
AGI	AWA	BRW	COO	INT	PER	WIL
+1	+2	+1	+2	+1	+1	+2

SKILLS			EARNINGS
Mandatory	Athletics	Ballistics	Resistance	2+1 
Elective	Medicine	Stealth	Tech	

GEAR: Light Combat Armour, Combi Rifle, 2 Pollock Grenades

HEXAS AGENT

The living embodiment of the Hexahedron's Strategic Security Division and an espionage fantasy made flesh, Hexas Agents safeguard PanOceanian interests throughout the Human Sphere. Equipped with bleeding edge tools, forward-thinking training, and the full support of the Hyperpower, a Hexas Agent has no boundaries, no moral code, and no conscience while in the field. The mission is all that matters, and the mission can change by the hour.

Able to infiltrate corporate facilities, capture the attention of hyper-elites, and pursue targets through adverse conditions, Hexas Agents are chameleons by necessity. Who they are today might not suit tomorrow's task. The spy fantasy both is and isn't everything it's cracked up to be, but the vids were right about one thing. Hexas Agents possess impeccable style.

ATTRIBUTES						
AGI	AWA	BRW	COO	INT	PER	WIL
+1	+2	–	+1	+1	+3	+1

SKILLS				EARNINGS
Mandatory	Close Combat	Persuasion	Stealth	3+2 Ⓝ
Elective	Hacking	Psychology	Thievery	

GEAR: Hexas Nightwear, 1 Malasartes Grenade, Wetspike

KNIGHT

Symbols of faith, collaboration, and unwavering dedication, Knights are living emblems for not only the military, but for PanOceanian society as well. Living beyond a soldier's ideals, a Knight must inspire others with their faith, even if they don't share it. Beliefs must be upheld, even if surrounded by those who flaunt them. Internal rivalries must be put aside, both figurative and literal, so that a united charge can be taken against PanOceania's enemies.

It's often said that Knights never truly retire, as they simply enter a new chapter of service. For a living embodiment of chivalry, piety, and holy warfare, there are no true days off, just new ways to serve.

ATTRIBUTES						
AGI	AWA	BRW	COO	INT	PER	WIL
+2	+1	+2	+1	+1	+1	+2

SKILLS				EARNINGS
Mandatory	Ballistics	Close Combat	Command	1+2 Ⓝ
Elective	See *Military Orders*			

GEAR: Blade of St. George, see *Military Orders*

SPECIAL: When taking this career for the first time, roll on the *Military Orders Table* to determine your Order. Once you've determined your Order, you no longer roll upon taking this career; but in either case, you can instead spend 1 Life Point to simply choose your Order.

MILITARY ORDERS

PanOceania's Military Orders each provide different resources, training, and experiences to their members. Rather than navigate separate careers, each Order has a distinct set of Elective Skills that it teaches its members. When working the Knight or Order Sergeant career, roll on the *Military Orders Table* below or spend 1 Life Point to select an Order, and then use its Electives. You may also use your Order's Elective Skills in place of the standard when choosing the Priest career, or at your GM's discretion, for other careers on a case-by-case basis.

MILITARY ORDERS TABLE

D20	ORDER	ELECTIVE SKILLS	GEAR
1–3	Calatrava	Discipline, Education, Science	Powered Combat Armour, Heavy Pistol
4–6	Dominican	Analysis, Psychology, Persuasion	Aletheia Kit, Medium Combat Armour, Nanopulser
7–9	Hospitaller	Lifestyle, Medicine, Persuasion	Powered Combat Armour, MediKit
10–12	Montesa	Acrobatics, Close Combat, Command	Powered Combat Armour, Breaker Pistol
13–15	Santiago	Extraplanetary, Hacking, Tech	Powered Combat Armour (Knight of Santiago Armour), E/M Grenade
16–18	Teutonic	Extraplanetary, Resistance, Spacecraft	Powered Combat Armour, Panzerfaust
19–20	Sepulchre	Close Combat, Discipline, Observation	Powered Combat Armour, Spitfire

CAREER PROFILE
LOBBYIST

The immense PanOceanian government, the largest in the Human Sphere, has ended the hypocritical separation between political and economic power. Old political parties have been abolished and replaced by a substantial number of lobbies. Lobbyists vie for political favour, coordinate the activities of lobby members, and engage in covert battles of influence with rival lobbies. An unprecedented level of transparency in modern lobbies means a Lobbyist can be practically anyone, from a citizen with a very active interest in the groups that preside over their area of concern, to a prestigious and influential leader intimately guiding the lobby's political fortunes. All Lobbyists are highly motivated and skilled in their chosen arena, as the lobbying game is both robust and demanding.

ATTRIBUTES						
AGI	AWA	BRW	COO	INT	PER	WIL
+1	+2	–	+2	+2	+2	+1

SKILLS				EARNINGS
Mandatory	Persuade	Psychoogy	Command	4+2 Ⓝ
Elective	Discipline	Lifestyle	Education	

GEAR: Negotiator's Suite (10 days rental credit), Geist Upgrade (+2 ranks in Psychology or Research Specialist talent for Education)

SPECIAL: Prerequisite (PanOceania Faction)

CAREER PROFILE
MAYACAST SUPPORT STAFF

Every star has bodies in its orbit, and the stars of Maya broadcasts are no different. Equal parts roadie, tech support, film crew, business manager, and personal security, these unsung heroes of the entertainment industry work tirelessly behind the scenes so that programmes can air without a hitch. Often ducking and diving just beyond a camera's view, their job is misunderstood, exhausting, and invisible. But these self-proclaimed "tech ninjas" wouldn't have it any other way. As any entertainer who's tried to make do without them will tell you, things just work out better when they're on your side.

ATTRIBUTES						
AGI	AWA	BRW	COO	INT	PER	WIL
+1	+1	+	1+	1	+2	+2

SKILLS				EARNINGS
Mandatory	Ballistics	Close Combat	Command	2+4 Ⓝ
Elective	Hacking	Pilot	Stealth	

GEAR: AR Eye Implants, Theia Orb, Powered Multitool, 3 Recorders

CAREER PROFILE
MAYA PERSONALITY

Would-be Maya Personalities number in the millions, but the real stars reach hundreds of millions of viewers and are fueled by devoted, fanatic fans. A Maya Personality might be a popular musician, a comedian, or spiritual speaker. Artists and life-casters broadcast their work and live sensory feeds across the Sphere. The Maya datasphere hosts a staggering variety of content, and talented Maya Personalities rise from the faceless multitudes to become somebody. Popular newscasters and public speakers can gain far more fame and influence through legions of followers than they would have experienced as a government official. Larger-than-life personalities create legions of fans who hang on their every feeling, perception, thought, or word. They spawn both blind conformance and vehement dissent, filling up forums and editorial screeds with endless debate.

ATTRIBUTES						
AGI	AWA	BRW	COO	INT	PER	WIL
+1	+2	+1	+2	+2	+2	–

SKILLS				EARNINGS
Mandatory	Persuade	Lifestyle	Observation	1+4 Ⓝ
Elective	Hacking	Discipline	Tech	

GEAR: Recorder (×3), High-Quality Clothing, Fake ID 1, AR Eye Implants

CAREER PROFILE
NEOTERRAN SPECIAL OFFICER

As one of the largest population centres in the Human Sphere, Neoterra is also arguably the safest. Exactly as intended. Whether it's the Tactical Operations Unit, Special Narcotics Force, the Territory Response Group's Hawk Brigade, or any of the countless other civilian police forces, Neoterra's Special Officers ensure stability is maintained at any cost.

Often working undercover or striking at a moment's notice, Special Officers live their lives on-call. They seek out the worst dregs of society and prevent them from causing harm, all without disrupting, terrorizing, or otherwise harassing the rest of the citizenry. If the wrong call is made, they must be fast enough to make up the difference. Balancing optimism and cynicism in equal measure is no small task, but these officers wouldn't trust anyone else with the job.

ATTRIBUTES						
AGI	AWA	BRW	COO	INT	PER	WIL
+1	+3	+1	+2	+1	+1	–

SKILLS				EARNINGS
Mandatory	Ballistics	Observation	Stealth	2+3 Ⓝ
Elective	Analysis	Hacking	Science	

GEAR: AR Eye Implants, Ballistic Vest, Banduk or Hacking Device or Stun Baton

SPECIAL: Cannot be selected by characters with a Criminal Record

CAREER PROFILE
ORDER SERGEANT

Not all members of a Military Order become Knights, which is no bad thing as logistics, bureaucracy, technical issues, and a thousand other factors mean the Orders have their hands full. Sergeants at Arms, colloquially known as Order Sergeants, provide the assistance and support necessary for the Military Orders to reach their full potential.

Ranging from earnestly pious, to opportunistic or even bloodthirsty, Order Sergeants are often temporary associates who have paid for the privilege of belonging to an Order. Regardless, they are the lifeblood in the Orders' veins once the call to action goes out. Conducting tactical support tasks and securing combat zones as part of the advance force, Order Sergeants represent the breadth of PanOceanian society for both good and ill. There are few defenders of faith and home as stalwart once the call to arms goes out.

ATTRIBUTES						
AGI	AWA	BRW	COO	INT	PER	WIL
+1	+2	+2	+1	+1	+1	+2

SKILLS				EARNINGS
Mandatory	Close Combat	Observation	Tech	1+4 Ⓝ
Elective	See *Military Orders*			

GEAR: Assault Pistol, Knife, Light Combat Armour

CAREER PROFILE
SENSORIUM MAYACASTER

The thrill of racing over Varuna's waves. The exhilaration of traversing Neoterra's urban environments via augmented parkour. The picoscale precision of an Acontecimento prima ballerina. Any Mayacaster can show their audience these things, but a Sensorium Mayacaster can make them feel it.

Communicating sensory data through their augmentations, these entertainers bring their audiences with them on remarkable journeys, letting the audience feel the exhilaration of success, the shock of despair, and every range of emotions in-between. Athletes are common, but all Sensorium Mayacasters provide their own unique perspective to their fans. For them, the concept of privacy is almost foreign, but the rewards are absolutely worth it.

ATTRIBUTES						
AGI	AWA	BRW	COO	INT	PER	WIL
+1	+1	–	+1	+2	+3	+1

SKILLS				EARNINGS
Mandatory	Acrobatics	Lifestyle	Persuasion	1+8 Ⓝ
Elective	Education	Hacking	Psychology	

GEAR: AR Eye Implants, High-Quality Clothing, Full-Sensorium Maya Integration

CAREER PROFILE
PRIEST

Whether pious or lackadaisical, religion is an integral part of daily life for most PanOceanians. The Hyperpower produces more clergy per capita than any other G5 nation. While the Church is overwhelmingly the dominant religion, there exist no small number of Hindu Pujari, Sikh Granthi, and other clerical representatives of their respective religions. Affiliations aside, Priests provide guidance, leadership, and hope to their clergy. With the advent of quantronic-assisted communion, modern Priests are frequently opinion leaders rather than liturgists or ritual leaders; a source of spiritual insight, a willing ear for confession, and a moral and spiritual compass — all reachable via comlog. Pillars of the community by default, it's no exaggeration that Priests are responsible for dictating large chunks of PanOceania's culture, whether they intend to or not.

ATTRIBUTES						
AGI	AWA	BRW	COO	INT	PER	WIL
+1	+2	–	+1	+2	+2	+2

SKILLS			EARNINGS
Mandatory	Command	Education	Persuasion	1+4 Ⓝ
Elective	Analysis	Lifestyle	Psychology	

GEAR: High-Quality Clothing, Geist Upgrade (+2 ranks in Education), Kirpan (if Sikh)
SPECIAL: Members of Military Orders may substitute their Order's Electives for this Career.

CAREER PROFILE
SPECIAL FORCES

The most elite soldiers in the Human Sphere carry out spec ops missions across known space… and sometimes upon unknown worlds. Special Forces units operate in covert missions of international warfare, hunting down war criminals, striking important assets, and retreating before anyone can blame their acting governments. These elite units also carry out the most difficult ops in the war for Paradiso, attacking Combined Army commanders and bases, rescuing allies caught far behind enemy lines, and countering the threat of elite enemy units. Governments deploy Special Forces when discretion is needed—all too common in the shadow warfare fought between nations of the Human Sphere—and when regular mercenaries or law enforcement simply aren't enough. A Special Forces soldier receives the finest training, equipment, and most important missions, demanding as much from themselves as their people do.

ATTRIBUTES						
AGI	AWA	BRW	COO	INT	PER	WIL
+2	+2	+2	+1	+1`	–	+2

SKILLS				EARNINGS
Mandatory	Survival	Resistance	Ballistics	2+1 Ⓝ
Elective	Close Combat	Hacking	Discipline	

GEAR: Medium Combat Armour, Combi Rifle or AP Rifle (with 5 Standard Reloads), Climbing Plus or Combat Jump Pack, Garrotte

CHAPTER 7
HELOTS

The amphibious native inhabitants of Varuna, Helots — or Omn, as they refer to themselves — have had an uneven time integrating into PanOceanian society. Indeed, a cursory look suggests that they might not have integrated at all, with hydrocultural workers labouring far from the eyes of most Varunans, and even those Helots who work among humans rarely opt to live alongside them. The average PanOceanian is unlikely to work with any Helots, less likely to count them as neighbours, and incredibly unlikely to see them in anything resembling their native habitat.

Even so, Helots have been gradually gaining a greater understanding of PanOceanian culture and the reverse holds true as well. Bit by bit, the two cultures are beginning to come to a greater understanding, as the refinement of pressure suit technology — allowing Helots control over their water-pressure induced mood alterations — has led to an increasing number of Helots venturing further into mainstream PanOceanian society (dipping their toes in the water, as it were).

HELOT CULTURE

The first thing that surprises most humans when meeting Helots for the first time, is how universally friendly they are. With expectations primarily set via news reports of Libertos attacks, many are surprised to find your average Helot to be a friendly, gregarious, and generally pleasant individual.

While this trait is probably most pronounced among those inquisitive young Helots most likely to interact with PanOceanian society, it's a reliably common thread throughout Helot culture. Typically, a Helot needs to dive to fairly deep waters before expressing introverted traits; and even then, those who return seem eager to seek out companionship.

Helots learn to be pleasant company at an early age but acting nice and being nice are very different things. Even a complete dastard who's planning to stab you in the back tends to be fun-loving company right up to the moment the knife goes in. However it's expressed, Omn culture teaches Helots

"SEMI-INTELLIGENT"

A Helot on land finds it difficult to focus; in the depths, they can become lethargic. Before pressure personalities were understood — and pressure suits allowed them to take the reins, so to speak — the general perception of Helots was that they were lazy, and a little slow. Early news reports branded them "semi-intelligent", a label they've had a difficult time shaking ever since. Even a recent study showing that suited Helots scored about the same as humans in culturally neutral intelligence testing has done little to dispel this notion.

Pressure Personalities – p. 302,
Infinity Corebook

HAPPY AS A WAVE

The Helot's native language, *Tetessom,* expresses concepts through simultaneous communication channels; when speaking a human language, they tend to be incredibly expressive, with sweeping gestures, and cascading colour shifts across their skin, designed to better illustrate the concept. While laughter isn't an instinctual response, it's caught on as a trend, especially with younger Helots. So while a happy Helot might titter, guffaw, or chuckle as the situation dictates, their mood is better understood through the cascading gradient colour shifts across their skin; fast, giggling ripples, broad, roaring waves, or a calm, cycling tide; all in shades of rich, warm browns.

"Pods? Pods! Beh, you're letting them call you fish. Can't you correct the humans? It's Padjj, not pods... you're not even listening, are you?"

– Kossomn Xima Wave-Glider, to a group of frys who were, in fact, not even listening

HELOT "TEARS"

An amphibious race, Helot's eyes don't secrete tears. In lieu of lacrimation, their eyes rapidly nictate, accompanied by a vivid change in iris colouration; black sorrow, turquoise relief, or whatever hue corresponds to the triggered emotional state.

to feel everything deeply, and imposes few restrictions on expressing it. To a human, Helot mood swings can come seemingly out of nowhere, as frequent as they are extreme. For their part, Helots simply feel things very deeply and most aren't shy about expressing that. It says something about their culture that even with the myriad threats and challenges that they face, the most frequently expressed sentiment tends to be joy.

PODS

The central feature of Helot culture is the pod. Usually consisting of twelve to twenty individuals – though both larger and smaller pods exist, they're an outlier – the pod is essentially a Helot's entire social network. Friends, family, lovers, colleagues, even rivals are all likely part of the same pod. Of course, nothing lasts forever, and pods are no exception. A given pod will split apart, join with other pods, and otherwise shift its membership several times over the course of its existence, though it's rare to see the *Pojju* – the half-dozen or so individuals who make up the core of the pod, it's heart and soul – fracture in this process.

Each pod has its own identity, name, and history, and they serve a socio-cultural function not dissimilar to a human's hometown and ethnic heritage. Due to the way that knowledge passes from generation to generation, each pod is like a micro-nation in its own right, with its own history, conflicts, biases, and idiosyncrasies; and just as complicated a relationship with other pods as any two human nations one cares to mention. Helots will often introduce themselves to outsiders of all stripes as hailing from a particular pod, as outsiders can't be expected to tell the vital context from sight alone.

One of the more divisive social developments in Helot history is currently unfolding; namely, the fact that some Helots, living in isolation from their people but surrounded by humans, have begun to "pod up" with them. This in itself isn't terribly controversial – every Helot should endeavour to make friends – but upon returning to their own waters, these "xenopods" maintain membership with and allegiance to their human companions, much to their elders' consternation. To some back home, it looks like turning your back on your own people. But to the Helots who form these bonds, it's the only natural course of action: these people are their family, their friends; their pod. Why would their species matter?

HELOTS ON THE SURFACE

Before the advent of the pressure suit, extended stays on the surface were simply less appealing to Helots. Twitchy, foul-tempered, and aggressive, early surface contact with Helots led to countless cultural misunderstandings; these conflicts shaped

Varuna's views on Helots in ways that the young race has yet to shake.

And they are, in many ways, a young people. Between the *kossomn*'s teachings, pod-legacies, and oral histories, it's difficult to put an exact timeline on the Helot's history, especially as these records tend to exist as living fables more than a record of historical peoples and events. Regardless of the length of their history, most Helots are relatively unburdened by it, seeing the lessons of the past as a good teaching tool: morality plays to keep in mind.

Most Helots tend to keep to themselves, with pods clustering in communities near or in the water and avoiding ever heading too far inland. Even with a pressure suit providing clarity of thought and the ability to enjoy living and working on the surface, Helots generally don't consider it a good day unless they've had time to go for a lengthy swim.

EPICURIOSITY

Helot culture places significant value on optimism, trust, and a willingness to see the best in others. To many humans, this often looks like naiveté; and the Helots themselves do little to dispel this notion. A young people culturally, if not necessarily evolutionarily or historically, Helots tend to approach the surface world with the wide-eyed wonder of a child, mixed with the easily-impressed novelty of a tourist, and tempered with the relentless cheerfulness that Helots have made their stock-in-trade. To their eyes, life on the surface is a never-ending parade of wonders; a magical adventure that they can barely keep pace with. It's not uncommon to find a pod "weeping" openly at a sunset, or cheering excitedly at the most trivial piece of good news.

To a Helot, novelty is no prerequisite to wonder, and familiarity rarely breeds contempt. In fact, subsequent exposure to stimuli tends to deepen, not lessen its emotional impact, leading to many pods creating ritualized habitual patterns, with the wonder and beauty of the world deepening with each pass. Given their desire to live a happy, tranquil life, their constantly refining experiential palates, and the grand, wondrous nature of their experiences, this Epicurean curiosity – dubbed "epicuriosity" by the Varunan media – has slowly worked its way into the PanOceanian zeitgeist. Epicuriosity is often cited as a reason why so few Helots venture beyond their home planet; after all, they literally understand it in a way that few others ever will.

HELOT SETTLEMENTS

In their native environment, Helots are strikingly communal. This extends to possessions, currency, and even property; a typical Helot settlement isn't

OMN FABLES

Every young fry is familiar with the mythologies and fables that make up their people's oral history, having heard them repeatedly from the moment they hatched. Lacking any major religious, political, or competing philosophical force, Helot society's understanding of morality is primarily communicated through these fables. Good and evil, right and wrong: all live in these tales of brave, compassionate heroes, and craven, selfish villains.

Less historical document, and more mythologized morality play, these fables provide the groundwork of Helot society; providing valuable lessons on virtue, companionship, and societal mores. While most fables are simply related from an adult to a group of frys, they're also an important part of both education and cultural exchange between pods. Members of a given pod will take on traditional roles in a dramatization of the events — a multisensory combination of aquabatics, acting, and coordinated pigmentation shifts to create "scenery," these performances are a primary point of cross-pod interaction, and are greatly anticipated events. While the full number of these fables has yet to be tallied, there are several common types of hero that routinely make an appearance:

- A steadfast friend, who constantly lifts the spirits of their companions. In the end of these stories, it is their relentless optimism, gentle hearts, and faith in their friends that carries the day

- The faithful, monogamous couple, who bravely rescue and care for their eggs in the face of considerable danger (it is not uncommon for storytellers to make these heroes the fry's parents in early tellings of the fable)
- The clever trickster. Helot heroes tend to be preternaturally savvy; these tales often deal with competition between tricksters of different depths; clashes between roguish speedsters from the uplands, and the patient, plotting schemers of sissolu depths are a frequent theme

In addition, there are several common types of antagonists:

- The greedy, impetuous youth, hoarding belongings for themselves, rather than sharing with their pod. They often wind up friendless; the cruelest fate in any fable
- The agitated workaholic. This antagonist has no understanding of, or sympathy for, anything besides their all-consuming drive to accomplish their goals. They are often rescued by their friends, who teach them to slow down and enjoy their lives
- The too-carefree, careless sort, floating through life, ignoring their kossomn's warnings. They are usually eaten by Water-Snakes.

While some Helots have embraced the spectrum of human religions and philosophical beliefs, most trace their moral compasses to these tales.

"owned" by any one person or group, but rather maintained by whomever's using it at the moment. Pods tend to exist in a constant state of motion; migrating from settlement to settlement, often hitching a ride on the *katallpeac* lilypads between destinations. Upon arriving in a new settlement, they find a vacant habitat, and take up residence in the structure, making it their home until it's time to depart once more.

A traditional habitat typically blends underwater caves with Helot gardening techniques; underwater vegetation can be cultivated to provide everything from bedding and cushions to doors and window "blinds," to say nothing of pods that tend to grow their own food. While constructed habitats have existed as long as Helots can remember, the modern aquatecture techniques that PanOceania has introduced have revolutionized Helot settlements, with new designs ranging from the utilitarian to habitable underwater sculptures. Businesses in industries (such as aquaculture) that rely on Helot migrant workers have taken to building particularly interesting habitats near their properties, in hopes of becoming a more attractive migrant destination, and gaining a competitive edge.

Regardless of the type of habitat, it's considered good manners to leave it in better condition than you found it. Helots traveling through human

territories are simultaneously comfortable with and confused by hotels; they're quite comfortable with temporary domiciles; but cleaning crews require an adjustment.

HELOTS IN THE WORKFORCE

It's no secret that PanOceania initially saw — and certainly still sees — the Helots as a low-skilled labour force, easily and efficiently exploitable, and a key economic factor in the feasibility of Varuna's industries, most notably aquaculture. Activists, primarily those hailing from Haqqislam and the Nomad Nations, have repeatedly likened the situation to slavery, and calls for reforms are a frequent talking point when these factions butt heads.

While few could deny that the situation is an exploitive one, calling the Helots slaves is an exaggeration. While their legal status is complicated, there exist opportunities, rights, and protections that defy the expectations of outside observers. Much like an old Earth commonwealth nation, Helots are considered quasi-citizens of PanOceania. They pay taxes, and can travel freely throughout the Hyperpower's territory, though they cannot join lobbies or otherwise participate in the governmental process. While eligible for demogrants, Helots only receive one-third of the disposable income portion, with the remainder going to a species-wide trust fund, accruing income at a steady rate.

CLUTCH HAVENS

During their young adult phase, female Helots travel to the shallow uplands to lay clutches of eggs, which they then leave to be fertilized and defended by males. While this seems strange to humans, to a Helot it's just a ritualized part of their adolescent mating rituals and certainly no stranger a human's first date. While their ancestors had to forage for whatever safe havens they could find, generations of Helots have left quite an array of clutch havens behind, ranging from the cosy and well-furnished, to the hidden, or highly-defensible. Recently, PanOceanian corporations have been trying to monetize this cultural phenomenon by offering custom-fabricated clutch havens; often with an array of security options for young males defending their claim.

PRESSURE PERSONALITY TRAITS

The intense biochemical reactions that Helots experience in response to pressure variations also influence their behaviour. This can manifest in several different fashions, but is roughly classifiable as deep, medium (or sissolu), and light pressure. Each level has its own associated modifiers, as well as a temporary trait that persists as long as the Helot is in the respective pressure level.

Deep Pressure: The deeper into the ocean a Helot goes, the more mellow, calm, and thoughtful they become. Generate 1 additional point of momentum on Psychology tests and Resolve Recovery tests, but increase complication range by +1 on all other actions. Gain Trait: Lethargic

Sissolu Pressure: Like the temperate waters of their youth, medium-pressure waters split the difference between light and deep. The primary venue for cross-pod cultural exchange, Helots in sissolu pressure find it easy to socialize. And while they're neither as lazy as in the depths, nor as unfocused as on land, they still suffer from both tendencies. Helots in sissolu pressure generate 1 additional point of momentum on Lifestyle tests, but increase complication range by +1 on all other actions. Gain Trait: Placid

Light Pressure: On dry land, the Helot is hot-tempered, twitchy, and expecting trouble around every corner. They generate 1 additional point of Momentum on face-to-face tests, but increase complication range by +1 on all other actions. Gain Trait: Twitchy

TETESSOM: THE HELOT NATIVE TONGUE

Language is always a barrier when first contacting a new culture, and the Helots proved no different. And while auto-translators made short work of the Helot's native language, it would be some time before its true depth would be fully appreciated.

As creatures of land, shallows, and incredible depths, Helots' language evolved to suit their unique needs. While *Tetessom* — literally, "tri-speak" — is a single, unified language, it's comprised of three separate sub-languages, working in unison:

A low-pitched, sibilant verbal component, known as *Lassom*

A semi-controlled photoreactive element, primarily observable in Helots' shifting eye colours, but also apparent in shifting patches of skin, known as *Erissom*

A fluid, expressive sign language reliant on the placement of bioluminescent skin patches, known as *Vadassom*

HELOT NAMES

Given the complexities of *Tetessom*, it should come as no surprise that Helots' names carry a layered complexity. Working alongside humans for generations has had a streamlining effect, however; while their names aren't (entirely) changing, the way they communicate them is.

A Helot's given name consists of a verbal component with an accompanying sign, while their surname is a *portmanteau* of both their parents' signs. Given the text-heavy nature of communicating with humans, this has been codified into a series of characters, usually accessed by motion detecting the speaker. So a Helot might be named Cessil in *Lassom* with a *Vadassom* placement of the hand over the heart, going from right to left to indicate a male gender. Cessil's surname, a combination of a crescent and a balled fist, would indicate the pairing that raised him, but would be stylised in animated slashes – like the strokes of a painter's brush – in text. Barring special characters, the directions are spelled out literally so our example Helot's name would be Cessil Crescent-Fist in plain text.

All of this takes much more time to explain than to actually do, and those who interact with Helots at any length often find themselves adding in the gestural part of their names on instinct.

Common Helot names include:
- Arrodiel, a popular hero figure in fables, known for their cleverness
- Lassit, meaning "beloved one"
- Sannay, meaning "sunbeam", one of the most successful diplomats during first contact with humanity
- Yisso, meaning "swift"
- Rose, meaning "rose", a popular name for young frys as PanOceanian culture becomes increasingly fashionable, and Helots adapt human names with strong visual or emotive motifs (another example of this is Aroha, a feminine Māori name meaning "love")

It's only by combining these three elements that the full richness of the language becomes apparent. While the interplay of the three is fairly complex, a general guideline is that *Lassom* is used to clinically explain concepts, *Vadassom* is used to express simple concepts, or to inform others of your feelings on the subject, and *Erissom* is used to add nuanced context. Helots can – and sometimes do – use a single linguistic element in their communication; hand signals are often sufficient for casual greetings, words alone are considered the best way to clinically communicate information, such as scientific data, and speakers are often given colour feedback, as its seen as less interruptive. But in general, using a single linguistic element is akin to speaking very slowly, as though you were explaining a concept to a child... or an idiot.

Given the interwoven nature of their language, a written analogue has never really developed. Simple, easy to read glyphs have served their purpose – Danger Ahead, Safe Harbour, These Are My Eggs (Back Off or I'll Kill You) – but even as increasing numbers of Helots become literate in human languages, a written *Tetessom* seems unlikely.

In fact, the evolution of *Tetessom* as it sees increased use on the surface has been a contentious one. Humans tend to focus primarily on *Lassom* vocalizations, without realizing that the excessive sibilance is essentially an accent, affected to make *Lassom* sound more natural when spoken in air, rather than water. The high-pitched sound waves of most consonants don't travel underwater; words like *sissolu* are humanizations of a vowel-primary spoken language, adapted to surface use. Many of the *Erissom* colours used are hyperbright hues more easily visible on the surface; to a *kossomn*, it's not only garish, but it entirely lacks nuance; akin to constantly shouting, rather than speaking respectfully. The increased use of surface forms is emblematic of a larger cultural conflict between the depths and the surface; a gap that is widening with each passing day, and leading increasing numbers of *kossomn* to lend their guidance to the Libertos movement.

To that end, anyone who's ever seen a pod of Helots break out laughing seemingly out of nowhere knows to look for the one with a smirk and an odd coloration; pigmentation-based sarcasm is considered the height of dry wit among Helots.

HELOTS IN THE HUMAN SPHERE

Despite their love for their homeland, the homeward pull of *Epicuriosity*, and the limited opportunities afforded them compared to other PanOceanians, there still exist Helots who seek their fortune among the stars. Venturing out into

HELOT PRESSURE SUITS

In their natural state, a Helot's temperament is largely a factor of environmental pressure; a phenomenon easily circumvented by wearing a pressure suit. Wearing a suit negates the effects of environmental pressure, allowing Helots to act normally, without any of the modifiers or temporary traits associated with different depths.

A sleek, skin-tight mesh, pressure suits provide no protection on their own, but can be worn under conventional armour with some modifications. Pressure suit-compatible armour either provides one less Armour Soak in all locations, or the added bulk restricts movement, negating the Strong Swimmer talent. Pressure suit modifications add +2 Ⓝ and +T2 to an item's cost, but the basic suits are subsidized by the Hyperpower, ensuring widespread adaptation.

PLAYTEST TIP
PRESSURE TRAITS

Rather than saddle Helots with a lengthy suite of negative modifiers, simply take advantage of their temporary pressure traits. Liberally invoking these traits is a good way to highlight when you have a fish out of water, so to speak.

TRUE COLOURS

While the nuances of *Erissom* tend to be expressed through gradients, some key colour associations — easily observable in the clear, uncontrolled hues of a Helot's eyes — are known to most Varunans:

Blue — Rage

Crimson — Calm

Green — Lust

Amber — Panic

Orange — Anticipation

Pink — Contemplativeness

Brown — Joy

Lavender — Curiosity

Black — Sorrow

Turquoise — Relief

"THEY THINK WE'RE STUPID"

"The thing you have to understand, is that they think we're stupid. They come to our home, kick us around, and call us slaves while laughing behind our backs! Well guess what. We can learn dead languages as well as you can. You call us slaves, and then have the gall to deny it? Well, these slaves just freed themselves; deal with it. The Libertos don't need your suits, your laws, your empty promises, and definitely not you! We won't stop until every last Omn is free, whether they know they want it or not. Sleep with one eye open, Conquistadores; we're coming for you." — Cinadon Arrow-Fist, founding Libertos member.

lands beyond Varuna — known to Helots as *kossala*, the deep uplands — requires a special sort of individual. Possessed of equal parts *Epicuriosity* and epic curiosity, these sidereal travellers exist in a near-constant state of wonder; as the new and the known constantly crash upon their senses like tidal waves of emotion.

Wide-eyed or not, Helots still need to eat. And since few are wealthy enough to finance a trip to the stars themselves, many find themselves employed as labourers, traders, or entertainers to make their way through the Human Sphere. Though there are relatively few Helot pilots, those who try their hand at crewing a ship find their natural inclination to think in three dimensions to be a boon to navigating in spacecraft, and all Helots gracefully adapt to zero-g conditions. For the most part, Helots present an interesting novelty; an honest-to-goodness alien, working and living alongside humanity as though it was the most natural thing in the world. Deserved or not, many of these Helots earn a reputation as ship's mascots; beloved figures who do more for morale than productivity.

Still, the number of Helots who venture beyond the shores of their youth remains quite small. It's hard for a Helot to consider it a good day if they don't get to go for a swim, and most starships don't have a public pool of appreciable depth. Even so, PanOceania is proud of these adventurous Helots — if for no other reason than to refute the accusations that their "client race" is nothing but disgruntled labourers and terrorists.

But ultimately, most Helot travellers do so for a simple reason; their pod. Their companions are one of the most important things in a Helot's life; and if those companions happen to be human, then travel might be in the cards. As it turns out, a Helot can put up with nearly anything if it means maintaining the relationships of those closest to them; and if that means venturing out into the void of space, they consider it a small price to pay.

LIBERTOS

Of course, not every Helot is happy with PanOceania's "stewardship" of their people. Formed in direct response to the colonisation of their homeworld, the Libertos — literally meaning "freed slave" in ancient Latin — see things very differently than most Helots. Students of human culture and history, they see PanOceania's role in Omn affairs as entirely exploitive; an invasion that they alone are still fighting.

To the Libertos, they're not terrorists, insurgents, or anything else the Mayacasts want to call them; they're the last bastion of free Omn, defending their

home. In their rage-blue eyes, they didn't start this war; they're the only ones who recognize it for what it is, and have the courage to fight back. Originally composed entirely of Omn, over time the group has added human members, from Ateks to full citizens, who either support their cause, or have their own bone to pick with the Hyperpower. Supported by activist groups, as well as PanOceania's many enemies, Libertos has become better-funded over time. And they pride themselves on putting their resources to efficient use.

Organized in a fault-tolerant clandestine cellular structure, Libertos has tapped into the Omn's natural inclination to form pods and used this as the basis for its internal structure. In a traditional cell organisation, neutralizing a given cell's leader would effectively cut it off from the rest of the organisation. Libertos sytmie the impact through a series of independent side links, paired dead drops, autonomous communication vectors, and custom cyphers that make good use of humanity's diffculties with Tetessom's nuances.

Libertos aren't much for peaceful protest; they prefer violent, disruptive action whenever possible, and rarely miss an opportunity to make a statement. Of particular note is their disgust at the existence of pressure suits, which they see as a fundamental subversion of their natural state, akin to brainwashing. Never mind the countless Helots who value the suits, saying they grant a hitherto unachievable focus; the suits are tools of the machine, and the machine has to burn. If some of their fellows get caught in the blaze, it's unfortunate, but can't be helped. To a Libertos, if you're not a part of the solution, you're part of the problem.

And no one else is a part of the solution.

LIBERTOS ACTIVITIES

Engaged in subversive actions all across Varuna — and very occasionally leaking out to the rest of the Human Sphere — Libertos operations tend to fall into one of four different categories: target destruction, intelligence acquisition, retributive actions, and political communication. Prefixed with the *Tetessom* word "B'akk" — a Libertos-coined word meaning violence, with an implied undertone of unnatural wrongness — all Libertos field operations are meant to send a message; every death, every explosion, every lost profit and frightened child are all designed toward one purpose, and one purpose only. The credo of Libertos, their desire for freedom from PanOceanian rule, must echo loudly through every strike. If the public is confused, then clearly, the mission was a failure, and in the future, the message should be clearer, and likely louder, to get the point across.

LIBERTOS B'AKK XHASSA (TARGET DESTRUCTION) MISSIONS

The loudest, and most public of Libertos' actions, there's nothing quite like a large-scale loss of property and life to send a message. While Libertos tend to eschew large-scale civilian casualties, the prevalence of Cubes in PanOceanian society has led them to adopt a *laissez-faire* attitude regarding collateral damage.

- Destruction of key military infrastructure, usually with improvised explosives
- Disruption of day-to-day life for PanOceanians: create power outages, disable transportation hubs, incinerate outgoing food shipments
- Removal of key personnel: anti-terrorism task force leaders, politicians, and media figures all feature prominently, but any enemy of the cause is fair game
- Destruction of an individual's Cube, removing any sensitive data they collected since their last backup

LIBERTOS B'AKK RHASSI (INTELLIGENCE ACQUISITION) MISSIONS

While it grabs fewer headlines, the Libertos' intelligence division is surprisingly robust, given the organisation's low-tech ethos. It has to be; PanOceanian counter-terrorism is a refined art, a chess match of traps, counter-feints, and false trails. To survive opposite such enemies requires skill, cunning, and no small amount of luck.

- Abduction of non-key personnel with access to closed systems; administrative assistants, dispatchers, and chauffeurs are common targets
- Low-tech, in-person surveillance by assets posing as civilians
- Favour-trading with Ateks, trading smuggled goods or other actions in exchange for information

LIBERTOS B'AKK B'AKKU (RETRIBUTIVE ACTION) MISSIONS

Varunan politicians are fond of appearing tough on the "Libertos issue," and often take widely publicised actions to "send a message" to them. The only message that the Libertos hear is "come and get me." Retributive actions are a form of targeted harassment designed to discourage powerful individuals from targeting the movement.

- Coordinated vandalism: the target never has a vehicle with unslashed tires, finds their Maya feeds awash in unwanted newsletters, and generally suffer in a thousand small ways over the course of the mission
- The acquisition of blackmail, and subsequent distribution to rival — primarily Yu Jing — news outlets
- *Riposte* actions: striking back publicly, and violently, at any forces who've enjoyed public success against the movement

B'AKK XHASSA: THE HELOT REBELLIONS

It was on the road to the NeoColonial Wars that Libertos first revealed its presence. Funded and equipped by unknown off-world sources, Libertos destroyed key infrastructure across the Atlantea Archipelago, leaving most of Akuna Bay without power for 72 hours while the government scrambled to figure out just what was happening.

B'AKK RHASSI: ONGOING MISSIONS

Varunan law enforcement estimates that at any given time, there are at least three high-priority Libertos Intelligence Acquisition missions, about a dozen medium-priority missions, and countless decoys. Counter-terrorism investigators have privately confessed confidence that they're wasting half their time chasing red herrings; they're just not sure which half.

LIBERTOS B'AKK PADJURA (COMMUNICATION) MISSIONS

While every Libertos mission is an act of political communication, targeted guerrilla messaging is a key component of every revolutionary movement. For their part, the Libertos could hardly be accused of neglect. Like many revolutionaries, they believe that if the world at large simply understood what they were saying, that the only rational response would be agreement; so they take every opportunity to get their message out, consequences be damned.

- Collaboration with off-world hackers — usually Nomads or Yu Jing — to flood citizens with graphic images of violent acts against Helots
- Strategic defacing of public places — covering religious statues with gallons of fish blood, wide-scale arson of public parks, or the introduction of invasive aquatic species to private beaches — anything to make the average Varunan feel the way that Libertos feel
- Any violent disruption of a public gathering

HELOT CHARACTERS

In contrast to the cornucopia of options presented to most PanOceanian citizens, the life of a Helot is comparatively restricted. Born on Varuna, most never stray too far from its oceans. A Helot's formative experiences are substantially different from other PanOceanians; Helot characters are created using the variant rules in this chapter, rather than those in the *Infinity Corebook*, or the variant rules for PanOceanian characters on page 80. The entries presented here supersede their counterparts in the corebook.

DECISION TWO: FACTION AND HERITAGE

All Helots are born PanOceanian citizens. Select PanOceania for both Faction and Heritage, and gain skills accordingly.

DECISION THREE: HELOT HOMEWORLD/HOMELAND

Helots, without exception, call Varuna their home; the next Helot hatched off-world will be the first, if it ever happens at all. While the *sissolu* that Helots hail from aren't tied to PanOceanian geography, the major archipelagos are the primary reference point when trying to find them on a map.

Select Varuna from the *PanOceania Homeworld Table* (p. 44, *Infinity Corebook*), add your attributes and skill as normally, then roll on the *Sissolu Waters Table* to determine their precise region, and what language(s) they speak.

SISSOLU WATERS TABLE		
D20	REGION	LANGUAGE
1–5	Atlantea Waters	*Tetessom*, and Spanish, English or Malay (choose one)
6–9	Gurindam Waters	*Tetessom*, and Tamil, Malayalam, or Malay (choose one) [1]
10–14	Hawaki Waters	*Tetessom*, and Māori or Malay (choose one) [1]
15–17	Kumari Kandam Waters	*Tetessom* and Tamil
18	Lemurian Waters	*Tetessom*, and Malay, Spanish, English, or Tamil (choose one)
19–20	*Katallpeac* Lilypad	*Tetessom* [1]

[1] Roll again on the *PanOceania Homeworld Table* (*Infinity Corebook*, p. 45) followed by the appropriate sub-table (p. 81) to determine a second fluent language.

HELOT SOCIAL STATUS TABLE			
2D6	SOCIAL STATUS	ATTRIBUTE	EARNINGS
1–4	Underclass	Agility	1
5–10	Demogrant	Personality	1
11–12	Middle	Willpower	3

THE ROLEPLAYING GAME

HELOT

ATTRIBUTES

AGILITY	–	AWARENESS	+1	BRAWN	–	COORDINATION	–
INTELLIGENCE	–	PERSONALITY	+1	WILLPOWER	-1		

Amphibious: Helots can breathe underwater, and possess the Common Special Ability Inured to Cold.

Strong Swimmer: Born underwater, Helots are naturally proficient swimmers; they begin with one rank of the Strong Swimmer talent.

Pressure Sensitive: A Helot's mood is strongly influenced by their environmental pressure; see *Pressure Personality Traits*, p. 117.

Pressure Modifications: While most Helots are unable to control their Pressure Suits, the more intrepid among them have discovered ways of tweaking their internal pressure levels to suit different situations. As a Standard Action a Helot may attempt a D1 Tech Test to adjust their suit's pressure, selecting the benefits – and drawbacks – of the associated Pressure levels.

Life Point Cost: 2

HELOT LIFE CYCLES

Every Helot goes through five stages of life: egg, fry, young adult, mature adult, and elder (or kossomn). This creates some distinct challenges. Notably, frys and elders are mermaid-like in appearance; without legs, navigating human environments is difficult to say the least.

Helot PCs are assumed to be mature adults by the time they reach play. Groups wishing to use the optional Step Six: Aging during Decision Nine of the Lifepath, or otherwise explore the transition through life stages, can use the following optional rules.

In addition to the normal effects of aging (p. 71, *Infinity Corebook*), when a Helot reaches the age of 45, and every three years thereafter, roll 1🅽. If an Effect is rolled, you have begun the transition into your kossomn stage. Gain the Common Special Ability Inured to Aquatic Pressure. Over the course of the next year, your legs will begin to atrophy; each month, make a D5 Resistance test. On a failure, you have lost the use of your legs. Barring replacement through augmentation, your movement speed is greatly reduced; it requires a Standard action to move to a point within Medium range, and all non-aquatic terrain tests are made at +3 difficulty.

DECISION FOUR: HELOT STATUS

Unlike their human counterparts, Helots find their social mobility extremely limited; there simply aren't that many opportunities, and the proverbial glass ceiling seems reinforced with Teseum; wealth is rare, and the next Helot Hyper-Elite will be the first. Helot characters roll on the *Helot Social Status Table*, but roll on the *Home Environment Table* as normally.

Note that nothing prevents Helot characters from advancing beyond middle class in play or later in the Lifepath. They can change status just like any other character; but none of them are born with a silver spoon.

DECISION FIVE: FRY EVENTS

Being a fry is both like and unlike being a human child. While Humans and Helots alike are routinely shocked by how much they have in common despite their obvious differences, fryhood tends to be a fairly dramatic time for Helots and their pods.

Roll 1d20 and 2d6, then reference the *Fry Event Table* below. Each event indicates a massive impact from your youth; something that shook you (and perhaps your pod) to the core. It might be something you've since moved past, or it may define you even into adulthood, but either way, you'll want to use the descriptions as a diving board for your imagination, and detail precisely what happened.

HELOT LIFEPATH DECISIONS

The Lifepath Decisions outlined on p. 38, *Infinity Corebook* should be followed with the following exceptions for Helot characters.

DECISION ONE—BIRTH HOST

In order to use this Lifepath your Birth Host must be a Helot. This may have been randomly determined or purchased with Lifepoints.

DECISION TWO—FACTION AND HERITAGE

Helot characters automatically take PanOceania for both Faction and Heritage, and gain skills accordingly.

DECISION THREE—HOMEWORLD/HOMELAND

Helot characters are born on Varuna; select Varuna as your homeworld, and roll on the *Sissolu Waters Table* (p. 98).

DECISION FOUR—STATUS

Helot characters roll on the *Helot Social Status Table* (p. 98).

DECISION FIVE—FRY EVENT

Helot characters roll on the *Fry Event Tables* (p. 100).

DECISION SEVEN—ADOLESCENT EVENT

Helot characters roll on the *Helot Adolescent Event Tables* (p. 101)

DECISION EIGHT—CAREERS

Instead of rolling on the PanOceanian Faction Career table in the *Infinity Corebook*, characters in the PanOceania faction roll on the *Expanded PanOceania Faction Career Table* (p. 84), as well as the PanOceania *Faction Career Event* tables.

HELOTS | 99

FRY EVENT TABLE

D20	2-5	6-8	9-12
1-4	Your pod clashed with a rival pod; the fighting was intense, and you lost someone close to you. Reduce your Resolve by 1.	Your pod clashed with a rival pod; the fighting was intense, and you lost people close to you on both sides. Gain a trait from the experience.	Your pod clashed with a rival pod; the fighting was intense, and despite your youth, you took a life with your own hands. Gain 1 rank in Close Combat.
5-8	Libertos came to your pod, trying to recruit it. Some left to join the cause, while others rebuffed the strangers; but everyone fought, and your *Pojju* split that day. Reduce your Vigour by 1 from the injuries you sustained.	Libertos came to your pod, trying to recruit it. Some left to join the cause, others rebuffed it, but either way, your *Pojju* split that day. Gain a trait from the experience	Libertos came to your pod, trying to recruit it. When it became clear that you weren't interested, they forced the issue. You didn't know how to fight, but that didn't stop any of you; your pod banded together to protect its own. Increase both your Resolve and your Vigour by 1 rank each.
9-12	Members of your pod were abducted. Your *Pojju* never really recovered, drifting apart over the next few years. Reduce your Resolve by 1. You can choose to take Libertos Member as your first career.	Members of your pod wanted to go to the surface, but as you didn't have legs yet, you stayed behind with a neighboring pod. Did they ever return? Did you rejoin them if they did? Gain a trait from the experience.	A group of human scientists traveled with your pod for a time. Were they friendly? Cold? Could you even communicate with them? Gain 1 rank in Awareness. You can select *Human Education* in Decision Six.
13-16	Your pod migrated to a beautiful, but empty, cave network. You soon discovered why; as the Varunan Water-Snakes were quite pleased you'd moved into their den, and much of your pod didn't survive. Reduce your Brawn by 1, as injuries and venom stunt your physical development.	Your pod migrated via the same *katallpeac* so often that it began to feel like home. An Atek shanty town floated on top; what were your relations like? Roll on the *Sissolu Waters Table*, and learn the associated language(s). Gain a trait from the experience.	Your pod welcomed back an old friend who'd served in the Helot Militia. Stories of their exploits captured everyone's imaginations, but they saw something special in you. Increase your Resolve by 1; you can choose to take Helot Militia as your first career.
17-19	Through circumstances beyond your control, your entire pod was wiped out, leaving you stranded and completely alone. Reduce Willpower by 1. Reroll any results other than *Human Education* or *Wild Pod* in Decision Six, accepting the new result.	Your pod reunited with an old member, who'd left to join. Libertos. While the pod was divided in their politics, your elders showered them in praise, ignoring you in the process. Reduce Willpower by 1, and gain a trait from the experience.	Whether through choice, tragedy, or circumstance, you joined the *Tete-Kulu*, relocating to the surface before your body was fully adapted. Reduce both Vigour and Willpower by 1, but increase Coordination by 1, and select *Wild Pod* in Decision Six.
20	Reroll Twice and Combine Results		

DECISION SIX: HELOT EDUCATION

When it comes to education, Helot characters do things a little differently. Even if a human school admits a fry for classes, their physiologies — legless, and requiring frequent submersion to properly develop into healthy adults — present a unique challenge, though not an insurmountable one. However, the overwhelming majority of frys are collectively taught by their pods, according to aptitudes they've shown, and the pod's own leanings and resources. They shadow adults in the pod, learning through kinesics, participation, observation, and good old-fashioned pedagogy. Given the communal nature of a pod's possessions, frys don't gain much in the way of gear in this process, but the knowledge gleaned will last them a lifetime.

As Helots transition from frys to young adults, the nature of their environment becomes much clearer; the type of education they receive says a great deal not only about the character, but about their pod as well.

If you roll a 20, your character is one of the few Helots to receive a human education; roll on the *Education Table* (p. 48, *Infinity Corebook*) as normally.

HELOT EDUCATION TABLE

D20	EDUCATION	EXAMPLE
1-6	Scout Training	Scavenger, Explorer, Raiding Scout
7-12	Hunter/Warrior Training	Shark hunter, Libertos military training, Pod Squire
13-18	Utility Training	Skiff Repair, Settlement Construction, Migrant Workers
19	Wild Pod	*Tete-Kulu* Surface Training, Off-Grid Survivalists, Remote Deep Fishers
20	Human Education	Religious monastery, Aquatic Research Institute, Quantronic Tutors

DECISION SEVEN: HELOT ADOLESCENT EVENT

As a Helot transitions to their young adult phase, changes are abundant. As their bodies change, their newly-grown legs open new opportunities, and they head to the shallow waters of the uplands, lay and fertilize eggs, and often have their first contact with humanity. It's a passionate, often violent season of their lives, and one that leaves them forever changed.

During Decision Seven, Helot characters roll on the *Helot Adolescent Event Tables* to determine which *Adolescent Event Table* they use to generate their adolescent event.

HELOT ADOLESCENT EVENT TABLES

D6	CAREER
1–4	Helot Young Adult Table
5–6	PanOceania Faction Adolescent Event Tables

DECISION EIGHT: CAREERS

As Helots transition into adulthood proper, myriad changes — both social and biological — come to pass. Most Helots form a monogamous pair-bond by this age, and travel back to *sissolu* waters to retrieve eggs that have reached *calassus,* raising the frys as their children. Even more so than with human characters, you'll want to think about your character's family life; do they have a pair-bond? Children? Why or why not? Any answer is viable, but having one is important.

During Decision Eight, Helot characters follow the normal procedures for performing their career phases, with the exception that they roll on the *Helot Career Table* whenever they would normally roll on the *Faction Career Table* in the *Infinity Corebook*; and whenever they would normally determine a career event they roll on the *Helot Career Event Table* to determine which *Career Event Table* to roll on.

HELOT CAREER EVENT TABLES

D20	CAREER
1	Career Event Table A[1]
2	Career Event Table B[1]
3	Career Event Table C[1]
4–6	Faction Career Table[2]
7–20	Helot Species Career Event Table

[1] *Infinity Corebook*, p.56–58

[2] If available. If not, roll on the *Helot Career Event Table*

HELOT EDUCATION BENEFITS—MANDATORY

EDUCATION	2	1	–1	MANDATORY SKILLS
Scout	Awareness	Coordination	Brawn	Acrobatics, Athletics, Observation, Stealth, Survival
Hunter/Warrior	Agility	Personality	Intelligence	Acrobatics, Athletics, Ballistics, Close Combat, Resistance
Utility Training	Personality	Intelligence	Brawn	Animal Handling, Education, Lifestyle, Psychology, Tech
Wild Pod	Brawn	Agility	Willpower	Athletics, Observation, Resistance, Survival

HELOT EDUCATION BENEFITS—SKILLS AND TALENT

EDUCATION	ELECTIVE SKILLS (PICK 2)	TALENT GAINED
Scout	Ballistics, Pilot, Thievery	Stealth: Scout
Hunter/Warrior	Medicine, Observation, Stealth	Acrobatics: Graceful
Utility Training	Analysis, Persuasion, Science	Lifestyle: Socialite
Wild Pod	Stealth, Survival, Thievery	Special: Gain 1 Life Point

HELOT CAREER TABLE

D20	CAREER
1	Unemployed[1]
2	Frontiersman[1]
3	Criminal[1]
4	Ship Crew[1]
5	Pilot[1]
6	Intelligence Operative[1]
7	Libertos Member
8	Aquatic First Responder
9	Bartender
10	Helot Militia
11	Labourer
12	Varunan Guide
13	Mayacast Support Staff[2]
14	Scuball Player
15	Omn Storyteller
16	Deep-Sea Explorer
17	Priest[2]
18	Trader[1]
19	Heavy Industry[1]
20	Starfish

[1] Career from *Infinity Corebook*, p. 59

[2] Careers from PanOceanian Characters, p 90

HELOT YOUNG ADULT TABLE

D20	ADOLESCENT EVENT	SUGGESTED CHARACTER TRAIT	OPTIONAL EFFECT
1	You fled the waters of your birth and the safety of your pod in search of adventure. It ended badly. How?	Once-Bitten	Reduce Resolve by 1.
2	Mimicking the trickster fables of your youth, you caused a problem you couldn't talk your way out of.	Too Clever by Half	Gain 1 rank in Thievery, but reduce Discipline by 1.
3	Eager to take your new legs out for a stroll, you visited Akuna Bay and were promptly beaten within an inch of your life by activists.	Xenophobic	Reduce Vigour by 1. Receive 2 Assets in reparations from the PanOceanian government.
4	You are kidnapped and experimented on. While the process was unpleasant, your insides are downright Silken.	Test Subject	Gain any Biograft or Silk augmentation that requires an action to use, but add +2 to its complication range.
5	Guilty or innocent, you were ripped from the waters, held without trial, and thrown in jail for Libertos terrorism.	The Usual Suspect	Spend 1d6 years in jail before starting your first career. Gain a Criminal Record (see p. 54, Infinity Corebook).
6	While exploring, you were separated from the rest of your pod. You haven't seen them since.	Orphan	Gain 1 Rank in Analysis.
7	During the mating season, you were nearly killed by a Varunan Water-Snake. You barely managed to escape, though your eggs weren't so lucky.	Traumatized	Reduce an attribute of your choice by 1 rank.
8	You took in a young injured creature, and despite its dangerous nature, nursed it back to health.	Critter Whisperer	Gain 1 rank in Animal Handling.
9	You discovered a human religion, and despite its alien assumptions, something about it took root.	Pious	Add 1 to your Resolve Stress track. You may choose Priest as your first career.
10	In the uplands, you chose a clutch haven that proved nearly – but not quite – impossible to navigate.	Daredevil	Gain 1 rank in Acrobatics.
11	During the upland mating season, you were swept away by a terrible current. Months later, you awoke in a human hospital bed. Your pod was gone, but the people who rescued you remained.	Fish Out of Water	Reduce Vigour by 1. You may take Aquatic First Responder (p. 104 as your first career.
12	Venturing into human territories, you discover that your pod has a reputation; and it's even a good one.	Vainglorious	You can reroll your first career but must accept the new career rolled.
13	Rivals, predators, or sabotage; whether you laid or defended them, none of your eggs survived to calassus.	Amber-Tinted Glasses	Reduce Willpower by 1.
14	You were stranded on dry land for months. What happened?	Xerophobia	Reduce Vigour by 1.
15	You are injured in a Libertos attack. While the burns eventually healed, your Errisom colours have never looked quite right.	Living Scars	Add +1 difficulty to social skill tests with other Helots due to damaged Erissom hues.
16	An encounter with automated farming equipment left you mangled. Your pod did what it could to fix you up.	Old Injury	Reduce Agility by 1.
17	During the upland mating season, you dragged your eggs to a shallow cove, spending your formative years in those hot-blooded shallow waters	Hair-Trigger Temper	You gain +2d20 to Surprise tests, but increase the difficulty of Discipline tests by+1.
18	Trapped in a dire situation, you were rescued by a Libertos cell. How did you react?	Nose for Trouble	Gain one rank in either Discipline or Thievery. You may choose Libertos Member as your first career.
19	Awakened by your pod in the still of night, you saw strange figures – human figures – with them. You left with them; willingly. Why?	Swimming Upstream	You defect to a new faction. Roll on the Faction Table (p. 41, Infinity Corebook), to determine your new allegiance.
20	A Kossomn entrusted you with a great secret. What is it, and why does it mean you can never go back to your old life?	Destined	Gain +1 Infinity Point refresh rate (max. 4). Increase the difficulty of social skill tests with other Helots by one step.

HELOT SPECIES CAREER EVENT TABLE

D20	CAREER EVENT	GAME EFFECT
1	While returning from a clutch haven, you're suddenly attacked; the eggs don't make it, and you barely do. Who or what was responsible?	Gain Trait: Bereaved.
2	Turns out that Epicuriosity doesn't preclude regular curiosity.	Gain 1 rank of training in a skill you currently have no training in.
3	While visiting the sissolu waters of your youth, you uncover some artifacts of unexpected value.	Gain 2 Assets.
4	Your bondmate (or someone similarly close to you) contracts a rare disease. An expensive cure exists, but you know you can do this.	Gain a debt worth 5 Assets. You are filled with determination; gain 1 rank in Resolve.
5	Your (or your pod's) new clutch of frys are smart. Real smart. The expensive kind of smart.	Gain a debt worth 6 🅝 Assets as you pay for the frys' education. Increase Social Status by +1 for each Effect rolled, as their accomplishments reflect well on your whole pod.
6	Your pod disbands suddenly. What happened? What do you do now?	Gain a character trait describing your newfound isolation.
7	Following a Libertos attack, you are taken in for questioning. What did they think you knew? And did you?	Gain a 1+5 🅝 Asset debt representing lost wages and court fees.
8	You save a tourist from a horrible fate. Little did you know they were Mayacasting at the time.	Gain Trait: Unlikely Celebrity. You may take Mayacast Support Staff as your next career.
9	A fryhood podmate has a bad injury, and turns to you for help. What happened?	Gain a debt worth 8 Assets, or gain the character trait: Pariah.
10	You are mistaken for a Libertos member who you clearly bear no resemblance to.	You must pass an Average (D1) hazard test for your current career or you are Fired (see p. 54, Infinity Corebook).
11	Other Helots think you're cursed; they might not be wrong.	Reduce your Infinity Point refresh rate by 1 (min. 0).
12	The sole survivor of a hurricane, people wonder if it's luck or savvy.	Gain +1 Infinity Point refresh rate (max. 4).
13	You're betrayed by a member of your *Pojju*, your bondmate, or some similarly intimate, trusted acquaintance. Who was it? What did they do to you?	Gain Trait: Deeply Cynical.
14	Both Libertos and the PanOceanian authorities are hunting you down. What do they think you know? Do you?	Gain both a criminal enemy and a police enemy. You must pass an Average (D1) hazard test for your current career or you are Fired (see p. 54, Infinity Corebook).
15	You survive a serious natural disaster. The person closest to you doesn't.	Gain Trait: Haunted.
16	You're singled out as a great employee; the example that other Helots should hold themselves to. Is it true?	Increase your Earnings by one (to a maximum of six), and gain the character trait: Toadie.
17	You discover a human language that works pretty well for you.	Learn a new language of your choice.
18	You are fired. What reason did they give, and why does it make no sense to you?	You are Fired (see p. 54, Infinity Corebook).
19	Other Helots think you're cursed; they might not be wrong.	Reduce your Infinity Point refresh rate by 1 (min. 0).
20	The tide comes and goes; but The Lavender Tide leads to curious – some would say interesting – times.	Roll again three times on the Career Event Table for this career phase. (When spending a Life Point to choose a specific event, you may not choose this result. If you roll duplicate events, it means some similar event has occurred. If you roll The Lavender Tide again, add additional rolls.

CAREER PROFILE
AQUATIC FIRST RESPONDER

EMTs, firefighters, lifeguards. Of the many career paths open to Helots, the First Responder is one that confuses humanity the most. Not that they aren't happy to see them, as any human EMT would be hard-pressed to match a Helot when navigating hazardous underwater terrain. For a species tarred as "lazy", however, many are confused to see how enthusiastically they take to the role.

What most Varunans fail to understand is that these Helots are living out their fryhood fantasies and following in the footsteps of the greatest heroes of Omn lore. Like Yisso-tal, they swoop into danger to save other's lives, and like Arrodiel, they risk their own skin to help strangers. This may be confusing to outsiders, but to a Helot First Responder it's simple. Who wouldn't want to be a superhero?

ATTRIBUTES						
AGI	AWA	BRW	COO	INT	PER	WIL
+1	+2	+2	+2	+1	+1	+1

SKILLS				EARNINGS
Mandatory	Athletics	Medicine	Tech	1+2 Ⓝ
Elective	Discipline	Observation	Pilot	

GEAR: Light Combat Armour (with pressure suit mod), MediKit (with 3 Serum)
SPECIAL: This career is not available to characters with a Criminal Record.

CAREER PROFILE
DEEP-SEA EXPLORER

Prideful as PanOceania are of their Explorers, it's curious that much of Varuna's depths remain unexplored. Of course, between the crushing pressure, aquatic predators, and omnipresent, oppressive darkness, most humans know better than to dive too deeply, undiscovered secrets or no. The Helots know better too. But they do it anyway.

No human could pilot a submersible craft, casually pop the hatch, and explore on their own the way that a Helot does. Whether in the employ of a corporation or government work programs, out on their own, or with their pod, Helots brave the deep sea with a bravado born of certainty, even if it literally ages them too fast. And while some never return, a fair number of them simply join the elder *kossomn* in the great depths, pondering life's mysteries among their own kind.

ATTRIBUTES						
AGI	AWA	BRW	COO	INT	PER	WIL
+1	+3	+1	+2	+1	+1	–

SKILLS				EARNINGS
Mandatory	Animal Handling	Pilot	Tech	1+3 Ⓝ
Elective	Analysis	Observation	Survival	

GEAR: Crashsuit (with pressure suit mod), Exo-Compass, D-Thread (3 charges), Knife
SPECIAL: If using the optional aging rules, roll 1d6 when working this career, subtracting the result from the age when you begin transitioning into your kossomn stage (45 by default).

CAREER PROFILE
BARTENDER

Across Varuna, particularly Ikatere, Helots indulge in the ancient role of barkeep, dispensing drinks and offering a friendly ear in equal measure. Legend states that early PanOceanian entrepreneurs revelled with a pod of Helots. They watched their hosts dive effortlessly beneath the waves, then resurface with various chilled liquors that were mixed with playful aplomb. An opportunity not to be missed.

Regardless of origin, it's difficult to dispute that Helots make exquisite bartenders. Their cooking involves a fair amount of mixing and chemistry, while a gregarious and cheerful disposition also serves them well. Beyond the exotic allure of *kotusum* drinks, several clubs have modified aquariums where Helot Bartenders retrieve chilled aquatic ingredients and mix beverages in a routine that's equal parts chemistry, aquabatics, and performance art.

ATTRIBUTES						
AGI	AWA	BRW	COO	INT	PER	WIL
+2	+2	+1	+1	+2	+1	+1

SKILLS				EARNINGS
Mandatory	Lifestyle	Persuasion	Psychology	0+1 Ⓝ
Elective	Education	Observation	Persuasion	

GEAR: Fashionable Clothing, Psychotropics (3 doses)

CAREER PROFILE
HELOT MILITIA

Considered little more than cannon fodder by PanOceania's command, Helot Militia specialise in amphibious operations and support the PanOceanian military in situations where amphibious natives provide a tactical edge. Primarily focused on internal security, though occasionally providing support in military operations abroad, these brave Helots have one of the highest casualty ratios in the PanOceanian military due to their primary deployment in high-risk situations. Despite abnormally high casualty rates, and even considering the risky situations in which they're typically deployed, many Helot Milita take pride in protecting their home and gain satisfaction in doing so in a fashion that the rest of PanOceania is sure to understand. If they escape with their lives, those serving in the Helot Militia always leave with some scars and stories to show for their trouble.

ATTRIBUTES						
AGI	AWA	BRW	COO	INT	PER	WIL
+2	+1	+2	+2	+1	+1	+1

SKILLS				EARNINGS
Mandatory	Ballistics	Observation	Resistance	1+1 Ⓝ
Elective	Close Combat	Discipline	Stealth	

GEAR: Light Combat Armour (with Pressure Suit mod) or Pain Filters, Rifle

LABOURER

When most people think of Helots, one of two things comes to mind. Either the terrorist actions of Libertos, or the many Helot Labourers working across Varuna. The advent of the pressure suit revolutionized the workforce, but even with this advancement, most Helots still make their living as semi-skilled Labourers. Primarily working in aquatic or amphibious farms, contributing to Varuna's primary aquaculture exports, or toiling in underwater mines, or performing equipment and facilities maintenance, Helot Labourers tend not to have particularly exciting or challenging professional lives, which suits many just fine. In a nod to Earth's early post-industrial workforce, many Helot Labourers have taken to colouring the collars of their pressure suits denim blue, in tribute to their human counterparts. But given the significance of the hue in Erissom, perhaps it's not a tribute at all. Perhaps it's a warning.

ATTRIBUTES						
AGI	AWA	BRW	COO	INT	PER	WIL
+1	+2	+2	+1	+1	+2	+1

SKILLS				EARNINGS
Mandatory	Athletics	Discipline	Resistance	0+3 Ⓝ
Elective	Discipline	Observation	Pilot	

GEAR: Locational Beacon, Powered Multitool or Repair Kit, Painkillers (5 doses)

OMN STORYTELLER

Owing to centuries of oral tradition as the primary means of recording their legends and history, the Omn ("those who speak" in *Tetessom*) are fantastic storytellers. Elder *kossomn* traditionally act as the primary lorekeepers, though everyone is encouraged to participate. Those with a talent for engaging, theatrical storytelling are singled out from fryhood. Recently, PanOceanian Cultural Integration Programs have made efforts to chronicle and highlight the art of the Omn Storyteller, with several popular Maya documentaries placing them on a stage unthinkable to their ancestors. For their part, Storytellers take this in their wake. Whether educating young Frys on the legend of *Vayyu* the Swift, explaining the intricacies of monogamous pair-bonds to a group of nodding scientists, or simply providing a sonorous voice-over for a new brand of deep-fried fish nugget, Omn Storytellers weave their narrative tapestries with luxurious precision.

ATTRIBUTES						
AGI	AWA	BRW	COO	INT	PER	WIL
+1	+1	+1	–	+2	+3	+1

SKILLS				EARNINGS
Mandatory	Education	Lifestyle	Persuasion	0+3 Ⓝ
Elective	Acrobatics	Persuasion	Survival	

GEAR: Cosmetics Kit, Recorder (x2)

LIBERTOS MEMBER

Libertos view themselves as change. To make change requires blood, violence, and confrontation. Faced with unacceptable conditions and convinced that there can be no change without violent upheaval, Libertos members take their destiny into their heavily-armed hands. Viewed as anti-human terrorists, they actually have very little issue with individual humans. Their insurgency rails against the intolerable treatment of their fellow Omn and the conquest of their planet. Sympathetic humans support the cause, but the heart and soul of Libertos will always be Omn. Trained in guerrilla tactics and sabotage, Libertos Members forego pressure suits unless used for infiltration purposes, preferring instead to bask in their natural agitation at being on land and using it to fuel the fires of revolution.

ATTRIBUTES						
AGI	AWA	BRW	COO	INT	PER	WIL
+1	+2	+1	+2	+1	+1	+2

SKILLS				EARNINGS
Mandatory	Ballistics	Close Combat	Stealth	0+2 Ⓝ
Elective	Hacking	Survival	Thievery	

GEAR: D-Thread, Fake ID 1, Malasartes Grenade (x2) or Heavy Pistol

SPECIAL: Criminal Career. Remove the pressure-regulating functionality of any pressure suits or pressure suit-modified armour upon starting the Libertos Member career

SCUBALL PLAYER

Unlike human players, who extensively use custom Scuball suits to better navigate the underwater environs, Helots are born swimmers. Unlike human athletes, who can't start seriously competing without organisational support, young Helots engage in different variants of the game before they reach maturity. Although it's among the more lucrative options available to them, the money hardly competes with the chance to enjoy their dream job. For applauding crowds. Whilst swimming. Helot Scuball Players constitute a significant portion of the league and include some of its top performers. For many, the comfortable glow of acceptance is even more addictive than the rush of competition and the thrill of victory. Much like with Dog-Bowl players, Helot Scuball Players have an accepted place in society. They are heroes even after the game. For some, that's worth any price.

ATTRIBUTES						
AGI	AWA	BRW	COO	INT	PER	WIL
+2	+1	+3	+1	–	+1	+1

SKILLS				EARNINGS
Mandatory	Acrobatics	Athletics	Lifestyle	2+3 Ⓝ
Elective	Athletics	Command	Observation	

GEAR: AR Eye Implants, Rippa X, Helot Jet Harness, Uniform

SPECIAL: In Decision Nine, set the value of your Rippa to the number of times you took the Scuball Player career.

STARFISH

After years of frustration in dealing with the Nomad Nations' cetacean pilots and their intrinsic understanding of three-dimensional spatial manoeuvres, the PanOceanian Armada snapped. The Star-Swimmer initiative hardly revolutionized the PanOceanian Navy, but recruiting the best, most tech-savvy, or reckless Helots available gave the Hyperpower an edge it had been sorely lacking. Whether maintaining the Acheron Blockade, hunting pirates, or giving the Nomads a taste of their own medicine, the Armada's Helot pilots — "Starfish" — possess a knack for sidereal manoeuvrability that is second to none. Less aggressive than a fighter pilot, but possessed of unmatched generational instincts, they're more a fraternity of Helots who've ventured into the deepest kossala and found the proverbial waters to their liking than formal unit.

ATTRIBUTES						
AGI	AWA	BRW	COO	INT	PER	WIL
+1	+2	+1	+3	–	+2	–

SKILLS				EARNINGS
Mandatory	Extraplanetary	Pilot	Spacecraft	1+2 Ⓝ
Elective	Ballistics	Lifestyle	Spacecraft	

GEAR: AR Eye Implants, Light Combat Armour with Pressure Suit mod) or Assault Pistol with 2 Reloads

VARUNAN GUIDE

From underwater mining in Damak, to scouting for new construction sites, to friendly neighbourhood tour guides, many Helots spend their time guiding their human neighbours around Varuna. Intricately tied to the tourism industry, outside of Labourers, more Helots find their employ as Guides than in any other vocation. Requiring not just extensive local knowledge, but the ability to explain its importance to a highly-educated populace, more than one Varunan Guide has needed to explain why and how eating a poisonous plant is a bad idea.

Equal parts sheepdog, tour guide, explorer, and local expert, many Helot Guides cluster around locations or phenomena that they know well, where their tendency towards *Epicuriosity* often translates the natural beauty and majesty of their home far better than any holo-pamphlet could ever hope to.

ATTRIBUTES						
AGI	AWA	BRW	COO	INT	PER	WIL
+1	+2	+1	–	+3	+2	–

SKILLS				EARNINGS
Mandatory	Animal Handling	Education	Psychology	1+2 Ⓝ
Elective	Athletics	Lifestyle	Survival	

GEAR: Adarsana Grenade, Lantern, Locational Beacon, Signal Flare, Survival Kit

CHAPTER 8

THE BEST & BRIGHTEST

Many people say that PanOceania is the Human Sphere — they couldn't be more right! PanOceania, being one of the two major Hyperpowers, has access to all the cutting-edge high technology currently on the market. Coupled with the fact that they receive logistical support from ALEPH, the benevolent AI, means there is nothing in the entire Sphere that can openly stand against them. The PanOceanian Military Complex (PMC), a sophisticated conglomerate of military forces intertwined with corporate assets, is one of the major discussion points during each year's budgetary meetings. Moreover, the church is another major actor within the Hyperpower, and its Military Orders are feared on the battlefield as they look to bring the Kingdom of God to PanOceania.

Separated into Corporate Assets, Knightly Orders, and Veteran Forces, this list of adversaries includes the typical kind of opposition one can encounter when facing the "Boys in Blue."

KNIGHTLY ORDERS

The contemporary Knightly Orders draw from historic traditions dating back to the Middle Ages. Created to protect church interests — which included individuals and groups — in the Holy Land, members of various orders such as the Templars and the Hospitallers were warrior-monks, scholars, tacticians and, sometimes, businessmen. Today, the ranks of the Orders concentrate on the warrior aspect — after all, that is why the church has brought them back. The on-going alien incursion means that there is no shortage of conflicts in need of advanced shock troops, and the Knights are happy to send these aliens back to the hellhole they crawled out from.

ELITE
KNIGHT OF MONTESA

Standard operating doctrine of the Military Orders requires reconnaissance duties to be carried out by trained specialists drawn from the ranks of the Order Sergeants. Due to the high scout attrition rates in hostile theatres, however, High Command decided to revise their approach; equipment, training, and faith superseded stealth and subterfuge. The Knights of Montesa are the pinnacle of this approach. Hulking individuals in lightweight power armour tasked with reconnaissance by fire actions, they are responsible for testing the enemy's resolve before other assets are committed. As mechanized deployment units renowned for reliability and stubborness, they are the first on and last off the field.

ATTRIBUTES						
AGI	AWA	BRW	COO	INT	PER	WIL
10	10	10	9	7	7	10

FIELDS OF EXPERTISE								
Combat	+2	1	Movement	+1	–	Social	+1	–
Fortitude	+2	1	Senses	+2	–	Technical	+2	–

DEFENCES						
Firewall	7	Resolve	10	Vigour	10
Security	3	Morale	2	Armour	3

ATTACKS
- **Combi Rifle**: Range C/M, 1+7 🅝 damage, Burst 2, 2H, Expert 1, MULTI Light Mod, Vicious 1
- **Chain-Colt**: Range C, 1+7 🅝 damage, Burst 1, 2H, Concealed 1, Torrent, Vicious 1
- **Pistol**: R/C, 1+6 🅝, Burst 2, 1H, Vicious 1
- **Sword**: Sword: Melee, 1+7 🅝, Parry 2, Vicious 1

GEAR: Powered Combat Armour (Montesa Variant), tabard emblazoned with Order heraldry

SPECIAL ABILITIES
- **Probationary Status**: The status of the Order of Montesa places each and every knight in the position where their actions could lead to the dissolution of their order. When faced with a Discipline test, the Knight can ignore any D1 or D2 test should failure bring their order into disrepute. Such tests are considered automatically successful.
- **Final Valour**: When a Knight of Montesa is killed by an enemy attack, they gain an immediate standard action to take one final attack at the enemy. This attack begins as a Dire [D4] test, and the enemy can react to the test as normal. In the unlikely event that momentum is rolled, this must be spent for extra damage.

ELITE
BLACK FRIARS

With beliefs turned upside down in the face of new revelations, various religions of Old Earth evolved to cope with the outcome of humanity's race to the stars. Many secret societies and sects formed, including the ancient Catholic order of the Dominicans, whose services were seemed even more necessary in these troubled times. Today, the Special Security Detachment of the Order of Preachers is made up of the Dominican Black Friars, so-called for the colour of the hoods that all the initiated wear. The Black Friars returned to their roots as Hounds of the Lord. The watchdogs of the Church and the Human Sphere. Most commonly found on Paradiso or places of high interstellar traffic, the Black Friars constantly search for enemies seeking to corrupt humanity from within and monitor the population for signs of alien interference.

ATTRIBUTES						
AGI	AWA	BRW	COO	INT	PER	WIL
9	9	9	9	10	9	10

FIELDS OF EXPERTISE								
Combat	+2	–	Movement	+1	–	Social	+2	–
Fortitude	+1	–	Senses	+3	1	Technical	+2	–

DEFENCES						
Firewall	10	Resolve	10	Vigour	9
Security	2	Morale	–	Armour	3

ATTACKS
- **MULTI Rifle**: C/M 1+6 🅝, 2H, Expert 1, Medium MULTI, MULTI Light Mod, Vicious 1
- **Pistol**: R/C, 1+5 🅝 damage, Burst 2, 1H, Vicious 1
- **Knife**: Melee, 1+4 🅝 damage, 1H, Concealed 1, Non-Hackable, Subtle 2, Thrown, Unforgiving 1

GEAR: Medium Combat Armour (Military Order), tabard emblazoned with Order heraldry, Multispectral Visor 2

SPECIAL ABILITIES
- **Biometric Visor**: Tasked with rooting out infiltrators, some Friars are equipped with specially designed biometric visors that aid their task. Black Friars can reroll 1d20 when making an Observation test, but must accept the new result. Additionally, Black Friars gain 1 bonus Momentum when making a face-to-face test against an opponent using stealth.
- **Watchers in the Dark**: As intelligence operatives first and foremost, the Friars make sure they are prepared for Infowar. They benefit from +1 Security Soak (included in their profile).

ELITE
ORDER SERGEANT

Order Sergeants are the lowest rank of troops that form the core fighting force of any Order. Contrary to popular belief, not all the members of the organisation are actual knights. Not all of them are official members of the clergy, either. Most are uninitiated servicemen, serving in this particular branch of the PanOceanian military just like they would in any other. Specialists in combat support, firepower handling, and advanced force operations, these courageous men and women excel in supporting the actions of their Brother Knights. All the Orders employ Sergeants, although within some of them, such as the Order of the Holy Sepulchre, the ratio of Sergeants to Knights is much lower as they do not perform many direct actions. Other Orders, such as the Teutons who have established their monastery-fortress on Paradiso, will employ more recruits to replace casualties in their fighting force.

ATTRIBUTES

AGI	AWA	BRW	COO	INT	PER	WIL
9	9	8	10	8	8	10

FIELDS OF EXPERTISE

Combat	+2	2	Movement	+2	–	Social	+1	–
Fortitude	+2	1	Senses	+1	–	Technical	+1	–

DEFENCES

Firewall	8	Resolve	10	Vigour	8
Security	2	Morale	–	Armour	3

ATTACKS
- **Combi Rifle**: Range C/M, 1+6 🅝 damage, Burst 2, 2H, Expert 1, MULTI Light Mod, Vicious 1
- **Pistol**: R/C, 1+5 🅝 damage, Burst 2, 1H, Vicious 1
- **Knife**: Melee, 1+3 🅝 damage, 1H, Concealed 1, Non-Hackable, Subtle 2, Thrown, Unforgiving 1

GEAR: Medium Combat Armour, tabard emblazoned with Order heraldry

SPECIAL ABILITIES
- **He Wills It So**: With God at their side, who would dare to stand against them? Through their faith, psycho-conditioning, or simple raw willpower, Order Sergeants ignore the effects of the Fear Common Special Ability. Any Intimidation Psywar actions targeting them are made at +1 difficulty.
- **Firing Drill**: Order Sergeants undergo daily trainings in the use of all firearms that the Complex has to offer. They may reroll two 🅝 when making a ranged attack but must accept the new results.

CORPORATE ASSETS

Money makes the world go 'round, and the megacorps have the money — from the relatively small, niche companies that provide goods no one ever needs, to transnational giants that use lobbys and Parliament to further their own agendas across entire star systems. Many Corporations utilize clandestine divisions that employ disposable assets for reconnaissance and corporate warfare — after all, accusations of spying and outright hostility are bad for business. Knowing how their employers view them means the mercs hold little loyalty to anything other than their pay cheque.

ELITE
CRISIS EXPERT SENIOR SPECIALIST

The CESS are a varied bunch. As implied, their employers hire them for specific problems or situations with the only stipulation being that the problem disappears. Usually jacks-of-all-trades, no two CESS are the same and usually tackle matters from differing angles; intimidation, bribery, or more lethal methods. Each CEO usually has at least one CESS on speed-dial, with a memo to file the expenses under 'miscellaneous'.

ATTRIBUTES

AGI	AWA	BRW	COO	INT	PER	WIL
9	10	8	8	10	9	9

FIELDS OF EXPERTISE

Combat	+2	–	Movement	+2	–	Social	+2	–
Fortitude	+2	–	Senses	+2	–	Technical	+2	–

DEFENCES

Firewall	10	Resolve	9	Vigour	9
Security	1	Morale	1	Armour	2

ATTACKS
- **Combi Rifle**: Range C/M, 1+7 🅝 damage, Burst 2, 2H, Expert 1, MULTI Light Mod, Vicious 1
- **Pistol**: R/C, 1+6 🅝 damage, Burst 2, 1H, Vicious 1
- **Hacking Device**: CLAW-1, SWORD-1, SHIELD-1, GADGET-2, IC-2, +2 🅝 damage

GEAR: Armoured clothing, Negotiator's SuiteGrenades; no Cube

SPECIAL ABILITIES
- **Jack-of-all-trades**: Most CESS have seen and done it all. They suffer no negative consequences from complications.
- **Master-of-none**: CESS struggle to master any of the topics they work on. PCs ignore any increase in complication range when making face-to-face tests against a CESS.

ELITE
CORPORATE DATA THIEF

Data thief is a name encapsulating all the hackers engaged in corporate espionage. Despite best attempts of the Corporations to stay ahead of the technological curve when it comes to breaching software and hostile intrusions, they must also face the reality that a highly motivated individual will eventually look on their servers. Many data thieves are still freelancers, but there are fewer of these due to the hard-handed punishments in cases of corporate espionage. Moreover, the Corporations began to put these hackers on their payroll as "advisors" to avoid them working for the competition. One would be mistaken, however, to assume that a data thief only sits in his basement looking at flowing data strings. These agents go out into the field and sometimes mingle with their targets at social gatherings, of which there are plenty in high society.

ATTRIBUTES

AGI	AWA	BRW	COO	INT	PER	WIL
8	9	7	8	11	9	11

FIELDS OF EXPERTISE

Combat	+1	–	Movement	+2	–	Social	+2	–
Fortitude	+2	–	Senses	+2	–	Technical	+2	1

DEFENCES

Firewall	11	Resolve	11	Vigour	7
Security	4	Morale	–	Armour	–

ATTACKS
- **Pistol**: R/C, 1+5 🅝 damage, Burst 2, 1H, Vicious 1
- **Knife**: Melee, 1+3 🅝 damage, 1H, Concealed 1, Non-Hackable, Subtle 2, Thrown, Unforgiving 1
- **Hacking Device Plus**: CLAW-2, SWORD-1, SHIELD-2, GADGET-3, IC-2, UPGRADE White Noise; +3 🅝 bonus damage

GEAR: Fake ID, Breaking & Entering Kit

SPECIAL ABILITIES
- **Blending In**: The best secrets are always well hidden, as are the best data thieves. The first sneaky action a Data Thief makes in a given scene does not provoke a stealth state test.
- **Master of Improvisation**: Data Thieves soon learn to work without access to their preferred toolbox. They suffer no penalties for Technical tests attempted without proper tools.
- **Master Hacker**: Data Thieves live and breathe Maya (and Arachne, for that matter). Their complex gear provides them with a Security rating of 4, included in the profile.

VETERAN FORCES

A key G5 player, PanOceania participates in many conflicts. Contemporary military operations rarely occur in the open, providing ample opportunities for operatives of all kinds to test their skills in CODE INFINITY situations. Commanders have a variety of experienced troops to draw on, from experienced alien hunters and civilian pacification specialists, to units trained for hostile environments. The ranks of the PMC will always provide..

PARADISO WAR VETERAN

With entire regiments exterminated, the First Paradiso Offensive proved to be a true crucible for the PanOceanian Military Complex. Survivors of these first skirmishes are treated with utmost respect, with many battle-scarred veterans still serving on the Paradiso frontline. They keep on fighting despite having been through hell and back and living to tell the tale, because they know that if you want something done right, you have to do it yourself. Who else will kick the aliens off planet?

ATTRIBUTES

AGI	AWA	BRW	COO	INT	PER	WIL
8	9	9	10	8	8	11

FIELDS OF EXPERTISE

Combat	+2	–	Movement	+2	–	Social	+1	–
Fortitude	+2	1	Senses	+2	1	Technical	+1	–

DEFENCES

Firewall	8	Resolve	11	Vigour	9
Security	2	Morale	1	Armour	3

ATTACKS

- **Combi Rifle**: Range C/M, 1+6 🄽 damage, Burst 2, 2H, Expert 1, MULTI Light Mod, Vicious 1
- **Light Flamethrower**: Range C, 1+5 🄽 damage, Burst 1, 2H, Incendiary 3, Munition, Terrifying 2, Torrent)
- **Knife**: Melee, 1+4 🄽 damage, 1H, Concealed 1, Non-Hackable, Subtle 2, Thrown, Unforgiving 1

GEAR: Medium Combat Armour, AutoMedikit

SPECIAL ABILITIES

- **Jungle Training**: When in a jungle environment, attacks targeting a Paradiso War Veteran from beyond Close range are at +1D. Additionally, they may reroll 1d20 when making Survival tests and gain 2 Momentum when making such tests in jungle environments.
- **Revered Veteran**: When leading a fireteam into action, the Veteran can reroll up to 2 🄽 for a ranged attack, but must accept the new results. Additionally, they benefit from a Morale Soak of 1.

SVALARHAIMA NISSE

In Nordic mythology, Nisse were house gnomes from folk tales, strong and friendly, but also moody and demanding a great degree of respect. Contemporary Nisses take their name from these fantasy creatures because they are experts at operating in hostile, winter environments and have an equally explosive temper. The regiment was created to operate where PanOceanian interests clash with those of Yu Jing, in the icy and desolate tundra of planet Svalarhaima. The Nisse are patient hunters and are completely immune to the cold that permeates the planet thanks to both the latest tech developments and rigorous training. Historically, Nisse regiments provided the best snipers in the PanOceanian Military Complex, and the Nisses are hard at work today to maintain that reputation.

ATTRIBUTES

AGI	AWA	BRW	COO	INT	PER	WIL
8	10	10	11	8	7	9

FIELDS OF EXPERTISE

Combat	+3	1	Movement	+1	–	Social	+1	–
Fortitude	+2	1	Senses	+2	1	Technical	+1	–

DEFENCES

Firewall	8	Resolve	9	Vigour	9
Security	2	Morale	–	Armour	3

ATTACKS

- **MULTI Sniper Rifle**: MULTI Sniper Rifle L 1+8 🄽, Unwieldy, Medium MULTI, Heavy, MULTI, Unforgiving 2
- **Pistol**: R/C, 1+6 🄽 damage, Burst 2, 1H, Vicious 1
- **Knife**: Melee, 1+4 🄽 damage, 1H, Concealed 1, Non-Hackable, Subtle 2, Thrown, Unforgiving 1

GEAR: Medium Combat Armour, Multispectral Visor 2

SPECIAL ABILITIES

- **Common Special Abilities**: Inured to Cold
- **Blizzard Born**: When in an arctic environment, any attacks targeting a Nisse at ranges beyond Close are made at +1 difficulty. Additionally, they may reroll one d20 when making a Survival test and gain +2d20 when making such tests in arctic environments.
- **Clear Shot**: The regiment's tradition as master snipers mean that each Nisse spends a considerable amount of time honing their skills. They may reroll up to three 🄽 when making a Ballistics test but must accept the new results. Additionally, they reduce the penalty for firing at a range other than the weapon's optimal range by one step (to a minimum of 0).

LOCUST, CLANDESTINE ACTION TEAM

Clandestine Action Teams are special Hexahedron units tasked with reconnaissance and HUMINT — intelligence gathered by means of interpersonal contact. Proficient in soft skills that allow them to gather the data they need without resorting to violence, CAT agents are also trained to handle explosives, hacking devices, and a plethora of deadly weapons. The technology they have access to supposedly doesn't exist, which makes it difficult to prepare for a fight with a Locust. Much like their namesake, they are bent on destruction, so the PanOceanian Military Complex often employs them in hostile theatres requiring specialised agents who accept any task, however gruesome it might be. After all, if the individual and organisation do not exist, how can they be charged with crimes against humanity?

ATTRIBUTES

AGI	AWA	BRW	COO	INT	PER	WIL
10	9	8	11	8	8	9

FIELDS OF EXPERTISE

Combat	+2	–	Movement	+1	–	Social	+1	–
Fortitude	+1	–	Senses	+3	1	Technical	+2	–

DEFENCES

Firewall	6	Resolve	10	Vigour	12
Security	–	Morale	–	Armour	3

ATTACKS

- **Breaker Combi Rifle**: Range C/M, 1+6 🄽 damage, Burst 2, 2H, Expert 1, MULTI Light Mod, Vicious 1, Breaker
- **Pistol**: R/C, 1+5 🄽 damage, Burst 2, 1H, Vicious 1
- **Knife**: Melee, 1+3 🄽 damage, 1H, Concealed 1, Non-Hackable, Subtle 2, Thrown, Unforgiving 1
- **Modded Hacking Device**: CLAW-1, SWORD-1, SHIELD-1, GADGET-2, IC-2, [UPGRADE – choose two] +2 🄽 damage

GEAR: Light Combat Armour, D-Charges, Optical Disruption Device, Garotte

SPECIAL ABILITIES

- **Common Special Skills**: Menacing 3.
- **You Don't Want to Do This**: Locust enjoy and utilise a fearsome reputation. They benefit from a Morale Soak of 1. Additionally, when attempting to intimidate an opponent, they gain 2d20 per Momentum spent, instead of the normal 1. (The normal limit of 3 bonus d20s still applies.)
- **Master Exploder**: Expert saboteurs, any ordnance rigged by the Locust *will* explode exactly when intended. Explosives prepared by the CAT Agent are at +2D to disarm.
- **Waiting for an Opening**: A Locust will always have the initiative in a Surprise situation.

INA MARIE (ORDER SERGEANT)

WASON LOUIE

NEMESIS

INA MARIE

ATTRIBUTES

AGI	AWA	BRW	COO	INT	PER	WIL
9	10	9	10	10	12	10

FIELDS OF EXPERTISE

Combat	+2	2	Movement	+1	–	Social	+3	3
Fortitude	+2	1	Senses	+2	1	Technical	+2	1

DEFENCES

Firewall	12	Resolve	14	Vigour	11
Security	1	Morale	2	Armour	2

ATTACKS

- **Combi Rifle**: Range C/M, 1+7  damage, Burst 3, 2H, Expert 1, MULTI Light Mod, Vicious 1
- **Pistol**: Range R/C, 1+6 damage, Burst 1, 1H, Vicious 1
- **Knife**: Melee, 1+4 damage, Concealed 1, Non-Hackable, Subtle 2, Thrown, Unforgiving 1

GEAR: Light Combat Armour, Order Sergeant Tabard

SPECIAL ABILITIES

- **Exultant (1 Heat)**: Ina's jovial nature can be infectious. She can spend 1 Heat to increase a target's complication range by 1 during face-to-face social tests.
- **Ordained**: Ina draws inner strength and determination from her faith. She has a Morale Soak of 2 and may reroll 1d20 when making a Discipline test.
- **Order Trained**: Ina has been trained to the exacting standards of the Order of Montesa. She may reroll 1d20 when making an Acrobatics test, or up to 2 when making a ranged or melee attack but must accept the new results. Additionally, she reduces the penalty for firing at a range other than the weapon's optimal range by 1 step (to a minimum of 0).

Smoke drifted up from behind the treeline. The Crusader Brethren had landed and established a beach head. Order Sergeant Ina Marie crossed herself, put on her helmet, and adjusted her displays.

She calmly surveyed the crammed vehicle, studying her comrades in arms: Father-Knight Miguel of the Montesa Order checking his holo-display, Sister Illeana readying her hacking device, Brothers João and Petru praying silently, and wide-eyed young Matteu gawking outside the transport.

She smiled under her helmet. "We are almost there, Brother Matteu. Think nothing of it and entrust yourself to God, and you will be delivered safely from your first battle," she reassured him.

Turning from the window, Matteu looked about to speak when the red deployment light flared. The other passengers quickly donned their helmets,

Father Miguel and the Sergeants drew their swords and made the sign of the cross as the vehicle's door powered open. "Brothers and sisters!" Father Miguel roared, rousing them. "We face our enemy! Trust your companions, your weapons, and most importantly your Faith! Miles Christi! In Hoc Singo Vinces!!"

Ina Marie thundered the battle cry of her Order and dismounted with her unit, firing short suppressive bursts at the few enemies still entrenched behind the smouldering remains of the alien communication towers as she ran. Originally five towers, the Crusader Brethren vanguard had destroyed three before being slaughtered by mercenary defenders. The few survivors were now pinned down behind a destroyed antenna.

As Father Miguel began to give an order, Ina noticed a snake-like smoke trail streaking towards the landing craft from the mercenary's position. "Incoming!" she screamed, though she was too late to do anything but take cover as the missile struck the transport and engulfed them in a ball of fire.

Disoriented, Ina Marie stood up. The explosion had claimed her rifle and helmet. Drawing her side arm, she took cover behind a piece of flaming wreckage and opened a communication channel.

"Marie here. Anyone else still standing?"

"Brothers Louis and Eliza at the north tower. The rest are with God now. Three hostiles at the west tower and one, a hacker we believe, at the south tower."

"We have to stop them. I'll take the south tower. Pray to God brothers, and we will be heard! Miles Christi!"

Ina jumped from behind her cover and charged through the breach, assured there was still much of God's work to be done.

APPEARANCE

A pretty, quietly spoken woman with an easy smile. Courteous towards civilians and strangers, Ina Marie is attentive and respectful with other members of the military. She wears a silver crucifix necklace on top of her bulletproof vest and Order regalia.

ROLEPLAYING

- She is very pious and frowns upon people cursing and swearing.
- When nervous or excited, she plays with her crucifix.
- Very polite to others, though righteous and fanatical in combat.

BACKGROUND

As a young woman toiling in one of Acontecimento's vast grain fields, Ina Marie fell from a huge harvester and hit her head, suffering several seizures thereafter.

Although scans detected no lasting damage, Ina swears she has visions during her episodes — fire, brimstone, and the impending doom of the End of Times.

Since then, her already faithful demeanour changed. She became more focused and fervent. Expected to join a nunnery, she surprised her family and joined the Acontecimento Regulars instead; Ina's plan did not include spending her life cloistered in a convent. Intending to bring her faith to where it was most needed, she volunteered for the Sergeants of the Order of Montesa as soon as her training allowed.

Once under the strict rules of the Order, her visions gradually subsided, only to be replaced by the reality an alien invasion. She knew then that Providence had delivered her right where she belonged. Moved entirely by her faith, she is a bulwark within her unit and a true leader ready to assist anyone in need. To continue her selflessness beyond death, she has recently begun researching how best to gain a Resurrection licence.

JAKUB PALM

NEMESIS

JAKOB PA-LEM

ATTRIBUTES

AGI	AWA	BRW	COO	INT	PER	WIL
9	11	10	9	12	9	10

FIELDS OF EXPERTISE

Combat	+2	1	Movement	+1	1	Social	+1	–
Fortitude	+2	2	Senses	+2	2	Technical	+3	3

DEFENCES

Firewall	15	Resolve	12	Vigour	12
Security	3	Morale	2	Armour	1

ATTACKS

- **Pistol:** Range R/C, 1+6 , Burst 1, 1H, Vicious 1
- **Knife:** Melee, 1+5 , Concealed 1, Non-Hackable, Subtle 2, Thrown, Unforgiving 1
- **Hacking Device:** CLAW-1, SWORD-1, SHIELD-1, GADGET-3, IC-1

GEAR: Light Combat Armour

SPECIAL ABILITIES

- **Educated Technician:** Jakob is intelligent and educated. He may reroll 1d20 when making an Analysis or Education, or any dice that did not generate a success on the initial roll of a Tech test, but must accept the new results.
- **Life Hack (1 Heat):** A rebel before being sepsitorized, Jakob's will is unerringly guided by the EI. He has 2 additional Security Soak and a Morale Soak of 2. Further, he may pay 1 Heat to inflict +1 difficulty to any attempts to detect his subversion (useable once each test affected). Additionally, he may reroll 1d20 or 2  when making a Hacking test but must accept the new results.

JAKOB PA-LEM (CA HACKER)

Jakob had never perspired so much in his whole life. He recalled hailing from Svalarheima. What had possessed him to get assigned to Paradiso? He had five Alguaciles escorting him for this mission, hacking alien-looking antennae to gain intelligence on the enemy. The antennae detected the incoming PanOceanian transports quickly enough for Jakob to easily warn the squad, yet he remained silent and observed them gathered around the northernmost antenna.

A loud whistle precluded one of the antennae exploding and crashing down to send one of the Alguaciles scrambling for cover. As expected, Jakob identified the vehicles as PanOceanian Crusaders. The vehicle's weapon loadout, however, was an unknown variable to collect data on. He reached out to the vehicle's command program. Shutting off the communications and power systems sent the transport crashing heavily into the surf a few metres from one of the towers.

The attacking humans had managed to destroy a second tower with only one loss so far. Two hostiles were heading to a third tower, so Jakob opened a channel and ordered the Alguaciles to fire a missile at its base. He then activated the same tower's security system, blasting the two Crusaders with electricity. The missile struck before they could recover, blowing both the structure and the humans to pieces.

Knowing the second aircraft would land in under 45 seconds, he acknowledged the attackers needed stalling for the mission to be considered complete so set to firing haphazardly at the remaining soldiers to make them aware of his presence. He also uploaded misleading information regarding Onyx Force positions into the antenna's memory bank for the humans to find.

Another explosion. This one from the recently landed transport vehicle. Jakob needed access to ALEPH. Arranging for this human vessel to be captured and interrogated by PanOceania was the best route to gain access to the humans' and their AI's cyber-space. Opening his eyes, he saw his comrades being cut down by a pair of furious Crusaders. Even more alarmingly, however, he saw the charging Sergeant headed straight for him. Bewildered, Jakob cursed the day he merged with the EI and threw up his hands in surrender. The following minutes were going to hurt like

hell and the EI would make sure he was conscious during every second...

APPEARANCE

A non-descript human wearing characteristic Nomad Clockmaker's attire, Jakob Pa-Lem's large eyes occasionally glaze, becoming emotionless and cold like those of a shark. He is quite inquisitive and is constantly interacting with any unattended technology.

ROLEPLAYING

- He is very shy and avoids social interaction as much as possible.
- He talks to himself about an "Episteme Monster" when nobody is watching.
- He avoids direct eye contact at all times.

BACKGROUND

A promising TAG engineer, Jakob was disdainful of wasteful PanOceanian projects. He criticised both military and entertainment ventures that had nothing to do with acquiring more scientific knowledge. He even denounced ALEPH as a diversion from true knowledge.

Chancing upon a data package from Paradiso, Pa-Lem discovered and became fascinated with the EI, even publishing a paper justifying its existence and ethical advantages over ALEPH. Naming this utilitarian thought the "Episteme Monster", he praised the EI for its Grand Pursuit. ALEPH removed all traces of his work and Pa-Lem defected to the Nomads. Growing to become his own named creation, he worked as a bounty hunter gathering information from Cube hacking.

Joining the EI seemed the only way forward for his pursuits, so he chose a mission on to get closer. The Shasvastii captured him soon enough, inflicting an induction process wiped his memory bar the vaguest ghosts. Ordained with the task of covertly damaging the cohesion of the Social Energy and gaining access to ALEPH, he has returned as one of the EI's agents. When not controlled by the EI, he understands that achieving its goals are as vital as keeping the VoodooTech implanted in his Cube hidden.

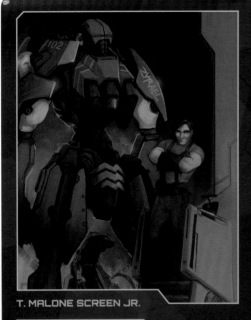

T. MALONE SCREEN JR.

NEMESIS

MALONE SKRYNE

ATTRIBUTES

AGI	AWA	BRW	COO	INT	PER	WIL
9	10	10	11	11	9	10

FIELDS OF EXPERTISE

Combat	+2	2	Movement	+2	1	Social	+1	1
Fortitude	+1	1	Senses	+2	2	Technical	+3	2

DEFENCES

Firewall	14	Resolve	11	Vigour	10
Security	–	Morale	2	Armour	1

ATTACKS

- **Pistol:** Range R/C, 1+6 damage, Burst 1, 1H, Vicious 1
- **Knife:** Melee, 1+5 damage, Concealed 1, Non-Hackable, Subtle 2, Thrown, Unforgiving 1

GEAR: Armoured Clothing, ECM 2, Survival Kit (Jungle), Tikbalang TAG (p. 78)

SPECIAL ABILITIES

- **In Tony's Footsteps:** Malone pushes himself hard to master his TAG. He can reroll 1d20 when making a Pilot test but must accept the new result. Additionally, he can reduce the penalty for damage by –2 difficulty when making a Pilot test with a damaged TAG (minimum of 0).
- **Swift & Silent:** Malone has an intuitive understanding of movement in the jungle, which he transfers to his TAG. He can reroll 1d20 when making an Acrobatics or Stealth test but must accept the new result. Additionally, he reduces the difficulty to move through, past, or over obstacles and difficult terrain by 2 steps, to a minimum of Simple (D0).
- **TAGged (2 Heat):** Malone has a knack for hitting enemy TAGs where it hurts with Zyrael. He can spend 2 Heat to reroll up to 4 when attacking other TAGs when using his own TAG.

MALONE "ZYRAEL" SKRYNE (TIKBALANG PILOT)

The crabbot remote handled itself very differently from Zyrael. The four clunky legs always made the remote tilt in weird ways, but this time, the PanOceanian engineers had demonstrated why they were the best in TAG technology. Malone placed the mine perfectly, without endangering Zyrael unnecessarily.

Grinning within the confines of his control pod, five kilometres away from the theatre, the pilot sent the little remote back to the awaiting TAG and eagerly switched control from the remote to the Stingray 3 TAG. The Tikbalang was identified in his regiment as Zyrael, an aggressive and cunning team of human cleverness and hyper-technological destruction machine.

"Zyrael online and ready to engage!"

"Copy that, Zyrael. Hostiles closing in your location. Defensive measures advised."

Malone checked his quantronic display. These were Morat, a totally different category above mere "hostiles," and defensive measures would not be enough. He had to take the battle to them, and that was precisely why he activated the crabbot.

Zyrael crouched in his hiding place, several metres behind the trees rigged with mines. The jungle fell silent. Malone's vitals rose in anticipation.

"Malone, your heart rate is spiking. Do you need assistance?"

"Negative. I'm fine."

At that precise moment, a series of coordinated detonations erupted in front of him followed by screams of fury and pain and then insults in Morat.

Malone grinned, switched on Zyrael's flamethrower and advanced upon the ambushed Morat.

"Just fine!"

APPEARANCE

Sergeant Malone "Zyrael" Skryne is a muscular man, though not very tall, and has an arrogant half-grin all the time. He moves with the confidence of a Holo-drama star, laughing out loudly and attracting the attention of all around him.

ROLEPLAYING

- He likes to be the centre of attention and constantly mentions his TAG.
- When frustrated, he behaves like a bully.
- He loves to bet on pretty much anything.

BACKGROUND

Malone and his TAG Zyrael came to Paradiso in the second wave of recruits after Tony Macayana's tragic death. Like hundreds of young volunteers from San Fernando de Dagopan, Malone had a crush with the ideal of Macayana and his heroic TAG Eduardo. Malone enrolled thinking he would ride into battle with his noble steed, avenging the honour of PanOceania.

Reality hit Zyrael's team during the follow up offensive to TAGLine where a brutal detachment of the Raicho Armoured Brigade swept through the rookie PanOceanian lines like a hot knife through butter.

The agile Zyrael managed to escape the main charge of the gargantuan alien TAGs thanks to Malone's understanding of jungle fighting. Later, during debriefing, Malone realized that even in a remote-controlled pod, the war in Paradiso was something terrible and deadly. He became more cynical in order to survive and to bring real vengeance to the alien army.

Zyrael and Malone quickly rose up the ranks of the regiment as a top TAG killer, with six confirmed TAG kills in its first twelve assignments. Zyrael, unlike the noble Eduardo, is a crafty, sneaky, and efficient jungle killer. They are less of a knight and steed and more a Tikbalang, a horse demon preying on the unsuspecting aliens.

RAMORA LEONHART
(HOSPITALLER KNIGHT—ROGUISH)

RILEY ESMOND

NEMESIS

RAMORA LEONHART

ATTRIBUTES

AGI	AWA	BRW	COO	INT	PER	WIL
10	10	11	10	9	11	9

FIELDS OF EXPERTISE

Combat	+3	2	Movement	+1	1	Social	+2	2
Fortitude	+2	2	Senses	+1	1	Technical	+1	1

DEFENCES

Firewall	10	Resolve	11	Vigour	13
Security	2	Morale	2	Armour	4

ATTACKS

- **Boarding Shotgun**: Range C, 1+7  damage, 2H, Knockdown, Medium MULTI
- **Pistol**: Range R/C, 1+6 damage, Burst 1, 1H, Vicious 1
- **Blade of St. George**: Melee, 1+7 damage, 2H, Grievous, Non-Hackable, Parry 2, Piercing 2, Vicious 1

GEAR: Heavy Combat Armour

SPECIAL ABILITIES

- **Devout**: Ramora draws inner strength and determination from his faith. He has a Morale Soak of 2.
- **Knightly Combat**: Ramora has been trained to the exacting standards of the Knightly Orders. He may reroll 1d20 when making an Acrobatics test, or up to 2 when making a ranged or melee attack, but must accept the new results. Additionally, he pays 1 less Heat to make Guard or Defence Reactions (minimum of 0).
- **Unconventional (1 Heat)**: Ramora can be unpredictable. If he spends Heat to seize initiative, he can spend 1 additional Heat to reroll 1d20 on any subsequent melee or ranged attack, but must accept the new result.

The monastery's halls were particularly cold this night. It certainly did not help the fact that the Hospitaller Order frowned upon using the knights' armour heating system for anything but strict survival.

Still, Ramora's spirit was up as he had finally finished the penance imposed on him for striking that Blizzard-6 officer.

"Officer," he blurted out. "A fancy title for that filthy mercenary!"

Ramora Leonhart of the Hospitaller Order chastised himself silently for his arrogance and headed to the monastery's infirmary. The Blizzard-6 team had entrusted the Order with guarding a crate of biohazardous material rescued from a crashed space shuttle that had the whole province on alert earlier that week.

Entering the infirmary, Ramora found the Brother in charge of the night shift was lying on the floor, murdered. The cameras were destroyed, and the doors to the biohazard storage were wide open.

Ramora drew his sword, praying to Saint John of Skovorodino. He had not come across anyone on the way there, and it was the only route, so the killer must still be inside.

Out of the corner of his eye, Ramora thought he saw movement. He swung his sword in a low cut while instinctively ducking and heard a loud bang near his head. The shot grazed his helmet, sending static and flashes up his retina display for a second. Ramora charged blindly, crashing into something and running straight through a glass door into a storage room.

He grappled with his enemy, shredding the optical disruption clothing just before he was shot again at point blank. Luckily, his helmet held one last time. By the time he took it off, his assailant was on the far wall of the infirmary, placing what looked to be demolition charges. Ramora grabbed his sword and hesitated before deciding to run for cover. After the charges exploded, Ramora rushed to the newly-made hole and his enemy was nowhere to be seen.

Ramora inhaled and immediately felt the icy cold of the planet.

"Oh well. I suppose I will be doing penance anyway." He grumbled as he activated the heating system of his battered armour.

APPEARANCE

Ramora is a tall man, with the characteristic fair hair of the Svalarheimans. He wears his armour comfortably. His demeanour is friendly, and he has a mischievous shine in his eyes.

ROLEPLAYING

- He is always happy and motivated.
- He is very impetuous, constantly getting into trouble with his superiors.
- He prays at least three times a day and constantly invites people to join him.

BACKGROUND

Ramora is one of the most popular members of the Holy Order of Hospitaller Knights of Saint John of Skovorodino. In one of the most serious and sober institutions of the Human Sphere, Ramora is always ready with a smile and a positive attitude that clashes with the sombre — and usually fatalistic — approach of the Knights Hospitaller.

Ramora's positivity is ironically both his best quality and his worst deficiency as he is constantly butting heads with his superiors on the strict following of the Order's Rules.

A pious and merciful soul, he tends to put orders on hold when innocents may suffer. He has taken his Order's main objective to heart but is unable to view the big picture when the safety of civilians is at stake. Thus, he is constantly praying and performing penance on account of his disobedience to superiors and their strict rules.

CRISTÓBAL HARRIS
(FATHER-KNIGHT HACKER)

CHRIS HARRIS

NEMESIS

CRISTÓBAL HARRIS

ATTRIBUTES

AGI	AWA	BRW	COO	INT	PER	WIL
9	11	10	9	11	9	11

FIELDS OF EXPERTISE

Combat	+2	1	Movement	+1	1	Social	+1	1
Fortitude	+2	1	Senses	+2	2	Technical	+4	2

DEFENCES

Firewall	15	Resolve	13	Vigour	12
Security	3	Morale	4	Armour	5

ATTACKS

- **Combi Rifle**: Range C/M, 1+7  damage, Burst 3, 2H, Expert 1, MULTI Light Mod, Vicious 1
- **Breaker Pistol**: Range R/C, 1+6  damage, Breaker, Burst 1, 1H, Standard, Vicious 1
- **D-Charges**: Charge, 2+6  damage, 1H, Anti-Materiel 2, Comms, Disposable, Piercing 3, Spread 1, Unsubtle, Vicious 2
- **Teseum Blade of St. George**: Melee, 1+10  damage, Unbalanced, Non-Hackable, Piercing 4, Vicious 2
- **Assault Hacking Device**: CLAW-3, SWORD-0, SHIELD-0, GADGET-0, IC-1

GEAR: Powered Combat Armour (Comms, Exoskeleton 3, Kinematika, Self-Repairing)

SPECIAL ABILITIES

- **Deo Vindice**: Cristóbal has a Morale Soak of 4.
- **Knightly Combat**: Cristóbal has been trained in the Knightly Orders. He may reroll 1d20 when making an Acrobatics or Discipline test, or up to 2  when making a ranged or melee attack, but must accept the new results. Additionally, he pays 1 less Heat to make Guard or Defence Reactions (minimum of 0).
- **Metaphysical Sword**: An expert hacker, Cristóbal can reroll 1d20 or up to 2  when making a Hacking test but must accept the new results.

Father Cristóbal contemplated the damage to the monastery's wall from the sabotage attack. He turned to face the sergeant in a hazmat suit.

"What do we have?"

"We retrieved one of the canisters intact, Father Cristóbal. It is some kind of bio-reactive component."

"A biological weapon?"

"A weapon, or a tool. It is constantly mutating, complimenting, and strengthening whatever it gets in contact with. There is no record of such a living organism, at least not in God's Sphere."

"Then we have no choice but to take that sample to the specialists. Sergeant, arrange for a shuttle to take me to Circular C1 before it makes the transit. Missio Dei!"

Father-Officer Cristóbal Harris entered his cell and studied the canister, wondering what demented and god-forsaken alien had produced the aberration. It was clear though, this was evil, and he would make sure all those involved would pay for their sins.

He turned on his terminal and looked up the monastery's records, carefully reviewing all the information regarding the canisters. The biohazard crate containing the samples was brought by a Blizzard team, whose leader had a spat with one of the Knights of the Order. The Blizzard team found the crates at the crash site of a private shuttle, which in turn was disengaged from the Circular currently passing through the Epsilon Eridani system.

He searched the cargo registries of the Circular, and things got more interesting. The registry of the shuttle stated it was private-owned and hailing from Dawn, but there was no clear reason for the shuttle to disengage. A safety alarm had gone off at the docking bay, and there was an increase in the Yu Jing armada's transmissions until the shuttle entered the planet's atmosphere.

Cristóbal's terminal started issuing security warnings, and he quickly logged off before he was discovered. Clearly, someone was covering their tracks regarding the organism, and that only told him those involved were guilty.

One way or another, Cristóbal swore, they would pay for their sins.

APPEARANCE

A stern looking man, Father Cristóbal has an intimidating countenance which, added to his field armour, makes him terrifying. He is clearly not comfortable wasting time talking and looks like he will explode at the smallest provocation.

ROLEPLAYING

- Harris has a deep voice that booms his favourite phrase, "God wills it."
- He is a fervent monk and will not tolerate any blasphemy.
- He is extremely impatient.

BACKGROUND

Cristóbal Harris is a man of unshakeable faith, a true soldier of God. He has a very traditionalist mindset even though he possesses highly advanced technological skills.

During his training as an acolyte, he received training from Father de Fersen, the most skilled hacker in the Order. The training cultivated Cristóbal's hacking abilities, but the young acolyte never grew accustomed to de Fersen's presence. There was something non-sanctus as he would put it to his confessor later, and that thought has never left Harris' mind.

Deep down, Cristóbal enjoys his labour as one of the Order's hackers, but he is aware that the theological implications of some technologies are downright heretical, and this makes him uncomfortable and quite intolerant towards new technologies.

THORBJORN HEIN

NEMESIS

THOR HEIN

ATTRIBUTES

AGI	AWA	BRW	COO	INT	PER	WIL
9	10	12	10	9	10	10

FIELDS OF EXPERTISE

Combat	+2	2	Movement	+3	2	Social	+2	1
Fortitude	+1	1	Senses	+2	2	Technical	+1	1

DEFENCES

Firewall	11	Resolve	11	Vigour	11
Security	–	Morale	2	Armour	1

ATTACKS

- **Pistol**: Range R/C, 1+6 🅝 damage, Burst 1, 1H, Vicious 1
- **Stun Baton**: Melee, 1+7 🅝 damage, Non-Hackable, Knockdown, Subtle 1, Stun

GEAR: Alethia Kit, Armoured Clothing, Bioscanner

SPECIAL ABILITIES

- **Energy Spike (2 Heat)**: All that sugar has to go somewhere. Once per scene, Thor can spend 2 Heat to immediately recover 2 Vigour.
- **On the Case**: Thor has taken to his new career like a Helot to water. He can reroll 1d20 when making an Analysis, Persuade, or Thievery test, but must accept the new result.
- **Sport Fusion**: Thor has enjoyed promising careers in both Scuball and the Fusiliers. He has a Morale Soak of 2. Additionally, he can reroll 1d20 when making an Acrobatics test, or up to 2 🅝 when making a melee or ranged attack, but must accept the new results. Additionally, he gains 2 bonus Momentum on Athletics tests.

THOR HEIN (PRIVATE INVESTIGATOR)

The small hologram Scuball figure slowly revolved, repeating the phrase, "To my biggest fan." The young girl watched it turn once more and thanked the man before running excitedly to her mother, just like the fans in the old days.

Thor Hein, former Scuball star, had business other than signing autographs at hand, however.

"Do you have any high-end Scuball gear?" The hologram in charge of the store, an attractive woman nodded. "Right this way, Mr. Hein. In the upper level."

Hein followed the lights, paying attention to where the security cameras and projectors were. He needed access to the store's warehouse — and do it discreetly.

Upstairs, he took the first piece he saw and asked to try it on. In the fitting room, he carefully put on the Scuball suit and produced an optical disruption device from his jacket, now hanging in the room.

Stealthily, he slipped out of the fitting room and found the almost invisible back-door heading to the store's warehouse.

Thor looked around and quickly what he was searching for, crates marked Switech Corp., unopened and way in the back, separated from the rest of the merchandise. He had been following the Switech lead for a while and this was good news. The only thing left to do was to get proof of the crates' contents.

As he pulled out his hacking gear, he wondered why Mikhail wanted him to follow up on sporting Hypercorp deals. He understood millions were always at stake with Scuball and Aristeia!, but this was not the reporter's usual line of research. But, his money was good, his contacts had paid off, and the only thing left to do was to get proof of the crates' contents.

Deftly, he hacked a lock on the nearest crate and opened it. The moment he lifted the lid, a security alarm activated, and his retinal projector flashed warnings. He was ordered to stay put and wait for the security team to pick him up. This level of security was over the top for even a Nitrocaine shipment. As he looked into the crate, he saw something worse than Nitrocaine, the inert bodies of several high-end Lhosts. Thor cursed himself quietly for not charging Mikhail more.

APPEARANCE

Thor is a huge athlete with the musculature of a Scuball professional and the observing gaze of a bird of prey. Of Scandinavian stock, he has a deep voice and a day-old beard. He has a confident smile and looks relaxed, as if he could take on anyone in the room and come out unscathed.

ROLEPLAYING

- Thor doesn't like to talk about his former life as a Scuball player.
- He likes to drink energy beverages constantly.
- He tends to be over-protective of his comrades.

BACKGROUND

After a tragic incident where an opponent drowned, Thor "The Bear" Hein, captain of the Neo-Canberra Sea Devils, left a promising career in sports and joined the Fusiliers where he distinguished himself in several operations against Libertos.

During the operations at Varuna, he became disillusioned by the way the Hyperpower was treating the Helots and was honourably discharged at age thirty-eight instead of continuing a potentially stellar career.

Currently, Bjorn makes his own rules, as a private investigator and bodyguard. He chooses his customers and assignments carefully, which allows him to be at ease with himself, knowing he is doing the right thing.

ANDREAS GRUBER

NEMESIS

ANDREAS GRUBER

ATTRIBUTES

AGI	AWA	BRW	COO	INT	PER	WIL
10	10	11	10	9	9	11

FIELDS OF EXPERTISE

Combat	+4	1	Movement	+3	1	Social	+1	1
Fortitude	+3	1	Senses	+2	1	Technical	+1	1

DEFENCES

Firewall	10	Resolve	14	Vigour	14
Security	–	Morale	3	Armour	1

ATTACKS

- **Combi Rifle**: Range C/M, 1+7  damage, Burst 3, 2H, Expert 1, MULTI Light Mod, Vicious 1
- **Pistol**: Range R/C, 1+5 damage, Burst 1, 1H, Vicious 1
- **Croc Mines**: Explosive Mine, 2+5 damage, 1H, Comms, Disposable, Fragile, Indiscriminate (Close), Unsubtle, Grievous
- **Knife**: Melee, 1+4 damage, Concealed 1, Non-Hackable, Subtle 2, Thrown, Unforgiving 1

GEAR: Light Combat Armour, Multispectral Visor 2

SPECIAL ABILITIES

- **Born Lucky (2 Heat)**: Once per scene, Andreas may spend 2 Heat to reroll any dice that did not generate a success on the initial roll of a test, but must accept the new results.
- **Sharp Teeth**: Andreas has a Morale Soak of 3 and may reroll 1d20 when making an Acrobatics or Stealth test, any dice that did not generate a success on the initial roll of a Resistance test, or up to 2 when making a ranged or melee attack, but must accept the new results. Additionally, he reduces the penalty for firing at a range other than the weapon's optimal range by 1 step (to a minimum of 0).
- **Unbreakable**: Andreas may reroll 1d20 when making a Discipline test, but must accept the new result. Additionally, he gains 2 bonus Momentum when taking the Recover action.

ANDREAS "LUCKY" GRUBER (CROC MAN)

Batroids were approaching Gruber's position in an unfortunate change of events. His mission was a simple recovery — locating and bringing back a prospector unit that had become lost in the southern swamp.

This far south of the frontline, a recovery was a reward mission, particularly after his last operation.

Still, as luck would have it, Gruber and the dark-haired Tech-Bee came directly across this CA patrol. Which also meant that for the past four days, he and the surviving engineer had been dodging Combined Army remotes left and right.

"How long until we reach the base, Lucky?"

"Don't call me "Lucky." Only my friends can do that. You'll jinx us," he whispered to the woman. The Croc Man paused, planning their next move. "If we manage to reach that hill over there, I can signal our location and call for an airlift. Then, we can return home."

It was noon by the time they reached the summit of the hill. On top of it, there was single sentry, a Unidron sniper next to a communication relay. It was surveying its unit's movements, oblivious to the danger a dozen meters from its feet.

Lucky slowly drew his knife — this would have to be quick and silent. The alien soldier screeched and fell to the ground.

"Sweet dreams, you filthy piece of alien trash!"

Breathing heavily, Lucky looked around and got a good view of the zone for the first time in days. Things weren't good, not good at all.

He opened his Comlog and sent a signal requesting not the rescue airlift but a full barrage bombardment on his location. The Combined Army was moving in force, and there was no one to warn the PanOceanians.

"I knew she'd jinx it!" he mumbled. Gruber returned to join the Tech-Bee and once more try to escape the incoming inferno. If only they were so lucky!

APPEARANCE

A rugged man covered in tattoos, he has several scars, both from combat and self-inflicted. He is light on his feet and has a full set of white teeth which he shows easily enough as he laughs a lot.

ROLEPLAYING

- He is very superstitious.
- He is constantly eating some kind of dry meat jerky.
- He gesticulates a lot when talking to someone he doesn't know.

BACKGROUND

Andreas "Lucky" Gruber got his nickname when the invasion began while he was still working as a tourist guide in Paradiso. Leading a tour through one of Paradiso's swamplands when the first landings occurred, he helped evacuate of a resort full of civilians in one of the CA's landing zones even though the boat he was steering got sunk by enemy fire.

Later on, after hearing about Ravensbrücke, Andreas volunteered as an auxiliary scout in the decimated Croc Men regiment, which was sorely in need of guides and people who knew their way around the Paradiso jungles. Andreas survived Basic Combat Training and a Shasvastii ambush during his first recon mission. After Advance Combat Training, he joined the regiment as one of the first Paradiso-born Croc Men.

Although fortunate, he is aware of having the "ability" to be in the right place in the right time during the worst situations. Andreas has become slightly superstitious, following the regiment's rituals and practices to the letter in order to keep his good luck intact.

JACK MILLS

NEMESIS

JACK MILLS

ATTRIBUTES

AGI	AWA	BRW	COO	INT	PER	WIL
9	11	10	9	11	9	11

FIELDS OF EXPERTISE

Combat	+2	1	Movement	+2	1	Social	+2	1
Fortitude	+1	1	Senses	+4	2	Technical	+2	1

DEFENCES

Firewall	13	Resolve	12	Vigour	11
Security	–	Morale	2	Armour	1

ATTACKS
- **Pistol**: Range R/C, 1+6 🟡 damage, Burst 1, 1H, Vicious 1

GEAR: Alethia Kit, Armoured Clothing

SPECIAL ABILITIES
- **Block Party**: Jack is a trained officer of the Block Forces. He can reroll 1d20 when making an Analysis or Thievery test, or up to 2 🟡 when making a ranged attack, but must accept the new results. Additionally, when making Education or Persuade tests relating to or interacting with the criminal element, he gains 2 bonus Momentum.
- **Gambler (2 Heat)**: Living life on the edge, Jack can spend 2 Heat to roll 1 🟡 when making a test. If a 1 or 2 is rolled, he adds that much Momentum to the test. If an Effect is rolled, he instead increases the complication range of the test by 2.
- **Tenacious**: Jack will dig deep to foil crime. He can reroll 1d20 when making a Discipline test but must accept the new result. Additionally, any time he is the target of a Persuade or Command test, Momentum paid to add dice to the Discipline tests provides 2 d20s, instead of 1. (Max 3 bonus d20s still apples.)

JACK MILLS (OFFICER OF THE LAW)

Jack Mills stepped into the room and something crunched under his feet. Lifting his boot, it looked like grains of sugar spilt all over the floor. Squatting, he scooped some of the substance into a sample vial. Jack then turned all his attention to the corpse lying on the floor as a nearby technician and a support Palbot stared at him inquisitively.

"I needed a sample of that," he explained.

"Of what? The glass?" the junior technician demanded impatiently.

"There are no broken windows..."

The technician sighed loudly, turned to the dead body, and began reciting.

"Female, in her twenties. No Cube, so it clearly was an Atek drug-related murder." He shrugged.

Detective Jack Mills's face turned red and took the technician's collar in his hands, shaking the young man violently.

"She was a human being, you imbecile! Get your sorry Cube and your 'bot out of my crime scene!"

The technician stumbled rapidly out of the room, the Palbot following.

Jack forced himself to breathe deeply and calmly kneeled beside the dead girl. She had a huge wound, right where her Cube would be stored. She had several electoos, the expensive ones, and her clothes were all clean and in fine condition. She was no Atek, this girl, she was the daughter of an important member of one of Neoterra's political lobbies. Her name was Camille, and Jack Mills had met her last night to discuss information regarding the human trafficking of the San Pietro Ateks.

The information Camille had would have saved a lot of lives and put some evil people in jail. Jack took the small vial and held it to the light.

"I'm guessing you got a holo-message telling you to meet me here, and you encountered someone you did not expect... Someone with very, very expensive nanopulser jewellery..."

APPEARANCE

A rugged looking detective in the service of one of San Pietro's larger Block Forces, he wears a greasy uniform and clearly hasn't had much sleep lately. He calmly observes every detail in the room before addressing the rest of his business.

ROLEPLAYING

- He likes to gamble on various sports, even though he seldom wins.
- His favourite meal is Lo Pan's noodles, but his local joint got closed recently.
- When stressed he develops a tick, touching his Comlog three times before entering a room.

BACKGROUND

A Neoterran detective, Jack is an honest cop with bad luck and no political friends. As it turns out, San Pietro is both one of the most pious cities in the Sphere and one of the most corrupt. Jack, believing he could make a difference in the Neoterran capital, began pursuing a crime syndicate involved in Atek slave labour. Jack, thinking this a simple crime ring using Ateks as cheap manpower, started following those involved and found a huge and disturbing web of corruption and crime that would shame any Submondo crime-lord.

An idealistic rookie, he went straight to his superiors who quickly put a lid on it and transferred Jack to Newton City where they expected he would either get in line or simply fade into oblivion.

To everybody's surprise, Jack adapted quickly to the provincial life of Newton City and continues his work, gathering more information on the Atek trafficking ring until the time is right to blow the lid on so many high-profile criminals.